SOCIAL PROBLEMS IN CANADA

Issues and Challenges

Second Edition

E. D. Nelson
University of Waterloo

Augie Fleras
University of Canterbury

Prentice Hall Allyn and Bacon Canada
Scarborough, Ontario

Canadian Cataloguing in Publication Data

Nelson, Adie, 1958–
    Social problems in Canada: issues and challenges

2nd ed.
Includes index
ISBN 0-13-955006-2
1. Social problems—Canada. 2. Canada—social conditions—1991–   .
I. Fleras, Augie, 1947–   . II. Title.

HN103.5.N45 1998 361.1'0971 C97-932209-X

© 1998, 1995 Prentice-Hall Canada Inc., Scarborough, Ontario
A Division of Simon & Schuster/A Viacom Company

Allyn and Bacon, Inc., Needham Heights, MA
Prentice-Hall, Inc., Upper Saddle River, New Jersey
Prentice-Hall International (UK) Limited, London
Prentice-Hall of Australia, Pty. Limited, Sydney
Prentice-Hall Hispanoamericana, S.A., Mexico City
Prentice-Hall of India Private Limited, New Delhi
Prentice-Hall of Japan, Inc., Tokyo
Simon & Schuster Southeast Asia Private Limited, Singapore
Editora Prentice-Hall do Brasil, Ltda., Rio de Janeiro

ISBN 0-13-955006-2

Vice President, Editorial Director: Laura Pearson
Acquisitions Editor: David Stover
Marketing Manager: Kathleen McGill
Production Editor: Kelly Dickson
Copy Editor: Susan Broadhurst
Marketing Coordinator: Dayna Vogel
Marketing Assistant: Kathie Kirschsteiger
Production Coordinator: Leora Conway
Cover and Interior Design: Sarah Battersby
Cover Image: PhotoDisc
Page Layout: B. J. Weckerle

1 2 3 4 5 RRD 02 01 00 99 98

Printed and bound in the USA.

Visit the Prentice Hall Canada web site! Send us your comments, browse our catalogues, and more at **www.ph-canada.com**. Or reach us through e-mail at **phabinfo_pubcanada@prenhall.com**.

Every reasonable effort has been made to obtain permissions for all articles and data used in this edition. If errors or omissions have occurred, they will be corrected in future editions provided written notification has been received by the publisher.

To Pat and Andrea, Megan and Theo

Table of Contents

Preface xiii

Chapter 1 Introduction 1

Social Problems: Private Troubles and Public Issues 3

Social Problems: Conditions and Processes 5
> A Problem Is Social in Origin When the Offending Condition Is the Result of Human Social Behaviour 6
> A Problem Is Social in Definition When It Is Defined as Such by a Significant Number of People 6
> A Problem Is Social in Treatment When Its Proposed Solution Resides within the Framework of Societal Practices or Institutions 7
> Case 1-1 The War Against Women 7

Approaches to Studying Social Problems 8
> Victim Blaming 8
> Enemy Blaming 9
> Institution Blaming 11
> System Blaming 12

Sociology and the Study of Social Problems 13
> The Functionalist Approach 14
> The Conflict Approach 15
> The Interactionist Approach 16

The Natural History of Social Problems 18
> Definition 18
> Mobilization 19
> Politicization 20
> Reaction and Response 20
> Treatment 20
> Case 1-2 Animal Rights as Collective Reform 21
> Impact 22

Working Assumptions 22
> A Sociological Framework 22
> Interplay of Actor and Structure 23
> Social Problems and Power 23
> Social Problems as Contested 23
> The Normalcy of Social Problems 23
> Social Problems as Moral Order 24

The Problem-Solution-Problem Conundrum 24
Policy Dimensions 24
The Problem of Bias 24
Evolving Discourses 24

PART 1 PRIVATE TROUBLES VS. PUBLIC ISSUES 27

Chapter 2 Addictions 28

Did You Know? 28

The Problem 29

The Costs of Addictions 33
The Crime Connection 33
The Economic Costs of Addictions 38
The Effect on Personal Well-Being 39
The Effect on Society's Well-Being 42

Analyzing the Problem 43
The Functionalist Approach 43
Case 2-1 The "Stages" of Drug Abuse 48
The Conflict Approach 51
The Interactionist Approach 53

Private Trouble or Public Issue: Confronting the Problem 57

Solutions and Questions 60

Summary 61

Chapter 3 Sex and Sexuality 62

Did You Know? 62

The Problem 63
Private Trouble or Public Issue? 66
Case 3-1 The Heterosexual Questionnaire 67

Analyzing the Problem 68
The Functionalist Approach 70
The Conflict Approach 71
The Interactionist Approach 73

Eroticism Scripts: Gender and Sexuality 75
The Double Standard 76
The Issues of Reproduction 78

Coercive Sexuality 86
Sexual Violence and Sexual Scripts 88
"Unfounding" Complaints 91
The Courts 91
Case 3-2 A Fitting Sentence or Criminal Neglect? 92

Summary 94

PART 2 STRUCTURAL PROBLEMS 95

Chapter 4 Crime 96

Did You Know? 96

The Problem 97

Read All About It: Crime and the Mass Media 99
    Case 4-1 The Mystique of a Murderer: The Case of Ted Bundy 100

Criminal Victimization and the Fear of Crime 102

What Is Crime? 103
    Crime as Harm 104
    No Crime without Law 105
    Actus Reus 105
    Mens Rea 105
    Concurrency 106
    Causality 106
    Sanctions 107

Who Commits Crime? 109

The Correlates of Crime 111
    Age 111
    Gender 115
    Race 116
    Socioeconomic Status 118

Crime Statistics and the "Dark Figure of Crime" 120

Analyzing the Problem 121
    The Functionalist Approach 122
    The Conflict Approach 123
    The Interactionist Approach 124

And Justice for All? Responding to Offenders and Victims 125

Summary 127

Chapter 5 Inequality and Poverty 129

Did You Know? 129

The Problem 131

Inequality as a Social Problem 133

Explaining Inequality 134
    Biology 135
    Psychology 136
    Culture and Socialization 136
    Social/Structural 136

Analyzing the Problem 138
    The Functionalist Approach 138
    The Conflict Approach 139

Class 140
    Class Counts 140
    Case 5-1 Caste Versus Class 142
    Counting Classes 143
    Class Mobility 144

Race and Ethnicity 144
    Case 5-2 Canada's Vertical Mosaic: Ethnicity as Inequality 146
    Rethinking Ethnic Inequality 149
    Re-imagining Equality 150

Regions and Regionalism 152
    Case 5-3 The Case of Atlantic Canada 153
    Explaining Regional Inequality 155
    Redressing Regional Imbalances 155

The Politics of Poverty 156
    The Scope of Poverty 157
    Fiddling with Figures 158
    The Art of Defining Problems Away 159
    Explaining Poverty Sociologically 160

Education and Schooling: Problems and Challenges 161
    Education in Crisis 163

Summary 169

Chapter 6 Gender 171

Did You Know? 171

The Problem 172

Two Perspectives: The Maximalist and Minimalist 174
    Case 6-1 University of Alberta Prof Responds to Student 175

Analyzing the Problem 176
    The Biological Background 176
    Psychoanalytic Theory: "Anatomy Is Destiny" 179

Feminist Theory and the Study of Gender 182
    Liberal Feminism 183
    Marxist Feminism 185
    Radical Feminism 186
    Socialist Feminism 186
    Cultural Feminism 187
    Inclusive Feminism 187
    Anti-Feminist Feminism 188
    Men's Liberation 189
    The Confusion of the Individual 190

Gender Socialization: Learning to be Unequal 191
    The Family 191
    Formal and Informal Education 192

Gender and Work 194

The Feminization of Poverty 199

Summary 206

Chapter 7 Race, Ethnicity, and Aboriginality 207

Did You Know? 207

The Problem 208
        Canada the Good 209
        The Bad and the Ugly 210
        The "In Between" 212

Race Matters: A Problem in Search of Substance 213
        Race as Social Construct 213
        Race Types and Typologies 214
        Case 7-1 Debunking Race 215

Racial Discrimination: A Social Problem 217
        Types of Racial Discrimination 220
        Solutions to Racism: Anti-Racism 223

Official Multiculturalism: Problem or Solution? 225
        Putting Multiculturalism to the Critical Test 226
        The Good, the Bad, and the Necessary 229

The Quebec Question 230
        Dueling Discourses 230
        The Problem with Federalism: Province or People? 232
        Sovereignty without Secession 235
        A Regrettable Necessity 237

The First Nations 238
        From Problem to Peoples 238
        The Problem with Problems 240
        Policy as Problem 242
        Aboriginal Solutions 243

Summary 247

PART 3 INSTITUTIONAL PROBLEMS 249

Chapter 8 The Family 250

Did You Know? 250

The Problem 251

The Changing Demographics of the Canadian Family 254

Home Sweet Home or the Ties That Bind? 256
        Case 8-1 A History of Control 260

Power within Intimate Relationships 261

Analyzing the Problem: Patriarchy and the Family 264

Functionalist Approach 264
The Feminist Challenge: The Conflict Approach 267
The Evolving Family 268

Canadian Families and Intimate Relationships Today 272
The Husband/Wife Dual-Earner Family 272
The Husband/Wife Single-Provider Family 274
The Single-Parent Family 275
The Common-Law Family 280
The Transitional Family 281
The Blended Family 282

Confronting the Problem 283

Summary 283

Chapter 9 The Media 285

Did You Know? 285

The Problem 286

Analyzing the Problem 289
"Mass" Media 289
The "New" Media 290
Unscrambling the Media 291

Media as Problem: Newscasting 293
What's News? 294
Case 9-1 Media and Fame: Spontaneous Combustion or Lethal Mixture? 295
Bias in Newscasting 300

Media as Problem: Television Programming 304
The Holy Codes 305
Reality Programming? 306
Case 9-2 TV Violence, Violent Society? 307

Media as Problem: Advertising 311
Advertising in Society: "Generating Discontent" 312
Case 9-3 Benetton: The Politics of Images 313
Problems in Advertising 315

Media as (Enlightened) Propaganda 316
Case 9-4 Media and Minorities: Couched in Compromise 318

The Networked Society 323
The Good: Anarchy Rules 324
The Bad: Electronic Alienation 325
The Banal: "Information Is Not Knowledge" 326
The In Between 326
Case 9-5 Globalizing the Internet 327
Towards a New (Cyber)World Order 329

Summary 330

Chapter 10 Work and Workplaces 332

Did You Know? 332

The Problem 333
Transforming Organizations 334
Diversifying the Workplace 335
Rethinking Work 336

From Crisis to Challenge 338
Rethinking Work: Workerless Factories and Virtual Workplaces 341

Humanizing the Workplace 344
Scientific Management: Workplace as Machine 344
Case 10-1 Conveyor Belt Burgers 346
Human Resources: Working in Circles 348
Case 10-2 Community Policing: Humanizing the Service 349

Organizational Change/Workplace Resistance 360
The Challenge of Change 361
Case 10-3 "Unbending Granite" 365

Summary 370

PART 4 GLOBAL PROBLEMS 373

Chapter 11 Globalization and Global Problems 374

Did You Know? 374

The Problem 376

Globalization: Problem or Solution? 378
Perceptions of Globalization 379
Defining Globalization 379
Case 11-1 Multinationals: Engines of Globalization 381

Globalization: Think Locally, Act Globally 383
From State to Market 384
From Local Production to Productive Loop 385
Case 11-2 Free Trade: Bonus or Bogus? 387
Whither Now Canada? Between Free Trade and a Free Society 392

Global Problems 394
Case 11-3 *Bon Appétit*: A Recipe for Bungled Development 396
Overpopulation 397
Urbanization 397
Poverty 398
Ethnic Nationalism and Ethnic Conflict 399
The Environment 400
Case 11-4 The Politics of Environmental Economics: Clayoquot or Clearcut? 402

Foreign Aid and (Under)Development 405
    Underlying Logic 406
    For Whom, for What? 407
    Perils and Pitfalls: "A Trojan Horse" 408
    What Next? 409
Summary 410

References 412
Index 455

Preface

It is sometimes said that with hindsight one becomes acutely aware of what one could or should have done differently. Although common in everyday situations, such feelings may be particularly pronounced for writers of textbooks who review their work when the euphoria of its completion has somewhat abated. However diligent and conscientious the authors have attempted to be, there are always more up-to-date statistics released, intriguing research published, and insightful commentaries located. And, when the absence of such materials are noted, the tendency may be marked for authors to pursue one of several options. They may elect to rail against their publisher, who bristled at projects taking slightly longer than anticipated (a year or two at most . . .) or who had the audacity to dispute the marketability of a 1700-page tome. "Those crass accountant types," it may be claimed, "understand nothing about Art." Alternately, they may wax indignant over heavy-handed copy editors, who recommended that their manuscript would benefit from "light editing" and then proceeded to wield their red pencil in a manner reminiscent of a slasher film. For those authors who share their task with a co-writer, other scenarios are additionally possible, since a collaborative effort, of course, allows each co-author to simply blame the other for any omissions or oversights that become apparent. It was one's co-writer, each may claim, who marred a perfectly splendid product by placing *their* Beefaroni next to the other's caviar. Within this battleplan, the quest for face-saving comfort encourages each author to represent the other as a goon of truly epic proportions; in even less friendly situations, fantasies of committing the perfect murder may be entertained. However, those writers who, like ourselves, have had the misfortune to find themselves bridled with a conscientious editor, an obliging publisher, and a co-author who is valued both as a friend and a scholar are placed in a markedly uncomfortable position. They must patiently gather the best of the new material that becomes available and simply hope for the chance to integrate it with the best of their original product in a subsequent edition of their work. And this is what we have attempted to do in this second edition of *Social Problems in Canada*.

In crafting this text, we have benefited from the many helpful comments of our students, colleagues, and reviewers. In consequence, we are pleased to note that new to this edition is an expansion of topic coverage, including, for example, education, the Quebec question, computer-mediated communication and the networked society, the environment, aging, child abuse, capital punishment, wrongful convictions, the "faint hope clause," and media-inspired "celebrity cults." We have also attempted to update our coverage of topics wherever possible and to add new, provocative examples to illustrate key concepts and ideas.

Once again, we recognize that during the lifetime of this book, certain problems will grow in importance while others will fade from public consciousness. Obviously, any textbook will be more "dated" than the evening newspaper or nightly news. However, we continue to hope that our contribution will fulfil those tasks earlier identified by Ian Robertson (1984) as salient challenges for a text devoted to the sociological study of social problems.

That is,

> specifically, a text should teach the theoretical approaches that provide the essential framework for analysis; it should emphasize the role of human action—particularly that of social movements—in creating and solving social problems; it should demonstrate the complexity and interrelatedness of social problems (for example, the recurrent tendency for an attempted solution in one area to create a new problem elsewhere); and it should instill a sense that they can indeed be solved, although this optimism should be tempered with a realistic awareness of the difficulties involved (vi).

Ultimately, our readers will judge how successfully we have accomplished our task.

ORGANIZATION AND CONTENT

We have produced a book in response to an identified need for a text on social problems confronting Canadian society as it approaches the twenty-first century. In setting out to produce a text both timely and relevant, we begin with the premise that social problems are socially constructed, relative to time and place, and respond to "treatment" in diverse ways. We would also stress that social problems cannot be understood apart from the social and cultural context in which they are located and from which they derive their designation as such.

The text will examine a variety of *conditions* in Canada that are widely perceived as social problems. The scope of our text is purposefully broad: we are concerned with various dimensions of the problematic condition, including antecedent causes, competing definitions, characteristics, proposed "cures," and the consequences of "solutions" previously attempted. The conditions chosen for analysis—from "microproblems" involving interpersonal relations to "macroproblems" with a focus on intergroup dynamics to "megaproblems" linking Canada to the world—may be inescapable in a society undergoing rapid technological change, increased racial diversity, and persistent inequality among gender, racial, regional, and class lines.

The text is simultaneously grounded in the belief that a focus on *processes* is also critical to the discussion of social problems. By directing attention towards how (when, where, and by whom) social problems are socially constructed and maintained, our intention is to suggest the dynamic quality of social problems. The designation of a social problem as a social process is not an "inevitable" consequence no matter how many casualties result from its occurrence. In the past, hunting buffalo to the point of extinction was not conceived to be a "social problem," nor was polluting of the environment recognized to result in disastrous consequences for every aspect of our ecosystem.

We argue that how social conditions become part of the public debate and the ways in which they are subject to competing interpretations, how aggrieved sections attract public attention and capture key resources for mobilization, how definitions themselves undergo revision in response to internal forces and external pressures, and how treatment—however well intended—may generate additional social problems are all crucial to understanding social problems. By directing attention to the processes through which social problems are defined, addressed, appropriated, contested, and "resolved," our intention is to provide students with a framework through which they can extend their investigations into other and future social problems.

The animating logic behind the construction of this book was to recognize that "social problems" are rarely so obliging as to follow the canons, arguments, reflexive logic, and transformations for one sociological perspective. Social problems are often unruly, despite the attempts of parent sociologies to contain them. Accordingly, we have attempted to identify some of the questions raised and answers forwarded within each of the three dominant sociological perspectives on social problems: functionalist, conflict, and interactionist. The production of knowledge on social problems must be recognized as a somewhat chaotic enterprise. Each perspective may raise questions that go unanswered, offer analyses that seem unreadable, and propose a framework that tumbles, like a house of cards, under the theoretical weight of another. On its own, each individual sociological approach to social problems may appear at times to be an unfinished work, offering mere conjecture and oblique solutions. However, when considered alongside of each other, the very eclecticism of the questions these approaches raise and the answers they forward may in itself be valuable.

Although we acknowledge that we each have our own ideas and opinions about the most pressing social problems facing Canada today, we have attempted to highlight the conflicting ways in which social problems—their development, their impact, and strategies for their resolution—have been conceptualized. Our objective is to ultimately foster understanding of the various dimensions of the phenomena under consideration, not to provide a forum for our opinions on a variety of topics of interest to us or to proselytize about the "correct" way in which specific social problems should be viewed.

The text is divided into five sections. Each of the sections contain one or more chapters about a central theme. In Chapter 1, Introduction, we provide an overview of the text, with particular emphasis on the conceptual frameworks for studying social problems from a sociological vantage point. We note the various theories academics and other social commentators have constructed to explain how social problems arise, and we discuss where these theories fit within the dominant sociological paradigms. We also explain the working assumptions that govern our treatment of the different chapter topics.

The second section, Private Troubles vs. Public Issues, focuses on how seemingly private issues may constitute social problems. We direct our attention to the issues of addictions and sexuality. In Chapter 2, Addictions, we note that in the 1990s the term "addiction" is increasingly used to refer to almost every type of personally or socially problematic behaviour. We observe that this trend trivializes the concept of addiction and discuss such topics as the definition of "addiction" and "co-dependency"; the relationship between addiction and crime; the individual, economic, and social costs of addiction; and the rise of the self-help or "recovery" movement. In Chapter 3, Sex and Sexuality, we focus our attention on the issues of the double standard in relation to male and female sexuality, the issues of reproduction (contraception, abortion, and the new reproductive technologies), "safe sex," and coercive sexuality.

The third section, Structural Problems, deals with social structures as sources of social problems. Social problems pertaining to lack of opportunity and social restraints are shown to exist within the structure of society. The structural causes of social problems may be especially evident in capitalist societies such as Canada, with their commitment to class relations and competitive consumerism. Structural problems dealt with include crime, inequality and poverty, gender relations, and race, ethnicity, and aboriginality. In Chapter 4, Crime, we show that the popular stereotypes and media presentations of "crime" and the "criminal" are contradicted by Canadian crime statistics and legal definitions. We discuss the correlates of crime in Canada, such as age, sex, and socioeconomic status, and various interpretations of why these associations exist. Topics of discussion include the fear of crime, young offenders, racism and gender bias in the administration of criminal justice, and the various solutions that have been proposed to win the "war against crime" in Canada. Chapter 5, Inequality and Poverty, focuses on inequality as a social problem that is manifest in matters of social class, race and ethnicity, gender, and geographic region. We explore the social problem of poverty in Canada and analyze the politics involved in defining the term "poverty" itself. Debates over the concept of equality as a set of entitlements (equal opportunity or fair shares) are examined in light of recent developments. As well, we examine the problems and challenges in Canadian education. In Chapter 6, Gender, we argue that our understanding of social problems in relation to gender depends on our understanding of the basis of gender, that is, whether we think of men and women as essentially similar or dissimilar. We highlight a wide range of opinions on this issue, including those that divide feminists and those in the growing men's movement. Topics of discussion include gender socialization, the intersection of work and family roles, gender stratification within the Canadian workplace, and the feminization of poverty. In Chapter 7, Race, Ethnicity, and Aboriginality, we note efforts to deal with the management of race and ethnic relations through official multiculturalism and include discrimination and racism as topics for discussion. We probe the myriad challenges posed to our system of Canadian federalism by those who seek sovereignty for Quebec and examine initiatives by aboriginal peoples to take ownership of the "Indian problem" by decolonizing their relationship with central authorities.

The fourth section, Institutional Problems, examines social problems from an institutional perspective. Institutions, as many sociologists have recognized, provide a fertile breeding ground for social problems because of the disjunction between structure and agency. This is especially the case as the forces of diversity, change, and uncertainty begin to undermine old solutions while redefining new problems. Institutions, in short, are sites of conflict and contradiction, and this alone makes them a subject for serious scrutiny. In this section, the institutional problems within the mass media, family, and work are examined. In Chapter 8, The Family, we show that our concept of the "ideal" form of family always influences how we respond to changes in family forms and intimate relationships. We explore the topics of power and violence within intimate relationships and the evolving families in Canada in the 1990s. Chapter 9, The Media, identifies several social problems inherent in newscasting, advertising, and television programming. Topics for discussion include propaganda, subliminal advertising, the treatment of minorities within the media, and the burgeoning world of the Internet. Chapter 10, Work and Workplaces, examines these institutions within the context of change, diversity, and uncertainty. Topics for discussion include the question of whether organizational problems are generated by the forces of bureaucracy, different styles of human resource management, and various initiatives for managing diversity.

The fifth and final section, Global Problems, looks at the concept of globalization and its impact on Canadian society. By examining issues ranging from the environment to the globalization of production, we direct attention to the "global picture" and Canada's positioning within it. Chapter 11, Globalization and Global Problems, discusses problems of globalization with respect to such issues as overpopulation, pollution and the environment, ethnic conflict, and urbanization. Special care is taken to examine the role and impact of multinational companies in Canada and the world at large. Canada's foreign aid and development programs are analyzed as both a problem and a solution.

Every author of a text on social problems is faced with the same two challenges: how to write a book that will not become too quickly dated, and how to make the topic coverage sufficiently comprehensive. In constructing this book, we have attempted to give attention to a wide variety of social problems but acknowledge that our work, of necessity, must be other than truly exhaustive in its coverage. We recognize that an undergraduate course on social problems is typically taught as a half-term course and that this factor, in itself, places limitations on both instructors and students. Similarly, we appreciate that to address all areas of interest to specific students and/or professors would necessitate an encyclopedia-length—and -priced—volume. We apologize for those omissions that become apparent to our colleagues and students but, at present, cannot amend them.

As our readers will undoubtedly note, many problems that currently exist in Canadian society straddle more than one specific area of our inquiry. For example, although we discuss the feminization of poverty in Chapter 6, Gender, it could arguably be placed in our chapters on social inequality or the family. Similarly, is violence against women best dealt with under the classification of crime? Gender? The family? The mass media? Or under yet another topic heading? In our placement of topics, we have often argued with each other over where a particular discussion would best belong. Therefore, we caution our readers against viewing such placements as sacrosanct or against inferring that we view the problem as properly belonging to only the chapter or section in which it appears. Rather, we stress the linkages of problems in contemporary Canadian society and encourage our readers to think broadly of the ways in which each social problem we discuss intersects with a myriad of others.

INTRODUCTION

We are a society of progress, paradox, inconsistencies, and pathos. As Canadians we can legitimately boast of our role as global pacesetters in the management of race and ethnic relations. We are proud to note that Canada is the first official multicultural society in the world, the first to constitutionally entrench aboriginal rights, and the first in terms of refugee acceptance rates. This last accomplishment was recognized by the United Nations when in 1986 it bestowed the Nansen medal on Canada, the first country ever to receive this prestigious honour. At the same time, we are a society whose past and present forbids complacent self-congratulation. For example, we are a country that holds the dubious distinction of being one of the world's largest mailing centres of hate literature (Sher 1983). Similarly, we stand accused of being a society of "polite racists," and of simply fostering a widespread myth that within our borders, aboriginal rights and human rights generally are respected.

For example, in 1983 the World Council of Churches wrote then Prime Minister Pierre Trudeau, charging that the Alberta provincial government and various multinational oil companies were engaging in action that could result in "genocidal consequences" for the Lubicon Cree. In 1989, after three years of consideration, the United Nations Committee on Human Rights agreed that the Lubicon Lake band could not achieve effective legal or political redress within Canada. Pending a hearing of charges that alleged that Canada had violated the rights of the Lubicon Cree under the International Protocol on Civil and Political Rights, the UN instructed Canada to do no further irreparable damage to the Lubicon's lands or way of life. The Canadian government elected to ignore this instruction, continuing oil company activity and announcing the sale of trees from a massive area of the contested land to a Japanese pulp mill (Goddard 1991). As of 1997, a settlement of the Lubicon Lake band's claim for recognition and settlement, a claim that dates back to the 1930s, had yet to be negotiated.

How are we to understand this inertia of the Canadian government in relation to the Lubicon, and what are we to make of the other contradictions that abound in Canadian society? We like to boast of our status as a democratic society in which justice for all is held to be a fundamental tenet; yet, investigations by government-appointed commissions during the late 1980s and early 1990s revealed a criminal justice system riddled with racism in both its composition and its workings (Ontario 1989, Cawsey 1991, Manitoba 1991). We are a country whose population is more than half female and in which traditionally women have been perceived (by men) to be in need of male protection. Yet, in 1980 when it was reported in the House of Commons that a study commissioned by the Canadian Advisory Council on the Status of Women had found that 1 in 10 Canadian women were the victims of wife abuse, our elected representatives responded with ribald laughter (MacLeod 1980, Wilson 1991). We are a country that champions the ideal of equality yet in which, like interwoven threads, strands of extreme affluence and power exist alongside those of dire poverty and powerlessness.

Despite all this, it seems that Canadians are divided when it comes to assessing the gravity of social problems within our borders. Some feel that, in comparison with our closest neighbour, the United States, there is much more that is admirable than socially problematic in Canadian society. These people usually point to our much lower crime rate (and, in particular, violent crime rate), our system of national health care, and so on.

For others, depicting Canada as "problem-free" is simply inaccurate. These Canadians observe that the three major political forces in Canada—aboriginal, charter groups, and racial/ethnic minorities—continue to engage in a competitive struggle for power and resources that they fear may spell the ruin of Canada as a sovereign and distinct society. They argue that the ongoing conflicts between French- and English-speaking Canada have created a society fraught with ambiguity and hostility. They note that visible minorities continue to experience prejudice and discrimination in employment, education, law enforcement, and housing. They observe that the socioeconomic status of aboriginal people in Canada is an international disgrace—that First Nations peoples often have a standard of living that is only marginally better than that experienced in many Third World countries. They direct attention to the pockets of poverty that coexist with affluence and prosperity, the high unemployment rates in the Atlantic provinces, the flight of industry and capital from Canada to the United States and Mexico, and the alarming numbers of children (one-quarter of Canadian children age 0 to 11) who live in households with an income below Statistics Canada's low-income cut-off line (LICO) (Pictor and Myles 1996). And, they prophesy, things can only get worse. Forecasting the debasement of Canada's natural beauty under an onslaught of acid rain and other forms of pollution, they predict a bomb-shelter lifestyle in the aftermath of ozone-layer depletion. The picture they paint is not very appealing, to say the least.

Mere parsimony may encourage us to select and choose one viewpoint or the other as the more accurate or correct way in which to view Canadian society. However, if we opt for the cheerier picture suggested in the former viewpoint, we cannot simply ignore the concerns enumerated in the latter. Nor can we simply toss our hands in the air, raise our eyes to the stars, and mutter that it really does not matter, that "time" will heal everything. As the late civil rights leader Martin Luther King, Jr. once observed, "Actually time is neutral. It can either be used constructively or destructively."

We believe that Canadians are, above all, a hopeful people, concerned with and committed to the attainment of social justice. We recognize that Canada's diverse composition often precludes consensus on social issues. However, we hope that sociology can contribute not only to an appreciation of the complex processes involved in the identification and resolution of social problems but, as well, to the cultivation of a sense of optimism that solutions are indeed possible.

SOCIAL PROBLEMS: PRIVATE TROUBLES AND PUBLIC ISSUES

Quickly now: provide a list of "social problems." At first the task may seem difficult, but the more you warm to the subject, the easier it becomes. After a while, the difficulty might lie in trying to silence you. However, if most of us are capable of compiling a list of social problems, we would still probably find that, even among our classmates, our designations and justifications for labelling phenomena as such would not be without controversy.

For example, Olmsted's 1988 study of controversial leisure activities noted that in the past, such diverse pastimes as billiards, parachuting, surfing, pinball, theatre, amateur archaeology, horse racing, butterfly collecting, motorcycling, target shooting, and dancing have all been identified as morally disreputable and socially problematic activities. In the 1920s, the tango was considered by many church and right-wing groups to be one of the greatest menaces to North American society. Thus, in Guy Lamphear's 1921 work, *The Modern Dance*, the author cautioned his readers that the average minister "knows the moral lapses and spiritual death are traceable too often to the ballroom, and that modern dance is the prolific source of domestic dissatisfaction, and therefore, is the nursery of the divorce court, and that as a social influence it weakens and destroys the best safeguards of virtue and purity" (Ramsey 1976, 26). In like fashion, the playing of Dungeons & Dragons has been labelled by various fundamentalist Christian sects in the United States and Canada and groups such as BADD (Bothered About Dungeons & Dragons) as "consorting with the Devil" and an "occult activity" that incurs "insidious and diabolical consequences, corrupting naive players who become involved in the game without knowing its dangerous side effects" (Martin and Fine 1991, 107).

More recently, in the summer of 1997, the Canadian tour of the horror or shock-rock group Marilyn Manson—whose members go by the names of famous serial killers, wear garters, ripped corsets, and black make-up, and offer a stage act that is "pretty basic Goth theatre, as tried-and-true as your average horror movie" (Williamson 1997)—became a fire-and-brimstone controversy that led to the group being banned in several cities, including Winnipeg and Calgary. In Calgary, city officials pointedly noted that the band's leader was an unabashed Satan worshipper, that the group produced albums with such titles as *Antichrist Superstar*, sang lyrics such as "I will bury your God in my warm spit," and sold "Kill Your Parents" T-shirts; they emphasized that the cancellation of Manson's concert should not be seen as censorship but as "stopping the damage before it occurs" (KW Record 1997a). In contrast, at various times and in various places, slavery, child labour, and the murder of a woman by her husband have all been defined as lawful and socially acceptable behaviour.

Similarly, racism, sexism, genocide, and myriad forms of inhumanity have flourished and been justified as natural and socially desirable.

Within contemporary Canadian society, the identification of social problems remains subject to ambiguity, confusion, and flux. Is the relative inability of women to walk in public bare-breasted testament to an underlying social problem? For some, the Ontario court ruling that women's breasts were not sexual when exposed in a "natural" setting (e.g., a beach) but were sexual when revealed in an "unnatural" setting (e.g., a shopping mall) was a partial and long overdue victory. For others, the ruling was construed as the height of legal sophistry (is an indoor swimming pool a "natural" or "unnatural" setting?) that, critics charged, would only lead to increased rates of skin cancer, sexual assaults, and traffic accidents.

Is "husband battering" a social problem? For some, the topic of husband abuse is subject to only the most superficial commentary, and may inspire little more than mirth. Indeed, some might offer the disclaimer that it only occurs within the world of comic strip characters. Others have dismissed the incidence of husband abuse as "minuscule" (Pagelow 1984), or argued that attention directed towards the existence of a battered husband syndrome is, in its very framing, a red herring (Small 1985). Thus, for example, for sociologist Walter DeKeseredy (1992, 247), the postulated existence of such a syndrome is thought simply to enable "patriarchal state officials to assert that since wives are as violent as husbands, new transitions houses are not necessary and existing shelters do not need expansion or refurbishing." He argues that researchers who would suggest that women are equally as or more violent than men within intimate relationships are guilty of victim-blaming by failing to contextualize why women use violence (that is, as a method of self-defence), while their findings "provide men with a discourse of legitimation" (1992, 249). In contrast, others have argued that the abuse of husbands is a topic that demands public attention and scrutiny (McNeely and Robinson-Simpson 1987; Steinmetz 1978; Straus and Gelles 1986).

Admittedly, it is highly tempting to respond to this muddle of contradictory visions and opinions by posing the questions, "Who is right?" and "Who is wrong?" However, the answer to both questions, if vexing, is of course, "It depends on one's perspective."

If we may stand accused of stating the obvious, it is evident that problems exist everywhere—from the minor and mundane to the monumental and potentially catastrophic. It is also evident that in judging certain social conditions to be social problems, a definitional process is involved, an active, evaluative, and dynamic component of human action and endeavour. An approach that lays emphasis on "just the facts" is insufficient to understand fully the complexities involved in deciding what is, and is not, considered to be a social problem in contemporary Canadian society.

C. Wright Mills' (1967) classic distinction between "personal troubles" and "public issues" suggests a useful starting point for consideration of what is and is not to be considered a social problem. According to Mills, if an individual is unemployed because of unacceptable work habits, he or she may be said to experience a "personal trouble." If, however, many are out of work, not because of their undesirable work habits but rather because of massive closures in industry due, for example, to a recession, then a "public issue" may be said to exist. In both cases, unemployment was identified; however, depending on its cause, it could variously signify a personal trouble or a public issue, a private trouble or a social problem.

For people who are out of work with little hope of finding employment, it may be of dubious satisfaction for them to note that there are others who are similarly situated or that, according to C. Wright Mills, they are but part of a segment of the population that is disadvantaged by a collectively experienced public issue. However, the distinction is nevertheless important. For Mills, if individualistic explanations can be employed to explain why a given person is unemployed, they are of little utility in understanding high unemployment within a country as a whole. Rather, the ability to recognize that private troubles may, in fact, be better understood as public ills, requires what Mills referred to as *the sociological imagination*—an appreciation of the essential link between the lives of individuals and the broader social, economic, and political forces that surround them. Moreover, a readiness to question the "naturalness" and "inevitability" of social life is what distinguishes sociologists from other theorists who have attempted to understand and respond to social problems.

SOCIAL PROBLEMS: CONDITIONS AND PROCESSES

Many sociologists have attempted to offer a definition of what is or is not a social problem. They have focused on social problems either as empirically observable *conditions that threaten a significant segment of society*, or as *processes of identification and definition* whereby the perspectives of members of society determine what can be called a social problem.

Some of those who subscribe to the former theory define social problems as conditions that affect a significant number of people in a negative manner, yet are amenable to treatment or correction through collective action. For example, Eitzen and Zinn (1992) define social problems as conditions that harm, exploit, exclude, or differentially control certain segments of society or that violate societal norms and values. Contained in this definition is the implicit assumption that, whether or not the "condition" is acknowledged by members of a society to be harmful, there is an objective basis for classifying it as a social problem.

In contrast, other writers have emphasized the *process* involved in the designation of a social problem (Spector and Kitsuse 1987; Best 1989). Thus, for these theorists, the role of cognition is considered to be central to the identification of social problems. A process-oriented approach emphasizes the acts of judging and defining and directs attention to such questions as: "Why and how do individuals begin to question certain activities within society? What mechanisms are brought into play for transforming passive spectatorship into active involvement? Which groups are resistant to changes in the status quo?"

In general, a problem assumes a sociological dimension when it is social in *origin*, social in *definition*, and social in *treatment*. A problem is social in *origin* when the offending condition is the result of human social behaviour. A problem is social in *definition* when it is defined as such by a significant number of people. Accordingly, the social reality must be perceived as contradicting cherished and widely held norms in some fundamental way. A problem is social in *treatment* when its proposed solution resides within the framework of societal practices or institutions. A true social problem must have the potential to be corrected, modified, or controlled by the means of collective action or institutional reform.

To illustrate how social problems can be conceptualized through this approach, let us examine the problem of Fetal Alcohol Syndrome (FAS) or Fetal Alcohol Effect (FAE). Can FAS/FAE be considered a social problem?

A Problem Is Social in Origin When the Offending Condition Is the Result of Human Social Behaviour

It has been established that almost every drug used by a pregnant woman will cross the placenta and enter the circulatory system of the developing baby. Moreover, it has been noted that certain drugs, called *teratogens*, produce malformations in the unborn child even though they may have no harmful effect on the mother. Although other factors, such as malnutrition (Crisis 1986), may be crucial in causing FAS and although only a small proportion of children of drinking mothers are born with this syndrome, the ingestion of alcohol during pregnancy has been identified as heightening the risk of fetal damage.

In Canada, it is estimated that the incidence of "full-blown FAS" is 1 to 2 per 1000 live births, with children exhibiting only FAE in 3 to 5 per 1000 live births (Sandor 1980). Although a major characteristic of children born with FAS is mental retardation, there may be significant differences in the visibility of the condition and the degree of retardation experienced by FAS children. Full-blown FAS affects all body systems, causing neurological problems (for example, seizures, hyperactivity, tremors) and anomalies and malformations of the musculoskeletal structure (spinal fusion, club foot, growth deficiencies), craniofacial formation (microcephaly, a short low-bridged nose, low- set ears, long upper lip), and internal organs (cardiac and kidney defects, problems of the genitals) (Winzer 1993, 58–59). In contrast, children with FAE may show relatively minor developmental defects and behavioural symptoms, such as irritability during infancy and hyperactivity in later childhood. Taken together, FAS and FAE would seem to qualify as a problem that is social in origin because they involve statistically significant numbers of mothers behaving in a way that seriously harms significant numbers of children.

A Problem Is Social in Definition When It Is Defined as Such by a Significant Number of People

Earlier, we noted that the definition of a social condition as a social problem is contingent on public perception of it as such and that the definition of a social problem has varied substantially over history. In the case of FAS, it is noteworthy that opinion on whether alcohol consumption during pregnancy harms the fetus has varied from age to age. In classical times, Aristotle raved against "foolish, drunken, or harebrain women . . . [who] for the most part bring forth children like unto themselves," while Plutarch thought that "one drunkard begets another" (Sandmaier 1992, 28). However, in marked contrast, in colonial America, alcohol was considered a popular cure for "'breeding sickness' . . . and both beer and rum mixed with milk were . . . regularly prescribed for nursing mothers" (Sandmaier 1992, 36).

The varying designations of alcohol use by pregnant women as unacceptable or acceptable, reprehensible or medicinally beneficial, are invaluable for our purpose because they alert us to the fact that *in spite* of the objective misery or suffering that may be caused by a social condition, harmfulness, in and of itself, is not sufficient to render it a social problem.

Rather, our recognition of the problem as a problem is based on information made available to us through immersion in our culture. We are unlikely to have personally conducted experiments to test the impact of alcohol use during pregnancy or to have read the clinical research on which media reports are based. However, if after "many years of research, it is still not known how much alcohol a pregnant woman can safely drink" (Canadian Social

Trends 1997), the results of studies indicating that abuse of alcohol during pregnancy, particularly around conception and during the first trimester, heightens the risk of birth defects, learning problems and other developmental delays, have now been reported widely enough to be regarded as common knowledge. In other words, the medical establishment and the media have cooperated in such a way that they have convinced a significant number of people that FAS should be defined as a social problem.

As evidence of this, Statistics Canada's Longitudinal Survey of Children and Youth (NLSCY) found that, in 1994, the majority of Canadian children (83%) had mothers who reported that they totally abstained from the use of alcohol during pregnancy; only 7 percent of children were born to women who reported using alcohol during their pregnancies (Canadian Social Trends 1997).

A Problem Is Social in Treatment When Its Proposed Solution Resides within the Framework of Societal Practices or Institutions

If one defines the birth of children afflicted with FAS in a fatalistic fashion, viewing such events as preordained either by the will of God or by the child's own "karma," then the existence of FAS children will be defined as other than a social problem. To be regarded as a social problem, the condition must be perceived not only as stemming from a social practice or arrangement that is harmful, but also as a condition that is amenable to social intervention. That is, the socially problematic condition must be considered correctable through the collective

---

CASE 1-1   The War Against Women

While it is surely not beneficial to a fetus for its mother to use drugs or drink heavily, such behaviour cannot be controlled by society, and no society should try to control it. Like men, women in despair, unhappy women, behave in self-destructive ways. A society that was really concerned about this behaviour would address the causes for the hopelessness. Most of the babies harmed by self-destructive maternal actions are part of the underclass that society condemns to death every time it chooses to spend money on weapons rather than social programs. We turn our backs on these babies when we move our families to the suburbs, snatch our children out of public schools, refuse to hire people of color, or simply see them as inferior

beings. We as a society do not care if these babies die—indeed, there are people who wish the poor and people of color would not procreate—yet we punish mothers whose actions acknowledge our indifference. Remember that in each minute that passes, the governments of the world spent $1.3 million of wealth produced by the public (between two-thirds and three-quarters of it by women) on military expenses. That government does not try to help but only to punish poor mothers; that it spends our money on weapons that kill children, not on nourishing them, is another sign of its war against women.

From Marilyn French, *The War Against Women* (New York, 1992), 146–147, by permission of the author and Summit Books.

action of a group of people. Moreover, as Marilyn French (Case 1-1) suggests, the individual can only do so much; the larger responsibility is society's.

APPROACHES TO STUDYING SOCIAL PROBLEMS

Is there one correct way of identifying disconcerting and upsetting conditions in society? Is there only one way of asking—and answering—the questions: "What is the problem? Why does it exist? How is it manifested? When and where did it emerge? Who or what is responsible? What should Canadians do to remedy its ravages?" Fatalists may attempt to sidestep these questions by maintaining that social problems are inevitable and that the situation cannot be remedied. Others may simply deny the existence of the problems. Such people continue to maintain that the Holocaust never occurred, that Blacks were not oppressed under the South African system of apartheid, and that political prisoners in Third World countries are not subject to torture and mysterious disappearances. More commonly, however, theorists show a marked tendency to blame one or more of four sources for society's ills: victims, enemies, institutions, and systems (Elias 1986).

Victim Blaming

In blaming victims, ultimate culpability for their misfortune is seen to rest in individuals or groups themselves. That is, characteristics or qualities possessed by the socially marginal are pointed to as causes of their victimization or oppression. With logic firmly grounded in Social Darwinism and theories of the "survival of the fittest," these theorists suggest that a natural sorting process has occurred, with those of superior stock achieving positions of eminence and affluence in society and others—those without the right stuff—doomed to marginal status. Whether the devalued quality is race, religion, ethnicity, gender, or biological or psychological inadequacies, the focus is typically narrow. However, as Parenti (1978, 24) has observed, "Focusing on the poor and ignoring the system of power, privilege and profit which makes them poor, is a little like blaming the corpse for the murder."

Although theories suggesting, for example, that certain races are inherently more or less intelligent, criminogenic, or moral have faded from popularity, there are still those who would invoke the arguments they contain and argue that social problems exist because we have, within our society, socially problematic or deviance-prone individuals. As an obvious example, one need only consider the platform of such groups as the Ku Klux Klan, the Western Guard, the Heritage Front, and other white supremacist groups. Maintaining themselves to be "pro-white" rather than racist, they suggest that many social problems can be best attributed to the presence of identifiably "different" groups. In consequence, they subscribe to an ideal Canada that seems reflective of George Orwell's *Animal Farm*, that is, a land in which "All animals are equal, but some animals are more equal than others" (1984, chapter 10).

In similar fashion, the current popularity of psychological explanations of troubling social behaviour suggests both the tenacity and continued support given to a "deficient person" approach to social problems. Assuredly, it is always possible to reduce the explanation of human behaviour to mysterious, dark forces that allegedly cause people to act in this or that manner. A common tendency exists today to automatically assume that different behaviour requires a different explanation. The more bizarre the observable difference seems, the more bizarre the underlying causes must be, according to many observers.

To assume automatically that the battering husband is simply a "sadist"or a "psychopath" who acts out his pathology on his "willing" and "deeply disturbed" wife immediately removes the participants from the mainstream of everyday life and excuses their actions. We do not believe that such an automatic assumption is justified. There is more to be observed in such phenomena than simple manifestations of pathology, and it would seem necessary to integrate these phenomena with the broader picture of social life. As Seymour Halleck (1971) has suggested in a discussion of "the politics of symptoms," treatments that focus solely on symptoms rather than on broader social or existential issues are likely to be efficient but unlikely to be effective.

The atrocities of the Holocaust and Canada's refusal of docking rights to ships carrying Jewish refugees may be seen as primary examples of victim blaming in this century. However, since that time, there has been continuing evidence to suggest the inhumanity possible when certain groups are viewed by others as "inferior" in one way or another. The vocabulary of inferiority has, in the past and present, been adopted to justify genocidal programs, involuntary sterilization, and the banishment, segregation, or warehousing of "deficient" persons within prisons and mental hospitals. As simply one example, consider Alberta's Sexual Sterilization Act, passed in 1928 and "inspired by the philosophy of the eugenics movement which believed mental retardation, criminality and much socially unacceptable behaviour (such as prostitution and poverty) were inherited" (Daisley 1996, 7). Daisley (1996, 7) notes that racism was a salient factor in the enactment of this legislation "as many people became concerned about increasing numbers of eastern and southern European immigrants to North America." The Act permitted the provincial government's eugenics board to order sterilization where "procreation by the person under consideration (a) would result in the transmission of any mental disability or deficiency to his progeny, or (b) involves the risk of mental injury either to such person or his progeny." Of the 2844 people sterilized by order of the province's eugenics board, "a disproportionate number were eastern European, Catholic or native" (Daisley 1996, 7). Although Alberta and British Columbia were the only provinces to pass sterilization laws, it is believed that hundreds of such operations were also carried out in Ontario. In Alberta, the Act was only repealed by the government in 1972.

Enemy Blaming

All designations of the "enemy," as well as the "threat" they are seen to pose, suggest a process of social labelling, subjective assessment, and social evaluation. Accordingly, who is viewed as an enemy and what is viewed as threatening reveal dominant ideologies held by a group or a society more generally.

An *ideology* refers to "a pattern of ideas (common-sense knowledge)—both factual and evaluative—which purports to explain and legitimate the social structure and culture of a social group or society and which serves to justify social actions which are in accordance with that pattern of ideas" (Abbott and Wallace 1990, 6). Composed of both taken-for-granted beliefs and common-sense wisdom, the knowledge provided by an ideology serves to shape our ideas about what is "natural," desirable, and unchangeable. Because it is espoused and reproduced by those in society who are in positions of power, a dominant ideology is best situated to portray its ideas *as if* they consist of universal knowledge. Nevertheless, all ideologies are socially produced and offer, at best, a partial and selective view of the social world.

At various times in Canada's history, the idea that certain populations were responsible for Canada's various social problems has enjoyed widespread popular currency. Melvyn Green's 1986 analysis of the early history of Canadian narcotics control has argued that "the public identification of opium smoking with a socially inferior Chinese population in the early part of this century allowed the passage of legislation which at first was deliberately directed to this immigrant culture" (37). Trasov (1962) similarly argues that the "menace" identified and targeted by early law reformers was more obviously concerned with the economic threat posed by Chinese immigrants than the problem of opium addiction, which was "generally regarded as an individual medical misfortune or personal vice, free of severe moral opprobrium" (Green 1986, 25). He suggests that hostility to the use of opium emerged in the context of a labour surplus that followed the completion of railway construction and the diminished intensity of the Gold Rush. Green notes that prior to this point, in the midst of a labour shortage, "the Chinese were regarded as industrious, sober, economical and law abiding individuals. They were highly regarded as domestic servants and gardeners" (25). However, as jobs became scarce and the Chinese were viewed as competitors for the positions that existed, "the earlier friendly feelings toward the Chinese changed to hostility . . . [and] [t]here was a great demand that Chinese immigration be restricted or discontinued" (25).

Despite the datedness of the example used, the enemy blaming approach should not be assumed to be a totally anachronistic approach. One of the continuing attractions of *scapegoating* certain persons or groups as the supposed cause of social problems is that it reduces complexity to simplicity. "Why are our young people doing all these drugs?" For an answer, choose any or all of the following: Because of the Communists, the Chinese opium pusher, the Colombian crack cocaine dealer, the Conservative Party (why not blame them for this, too?). Whatever.

In contemporary Canadian society, the fear of AIDS may be seen to have refurbished *homophobia*, the fear and hatred of homosexuals, and the threat homosexuals are accused of posing for Canadian society. Fear of a disease for which there is no known cure and identification of homosexuals as a high-risk group have prompted suggestions that quarantine and confinement of suspected homosexuals be adopted as possible "solutions" to the "gay plague." Indeed, Lorne Razovsky, a Halifax lawyer, has pointedly noted that quarantine may be legal, despite the provisions of the Canadian Charter of Rights and Freedoms, when those held in quarantine are not "compatible with the interests of society" (Allen et al. 1985, 48). In our society, the label "gay" would surely seem an ironic misnomer; a stigma has been applied to both the actor and the activity.

While there are similarities between victim blaming and enemy blaming, it is important to point out that the enemy is not always a victim, but in some cases may be one who benefits from the problem or who is *perceived* to benefit from the problem. For example, according to VOCAL (Victims of Child Abuse Laws), an international organization dedicated to making it more difficult to prove child abuse charges, child abuse is little more than a colossal hoax. Thus, according to VOCAL's executive director, Graham Jeambey, only 1 to 2 percent of child sexual abuse allegations are truthful. The remainder, it is argued, are largely the result of claims made by quota-conscious child-protection workers in an effort to get large amounts of money—supposedly $40 000 per family—from the coffers of the federal government. Jeambey additionally claims that children are routinely coached to make false allegations, and he blames women, who are "down on males," for the emergence of most false allegations (Vanderbilt 1992, 66).

Institution Blaming

Some have argued that within Canadian society, social problems can best be viewed as attesting to the failure of specific societal institutions. Thus, the inadequacies of, for example, social services, the police, correctional services, human rights agencies and legislation, and so on, may be identified as responsible for the emergence or continuation of certain social problems. Even though the agency or institution targeted may vary, this approach assumes that all we need to do is supplement or modify existing social institutions so that they function efficiently and effectively. Even though on the surface this approach assumes a critical attitude towards social institutions, it can actually be seen as highly supportive of existing social structures.

For example, some critics have suggested that police violence against minorities currently constitutes a pressing social problem in Canada. However, Canadian commissions that have studied this and similar claims over the past 20 years have typically reported that the problem is simply attributable to organizational failures: improper training, inadequate screening measures to combat racism at the recruitment stage, lack of education on such topics as race and ethnic relations, and so on. Rather than locating the existence of racism and discrimination within systemic structures that serve to favour certain groups at the expense of others, the solutions proposed by an "institution-blame approach" advocate a more limited strategy. In consequence, the proposed solution to the problem of police brutality could simply consist of altering certain hiring and advancement procedures within individual police forces through the introduction of such measures as employment equity programs.

Consider, for example, that in 1995 the RCMP voluntarily agreed with the Human Rights Commission to embark on an employment equity program; of 630 RCMP cadets hired during 1995–96, 32 percent were female, 18 percent were aboriginal, 22 percent were other visible minorities, and 33 percent were Caucasian males (Mofina 1996). Moreover, in an attempt to ascertain why female, aboriginal, and other minority members leave the RCMP at a higher rate than Caucasian males, the RCMP's Research Branch Personnel Directorate conducted a survey involving a random sample of 525 officers of all ranks across Canada. Although the RCMP initially attempted to keep the findings of the study confidential, the *Calgary Herald* sought the public release of this study under the federal Access to Information Act—a request initially denied in 1995 and then, after a formal complaint by the *Herald* to the Office of the Information Commission, granted the following year. The findings of this study were disquieting: 60 percent of female officers reported some form of sexual harassment within the force; approximately half (49%) of aboriginal members and 45 percent of visible minorities had seen racist material in RCMP offices; 55 percent of male members felt there were assignments for which women were not suited (particularly emergency response or SWAT teams); and over half (51%) of Caucasian male officers felt that female, aboriginal, and visible minority members "see discrimination where it doesn't exist." Nevertheless, when asked for comment, a spokesperson for the RCMP remarked, "We asked candid questions because we wanted the answers" and emphasized that the study's findings "could result in the force being reshaped."

Thus, there is a paradox to be noted in the dynamics of the institution-blame approach. That is, although specific institutions may face a tarring of both their members and their practices, the legitimacy and credibility of the institution itself may be refurbished or restored. If criticisms are acknowledged and addressed, there is the tacit assumption that the institution is indeed accountable and responsive to the public it serves and capable of self-correction and progress in socially desired and defined ways. There is also the implicit assumption that the underlying structures of society do not themselves require major transformations. In stressing that social problems arise from operational flaws in the workings of discrete social institutions, there is the tacit suggestion that such flaws are intrinsically identifiable and correctable.

Within each of the approaches to social problems discussed so far there exists some common ground. All implicitly assume that social order is maintained by consensus and that the identification of inadequate persons or groups, sinister enemies, or inept institutions is relatively unproblematic. However, for others, social problems are not the fault of inadequate persons, sinister enemies, or the minor and correctable flaws of varied institutions. These critics, moreover, would argue that contemporary societies are not characterized by consensus, but rather by conflict and dissension. "Conflict" in this sense does not necessarily refer to armed rebellion and violence but rather to "both disagreement over values and competition for scarce resources such as power, wealth or privilege" (Robertson 1980, 16). This conflict between competing groups and perspectives is seen as central to the emergence of social problems by those who would favour a system-blaming approach; and it is important to note that, within this perspective, it is the system itself that is criticized.

System Blaming

A system-blaming approach suggests that achieving a just society will not be accomplished if we simply rely on containment methods to "restrain" persons who are identified as "problematic" or through piecemeal changes to social institutions. Rather, theorists who favour this approach stress that the eradication of social problems can only be accomplished through fundamental social, political, and economic change.

Those who favour a system-blame approach have suggested that we focus our attention on such systemic structures as "nationalism and the structure of international relations . . . legal and bureaucratic structures . . . foreign and domestic policy goals . . . international economic dependence, business objectives, and corporate capitalism" (Elias 1986, 212). Similarly, rather than focus exclusively on lawbreakers, we are directed to examine laws themselves because "the law may institutionalize classism, racism, and sexism, and provide fundamental support for corporate capitalism, a system to which many attribute considerable political and economic oppression" (Elias 1986, 212). System-blame theorists insist that we look far beyond the conventional windows of social problems if we wish to resolve them.

For example, if victim-blame theorists explain rape as the result of provocative victim behaviour, radical feminism argues that rape is "normal sexual behaviour in a male-dominated world" (Kaminer 1992, 42). Similarly, if the term "violence against women" may be narrowly conceptualized as the problem of "dysfunctional families" or "dysfunctional, aberrant, violence-prone individuals," "[f]or feminists, all violence is a reflection of unequal power relations between men and women" (see Smith 1989). Thus Dworkin (1974; 1981), in coining the term *gynocide*, refers to "the systematic crippling, raping, and/or killing of women by men . . . the relentless violence perpetrated by the gender class men on the gender class women" (16). For Dworkin, "under patriarchy, gynocide is the ongoing reality of life lived by women" (19). In like manner, Caputi and Russell's (1992) use of the term *femicide* suggests that the murder of women is only fully understandable with reference to the pervasive presence of *misogyny* (the hatred of women) in sexist societies. Accordingly, the term links the killing of women by serial killers, abusive husbands, cultural traditions such as the once-expected and now-banned Hindu ritual of *suttee* (in which a widow throws herself on her husband's funeral pyre), and the abortion of female fetuses following the determination of the sex through amniocentesis. All are seen as evidence of women's oppression under patriarchy, in which violence is the norm rather than a deviation.

It is evident that the term "violence against women" can be defined narrowly or very broadly. Indeed, for some it may even be employed to signify a structural problem of society whose consequences are translated into inequitable treatment within education, the family, the workplace, the law, and politics. Accordingly, employing the term "victim" to describe women's experiences is thought by some to be misleading and inaccurate. That is, for certain groups of feminists, the term "victim" is inappropriate because its gender-neutrality juxtaposes the misfortunes of women with those of men who are victimized by criminal violence (Rock 1992).

It is evident that there are a number of ways of conceptualizing social problems. Our next question is, How can the discipline of sociology assist us in understanding social problems?

SOCIOLOGY AND THE STUDY OF SOCIAL PROBLEMS

All theories of human social behaviour, whether sociological or common-sensical, represent attempts to understand what one observes. However, although sociologists try to be objective about what they study, all theories reflect preconceptions about the reality of our social world, and they influence what we select to examine as problematic. For example, if we accept women's role as primary caregivers of children as natural, biologically impelled, or divinely ordained, we do not ask questions such as "Why don't men look after children?" Similarly, if our theory assumes that all women have a deep, innate maternal instinct, we might conclude that women who decide to forego childbearing and child rearing are deviant or deficient in some fundamental way. Even though sociologists attempt to be reflective, to question taken-for-granted assumptions, and to critically assess what evidence exists to support or challenge the positions they hold, sociology as a discipline is not immune to criticism of bias (see Oakley 1972; 1974; 1981).

From the time of its inception, sociology has been concerned with both the identification and the resolution of social problems. Sociology as a discipline emerged in the aftermath of two great revolutions, the Industrial Revolution and the French Revolution of 1789. As Nisbet (1965, 20) has observed, "[i]n terms of immediacy and massiveness of impact on human thought and values, it is impossible to find revolutions of comparable magnitude anywhere in human history." It is perhaps not surprising that sociology flourished amidst attempts to understand the formidable social changes that were occurring, "to construct a rational society out of the ruins of the traditional one" (Vold and Bernard 1986, 144) and to "mastermind the political course of 'social regeneration'." For these reasons, practical concerns and social utility were the underpinnings and justification of sociology as a discipline; it was to be both useful and analytically potent, providing a basis for both social control and social reform.

We can distinguish three primary approaches to the sociological study of social problems: the functionalist approach, the conflict approach (within which we include feminist theory), and the interactionist approach.

The Functionalist Approach

In their attempts to understand political and economic changes, early sociologists such as Herbert Spencer (1820–1903) found it useful to view societies through an organic analogy. Just as each organ within a living creature is necessary and vital to the functioning of the whole, each part of society—the state, the economy, the family, religion, education—was viewed as interdependently contributing to its survival. Similarly, for Emile Durkheim (1858–1917), it was important to determine what function the existence of any feature of society had on the maintenance of society as a whole. Durkheim considered it pointless to study the parts of systems such as education or the family in isolation; rather, they were to be studied in terms of their interrelationships and contributions to the larger society.

For example, in arguing that crime was "normal," and "a factor in public health, an integral part of all healthy societies" (1966, 67), Durkheim suggested that a latent function of crime was to clarify and reinforce the boundaries of acceptable behaviour, "heighten collective sentiments" of moral imperatives, and integrate the community against the offender. While "excess [an unusually high rate of crime] is undoubtedly morbid in character"—inasmuch as social cohesion is at risk—too little crime is also seen as pathological: "There is no occasion for self-congratulation when the crime rate drops noticeably below the average level, for we may be certain that this apparent progress is associated with some social disorder." That is, Durkheim regarded an exceedingly low crime rate as evidence that the forces of social control had become so strong that social stagnation had resulted. He thought a "normal" degree of crime was necessary to allow, through the challenge it posed, for progressive social change. Thus, something like crime, which at first glance seems to disrupt the structure of society, actually serves a functional role in strengthening it.

In like fashion, the American sociologist Talcott Parsons (1902–1979) argued that under ideal conditions each interrelated part of a society works to maintain the stability of society as a whole. He likened this "law of inertia" to the concept of homeostasis in physiology and argued that society has a natural tendency towards maintaining a state of equilibrium. That is, the structure of society—its *institutions* (law, education, family, etc.), *norms* (formal and informal rules governing behaviour), and *roles* (behaviour expected of an individual occupying a particular social status in society such as "mother," "doctor," "teacher," "prime minister")—should, in an interdependent manner, function to preserve the integrity and stability of the whole. However, under certain conditions such as rapid social change, *strain,* a disturbance to the expectation systems of individuals within society, or *social disorganization,* an upset to the normal equilibrium that a society maintains, could occur.

This approach suggests that social problems emerge when one or more parts of the system become *dysfunctional* in some way and no longer positively contribute to the smooth functioning of the system as a whole. And, because society is considered to be an interdependently functioning system, changes in one aspect will, in domino fashion, have negative effects on other aspects of that system. Accordingly, to resolve social problems, efforts must be made to mold society into a once again stable, well-organized system. This approach is termed the *structural functionalist* approach or, more simply, *functionalism.*

A functionalist approach to the study of social problems directs us to ask what the functions of an institution, practice, or social arrangement are—both *manifest* (intended) and *latent* (unintended). For example, the manifest functions of a jail system are to provide punishment and a form of retribution. However, a latent function of a jail system is to provide food, shelter, clothing, and a routine structure of life to the point where the jail system becomes attractive to some people. Thus, for example, while a homeless person may feel that life on the streets is tolerable during the spring through fall seasons, the comfort of a warm jail cell during winter months may be considered a sufficient inducement to commit an offence that will result in a short period of incarceration. Moreover, some people may become *institutionalized* to the degree that they cannot function without the support available from the prison system. In such ways, the institution in essence becomes the source of its own problems and the progenitor of its future clientele.

A functionalist approach also encourages us to examine both the intended and recognized functions as well as the unintended and unrecognized functions of a particular set of social arrangements and to ask these questions.

1) What is the normal functioning state of equilibrium within a particular society at a particular point of time?

2) How do existing conditions differ from that equilibrium state?

3) Does the condition under consideration contribute to or detract from the stability of existing social structures?

Functionalism has long dominated the study of social problems but has increasingly been challenged. Feminist sociologists have identified functionalism as a primary example of mainstream or "malestream" sociological theories that "underpin and justify the subordination and exploitation of women by men" and that are "at best, sex-blind and at worst sexist" (Abbott and Wallace 1990, 5–6). Thus, they argue that functionalist approaches favour the reproduction of *androcentric* or male-defined knowledge as "universal knowledge" while marginalizing the views and experiences of those who are not in a position of power. For example, slavery as a social practice was not experienced or viewed similarly by those who kept slaves and those who were enslaved. Moreover, because of functionalism's focus on social stability, critics have charged that it contains an inherent conservatism, an implicit and uncritical nostalgia over how society was structured in the past, and a tendency to see change as dysfunctional and unwelcome.

The Conflict Approach

While functionalist theorists assume a consensus of norms and values at the core of society, conflict theorists presume that society is shaped by conflict among competing interest groups. Accordingly, the challenge posed by conflict and Marxist theorists to discussions of the causes of social problems is substantial. Unlike consensus theories, which assume that society is characterized by shared values, beliefs, and like-minded members, conflict theories rest on the presupposition that society itself must be changed and that conflict is therefore inevitable.

For example, Sellin (1938) suggests that different cultures establish different *conduct norms* or rules requiring that their members act in a specified way in certain circumstances. If these members live within homogeneous, self-enclosed groups, conduct norms may be expressed in laws that are formal embodiments of consensually defined values and interests. However, as a society becomes more complex, there is an increased likelihood of contradiction between the conduct norms of the various groups that compose it. A type of *cultural conflict* is said to exist within a single society in which disparate *subcultures* or smaller groups have emerged, each characterized by its own unique set of conduct norms.

According to George Vold (1958), society is a collection of disparate groups, or sub-cultures in which there are conflicting interests, purposes, and loyalties. Conflict intensi-fies as each group attempts to seek or protect its own interests and gain access to power. Those groups that lack power, legitimacy, and authority in society are more likely to find their actions viewed as deviant or socially problematic than those who are able to negotiate from a position of strength.

Marxist Theories

All theories based on the writings of Karl Marx (1818–1883) share the common assumption that the principal conflict in society is between two polarized groups: capitalists, the own-ers of the means of production who become richer and more powerful as their numbers de-crease, and proletarians, who sell their labour for a wage and who become poorer and poorer as their numbers increase. Marx referred to this trend towards polarization as the "contra-diction" inherent within capitalism. He prophesied that this polarization would inevitably re-sult in a revolutionary restructuring of the social relations of production.

A discussion of the various forms of Marxism is beyond our scope here. In general, Marxists tend to focus on the ways in which existing ideologies and corresponding cultural practices exist to support and reinforce relations of inequality between members of the dif-ferent social classes. They refer to this power of the privileged classes as *hegemony*. Regardless of whether the external identifying differences between groups appear to be those of race or gender, the key element, according to Marxists, is the underlying element of social class. Therefore, Marxists share the assumption that the root cause of social prob-lems rests within the system of capitalism.

Feminist Theories

Just as Marxist theories presuppose a class structure and class dominance, feminist theories presuppose the existence of institutions and ideologies that justify the oppression of women. Although feminism is not, as we will see in Chapter 6, Gender, a unified movement with a monolithic theory, all feminists would agree that women have been subordinated by men in society, and that it is necessary to develop strategies by which they may be liberated.

In summary, the conflict approach directs attention to the relative *power* or disparate abilities of certain groups to control the behaviour of others in society, and directs us to ask "who benefits?" from the persistence of social problems (Robertson 1980, 16).

The Interactionist Approach

Sociologists working in the interactionist tradition emphasize that through interaction, peo-ple develop definitions or "social constructions" for the people, behaviour, and events around them. For interactionists, *deviance* refers to "any behaviour that violates important social norms and consequently is negatively valued by large numbers of people" (Robertson 1980, 17). The term is not meant to convey a moral judgment about the wrongfulness of the act or the reputability of the actor; rather, it simply recognizes that the act does not con-form to or follow the norms of the dominant culture.

In the 1950s, Howard Becker argued that things we consider deviant or socially problematic are best conceptualized as by-products of power relations among people in society. It is Becker's contention that "social groups create deviance by making the rules whose infraction constitutes deviance, and by applying those rules to particular people and labelling them as outsiders" (1973, 9). According to this approach, termed the *labelling* perspective, "deviance is simply any form of behaviour that people so label." That is, "[d]eviance is not a quality of the act a person commits, but rather a consequence of the application by others of rules and sanctions to an offender" (Becker 1963, 9). For this reason, labelling theory has been called "relativistic in the extreme" (Gibbs 1966, 10) "since nothing is intrinsically deviant, anything could be called deviant and nothing has to be" (Plummer 1979, 96). Nevertheless, in departing from approaches that would restrict analysis to taken-for-granted categories of deviant types and stressing the elasticity and variability of what may be regarded as deviant, the labelling perspective directs attention to the processes involved in both rule-making and the application of rules. As such, labelling theory serves the purpose of challenging status quo definitions of what is and is not socially problematic.

According to Plummer (1979, 88), the labelling perspective centres attention on four primary questions:

1) What are the *characteristics* of labels, their variations and forms?

2) What are the *sources* of labels, both societally and personally?

3) How, and under what *conditions*, do labels get applied?

4) What are the *consequences* of labelling?

The history of sociologists' attempts to understand social problems is itself illustrative of the numerous perspectives through which social problems can be filtered. But rather than showing a linear and cumulative development of theory, this history reveals a somewhat fitful enterprise. Each perspective on social problems offers a discrete intellectual discourse that has inherited little from its predecessors and has bequeathed little to its heirs. Although presenting them chronologically may suggest an accumulation of knowledge in which ideas, once championed, are eventually discarded as less useful or adequate than others, what emerges may be more accurately described as the product of historical succession. It is open to debate whether later theories are more—or less—useful than those earlier championed. Similarly, to suggest that there is but one perspective through which contemporary sociologists view social problems would be little less than mischievous. Indeed, if our readers also read other sociological texts, they might find it jarring to note the extent to which sociologists are themselves divided in their approaches to social problems. Nevertheless, it would be premature to assume that each perspective is irreconcilable with all others or that the offering of differing perspectives—which begin with different assumptions, ask different questions, and focus on different aspects of social reality—is disadvantageous and to be deplored. We would discourage the student from asking or worrying about which perspective is "right." Here, we take a very pragmatic approach and simply use the theory that works best to enhance our understanding of any particular social problem.

THE NATURAL HISTORY OF SOCIAL PROBLEMS

Social problems are not static realities that appear full-blown, persist over a certain period of time without much adjustment, and then vanish once their shelf-life has expired. Rather, they are perceived as possessing a "history" in the sense that they reflect movement through stages of:

1) definition,

2) mobilization,

3) politicization,

4) reaction and response,

5) treatment, and

6) impact.

Definition

A social problem emerges when people become aware of a condition that disturbs them and perceive that a gap exists between the ideals of their society and the social reality that confronts them. This primary stage within the history of a social problem stresses that its definition entails an interpretive and evaluative assessment—a judgment shared by many people that something is undesirable.

Although such behaviours as wife battering, child abuse, racism, and sexism have existed for centuries, it is only relatively recently that they have been defined as social problems. For example, under English Common Law, the "rule of thumb" allowed a man to beat his wife with a rod no thicker than his thumb; until 1983, a man was, by law, considered incapable of raping his wife; until 1967, racism was formally enshrined within Canada's Immigration Act in its listing of "non-preferred" countries for applicants seeking immigration into Canada. Not only were such acts not defined as social problems, those disadvantaged by them were seen as "culturally legitimate victims" (Weis and Borges 1973).

In various ways and to varying degrees, our current definitions of certain phenomena as social problems remain somewhat contradictory and ambiguous. Thus, although child abuse is now widely recognized to be a social problem, Canadians are nevertheless equivocal as to what is considered to be abusive. For example, a Decima poll reported that one in three Canadian parents admitted to slapping or spanking their children and that parents who had children under the age of six were twice as likely to use physical punishment as parents of older children (Conway 1990, 82). Is this evidence of child abuse? The answer is, yet again, less clear than we may suppose: it might or might not be. Section 43 of the Canadian Criminal Code specifically allows parents, guardians, schoolteachers, or those acting in place of parents, to use a "reasonable degree of force by way of discipline or correction" on a child in their charge. Unlike such countries as Austria, Cyprus, Denmark, Finland, Italy, Norway, and Sweden where the use of corporal punishment in the home or school is against the law, Canadian law specifically allows for the corporal punishment of children and recent court rulings have deemed punishment that results in temporary marks on the skin of a child or discolouration lasting for several days to be "reasonable." For example, in a case in which a Manitoba stepfather, during an argument over sunflower seeds, had kicked his stepson downstairs and pulled a clump of hair out of the child's head, a Canadian judge commented that the punishment imposed was "mild, indeed, compared to the *discipline* I received in my home" [emphasis added]; in New Brunswick, the actions of a teacher who directed karate blows, including ones to the faces of four teenage boys, were deemed acceptable by a second Canadian judge who remarked that the behaviour "would instill respect in the students"; in B.C., a teacher was acquitted of assault "even though he had hit a 13-year-old male student in the head with a hammer" (Reform Watch 1997). Accordingly, while some might argue that corporal punishment is in and of itself "abusive," others might blithely invoke the adage of "spare the rod and spoil the child."

Moreover, even when the use of corporal punishment is judged to be other than reasonable, Canadians would still seem equivocal about what should be done about it. In a Gallup poll, 14 percent of those surveyed reported "*personal* awareness of a *serious* instance of physical abuse of children by a parent." However, 37 percent of these people took no action whatsoever to intervene (Conway 1990, 83). Similarly, although a publicity campaign initiated by the Department of Health has promoted what they term constructive, non-violent alternatives to corporal punishment, and the Institute for the Prevention of Child Abuse has called for the repeal of Section 43, attitudes towards children as the property of parents as well as religious prescription of harsh child rearing practices may suggest that corporal punishment is not only acceptable but desirable. For example, research conducted by Grasmick, Burskil and Kimpel (1991) on Protestant fundamentalist groups observed that within such groups there was a pervasive belief that corporal punishment was a useful and appropriate tool for the socialization of children and that their views on abortion and sex before marriage were more open or flexible than were their views on the use of corporal punishment. Obviously, while we would seem generally to agree that child abuse is unacceptable, we are less than precise in our definition of abuse or in delineating what measures must be pursued in order to combat it.

Mobilization

In an effort to transform "private troubles" into social problems, a dedicated core of people must mobilize affected persons and others concerned with the problem. Aggrieved sectors must marshall resources, galvanize support, mobilize membership, create conviction, and attract attention. To ensure widespread dissemination of one's cause both to the general public and to government agencies, it is critical to procure widespread media coverage. To transform a group issue into a social problem, the aggrieved parties must be able to convince a significant number of people or a number of significant people of the need for collective action.

For example, following the murder of their son by serial killer Clifford Olson, Gary and Sharon Rappoport directed their energies towards alerting Canadians to what they perceived as a need for changes in Canadian criminal law and the administration of criminal justice. In time, their efforts resulted in the formation of the group Victims of Violence, a national lobby group that devotes itself to victim-centred aims. In like fashion, the mother of murder-victim Nina de Villiers helped create CAVEAT (Citizens Against Violence Everywhere Advocating its Termination), another Canadian victims-rights advocacy group. In each case, the horrific nature of the crime itself ensured widespread media coverage and therefore was focal in directing attention to the perceived need for changes in the Canadian justice system.

Politicization

Although many social problems have existed for a long time, discussion of their existence was muted. Spector and Kitsuse (1977) have suggested that to understand social problems, we must recognize the process of "claims-making" as important. It is their contention that social problems emerge as "the activities of individuals or groups making assertions of grievances and claims with respect to some putative conditions" (75). Best (1989, xvi) notes that until the 1970s, when the contemporary feminist movement encouraged women to "make the personal political," the problems of wife battering, sexual harassment, pay equity, and gender stratification in the workplace were largely ignored. In suggesting that these issues should be regarded as other than private troubles, "[f]eminists began bringing these issues before the public; they held demonstrations, gave press conferences, wrote books and articles, and lobbied government officials." In doing so, they made terms such as sexism, violence against women, job segmentation, and the feminization of poverty part of the common language, thus helping to shape and frame further discussions of these topics.

Reaction and Response

It is evident that some conditions identified as social problems are less successful at achieving widespread acceptance than others. Clearly, many social problems evolve into contested sites involving a struggle among competing groups as each one tries to impose its own definition of reality as the most sagacious, well-informed, or socially desirable. A process-oriented approach such as ours promotes investigation of why some groups, but not others, are able to mobilize attention and support for their demands. As well, it focuses attention on how other sectors may attack the claims made by those who would identify certain conditions as socially problematic.

Treatment

Identifying a condition as socially problematic—be it sexism, racism, the depletion of the ozone layer, or the vivisection of animals—seems automatically to invite recommendations for its immediate and complete eradication. However, the solutions that end up being implemented are rarely so swift and simple. This is largely because in a democratic society all such treatment plans are negotiated between opposing parties. The negotiation process can seem painfully slow and the solution, in the end, may leave no one party happy with the result. As an example, one need only consider the diametrically opposed solutions to the problem of street prostitution in Canada offered by various interest groups. As Carrington and Moyer (1991, 3) observe, "Municipal politicians, police, and community groups viewed the phenomenon of street prostitution primarily as a social control problem, and pressed for strengthened laws; whereas women's groups, gay rights, and civil liberties organizations viewed it primarily as a social problem, requiring socio-economic solutions rather than criminal justice control measures." None of these groups, it would seem, viewed the 1972 introduction of the "soliciting" offence into the Criminal Code as a truly satisfactory "solution."

CASE 1-2 Animal Rights as Collective Reform

For at least the last 20 years, philosophers, ethicists, and journalists have argued that animals should have legal rights (Singer 1976, Reagan 1983), exposed animal abuse in biomedical research (Ruesch 1985), and written guidelines for the ethical treatment of animals (Besch 1985). In these works, "animal rights" emerges as a philosophy of formal, moral prescriptions. Historians inform us that the animal rights movement began in England during the nineteenth century when urban Victorians changed their views of animals from beasts of burden to nostalgic symbols of a less complicated rural existence (Sperling 1988). Today, as a result of growing activism and collective protest, people everywhere have come to rethink their relationship with the animal world.

Animal rights activists claim that it is necessary for them to direct attention to cruelty against animals simply because the animals are incapable of doing so themselves. The very designation of the group as being engaged in an animal "liberation" movement would seem important. By referring to liberation, the movement symbolically allies itself with, and draws strength from, the more established civil rights movement. That is, this one word invokes a precedent for the behaviour of animal rights activists, no matter how radical, and conceptually forges a link with a group that is now accepted and respected by mainstream society. Moreover, for animal rights activists, "cruelty to animals" is seen to encompass far more than a denunciation of individual acts of deliberate or accidental cruelty. It is broadly viewed as symptomatic of contemporary society,

part of the spirit of the times, which is characterized by greed, consumerism, materialism, and elitism. Within this framework, the institutions identified by animal rights activists as problematic—scientific bodies, factory farms, fur retailers—are seen to embody and perpetuate these social ills.

Is the wearing of fur a social problem? For animal rights activists the answer is yes, and they have mounted successful campaigns to dramatize the plight of fur-bearing animals and the brutality of trapping and hunting methods. In their opposition to *species-ism* (the objectification of animals as qualitatively different from humans so as to justify their exploitation), this movement has effectively eliminated Canada's seal industry and come close to eliminating the demand for fur coats. Activists have engaged in raids, vandalism, and such flamboyant gestures as hurling eggs and spraying blood-coloured paint at celebrities who wear fur coats. Activists have also become more sophisticated in politicizing animal rights through filing courtroom litigation, lobbying for changes to legislation, attending shareholder meetings, and drafting educational programs for primary and high school students. Their success is evident not only in an increased public awareness of the issues involved but also in their demonstrated ability to modify government policy in Canada and in various European countries.

Those who depend on the fur trade as their primary source of livelihood, however, denounce animal rights activists as hypocritical sentimentalists. For many

> **CASE 1-2**   **Animal Rights as Collective Reform (continued)**
>
> aboriginal peoples, hunting and trapping not only provide a means of support for themselves and their families, but also have a cultural and spiritual significance.
>
> As sociologists we are less than qualified to act as judges, assessing the relative merits of each submission and rendering a verdict, or as fortune-tellers predicting the most probable outcome of events. However, we can focus our attention on questions of conditions and processes within not just the designated solution itself but also the debates that surround it.

Impact

The implementation of policies and programs designed to redress social problems is a necessary but insufficient condition to ensure the eradication of these problems. In certain cases, initial intervening efforts may cause the problem to be solved and to seem to disappear. In other cases, inadequacies in official responses may ensure the survival of the problem in a modified form or, alternatively, create entirely new problems.

An enduring "problems-solutions" conundrum is that some peoples' solutions to a particular social problem frequently become other peoples' problems. Since this is so, it is obvious that a linkage of problems exists within a modern society such as Canada's. To the extent that this linkage becomes apparent to members of the society, including social scientists, solutions may become tempered or even ultimately voided by all or some of the population. The solution to the problem of cruelty to animals is, in part, to ban hunting and trapping of all animals. This solution in turn creates a problem for aboriginal peoples, who subsequently face a loss of livelihood, greater unemployment, and further reliance on social assistance. In a complex industrial society, problems do not exist in isolation.

It is worth noting that often the aggrieved group will be unhappy with the formal solution to the problem it helped to identify. Consequently, the process outlined above may itself be capable of infinite resurrections as discontented parties are again mobilized, an agenda formulated, and negotiations resumed.

WORKING ASSUMPTIONS

A sociology of social problems is guided by a number of key assumptions that furnish a certain style and substance to the subject matter and impart a degree of coherence to the organization and content of this text.

A Sociological Framework

A sociology of social problems cannot proceed without the acceptance of core sociological assumptions (Eitzen and Zinn 1992). First, sociologists acknowledge the existence of social forces that account for patterns of stability and consensus as well as conflict and change. These forces are not only real and powerful in shaping human behaviour, but also are amenable to scrutiny and analysis by sociologists. Second, individuals as social actors are seen as the by-product of their environment. This does not mean that individuals are excused from all responsibility for their actions; however, it does mean that society cannot be simply envisaged as the unproblematic backcloth against which "pathology" is discussed. Third, sociologists believe that discussions of the causes, consequences, and solutions of social problems cannot be divorced from social organization and intergroup dynamics. This puts an emphasis on a more critical approach to the study of society.

Interplay of Actor and Structure

Sociologists are, by definition, interested in the study of society, with particular emphasis on the social determinants of behaviour. At the core of this orientation is an awareness that these determinants, which originate in the structures of society, are just as compelling in motivating an individual's behaviour as psychological and spiritual determinants, and that they create just as many problems.

Social Problems and Power

Consideration of the distribution of power is central in understanding the origins, consequences, and proposed solutions to problem conditions. Those with power and wealth possess the resources and resourcefulness to define situations as problematic, as well as to advance a line of treatment. They determine the problems for discussion and debate, what will come to political attention and what will not, and the type of solutions deemed to be appropriate (Eitzen and Zinn 1992).

Social Problems as Contested

Social problems are not a clearly defined category with unanimous agreement over their causes, consequences, or solutions. They are not only constructed, they are also contested. Differences in interpretation reflect the diverse interests and experiences of people in society, as well as a desire to promote competing interests and opposing agendas.

The Normalcy of Social Problems

In a field strewn with fallacies and so-called common-sense wisdom, few misconceptions are more dangerous than a belief that all social problems are intrinsically evil. Social problems are not necessarily the handiwork of corrupt people who deliberately explode into wanton acts of destruction. Many social problems stem from the logical and inevitable consequences of normal behaviour and traditional values. They may also spring from well-meaning actions that are rooted in miscalculation or incorrect assumptions. Even conformity, when blindly adhered to, can pose as much of a problem as disobedience or defiance (Janis 1972). The same values that induce prosocial behaviour (consumerism, competition, and individualism) can also be considered antisocial when taken to an illogical extreme. When employed as a short cut to achieve widely accepted goals, cutthroat competition may lead to material affluence, yet also induce personal stress, social dislocations, and environmental destruction.

Social Problems as Moral Order

Any discussion of social problems implies a set of tacit assumptions about right and wrong. This, in turn, suggests that such a discussion can only be understood when that which is regarded as "unproblematic" is made explicit. Put simply, references to social problems are rooted in a vision of an ideal state of affairs; when reality is compared to this ideal, it is usually judged to be lacking. Understanding that there is always a norm is critical: the ideal state of affairs sharpens an understanding of the contours of the social problem. It can also point to solutions that are relatively consistent with the definition, nature, and scope of the social problem.

The Problem-Solution-Problem Conundrum

As earlier noted, an emphasis on the interconnectedness of problems and solutions is essential to an understanding of social problems in contemporary Canadian society. Like the Hydra in Greek mythology, social problems tend to be many-headed. For example, while Canadian society in the 1990s has become more sexually liberated than in former decades, some would argue that the consequences (increased rates of teenage pregnancies, illegitimacy, abortion, and sexually transmitted diseases) are more problematic than liberating.

Policy Dimensions

Social problems are inextricably linked with policy since policies are formulated, implemented, and modified in response to public demands and minority claims. Accordingly, this text focuses partly on the interventionist strategies and social actions taken by those with the power and resources to address recognized social problems.

The Problem of Bias

Most sociological theories, both past and present, have suffered charges of bias. Becker (1971) has distinguished two forms of bias that are of specific concern to sociological writings:

1) when writers present as statements of fact findings or arguments that are actually incorrect or misrepresented, and

2) when writers present their results in ways that would appear to favour one party or another in a controversy.

He suggests that "we cannot avoid being subjected to the charge of bias in the second sense," but maintains that until sociologists are able to grasp all sides of a situation, good objective work may still be done.

Evolving Discourses

The type of social problems that are selected for discussion and debate can vary enormously over time. Similarly, the way in which sociologists have framed their discussions of social problems has itself been subject to competing definitions. If traditionally social problems have been framed using such terms as "pathology" and "dysfunction," the proliferation of social problems in Canada need not necessarily be viewed as a sign of decay or disintegration. The apparent ubiquity of phenomena designated as socially problematic may be, instead, interpreted as a healthy indicator of progressive change. If we live in a society seemingly riddled with social problems, we have also, over the last several years, enlarged the parameters of justice, equality, and fairness.

Perhaps the concept of the social problem is overdue for conceptual refurbishing. Rather than view shortcomings in Canada as social problems per se, perhaps we should reconceptualize them as "issues" and "challenges" intrinsic to a liberal, democratic, and capitalist society that is complex, diverse, and changing. Perhaps we should view the contradictions and disjunctions that we are witness to as the price we pay for a society in which an older system of rules, roles, and relationships is reluctantly conceding ground to a newer, more equitable one. Perhaps our awareness of the number of social problems, coupled with a growing willingness to address and resolve them, is in itself a hopeful sign.

PRIVATE TROUBLES VS. PUBLIC ISSUES

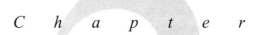

ADDICTIONS

DID YOU KNOW?

- For leaders of the Adult Child and co-dependency movement, such as Anne Wilson Schaef and John Bradshaw, almost all of us (over 95%) can be considered addicts of one sort or another.

- For every 100 000 male and female smokers now age 15, the following deaths will occur before they reach the age of 70: 1200 will die in car accidents, 900 will commit suicide, 130 will be murdered, and 70 will die of AIDS. Only 10 will die as a result of illicit drug use. Tobacco-related diseases will kill 18 000 of these children before the age of 70, 8 times the combined total of premature deaths due to car accidents, suicide, murder, AIDS, and drug abuse.

- In Canada, about one in five deaths during the early 1990s were attributable to smoking— a fact that makes smoking the single most important cause of preventable illness, disability, and premature death in this country.

- In 1990 Alcoholics Anonymous claimed a worldwide membership of 1.8 million people and 87 696 groups.

- In 1992 an estimated 1600 Canadians lost their lives in alcohol-related motor vehicle accidents; among those drivers killed, almost half (48%) had been drinking.

- An RJR Macdonald cigarette company poll indicated that 97 000 more young Canadians were smoking at the end of 1996 than before the federal government cut cigarette taxes in 1994.

THE PROBLEM

Although addiction has long been recognized to be a social problem, when we try to define the term today, we find it has been diluted in popular usage to the point of meaninglessness. For example, in the late 1980s one popular women's magazine was devoted to the topic of "Addictions: The surprising dependencies of independent women." The magazine cover announced that the discussion would include such addictions as "the man-junkie factor" and "compulsive shopping." The author of the article noted that among the thousands of respondents who had completed the magazine's questionnaire, the term "addiction" was employed in a somewhat elastic way. "Women said they felt addicted to walking, running, yoga, exercise, cleaning, sleeping, work, daily routines, 'keeping busy,' shopping, credit cards, religion, nail biting, doodling, and the phone, among other things . . . One woman felt addicted to her cat . . . [a]nother woman said she 'mainlined' books" (Gelder 1987, 45). When the term is employed in this manner, there can be little doubt that almost everyone in Canada can be said to be suffering from some sort of addiction, that is, to be debilitated by a craving so strong that it results in personal behaviour that is socially problematic.

Many sociologists, however, have elected to retain the earlier, more delimited focus of addiction and restrict their discussion to the problems posed by drugs and alcohol. Whether the term is used to refer to a finite or seemingly infinite list of social behaviours, it connotes behaviour that is reckless, personally debilitating, and socially injurious. Giddens (1992, 71) defines an addiction as "a prepatterned habit that is compulsively engaged in, withdrawal from which generates an unmanageable anxiety," and he stresses that "[a]ddictions are compulsive, but are not minor rituals; they colour large areas of an individual's life." The addict is described as being overcome by passions, impotent to resist them, and powerless in their wake. Addiction to a large extent becomes the secular equivalent of demonic possession, but with this difference: that the addict is portrayed as simultaneously sinner and sinned against, victim and criminal, the problem and the patient. As Szasz (1992, 45) wryly observes, only in our society "can people drink, smoke, and use drugs to their hearts' content; claim to be suffering from alcoholism, tobacco dependence, and drug addiction; demand treatment from the state and damages from the companies that sold them the substances they craved; and enjoy the approval of a society eager to authenticate their excuses as the valid complaints of victim-patients, and their expectations as the rightful demand for "health care rights'."

Estimates of the pervasiveness of addictions have varied considerably, but some recent survey results demonstrate that addiction to drugs and alcohol is not as widespread in Canada as the mass media would have us believe. For example, using data collected by the National Alcohol and Other Drugs Survey (NADS) conducted by Health and Welfare Canada in 1989, Eliany (1991) notes that although some degree of underreporting may exist, only "a small minority of Canadians use illicit drugs, and an even smaller proportion use them regularly." Cannabis (marijuana, hashish, and hashish oil) was the most widely used illicit drug in Canada, with 6.5 percent of survey respondents age 15 and over identified as current users (that is, they identified themselves as having used this drug at least once in the year before the survey). Of these people, less than one-quarter (22%) reported weekly use. In 1989, Eliany notes, merely "1.4 percent of people aged 15 and over were current users of cocaine or crack, and fewer than half of one percent reported using LSD, speed, or heroin." In Canada, persons living in British Columbia were most likely to report using illicit substances. More recently, the Health Promotion Survey (1990), the 1993 General Social Survey (GSS) and the Canadian Alcohol and Drug Survey (1994) found that the proportion of Canadians age 15 and over who reported use of LSD, speed, or heroin remained low (ranging from 0.3 to 1.1%). Similarly, cocaine use was only reported by a small percentage of Canadians in these surveys (ranging from 0.3 to 0.7%). These surveys also note that although cannabis remained the "drug of choice" for most Canadians, the proportion reporting its use ranged from a low of 4.2 percent in the GSS to a high of 7.4 percent in the Canadian Alcohol and Drug Survey (1994). Within surveys conducted in the 1990s, men and women showed comparable percentage increases, although the ratio of male to female users reported was roughly 2:1. Thus, while the Health Promotion Survey (1990) reported that 7 percent of males age 15 and over reported cannabis use in the past year, only 3 percent of Canadian women reported cannabis use. The comparable figures reported in the GSS (1993) were 5.9 percent versus 2.6 percent and in the Canadian Alcohol and Drug Survey (1994) were 10.1 percent versus 5.1 percent (CCSA/ARIF 1997).

Although most Canadians partake of alcohol from time to time, since the late 1970s there has been a trend towards moderation: "[a] smaller proportion of people are drinking, those who do drink are consuming less, and many have stopped drinking" (Eliany 1991, 20). Although Canadians in 1993 were less likely to report that they had never had a drink than in 1978 (12% versus 8%) and there has been little variation in the average amount of alcohol consumed by current drinkers (4 drinks a week in 1993 versus 5 drinks in 1989), there were some encouraging signs. For instance, although in 1978 82 percent of Canadians age 15 and over reported having had at least one alcoholic drink in the previous year, in 1989 this figure had decreased to 78 percent (Eliany 1991) and in 1993 it had decreased further to 74 percent (Canadian Social Trends 1995). Moreover, according to the GSS (1993), the proportion of Canadians who used to drink but had stopped rose from 3 percent in 1978 to 18 percent in 1993 (Canadian Social Trends 1995). Heavy drinking has also become less common; although the 1989 National Alcohol and Other Drug Survey reported that in 1989 over half (51%) of Canadians had consumed 5 or more drinks on at least one occasion that year (Eliany 1991), in 1993 the respective figure was 46 percent (Canadian Social Trends 1995). In 1993, frequent heavy drinking was more common among Canadian men and women with only some postsecondary education and among those with lower incomes (Canadian Social Trends 1995).

In 1993, young Canadians age 20 to 24 were the group most likely to have consumed alcohol. While 85 percent of this age group reported some alcohol consumption in that year, the proportion dropped for successive age groups (82% of those age 25 to 34 and 55% for those age 65 and over). For young people age 15 to 19, many of whom are below Canada's legal drinking age, approximately 6 out of 10 (65%) reported that they had consumed alcohol in 1993. Canadians age 20 to 24 were those most likely to drink heavily, and to do so more frequently than individuals in other age groups; "in 1993, 69% of current drinkers aged 20 to 24 and 66 percent of current drinkers aged 15 to 19 reported drinking 5 or more drinks on at least one occasion." In comparison, only 15 percent of current drinkers age 65 or over were heavy drinkers. Similarly, while the number of heavy drinking occasions ranged from 14 to 17 for heavy drinkers in other age groups, Canadians age 20 to 24 drank heavily on an average of 19 occasions in 1993 (Canadian Social Trends 1995). While men in all other age groups are more likely to consume alcohol than women, among Canadians age 15 to 19, a larger proportion of women (69%) than men (64%) drank in 1993.

Eliany (1992, 12) notes that despite the pervasive media imagery of Canadian youths hooked on drugs and school corridors infested with teenage junkies, the majority of Canadian youths do not use illicit drugs. According to Health and Welfare's Alcohol and Other Drug Use by Canadian Youth Survey, only 16 percent of young Canadians had ever tried illicit drugs on at least one occasion—a reported decrease over the past decade. Table 2-1, based on provincewide surveys of Ontario students conducted from 1981 to 1995, suggests that after a relatively steady decline in the percentage of students reporting that they had used selected drugs on at least one occasion during the prior year, increases in drug experimentation occurred, most markedly in relation to cannabis, LSD, and other hallucinogens. More recently, based on the results of their 1997 survey, the Addictions Research Foundation reported that, after a spike in the early 1990s, drug use among 12- to 17-year-olds had stabilized and that about a third of all students surveyed had reported no use of any drug, including alcohol and tobacco. They reported that over-all drug use had declined since the late '70s and early '80s. About one-quarter of the 3,990 students surveyed reported using marijuana in the previous year (up from approximately 23 percent in 1995 but down from a reported 32 percent in 1979). Fewer Ontario students were using heroin, crack or PCP. However, there were increases in the use of such hallucinogens as mescaline and psilocybin (magic mushrooms) with OAC (Ontario Academic Credit) students showing an increase in use from 7 percent in 1995 to 13 percent in 1997. These drugs, along with ecstasy, are closely associated with both the dance culture and "retro" revival of the late 1990s. Moreover, the survey found greater

TABLE 2-1	Percentage of Students Reporting Drug Use at Least Once During the Prior Year, Ontario							
Type of Drug	1981	1983	1985	1987	1989	1991	1993	1995
Cannabis	29.9%	23.7%	21.2%	15.9%	14.1%	11.7%	12.7%	22.7%
Glue	2.3	3.2	2.0	2.4	1.9	1.1	1.6	2.4
Other solvents	3.2	4.1	2.7	3.7	3.1	1.6	2.3	2.9
Barbiturates[1]	12.5	11.0	9.0	7.8	7.8	4.4	5.6	4.8
Barbiturates[2]	8.1	6.0	4.4	3.3	2.2	2.2	3.0	2.7
Heroin	1.5	1.6	1.5	1.4	1.2	1.0	1.2	2.0
Speed	3.0	3.9	3.1	3.1	2.5	1.8	2.0	4.6
Stimulants[1]	6.1	5.2	4.3	4.3	3.3	2.6	4.0	4.1
Stimulants[2]	12.1	15.4	11.8	7.9	6.5	4.0	5.4	6.3
Tranquillizers[1]	7.5	6.5	4.7	4.9	3.1	2.9	2.2	1.8
Tranquillizers[2]	4.9	5.0	3.3	3.0	2.4	1.6	1.1	1.6
LSD	10.2	8.6	7.4	5.9	5.9	5.2	6.9	9.2
Other Hallucinogens	4.7	6.0	4.8	4.5	4.3	3.3	3.1	7.6
Cocaine	4.8	4.1	4.5	3.8	2.7	1.6	1.5	2.4
PCP	2.5	2.0	1.7	1.3	1.1	0.5	0.6	1.7

[1]Prescription
[2]Non-prescription

Note: Based on a provincewide survey of approximately 3270 Ontario students in 1981; 4737 in 1983; 4154 in 1985; 4267 in 1987; 3915 in 1989; 3945 in 1991; 3571 in 1993; and 3870 in 1995 in Grades 7, 9, 11, and 13.

Source: Adlaf, E.M., F.J. Ivis, R.G. Smart, and G.W. Walsh, *The Ontario Student Drug Use Survey: 1997–1995* (Toronto: Addiction Research Foundation, 1995).

acceptance of drugs, with fewer students believing regular marijuana use poses a great risk (Chamberlain 1997).

From a sociological point of view, theorists have long been fascinated by the question of why particular societies view certain substances and activities as problematic while other substances or patterns of consumption are considered unproblematic. For example, until relatively recently, it was significantly easier to obtain alcohol in the Yukon Territory than in any of Canada's provinces. Until 1979 one could legally stroll down the main street carrying an alcoholic drink, until 1985 drinking while driving a car or truck was not illegal, and until 1986 liquor could be purchased 24 hours a day through off-licensed establishments. In consequence, it is perhaps not surprising that the Yukon Territory used to have the highest proportion of current drinkers in Canada or that since the introduction of legislative changes, drinking behaviour has changed. According to the 1990 Yukon Alcohol and Drug Survey, the proportion of adult men and women in the Yukon who reported drinking in that year (78 and 76% respectively) was about the same as the national average (78%) (Canadian Social Trends 1995).

Almost all human societies exhibit some form of drug use, with the exceptions of communities that are bound by religious conviction to abstinence or those who live in an area in which there is an absence of drug-yielding plants (Robertson 1980). However, the specific drugs that are viewed as legitimate or illegitimate may vary enormously over time and place. For example, prior to the enactment of the Opium Act in Canada in 1908, the consumption of opium was legal and its manufacture, distribution, or purchase regarded as innocuous acts. In marked contrast, following the enactment of the Narcotic Control Act in 1961, the specified maximum penalty for trafficking in narcotics was life in prison with a minimum sentence imposed, in the case of importing or exporting narcotics, of seven years. As Solomon and Green (1988) have noted, only those convicted of murder or treason were subject to more severe sentences.

In contemporary times, the use of anabolic steroids in sports has been denounced as deviant, unethical, and dangerous. However, as Nuwer (1990, 25) has noted, during the 1950s the perception of steroids as "wonder drugs that could fatten cattle quickly . . . [that were] thought to be a long-awaited cure to cancer . . . [and were] given to sick and malnourished people to make them bigger and better" encouraged the Soviets to ask—or order—"their male and female athletes to take straight testosterone as part of the conditioning process to prepare for the 1956 Olympic Games." It was arguably not until 1988 when Canada's Ben Johnson lost his gold medal at the Seoul Olympics (for taking a performance-enhancing drug) that many Canadians became aware of the abusive aspects of this type of drug. But even now, public opinion polls suggest that Canadian society is equivocal as to whether steroid use should be considered as serious as the use of such street drugs as marijuana, cocaine, and amphetamines (Nuwer 1990, 23).

Our equivocal responses to the identification of steroids as dangerous suggests yet another area of interest for sociologists, that is, the social reactions to various forms of addictions. Why are certain types of behaviour or patterns of consumption viewed as socially problematic and others not? How does the status of individuals (that is, whether they are rich or poor, socially prominent or obscure) affect the likelihood of their conduct or patterns of consumption being viewed as legitimate or criminal? In our society, the social response to the issue of addiction is greatly influenced by the institutions of medicine and the law. In the end, the designation of certain addictions and not others as social problems may hinge on what these two institutions determine to be the economic costs to Canadian society.

THE COSTS OF ADDICTIONS

Addiction in Canada is perceived to be a social problem whether it is narrowly defined with reference to the social costs and consequences of drug and alcohol use or expanded to include a broad inventory of postulated addictions. In particular, three themes may be seen as motivating the "war" against addictions: the connection of addiction to crime, the economic costs to society of addictions, and the risk posed by addictions to personal and social well-being.

The Crime Connection

It is common for the social problem of addictions to be discussed with reference to organized crime and other forms of criminal activity. For example, speaking at the third Health Futures Conference in Ontario in 1989, Ken Black (1991, 11), who headed up a provincial task force on anti-drug strategy and later became the minister in charge of its implementation, emphasized the "serious problem" of illegal drug use in Canadian society and its connection to various forms of criminal activity. He noted that "[t]he illegal drug trade is the biggest single drug trade in the province of Ontario," that "75 percent of the street crime and the crimes against property in [Ontario] . . . are directly related to the illegal drug trade," that "a good deal of the prostitution that occurs in our major centres is either directly or indirectly linked to the use of drugs," and that "a lot of the family violence, the sexual abuse and many other social problems also have some very clear linkages to illegal drugs" (11). Not least of all, he commented, "you and I as taxpayers spent . . . another $9 to $10 billion in the cost of extra law enforcement, extra health care, loss of time from work and loss of productivity." It is evident that the social problem of drug addiction is seen by some to be wide ranging in its effects and to stem principally from consumption of various illegal drugs, not from legal drugs such as alcohol and tobacco.

Although media reports have tended to focus on such substances as crack cocaine and heroin, there are literally hundreds of psychoactive drugs that are either illegal or controlled in Canada in the 1990s. Some, like cocaine and amphetamines, are "uppers" that act as *stimulants* of the central nervous system and provide an increased energy level. Others, such as heroin, morphine, and barbiturates, are "downers" that act as *depressants* to slow down or desensitize the central nervous system, encourage sleep, reduce pain, and alleviate anxiety. A third type of illegal drug is *hallucinogens* or *psychedelics* and includes such drugs as marijuana and LSD. These drugs temporarily alter the user's consciousness or perception of his or her surroundings. A fourth category is *dissociative anesthetics* and includes such drugs as PCP (angel dust), which was originally used as a tranquilizer on large animals and causes schizophrenic-type separations from reality for extended time periods.

The RCMP Approach

According to the RCMP National Drug Intelligence Estimate 1992, heroin and cocaine were widely available in the urban centres of Vancouver, Toronto, and Montreal in 1991, and, as measured by seizures and arrests, the use of these illegal substances seemed to be increasing rather than decreasing. For instance, more than 99 kilograms of heroin were seized by federal officials in 1991, a 60 percent increase over the amount seized in 1990. As well, arrests for heroin-related offences climbed by 15 percent.

The RCMP report takes issue with statistics that suggest fewer Canadians are using drugs, principally because its authors doubt that heavier users would participate in surveys. For example, it notes that "[a] young person of high school age who is a serious cocaine user is likely to drop out of school and thus become unreachable by conventional survey methods" (18). Citing the 1989 Street Youth Drug Survey, it reports that up to 64 percent of the homeless young people in Toronto surveyed reported use of cocaine during the previous year. The RCMP report goes on to point out that the abuse and availability of crack, formerly associated only with the larger metropolitan centres in Canada, "is spreading from its urban stronghold into outlying communities" (19) such as Prince George, British Columbia; Yarmouth, Nova Scotia; and Regina, Saskatchewan (where the first known seizure of crack occurred in 1991). It states that "[t]he violent crime rate has risen in the inner city neighbourhoods and housing projects where the crack trade has taken roots" (19).

The report also refers to the increased availability and abuse of chemical drugs such as methamphetamine, barbiturates, and LSD. But far and away, the illicit drugs of choice for Canadians in 1996 continued to be cannabis-based products such as marijuana and hashish. In 1996, the RCMP alone laid cannabis-related charges against 8435 persons; of this figure, 5316 were charged with simple possession, 1747 were charged with trafficking or possession for the purpose of trafficking, 355 were charged with importation, and 1017 were charged with cultivation (unpublished statistics provided to the authors courtesy of the RCMP Intelligence Directorate). In addition, Canadian-related cannabis seizures during 1994 resulted in the diversion of 43 194 kilograms of marijuana, hashish, and hashish oil from Canadian consumers.

For the compilers of the RCMP report and for many other Canadians, it is evident that a strong link exists between addictions and crime. One need only consider the number of laws and programs that have been enacted over the past several years to realize that the government feels it enjoys popular support for targeting traffickers and users of illegal drugs with heavy fines and sentences. In 1991, The Proceeds of Crime Act was passed to penalize those involved in laundering drug profits, and there have been a number of amendments to the Criminal Code, the Narcotic Control Act, and the Food and Drug Act that have targeted the possession and laundering of proceeds from drug crime. The RCMP's Anti-Drug Profiteering Program seized money and assets of $21 262 287 in 1996 alone.

For many Canadians then, there is at least a tacit perception that illegal drugs are responsible for the most grievous social consequences or demonstrate the most toxic pharmacological effects. This is one major approach to the problem of addiction in Canada, and we may term it, for the sake of argument, the RCMP approach. Nevertheless, as Boyd (1991, 136) has noted, "Legal and illegal drugs cannot be neatly classified . . . in terms of their potential for inflicting individual and social harm." Many of the most dangerous drugs may be legal or legally available, or their "illegality" may depend on their mode of distribution or possession. Consider, for example, over-the-counter drugs such as Aspirin, ipecac, diuretics, and laxatives. Each of these can be abused and cause physiological harm. The ingestion of any purgative or laxative, for instance, may be abused by someone suffering from bulimia and result in disturbed electrolyte levels, damage to the liver and the heart, and even death. However, the government does not control such products. The person who buys these products is not a "criminal" but merely a "customer;" the seller is considered a "merchant," not a "pusher."

Similarly, some drugs may be legally used by a person who is considered an adult for the purposes of their consumption under Canadian law, as is the case with alcohol and tobacco.

Also, a patient who possesses a prescription for the use of a controlled drug, such as Valium, Librium, or Ritalin, is not considered a criminal. There is no criminal penalty in Canada for simple possession of amphetamines, even though the effects of amphetamines are arguably more potent and more toxic than some illegal drugs such as marijuana and cocaine (Boyd 1991).

It is also worth noting that the consumption of an illegal drug may be legal in some cases if the consumer is an addict who uses the drug as part of a treatment program. For example, methadone hydrochloride is routinely used as a substitute for heroin in clinics in Canada, the United States, and England. This is justified by the claim that methadone not only satisfies the heroin addict's craving for an opiate without incurring the disabling side-effects of heroin, but that it also blocks the "high" produced by heroin and in this way reduces the likelihood that addicts will return to using heroin. A methadone fix, therefore, is seen as a "necessary evil" rather than as the replacement of one addiction with another.

The Turn-the-Tables Approach

In a second major approach to the addiction problem, some have suggested the need for Canadians to move away from the crime-fighting view of addictions and recognize that Canada's most significant problem with addictive behaviour actually centres on legal drugs, specifically alcohol and tobacco. We may term this the turn-the-tables approach. Theorists who subscribe to it maintain that our current villains of choice—illicit drugs such as cannabis, cocaine, and heroin—and our customary depiction of the problem as stemming from gangsters, organized crime, and the South American cocaine cartels misinforms the Canadian public about the reality of drug abuse in Canada and what should be done to combat it.

Thus, for Solomon and Constantine (1991, 81) "Canada's alcohol and drug policies represent a curious blend of good intentions, myths, hypocrisy, ad hoc crisis management, and political posturing. We are targeting the wrong drugs, employing the wrong mechanisms to combat them, and giving dangerously misleading messages to young people." They suggest that although "Canadian narcotics enforcement probably consumes well over $100 million a year" it has largely functioned to saddle "over 700,000 people—the overwhelming majority of whom are in their late teens or early 20s—with permanent criminal records for possessing relatively small quantities of cannabis. Despite the rhetoric of focusing on 'hard' drugs and large-scale traffickers, 80 percent of all federal drug charges in the past decade have been for cannabis possession" (82). Similarly, they argue that "there is little evidence to suggest that the criminal justice system is capable of reducing the influx, distribution or consumption of illicit drugs in Canada" (83), and that the American experience suggests that drug enforcement is a "bottomless pit" that will absorb our money and resources with little real practical benefit. The real drug problem, they suggest, is alcohol and tobacco abuse, and the ravages are enormous.

It should not be surprising, they suggest, that "most young people smoke or drink underage, that millions of Canadians are addicted to tobacco or have serious drinking problems, that drinking and driving is endemic, and that tens of thousands of Canadians die, are injured or become sick each year as a result of alcohol and tobacco use" (86). Encouraged to view the use of alcohol and tobacco as a sign of maturity, a social lubricant, and a symbol of the "good life," young people may easily fall from simple use of these drugs into patterns of severe abuse. Clark (1996, 3) points out that for many young people, "smoking is an 'initiation' . . . a way to appear more mature, to cope with stress, to bond with a group of peers or to display independence from their families." According to the 1994 Youth Smoking Survey, approximately 15 percent of young Canadians age 10 to 19 were current smokers (i.e., "has smoked 100 or more cigarettes in his/her lifetime and has smoked in the 40 days preceding the survey"), an additional 7 percent were beginning to smoke ("has smoked between 1 and 99 cigarettes in his/her lifetime and has smoked in the 30 days preceding the survey"), and 12 percent were past experimenters ("has smoked between 1 and 99 cigarettes in his/her lifetime, but has not smoked in the 30 days preceding the survey"); according to the 1994 Smoking in Canada Survey, among Canadians who had ever smoked, 84 percent began before reaching the age of 20. While no difference was found in the percentage of boys and girls who smoked, boys were more likely to be heavy smokers; boys who smoked daily consumed an average of 13.2 cigarettes versus an average of 11.5 among girls (Clark 1996, 3).

Pollay (1997) observes that tobacco companies such as Imperial Tobacco Ltd. and R.J. Reynolds-Macdonald have conducted dozens of research studies in their attempt to identify the risks and rationalizations of pre-teens and teens when they begin to smoke. In turn, they have used these findings to make their advertisements and products specifically appealing to the young. Export A, for example, was recognized to have a "special appeal for young adolescents . . . because it provides them with an instant badge of masculinity, appeals to their rebellious nature and establishes their position amongst their peers." Accordingly, the image of Export A smokers cultivated was of a "breed of men who are masculine, independent, adventurous and possess the qualities of natural leadership . . . Women are attracted to these men because of their youthful virility, independence and spirit of adventure" (in Pollay 1997, 10).

Clark (1996, 6) observes that while "there are many influences on youth smoking behaviour . . . some appear to be more powerful than others." For example, controlling for age and parental smoking behaviour, "friends are the most important predictor of a young person's smoking behaviour," with teenagers whose friends smoked 16 times more likely to smoke than those whose friends did not. The presence of nonparental smokers in the home was also significant; while having at least one parent in the home who smoked increased the likelihood that a young person would smoke by 40 percent, young Canadians exposed to nonparental smokers in the home were approximately four times more likely to be current smokers. In addition, school and work programs that teach the risks associated with smoking and policies that restrict or ban smoking entirely must be recognized as significant. For example, while 20 percent of teenagers at schools that had restricted areas for smoking were current smokers, only 13 percent of young people who attended schools that banned smoking entirely smoked. Similarly, about one in four young or current smokers (23%) employed in a workplace that had a partial or total ban on smoking reported that the restriction had prompted them to reduce or quit smoking altogether (Clark 1996, 6).

In 1992, Ralph Nader et al. (1992, 87) observed that "Canada leads the countries of the world . . . with its push to kick the tobacco habit." They noted that in 1972 Canadian companies had voluntarily withdrawn from the use of TV and radio to advertise tobacco. Moreover, Air Canada's 1986 announcement that it would offer smokeless flights between three Canadian cities made it the first major North American airline to do so. On October 1987, and in accordance with government regulations, smoking within federal government offices was restricted to designated smoking areas; on January 1, 1989, smoking was banned outright within all federal workplaces. The February 1988 Olympic games, held in Calgary, were also reputedly the "world's first tobacco-free Olympics" (Nader 1992, 88), with smoking banned in the athletes' villages, at all events, and in vehicles transporting the athletes to and from competition sites. The Canadian federal government also instituted a national anti-smoking campaign that has as its explicit goal to usher in a "new generation of non-smokers" by the year 2000. Its target audience is young Canadians and includes "a smoking-prevention program for pre-adolescents, an eight-part public relations kit to guide local and provincial prevention efforts, and a newsletter highlighting anti-smoking initiatives by governments and health organizations" (88). It has also developed a $33.5 million "tobacco diversification program" that compensates tobacco growers who elect to leave the industry.

On April 30, 1987, Bill C-51, the Tobacco Products Control Act, was introduced by Canada's Health and Welfare Minister Jake Epp. This law sought to "ban or restrict all tobacco advertising, promotion and brand sponsorship in Canada" (Nader 1992, 88). Despite a multimillion dollar lobbying campaign by tobacco manufacturers, Bill C-51 was passed in the House of Commons and came into effect on January 1, 1989. As a result, the advertising of tobacco was banned in newspapers and magazines, on billboards and transit posters, and through point-of-sale ads. Corporate sponsors were additionally prohibited from using any depictions of cigarettes or emblems depicted on cigarette packages at events. Some tobacco companies have been crafty, however. As Nader (1992, 89) has reported, "many tobacco companies have set up new corporations with the cigarette brand name as the corporate name and with similar emblems as the corporate logo, and have used these corporations to sponsor events." In 1993, Health Minister Benoit Bouchard introduced the Sale of Tobacco Young Person's Act, which increased the legal age for the purchase of cigarettes from 16 to 18, placed restrictions on the location of vending machines that sell cigarettes, and imposed fines of up to $50 000 for the sale of tobacco to minors. In Canada, all cigarette packages now carry health warnings that occupy approximately one-quarter of the front and back of the package. The messages they convey are stark and pointed: Cigarettes are addictive; Cigarettes cause strokes and heart disease; Cigarettes cause cancer; Tobacco smoke can harm your children.

Charlotte Schoenborn (1993) also observes that Canada's participation in the World Health Organization's "Health for All by the Year 2000" initiative, national anti-smoking campaigns that have publicized the hazards of smoking, introduction of higher insurance premiums for smokers, and increasing number of non-smoking public areas and workplaces have all discouraged Canadians from smoking and led to a decline in the rates of tobacco use.

However, noting that smoking among Canadian teens since 1979 has been inversely related to the price of cigarettes, some anticipated that Ottawa's 1994 decision to cut federal taxes on cigarettes would encourage at least some Canadians to start or to resume smoking— a prediction that, unfortunately, seems to have been proven correct. Leiss (1997) notes that although the prevalence of youth smoking fell by almost 25 percent between 1985 and 1990, by 1994 it had rebounded to its 1985 levels, "an outcome that most observers would attribute to the price reduction stemming from tax changes" (7). In 1994, in an attempt to reduce cigarette smuggling, the federal government decreased tobacco taxes dramatically, an action that was followed by several provincial governments. The Survey on Smoking in Canada, conducted by Statistics Canada on behalf of Health Canada, measured changes in smoking behaviour among respondents age 15 and over following the tax reduction in early 1994 and four times between May 1994 and February 1995. The survey reported that 5 percent of 15- to 19-year-olds increased their level of smoking because of the price decreases and 19 percent of those within this age group began smoking because of the reduced cost of doing so (Clark 1996, 5). Similarly, cigarette company polls indicate that 97 000 more young Canadians were smoking at the end of 1996 than before the federal government cut cigarette taxes in 1994. It would seem that price is the key determinant in selling cigarettes, regardless of what goes on billboards or race cars. A poll conducted by Thompson Lightstone and Co. reported that the percentage of young adults age 19 to 24 who smoke rose to 32.3 percent in December 1996, up from 28.3 percent in 1994. This 4 percent increase represents 97 000 smokers. It was also estimated that underage smokers accounted for an additional 3 percent of the industry's sales (KW Record 1997b). However, Hamilton et al. (1997, 18) argue that raising taxes on cigarettes only results in increased hardship for low-income smokers and "leave[s] low-income persons who continue to smoke with less to spend on food, clothing and other necessities."

It should be evident that discussion of our "drug problem" need not be narrowly restricted to those drugs that are illegal or distributed by members of "posses" or organized crime. In addition, it should be noted that Black's suggestion that "a lot of the family violence, the sexual abuse . . . have very clear linkages to illegal drugs" would seem overly bold and somewhat misleading. Certainly not all illegal drugs result in evidence of aggressive behaviour; marijuana users, for example, are noted more for their passivity than aggressiveness. Also, Robertson (1980, 434) notes that "LSD and other hallucinogenic drugs . . . have little or no relationship to violent or criminal behaviour." Research has, however, demonstrated a very high correlation between alcohol and violent crime (Janson 1989; Toch and Adams 1989) and violent behaviour that does not lead to criminal charges. Fedorowycz (1994) reports that of the 600 homicide incidents reported to police during 1993, over half of the suspects were known to have consumed alcohol and/or other drugs at the time of the offence. Koenig (1996, 6) emphasizes that "[o]f those using substances, two-thirds had used alcohol alone, while one-quarter had used alcohol in combination with other drugs; fewer than 1 in 10 had taken other drugs without alcohol." Based on research on a representative sample of Canadian penitentiary inmates, Hodgins and Cote (1990) report that among inmates who had never suffered from a major mental disorder, 67 percent had formerly or currently met the medical criteria for alcohol abuse and/or dependence. Johnson (1996, 11) additionally reports that according to Statistics Canada's 1993 Violence Against Women Survey, "women who are married to or living with heavy drinkers are five times more likely to be assaulted by their partners than are women who live with nondrinkers." She notes that half of all wife batterers were drinking at the time they assaulted their wives and that women who suffered very serious abuse were approximately twice as likely to report that their spouse had been drinking at the time. According to this survey, "the more a man drinks the greater the likelihood that drinking will be involved in incidents of assault against his wife." (11).

The Economic Costs of Addictions

As we have seen, whether the problem of addictions is thought to stem from the consumption of legal or illegal drugs, both approaches to the problem direct attention to the economic losses to society caused by addiction. Thus, in stressing the extreme profitability of pandering to those who desire illicit drugs, Black (1991) reminds us that the profits enjoyed by drug sellers generate a huge, untaxed income that goes unrecorded as part of Canada's gross national product. Similarly, Stamler (1992, 408) has written of "[t]he cost of corruption for bribes and payoffs, and contracts for intimidation and extortion . . . [a]s the only price crime organizations will pay directly to maintain their base of control. In this environment the consumer will pay the highest price for the lowest-quality product that the market will bear, and the crime organization will achieve its prime objective, which is to accumulate profit and power." According to the National Drug Intelligence Estimate 1992, although an illicit opium dealer may pay merely $2900 to $3900 for a kilogram of injectable heroin from a laboratory in Southeast Asia's Golden Triangle, this same kilogram sells for $120 000 to $200 000 on the Canadian market. To fully appreciate the enormity of the potential profits available, one must also consider that a capsule dosage unit of heroin may contain, after being cut and diluted, only 5 or 6 percent pure heroin (Stamler 1992, 408).

Moreover, some have argued that the social and economic costs of drug abuse extend beyond the parameters of the criminal justice system. There are, for instance, the hidden costs of drug abuse—"lost productivity, accidental injuries and death, disruption to families and communities, and public expenditure needed to maintain health care and social systems" (Johnson 1988, 8). Consider that in 1992, Canada's medical system was confronted with no fewer than 5369 cases of alcoholic psychoses, 12 316 cases of alcohol dependence syndrome, 3129 cases of alcohol polyneuropathy, 2053 cases of alcoholic gastritis, 5220 cases of alcoholic liver cyrrhosis, 634 cases of alcoholic toxicity, 1207 cases of drug psychoses, 1151 cases of cocaine dependence/abuse, 1151 cases of cannabis dependence/abuse, 192 cases of cocaine poisoning, 439 cases of psychotropic poisoning, and 222 cases of alcoholic cardiomyopathy (Addiction Research Foundation 1997).

The Effect on Personal Well-Being

Many authors have written of the personal costs of addictions. Solomon and Constantine (1991) point out that drinking and driving is the largest single criminal cause of death in Canada, that almost half of all traffic fatalities involve someone who has been drinking, and that between a quarter and a third of all drivers injured in accidents are impaired. In 1992 it was estimated that over 1600 Canadians lost their lives in alcohol-related motor vehicle accidents; among Canadian drivers killed on the roads, almost half (48%) had been drinking. While the rate of Canadians charged with impaired driving has declined significantly (from 588 of every 100 000 Canadians in 1978 to 322 in 1993), in 1993 almost 6 out 10 (59%) of Canada's 197 800 reported traffic offences involved impaired driving. Consider, as well, that in 1993 13 percent of current Canadian drinkers reported that they had driven within one hour of drinking two or more drinks, with men three times as likely as women to do so. Those most likely to drink and drive were Canadians age 25 to 34 and those in the highest income group (Canadian Social Trends 1995).

Despite the fact that smoking is identified as "the greatest single preventable cause of disease, disability and death in Canada," rates of smoking in Canada remain "intolerably high." Citing data presented by the National Clearinghouse on Tobacco and Health, Solomon and Constantine (1991) observe that:

> For every 100,000 male and female smokers now age 15, the following deaths will occur before they reach the age of 70: 1,200 will die in car accidents, 900 will commit suicide, 130 will be murdered, and 70 will die of AIDS. Only 10 will die as a result of illicit drug use. Tobacco-related diseases will kill 18,000 of these children before 70, 8 times the combined total of premature deaths due to car accidents, suicide, murder, AIDS and drug abuse (87–88).

Belliveau and Gaudette (1995, 3–4) observe that although lung cancer is "one of the most preventable cancers, with almost 90% of deaths due to this type of cancer attributable to smoking," it is now the most common cause of cancer death, accounting for 33 percent of the estimated 33 700 male cancer deaths and 21 percent of the estimated 27 000 female cancer deaths in Canada in 1995. Moreover, while there has been a recent decline in lung cancer among Canadian men, the rate of lung cancer among Canadian women has been rising. Villeneuve and Morrison (1995, 9) note that while deaths due to smoking-related cancers (defined as those cancers that are at least 70 percent attributable to smoking or other forms of tobacco use), such as cancer of the pharynx, esophagus, larynx, lung, and mouth, have been rising since the 1950s, the increase in the death rate among females has surpassed that among males. In contrast, the death rate from non-smoking cancers among women declined during the same period. While the proportion of men who are regular smokers has undergone a considerable decline since the late 1960s, the proportion of women who were regular users peaked in the 1970s and has only declined "relatively slowly since then" (9).

Inasmuch as statistics on lung cancer mortality may be seen as "a reflection of the smoking habits of people at least twenty years earlier" (Villeneuve and Morrison 1995, 10), the fact that the "average lag time between starting to smoke and developing lung cancer is over twenty years" (Villeneuve and Morrison 1995, 10), coupled with youthful feelings of invulnerability, may explain why the rate of young Canadians who smoke remains substantial. As Pollay (1997, 8) notes, many young Canadians "no longer disbelieve the dangers of smoking, but they almost universally assume these risks will not apply to themselves because they will not become addicted."

Various authors have highlighted the potentially dangerous consequences of illicit drug use. Although rates of heroin use have not increased significantly in recent years, the availability of newer and purer forms of the drug have been associated with a series of lethal "Welfare Wednesdays" in Vancouver when, following the receipt of welfare checks, addicts used their newly acquired funds to obtain a particularly potent form of heroin known as China White. The dangers of any addiction can vary with the specific drug used or behaviour engaged in, but the dangers associated with illegal drugs include overdosing, infections from unsterilized needles, and unanticipated consequences due to impurities in the drugs. Opiate users may suffer infections of the heart lining and valves, skin abscesses, and congested lungs. Amphetamine injection may lead to various forms of kidney, blood vessel, or heart disease. Prolonged use of amphetamines may result in "amphetamine psychosis," in which irrational thoughts, hallucinations, paranoia, and delusions are experienced in conjunction with permanent brain damage and attendant disturbances of speech and thought patterns. In some PCP users, "flashbacks" leading to recurrent attacks of bizarre, unpredictable, and sometimes violent behaviour may occur. Large doses of PCP may lead to convulsions, coma, and death. In like fashion, attempting to drive or operate machinery while using sedatives may be lethal. Moreover, when taken together, a combination of drugs (such as alcohol and sedatives) can kill.

The personal costs of addictions are many and varied, even among young Canadians. For example, Canadian Social Trends (1995) notes that although "moderate drinking may have some health benefits" (e.g., providing protection against some forms of cardiovascular disease and cancer), the number of problems related to drinking increase with the number of occasions on which heavy drinking occurs. They note that 1 in 20 Canadians who drank in 1993 reported that their drinking had negatively affected their finances and personal health, and 1 in 50 reported that their drinking had negatively affected their marriage and home life, their social life, and their relationships with friends. While 9 percent of Canadians who drank alcohol reported at least one problem related to their drinking, people who frequently drank heavily were significantly more likely to have drinking-related problems. Among Canadians who had 365 or more drinks in 1993 and drank heavily on at least 7 occasions during that year, over 1 in 3 (35%) reported having problems related to their drinking. In general, drinking-related problems were more common among men, young people age 20 to 24, and those with low incomes.

Given that people who drink tend to socialize with others who also consume alcohol, it is perhaps not surprising that Canadian drinkers and, in particular, heavy drinkers are also more likely to report problems that arise from others' consumption of alcohol. For example, among those who drank heavily on seven or more occasions during 1993, two-thirds reported at least one problem that resulted from another person's drinking. In comparison, among those who never drank heavily, just over a third (39%) reported problems with other people's drinking. In 1993, over 4 out of 10 (44%) Canadians reported having problems as a result of someone else's drinking, with the most common complaints related to loud parties and being insulted. Less common were problems of being in a car with someone who had been drinking or being assaulted by someone who had used alcohol; however, current drinkers were more likely to report these relatively uncommon but potentially serious problems. In 1993, current drinkers were more than twice as likely as former drinkers and lifelong abstainers to have travelled in a car with a driver who had been drinking; similarly, while 6 percent of Canadians who drank reported being assaulted by someone who had been drinking, the comparable figures for former drinkers was 4 percent and for lifelong abstainers was 2 percent. While similar proportions of Canadian men and women reported being bothered by loud parties, being insulted, and arguments related to others' drinking, men were more likely to report that they had been assaulted or had been a passenger in a vehicle driven by someone who had been drinking. Canadian women were twice as likely as Canadian men to report problems with their marriage or home life (12% versus 6%) and financial problems (2% versus 1%) due to another's drinking (Canadian Social Trends 1995).

In addition, Eliany (1992) notes that according to the Alcohol and Other Drug Use by Canadian Youth Survey (1989), 23 percent of current alcohol drinkers age 15 to 24 reported having experienced an alcohol-related problem. These included problems with physical health (11%), friends or social life (9%), finances (9%), happiness or outlook (6%), work or education (5%), and home life (5%). Similarly, he notes that among adult Canadians, heavy alcohol use is associated with a relatively high incidence of problems with health, finances, family, and friendships. Twenty-two percent of Canadian adults who reported having had 15 or more drinks in the week preceding the 1989 National Alcohol and Other Drug Use survey also reported having a health problem during the previous year (versus 5 percent of those who reported no consumption of alcohol). In addition, 17 percent of heavy drinkers reported financial difficulties in the year preceding the survey (versus 2 percent of non-drinkers), and 13 percent reported problems with friends or home life during the year preceding the survey (compared with 3 percent of non-drinkers).

The consumption of certain substances may also result in criminal sanction. In comparison with other types of crime, a large proportion of drug offences result in charges. In contrast to violent offences (where only about 45 percent of those arrested were charged), 75 percent of drug offences resulted in charges in Canada. However, the likelihood of a convicted drug offender being sent to jail varied for different drugs. Thus, 75 percent of heroin convictions,

42 percent of cocaine convictions, 40 percent of convictions involving controlled or restricted drugs, 30 percent of convictions involving other narcotics, and 20 percent of cannabis convictions resulted in jail terms. Over one-half of drug convictions in Canada resulted in fines, fewer than one-quarter (23%) resulted in jail sentences, while slightly less than one in five (19%) resulted in probation or were discharged (Johnson 1988, 5). Once a person is convicted of a drug offence, he or she may have to face "the disadvantages of having a criminal record, including social stigma, job loss, employer discrimination, and passport restrictions" (Gomme 1993, 310).

The Effect on Society's Well-Being

In the last decade, a series of well-publicized incidents in Canada and the United States drew attention to the risks to society at large of addicts and their addictions. For example, the collision of a freight locomotive into an Amtrak passenger train that killed 16 people and injured more than 170 others became additionally jarring when later investigation revealed that the engineer of the freight train, who had ignored a stop signal and steered his locomotive onto the wrong track, had used marijuana and other drugs. Similarly, the trial of three Northwest Airline pilots charged with flying passenger jets while under the influence of alcohol became particularly newsworthy when it was revealed that, according to the records of the Federal Aviation Administration, 1200 active pilots had received treatment for alcoholism since 1975. As McMillan (1991, 30) comments, "people begin to question whether other workers—perhaps even those in the most sensitive jobs, such as air traffic controllers or police officers—might be using drugs on the job, too. What about technicians at nuclear power plants or military installations? Doctors, nurses, school-bus drivers?"

In addition to these incidents of alcohol and drug abuse that posed risks to specific segments of society, a more amorphous threat to Canadians materialized in the early 1980s when it was discovered that intravenous drug users were among those "high-risk" people who stood an increased chance of acquiring AIDS and then passing it on through their bodily fluids. Suddenly, AIDS was no longer "merely" a homosexual disease, and the threat of being exposed to AIDS-tainted blood, especially through transfusions, became especially pronounced. Health-care workers, social workers, and the police—professionals whose occupations brought them into routine contact with groups identified as high risk—all at once realized how vulnerable they were to HIV infection.

The tragedy visited on Canada's hemophiliac population—80 percent of whom received blood transfusions tainted with the AIDS virus—offers a telling illustration of the threat AIDS poses to public health. In March 1983, approximately one year after the first AIDS patient was identified in Canada, the first hemophiliac died of AIDS. Despite evidence of the connection between blood transfusions and HIV, the majority of Canadian agencies refused to act until they had "absolute proof." In consequence, the Canadian Red Cross delayed efforts to discourage high-risk donors and, from December 1984 to June 1985, continued to stockpile tainted blood. Furthermore, persons who had received tainted blood during transfusions were not notified by their doctors of the possible danger they faced. As a result, spouses and babies were unwitting recipients of the disease. As Parsons (1995: C21) observes, "Months after a reliable screening test could have been used, thousands more were infected by HCV, hepatitis C, a virus more common than HIV and a cause of cirrhosis of the liver.

Seeking compensation from the federal and provincial governments, victims and their families once again faced ignorance and stonewalling."

Although by 1994, more than 900 Canadians who had been infected with the AIDS virus through blood transfusions were eligible for provincial compensation packages that would provide them with immediate payments of $22 000, and then $30 000 a year for the rest of their lives (*The Globe and Mail*, March 15, 1994: A1, A6), it is obvious that no amount can truly compensate those who became infected. Consider as well the additional enormous economic costs incurred by HIV and AIDS. Frank (1996, 5) observes that "[t]he annual cost to the health-care system of treating people living with AIDS has been estimated at over $200 million" and that other costs, "including those related to lost productivity, insurance settlements and social services, could be as high as $800,000 per person living with HIV."

Estimates suggest that by the end of 1994, 16 000 cases of AIDS had been diagnosed in Canada. Although only 15 percent of AIDS cases among women and 3 percent of those among men were contracted through injection use, the association between addiction and AIDS has become focal for at least some Canadian activists. According to members of the Killing Fields Campaign, Vancouver's skid-row neighbourhood in the downtown east side has the highest rate of HIV infection in the Western world; reportedly, more than 1000 people have died in this area since 1994. A study conducted in 1996 to track 1000 drug users in the area found that 1 in 4 were already infected with HIV, while another 20 percent were expected to become infected in 1997. Although members of the Killing Fields Campaign have called on the federal government to stop the rising death toll among intravenous drug users by introducing legislation that would provide for the controlled and legal distribution of narcotics by doctors and the provision of safe places for addicts to inject their drugs (Canadian Associated Press 1997), not all Canadians agree with this proposed solution. Heroin junkies are stereotypically viewed as crazed individuals who commonly share needles and who, in the U.S., sell their blood for the price of a fix or, in Canada, donate blood without appreciation of the risk posed to others; to the extent that this stereotype is believed to be true, the threat posed by addicts may be seen to warrant more draconian measures. Intravenous drug users, like homosexuals and promiscuous heterosexuals, may be subject to high levels of vilification because they are seen to engage by choice in behaviour that has potentially deadly consequences not just for themselves but for others.

ANALYZING THE PROBLEM

The Functionalist Approach

Functionalists assume that persons within a society agree on which values and behaviours are appropriate and inappropriate. At a micro level of analysis, functionalists may favour a social pathology approach, which suggests that addicts are simply weak-willed people who have failed to internalize social norms that govern patterns of behaviour. However, a latent function of addictions may be to build social cohesion through the identification and censuring of those who engage in rule-breaking behaviour. In this way, those who are labelled "addicts" serve to illustrate, by their breach, the boundaries of normal and acceptable behaviour and to reiterate social values and goals. Accordingly, the apparently deviant activities of addicts are seen to have functional consequences for society.

As a contemporary illustration of this type of reasoning, in *Blessed Are The Addicts*, John A. Martin, a Catholic priest described as a "spiritual consultant and lecturer at local alcohol and drug rehabilitation centres," writes that the sight of the addict "stirs one's soul: it makes one want to reach out and hug the suffering addict in the same way that one wants to feed the skin-stretched bodies of starving children with the oversized and pleading eyes that one sees in haunting photos" (xi). Evidently Martin has little problem with the popularization of the concept of addiction or with the fact that an increasing number of phenomena are now being identified as addictions. Indeed, he writes of his belief "that in the next century we will discover thousands more" (xii). Why? "All addictions," he maintains, "are the same. . . . I used to say that this disease is 90 percent spiritual. I now say without any doubt that it is 100 percent spiritual. . . . Addiction is primarily a spiritual malfunction . . ." (xiii, 4, 10, 21). Martin suggests that the cause of addiction resides in an individual's early feelings of alienation, "a kind of disconnection that is deep, persistent . . . progressive . . . [and] embedded in the being of the person" (21). Accordingly, rather than being discouraged by the seemingly vast numbers of addicted persons afflicted with spiritual malaise, Martin stresses that "to experience the change in a person from addiction to recovery is to witness a miracle. In front of one's very eyes, the liar becomes the lover of truth, the thief becomes the trusted servant, the violent and destructive person becomes the peacemaker, the irresponsible . . . becomes responsible, the uncaring becomes the lover of this world." Suggesting that none can fail to be profoundly affected by the witnessed transformation, Martin extols the functional benefits of addictions to society and its members:

> And thank God that there are addictions! For it is through the experience of addiction that one can become aware of the call of life. Through addiction, one is given the opportunity to wake up, to mature, to respond to that call in a positive and creative way. One can finally say a conscious yes to one's destiny and become one with oneself, one's world and one's God. (xiii)

Although this perspective on addictions would undoubtedly be phrased in different terms by sociological functionalists, there is a rough congruence between Martin's depiction of addiction and Durkheim's suggestion that two latent functions of deviance are to permit those who conform to conventional behaviour to feel virtuous and to clarify social norms. Moreover, on a macro level, functionalists have argued that the concepts of alienation and anomie may help explain the root causes of drug use, alcoholism, and various other forms of addictions. Functionalists might note that drugs, when properly used, may have many functional benefits for society. As a treatment for illness, a prescribed part of a ceremonial practice, or a "social lubricant," drugs may be beneficial and contribute to the smooth functioning of society as a whole. However, in the event of social disorganization, society itself may become structurally dysfunctional and produce addictions as a form of stress adaptation.

In Chapter 4 we will discuss Robert Merton's suggestion that criminal behaviour could, in part, be seen as a stress adaptation to a society in which the culturally induced aspirations of many are doomed to failure. It could be argued that some addictions may also be seen as an innovative type of stress resolution in which goals and means are accorded different weight. For example, it has been suggested that the use of performance-enhancing drugs by athletes is nothing more than the logical consequence of a "winner takes all" mentality. Whether the addict is a bodybuilder who desires more lean mass and less body fat, a weightlifter who wants to "bulk up," or a field athlete who wishes to throw a javelin, discus, or hammer as far as possible, the desire to win may be more essential than the health risks or potential social sanctions that might result from the steroid use. As Yesalis (1993, xxvi) points out, "The use of drugs to enhance physical performance has been a feature of athletic competition since the beginning of recorded history." Noting that the specific drugs used over time have included hallucinogenic mushrooms, stimulants, alcohol, digitalis, nitroglycerine, cocaine, ether, strychnine, opium, and heroin, he observes that the term "doping" was already used in the 1930s as a title of an article that, in part, stated:

> There can be no doubt that stimulants are to-day widely used by athletes participating in competitions; the recording-breaking craze and the desire to satisfy an exacting public play a more and more prominent role, and take higher rank than the health of the competitors itself. (Yesalis 1993, xxviii)

If in using anabolic steroids the athlete may be seen to be addicted to achieving perfection at any cost, this same type of imagery has been adopted by various feminist authors in explaining "food addictions" and the compulsive control of food intake evidenced by anorexics and bulimics. For example, noting that thinness is an important component of contemporary cultural ideals of female desirability, certain writers have argued that the "tyranny of beauty" may encourage some women to adopt extreme measures in its pursuit. They note that the relentless quest for perfection (as embodied in the waiflike appearance of such "heroin chic" supermodels as Kate Moss) encourages compliance to the former Duchess of Windsor's dictum that "one can never be too rich or too thin." Within this milieu, it is not surprising that "[f]or the past three decades the public perception has been that a woman is attractive, desirable, and successful when she is thin" (Abraham and Llewellyn-Jones 1992, 1). "Obesity," Valette (1988, 2) observes, "has become a 'national phobia' that outranks the fear of death and aging."

Merton suggested that addiction could additionally be seen as a form of retreatism in which individuals who find their access to social goals blocked and opportunities for "success" remote adapt to frustration by goal de-escalation. In his attempt to explain addictions among young, urban, non-white males, Merton postulated that addictions could be seen as a retreatist response to structured inopportunities. Elaborating on Merton's thesis, Cloward and Ohlin (1960) have suggested that addicts may be considered double failures who not only lack legitimate opportunities to achieve social goals but are also prevented by internal prohibitions from engaging in illegitimate means of achieving social goals. Unlike both the innovator, who replaces legitimate means with illegitimate means to achieve socially desirable goals, or those individuals who express their frustrations in a violent fashion, double failures may only retreat into their own misery. Coupling Merton's analysis of social structure and anomie with the elaborating work of Cloward and Ohlin, we may portray addiction as a consequence of the discrepant opportunities provided within society to achieve valued goals through institutionalized means.

Others, evidently sympathetic to the underpinnings of functionalism, have found the theory of differential association useful in understanding addictions. This theory suggests that addictions may stem from involvement in a subculture that lacks adequate social norms to govern human behaviour or, alternatively, that promotes maladaptive patterns of use. For example, Robertson (1980, 437) observes that among Italians and Jews, there are norms to govern the use of alcohol that reduce the likelihood of alcoholism or drunkenness. Within the Italian subculture, he notes, the use of wine at meals, even by the young, is unlikely to produce drunkenness both because of its low alcoholic content and because of the presence of food in the stomach. Similarly, he notes that alcoholism among Jews is rare and attributes this to the strong norms that govern the use the alcohol within the Jewish community (that is, as part of religious rituals). For the Irish, he suggests, "there is no such custom of closely regulated alcohol consumption within the family, but the culture tolerates periodical bouts of excessive drinking by single males as a way for them to relieve frustration and tension" (438).

It may additionally be noted that the medical or disease model of alcoholism implicitly adopts the functionalist belief that under normal situations and in normal persons, alcoholism should not occur. Accordingly, the medical model views the addict as sick and in need of treatment. The addiction becomes the illness and the addict becomes the patient. In its purest form, the medical model suggests that addictions are caused, to a greater or lesser degree, by some form of physical deficiency or aberration. For example, Jellinek's classic 1945 article, "Heredity of the Alcoholic," resurrected an age-old view that alcoholism is hereditary and modified it somewhat by claiming that it was "not a disposition toward alcoholism [that] is inherited but rather a constitution involving such instability as does not offer sufficient resistance to the social risks of inebriety. The inherited constitution is merely a suitable breeding ground for inebriety" (in Lester 1988). Such subtleties notwithstanding, in his 1960 book, *The Disease Concept of Alcoholism*, Jellinek argued that:

1) alcoholism is a disease rather than a moral weakness;

2) alcoholism is a progressive, irreversible process in which problems continuously accumulate over time; and

3) alcoholics should never be given alcohol to drink because they experience loss-of-control drinking.

Although Jellinek's 1945 article displays an awareness that "even a perfectly heritable trait could be substantially changed by an environment," this point seems to have been somewhat neglected by many of his successors. Indeed, some who have favoured an all-encompassing hereditary theory of alcoholism have suggested that alcoholism be renamed "Jellinek's Disease" (Fitzgerald 1983). Various writers have suggested that there is a neurobiological basis of alcoholism or, in a modified form, a mechanism through which genetically determined physiological factors combine with environmental factors to produce positive feedback loops that promote alcoholism (Tabakoff and Hoffman 1988). For Tarter, Alterman, and Edwards (1988) the research finding that certain behavioural disturbances such as hyperactivity, behavioural disinhibition, restlessness, and impulsivity in childhood and adolescence increase the likelihood of alcoholism in adulthood suggests that alcoholism may stem from a dysfunction of neural systems in the brain. It has also been suggested that alcoholics possess a specific gene affecting dopamine receptors that is not present in non-alcoholics.

Cloninger et al. (1981, 867) have emphasized that "the demonstration of the critical importance of the sociocultural influences in most alcoholics suggest[s] that major changes in social attitudes about drinking styles can change dramatically the prevalence of alcohol abuse regardless of genetic predisposition." Despite this observation, the title of a pamphlet published by the U.S. National Institute on Alcohol Abuse and Alcoholism, "Alcoholism: An Inherited Disease," suggests the continuing popularity of genetic-based models of alcoholism. According to this source, "Knowing that alcoholism is hereditable should make it easier for us to rethink our cultural attitudes toward alcoholism and to accept it for what it is"—that is, "a disease with a molecular basis" (v). The solution to the problem of alcoholism is seen to lie in "specific pharmacological interventions to prevent it and treat it" (36). With the identification of the single culprit that is presumed to turn alcoholism "on and off," the problem of alcoholism, it is suggested, will be solved.

With this medical or disease model of addiction in mind, our understanding of human behaviour has been transformed from one underwritten by assumptions of free will, personal choice, rationality, and individual responsibility to one that has as its underpinnings presumptions of pathology and disease. Accordingly, the "addict" within this discourse is transformed from being purposefully engaged in an activity into a passive victim deprived of agency by forces beyond his or her control. While the person may be viewed as impotent in the grip of overwhelming temptations, the source of the "problem" may, somewhat paradoxically, be granted a type of personhood—the "demon rum" (alcohol in general), the "panty remover" (gin), "mother's little helper" (Valium), the "white lady" (cocaine), the "ladykillers" (cigarettes), "Bennies" (amphetamines), "Maryjane" (marijuana), and "Shermans" (small cigars dipped into a PCP solution and smoked). Personifying the problem performs a useful service: it permits moral evaluation and facilitates the identification of villains and victims. Within this depiction, addiction is portrayed as a hostile enemy who occupies foreign lands and is to be "attacked," "expelled," and "eliminated;" simultaneously, the addict is portrayed as the blameless victim whose body is "under siege" by hostile forces. The addict is "sick" and must accordingly be considered a nonculpable agent to his or her misfortunes. Just as nobody chooses to be a diabetic, the medical model of addictions informs us, nobody chooses to be an addict.

Paradoxically, within the model of addict as victim-patient the individual is called on to take full responsibility for his or her addiction. The medical model ignores social, political, and economic factors as causes of personal and social problems. This extreme emphasis on individual responsibility (despite personal powerlessness) is accompanied by the belief that what the addict truly needs is best achieved through individual change, not through social or political activism. It would appear that addiction theorists generally believe that the factors that underlie substance abuse are far less intellectually intriguing than the dynamics of the addiction itself. One finds a whole industry devoted to the solution of a problem whose etiology is mystical.

In suggesting that addicts require "treatment" or that the problem of addiction writ large requires a "spiritual revolution" (rather than, for example, social change or the transformation of society), the medical model may be seen to encourage self-preoccupation rather than social activism. It promotes as necessary rites of passage the acts of confession, self-surrender, submission to the authority and direction of a Higher Power (whether secular or sacred), and, implicitly, acceptance of the political-economic status quo. There are a number of homilies, aphorisms, and slogans that reiterate this individualistic focus: One Day at a Time; Easy Does It; Let Go and Let God; Keep It Simple Stupid (KISS); Utilize, Don't Analyze; Fake It Until You Make It; One Drink, One Drunk (Bufe 1991, 59). Self-change in accordance with the dictates and standards of an authoritative voice is championed, not social activism. The medical model of addiction as expressed in the psychiatrist–patient relationship, the addiction counsellor–patient relationship, or the recovery movement accordingly may be seen to encourage a posture of anti-intellectualism. Unquestioning faith in the abilities of "the expert" (be it a psychiatrist or the person sitting beside you at a 12-step group) is an essential part of the therapeutic process. Unless the individual truly wants to be healed, we are informed, salvation can never be attained. Thus, would-be supplicants must confess their sins and identify themselves as "sick" as a precondition of "therapy," then accept and religiously follow the treatment program prescribed.

CASE 2-1   The "Stages" of Drug Abuse

There is, assuredly, an aura of precision that may be invoked by the nomenclature that surrounds the medical model's depiction of addiction. For example, drawing on the American Medical Association's attempts to produce a "clear and uniform terminology," Stimmel (1991) offers an eight-stage continuum of drug use that ranges from:

1) nonuse,

2) appropriate use ("using a substance for sound reasons in an accepted and approved manner" [21]),

3) misuse ("taking a drug for its prescribed purpose but not in the way it is supposed to be taken" [22]),

4) experimental use ("trying a drug only once or twice to see its effect"),

5) abuse ("taking a drug for other than its intended purpose and/or in a way other than that prescribed . . . [or] use of any illicit drug that can result in physical, psychological, economic, legal, or social harm, either to oneself or to others" [22]),

6) habituation ("the need to take a drug at given times to avoid the anxiety associated with not taking it" [22]),

7) psychological or physical dependency (characterized by three responses: "the need to take a drug to experience its pleasurable effects, the appearance of behavioral changes—psychological and/or physiological—when the drug is abruptly discontinued, the need continually to increase the dose and/or frequency of use to sustain its initial effects" [23]), and

8) addiction ("characterized by the compulsive use of a substance resulting in physical or psychological dependency . . . usually accompanied by increased tolerance. The person is unable to restrict drug use" [24]).

However, for a number of reasons, even the terminology of the medical model of addiction may be considered problematic. First, the suggestion that patterns of drug use conform to an eight-stage continuum is vexatious inasmuch as it supposes that once individuals cross the fateful divide between "nonuser" and "user" status, they proceed, like lemmings, to an ignominious end. Plummeting into the depths of addiction, the addict is portrayed as powerless to voluntarily disengage from "compulsive use of a substance" and is transformed into one unable to exercise personal autonomy.

Second, it may be noted that the assignment of distinctive labels in the addiction continuum is, at least arguably, somewhat meaningless and arbitrary. For example, the distinctions between "appropriate use," "misuse," and "abuse" are riddled with subjective terms ("sound reasons," "accepted and approved manner"). The medical model of addictions encourages us to ignore the fact that the distinction between "use" and "abuse" is often unclear to experts themselves. For example, "drug abuse" exists on a continuum with drug use and there is nothing magical or axiomatic that separates the two. Indeed, psychoanalyst Sandor Rado's classic 1933 article, "The Psychoanalysis of Pharmacothymia [Drug Addiction]," contrasted the severe "psychopathology" of the individual who

| CASE 2-1 | The "Stages" of Drug Abuse (continued) |

suffered the disease of "pharmaco-thymia" with the "*normal* person who makes *daily* use of stimulants in the form of coffee, tea, tobacco, and the like" (23, emphasis added). This statement today seems at least somewhat ironic. Some would undoubtedly argue that the daily use of a stimulant is testimony to an "addiction" and that the problem of tobacco use is one of our most socially and personally injurious addictions.

Third, when the term "addiction" is applied, as we have seen, to an ever-expanding inventory of behaviour, the problems of bias and rampant sub-jectivity become acute. The distinctions between "acceptable dieting" and food "addictions," being a "glutton" versus a "food junkie," demonstrating "loyalty" and "commitment" to a partner instead of being "addicted" to a bad relationship, or evidencing "ambition" and "industry" versus being a pathological "workaholic" are not simply problems of semantics. As Thomas Hobbes suggested, "the power to name and diagnose, the power to make definitions, is the ultimate authority" (Tavris 1992, 173). Based on an evaluator's drawing of a line to demarcate "acceptable" and "unac-ceptable" behaviours or patterns of consumption, the "addict" is defined. The standard itself may be problematic, especially when it is couched within a type of medicomystical jargon that obscures as much as it reveals.

On occasion, however, challenges may be forthcoming. The uncontrite may be unwilling to agree to the definition of their behaviour as an "addiction," and argue that they do not have a problem. However, this disclaimer may in itself be construed as consistent with a "stage" in the addictive process—that is, denial—and testimony to the existence of the problematic "condition." Similarly, it might seem heretical to point out that battling one drug with another (for example, heroin with methadone, alcohol with disulfiram or Antabuse, or tobacco with Nicorette) would seem based on a specious type of logic that employs a somewhat arbitrary notion of "drug abuse" or socially problematic behaviour. After all, the unenlightened might note, both the problem and the solution adopt similar processes—that is, the consumption of drugs. Why is it that one is viewed as legitimate and its use as innocuous while consumption of the other is cloaked in disreputability? The image of drug addicts furtively ducking into a crack house for their fixes stands in marked contrast to that of addicts in recovery who dutifully appear at their appointed time for their prescribed treatment. Both "addict" and "patient" are consuming drugs and some might query why their drug-of-choice is deemed illegal or dangerous while the selection of the practitioner is deemed acceptable and legitimate. Nevertheless, it would seem that experts in the realm of addiction are granted a type of benefit-of-clergy. It is taken for granted that the actions of the expert are logical, informed, and sagacious, and that those of the addict are not. The idea that experts can always discern deep truths that evade their reluctant patients is both paternalistic and authoritarian.

Consider, for example, the definition of "co-dependency" offered by one guru of the burgeoning self-help or recovery movement. To Anne Wilson Schaef, a best-selling author whose *Co-dependence: Misunderstood—Mistreated* sold 300 000 copies and whose 1990 *Meditations for Women Who Do Too Much* sold over 400 000 copies, co-dependency is "a disease process whose assumptions, beliefs, and lack of spiritual awareness lead to a process of nonliving which is progressive" (Kaminer 1992, 10). If the reader is baffled at this definition and wonders how a disease process may have cognitions or questions how a process of nonliving (which would seem to suggest death) may be progressive, such psychobabble is a stock-in-trade of many such authors. Thus, Wendy Beattie, author of *Co-Dependent No More* (which sold more than 2 million copies) and *Beyond Co-dependency* (which sold over half a million copies), offers her own personal definition of the "co-dependent person" as "one who has let another person's behaviour affect him or her, and who is obsessed with controlling that person's behaviour." As Tavris (1992, 193) has observed, this definition is so broad that it "excludes only a few saints and hermits." Apparently recognizing this oversight, Beattie has noted, "Some therapists have proclaimed: 'Co-dependency is anything, and everyone is co-dependent.'"

As Tavris points out, this generosity of definition makes for a "curious type of disease; what physician would write a book on diabetes, saying: 'Diabetes is anything, and everyone is diabetic?'" (194). Nevertheless, the authoritarian overtones of the "disease" model of addiction that would label certain persons as "sick" or as "addicts" are no less apparent within its popularized form. Indeed, scepticism and "judgmentalism" (that is, viewing such works in a critical manner) are also seen as "characteristic" of those suffering from the "disease" (of denial). In a society in which the recovery or self-help movement is currently in vogue, "co-dependency is advertised as a national epidemic, partly because every conceivable form of arguably compulsive behaviour is classified as an addiction" (Kaminer 1992, 10). Such is the spirit of the times, she argues, that there are only two states of being—recovery and denial—that are recognized.

In marked contrast, Szasz (1992) would repudiate both the wisdom and the scientific validity "of placing rule-breaking behaviour in the same category as bodily disease" (ix–x). For Szasz, our liberty, our right to property (including that of our body), and personal happiness "entails opportunities as well as risks." "The essence of freedom," Szasz writes, "is choice, and that choice implies the option to make the wrong choice, that is, to 'abuse' freedom and suffer the consequences." He notes that some would view the right to property as having given us the right to comfort, prosperity, and the legitimate employment of numerous individuals within our society (for example, builders, contractors, engineers, architects, real estate agents, and landlords). For others, however, the right to property has given us "unscrupulous moneylenders and greedy slumlords to exploit people's homelessness." "Both images," he maintains, "are real. Both are true. And the *choice* is ours" (emphasis in original).

Szasz chides those who suggest that our consumption of drugs is different from our consumption of other products or our participation in other social activities and notes that it is theoretically possible to view all social interchanges as infused by the forces of cabalism and conspiracy. Thus, he suggests, it could be argued that those who staff or own our supermarkets exist to "prey upon" and "exploit" the troubled persons in our society who suffer from eating disorders. However, in stark contrast to our vilification of those who would sell us "dangerous drugs," we do not typically blame farmers or grocers for the conditions of those who are obese or anorexic. Nevertheless, he points out, "we do blame the drug habits of addicts on the people who sell them drugs." He argues that "if we try to redefine liberty in such a way that it is not liberty unless its results are individually and collectively 'healthy' . . . we fool only those foolish enough to believe in miracles. Sometimes, this category includes the majority. We then speak, usually in retrospect, of a crowd madness" (12–13). Rather than speak of "addictions" and "dangerous drugs" that cause "epidemics" and necessitate a holy war against the use of certain products or the engagement of persons in certain activities, Szasz forwards the existentialist's views on freedom and responsibility, of making choices and bearing responsibility for them: "Life is full of risks. Faced with risks, we must make decisions." He acknowledges that there are tragedies of human existence, but suggests that we blunder when we assume that all tragedies are diseases conducive to treatment and when, consequently, we confuse hubris and dogma with real science.

The Conflict Approach

In posing the fundamental question of "Who benefits?" to the problem of addictions, the conflict approach requires that we suspend the taken-for-granted assumption that addiction should be seen as a medical problem and treat the concept instead as a social construct that has shown a good deal of elasticity. Why is it, conflict theorists ask, that certain behaviours or consumption patterns are viewed as "addictions" and their practitioners as "addicts" while others escape designation as such? They stress the heterogeneity of meanings and values in society in responding to patterns of behaviour and argue that we should view the concept of addiction in light of the constant conflict between different levels of society. The identifications of drug abuse as a social problem and of certain drugs as intrinsically more dangerous than others are not regarded as sacrosanct "facts" by the conflict theorist. In their efforts to deconstruct why certain drugs are considered dangerous and how some may come to be formally prohibited within criminal law and their consumers punished by agents of social control, conflict theorists maintain that a discussion of power is more important for understanding the problem of addiction than a discussion of personal pathology would be.

Szasz (1992) says it is significant that the Greek word for scapegoat is *pharmakos* and contends that the concepts of "drug abuse" and the "War on Drugs" are merely "pretexts for scapegoating deviants and strengthening the power of the state" (62). Although in the early 1900s alcohol, cocaine, and morphine were the main ingredients of patent medicines, Szasz writes, "now these drugs are our favourite scapegoats" (62). Just as in the past when an animal would be offered as a ritual sacrifice to the gods, to appease them and win their blessing, now a particular behaviour or drug is held out to be "the embodiment of transcendent disease-producing evil and, presto, we have the perfect modern medico-mythological scapegoat" (29). If long ago Marx referred to Western religion as the "opiate" of the people, it would seem that today it is the mere concept of addictions that succeeds in stultifying the people.

Szasz argues that our perception of the "drug problem" as the private addictions of dysfunctional individuals signifies that the disinformation tactics sponsored by the government have succeeded. We are asked to believe that the drugs we ingest (either for recreational or therapeutic use) are more dangerous than those imposed on us, such as the radioactive wastes that have been introduced into the environment (Szasz 1992, Douglas and Wildavsky 1982). How does one "Just Say No" to things that we cannot see, smell, or taste? Szasz (1992, 73) argues that the "truth" of what is a "dangerous drug" "has been so radically wrenched from its proper pharmacological and social context that it has become a big lie. . . . [O]f all the potentially dangerous chemicals in our environment, none is more difficult to avoid than a radioactive element in the air, water, or soil—and none is easier to avoid than cocaine or heroin."

In like fashion, some say that what we define as an addiction and whom we define as an addict both offer testimony to the varying degrees of power possessed by persons within our society. The associations of opium use with the Chinese, of marijuana with Blacks, and of alcohol abuse with the "dangerous classes" (that is, immigrants and the urban poor) are not coincidental factors in the identification of these products first as dangerous and subsequently as illegal. Green (1986) employs Duster's concept of the moral centre to illustrate that "behaviour primarily engaged in by those occupying the centre of society's moral order cannot long sustain a deviant label, while ethically equivalent conduct engaged in by socially inferior and thus morally vulnerable classes will attract and support a designation of immorality" (37). He notes that in the United States, the temperance ideology prevailed "so long as its advocates were identified with the middle classes, but was doomed to moral (and subsequently legal) reappraisal when these same classes began to consume alcohol in public in the face of Prohibition" (26).

In various ways, the reconceptualization of certain patterns of social behaviour as "addictions" invites reconsideration of the question raised at the beginning of this section: "Who benefits?" For example, who does benefit from creating the concept of a sexaholic and the attendant addiction? Some might say that by deliberately narrowing the dividing line between mental health and mental illness in this way, that is, by constantly proliferating the number of possible addictions, those involved in the mental health industry and those who profit by popularizing its jargon are involved in a massive process of empire-building and power-grabbing. Needless to say, they are also profiting by capitalizing on people's insecurities and fears. Moreover, Christie (1993) notes that drug control may be seen as an "inroad to the totalitarian state," which, by breaking down borders between the public and private and controlling categories of people rather than behaviours, increases the number of people under state control (see also Riley 1993).

The Feminist Approach

In various ways, feminist authors have directed attention to the limitations of a "disease framework" for understanding addiction and stressed how social factors (rather than personal weakness or pathology) may encourage women's apparent addictions to smoking, alcohol, dieting, bad relationships, and so on. For example, in the early 1980s Erin Pizzey and her husband Jeff Shapiro drew considerable fire with the publication of a book entitled *Prone to Violence* that claimed that some women are addicted to violence and, despite the existence of viable and attractive alternatives, seek out abusive men or remain in abusive relationships because they are violence-prone. They distinguish between the woman "who accidentally becomes involved with a violent partner and who now wishes to leave and never return again and a woman who, for deep psychological reasons of her own, seeks out a violent relationship or a series of violent relationships with no intention of leaving." The latter, they suggest, is an "addict" and "it is the addiction that explains . . . why, when the violent relationship ends, these violence-prone women quickly find other abusive partners" (Fattah 1991, 177).

In contrast, feminists say that analyses like Pizzey's and Shapiro's ignore the larger social complexities of women's lives. Lundy (1991) argues that women's addiction to alcohol, for example, cannot be understood unless "women's reality: a life of subordination" (60) and the aftermath of this life (underpaid work and spousal violence) are acknowledged. Thus, Sandmaier (1980) suggests, "Women are driven to all kinds of self-destructive escapes from their powerlessness and their conflicted visions of themselves: depression, compulsive eating, other drug addiction, obsessive housekeeping, suicide . . . alcohol is only one escape of many."

Some feminist authors focus on the social forces that underlie specific patterns of addiction among women, such as smoking (Jacobsen 1988), prescription drugs and cocaine (Peluso and Peluso 1988), or the ideal of beauty itself (Wolf 1991). In particular, the phenomenon of eating disorders has attracted much attention from feminist authors, who note that the "overwhelming preponderance of female patients confers on eating disorders the distinction of having the most lopsided sex ratio of any known to psychiatry" (Gordon 1991, 32). The analysis of what eating disorders mean may varies. For Lawrence (1982, 104), "[w]e must see this statistic and this dramatically painful and potentially harmful adaptation to life as a scathing criticism and a raging protest of what it means to be a woman today." Some, such as Orbach (1986), direct attention to the "precondition" of supposedly pathological relationships between ambivalent, needy mothers and their suffering daughters or, such as Friedman (1985, 63), discuss the "narcissistic injury" done to daughters within dysfunctional mother–daughter relationships. For others, however, such as Bepko and Krestan, "addiction . . . [is] a metaphor for the ways that stereotypes of maleness and femaleness deprive both men and women of their full humanity. Addiction, eating disorders, phobias, depression, codependency—all began to make some large sense as metaphors for unworkable gender arrangements" (in Tavris 1992, 204).

For this latter group of feminists, both the increasing number of postulated addictions and the surge in popularity of self-help books and groups are considered problematic. As Kaminer (1992, 31) observes about the self-help movement, "Feminists did say that the personal was political, but they meant that private relations between the sexes reflected public divisions of power, that putatively private events, like wife beating, were public concerns. They didn't mean that getting to know yourself was sufficient political action."

The Interactionist Approach

Interactionist theorists are fascinated by the process through which a person comes to be identified as an addict and by the consequences of such labelling on the self and others. Unlike those who would adopt an objectivist position on the reality of addictions, symbolic interactionists stress that becoming an addict signifies a process of continuous action and reaction between the addict and those around him or her. Despite popular acceptance of what Blackwell and Erickson (1988) have termed "the enslavement hypothesis of addiction" (that is, that certain substances are so overwhelmingly potent or "addictive" that once used, they enslave their unwitting victims for the rest of their lives), Gomme (1993, 317) maintains that "scientific evidence supporting this . . . hypothesis is extremely shaky." Similarly, he points out that "the assumption that any drug has an invariable chemical effect on anyone who takes it is false. The attitudes, motivations, and expectations of users affect the manner in which the drug experience evolves. Moreover, the setting in which a user partakes of a substance has important impacts" (317). Symbolic interactionists argue that the strict adoption of the disease model of addiction promotes tunnel vision. They would rather discuss behaviour patterns in dramaturgical terms, that is, with the individual as an actor playing various roles (Goffman 1971). In this way, Lurie (1971) describes the use of alcohol by North American aboriginals as "the world's oldest on-going protest demonstration." Similarly, Braroe (1975) has suggested that the stereotype of the "drunken Indian" became a strategic resource that aboriginals used to manipulate whites when they had dealings with them in town.

As Heath (1988) points out, a theory of alcoholism as a genetically inherited addiction fails to consider the importance of research findings that indicate:

- Drinking is almost always a social act—in many cultures, drinking alone is unthinkable, and in most, drinking together is an act endowed with strong positive meanings.

- People are rarely neutral about drinking—it is often hedged about with a varied lot of norms, to a far greater extent than many other kinds of activity.

- Those norms are often endowed with a strong emotional charge, again more than is the case in many other sets of norms.

- Such affectively loaded norms include expectations about the results of drinking that are regularly patterned among most members of any given population.

- Actual drunken comportment conforms to such patterns, and the fact that it rarely exceeds widely shared limits of propriety indicates that it is strongly affected by social learning.

- In most of the cultures where drinking occurs at all, most drinkers have few, if any, alcohol-related problems in physiological, psychological, social relational, economic or other terms.

- The phenomenon of dependence or addiction is rare with respect to alcohol, on a worldwide basis.

- Among those who develop drinking problems, aspects of the cultural context in which they live often play a major role in the aetiology of their problem.

- There is no uniform developmental sequence that applies cross-culturally with respect to the way in which various kinds of alcohol-related problems (with the possible exception of certain organic pathologies) manifest themselves.

- For those individuals who seek help in relation to drinking problems, cultural differences can result in potentially harmful misunderstandings; cultural differences can also be helpful in identifying potentially fruitful adaptive strategies for individuals and populations (397–398).

In other words, the beliefs, attitudes, and values held by a group with respect to alcohol (or any other potentially addictive substance or behaviour) largely shape the reactions of individuals to it.

In his classic work "On Becoming a Marijuana User," Howard Becker illustrated the developmental process wherein a person learned the techniques, interpretive framework, and rationale necessary to become a marijuana smoker. There is, after all, nothing intrinsically pleasurable about the sensations that accompany drug use; rather, he suggests, the participant must learn how to interpret them as such, to recognize certain feelings or sensations created by the drug, and to experience them as desirable enough that the behaviour is sustained. He stresses that even "scientists no longer believe that a drug has a simple physiological action, essentially the same in all humans" and argues that any drug has a "protean [changeable] character, varying from person to person and place to place" (1973, 26). Among his sample, Becker observed that the novice marijuana user did not simply inhale the drug and get "high;" indeed, the language of "smoking up" or taking a "drag" on a "joint" itself suggests insider knowledge that is not commonly shared among all members of a society. Similarly, the term "chasing the dragon" for smoking heroin may be recognized by users (and police) but be meaningless to outsiders. Noting that the neophyte is typically introduced to marijuana use through members of a peer group, Becker suggested that the existence of the group and their evident approval of engaging in an "illicit" activity helps the novice to overcome any reservations.

If engaging in marijuana use is regarded by some as discreditable behaviour, Becker's analysis reminds us that the label of respectability is not conferred on acts or behaviours by a monolithic social apparatus. The acceptability of "doing drugs" may be based on a logic that is dictated less by the illegality of the behaviour than by the group norms that legitimate it. Moreover, the application of the "pothead" label by unfriendly others and the formal "status degradation ceremony" of criminal justice proceedings are not always sufficient to shame the person into stopping the activity. As Tangri and Schwartz (1967, 187) observe, "a delinquent self-concept is not necessarily a negative self-concept."

In arguing his structuration theory of addiction, Giddens (1992) attempts to marry functionalist and Marxist theories with symbolic interactionism to discuss the issues of both structure and agency. He begins by noting that the term "addict" dates back no further than the mid-nineteenth century and argues that "[t]he invention of the addict, in Foucault's terms, is a control mechanism, a new network of 'power/knowledge' . . . The addict, after all, is someone who is 'intemperate,' a word that does not relate only to public order but to a refusal, a disinclination quietly to accept one's lot" (74). He advances the implicitly functionalist claim that "[a]ddiction signals a particular mode of control over parts of one's day-to-day life—and also over the self" and that "addiction has to be understood in terms of a society in which tradition has more thoroughly been swept away than ever before and in which . . . the individual is continually obliged to negotiate life-style options" (75). Then, somewhat abruptly, Giddens announces that it is crucial to appreciate that "such choices are not just 'external' or marginal aspects of the individual's attitudes, but define who the individual 'is.'" He writes:

> In a post-traditional order . . . [p]rocesses of self-actualization . . . are very often partial and confined. Hence it is not surprising that addictions are potentially so wide-ranging in nature. Once institutional reflexivity reaches into virtually all parts of everyday social life, almost any pattern or habit can become an addiction. Every addiction is a defensive reaction, and an escape, a recognition of lack of autonomy that casts a shadow over the competence of the self. In the case of minor compulsions, feelings of shame may be limited to mild self-disparagement . . . In more pronounced forms of compulsive behaviour the integrity of the self as a whole is menaced (75–76).

In his discussion of "love, sex and other addictions," Giddens (1992) argues that while the idea of sex addiction "might at first sight look like just another eccentricity—or perhaps a new mode of exploiting a gullible populace" (66), it can, despite its lack of a definite physiological base, be conceptualized as an addiction. Giddens points out that while the concept of addiction originally focused on chemical dependency, all addictions involve compulsive behaviour and "addiction is measured de facto in terms of the consequences of the habit for an individual's control over his or her life, plus the difficulties of giving up that habit" (66–67). He notes that while all individuals have made certain patterns of behaviour routine (for example, eating a meal at a certain time), habitual activities are characterized by the use of the word "always" (for example, "I always have a martini before supper") and signify a "more psychologically binding form of repetitive behaviour" that requires a concerted effort to break. He says that compulsions are patterns of behaviour "which an individual finds very difficult, or impossible to alter through will-power alone" (71), inasmuch as their enactment—be it washing one's hands 42 times, slashing one's body with a sharp object, or sticking one's fingers down one's throat to induce vomiting—allows the individual to feel a release of tension. Even if the behaviour is time-consuming, disgusting to enact, or painful to endure, a failure to engage in it is accompanied by withdrawal-like symptoms.

According to Giddens (1992, 72–74) all addictions, whether they incur a physiological or psychological dependence, are "essential narcotising." He describes seven of the specific characteristics of addictions:

1) The high: "an experience which is set apart from the ordinary, from the mundane characteristics of everyday life . . . [A] momentary feeling of elation . . . when a 'special' sensation is produced."

2) The fix: "eases anxiety and introduces the individual into the narcotising phase of the addiction. The fix is psychologically necessary but sooner or later is succeeded by depression and feelings of emptiness; and the cycle begins again."

3) The time out: both the "high" and the "fix" are part of a "time out" in which the normal and mundane are temporarily suspended; "the person, as it were, is in 'another world' . . . [T]hese feelings are often subject to an abrupt reversal, and might turn to disgust with the addictive pattern," especially if the individual feels impotent to control the addictive behaviour.

4) The giving up of self: "the feeling of displacement of self . . . intrinsic to the sensation of release from anxiety."

5) The loss of self, followed by shame and remorse: "[a] negative feedback process . . . in which a growing dependence upon the addictive behaviour generates not increasing feelings of well-being, but panic and self-destructiveness."

6) Feeling that the addictive experience is special: a person may overcome one addiction and replace it with another; there may be two or more multiple addictions with one used to fend off the craving for another; "addictive behaviour may be layered . . . such that more minor addictive traits, or compulsions, cover over the core addictions." In that addictions "tend to be functionally interchangeable this lends strong support to the conclusion that they signal an underlying incapacity to cope with certain sorts of anxiety."

7) Addictions as pathologies of self-discipline: both the fasting of the anorexic and the bingeing of the bulimic are thought to be "two sides of one coin" with "letting go" and "tightening up" functional equivalents.

Despite his stated intentions, Giddens' analysis remains anchored in a discussion of addictions as the private misery of individual addicts. Within his treatment, the problem of addictions ultimately remains the problem of individuals that necessitates "recovery" through an individualized form of "treatment" program.

PRIVATE TROUBLE OR PUBLIC ISSUE: CONFRONTING THE PROBLEM

Perhaps no other topic more seriously challenges us to consider the "private troubles/public issues" distinction than the topic of addictions. The image of the down-and-out alcoholic, the skeletal anorexic, and the emaciated junkie all suggest that the "problem" is that of troubled individuals. This narrow focusing of attention is also reinforced by any number of self-help books dealing with any one of an expanded list of addictions. As simply one example, consider that self-mutilation has been called "the addiction of the '90s," with the growing popularity of tattooing, bodypiercing, scarification, and branding suggesting a "disease" of "epidemic" proportions (Egan 1997, 22).

There is little doubt that addicts—be they addicted to alcohol, drugs, sex, or chocolate— experience a variety of troubling or even lethal consequences as the result of their addictions. An individual addict may also find comfort or benefit from any one of several approaches that attempt to treat the problem of addiction, either through drug therapy, psychotherapy, a 12-step program, or a self-help book. However, unlike treating an individual diagnosed as suffering from diabetes, attempts to treat the problem of addiction may give rise to a host of social conditions that others would regard as socially problematic.

Consider, for example, the implications for self-labelling suggested by adherence to the philosophy of 12-step models that emphasize that:

Step 1. We admitted we were powerless over alcohol . . . that our lives had become unmanageable.

Step 2. Came to believe that a Power greater than ourselves could restore us to sanity.

Step 3. Made a decision to turn our will and our lives over to the care of God as we understood Him.

Step 4. Made a searching and fearless moral inventory of ourselves.

Step 5. Admitted to God, to ourselves, and to another human being the exact nature of our wrongs.

Step 6. Were entirely ready to have God remove all these defects of character.

Step 7. Humbly asked Him to remove our shortcomings.

Step 8. Made a list of persons we had harmed, and became willing to make amends to such people wherever possible.

Step 9. Made direct amends to such people wherever possible, except when to do so would injure them or others.

Step 10. Continued to take personal inventory and when we were wrong promptly admitted it.

Step 11. Sought through prayer and meditation to improve our conscious contact with God as we understood Him, praying only for knowledge of His will for us and the power to carry that out.

Step 12. Having had a spiritual awakening as the result of these Steps, we tried to carry this message to alcoholics and to practise these principles in all our affairs. Made a decision to turn our will and our lives over to the care of God.

There is no doubting the popularity of 12-step self-help programs such as Alcoholics Anonymous (AA). In 1990, AA claimed a worldwide membership of 1.8 million and 87 696 groups. Such is the widespread support of AA, Bufe (1991, 54) notes, that participation in one of its groups is "either a voluntary or mandatory aspect of virtually every institutional alcoholism program" (52) within the United States. A similar situation exists in Canada, where prisons afford inmates the assistance provided by groups such as AA, and attendance at AA meetings is frequently recommended by parole officers as a condition of a prisoner's release.

Despite their widespread popularity, groups such as AA encourage self-labelling as an "alcoholic" or "addict"—albeit a recovering one. As Bufe (1992, 72) points out, "Step 12 clearly indicates that A.A.'s program is a program for life—no one ever graduates from it." Whether one is a recovering chocoholic, alcoholic, or sexaholic, the key word is less "recovering" than identification of oneself as a "-holic" of some kind. Once an addict, the program suggests, one is always an addict; there is no cure. The individual is "sick" and remains so. In consequence, some would suggest that 12-step programs perpetuate within the individual a sense of being a victim in some way.

In his history of AA, Charles Bufe (1991) poses the question of whether the group should be seen as a "cult" or a "cure." He observes that the atmosphere of the self-help meeting is cozy, warm, and intimate. In some ways, the meetings would seem equivalent to the old tea group or the sensitivity sessions of the 1960s in which fellowship and camaraderie were held to be of primary importance. However, he suggests that its message is not particularly benign and that AA is selective about those it believes to be worthy of salvation. The sceptics or "one-steppers," he claims, are despised. "Rather than attempt to see why so many alcoholics reject A.A. (remember, these are oftentimes desperate individuals urgently seeking help), and whether anything—changes in the A.A. program, development of alternative programs—can be done to help them, A.A. blames them and maintains that the reason they can't stand A.A. is their 'character defects,' their lack of 'honesty,' or their lack of a genuine desire to stop drinking . . . To members, the A.A. program is perfect; the problem lies solely with those who reject it" (95). He argues that, despite the obvious religiosity of AA and the provision of groups that cater specifically to gays, lesbians, non-smokers, atheists, and agnostics, AA is nevertheless dogmatic and authoritarian. "Members of A.A. are not urged to help others overcome alcoholism regardless of their belief or disbelief in A.A.'s program. Rather—because A.A. has the answer—they are urged to 'carry this message to alcoholics,' and if those alcoholics don't want to hear the message, screw 'em" (72). For Bufe, this attitude is indicative of a "dogmatic religious sect, not that of a rational, humanistic organization concerned with the treatment of what it insists is a deadly 'illness'" (95).

Bufe concludes that AA is not a cult because it does not engage in mind-control techniques, employ deceptive recruitment techniques, provide a closed, all-encompassing environment for its members, economically exploit its members, or engage in violence in harassment of its critics. It does not have a charismatic leader nor an authoritarian hierarchy;

it makes no organizational attempt to retain members nor does it preach that the world is coming to an end (millenarianism) and that only its members will be among those fortunate few saved. Despite this, Bufe argues that AA does have within its ideological system "dangerous cult-tendencies" inasmuch as "A.A. is religiously oriented, self-absorbed, irrational, dogmatic, insists on the submission of the individual to the will of God, and views itself as the exclusive holder of truth (at least in regard to the treatment of alcoholism)" (101).

If a person learns the behaviours and justifications that lead to addiction through social interaction with others, Bufe suggests that the process of learning to be a "recovering addict" through 12-step models may also be maladaptive and result in socially problematic patterns of behaviour. He says that while the first step of confessing personal powerlessness may be useful in overcoming denial, it may contribute to lowered self-esteem. Similarly, it is Bufe's contention that the idea of powerlessness is reinforced by the "one-drink, one-drunk" assumption that a single drink is catastrophic and leads to "full-blown" relapse into addiction. He cautions that the aphorism itself might encourage a self-fulfilling prophecy in which the individual feels impotent to regain control after indulging in one drink. In addition, although the customary goal of rehabilitation stresses independence and self-directedness, the 12-step philosophy educates its members into a position of perceived helplessness and dependency. Steps 6 and 7 expressly emphasize the personal powerlessness of the individual.

For Bufe, the expansion of 12-step programs to cover an increasingly widespread range of behaviours is disconcerting. In particular, he suggests that its adoption by Incest Survivors Anonymous "would seem grotesque." He asks, "Should victims really adopt guiding principles which emphasize that they make 'amends' to those they've 'harmed', take a moral inventory of themselves, and admit their 'wrongs?'" (118). Moreover, Bufe contends that a "private trouble" approach to the problem of addictions is encapsulated within programs such as AA; indeed, he speculates that "given the inherent anti-political bias in A.A.'s program, with its inward focus, its total neglect of social factors involved in the production of alcoholism, its emphasis upon individual powerlessness, and its insistence upon divine guidance as a panacea," it and other 12-step programs will undoubtedly flourish "as a buttress for the inequitable social system within which alcoholism flourishes" (117). Commenting on AA's expansion into Latin America, Bufe argues that "[g]iven the dimensions of the alcohol abuse problem, the lack of alternative treatment programs, the presence of repressive regimes which welcome a message of political quietism, and the religion-soaked atmosphere in these countries (a not-surprising reality in lands where social misery reigns), it seems a near certainty that, for better or for worse, A.A. will continue to expand rapidly in Latin America" (117–118).

In accounting for the growth and widespread popularity of 12-step programs in North America and elsewhere, Bufe is critical of attempts to contain the social problem of addictions to troubled individuals suffering from a seemingly inexhaustible list of "addictions." He suggests that, in part, the religiosity of 12-step programs appeals to so many because they have been taught, since childhood, "that God and religious faith are the very essence of goodness" (118). Second, he suggests that the problem of loneliness is so acute in contemporary society that "people will flock to almost anything which relieves it—even 12-step meetings" (119). That is, the site occupied by the self-help group may provide a meeting place where the lonely can congregate without fear of social rejection. Moreover, if in the not-so-distant past identification of oneself as an "addict" was considered to be a stigma, it would seem that today it is considered to be a badge of self-knowledge and courage ("Oh, you're finally facing up to your problem. I really admire you for that.").

Third, Bufe argues that the anti-intellectualism of 12-step groups contributes to their popularity. The individual does not have to explore the ambiguous labyrinth of social inequities and structural problems. Fourth, the popularity of 12-step programs suggests that for many in our society, there is rampant psychological pain and problems that are "all too real." He writes:

> Unfortunately, it's a virtual certainty that, for the foreseeable future, the socioeconomic system will continue to act as a human meat grinder, churning out generation after generation of emotionally damaged people replete with "addictions" and other "dependencies." If the current trends toward regressive distribution of wealth and income, and sadistic, punitive "solutions" continue—jails rather than job training, savage drug laws rather than a socially tolerant legal code, etc.—it seems likely that the social meat grinder will accelerate the pace of its grisly work (119).

For critics of the recovery movement, the tendency of AA meetings to degenerate into a "drunkalogue" (that is, recitations of drunken escapades) may severely limit their efficacy. If the addiction itself is conceived to be the problem (rather than social stratification or the conditions that create social pressures or frustrations), only personal change—not social change—is advocated. Within this context, there is no praxis, no analysis, but rather the provision of a metaphorical emotional womb that contains and manages both the problem and the sufferer.

SOLUTIONS AND QUESTIONS

In many ways, confronting the problem of addictions is somewhat akin to describing the images produced within a hall of mirrors. One is challenged to consider whether addictions are personal or public, the problem of dysfunctional individuals or inequitable social conditions; whether the term itself should apply only to those substances that induce a physiological dependence, or be broadened to include an expanded repertoire of troublesome conditions. In addition, one might be disconcerted to note that, unlike arithmetical problems that lend themselves to unequivocal solutions, social problems frequently defy our benevolent intentions to "solve" them.

It is obvious that for Bufe, the would-be solutions of 12-step programs create a new set of social transactions and personal behaviours that can be considered socially problematic. In like fashion, it could be argued that all of the various strategies that have been promoted as solutions to the problem of addictions have created, somewhat inexorably, new sets of social problems. For instance, law-and-order advocates might urge us to increase the legal powers of police and adopt a get-tough policy with respect to addicts. For civil libertarians, however, this suggestion would not be desirable, as it would necessarily entail limiting the civil rights of Canadian citizens. In addition, the economic costs of an expanded drug enforcement role could become astounding.

There are those, too, who would have us subject everyone to drug tests so that we can "know what we're up against and minimize the risks." At present, our systems of drug testing can hardly be claimed to be foolproof. The dangers of false positives are significant. Szasz (1992) has noted various cases in which, despite evidence furnished by follow-up testing that he or she did not, in fact, take drugs, an employee could be ordered to attend in-patient therapy programs or face dismissal by an employer. Moreover, the spectre of random drug testing or making drug-testing compulsory suggests an encroachment of our rights to bodily integrity and sanctity of person. Although testing may be conducted to determine the presence of a specific drug, the investigator is furnished with additional evidence that, for whatever reasons, we may prefer to conceal (for example, that a woman is pregnant or that a man has diabetes). Testing itself could become a tool of harassment, discrimination, or exclusion.

Others have urged us to solve the problem of addictions by simply banning everything they consider to be dangerous. As we have seen, however, the identification of a drug as "dangerous" is seldom unproblematic. Is it socially desirable or socially vexatious to impose a totalitarian system of control on Canadians in order to mitigate against the potential dangers of addictions? Given that some have suggested that a variety of sources promote compulsive or "addictive" behaviour, the solution would seem to necessitate censorship on a massive scale.

SUMMARY

1. In the 1990s, we are witnessing an expanding list of "addictions" from which people are thought to be suffering.

2. In the original use of the term, "addiction" was narrowly restricted to discussions of drug and alcohol use. Some would retain this focus and argue that the use of illegal drugs and alcohol constitute the basis of the majority of our social problems. In contrast, others have suggested that virtually all of us should be acknowledged as "addicts" of some sort or another.

3. Whether the term addiction is used in a limited or expanded sense, the problem posed by it is generally linked to its association with crime, and it is seen to register costs in three areas: with the person, with the economy, and with society as a whole.

4. There are two common "approaches" to the concept of drug addiction. We termed the first the RCMP approach because it assumes that the greatest threat to society is posed by illegal drugs such as heroin, cocaine, and marijuana. We called the second the turn-the-tables approach because it argues that the most serious threat comes from drugs like nicotine and alcohol that are legally available and approved by society.

5. We have suggested that the popular conception of the "drug problem" may simply signify the success of "disinformation" techniques that discourage us from confronting those drugs and substances—in our environment, our workplace, or our supermarkets—that may be equally or more harmful.

6. The vast majority of social problems do have repercussions, often painful ones, in the lives of individual people. It would appear, however, that in the majority of the attempts to understand the problem of addiction, the recommended solutions have been so person-centred or solipsistic that the efficacy of social change has been completely ignored.

SEX AND SEXUALITY

DID YOU KNOW?

- It is estimated that over 4.5 million AIDS cases have occurred worldwide since the late 1970s. Although few Canadians had heard of AIDS when the first case in Canada was reported in 1982, by 1997 an estimated 20 000 had been diagnosed with AIDS (of which half had already died from AIDS-related causes) and 45 000 to 50 000 had been infected with HIV, the virus that causes AIDS.

- In 1997, a B.C. human rights tribunal ruled that prohibiting breast-feeding at work is a form of sexual discrimination and that discrimination against women who are breast-feeding is prohibited by the Human Rights Code.

- According to 1992 statistics from Ontario's health ministry and the City of Toronto's department of public health, more than half of sexually active 16- to 24-year-olds say they never use condoms to protect themselves from sexually transmitted diseases. Perhaps it is not surprising, then, that in Ontario the rate of chlamydia for females age 15 to 19 has increased fivefold in seven years, and for males of the same age has more than doubled.

- A 1993 study conducted by Jaffe and Suderman on more than 1500 students in grades 9 through 13 found that approximately 20 percent of male students in grades 9 and 10 believed that forced intercourse was acceptable if the female had aroused her date or had "led him on." Among female students, 7 percent felt that forced intercourse was all right in those circumstances.

THE PROBLEM

There is a commonly held belief that sexuality is nothing more than "doing what comes naturally;" after all, as Mary McIntosh (1978, 55) has pointed out, "you do it with little or no equipment and with no clothes on." Nevertheless, McIntosh stresses that while "there may be a generic 'sex' drive that is natural . . . the specific ways in which it will be expressed, and indeed whether these will be recognizably 'sexual' at all" requires that we understand the cultural definitions involved, definitions that often include prohibitions against specific forms of conduct. It is also important to understand that what we, in our particular culture, consider socially problematic in relation to sexuality is often subject to competing and sometimes contradictory evaluations.

Consider, for example, the case of *R. v. Chase*, heard in a New Brunswick court during the mid-1980s, in which the court ruled that to qualify as a "sexual assault," genital contact must have occurred. In this case, a 15-year-old girl had been forcibly touched on her shoulders and breasts by her 40-year-old male neighbour. The court found that man guilty of common assault and maintained that his actions did not constitute a sexual assault. The New Brunswick Court of Appeal agreed with the lower court, maintaining that a woman's breasts were merely "secondary sexual characteristics" and not a "primary sexual organ." In the opinion of the Court of Appeal, to rule otherwise would mean that pulling a man's beard (in their opinion, a similar "secondary sexual characteristic") would also qualify as a sexual assault. In 1987, however, the *Chase* decision was overturned by the Supreme Court of Canada; breasts were to be regarded as sexual, and sexual assault was recognized as an assault "committed in circumstances of a sexual nature, such that the sexual integrity of the victim is violated" (in Comack 1996, 149). This definition of female breasts as inherently "sexual," however, has been called into question. On the heels of topless trailblazer Gwen Jacobs and the Ontario Court of Appeal decision in 1996 that overturned her conviction for committing an "indecent act" (that is, baring her breasts in public), women activists in Canada are increasingly involved in campaigns to bare their breasts. They challenge societal definitions of female breasts as "sexual objects" and reject a male-defined aesthetic that considers the baring of breasts by certain women (e.g., Baywatch beauties, exotic dancers, etc.) as alluring but as "unacceptable" or "disgusting" by other women. All men enjoy the right to go topless, it is pointed out, regardless of how visually appealing they may be to onlookers.

A precedent-setting case heard before the British Columbia human rights panel in 1997 further challenged the notion that breasts are "sexual." Rather, the case stressed the biological function of female breasts in providing milk for infants and a woman's right to bare her breasts in public for the purpose of breast-feeding. Michelle Poirier, who worked as a speech-writer in the Ministry of Municipal Affairs, gave birth to a child in August 1990 and returned to work after her maternity leave in December of that year. At lunch-time, her daughter was dropped off at her office and breast-fed in Poirier's work cubicle; neither her supervisor nor the employees in adjacent cubicles objected to this. However, in March 1991, during a public, lunch-time presentation sponsored by the ministry's woman's program branch and held as one in a series of events related to International Women's Day, several women objected to Poirier's breast-feeding in mixed company in public, claiming it was "indecent" and "disgusting." In response, the ministry issued a new policy that prohibited employees from bringing children to the workplace. Several weeks later, Poirier wanted to attend a luncheon that was directly related to her work, but was told that the new policy prohibited her from bringing her daughter. Poirier noted that she desired to continue breast-feeding at lunch-time to avoid the physical consequences of not breast-feeding: "It hurts," she said. "It's messy. It's embarrassing and damaging to the whole process of breastfeeding." In consequence, she filed a complaint with the human rights commission in what was to become the first case in Canada to deal with breast-feeding in public. In 1997, the B.C. human rights tribunal ruled that prohibiting breast-feeding at work is a form of sexual discrimination and that the government's actions had imposed burdens on Poirier that were not imposed on other employees; the ruling also makes it clear that discrimination against women who are breast-feeding is prohibited by the Human Rights Code (Matas 1997).

Beginning early in our childhood, through direct and indirect messages, we learn about social norms surrounding sexuality—the who, what, when, and where of sexual conduct. However, the specific content of the messages we receive may vary according to such factors as our religion, our cultural background, and the time, place, and circumstances in which we live. As Masters, Johnson, and Kolodny (1985, 9) have emphasized, "*There is no sexual value system that is right for everyone and no single moral code that is indisputably correct and universally applicable*" (emphasis in original).

Anthropological research on sexual behaviour has revealed a wide variation in the cultural meanings assigned to various forms of sexual behaviour. For example, despite the Judeo-Christian ideal of monogamy and fidelity within a heterosexual union, neither of these are universal social norms. Ford's and Beach's (1951) classic study of 183 societies found that only 16 percent formally restricted infidelity, and within that percentage less than a third totally disapproved of both premarital and extramarital liaisons. Outright approval of specific types of extramarital liaisons existed in 39 percent of the societies. They also reported that in their research on 76 simpler societies, 64 percent regarded homosexuality as acceptable for some groups. Gebhard's (1965) survey of 193 cultures worldwide showed that only 14 percent rejected homosexuality. Obviously the determinants of "deviancy" are created within the limits of a specific sociocultural context. As Ford and Beach (1951, 49) pointed out, "When the Thonga first saw Europeans kissing they laughed, expressing this sentiment: 'Look at them—they eat each other's saliva and dirt.'"

The terms "sexual deviance" and "sexual perversion" are used interchangeably to refer to what others might define in a less value-laden way as "sexual variance." Although the stereotype of the deviant has often been mired in discussions of "nuts, sluts and perverts" (Liazos 1972), there has been much disagreement as to who we should regard as a "sexual deviant." In actuality, the distinction between sexual deviance and sexual normalcy is less precise than one might suppose. The criteria used in judging certain conduct as perversion or sexual deviance may be based on moral, medical, legal, or statistical grounds and result in widely divergent definitions of similar conduct. For example, a clinician might view a man's desire to observe women partially or totally nude as evidence of tendencies towards voyeurism or scoptophilia. If the man engages in such behaviour in a clandestine manner and uses it as a primary form of sexual gratification, the clinician may classify the desire as a paraphilia or fetish. However, others might dispute the wisdom of these definitions and argue that the man's behaviour is "normal" rather than perverse. They might point to the widespread presence of exotic dancers, male and female, in taverns, nightclubs, and bars, and suggest that such forms of entertainment attest to the normalcy and acceptability of the man's desire.

Evidently, reactions to the varied forms of sexual behaviour are multivocal. Although in the 1990s there are an impressive number of books, both popular and scholarly, that instruct readers on ways to improve their sex lives, some people remain convinced that only certain forms of conduct are acceptable and that those who deviate from these standards are morally disreputable. For example, research conducted by Allgeier and Fogel (1977) revealed that when unmarried college students were shown pictures of couples having sex in various positions, the women, but not the men, showed real distaste for the couple in the woman-above position. They rated the woman as "dirtier, less respectable, less moral, less good, less desirable as a wife, and less desirable as a mother when she is on top than when she is beneath the man during intercourse." This reaction may reflect negative attributions given to someone who engages in what appears to be, according to the new Kinsey report on sex, simply a less frequently used sexual position (Reinisch and Beasley 1990).

Although some forms of sexual conduct may, if acted upon, be indictable under Canadian criminal law (for example, pedophilia, exhibitionism, or soliciting for the purpose of prostitution), changes within the law reveal shifting attitudes as to what should be regarded as socially problematic in relation to sexual behaviour. For example, until 1983 "marital rape" did not exist under Canadian law. The omission of marital rape as an offence was consistent with laws and customs dating back to the world's earliest civilizations, which held that a woman had only the status of a chattel, or a piece of property, first of her father, then of her husband, and then of her son. Virginity until marriage and fidelity within it were inexorably bound to what was considered a normal measure of obedience; the dutiful daughter was virginal until marriage and the good wife was faithful and sexually receptive to her husband.

For example, in Athens, women had no more political or legal rights than slaves and were under the absolute authority of their male next-of-kin. To the Greeks, a woman was *gyne*, a "bearer of children," regardless of her age or marital status. Similarly, under English common law, the status of women as property of their husbands within marriage was illustrated by criminalizing the act of *criminal conversation*, defined as one man having sex with another man's wife. The cuckolded husband was permitted to sue his wife's lover for damages to compensate him for the infringements against his honour and for the loss of his monopoly over his wife's sexual services.

One way of defining "deviancy" is to limit it to behaviour that is statistically rare. But if we do this, it is difficult to maintain that many of the departures from Judeo-Christian teachings on sexuality are, in fact, "deviant." Thus, the research of Kinsey et al. (1948; 1953), the first major study of sexual behaviour, showed the wide range of sexual conduct engaged in by North Americans, reporting that 70 percent of men had patronized prostitutes, that 40 to 50 percent of males raised on farms had engaged in sexual activities with animals, that 92 percent of men and 58 percent of women had masturbated, and that 59 percent of men and 43 percent of women had engaged in oral-genital activity within a heterosexual relationship.

Kinsey's research also suggested that homosexual behaviour was relatively common. His findings reported that 60 percent of males had had some form of homosexual experience prior to adulthood and that approximately 37 percent of all males had had at least one adult homosexual experience leading to orgasm. Only 4 percent went from those experiences to permanent homosexual roles. Kinsey et al. (1953) estimated that approximately 13 percent of women had experienced at least one same-sex experience leading to orgasm and that only 2 to 3 percent of females were mostly or exclusively homosexual on a lifelong basis. For women, bisexuality (having sexual relations with both males and females) was much more common than exclusive homosexuality.

The research of Kinsey et al. (1948; 1953), and others to follow, demonstrates the futility of attempts to divide human beings into only two dichotomous, polar-opposite categories—"heterosexual" and "homosexual." Rather, the Kinsey findings and the subsequent development of a seven-point scale of sexual behaviour emphasize the fluidity of human sexual experience. "Bisexuality" (positions 1 through 5 on the scale) was much more common than exclusive homosexuality (position 6). Six to 14 percent of unmarried women, 2 to 3 percent of married women, and 8 to 10 percent of previously married women were found to have had more than incidental same-sex experiences along with predominantly other-sex experiences. The comparable statistics for men were 2 to 6 percent of unmarried men, 1 percent of married men, and 1 to 6 percent of previously married men. All of these statistics refer to sexual behaviour only and do not include sexual feelings that were not acted on nor sexuality identity.

More recently, the nationwide research of Michael et al. (1994, 174–177) on 3432 American adults age 18 to 59 focused attention in part on three different aspects of homosexuality: sexual attraction to others of the same sex (a desire measure); engaging in same-sex sexual acts (a behavioural measure); and identification as being homosexual. "The three categories are distinct . . . and produce three different estimates of homosexuality. . . . [E]stimates of the prevalence of homosexuality depend very much on what questions you ask and what you think it means to be a homosexual" (Michael et al. 1994, 174).

Their research, not unexpectedly, notes that there are more people who find others of the same sex sexually attractive than there are people who actually engage in homosexual acts. Thus, while 5.5 percent of women reported that they found the thought of a lesbian sexual experience very appealing or appealing, only 4 percent reported themselves to actually be attracted sexually to other women, and less than 2 percent reported having had a sexual encounter with another woman in the preceding year (Michael et al. 1994, 174–175). Among the women in their sample, slightly over 4 percent reported having had a sexual experience with another woman at some point in their lives. Such experiences rarely occurred prior to age 18 (Michael et al. 1994, 175, 176). However, only 1.4 percent of the women in their sample identified themselves as homosexual or bisexual.

Among the men, approximately 6 percent indicated being attracted to other men, although only 2 percent reported having had a sexual experience with another man in the past year. Nine percent of the men had had a homosexual encounter at some point in their lives since puberty. Sixty percent of the men who reported having had a sexual experience with another man prior to the age of 18 continued to engage in homosexuality during their adult years. Only 2.8 percent of the male sample identified themselves as either homosexual or bisexual (Michael et al. 1994, 176). In general, men who find other men sexually attractive are more likely than women to act on their desires and to identify themselves as homosexual. Nevertheless, The Heterosexual Questionnaire (Case 3-1) offers a telling commentary on the relative acceptability of heterosexuality and homosexuality within contemporary society.

Private Trouble or Public Issue?

It seems as if we are confronted daily with evidence of how the private sexual conduct of Canadians enters the *public* domain of commentary and debate. Perhaps the most obvious example in recent years is AIDS, which early on was associated with homosexuality, prostitution, and promiscuity, and in this way came to be popularly thought of as a disease of retribution for deviant sexuality. Similarly, at various times, the practices of masturbation, birth control, premarital or extramarital sex, divorce, and wife-swapping have all been viewed as symptomatic of a social malaise that, if unchecked, would precipitate widespread moral degeneration and societal collapse. For some social commentators, the viewpoint

---

CASE 3-1   The Heterosexual Questionnaire

1. What do you think caused your heterosexuality?

2. When and how did you decide you were a heterosexual?

3. Is it possible that your heterosexuality is just a phase you may grow out of?

4. Is it possible that your heterosexuality stems from a neurotic fear of others of the same sex?

5. If you have never slept with a person of the same sex, is it possible that all you need is a good gay lover?

6. Do your parents know that you are straight? Do your friends and/or roommate(s) know? How did they react?

7. Why do you insist on flaunting your heterosexuality? Can't you just be who you are and keep it quiet?

8. Why do heterosexuals place so much emphasis on sex?

9. Why do heterosexuals feel compelled to seduce others into their lifestyle?

10. A disproportionate majority of child molesters are heterosexual. Do you consider it safe to expose children to heterosexual teachers?

11. Just what do men and women do in bed together? How can they truly know how to please each other, being so anatomically different?

12. With all the societal support marriage receives, the divorce rate is spiraling. Why are there so few stable relationships among heterosexuals?

13. Statistics show that lesbians have the lowest incidence of sexually transmitted diseases. Is it really safe for a woman to maintain a heterosexual lifestyle and run the risk of disease and pregnancy?

14. How can you become a whole person if you limit yourself to compulsive, exclusive heterosexuality?

15. Considering the menace of overpopulation, how could the human race survive if everyone were heterosexual?

16. Could you trust a heterosexual therapist to be objective? Don't you feel s/he might be inclined to influence you in the direction of his/her own leanings?

17. There seem to be very few happy heterosexuals. Techniques have been developed that might enable you to change if you really want to. Have you considered trying aversion therapy?

18. Would you want your child to be heterosexual, knowing the problems that s/he would face?

From M. Rochlin, "The Heterosexual Questionnaire," in *Changing Men*, Spring 1982.

that equates deviation from Judeo-Christian norms with social disorganization seems especially warranted in the 1990s. Exotic dancing, telephone sex lines, escort services, and personal ads for sexual services are all pointed to as evidence of a society in a perilous state. In addition, the intensity of the debates generated by topics related to reproduction (for example, illegitimacy, contraception, and abortion), also serves to remind us how society impinges on the most private or intimate of acts.

Although historically, intimacy, sexuality, and procreation were seen as inextricably bound together with the family, increasingly there has been a fragmentation and separation of these assumed functions of the family. Thus, even though sexuality was never *exclusively* the property of the family, it has become increasingly separate from both marriage and reproduction. Similarly, if reproduction was held to be the *sine qua non* of the family in former times, the availability of adoption and the new reproductive technologies make the possibility of the homosexual family—and particularly the lesbian family—increasingly viable. Accordingly, in seeking to understand the social problems of sexuality in contemporary Canadian society, we are forced to examine our notions of what constitutes a "private trouble" or a "public issue" and to challenge taken-for-granted classifications of what formerly may have been considered "sexual deviance" or, less judgmentally, "sexual variance."

ANALYZING THE PROBLEM

For conservatives past and present, the problems identified in relation to sexuality are attributable to the rejection or ignorance of the social norms that traditionally regulated "appropriate" sexual, marital, and family behaviour. In the Christian tradition, following St. Paul, sex was redeemed only if it occurred within the confines of marriage for the purposes of procreation. From the fourth-century writings of St. Augustine to the thirteenth-century writings of St. Thomas Aquinas, one finds evidence that the proposed ideal state was total celibacy, advocated for all who could practise it and a view of sex that can best be described as fearful. Even within marriage, sex was controlled—taboo on Sundays, Wednesday, and Fridays; for the 40 days preceding Easter and Christmas; during penance; and for the three days before attending Mass. Marital intercourse was to be endured rather than enjoyed if women wished to be strictly virtuous. Indeed, a sixth-century pope, Gregory the Great, decreed that married couples "not befoul their intercourse with pleasure" (Masters, Johnson, and Kolodny 1985; see also Tannahill 1980).

Thus, sexual deviance was identified as behaviour discontinuous with the "code ethics" (Pike 1967a; 1967b) of Judeo-Christianity (for example, "If a man also lie with mankind as he lieth with a woman, both of them have committed an abomination: They shall surely be put to death and their blood shall be upon them" [Leviticus 20: 13]). Accordingly, engaging in actions other than heterosexual intercourse within the boundaries of marriage was thought sufficient to adjudge a person as a "deviant," a type who was sexually loose, promiscuous, immoral, or sinful. The act that contravened the norm became a "master status" (Becker 1963, 33) thought to provide conclusive information about the character of the person. For example, in the past, discussions of prostitution often employed a medical analogy to depict it as dysfunctional or debilitating to society's "moral fibre." Thus, Sanger (1910, 3) described prostitution as "a moral pestilence which creeps insidiously into the privacy of the domestic circle, and draws thence the myriads of its victims and which saps the foundation of that holy confidance, the first, the most beautiful attraction of home." Similarly, Acton (1857, 161) decried "this plague . . . now eating into the heart of society . . . the very worst form which human wretchedness and degradation can assume . . . the worm that never dies."

Admittedly, both Acton and Sanger represent rather antique sources. However, the tendency remains for prostitution to be termed dysfunctional, if not for society as a whole than for the individual prostitute him- or herself. Indeed, perhaps the most significant change that has occurred in recent times is in the types of metaphors employed to describe the "deviant." Thus, rather than viewing the prostitute as "evil" or "spiritually depraved," the prostitute may be described in the language of sickness or pathology (Greenwald 1958). Accordingly, whereas Acton recommended purging British society of moral pestilence by sending its prostitutes to Canada, conservative writers now extol the wonders of psychological intervention to cure the "prostitute," the "homosexual," or other so-called "sexual deviants."

In addition, conservative social critics, past and present, have suggested that "profane sex" (Gairdner 1992, 87) can only lead to the deterioration of society as a whole. For example, Murray (1990) assigns culpability for many social ills to the presence of an "underclass" who are largely distinguishable by their sexual behaviour. For Murray, of the three principal "indicators" of the "underclass"—illegitimacy, violent crime, and wilful unemployment— illegitimacy is primary.

While Murray views all types of single parenthood as having potentially harmful effects, he considers unwed mothers to be particularly problematic. According to him, the problem of illegitimacy is primarily a lower-class phenomenon, with unwed mothers likely to live most of their lives on welfare. Supposedly, for women of the lower classes, the prospect of living on welfare offers less of a deterrent than it might for women of higher socioeconomic classes; indeed, Murray suggests, it may even prove a powerful incentive for unmarried women to become pregnant. Accordingly, he argues that unless women are confronted with financial deterrents or suffer from acute social stigma for bearing children out of wedlock, they will be cheerfully promiscuous and bear large numbers of children because "sex is fun and babies are endearing." Portraying lower-class women as promiscuous and opportunistic, Murray views the rise in illegitimate births as directly related to the benefits available to single women with children and the availability of public housing. Unless they are made to suffer the consequences of their actions, Murray warns, such women will not only incur vast amounts of public debt but also set in motion a host of socially injurious consequences.

First, the unwed mother who is part of the underclass is depicted as wholly self-absorbed and, in consequence, a negligent and inept mother. Moreover, because the underclass is thought to congregate largely in lower-class neighbourhoods where dysfunctional attitudes become entrenched, Murray predicts that the rise in illegitimate births will actually increase the incidence of social ills such as child abuse, delinquency, drug use, and crime. He maintains that in communities where single-mother households predominate, "the kids tend to run wild. The fewer the fathers, the greater the tendencies" (in Abbott and Wallace 1992, 85).

Second, deprived of positive male role models, and confronted with "independently wealthy" welfare mothers, young men are emasculated. They see little reason to take jobs or seek higher education, or later to support their families. In consequence, they are portrayed as prone to take up deviant and criminal lifestyles. Championing the view that hard work is good for the soul and that marriage acts as an "indispensibly civilizing influence" on men, particularly young men who "are essentially barbarians," Murray warns, "Men who do not support families find other ways to prove that they are men, which tends to take various destructive forms" (in Abbott and Wallace 1992, 85).

In this way, the unwed mother becomes an ideal-typical folk devil (Cohen 1980), who is assigned culpability for a host of social ills. Moreover, as Abbott and Wallace (1992, 89) observe, even if Murray's arguments are "intellectually fallacious and his use of statistics highly selective," they give a pseudo-intellectual authority to the "victim-blame" approach, which identifies the poor—especially female-headed households and black people—as the causes, not the victims, of poverty, crime, and child abuse. In addition, by suggesting that children of the "underclass" are "undersocialized" as the result of their inept, selfish mothers and absent, emasculated fathers, Murray implies that the "seeds" of crime are contained within the "dysfunctional" home.

The Functionalist Approach

For functionalists, many of the prohibitions against various forms of sexual practices are only truly explainable by reference to the past. Functionalists point out that in traditional, preindustrial societies, a high birth rate was necessary to ensure a stable population and to offset the ravages of a high mortality rate due to wars, diseases, famines, and plagues. Children born within families were thought to have the optimal chance of survival; moreover, the agrarian lifestyle of times past often demanded the energies and availability of a sizeable pool of workers. Accordingly, an insistence on heterosexual practices that favoured procreation was highly functional; practices that discouraged the likelihood of procreation, such as homosexuality, masturbation, and birth control, were viewed as dysfunctional. Moreover, given the fact that "maternity" is evident but "paternity" less certain, the greater social control of female sexual behaviour was justified by concerns over family lineage and inheritance.

In like fashion, functionalist theorist Kingsley Davis (1936) has argued that prostitution has always functioned to offer society a "safety valve" by providing a readily available sexual partner for potential rapists, dissatisfied husbands, and sexually hyperactive youths. Davis' article is interesting if only because he maintains that a latent function of prostitution is the promotion of marriage as a social institution. That is, patronizing a prostitute is seen as a form of painless adultery that does not disrupt a legal marriage. In this way, prostitution becomes functionally bound to other social institutions. According to Davis, there is a "natural imbalance" between male and female sexual appetites, with males supposedly possessing a greater sex drive than women. As a result of "a simple biological appetite" that makes a man "naturally" more interested in sex than a woman, "[w]hen all other sources of gratification fail, due to defects of person or circumstance, prostitution can be relied on to furnish relief " (1936, 750).

It is noteworthy that Davis nowhere considers a woman's desire for sexual variety, indulgence, or perversion. As Mary McIntosh (1978) observed in her article, "Who Needs Prostitutes Anyway?" functionalist sociologists seldom expressed concern over the provision of a readily available partner for the sexually desirous female. Rather, by positing male sexuality as different from female sexuality, functionalists cast women into one of two roles: the "decent woman" who is to be protected from male lust and the "prostitute" who exists to expressly satisfy it. Similarly, Davis approvingly cites Flexner's commentary as to why the prostitute, rather than the patron, should bear the social stigma of what is assuredly a mutual act:

> Being a social outcast [she] may be periodically punished without disturbing the usual course
> of society; no one misses her while she is serving out her turn—no one, at least, about whom

society has any concern. The man however, is more than partner in an immoral act: he discharges important social and business relations. . . . He cannot be imprisoned without deranging the usual course of society (Davis 1936, 754).

As Lowman (1992, 58) has commented, the belief that prostitution is latently functional rests on the unchallenged assumption that males possess a more urgent sex drive than women and that this desire must be satisfied. In his words, "once that belief is problematized, the question 'functional for whom?' is bathed in a different light; male interests seep from the shadows."

The Conflict Approach

The conflict approach emphasizes and questions the competing interests and sometimes hidden value systems that exist in relation to sexual behaviour. As an obvious example, conflict theorists would maintain that the controversy surrounding the issue of pornography reveals the numerous disagreements possible in responding to a sexually charged issue. Even though the terms pornography and obscenity are often used in everyday language as synonyms, conflict theorists would note that it is important to remember that the two are legally distinct. *Pornography*, derived from the Greek word referring to writings by or about prostitutes, is legal in Canada. *Obscenity*, defined as work or material that has as its dominant characteristic "the undue exploitation of sex" and that thereby violates "community standards of tolerance," is illegal. The depiction of explicit sex in and of itself is not obscene unless children are used in the presentation. However, material that exploits sex in a "degrading or dehumanizing manner," or the portrayal of sex coupled with violence, is considered evidence of obscenity.

Even though all reasonable people would agree that snuff porn, which captures the murder and torture of a woman on film, is obscene, in other cases the task of distinguishing and defining obscenity is more controversial. As Mr. Justice John Sopinka noted in a 64-page 1992 Supreme Court of Canada ruling that upheld the constitutionality of the federal obscenity law, "the community standards test is concerned not with what Canadians would not tolerate being exposed to themselves, but what they would not tolerate other Canadians being exposed to" (The Globe and Mail, February 28, 1992). In other words, while we may personally view certain depictions of sex as repugnant or offensive, we may at the same time support the rights of others to pursue what they find erotic, stimulating, or pleasurable.

There has also been debate over what specific acts are "degrading or dehumanizing." Mr. Justice Sopinka observed that "degrading or dehumanizing materials place women (and sometimes men) in positions of subordination, servile submission or humiliation" and, as such, "run against the principle of equality and dignity of all human beings." In practice, such guidelines can be difficult to apply, but again most reasonable people would agree that the depiction of bestiality or sex with animals would qualify as "dehumanizing" and therefore obscene, as would depictions of violent sado-masochistic activities.

From the 1960s through the 1980s, feminists waged war against pornography, guided in part by Steinem's (1978) distinction between *erotica*, characterized by depictions of mutually consenting adults participating in egalitarian sexual encounters, and *pornography*, sexual relations characterized by dominance, exploitation, and violence. "Good" sexuality is thus differentiated from "bad" sexuality by virtue of the distribution of power between participants. Women presented in pornography were held to be without power while male participants in and viewers of pornography possessed power. Fueled by a strong belief that pornography, broadly and vaguely defined, causes men to commit sexual and nonsexual violence against women, feminists lead by Dworkin (1981) and MacKinnon (1987) fought to ban, by legal or other means, virtually all explicit depictions of sexuality.

The efforts of the anti-pornography movement have met with resistance from both outside and within feminism, since the issues involved are more than the objectification and commodification of women depicted in positions of unequal power but also censorship in general and censorship of sexuality in particular. Some feminists are against censorship but not necessarily pro-pornography (see Burstyn 1985) while others are pro-pornography (see Strossen 1995). The latter groups of feminists use the term "pornography" to refer to any explicit depictions of sexuality and do not consider power to be either a central or a contentious issue. Any objections they raise against existing pornography pertain to poor quality in all facets of production and an orientation directed solely towards promoting and satisfying male interests in sexuality. Pro-pornography feminists advocate for better-quality pornography written, produced, and directed by women for women and designed to appeal to, explore, and extend female sexual fantasies, along with discussion and debate about female sexuality—in other words, females literally writing, performing, and disseminating their own sexuality scripts.

The pro-pornography movement emphasizes the importance of women gaining power and control over their sexuality and their roles in sexual scripts. Without the power to explore their own sexuality, to name, understand, and express sexual desire, women's sexuality will remain bounded by limitations created and enforced by men and, through socialization conditioning, by women themselves. The "feminist sexuality wars" between anti- and pro-pornography adherents, and between feminists who insist that only egalitarian, consensual, nondirected sexuality is acceptable for women and other feminists who reject such "vanilla" sexuality and argue that women should be encouraged and permitted to pursue any and all forms of sexual pleasure, including sado-masochism, have persisted for over two decades and promise to continue into the next millennium. As well, how successful women will be in renegotiating existing heterosexuality scripts or gaining acceptance of new scripts is debatable. Clearly issues surrounding sexuality, gender, and power have yet to be resolved.

Consider as well that while most discussions of pornography centre on materials that appeal to men, there is, as Robert Stoller (1985) observed, "a pornography just for women," that is, modern day romance novels. Conflict theorists would suggest that the impact of this sort of material on society, though more subtle, is no less vexatious than that of material that could be defined as legally obscene. Conflict and feminist theorists would observe that romance novels only serve to reinforce the patriarchal structure of society—so-called romantic fulfilment is just another inducement for women to sign over control of their lives to the men with whom they get involved.

In the early years, Harlequin Romances, a spectacularly successful Canadian publisher of romance novels, followed a readily recognizable format. Its books were avowedly "clean, easy to read love stories about contemporary people, set in exciting foreign places" (in Kaplan 1991). Over the last two decades, the range of Harlequin romantic fantasies has expanded. Although incest, adultery, and abortion remain taboo, there is an assortment of "bodice rippers," as they are termed in the publishing industry, to appeal to differing female erotic tastes. As Louise Kaplan has commented, "Harlequin is now capable of providing loyal readers with an inviting assortment of romantic delights." She notes that while the "basic Romance series stresses a clean, fresh approach to sex, where heroines are virtually innocent to start with and metaphorically so after the seduction," other series, such as "Superromance" are designed to "appeal to the more passionate reader" or offer "the promise of love—the guarantee of satisfaction" (1991, 325).

In other words, when it comes to sex scenes these books run the gamut from a sort of frilly, perfumed erotica to graphic descriptions that border on the pornographic. Still, at the end of the story, Harlequin and other erotic romances provide the female with a husband. The importance of this message for women, namely the need for an intimate relationship, remains constant. This message, feminists have suggested, is vexatious, for it functions as an informal system of social control on women, tying the expression of female sexuality to a normative framework of heterosexual love, romance, marriage, and procreation.

But this question remains: Could this material actually qualify as obscene under Canadian law? Conflict theorists would maintain that although romance novels are not legally obscene, they function to promote arrangements in society that should be considered obscene. Even though the heroines in contemporary Harlequin Romances are portrayed as being more erotically and financially self-assertive than they used to be, romantic love is still held out to be the highest good in life. In this way, they obscure the need for radical social change and for a realignment of power relations between the sexes.

The Interactionist Approach

The interactionist approach focuses on the social process by which people come to learn sexual conduct, conventional or otherwise. For example, the socialization process involved in becoming a homosexual is thought to begin with a person's perception of himself or herself as possibly being gay. This perception may arise in a number of ways: from erotic fantasies about people of the same sex, from an actual physical encounter, or from something as vague as feeling a sense of "differentness" about oneself. For men, finding oneself to have "feminine tastes" or a "feminine" body build may be sufficient cause for considering oneself a homosexual.

The label "homosexual" can also be foisted on one through the reactions of others. Thus, if a child is discovered engaging in same-sex exploration or play, a parent or peer may accuse the child of being a "fag," "dyke," or "queer." Pogrebin (1983, 39) has observed that in a sexist and homophobic society, many parents feel the need to "protect" their children from becoming homosexuals, viewing homosexuality as one of the worst things that could happen to their children—worse even than drug addiction.

In an attempt to distinguish homosexuals by

1) the extent to which homosexuality is important to the individual's self-concept, and

2) the degree to which the individual's homosexual experience is socially organized,

Plummer (1975, 98) constructed a fourfold classification of the forms of homosexual experience. He used the term *casual homosexuality* to indicate brief homosexual encounters (real or imagined) that have no profound significance for the individuals involved. For example, Kinsey et al. (1948, 610) reported that 60 percent of pre-adolescent males engaged in some type of homosexual activity but that only 2 to 3 percent were homosexual on a lifelong basis. Plummer coined the term *personalized homosexuality* to refer to those instances in which the homosexual experience is regarded as important, but the individual is isolated from any pro-homophile movements or group structures that would provide positive support for the experience. For example, Humphreys (1970) has suggested that the "closet queen" (that is, the homosexual who purposefully attempts to deny his homosexuality or keep it hidden) is apt to be politically conservative and a "moral crusader" who, at least publicly, supports such activities as police intimidation of those who engage in homosexual activity. This is one way in which the closet queen attempts to pass as "straight" within conventional society.

For Plummer, *homosexuality as a situated activity* refers to those people for whom homosexual behavior may be expressed within specific settings or groups but in which the individual does not see himself as being gay nor view homosexuality as being of pivotal importance to his life. Thus, in a study of adolescent male prostitutes, Reiss (1961) noted that they were able to retain a heterosexual self-image by following a strict code that separated their "work role" from their self-concept as heterosexual. The adolescent males did not associate with homosexuals other than for payment, refused to participate in specific types of sexual encounters, confined their participation to the "male" (insertor) role during sexual intercourse, and were indignant and hostile when approached by homosexuals in an "off situation." Similarly, Kirkham (1971) notes that when incarcerated men face the limited sexual choices available within prison—celibacy, masturbation, or homosexuality—the decision to engage in homosexual conduct need not entail a fundamental restructuring of the person's identification as heterosexual.

Plummer's fourth category, *homosexuality as a way of life*, refers to people for whom homosexuality is a lifestyle and who embrace the homosexual subculture in which individuals have defined themselves as gay and made this central to their lifestyle. According to Simon and Gagnon (1967, 181), "coming out" refers to the point in time when the individual identifies him- or herself as a homosexual or lesbian and the first major explorations are made of the gay community. Through the process of coming out, personalized homosexuality may be redefined from something shameful or guilt-inducing to something positive and acceptable. The individual may gain access to role models or to those who will instruct him or her in social and sexual roles. As well, immersion in a community of like-minded others may encourage the perception that the individual is not an isolated "deviant."

In addition to concentrating on the socialization process by which a homosexual becomes aware of his or her sexual orientation, interactionists also focus on the process by which homosexuals are labelled as "deviants" and on the difficulty they experience in trying to convince mainstream society to repudiate this label.

Since 1969, Gay Liberation Front organizations have attempted to challenge pejorative legal and social evaluations of homosexual and lesbian behaviour. Although in Canada there is no national Gay Liberation Front per se but rather a series of fragmented organizations ranging from the unstructured to the highly organized and bureaucratized, Kameny (1972, 185) suggests that there are two basic tenets of the homophile movement:

1) homosexuals are the equals of heterosexuals, and

2) homosexuality is fully the equal of heterosexuality.

Therefore, the movement is dedicated to the denunciation of the "pathological" model of homosexuality and determined to enhance the lives of homosexuals as homosexuals. The struggle over the moral meaning of homosexuality is fought simultaneously on several fronts. Employment, housing, cultural representations in mass media, and familial rights all provide arenas in which the moral appropriateness of homosexual and lesbian conduct is debated and negotiated.

It should not be supposed that the process of "coming out" is simple or painless. Interactionist critics will often focus on this process to explain why there seems to be a preponderance of admitted homosexuals in some professions and not in others. First, it may be assumed that homosexuals may gravitate to those professions that have already been integrated and therefore offer situations in which they will feel supported instead of condemned. Second, Green and Money (1966) have suggested that homosexuals are drawn particularly to professions such as acting because they have had to hone their role-playing skills as a means of self-defence. Rather than viewing the selection of a theatrical career as a response to some form of innate "propensity," we should understand that acting is a logical extension of "passing" strategies through which the homosexual attempts to avoid negative social sanctions by pretending to be straight (Williams and Weinberg 1971). While there are in fact homosexuals and lesbians in every profession, it is obvious that certain professions afford greater laxity or freedom of choice with respect to their members' sexual orientations than others. Thus, a "self-fulfilling prophecy," or the illusion of one, may occur. Stereotypes may be inadvertently reinforced because gays and lesbians in atypical professions may be hesitant or fearful about "coming out" and thus remain socially "invisible."

Finally, interactionists note that the militant tactic of "outing" or exposing prominent closet queens, particularly those who have publicly condemned homosexuality, is designed, in part, to furnish positive role models for homosexuals and to force closeted gays to address their own homophobia. The exposure of such persons is thought to encourage an awareness that homosexual feelings and behaviours are not confined to persons who fulfil only the most florid of stereotypes.

EROTICISM SCRIPTS: GENDER AND SEXUALITY

Sprecher, McKinney and Orbuch (1987, 30) observe that "men and women are socialized to different sexual scripts . . . which are norms and beliefs about the when, why, what, where and with whom sex is appropriate for a particular gender." Needless to say, the contents of these sexual scripts have varied over history and continue to differ in important ways for males and females.

As we shall see, the social changes that have occurred in relation to sexuality in Canadian society have been overlaid on old beliefs, attitudes, and values about sex in general, and in particular about the normative sexual scripts of male and female sexuality. The result is a confusing and contradictory mixture of bold new expressions and vestiges of the old. Some in our society exemplify a new eroticism; however, they coexist in sharp contrast to their neighbours who embody the traditional. Other individuals contain within themselves a personally constructed combination of both new and the old elements. Indeed, even media images of the heroes of pop music exemplify the array of female and male erotic roles: from the self-advancing and raunchy sexuality of Madonna and Mick Jagger, to the homosexuality of k.d. lang and the ultimate gender-blender "Gynan" (a.k.a. Prince), to the down-home, wholesome images of Anne Murray and Garth Brooks.

As Nelson and Robinson (1994) note, the history of changes in sexual values over the past century and a half in Western societies is largely a history of changes in female erotic patterns. That is, the erotic "script" for females has undergone the most significant alterations over time, while the male script has remained largely unchanged (Long Laws and Schwartz 1977; Ehrenreich, Hess, and Jacobs 1987). After examining the ways in which the scripts have changed, we will also consider some of the contemporary social problems these changes have created.

The Double Standard

From the nineteenth century onwards, the medical empire of general practitioners, gynecologists, obstetricians, mental health professionals, and asylum workers defined female sexuality in a way that affected the lives and liberties of women in everyday life (Edwards 1981; Ehrenreich and English 1974; 1978). As "experts," their opinions served to legitimate the suppression of women and their eroticism by viewing any behaviour that contradicted the norms of chastity or marital fidelity as indicative of mental illness. Moreover, as Taylor (1956) has pointed out in his history of sexuality, in former times, a single episode of sexual intercourse outside the confines of marriage was sufficient for a woman to be labelled a "prostitute."

Based on their content analysis review of "marriage manuals," sociologists Gordon and Shankweiler (1971) documented a change in the opinions and beliefs of the medical profession beginning around the turn of the twentieth century. Slowly, "good" and "virtuous" women were granted by professional experts a right to be sexual so long as their sexuality was confined within the institution of legal marriage. Nevertheless, female sexuality was believed to be characterized by two major qualities: dormancy and monogamy. Women were believed to be monogamous by nature and therefore naturally prone to saving their sexuality for one man only, namely their husbands. Men, in contrast, were not considered to possess this monogamous quality, and this provided an apparent justification for a "double standard" of expectations for male and female sexuality. In addition, it was also widely believed that female sexuality was essentially dormant, quietly residing under the surface, until awakened in true Sleeping Beauty fashion by a man—again, her husband. However, in contrast to the practice in previous centuries, a "good" woman could now be sexual and actually enjoy the erotic activity that took place in her marital bed. Within this framework, it is not surprising that the topic of lesbianism was generally ignored; when female sexuality is defined as a response to male sexual need, rather than as aggressive or purposeful, lesbian behaviour becomes a theoretical non sequitur.

Although these official revelations appear to have had a liberating impact on both marital and nonmarital eroticism of the time, the next significant attitudinal change did not occur until the "sexual revolution" of the mid-1960s. At this time, the supposedly monogamous character of female sexuality was altered further by numerous scientists and social critics to permit, even advocate, premarital sexual experiences. Research on college and university undergraduate students documented the steady increase in the proportion of women experiencing eroticism (not only sexual intercourse, but also oral and anal sex) while still unmarried and typically with no intention of marrying their current sexual partner. (For one summary of the changes in erotic practices and attitudes since the 1960s, see Rubin 1990.)

Although these changes have often been attributed to the invention of oral contraceptives, various forms of contraception were available and used in the past without initiating similar changes in attitudes. It is noteworthy, for instance, that the condom was invented over 150 years ago when the vulcanization of rubber made the mass production of condoms possible, but that this device had no liberalizing effect on Victorian attitudes towards sexual self-expression. Moreover, as Nelson and Robinson (1994) point out, "an inert object—a pill—cannot by itself, bring about significant changes in behaviour. Behaviour itself must first change, including, at the very minimum, creating the behaviour of actually taking the pill." Among the many other changes occurring during the 1960s and 1970s were the growing financial independence of women and the growing sense of female empowerment that has continued to this day. Reiss (1986) has noted that "the greater the power of one gender, the greater that gender's sexual rights in that society." A growing economic independence, coupled with a more effective form of contraception that permitted greater control over reproduction, further weakened the previously necessary link between sexuality and legal marriage.

In Canada, the most dramatic increases in female premarital sexual behaviour occurred during the period from the mid-1960s through the 1970s. However, by the mid-1980s the rates of increase began to slow down. Similarly, national survey data collected in the United States on American teenagers found the same trend of a dramatic increase in the proportion of females experiencing sex during their teenage years during the 1970s and the levelling off of the rates of increase during the early 1980s (see Hofferth, Kahn, and Baldwin 1987). This development has been interpreted by some in both Canada and the United States to indicate a "trend towards conservatism," or a "resurgence in traditional family values." However, others such as Robinson et al. (1991) have suggested that the slowing down of rates during the 1980s simply indicates a "ceiling effect." That is, they argue that we have now reached the level where the vast majority of those interested in sexual experimentation prior to marriage are now engaging in it. Those still abstaining, termed *committed virgins*, who prefer for different reasons to wait until marriage before having sexual intercourse, are thought to comprise approximately 15 percent of the younger population.

Although the problem of how best to interpret the levelling off remains subject to debate, what is less arguable is that we have been witnessing a "*trend towards convergence*" (see Darling, Kallen, and Van Dusen 1984) in the sexual behaviour patterns of young unmarried males and females. That is, there is less and less of a statistical discrepancy in the numbers of young women and young men who are sexually active. To this extent at least, the double standard is crumbling.

However, in a person-perception experiment conducted to examine the effect the "double standard" has on judgments young people form about their peers' sexual experiences, Sprecher, McKinney, and Orbuch (1987) discovered that the double standard still exerts a measure of control even over the minds of sexually active youths. They provided 233 males and 320 female undergraduates with information about the first coital experiences of fictitious persons, both male and female. Their findings indicated that more negative evaluations were made of the female if she first had sexual intercourse within a casual rather than a steady relationship and if she was a teenager (age 16) rather than an adult (age 21). As the authors noted, one consequence of sexual socialization in which men and women are taught two sets of standards about sexuality—one for men and one for women—is that this "results in men and women interpreting and evaluating the same sexual behaviour differently depending on whether the actor is male or female and whether this actor is violating his/her appropriate (gender based) sexual script. The fact that both men and women hold this conditional double standard follows the notion that both men and women are socialized to know the different sexual scripts for the genders" (29).

These attitudes would seem consistent with older sexual scripts that suggested "sex is bad, except in marriage, and then you should not enjoy it too much, especially if you are a woman" (Hacker 1992, 1, emphasis in original). Hacker argues that our culture is not truly sexually permissive; rather, she sees the contemporary era as one "of transitions in which there are two moralities existing uneasily side by side: one which encourages more sexual freedom; and the other which is characterized by considerable discomfort with being sexual" (3). She observes that while "truly permissive cultures . . . have an accepted norm of permissiveness . . . [o]ur culture, however, is presently without a clearly identifiable sexual norm." She suggests that the failure of teenagers to use contraception stems from their not accepting themselves as fully sexual beings and from their feeling that to plan for intercourse "would be akin to planning for sin." At the same time, gendered stereotypes that discourage the use of contraception may persist. For example, psychologist-sociologist Lillian Rubin (1990) quoted one of her 18-year-old male respondents as saying, "You always know the bad girls; they're on the pill. . . . It means they're always ready for sex; that's why they're taking it" (177).

The Issues of Reproduction

Contraception

Since 1969, birth control measures have been legal in Canada. Prior to 1969, these measures "were illegal if practised for birth control rather than for an acceptable 'medical' reason—to prevent venereal disease or to deal with problems of menstrual irregularity" (Conway 1990, 213). However, even within contemporary society cultural inhibitors remain that would seem to discourage women from acknowledging their participation in sexual activities. Often, teenaged girls fail to use contraceptives simply because in order to obtain most methods they have to acknowledge their "bad" behaviour either to strangers like pharmacists or doctors or to their parents (Nelson and Robinson 1994). Similarly, Hacker (1992, 16) has observed that "most teenage pregnancies occur in the first six months of sexual activity, and . . . seeking contraception typically is delayed from nine to 12 months after intercourse has been initiated."

Traditionally, both contraception and conception have been seen as the woman's responsibility and the woman's problem. In part this is because it is the female who most directly suffers from an unwanted pregnancy, but it is also partly due to the still commonly held belief that women do not possess sexual urges that are as powerful as a man's. As a consequence, women are believed to be capable of more rational thinking regarding things sexual. In contrast, Pfuhl (1978) observes that a man who impregnates a female to whom he is not married has the ability to "negotiate from a position of strength;" the double standard reduces his culpability. Rather than being seen as a "sexual exploiter," the unwed father is seen as a "non-deviant rule breaker."

The most recent research on a representative sample of American women 15 to 44 years of age noted that while the vast majority of them did use some form of contraception, the "pill" was still by far the leading method (Mosher 1990). In Canada, earlier research by Balakrishnan, Krotki and Lapierre-Adamcyk (1985) reported that the pill had been replaced by sterilization as the most popular form of birth control among Canadian women age 18 to 49. It is interesting to note that 35 percent of the women surveyed, compared to 12 percent of the men, had undergone sterilization.

Despite the availability of the pill and the increasing use of the more radical technique of sterilization, statistics show that the rate of illegitimate births is rising. Between 1931 and 1960 out-of-wedlock births accounted for approximately 4 percent of births in Canada; in 1983 they accounted for 16 percent, and in 1990 they accounted for 22 percent (Gairdner 1991, 164). In particular, the rise of illegitimate births to teenage mothers is viewed by many with concern. While the pregnancy rate among every other age group of fertile women is decreasing, teenage pregnancy is growing. From 1985 to 1993, pregnancy rates for Canadian teenagers 15 to 19 increased from 41 to 48 per 1,000. By 1997, the teen pregnancy rate had increased to 59.2 percent. In 1995, 23 416 babies were born to teenage mothers in Canada (Crawford 1997a).

Although various authors have argued over whether teenage pregnancy causes poverty or grows out of poverty, it is noteworthy that groups in our society that are marginalized and that experience social disadvantage demonstrate higher rates of illegitimacy than those groups that enjoy a higher social status. Thus, in Canada, the rate of illegitimacy among aboriginals is 60 percent greater than the national average (Fleras and Elliott 1992, 17). In the United States (where the fastest rise in out-of-wedlock births has been among whites), "90 percent of teenage births in blacks now take place out of wedlock (compared with 47 percent 20 years ago)" (Allen 1992, 146).

There are many possible solutions to the problem of illegitimacy; however, because sexuality and its regulation are not simply technical details to be worked out but instead form a strategic site at which history, ideology, and politics meet, we should not expect these answers to be simple.

> Birth control is a topic laden with tension . . . particularly for nonwhites. . . . Federal birth control programs began with nonwhites. . . . [Among aboriginals] the memory of genocide and tribal extinction is a raw unhealing wound. Fear persists that the desire for the "ultimate solution to the Indian Problem" . . . still lives (Witt 1984, 30).

Similarly, feminist research reminds us that the actual design of birth control devices and their consequences necessitate a cautious approach to their use. For example, Marshall (1987) observes that although the Dalkon Shield, an intrauterine device (IUD), was linked to sterility, pelvic inflammatory disease, septic abortions, and in some cases the death of the user, neither the Canadian nor American governments ever demanded its recall. Similarly, although with the 1997 approval of Depo-Provera for use as a birth control method in Canada, women can use just four injections of the drug each year to prevent pregnancy, there have been concerns expressed over side effects of this drug, which range from bleeding and weight gain to a possible connection with osteoporosis (Crawford 1997b).

Adding to the polyphony of voices, some have argued that although the rise of these new forms of contraception may decrease the rates of illegitimacy, they will only do so at the cost of further privatizing and medicalizing the issues of sexuality and reproduction, marginalizing men's role within the decision-making process, and decreasing, rather than encouraging, the shared responsibility for reproduction between the sexes (Shostak 1991, 45). And, of course, there are those who would sombrely remind us that throughout history, a host of characters from eminent physicians to carnival hucksters have proclaimed that they have available (for a "nominal fee") some type of easy-to-use product, strategy, or elixir that can cure, counteract, and prevent every conceivable ailment that plagues us—be it social, emotional, or physical. Unfortunately, it often turns out that what is dispensed is simply a spurious nostrum, snake oil for those who are gullible or desperate enough to believe in instantaneous cure-alls. However, because of the complexity and interconnectedness of social problems, it would seem unlikely that the introduction of any single product can, in and of itself, solve all the social problems identified within the arena of sexuality and intimacy or fully satisfy all the disparate groups in society.

Abortion

For feminists, the availability of birth control has long been seen as central in campaigns for equality between the sexes. Similarly, since the second wave of feminism began during the 1960s, the issue of reproductive choice has been pivotal. Thus, Conway (1990, 213) maintains, "Women's reproductive choice, including the unfettered access to abortion services, is not a family issue. It is an issue of women's rights and freedoms. Indeed, it is arguably one of the most profound issues of women's rights at the present time in Canada." Similarly, Jacobson (1992, 136) argues that "[t]he struggle for abortion rights cannot be separated from the broader struggles of women to gain equality in all facets of life, from family and domestic issues to parity in the workplace."

There can be no doubt that in contemporary society the issue of abortion remains highly controversial. As Faludi observes, "[i]n the last two years of the '80s alone, more than fifteen hundred articles on abortion appeared in the major [U.S.] dailies, and the newsweeklies devoted more space to abortion than any other social policy issue." It is Faludi's contention that "[i]n periods of backlash, birth control becomes less available, abortion is restricted, and women who avail themselves of it are painted as 'selfish' or 'immoral'" (1991, 55). She argues that the media depiction of abortion as a social problem reflects an androcentric vantage point and charges that "[t]hese articles rarely explored the needs or views of the millions of women hurt by the . . . attack on abortion; instead, they moralized, wondered if female reporters should even be allowed to cover the abortion debate, and worried about how the abortion battle might 'hurt' various politicians" (Faludi 1991, 414). For others, however, the issue is framed quite differently.

In particular, three decisions rendered by Canadian courts during the 1980s and early 1990s became highly controversial, for they were variously thought to indicate the lack of serious consideration of "fetal rights" versus recognition of women's rights to bodily integrity (the case of Lemay and Sullivan), the state's intervention and usurpation of parental autonomy (the decision of Justice Karswick in ruling on a 13-year-old pregnant girl's right to have an abortion), and paternal rights (the case of Chantale Daigle). Each could be regarded quite differently, celebrated as a "victory" or castigated as a "defeat" for men, for women, for the family, or for Canadians in general, depending on a group's point of view.

In the first case, that of Lemay and Sullivan, the Supreme Court of Canada ruled that a child whose head was out of the birth canal was not a legal person. If the ultrasonic imaging of the fetus in the uterus provides a particularly powerful visual incentive to view the fetus as a "person" (rather than as embryonic tissue), the visibility of the fetus in this case made the issue particularly combative. For those who believed that the application of rights to the fetus was potentially dangerous to the mother's health and a "legal nightmare," the decision was hailed as wise and thoughtful. To those who argued that life begins at conception, the decision was viewed as a travesty of justice and an example of Canada's "criminal" refusal to acknowledge fetal "personhood."

The question of fetal "personhood" is a critical element within the abortion debate, and we certainly cannot offer any definitive solution to this question beyond noting that the opinions offered in the past few decades by researchers, embryologists, obstetricians, ethicists, philosophers, medico-legal theologians, and feminists suggest that there are no easy answers. The debate over whether a human fetus is a person is highly contentious, and it is doubtful that it will become less so in the immediate future. The questions of when life begins, when an individual is to be regarded as a legal person with the protection that this conveys under the Charter of Rights and Freedoms, under what circumstances abortion should be recognized as "justified," and who should have control over a pregnant woman's body are not simply "legal" questions. Indeed, the contrasting positions held by pro-choice and pro-life groups are so intractable that the struggle over meaning in the abortion debate has been described by one observer as the "clash of absolutes" (Shostak 1991, 20).

Similarly polarizing was the July 1990 decision of Judge Karswick of the Ontario Provincial Court, who ruled that a 13-year-old girl, who was 17 weeks pregnant, could have an abortion despite the objections of her parents, who belonged to a Pentacostal religious sect. In reporting this ruling, *Reality*, the newsmagazine of REAL Women Canada, noted that

> [t]he [girl's] parents . . . had offered to look after their grandchild after its birth and told the court that they cared deeply for their daughter. The unborn child in question appeared to be normal and active during an ultrasound procedure. The young mother, however, had been treated with tetracyclines for a sexually transmitted disease called chlamydia and this treatment according to her doctor's testimony posed a risk to the unborn child's *tooth* development! (Emphasis in original.)

It is obvious from this excerpt that the court's decision, hailed by some as "progressive," was viewed by REAL Women as an unwarranted intrusion in parental autonomy. In stressing that the girl's decision to abort was based, in part, on the possibility of damage to the unborn child's teeth, the article suggests that the girl was literally "throwing the baby out with the bathwater." Because of the perceived ill logic of her decision, the article implicitly suggests that the wishes of the girl's parents should have been accorded greater weight than those of the girl herself. (See Sullivan 1992, chapter 2, for an extended discussion of the issue of parental rights versus the rights of their children in the case of abortion.)

This issue of parental control versus the rights of underage daughters to receive an abortion will likely continue to be an important one for activists on both sides of the abortion debate, if only because at present the majority of women who receive abortions are relatively young. In Canada, one in five therapeutic abortions were performed on women under age 20 and almost one in three therapeutic abortions were performed on women age 20 to 24. Moreover, therapeutic abortions as a proportion of live births have doubled in the youngest age groups since the mid-1970s. In the 15- to 19-year-old age group, there were two therapeutic abortions for every three live births (MacKenzie 1990). Expressed as a rate per 1000 women, the highest rates of abortion in Canada are among women between the ages of 18 and 24. After age 24, rates of abortion decline steadily to less than 2 abortions per

1000 women age 40 to 44. The rates of therapeutic abortions among all age groups have been relatively stable, albeit with some minor fluctuations, since the 1970s.

Finally, the 1989 case of 21-year-old Chantale Daigle from Chibougamau, Quebec, generated a storm of controversy. For some it was seen as illustrative of the erosion of "paternal rights" within Canadian society. For others, it suggested the need for women to have unfettered autonomy in deciding whether they wished to undergo an abortion. According to Conway's (1990, 30) summary,

> Jean-Guy Tremblay began pursuing Daigle in November 1988, and within weeks the couple were cohabiting. Two months into the union, Tremblay suggested marriage and urged Daigle to stop using birth control; by March 1989 she was pregnant. Daigle says that Tremblay then became physically and verbally abusive. Tremblay insists that he never hit her "hard enough to leave marks." In early July 1989 Daigle left Tremblay and decided to have an abortion.

As a result of Daigle's decision, Tremblay obtained first a temporary and then a permanent court injunction that prohibited Daigle from having an abortion. Exactly what Tremblay envisaged as the aftermath of his actions is less clear.

> First he told the press that he would care for the baby himself, then decided that his father would, and then suggested that he would allow Daigle to keep and care for the child. In an interview, Tremblay revealed his dream—a traditional family with him out at work and Daigle at home with the child. Daigle's response was simply, "I don't even want to see that guy again" (Conway 1990, 31).

The Quebec Superior Court's injunction was subsequently overturned by the Supreme Court of Canada on August 9, 1989. However, before this decision was made, Daigle had the child aborted in the United States, "afraid that Canada's highest court would require her to carry through with the pregnancy" (Thorne-Finch 1993, 199).

For various fathers' rights groups, Daigle's actions and the ruling of the Supreme Court of Canada were thought to illustrate the marginal role into which fathers have been cast in contemporary society—as "ghost lovers" and "ghost fathers" due to "prejudice against men." For others, however, the fact that Daigle had been emotionally abused during her relationship and physically battered by her ex-lover, a former nightclub bouncer, cast a different light. Tremblay's motivation for seeking to prevent Daigle from aborting the child was held as highly suspect. Rather than being viewed as an issue of the "rights of fatherhood," his actions were construed as a telling illustration of coercive male efforts to control women.

Recently, the so-called "abortion pill" RU-486 has been hailed by some as "a safe, reliable, and relatively inexpensive alternative to surgical abortion" that "may be an effective treatment for aging, brain and breast cancers, diabetes, obesity, and more" (Shostak 1991, 43). Indeed, in promoting the drug's wide-ranging potential, some in the United States have strategically "downplayed its role as an abortifacient and couched the battle over importation as a test of U.S. primacy in biomedical medical research" (Werth 1993, 128). Although denounced as the "French death pill" by the anti-abortion New Right, RU-486 is celebrated by many in the pro-choice movement as an alternative to abortion that is "safer, easier, more user-friendly" (Werth 1993, 131), and that effectively removes the possibility of confrontations at abortion clinics between women who would undergo abortions and "rescue" workers of the pro-life movement. Similarly, Norplant, a long-term device implanted under the skin, has been described as "what many women have been waiting for: it is more than 99 percent effective, and its five-year cost is about $350 (compared with about $900 for the pill)" (Shostak 1991, 43). However, although in 1992 in the United States, Eleanor Smeal, former president of the National Organization of Women, organized a multi-fronted "Web of Influence" to demand the marketing of RU-486 and announced that "[f]ascism and control of the womb go hand and hand" (in Werth 1993, 130), many other feminists advocated a more cautious approach. As Rowland commented, "Have we learned anything from experiences like those associated with the pill and the Dalkon Shield? . . . Who invented it, who manufactured it, who licensed it, who dispenses it? But who dies from it?" (in Mackie 1991, 119).

In 1993, a Gallup poll based on telephone interviews with a stratified random sample of Canadian adults, age 18 or over, reported that almost one-third (31%) of respondents believed that abortion should be legal under any circumstance while 56 percent of respondents felt that abortion should be legal under certain circumstances. Only 1 in 10 Canadians felt that abortion should be illegal in all circumstances. The survey noted that regional differences existed in the positions held on the abortion issue. For example, 5 percent of those living in Quebec felt that abortion should be illegal in all circumstances, compared to 16 percent of Canadians living in Atlantic Canada. Similarly, while 37 percent of those living in Quebec felt abortion should be legal under any circumstance, 16 percent of those living in Atlantic Canada, 23 percent of those living in the Prairies, 33 percent of those living in Ontario, and 38 percent of those living in B.C. believed that abortions should always be legal. The results of the 1993 Gallup poll additionally suggest that support for abortion is associated with higher levels of education. Among the Gallup poll sample, 25 percent of those with only a public school education believed abortion should always be legal, compared to 28 percent of those with a high school education, 32 percent of those with a community college education, and 35 percent of those with a university education.

Among the Gallup poll respondents who believed that abortion should be legal only in certain circumstances, 81 percent felt that abortion should be legal if the mother's health was endangered by the pregnancy, 70 percent felt that abortion of a pregnancy that resulted from rape or incest should be legal, and 64 percent supported legal abortion where a strong likelihood of "serious defect" in the child existed. Slightly more than 4 in 10 (42%) Canadians believed that agreement between a woman and her doctor was sufficient to justify abortion; less than one-fifth (19%) believed that abortion should be legal if the family had a very low income. In general, Canadians were more likely to view abortions conducted during the first trimester rather than during later stages in the pregnancy as acceptable. While one-third (33%) of Canadians supported abortions conducted within the first three months after conception, only 12 percent felt that abortions should be legal if they occurred within the first five months following conception (Hughes 1993).

As of 1997, Canada had no law covering abortion; as French (1992, 93) has observed, Canada may be "the only nation in the world so situated." And, because of the heterogeneity of opinion on the issue of abortion, all legislative and judicial outcomes are victories to one group and defeats to the other. For example, the goal of the pro-life groups came close to becoming reality when, in the early 1990s, the Conservative party sought to pass Bill C-43, which would have made abortion criminal, enabled third-party intervention from husbands or male partners, and further restricted access to abortion. When the bill was narrowly defeated in the Senate by a tie vote of 43–43, its demise was regarded quite differently by different groups, celebrated as a "victory" or castigated as a "defeat" for women, for men, for the family, or for Canadians in general. In a similar way, the 1994 bombing of the Vancouver home of a physician who performed abortions was denounced by some as the work of pro-lifers who would wilfully use "terrorist tactics" to suppress women and the physicians who would assist them. For others, of course, the event was framed as "regrettable, but necessary" to "end the murder of babies." Nothing, then, is ever complete, with each action only a way station in a moral struggle. For feminists, "women's struggle for the body" (Currie and Raoul 1992) is of central importance, whether expressed in relation to the abortion debate, efforts over the control of new reproductive technologies, or within the area of health and child care (21). That is, "[b]oth metaphorically and literally, the body is at the centre of political life" (Currie and Raoul 1992, 21).

Safe Sex?

In recent times, controversy over whether condom dispensers should be placed within high school washrooms illustrates the marked increase in premarital sexuality, the increasingly younger ages at which sexual behaviour now occurs, and the concern over both pregnancy and sexually transmitted diseases. For conservatives, the placement of condom dispensers within school washrooms coupled with sex education is seen to encourage sexual behaviour at increasingly younger ages. Thus, a frequently used analogy is that "if you give a kid a bike, he or she will learn to ride it." However, more liberal social critics would counter this analogy by arguing that kids today are likely to already know how to ride a bike; the "problem," they would suggest, is getting them to ride with a helmet for protection.

Although recent years have seen the widespread promotion of "safe sex," "venereal diseases are sweeping through the teenage population" in what has been termed a "sexually transmitted disease epidemic." Citing 1992 statistics from Ontario's health ministry and the City of Toronto's department of public health, one news report noted that more than half of sexually active 16- to 24-year-olds say they never use condoms as protection from sexually transmitted diseases; the rate of chlamydia for 15- to 19-year-old females has increased fivefold in seven years; reported cases of chlamydia in girls age 10 to 14 increased from 29 cases in 1985 to 148 in 1992; and the chlamydia rate has more than doubled for males age 15 to 19. Chlamydia and gonorrhea—the two most common sexually transmitted diseases in the adolescent population, and both of which are asymptomatic—account for 6300 cases a year among young persons in Ontario; more than 3000 cases of hepatitis B (which can lead to liver cirrhosis and cancer) occur every year in Ontario; and an estimated 25 percent of Canadian adults are infected with the human papilloma virus (which causes genital warts) and don't even know it (The Toronto Star, August 15, 1993: A4).

Although few Canadians had heard of AIDS when the first case in Canada was reported in 1982, by the end of 1994 an estimated 16 000 had been diagnosed with AIDS (of which half had already died from AIDS-related causes) and 45 000 were infected with HIV, the virus that causes AIDS. While the rate of AIDS is notably lower in Canada than in the United States (380 cases per 1 million population in Canada versus 1542 per 1 million in the U.S.), there can be little doubt that this disease, for which there is no vaccine or cure, represents one of the most pressing health and social issues in Canada today. In Canada, as of 1994 the rates of adult AIDS were highest in British Columbia (75 per 100 000 adults), Ontario (73 per 100 000 adults) and Quebec (69 per 100 000 adults). Among adult women, almost one-half (49%) of AIDS cases were in Quebec. It is estimated that over 4.5 million AIDS cases have occurred worldwide since the late 1970s (Frank 1997).

In recent years, the proportion of annual AIDS cases attributed to specific risk factors has shifted. Men who have sex with men still account for the largest risk group, although the proportion of AIDS cases attributable to this factor have declined since 1987 from 8 out of 10 to 7 out of 10. Moreover, due to improvements in blood screening, the risk of infection through blood products or transfusions has declined, with the proportion of AIDS cases involving blood product recipients decreasing from almost 6 percent in 1988 to 2 percent in 1994. In contrast, while injection drug users accounted for simply 1 percent of AIDS cases in 1987, this risk factor has increased in importance and, in 1994, accounted for 6 percent of AIDS cases. In marked contrast to the experience of the United States, where AIDS cases in females account for 48 percent of all reported cases, women account for only 6 percent of all diagnosed cases of AIDS each year in Canada. Heterosexual contact with a person at risk is the most frequently identified factor (38%) for AIDS transmission among Canadian women (Strike 1991; Frank 1997).

Although in 1993 HIV/AIDS was the third leading cause of death among men age 20 to 44 in Canada (exceeded only by suicide and motor vehicle crashes), research conducted by the University of Alberta's Population Research laboratory suggests that many are unprepared to make significant changes in their sexual practices. Although approximately 17 percent of Albertans participated in high-risk activities (for example, unprotected sexual contact or intravenous drug use), fewer than 2 percent felt their chance of getting AIDS was "high," while 5 percent thought their risk was "medium." For the rest of Albertans surveyed, their perceived risk of getting AIDS was low or non-existent and even those Albertans who reported participation in high-risk activities did not believe that they were placing themselves at greater risk of HIV infection and AIDS. As McKinnon (1991, 25) observes, "There are indications that sexual behaviour among adult Albertans has not changed appreciably in response to the potential threat of AIDS. For example, those at high risk were not more likely to use condoms during sexual intercourse."

Research does indicate, however, that condom use significantly increased among teenagers and never-married women between 1982 and 1988 (Mosher 1990). Indeed, journalist Wendy Dennis (1992) reported that in 1988 "industry estimates indicated that women represented some 40 percent of the . . . American condom market." She notes that in recent years manufacturers have targeted the female market with "whisper-thin condoms, rose-petal-embossed condoms, mint-flavoured condoms and condoms in tasteful carrying cases. . . ." (140–141). However, "being prepared" may be perceived as being "experienced," overly "pushy," or "unfeminine." Although the prospect of sleeping with one's partner's entire past sexual history may be frightening, "young females, who often say they are not sure they want to 'touch that thing'" (Hacker 1992, 27), may be discouraged from incorporating condom use into sex play prior to intercourse or from insisting on its use.

The increased incidence of females with sexually transmitted diseases has been attributed to the power imbalance between men and women, which is especially pronounced among teens. Accordingly, if some adolescent boys scoff at the notion of wearing a condom because it is thought to "reduce the sensation," women may lack the power in a relationship to insist on it. In various ways, the cultural script of "men as pursuers, women as pursued" is still widely held as an ideal and reiterates the notion of female sexual passivity. While women appear to be more knowledgeable than men in the strategic use of flirtation, well-versed in the subtle attempts by which one can suggest or signal sexual interest and receptivity, men still appear to be the principal architects of sexual relationships. Thus, even today, a man more frequently asks a woman out on a date rather than vice versa; similarly, it is more frequently the male, rather than the female, who initiates sexual activity and directs its type and frequency. One major exception to this appears to occur in cases where a dating couple has decided to abstain from sexual activity. In this situation it is typically the woman whose veto constitutes the major restraining influence. Thus, in accordance with older scripts, males hold the basic power of observable initiation while females hold the power of refusal, a power that is manifestly ignored in cases of rape.

COERCIVE SEXUALITY

During the last 20 years, increased public attention has been directed to the social problems of sexual assault, incest, and the sexual abuse of children. In particular, the women's movement has sought to challenge the stereotypes of the rapist as a psychopathic stranger and the child molester as a pervert who preys on children in playgrounds. They have also directed attention to the plight of sexual assault victims and campaigned for greater sensitivity and education among professionals working within fields such as medicine, social work, the law, and the criminal justice system.

In a strictly legal sense, the crime of rape has not existed in Canada since 1983, when it was changed to the tripartite offence of sexual assault, sexual assault with a weapon, and aggravated sexual assault. According to Section 143 of the Canadian Criminal Code, rape was a gender-specific offence: only men could rape and only women could be victims of rape; a woman could only be found guilty of rape if she aided or abetted a man to commit the rape of another woman. Despite its reported commonality in male prisons, homosexual gang rape was not, under this definition, legal rape (although it was an "indecent assault upon a male," an offence formerly covered under a separate section of the Criminal Code). As previously noted, the former law of rape contained a "marital exemption;" in law, a man could not rape his wife. Our former rape law also contained the specification that the man had "sexual intercourse" with the woman. It was sexual intercourse ("penetration to even the slightest degree, notwithstanding that seed is not emitted") that turned "indecent assault" into rape and distinguished one sexual offence from another. Prior to 1983, the sexual components of the act—rather than its violence—were what distinguished the crimes. Section 143 also specified that no male under 14 years of age could be found guilty of rape or attempted rape, regardless of what, in fact, he did.

The passage of Bill C-127 in October 1982 (which came into effect January 1983) amended and/or replaced a number of sexual offence provisions. Similarly, the passage of Bill C-15 (which received Royal Assent on June 30, 1987, and was proclaimed as law on January 1, 1988) amended many substantive and procedural provisions of the Canadian Criminal Code in relation to sexual offences. These Bills "modernized" the law, repealed and replaced various laws governing sexual offences, and introduced substantive changes both procedural and evidentiary. Unlike the old law of rape, the offence of sexual assault is not narrowly restricted to acts of nonconsensual sexual intercourse. While the former law of rape was included in a section outlining "sexual offenses," the law of sexual assault is included in the "assaults" section of the Canadian Criminal Code. The laws prohibiting sexual assault are distinguished by the degree of violence that accompanies the act. The term "sexual assault" is thought to capture and focus attention on the violence that is an essential component of the act rather than the type of sexual violation imposed on victims.

The new laws create three levels of penalties that reflect the degree of violence used in the commission of the offence. A charge of sexual assault can be dealt with as either a *summary conviction offence* or as an *indictable offence*. A person convicted of a *summary conviction offence* faces a maximum penalty upon conviction of a fine of not more than $2000, a term of imprisonment of not more than six months, or both. The punishment for an *indictable offence* is more severe, and may include "life imprisonment" (or, more accurately, 25 years imprisonment). The offender may be a stranger, an acquaintance, or a family member of the victim.

Although Canadian law gives a distinct status to the crime of incest (Section 155 of the Criminal Code), the requirements that the offender and victim be specific types of blood relatives (e.g., a parent, child, brother, sister, grandparent, or grandchild) *and* that the act engaged in was vaginal intercourse makes this charge relatively rare. While we might define a stepfather's sexual fondling of his stepson or stepdaughter as incest, the law does not yet reflect the changing demographics of the family within Canadian society. Accordingly, those found guilty of "simple sexual assault," as it is termed, are a hybrid category whose actions are varied; some offenders may have been strangers to the victim, while others may have engaged in acts that involved a more flagrant breach of a trust relationship.

The second tier of sexual assault with a weapon applies if bodily harm occurs to the victim, if the attacker carries, uses, or threatens to use a weapon or an imitation thereof, if the attacker threatens to cause bodily harm to a third person, or if there is more than one party to the assault. The maximum penalty for this type of assault is imprisonment for a term not exceeding 14 years. The most serious form of sexual assault involves circumstances wherein the sexual assault is accompanied by wounding, maiming, disfiguring, or endangering the life of the victim. This type of conduct is referred to as aggravated sexual assault. Upon conviction, the offender is liable to life imprisonment.

Unlike the old law of rape, both males and females can be victims and both males and females can be charged and convicted of any of the three types of sexual assault. Women can be charged with sexually assaulting women or men, and men can be charged with sexually assaulting men or women. Moreover, the spousal exemption has been removed and a spouse of either sex can be charged with the sexual assault of his or her partner. In theory, the laws on sexual assault in Canada are now inclusive enough to protect women and men, and adults and children from sexual victimization. However, as Roscoe Pound noted long ago, there is a difference to be observed between the "law in the books" and the "law in action."

Although Canadian criminal law clearly announces society's condemnation of sexual violence, its reporting by an adult—or child—can engender profound disbelief. In the seventeenth century Lord Hale cautioned against the adoption of anything but a sceptical poise in his oft-quoted comment that "rape is an accusation easily made and hard to prove and harder to be defended by the party accused, tho' never so innocent." Similarly, Lord Wigmore, whose learned treatise on evidence was to have a profound influence on the development of British jurisprudence and whose work was acclaimed as "the greatest treatise on criminal law ever produced" (Radzinowicz 1961, 115), commented that it was the "behaviour of errant young girls and women" who made allegations of sexual violence that required examination and suggested that "[t]heir psychic complexes are multifarious, distilled partly by inherent effects. . . . diseases derangements, or abnormal instincts, partly by bad social environment, partly by temporary physiological or emotional conditions (1940, 459–460).

According to Wigmore, "one form taken by these complexes" was the bringing forth of false allegations of sexual violence and he cautioned that "no judge should ever let a sex-offense charge go to the jury unless the female complainant's social history and mental make-up have been examined and testified to by a qualified physician" (2061). Moreover, there is evidence that equivalent views are not the province of antiquity. Various recent writers (Fekete 1994; Roiphe 1993) have suggested that allegations of sexual assault may be made to appease a woman's parents, husband, or lover, to account for venereal disease or pregnancy, to enact revenge or blackmail on a dismissive ex-lover, or to satisfy the "demands" of "feminist counsellors" and other "agents of political correctness." Invoking the images of cabals and conspiracy, Fekete (1994, 56) emotively writes that "[i]t is a sinister coalition which joins up the biofeminist hostility to men. . . . [o]nce a panic atmosphere comes to reward accusers with moral honours and sometimes celebrity status and . . . major financial incentives are made available for successful claimants."

In the early 1990s, attempts by researchers to identify the incidence of sexual assault on university campuses spurred considerable controversy in both Canada and the United States. This was partly because the definition of sexual assault (which, akin to its legal definition, was far broader than rape) used seemed, for some, more elastic than rigorous. If everything is sexual assault, critics argued, then nothing is sexual assault. Moreover, it was suggested that by defining "sexual assault" so loosely, the researchers had simply revived Victorian notions of women as frail, delicate beings who had to be "sheltered" and "protected" from uncouth individuals and "ungentlemanly behaviour." For example, Roiphe (1993) argued that "[w]e all agree that rape is a terrible thing, but we no longer agree on what rape is." According to Roiphe, "[r]ape is a natural trump card for feminism. . . . By blocking analysis with its claims to unique pandemic suffering, the rape crisis becomes a powerful source of authority" (28).

Despite Roiphe's suggestion that "[a]rguments about rape can be used to sequester feminism in the teary province of trauma and crisis" (28), various feminist scholars have documented gender bias in both the substantive and procedural laws governing sexual offences (Edwards 1981). They have demonstrated, for instance, that when the act of sexual assault is reproduced through testimony in the courtroom, the victim's experience of violation is often transformed into an act of "routine, consensual sex" (Lees 1996). For the victims, it is condescending, to say the least, to refer to their suffering as a "trump card" they play to gain an advantage in an ideological battle.

Sexual Violence and Sexual Scripts

Feminists have argued that the combined features of the male sexual role—aggressiveness, frequency, heterosexism, and performance—create the social problems of sexual harassment, homophobia, sexual assault, and in particular, date rape and marital rape. Sexual violence is seen as a caricature of masculinity that is logically consistent with its underlying dimensions. Thus, Schur (1989, 148) asserts that "forced sex is the ultimate indicator and preserver of male dominance" and that sexual harassment can be seen, in the words of legal scholar Catherine MacKinnon, as "dominance eroticized." Schur argues that "we live in a 'rape culture,' in which sex and force are inextricably linked . . . so that a continuum of coercion is created in which the difference between rape and normal sexual aggression is only one of degree" (149). Moreover, it is odd that rape by a stranger remains the dominant stereotype of sexual assault in the popular imagination (Kelly and Radford 1996), odd because "estimates of the percentage of rapes committed by a perpetrator known to the victim [now] range from 50 percent . . . to 88 percent" (Bridges 1991, 291).

While the stereotype continues to focus on the rapist as a victim of some form of psychosis or other pathology, the sex-role socialization theory of rape suggests that rape, and particularly acquaintance rape, occurs because of traditional heterosexual role behaviours and rape-supportive beliefs. That is, in some situations men feel that they are expected to act in a sexually aggressive manner; if they don't, they are somehow denying their manhood. Thus, Koss et al. (1988) have suggested that perpetrators of acquaintance rape may show an "oversocialized masculine belief system" (991).

Childhood and High School

Russell and Finkelhor (1984, 237–238) maintain that the overrepresentation of males as sexual offenders against children can be explained, in part, by reference to the contrasting scripts of males and females within society. They (1984, 237) have suggested that male sex-role socialization in accordance with the social ideal of "masculinity" and the "virility mystique" may actually facilitate the development of sexual attraction towards children. They argue that "[m]ales are socialized to be initiators, aggressors and seducers of women and adolescent female partners, whether or not they are willing. . . . Females, on the contrary, are socialized to be passive and to wait for male initiative. . . . This attitude difference increases both the likelihood that males will sexually abuse children and that females will not."

Feminists often focus on discussions of sexual violence and "sexual scripts" because, by highlighting stereotypes, these discussions can help us to arrive at fuller definitions for terms like "sexual assault," "victim," and "offender." For example, a 1993 study conducted by Peter Jaffe and Marlies Sudermann on more than 1500 students in grades 9 through 13 at two London, Ontario, high schools found that approximately 20 percent of male students in grades 9 and 10 believed that forced intercourse was all right if the female "gets her date 'sexually excited' or has led him on;" among female students, 7 percent felt that forced intercourse was all right in those circumstances. The study also noted that male students stated that forced intercourse was acceptable if "he spends money on her," if "he is stoned or drunk," or "if they had been dating for a long time." Their findings noted that "40 percent of the female students reported having experienced emotional or verbal abuse from boys they were casually dating, while 59 percent reported having experienced physical abuse and 28 percent sexual abuse in a steady dating relationship. In Grades 9 to 13, 22 percent reported sexual or physical abuses" (*The Globe and Mail*, August 23, 1993: A8).

On Campus

In a two-phase study of women students conducted at the University of Waterloo in 1985, McDaniel and Roosmalen (1992) found that sexual harassment was a common experience and one structured by power differentials. Their findings indicated that 74 percent of female university students had experienced sexual insults ("an uninvited, sexually suggestive, obscene or offensive remark, stare or gesture"), 29 percent had received a sexual invitation ("a sexual proposition without any explicit threat or bribe by a person in a position of power or authority"), 7 percent reported sexual intimidation ("a threat or a bribe by a person in a position of power or authority to coerce sexual contact"), and 10.8 percent had been sexually assaulted ("sexual contact through the use of force, threatened force or a weapon, without consent as inferred from refusal, helplessness or incapacitation"). They argue that "[t]he behaviour is so pervasive that some might suggest that it has been seen as almost 'natural', a part of 'normal' male culture . . . an inevitable part of male-female relationships" (4). They note that reactions to allegations of sexual harassment may be dismissive, "laughing it off as humorous and flattering, or broadening the definition to the point of absurdity" (5). However, citing MacKinnon, they emphasize how sexual harassment, "the presumption that women workers can be pressured into complying with the harasser's wishes," (4) undermines women's potential for social equality in two notable ways: "by using her employment position to coerce her sexually, while using her sexual position to coerce her economically" (5).

Violence and sexual exploitation have been called the "dark side" of courtship and dating. Although specific figures vary from one study to another, generally between 15 and 40 percent of university student samples indicate they have either inflicted or incurred violence while dating (e.g., Stets and Straus 1989), while the figures for sexual aggression alone are usually much higher (e.g., Burke et al. 1988). University women report a higher incidence of having been raped by a steady date than by an acquaintance or a stranger (Koss and Cook 1993). Twenty percent of the women in one American university indicated they had been raped while on a date. The incidence of actual rape itself is just the tip of the sexual aggression–violence iceberg. A review of studies conducted in the 1980s concludes that "fully one half to three quarters of college women report experiencing some type of sexual aggression in a dating relationship" (Lloyd 1991, 17). Ward et al. (1991) found that, in dating situations during that year only, 34 percent of their American female university students had experienced some form of forced sexual contact, 20 percent had had a partner forcibly attempt intercourse, and 10 percent had experienced forcible vaginal, oral, or anal intercourse. An all-female Ontario university study indicated that, while less than 1 percent of the sample acknowledged being raped on a date during the previous year, 22 percent acknowledged having had intercourse when they did not want to because they felt "it was useless to attempt to stop him," and an additional 9 percent had had intercourse when they did not want to because they "felt pressured by his continual arguments" (DeKeseredy et al. 1993, 267).

Being raped by a stranger is more likely to be defined as a criminal act and reported to authorities (Hills 1980/1995) than is being raped by an acquaintance or, especially, by a partner in an ongoing intimate relationship (Russell 1982; Finkelhor and Yllo 1985; 1988; 1989). Since women are socially held responsible for the maintenance and regulation of intimate relationships (Belensky et al. 1980) and are still likely to be held blameworthy when an encounter exceeds acceptable boundaries, many women are reluctant to acknowledge to themselves or others that the unacceptable has happened. The figures noted above from available studies likely are underestimates of the full extent of "date rape."

In this vein, consider that in Ontario, some male students at Queen's University reacted to a sexual abuse, "No Means No" campaign by posting signs in dormitory windows boldly proclaiming that "No Means Tie Her Up" and "No Means More Beer" and by selling boxer shorts that read "No Non" in daylight but "Yes Oui" in the dark (Motherwell 1990, in Benokraitis 1996, 222). At least some of these students felt they had the support of their male peers, or felt they needed such bravado to seek support from their peers, in denigrating a campaign designed to heighten sensitivity to women's rights of refusal and to lessen men's perceived right to force their will.

In similar fashion, in October 1990 20 to 30 male students who lived in the all-male Caribou House residence at the University of British Columbia sent "party invitations" to 300 women in another nearby residence. The invitation-writing, which turned into a competition among the male students, featured such "enticements" as: "Come to the tug-of-war—we'll fuck the shit out of you;" "What's the best thing about fucking an advisor? Killing her afterwards and giving her 2 points for screaming;" "We'll crush your cervix to oblivion;" "We'll suck your nipples bloody;" and "What's the best thing about fucking a 12-year-old? Killing her afterward" (Hookham and Merriam 1991, 58). Nevertheless, at least some observers are moved to downplay such incidents with comments such as "lighten up, it's just guys havin' fun."

"Unfounding" Complaints

In Canada, the research of Clark and Lewis (1977) paved the way for analysis of the neutralization of sexual assault allegations by police. Their research suggested how informal case-screening criteria became tantamount to a "formal" policy that redefined the legal definition of rape and substituted, in its place, a series of implicit notions about the "type" of woman who was viewed as a credible complainant. Clark and Lewis contended that the "unfounded" status that police assigned to many sexual assault complaints was simply inaccurate as an assessment of complainant credibility. In reality, the identification of a complaint as "unfounded" was thought simply to signify the police officer's belief that it would be impossible to obtain a conviction against the alleged rapist. Although the police labelled 64 percent of reported rapes to be "unfounded," the researchers' independent analysis of police records suggested that in only 10 percent of cases could it be concluded that no rape had, in fact, occurred.

Because of our taken-for-granted constructs of "real rape" (Estrich 1987), we may fail to recognize or legitimate cases that fall within the legal definitions. Dominic and Check (1986) reported that in their research, less than half of their respondents (48%) labelled a scenario of acquaintance rape that fell within the legal definition of rape as actual rape. Only when the level of violence escalated to the point where the offender was depicted as slashing his victim with a knife were all respondents convinced that the depiction was one of rape. The consequences of these taken-for-granted "unrealities" of sexual violence are enormous. It must be remembered that in cases heard in criminal courts in Canada, guilt must be proven beyond a reasonable doubt. If a member of the jury or the judge is one of the 52 percent who holds "a reasonable doubt" that a crime has taken place, there will be an acquittal.

The Courts

Since the 1970s, feminists have increasingly challenged the conventional wisdom that minimizes the seriousness of various forms of coercive sexuality. The "she must like it" rationalization for marital rape, the "precociously sexual child" vision of child sexual abuse, and the "sleeping her way to the top" view of sexual harassment have all come under scrutiny. However, there is evidence to suggest that gender bias may still occur within Canadian courtrooms in adjudicating cases of coercive sexuality.

A study conducted by METRAC, a Toronto group concerned with violence against women and children, amassed more than 1000 sentencing reports that suggested that judges often blamed victims for "provoking" their assailants, minimized the seriousness of such crimes, and accepted such factors as the offender's family background and employment record as grounds for leniency. According to Patricia Marshall, chairperson of METRAC, "Judges see real rape as [happening when] a blameless virgin or older woman at home behind locked doors crocheting a flag . . . is raped when a man breaks in wearing a balaclava. Anything else is just bad sex."

In 1993, a federal–provincial study on gender equality concluded, in part, that the legal system in Canada was male-dominated, sexist, and placed women at a heightened risk of violence. Their recommendations included toughening anti-pornography laws and improving the way in which courts treat female victims and offenders. The federal panel, which studied violence against women across Canada, linked inequality and violence against women, maintaining that an end to violence could not be attained without the achievement of true gender equality. Among other suggestions, the writers of the report asked for men to:

1) make a pledge not to be violent;

2) relinquish their need for power and control;

3) ask women about their experiences, fears, and the equality barriers they face;

4) share in child care and home maintenance;

5) challenge any tolerance of violence or sexist behaviour; and

6) give financial and political support to services for victims and survivors.

All of these were thought necessary to eliminate the soaring amount of violence against women. Nevertheless, at least some Canadians were unconvinced that violence against women represented a significant social problem and some suggested that the problem had simply been magnified for political effect (Fekete 1994).

CASE 3-2   A Fitting Sentence or Criminal Neglect?

A judge in Manitoba noted that a former teacher who was convicted of sexually assaulting a female student had attracted negative publicity and had been fired. In handing down a suspended sentence, the judge noted that the man had received "glowing" character references, including one from the pastor of his church that read, "Winnipeg needs one hundred more like him. Give him a citation for good citizenship. He has my unqualified admiration."

During a case involving a man charged with sexual assault, a Manitoba provincial judge told a Crown attorney "he would have to have grown up in a vacuum not to know women often at first resist sexual advances only to give in to their instincts eventually."

CASE 3-2   **A Fitting Sentence or Criminal Neglect? (continued)**

A Quebec judge, during an argument over a point of law in an assault and weapons trial, interjected, "Rules are like women, they are made to be violated."

A British Columbia judge stated in his written decision, ". . . the mating practice, is less than a precise relationship. At times no may mean maybe, or wait awhile."

A judge commented that a prostitute who was raped, urinated on, and had a plunger used on her vagina, "suffered no long-lasting psychological injury."

A judge ruled that the stress of being charged was sufficient punishment for a prominent businessman who was convicted of sexually assaulting his children's babysitter.

A man was sent to prison for 3 years for forcing sexual intercourse on his daughter 500 times over a 9-year period and attempting to rape his niece. The judge commented that "there was no physical coercion."

A social worker convicted of sexual abuse was given a suspended sentence with the judicial comment that "to err is human." The judge also commented that the crime was "completely out of character"—not knowing that the same man had been in court twice that same week on similar charges.

A judge reduced a two-and-a-half-year sentence for a sexual assault to two years less a day. Sentences of two years and longer are served in a federal penitentiary; sentences of shorter duration are served in a provincial jail. The convicted man carried a gun as he abducted the woman, threatened her with death,

and raped her, yet the judge said that the attack was "not accompanied by many of the unpleasant features that normally surround such an offence."

A 22-year-old man from Sault Ste. Marie, Ontario, was sentenced to a 90-day jail term to be served on weekends after he was convicted of following a woman out of a hotel where she was celebrating her birthday, dragging her into a nearby garden, punching her in the face until she passed out, and sexually assaulting her. The judge said the man came from a "good family" and had learned his lesson. He also commented that the assault was not premeditated and "had an element of impulsiveness, of spontaneity." When the defence lawyer informed the judge that the offender coached a soccer team on Friday nights, the judge granted a two-hour extension to the time the man had to report to jail. The Crown successfully appealed the sentence and the man was given a jail term of two years less a day.

A man who admitted a sexual incident with a 3-year-old girl was given a suspended sentence because the judge found that the victim was "sexually aggressive." A second factor the judge considered was that the defendant was "under the influence of alcohol to a fair extent at the time," and also suffering from fatigue. The defendant was placed on probation for 18 months and directed to take alcohol counselling and to "make all reasonable efforts to obtain and keep employment."

Sources: Marshall and Barnett (1990); Comack (1991; 1996).

SUMMARY

1. Images of social problems in relation to sexuality rest on assumptions about the purpose sexuality is thought to serve. For traditionalists, the linkage between sexuality, marriage, and the family remains of considerable importance.

2. Despite a trend towards convergence in the sexual freedom and behaviour of men and women, it would seem that both men and women are still reared in accordance with different erotic scripts, and that a "double standard" remains in effect for assessing the acceptability of female and male sexual behaviour.

3. The issue of abortion illustrates the varying positions possible in relation to judging conduct as socially problematic. For instance, some writers argue that it is inconsistent for feminists to claim abortion as a woman's right but at the same time to view the aborting of a female fetus as an act of patriarchal aggression in the "war against women." The abortion issue often serves as an indicator of the positions we take on when life begins, on the nature of sexuality and the roles of men and women in society, and on the nature of the family and its function in society.

4. Feminist social critics argue that the problem of coercive sexuality must be recognized as other than the private troubles of those people who are victims of it. They have insisted that sexual violence be seen as a logical extension of the masculine erotic script.

Part

2

STRUCTURAL PROBLEMS

CRIME

DID YOU KNOW?

- In 1997, an Angus Reid–CTV News poll reported that almost 6 out of 10 Canadians (59%) believed that violent crime was on the increase—even though the police-reported crime rate decreased for the fifth consecutive year in 1996 and the rate of violent crime decreased (by 2%) for the fourth consecutive year.

- In contrast to the United States, where in 1994 there were approximately 9 murders per 100 000 people, the Canadian rate in 1995, at 1.98 per 100 000, reached its lowest level in 25 years. The 1995 rate was 3 percent lower than the 1994 rate of 2.04 while the latter figure was itself 51 percent lower than the 1975 rate of 3.02.

- In the first six months after the double murders of Nicole Brown Simpson and Ron Goldman, there were 39 261 articles written in major U.S. and Canadian newspapers or magazines on the "O.J. killings."

- According to statistics released by the Center for Media and Public Affairs, which scrutinized the ABC, NBC, and CBS nightly newscasts from 1990 through 1996, while coverage of crime ranked sixth from 1990 to 1992, it skyrocketed to first place after that with 7448 stories devoted to crime in a four-year period. Approximately 1 out of every 20 American network news stories during that four-year period was about a murder—suggesting an unprecedented electronic crime wave.

- Although aboriginals comprise 2 percent of the Canadian population, they account for 24 percent of those incarcerated upon conviction for a crime. In Manitoba, where aboriginal people constitute a mere 6 percent of the total population, aboriginals account for over half of the inmates in correctional institutions. In Alberta, aboriginal young offenders are less likely than nonaboriginal youths to be referred to alternative measures programs and more likely to be charged, to receive a custodial sentence, and to spend a longer period of time in custody.

- Since the 1970s, Gallup polls have consistently noted that the majority of Canadians believe that the courts are too lenient with lawbreakers. In 1995, approximately 85 percent of a national, random sample of Canadians maintained that the courts did not deal harshly enough with criminals. Moreover, about 82 percent of Canadians expressed the belief that the death penalty should be exercised in some instances—a figure that has been remarkably consistent over time.

- Despite the fact that from 1990 to 1991, approximately $7.79 billion was spent on funding for police, courts, and correctional services in Canada (about 2.5 percent of the combined total of federal, provincial, and municipal government expenditures), and that in 1994 to 1995, the cost of policing in Canada alone was $5.78 billion, many Canadians still believe that we are losing the war against crime.

THE PROBLEM

The issues of why some people commit crimes, the impact of crime on society, and the most desirable way in which to respond to criminals have preoccupied humankind since antiquity. In the 1990s, these topics remain of salient concern to Canadians. Indeed, the focal importance of crime as a social problem becomes especially apparent when, in the weeks leading up to a federal election, campaigning politicians routinely note that *their* party, if elected, will tackle the issue in a more effective way than their opponents. If some within the media caustically observe that "pushing the crime button" and "exploiting people's fear is a political trick as old as the hills" (The Toronto Star, August 15, 1993), conducting a "war against crime" is often central to the campaign promises of the various Canadian political parties, whether couched in the rhetoric of social reform or in calls to "hang 'em high."

With the results of public opinion polls reporting that approximately 80 percent of those surveyed believe crime to be a major problem in their communities, this focusing of political attention would not seem misplaced. Indeed, according to a review of Environics polling data, although Canadians ranked the economy far ahead of crime when asked what issue concerned them most from 1983 to 1992, the fear of crime emerged as the fastest growing concern of Canadians—surpassing even the growing rate of concern about the economy. It was also noteworthy that from 1983 to 1992, the number of Canadians who reported that they feared walking alone at night in their neighbourhood increased from 29 to 40 percent.

Public opinions polls have repeatedly noted that many Canadians sincerely believe that the crime rate, in particular the rate of violent crime, is rising rapidly and reaching the levels that plague American society. Despite this perception, however, the crime rate in the United States in much higher than in Canada. For example, the murder rate in Canada has remained constant and relatively low when compared to other Western countries. In contrast to the United States, where there were approximately 9 murders per 100 000 people in 1991, the Canadian rate in 1995, at 1.98 per 100 000, reached its lowest level in 25 years. The 1995 rate was 3 percent lower than the 1994 rate of 2.04 while the latter figure was itself 51 percent lower than the 1975 rate of 3.02. The 1992 International Crime Survey noted that the Canadian murder rate has been consistently 3.5 to 4 times lower than that of the United

States during the last 10 years (Department of Justice 1993). Similarly, although a 1995 Canadian survey, conducted during the highly publicized trial of Paul Bernardo, found that 85 percent of respondents reported a belief that there had been an increase in crime in Canada over the past five years (Bibby 1995, 61) and a 1997 Angus Reid–CTV News poll reported that almost 6 out of 10 Canadians (59%) believed that violent crime was on the increase, the national police-reported crime rate has actually fallen, decreasing in 1996 for the fifth consecutive year while the violent crime rate declined for the fourth consecutive year. Although the violent crime rate in Canada has increased significantly over the last 15 years, it seemed to peak in 1992, and has declined every year since that time. For example, the 1995 rate of 995 incidents per 100 000 population is 4 percent lower than the 1994 rate, which in itself was 3 percent lower than the rate in 1993. With the exception of Vancouver and Calgary, most major cities across Canada saw a decline in the incidence of violent crime. Recent victimization surveys also suggest a decline between 1991 and 1995 in most crimes with the exception of motor vehicle theft, theft of personal property, and residential breaking and entering (Kong 1997).

While Canadian society has witnessed an increase in violent crime of almost 47 percent during the past decade, at least part of this increase is attributable to an increase in people reporting such crimes as family violence and sexual assault—crimes that previously were endured in silence. Thus, some have identified public and professional education as well as specific policy initiatives as having led to a heightened sensitivity on the part of the police and the judiciary system that is reflected in an increase in the number of charges laid in relation to these types of offences. For example, a study conducted in London, Ontario, that sought to determine the effects in the police department of a new mandatory-charging policy in cases of domestic violence noted that between 1979 and 1990, the rate of charging increased from 2.7 to 89.9 percent. During this period, officers became "significantly less inclined to leave the responsibility for laying charges with victims. . . . The trend in court response to the charges laid was evidenced by the fact that fewer cases were being dismissed or withdrawn than in previous years. In addition, increased charging led to a marked rise in the number of more serious court sentences, such as probation and incarceration, especially in comparison with victim-laid charges" (Biesenthal 1993, 8–9). Increased public education on family violence may also have lowered social tolerance for such behaviours and, in turn, encouraged victims and witnesses to report these crimes to police. Accordingly, the increased number of charges laid in relation to these types of offences may, somewhat paradoxically, be considered a positive sign rather than an ominous spectre of an exponentially increasing crime rate. Nevertheless, it would seem that any reported increase in crime is often viewed as if only one explanation is possible—that a "crime wave" is upon us and we must take punitive measures to forestall catastrophe.

The danger, of course, is that the answers that emerge in the context of an ostensible crime wave are likely to suggest solutions that blame easily identifiable "enemies." For example, in their 1992 book, *Leaders and Lesser Mortals: Backroom Politics in Canada*, Laschinger and Stevens charged that the 1991 election of Toronto mayor June Rowlands was largely a result of her contention that young blacks were responsible for a disproportionate number of crimes and of the manner in which she "talked tough" about what was needed to be done to combat this problem. A call to arms to fight the war against crime often succeeds only in painting the villain to be opposed in stereotypic and simplistic ways. It is seldom an invitation to consider rationally the complexities and sources of crime or to evaluate in a critical fashion the strategies for its solution.

READ ALL ABOUT IT: CRIME AND THE MASS MEDIA

The perception that violent crime is rampant would seem attributable in part to the selective attention given by the media to reporting on crime in Canada. One of the functions of the media apparently includes dissemination of knowledge about criminals and deviants, "furnishing a landscape of evil-doers and villains which seems to be as real as anything known to limited immediate experience" (Downes and Rock 1982, 42). Consider, for example, that in the first six months after the double murders of Nicole Brown Simpson and Ron Goldman, there were 39 261 articles written in major U.S. and Canadian newspapers or magazines on the "O.J. killings"—not to mention the air time devoted to it, the books on the best-seller list, or the movies of the week (Nelson 1997). The pervasive presence of television programs from the United States may give Canadians a false impression of the rate and nature of crime in their own country. Consider as well that according to the Center for Media and Public Affairs, an analysis of the ABC, NBC, and CBS nightly newscasts from 1990 through 1996 revealed that while coverage of crime ranked sixth from 1990 to 1992, it skyrocketed to first place after that with 7448 stories devoted to crime in a four-year period. Approximately 1 out of every 20 American network news stories over that four-year period was about a murder—suggesting an unprecedented electronic crime wave.

It is obvious that such programs as *America's Most Wanted, Cops*, and *Rescue 911* are part of the private media that exists first and foremost for the pursuit of profit, not to educate viewers about a very complex topic. As Richardson (1988, 69) notes, "To violate conventional thought—producers feel—would cost the media and its advertisers the mass market's dollar." Profit derives from advertising revenues, which, in turn, derive from the share of the potential audience that can be captured by an appealing show. In this respect, it is interesting to note that economic analysts have estimated that the annual Canadian costs of *white collar crimes* (Sutherland 1940; 1949) such as embezzlement, stock fraud, bid rigging, and computer crime, exceed $4 billion (Gomme 1993, 398). But as Schlesinger and Tumber (1993, 26) have observed, "'[w]hite collar crime' is generally judged to have less visual appeal than violent crime. . . . Action stories are regarded as more attractive for a programme conceived as popular television." One of the consequences of a steady diet of violent TV programs is that our ideas both about violent crime and the dangers we face in contemporary Canadian society may become grossly exaggerated.

Another consequence of this sort of fare is even more disturbing. The widespread popularity of biographies of serial murderers, the news that rapist-murderer Ted Bundy received hundreds of marriage proposals after his conviction, and the marketability of autographed pictures of clowns drawn by pedophiliac murderer John Wayne Gacy may all be construed as disconcerting social facts. Indeed, the commercial availability of "killer cards," which, adopting the format of baseball or hockey cards, feature notorious killers on collectible cards, suggests that, at least for some people, the infamous have attained the status of celebrities, with all that implies. If traditionally we expected our heroes and heroines to behave in a more ethically rigorous fashion, the commercialization of crime and its treatment in the media has apparently allowed murderers and child-rapists to become figures of fantasy and romance, endowed with memorable—if chilling—nicknames (e.g., the "Night

Stalker" (Richard Ramirez); the "Hillside Strangler" (Kenneth Bianchi); "Son of Sam" (David Berkowitz); the "Yorkshire Ripper" (Peter Sutcliffe); and the "Barbie and Ken" of Canadian crime (Bernardo and Homolka)). As but one example, consider that during the trial of Paul Bernardo, following evidence of his ex-wife Karla Homolka's participation in the sexual assaults and torture of the victims, one daily newspaper in Toronto polled its male readers to determine what percentage would favourably regard the opportunity to "sleep" with Homolka. It would seem fair to say that the media finds the perpetrators of violence infinitely more intriguing and newsworthy than their victims (see Case 4-1). Indeed, Loftus and Ketcham (1991, 62), in referring to the many victims of serial killer Ted Bundy, have remarked that when, "[b]eginning in January 1964, young women in their late teens and early twenties, all pretty . . . began to disappear . . . [t]he media, in a hideous display of insensitivity, began referring to the missing women as 'Miss February,' 'Miss March,' 'Miss April,' and 'Miss May.'" All were considered somewhat interchangeable and as forgettable as the women illustrating the last month of one's calendar.

In the quest for profits, television and publishing executives have made a point of capitalizing on stories that feature the grotesque and the out-of-the ordinary instead of the mundane and everyday. For example, the rape-murder of 11-year-old Christopher Stephenson

---

CASE 4-1 The Mystique of a Murderer: The Case of Ted Bundy

Robert Ressler, a former FBI agent who coined the term "serial killer" and who is regarded as a leading authority on this type of criminal, describes the discrepancy between the media-constructed image of Ted Bundy, "the most celebrated murderer of his time," and the reality of Bundy's deeds.

A handsome, intelligent young man who seemed to some people to have considerable sex appeal, Bundy was painted by the media as a smooth guy, respected, clean, a former law student, a Mr. Nice Guy, almost a benign killer, a good lover who would kill his victims quickly.

Far from being the Rudolph Valentino of the serial killer world, Ted Bundy was a brutal, sadistic, perverted man. His last victim was a twelve year-old girl whom he suffocated by shoving

her face in the mud during his sexual assault. By his verbal skills, Bundy would habitually lure girls and young women into a position of vulnerability, then bludgeon them with a short crowbar that he had concealed in a cast on his arm, or hidden under the seat of his car. He would then commit gross sexual acts with the unconscious or semiconscious women, his favourite practice being anal assaults. After that, he'd kill them by strangulation, then transport the bodies, often several hundred miles. Before leaving them, he would mutilate and dismember them, and sometimes commit necrophilic acts. . . . This guy was an animal, and it amazed me that the media seemed unable to understand that.

From: Robert Ressler and Tom Schachtman, *Whoever Fights Monsters: My Twenty Years Hunting Serial Killers For The FBI* (New York: 1992), 63–64, by permission of St. Martin's Press.

in Brampton, Ontario, by a repeat sex offender who had been released from prison on mandatory supervision attracted substantially more media attention than did the fact that the vast majority of parolees, even those convicted of violent offences, do not reoffend. Erwin (1992) has noted that between January 1, 1975, and March 31, 1990, 658 offenders convicted of murder were released on full parole; more than 77 percent of them did not reoffend while on parole and less than 10 percent had their release revoked for an indictable offence. Only five of the released offenders were convicted for committing a second murder while on full parole.

Similarly, if the abduction murders of teenagers Leslie Mahaffy and Kristen French in 1992 seemed for many the enactment of a collective parental nightmare, the media's reporting of these tragic crimes could also be seen to promote the fear of crime, particularly of child abduction, and to heighten a sense of omnipresent danger. The depiction of accused murderer-rapist Paul Bernardo as the "handsome" and successful "boy next door" who had married his "stunning" blonde wife Karla Homolka (co-accused and convicted of two counts of manslaughter) in a "fairy tale ceremony" seemed to legitimate an amorphous fear that anyone was capable of the most heinous acts and that no one, no matter how superficially appealing, could be trusted. Beyond a doubt, the killings of Stephenson, French, and Mahaffy were heinous and tragic. However, as Moore and Trojanowicz (1988) have observed, while reasonable fears may be harnessed to fight the threat of crime, fears that are unreasonable can become a counterproductive force and a social problem in their own right.

In all of the above instances, the suggestion is implicitly conveyed that the stereotypical murderer is a *serial killer* who preys on strangers, selecting victims at random or because of some characteristic they innocently share, such as blonde hair. It is important to note, however, that in the majority of murder cases, Canadians are not murdered by homicidal stalkers. Even though 4 out of 10 Canadians identify violent assault as the crime they fear most, in the majority of crimes involving violence the offender and victim are acquainted, with approximately 30 percent involving family members (Sacco and Johnson 1990). Similarly, the majority of homicides involve victims and offenders who are known to each other: in one-third of homicides solved in 1993, the victim was killed by an immediate family member or relative, and in just over one-half the victim was killed by some other acquaintance. Female homicide victims were more likely than male homicide victims to be killed by a spouse (39% versus 7%), another family member (21% versus 13%), or a person with whom they are involved in an intimate relationship (11% versus 4%) and less likely to be killed by a nonintimate acquaintance (23% versus 56%) or by a stranger (6% versus 19%) (Koenig 1996, 393–394).

Despite the lurid stereotypes promoted by the media in discussions of crime, Fattah (1991, 53) noted that "when compared with many other risks to which we are daily exposed in the modern, technological society in which we live, criminal victimization proves to be less injurious than other types of victimization." He noted that with the obvious exception of such statistically rare crimes as murder, rape, or aggravated assault, "most victimizations, even the ones usually called serious, are actually trivial in nature, as well as consequences" (53). Arguably, however, no incident of crime, no matter how atypical or statistically infrequent, is ever insignificant. The harm incurred, the pain endured by victims, their loved ones, and society as a whole is never a factor to be ignored, discounted, or trivialized. However, as Elias (1986, 119) has observed, "In a way, many people have become victimized more by their fear of crime than by crime itself, [which is] particularly tragic since many of those fears are misplaced."

Quinney (1970), noting that the context in which news is presented may vary substantially from one newspaper to another, has suggested that a person's perception of crime may depend on the newspaper he or she reads. Indeed, Fishman (1978) has described how a crime wave against the elderly in New York was created by reporters who began to search for and highlight more and more cases of attacks on the elderly. The media may be identified as particularly influential in promoting a polarized view of a conforming majority and a deviant minority, buttressed with stereotypical images of "crime" and the "criminal." These conceptions "may serve ideological purposes, including providing misleading cues about who and what endangers us the most" (Elias 1986, 120).

CRIMINAL VICTIMIZATION AND THE FEAR OF CRIME

Victimologist Ezzat Fattah (1991) has noted that, in general, four rules apply to most forms of criminal victimization.

1) The frequency of a type of crime is inversely related to its seriousness. Less serious criminal offences such as shoplifting and other forms of minor property offences occur more frequently than offences such as aggravated assault or murder. Of the 2.6 million Criminal Code incidents (omitting traffic offences) reported in 1996, 59 percent were property crimes, 30 percent were other Criminal Code offences (e.g., bail violations, disturbing the peace, mischief), and 11 percent were violent crimes (Kong 1997).

2) With the exception of sexual assaults, the more serious a criminal offence is, the more likely it will be reported to the police. For example, a 1994 Statistics Canada study found that 90 percent of sexual assaults were not reported, while only a third of home break-ins were not (Bindman 1997: A3). In general, however, an assault causing bodily harm or a case of aggravated assault, in which a victim is wounded, maimed, or disfigured, is more likely to be reported than a common assault.

3) The greater the social distance between victim and offender, the greater the likelihood that the offence will be reported. A "date rape" is less likely to be reported than a sexual assault committed by a stranger; intrafamilial violence is less likely to be reported than extrafamilial assault.

4) In general, the likelihood of criminal victimization in Canada peaks during the teen and young adult years and declines quite sharply after age 24. Exceptions, of course, do exist. For example, it has been noted that the elderly and the infirm have often been the preferred targets of "tele-sharks"—confidence artists who through telephone sales inform their "marks" or "targets" that they have won an expensive prize, but that before they can collect they must make a purchase or payment. Perhaps because of loneliness, reduced mobility, or social isolation, the elderly are more likely to listen to the tele-shark's pitch of instantaneous wealth and luxury without scepticism.

Although victimologists emphasize that our chances of experiencing criminal victimization are relatively rare, no proportional relationship links our *fear of crime* with our probable likelihood of criminal victimization (Fattah 1991). Rather, the opposite would seem to be true.

Although overrepresented as victims of criminal acts relative to their proportion of the population, young males as a group demonstrate a fear of crime that is markedly lower than that of women or the elderly—groups whose rates of victimization are considerably lower than those of young males. Elias (1986, 119) has observed that "people . . . tend to fear the wrong crimes, or generally have fears that contradict their objective danger." He notes that although people in the middle and upper socioeconomic classes commonly fear violent crime, they are "relatively immune" from violent criminalization compared to the lower classes.

The fear of crime may act as a galvanizing force leading to calls for an increasingly punitive response to the problem of crime. Championing the return of the death penalty, dismissing educational programs for offenders as a "waste of tax dollars" and an "insult" to the law-abiding citizens who must pay for such privileges themselves, and deriding various procedural safeguards to ensure defendants' rights as forestalling rather than promoting the attainment of justice, some conservative critics have suggested that those who contravene society's laws are due little empathy or concern.

Earlier, we suggested how media representations of crime may influence and distort public perceptions. However, it would be overly simplistic to suggest that the media is the only source of the public's misperception of crime and of criminals. It is evident that, as Elias notes, "[w]hether politically motivated and directed, or simply happenstance, we have historically designated certain people and certain groups as scapegoats for our problems" (1987, 122). Accordingly, he argues that our fear of crime and whom we conceive to be dangerous "may have less to do with objective dangers or bad experiences and more to do with culturally inculcated stereotypes" (120). He suggests that the middle and upper classes have been socialized to identify the lower class as an enemy who threatens their social status, opportunities, and economic and social well-being. In consequence, he says, the perception on the part of these higher socioeconomic groups that crime is a "lower-class phenomena" simply serves to intensify the corresponding perception of the lower classes as the so-called "dangerous class." Moreover, noting that the economy and crime tend to vie with each other as the social problem the public views with greatest concern, he also suggests that these two may be related. "Concern about crime may have more to do with economic insecurity than criminal insecurity. Crime concerns may, in fact, have less to do with victimization's impact and more to do with its symbolic importance" (121).

WHAT IS CRIME?

We are sometimes told that certain things are—or should be considered— "criminal;" but the basis for such judgments often moral, not legal. For example, for some fundamentalists, homosexuality is a social evil and a "crime against God," if not against the Canadian Criminal Code. Despite the fact that homosexual acts committed between consenting adults are legal in Canada, many Canadians remain intolerant of homosexuality.

There is assuredly a link between a society's moral belief system and the practices or behaviour sanctioned in its laws. It is worth remembering that the modern symbol of the homosexual rights movement, the pink triangle, originated as a symbol used to identify homosexuals within the Nazi concentration camps, where tens of thousands of homosexuals were killed. The persecution and extermination of homosexuals were justified in a 1936 speech by Heinrich Himmler, head of the Gestapo: "Just as we today have gone back to the ancient Germanic view on the question of marriage mixing different races, so too in our judgement of homosexuality—a symptom of degeneracy which could destroy our race— we must return to the guiding Nordic principle: extermination of degenerates" (Jackson and Persky 1982). During the period of the Nazi regime, approximately 50 000 men were convicted of homosexuality in Germany; "protective custody" was also extended to those who had come to the attention of the police prior to the Third Reich and to homosexuals from Nazi-occupied territories. Obviously, not all laws are unbiased, equitable, or humanistic. Unjust or discriminatory ideologies may become embodied and fortified within a nation's governing laws. However, moral indignation by itself does not make certain conduct criminal. As Brannigan (1981) has pointed out, for any behaviour to be considered a crime, seven distinguishing elements of criminal conduct must be fulfilled. Adopting his framework, let us examine each of these elements in turn.

Crime as Harm

The notion of crime as behaviour that causes harm to persons or property is the most readily recognizable element of criminality. That is, the majority of us would acknowledge and appreciate that behaviour that results in murder, sexual assault, assault, or armed robbery cannot be socially condoned. However, if common sense and the popular imagination favours a depiction of crime that readily identifies a victim and offender, our understanding must be expanded to recognize that "criminal" behaviour does not always result in immediate or graphic forms of injury. Victims may be groups of people who, at least on the surface, do not bear the wounds or scars of an immediate attack.

An example of harm that is more diffuse than concrete is illustrated by prohibited conduct that is sometimes referred to as *victimless crime*. This term is used to refer to consensual behaviour such as drug and alcohol use, prostitution, suicide assistance, public nudity, abortion, pornography, and gambling. Inasmuch as parties to these acts knowingly and willingly engage in these behaviours, some have argued that these types of behaviour should not be under the state's control and that in criminalizing these forms of conduct we witness the *overcriminalization* of the law.

Consider, for example, the issue of illegal drug use. Those supporting unrestricted use of alcohol and drugs have argued that enforcing drug laws, particularly those prohibiting possession of cannabis, is misguided. For example, Robertson (1980, 384) argued that "organized crime in the United States owes its existence largely to laws against victimless crimes, since it makes the bulk of its money by satisfying consumer demands for goods and services that have been made illegal in the supposed interests of the moral regulation of society." He further suggested that enforcement of victimless crime has led to corruption of the police at both an organizational and individual level. "Few police are willing to accept bribes from murderers, burglars, or other criminals whose acts are patently harmful and have identifiable victims. However, many police officers feel that victimless crime is not particularly serious and that, in any case, it is impossible to eradicate" (394). It may also be noted that, in Canada, it costs $51 000 a year to keep a person in prison and that Canada currently has the second highest incarceration rate in the Western world with 112 inmates per 100 000 people.

Maintaining that the social harm of marijuana is dwarfed by the ravages associated with alcohol and tobacco use, others have argued that it is hypocritical to impose criminal penalties for marijuana possession while the sale or possession of tobacco and alcohol to persons over a certain age is lawful. At the moment it would appear that well-funded lobbyists in the tobacco industry have been successful in keeping their products from coming under the jurisdiction of the Narcotics Control Act. No such powerful lobby exists for marijuana decriminalization.

No Crime without Law

This element of criminal conduct reminds us of the distinction we must make between our common-sense definitions of crime and those behaviours that are specifically prohibited by law. We can distinguish, at least analytically, two types of criminal conduct. The first type, termed *mala in se* (evil in themselves), involves acts that are almost universally recognized as criminal in that they involve behaviours that would, if condoned, make orderly social life impossible. The second type of criminal conduct, termed *mala prohibita*, involves acts that are considered crimes because there are laws that forbid their commission but that are not construed to be intrinsically serious or significant. We can note differences between provinces in relation to these types of offences—for example, whether cyclists are required to wear helmets. Nevertheless, the stipulation that there is "no crime without law" reminds us that the definition of crime is dependent on the prohibition of the conduct within penal law.

Actus Reus

Actus reus or "the forbidden act" refers to the physical nature of the crime, that is, to the criminal act itself. It is evident that the precise actions prohibited by law may vary by time and place. For example, until August 1993 it was not a criminal offence in Canada to possess child pornography, although it was illegal to import or sell it. Since then, amendments to the Canadian Criminal Code have made simple possession a criminal offence that is punishable by a maximum of five years imprisonment. In Canada, crime may also involve the *failure* to act in a certain way (failing to file one's income tax return or failing to maintain one's vehicle in proper working condition).

Mens Rea

Mens rea or "the guilty mind" refers to the requirement that to be convicted of a criminal act, one must be wilfully engaged in the commission of the act. In law, the mental element or *mens rea* is construed in three ways: intent, knowledge, and recklessness.

Intent

Specific intent "means purposefully and knowingly wanting to act and accurately foreseeing the act's immediate consequence" (Gomme 1993, 24). If a professor informs her student that his mark will benefit enormously if he is sexually receptive or that it will suffer if he is "unfriendly," it is evident that these demands are not uttered inadvertently. On the other hand, *general intent* may be inferred if, for example, an individual is engaged in the commission of a lesser crime, such as armed robbery, and a more serious crime is committed, such as killing a bank teller.

Knowledge

A person may be judged to have *mens rea* even if he did not set out to commit a criminal act but finds that his subsequent conduct is in violation of the law. For example, if a father upon leaving a jewellery store discovers that his child has absconded with a Rolex watch and makes no effort to return it, *mens rea* to commit theft could be shown.

Recklessness

Persons who, in a manner inconsistent with that of any "reasonable person," disregard the potential consequences of their actions, can be held accountable. For example, a driver's failure to insist that her passengers wear seat-belts may, in the event of an accident that results in their death, lead to criminal charges of recklessness.

Certain Canadian Criminal Code offences are *absolute liability* offences that do not require demonstration of *mens rea* but simply proof of *actus reus*. Osborne (1991, 63) commented that "there are a staggering number" of such laws and estimated their number within both federal and provincial legislation to be "in the tens of thousands." She noted that "[m]any of our highway traffic laws, for example, make liability strict, as do antipollution enactments and fishery regulations." The rationale for this is "that intention or knowledge in these areas would be difficult to prove. How would you establish, for example, that a person intended to exceed the speed limit or to catch undersized lobster? In such situations, the protection of the public should be paramount, with those engaged in the activities assuming responsibility for them" (64).

Canadian criminal law does recognize that not all persons can or ought to be regarded as equally blameworthy. Thus, the law allows for certain exemptions to be made that acknowledge the possibility that due to youth, legal insanity, or situations involving duress or necessity, certain people may not possess the necessary element of *mens rea*. However, these exemptions themselves testify to the often equivocal evaluations Canadians hold of who should be considered a culpable agent.

Concurrency

For an act to be considered criminal, the physical element (or *actus reus*) and the mental element (the *mens rea*) must be *concurrent* or fused together. If, during the course of writing this text, one of us feels tempted to kill the other on Thursday, resolves the difficulties that led to this feeling on Friday, and then accidentally causes the death of the other by serving a can of botulated chili as a meal on Saturday, there is no crime if the expressed desire on Thursday was not the responsible factor behind the act on Saturday. The unfortunate incident is only a coincidence, not a crime.

Causality

The sixth element of criminal conduct is that of *causality* or the relationship between conduct and harm. This issue is generally not raised in most situations because the relationship between one individual's conduct and another's injury is usually obvious. On occasion, however, the relationship can be problematic, especially in determinations of injuries that are thought to result from corporate activities. For example, the warnings on cigarette packages alert us to the link between tobacco use and lung cancer and heart disease. However, if a person who smokes dies of lung cancer, can the tobacco manufacturer be found guilty of any criminal act?

This question is a complicated one for many reasons. To begin with, Canadian law recognizes two types of persons. The first type, a *natural person*, is a living, breathing individual, and the second type is a *juristic person*, that is, a corporation. IBM, Ford, and General Electric are examples of juristic persons. The trouble with seeking to apply criminal penalties to a juristic person is that it is often difficult to identify who within the anonymous corporate structure should be held accountable for the actions of the corporation. Returning to our example of the tobacco manufacturer, who would be assigned criminal responsibility? The president of the company? The chief executive officer? The chief engineer? The head of research? Tracing the responsible person or group of people can be extremely difficult.

A second problem that arises concerns the issue of causality. Even though cigarette smoking is recognized as a contributing cause of cancer, hordes of tobacco company lawyers have continued to maintain that the chain of effects is questionable. Some who do not smoke get cancer, and some who do smoke do not get cancer. It should be noted that in cases heard in criminal court, guilt must be proven *beyond a reasonable doubt.* Even if one isolated an individual in a room with her cigarettes for 30 years, safeguarding her from all other possible contaminants, it could still theoretically be possible to argue that she developed cancer because of a genetic weakness. And, if the defence could create a reasonable doubt in the minds of a judge or jury, no guilty verdict could be brought forth. For this reason, one often finds that attempts to obtain redress or compensation for actions perpetrated by companies are heard in civil court, where the test for truth depends on the *balance of probabilities* that either supports or fails to support the complaint.

Sanctions

The last criterion of criminal behaviour is that some form of *sanction* is attached to the commission of the prohibited behaviour. However, even if we agree that criminal acts warrant punishment, the nature of that social sanction and its severity are subjects that are less clear-cut. Our response to criminals has been mixed, with some advocating *restraint* and others stressing *retribution* or *rehabilitation*. All of these strategies are thought to deter individuals from committing crime and to ensure the right of Canadians to be free of danger to themselves, their property, their loved ones, and their community.

Deterrence operates on two levels. The first level, individual or specific deterrence, refers to the possible effect of punishment on an offender's future behaviour. The second level, general deterrence, refers to the symbolic impact that punishing an offender has on others in society who may be contemplating replicating the offender's deed. In the past, burning at the stake, public hanging, flogging, and the branding of offenders were thought to be not only fitting punishments for certain offences but also useful in deterring others from committing the same offences.

The goal of *retribution* is probably the oldest and most obvious objective of criminal law. In earliest times, the practice of lex talionis (literally, "the law of the same kind") illustrated this goal most graphically by requiring judges to "let the punishment fit the crime." In consequence, the tongue of a perjurer or a slanderer would be cut out, the hand of a thief or the penis of a rapist would be amputated, and so on. Similarly, many who argue for the return of the death penalty, especially in cases of murder, often cite the goal of retribution when they demand that the offender pay with his or her life for that of the victim.

Canada inherited the death penalty from England and France. Under England's "Bloody Code," for example, literally hundreds of crimes were deemed to be capital offences and executions were public events with dramatic processions from jail to the gallows and assorted degradations performed on the corpse, which was typically left on display. In Canada, where French or English law was adopted, these practices continued. As Engels (1996) has observed, the annals of Canada's prehistory are littered with references to the use of capital punishment; in Upper Canada, where there was an exalted respect for property, it was a capital offence in the nineteenth century to move a boundary marker from one place to another without approval. In New France, there were 11 legal methods of execution, including being "broken on the wheel," being shot, having one's head crushed, or, if a member of the nobility, being decapitated; disembowelment and dismemberment were used for those convicted of treason, while offenders who escaped were hanged in effigy. Although the precise number of people hanged in early Canada remains unknown inasmuch as accurate records date only from 1867, the first person executed for a crime is reputed to have been a young girl hanged at the age of 16 for the crime of petty theft; the last was a double execution in 1962 at Toronto's Don Jail. Capital punishment was formally abolished in this country in 1976; however, the state, as the holder of "legitimate force" in our society, retains the right to bring it back.

Since the 1970s, Gallup polls have consistently noted that the majority of Canadians express the belief that the courts are too lenient with offenders; in 1995, approximately 85 percent of a national, random sample of Canadians maintained that the courts did not deal harshly enough with criminals and about 82 percent expressed the belief that the death penalty should be exercised in some instances. While support for the reinstatement of capital punishment is somewhat lower in Quebec and marginally higher in the Prairie provinces, on a national level, support for the death penalty has been remarkably consistent over time (e.g., in the fall of 1943, Gallup reported that 80 percent of Canadians were in favour of capital punishment) and there are only small reported differences between women and men, and younger and older Canadians in their level of support for capital punishment (Bibby 1995).

The goal of *rehabilitation* is predicated on the optimistic premise that criminal offenders are not inherently wicked or evil but can be reformed and reintegrated into society. For example, the controversial "faint hope clause," Section 745 of the Criminal Code, which became law in 1976 (after the death penalty was abolished and the life sentence for first-degree murder was set at 25 years for eligibility to apply for parole), allows first- and second-degree murderers who have served 15 years of their life sentence to apply for a reduction in their parole eligibility dates. It is suggested that the measure, which allows offenders the right to apply for a judicial review before a jury (that considers factors including the inmate's character, conduct in prison, the nature of the offence, and other matters the judge considers relevant), is important as an incentive for rehabilitation. It is also believed to discourage the likelihood of prisoner suicide and to lessen the risks to guards from prisoners who may feel they have nothing to lose. It should be noted that not all murderers can benefit under this section of the Criminal Code. In 1997, the federal government tightened the provision so that its use is denied to multiple murders. In addition, judges are allowed to screen out applicants with no hope of early parole and juries are required to agree unanimously on a sentence reduction. Nevertheless, opponents contend that the clause offers serious offenders much more than a faint hope. Since the first judicial review was heard in 1987, 76 decisions have been handed down; of these, 60 parole reduction requests were granted and 16 were denied. Although the parole board is not bound to grant parole in those cases where requests are granted and approximately 25 of those granted a reduction remained incarcerated, the 1997 parole review of serial killer Clifford Olson, sentenced in 1981 to life imprisonment without parole for 25 years for the brutal murders of 11 children across B.C.'s lower mainland (and who had applied for parole reduction before the more stringent provisions came into effect), was seen by many as "an exercise in law, but not in justice" (The Toronto Star 1997). In general, Canadians seem to regard the goal of rehabilitation in a paradoxical manner. Thus, while the need for treatment and therapy is often championed, at the same time Canadians seem to hold a rather jaundiced view of the efficacy of such measures, particularly in the cases of sexual and violent offenders.

It is evident that the goals of punishment are not simple, clear-cut, or easy to realize in practice. Nevertheless, the notion that the punishment for criminal behaviour should involve a measure of deterrence is the seventh distinguishing characteristic of a crime.

WHO COMMITS CRIME?

The notion that persons who commit crime are readily recognizable and distinguishable from people who are law-abiding is one that can be traced back to antiquity. This fallacy is buttressed by images in the media that present the criminal as "wild-eyed" and "sinister." The result is that discussions of criminality often become anchored in a "type-of-person" approach to crime. The human implications of such stereotypes are vast. Our understanding of criminals and our assessment of the threat they pose may mirror these common-sense understandings more fully than they reflect the reality of crime within Canadian society.

If the mass media's coverage of crime encourages a distorted perception of criminal justice issues, the image it constructs of the offender is particularly problematic. That is, by offering depictions of the "criminal" that tend to the bizarre and that concentrate on the lawbreaker-as-sociopath, the media encourage the public to generalize this information as if the description of a particular offender were reflective of every offender in the country. As Roberts and Gabor (1990, 293) observed, "[T]o the average member of the public, crime is a relatively unidimensional phenomenon: it usually involves violence, loss of property, and is a consequence of a 'criminal disposition.' Members of the public tend to regard offenders as a relatively homogenous group . . . varying somewhat in their actions but not in their motivations." Although criminologists generally recognize the naïveté of assuming that there is one explanation that accounts for all possible forms of crime, this doesn't stop the media from favouring just this type of reductionist argument.

For example, in 1989 the Canadian news media devoted unprecedented attention to the claims of psychologist Phillipe Rushton, a professor at the University of Western Ontario, that his research demonstrated a genetic influence on crime rates, specifically evidence of significant interracial differences. In a paper delivered at a conference of the American Association for the Advancement of Science, Rushton outlined a "genetic hierarchy" of crime and suggested that Blacks (whose evolution, Rushton maintained, preceded that of Whites or Asians) were less intelligent and law-abiding than the White or Asian racial "types." Disdaining to define "race," treating crime as a unitary phenomenon, and assuming racial purity as a given, Rushton used aggregate statistics of *index offences* such as homicide, rape, aggravated assault, and robbery to argue that Blacks are more criminal than, in descending order, Whites or Asians.

A review of Rushton's research suggests that it was guided by Maier's law, that is, if the data contradict your theory, dispense with the data. Thus, his presentation failed to explain why, in the United States, Blacks are overrepresented in crimes such as robbery and murder but underrepresented in white collar offences such as embezzlement and tax fraud; why, in the United States, Blacks are also overrepresented as victims of violent crime; and why, in Canada, natives (being Asian or Mongoloid) display higher rather than lower rates of crime than non-natives (Roberts and Gabor 1990). Although, as Roberts and Gabor (1990) argue, the scholarly merit of his assertions is far less than convincing, it is nevertheless worth noting that "Rushton's speculations about race and crime . . . achieved national coverage exceeding that accorded any research project undertaken by criminologists." This focusing of attention, Roberts and Gabor suggest, has potentially serious ramifications. As they note, lay persons are less likely to attend to the fact that Rushton has simply presented correlational data on race and crime and that *causality* cannot be presumed. In consequence, they argue that the popularization of Rushton's research may have the invidious effect of inflaming racism within Canadian society, particularly among those who are already receptive to a "person-blame" approach.

A "person-blame" approach to the social problem of crime is often tempting; indeed, our legal system is built on a foundation that stresses individual free will and personal responsibility. As Parker (1991, 42) notes, "Modern psychological and sociological views of crime have little relevance to the way in which the law defines crime and determines guilt (although those disciplines do make some contribution to the sentencing process)." However, when coupled with a view of criminals as a homogenous group, the temptation to view all criminals as "dangerous" may be marked. For example, in 1993, in response to the construction of a federal prison for women in the Doon Pioneer Park section of Kitchener, Ontario, a group of residents formed a lobby group to demand that the facility be located somewhere else and distributed flyers with Karla Homolka's picture prominently featured on the cover page under the headline "MOST UNWANTED."

The suggestion that Homolka could be depicted as representative of Canada's female offenders would surely seem misplaced. Although women's share of criminal charges has been gradually rising since the late 1980s, women still account for only 16.5 percent of all charges, with theft under $1000 the most common criminal charge laid against them. While the murder rate for Canadian males has fluctuated, the murder rate for women has been rather stable, with an average offender rate of approximately 0.45 per 100 000 women. In 1993 women represented 12.7 percent of all adults charged with assaults other than sexual assaults, 14.1 percent of all adults charged with homicide, 14 percent of all adults charged with attempted murder, and 1.6 percent of all adults charged with sexual assault. Moreover, Homolka was a highly atypical offender even among those who commit violent crimes. Silverman and Kennedy (1993) have noted that almost 9 out of 10 (89%) women who kill do so on their own, 95 percent kill a single victim, and "[o]verwhelmingly, female offenders kill members of their own family (75 percent)" (146). In their examination of the 1314 killings committed by females in Canada between 1961 and 1990, 40 percent of the victims were the woman's legal or common-law husband, while 22 percent were the woman's child. Nevertheless, at public meetings and in numerous letters to the editor of the local newspapers, the suggestion that a prison for women would house a uniform population of Homolka-clones seemed potent as anti-prison spokespersons detailed the "threat" posed by "dangerous" offenders.

Here again we witness the distinction between common sense and legal constructions of what constitutes a "dangerous offender." It should be noted that according to Canada's Criminal Code, a person can only be labelled a "dangerous offender" and given an indefinite sentence (versus a sentence for a fixed period of time) if that person has been convicted of a "serious personal injury offence" and there is strong evidence to suggest that the person constitutes a threat to others. Since 1977, when the law was enacted, only 93 people (92 men and 1 woman) have been designated dangerous offenders. For some, this type of law is necessary to ensure the protection of the public. However, others feel it represents "the most draconian measure the government has at its disposal for dealing with violent criminals" because it requires judges to *predict* who will reoffend (Kershaw and Lasovich 1991, 118). Accordingly, critics suggest, the end result may be the detention of those whose characteristics are congruent with the popular stereotypes of the "criminal" already in effect.

For example, in her summary of the research of Esses and Webster (1986), Jackson (1991, 185) has shown how stereotypes of the "criminal" may result in bias in the courtroom. In their Canadian research, the investigators furnished 284 adults with information about hypothetical offenders that included facial photographs and a description of identifying features. Their research subjects were then asked to review summaries of the offenders' backgrounds. The different offenders were distinguished primarily by their looks and their conviction records. As Jackson notes, "Physical attractiveness was varied at three levels: descriptions were given of features suggesting both abnormality and normality; the conviction record had two different listings, sexual or nonsexual, for each of two levels: one present conviction and five previous convictions." Respondents were then asked to evaluate the offenders in relation to the Canadian Criminal Code definition of a "dangerous offender." The results of this research indicated that, for their subjects, the physically unattractive sexual offender was perceived as significantly more likely to fulfil the Canadian dangerous-offender criteria than were the average-looking and attractive sexual offenders. As Jackson notes, although the assumption that criminal offenders are identifiable by their physical characteristics "has no proven validity in reality," the stereotype could become real enough in its consequences.

THE CORRELATES OF CRIME

In this section we will review some of the major correlates of criminal behaviour. However, we would caution the reader against assuming that these are causal factors. As we shall see, these factors have been identified through statistical analyses of convicted criminals; however, the precise nature of how these factors are related to criminal activity continues to inspire controversy and debate.

Age

Although Hartnagel (1996, 96) has noted that "[w]ithout much exaggeration, crime can be said to be a young man's game," there are, of course, exceptions to this rule. For example, white collar offences are rarely committed by juveniles, and few figures in the world of organized crime have been noted for their youth. Similarly, prior to 1972 the crime of prostitution was a gender-specific offence and currently the crime of infanticide remains by statutory definition a female offence. Nevertheless, in general terms, the emphasis on youth and gender implied in Hartnagel's comment is literally correct.

As Hartnagel (1996, 97) notes, although youths age 12 to 17 account for approximately one-eighth of the Canadian population, this group accounts for 13 percent of persons accused of violent incidents and 27 percent of persons accused of property incidents. Moreover, young adults age 18 to 24 account for 22 percent of persons accused of violent incidents and 28 percent of those accused of property incidents, while Canadians age 25 to 34 account for 33 percent of persons accused of violent incidents and 24 percent of persons accused of property offences. In general, he remarks, "the percentage of persons accused of crime increases from early adolescence to young adulthood and then declines" (97). Indeed, some attribute the overall drop in our national rate of crime to the fact that the sector of the population responsible for most crimes, those in the 18 to 29 age bracket, has been shrinking.

Although the rate of youths charged in 1996 decreased across all crime categories, including a 4 percent drop in violent crime, this represented the first notable decrease since comparable data on young offenders became available in 1986. Nevertheless, the rate of juvenile crime in this country has struck many Canadians as particularly problematic and various social commentators have pointed to changes within the family, specifically the rise in divorce and single-parent families, and the increased mobility of Canadians (for example, the average Canadian family now moves once every five years) as influential. Others have focused on the use of television as the "electronic babysitter" and suggested that "television can only feed the malignant impulses that already exist in some children" and "that a society which finds violence so fascinating is also a society that can anticipate its wider use by people in all walks of life, be they policemen, robbers, hockey players, drunken husbands, or juveniles" (Hackler 1978, 196). If Nettler (1984) has suggested that the visibility of juvenile crime simply suggests that, compared to adults, juveniles engage in relatively unsophisticated methods of crime and, in consequence, are detected more frequently, others have argued that the relationship between youth and crime is far more complex.

Greenberg (1979) has identified age stratification within contemporary Western societies as a crucial factor in accounting for high rates of juvenile crime. In particular, he suggests that the ambiguous social dictates of "adolescence" in themselves may be seen to encourage defiant, deviant, or criminal behaviour. It may be noted that the recognition of "adolescence" as a distinct period in the life course is relatively recent.

It is this limbo status of adolescence—between childhood and adulthood— Greenberg argues, that may explain the high involvement of youths in criminal activities. He suggests that nonutilitarian crimes such as vandalism or seemingly senseless acts of violence may be ways in which disenfranchised youths can attain status among their peer groups. Similarly, encouraged to act in an "adult" manner by peers and the media in terms of conspicuous consumption, yet simultaneously excluded from adult responsibilities, social status, and employment income, these youths may in the end succumb to the enticements of profitable forms of crime.

Moreover, Greenberg suggests that the existence of *maturational reform*, in which people "age out" of crime and become more law-abiding as they grow older, can be explained by reference to the lower legal and social penalties experienced by young offenders compared with those of adults. In other words, faced with the increased penalties for criminal misconduct once they are adults, individuals acquire a greater "stake in conformity." In this vein it may be noted that Canadian social commentators frequently have suggested that the Young

Offenders Act, which governs the conduct of Canadian youths under the age of 18 and which shields them from the penalties given to adults for the same sort of conduct, may in itself encourage juveniles to engage in criminal behaviour.

The shifting and evolving notions of what young people are capable of and of the most beneficial way in which to respond to youthful crime can be illustrated by the different definitions used within the two major laws that have been enacted in Canada to respond to crime committed by youths. Both the Juvenile Delinquency Act (1908) and the Young Offenders Act (1984) recognize that young people do not have the same capacity for forming *mens rea* as do adults, but aside from that, they offer quite dissimilar suggestions as to how we should respond to youth crimes.

Bala (1988, 3, 11) notes that during the 1800s and continuing in Canada until 1984, "the English common law standard was applied" with children under the age of 7 held to be *doli incapax* (incapable of doing wrong). In relation to children between the ages of 7 and 13, "there was a presumption of diminished capacity, but this could be rebutted if there was evidence to establish that the child had sufficient intelligence and experience to 'know the nature and consequences of the conduct and to appreciate that it was wrong'" (11). Bala points out that "those children who were convicted faced the same penalties as adult offenders, including hanging and incarceration in such places as the old Kingston penitentiary" (11).

Largely as the result of efforts made by social reformers who sought to promote more humane treatment, the Juvenile Delinquency Act (JDA) of 1908 provided for a court and correctional system that was to be separate and distinct from that of the adult system. Moreover, the philosophy underlying the JDA "clearly had a child welfare, or *parens patriae* [father or parent of the country] philosophy." As Section 38 of the JDA directed, "The care and custody and discipline of a juvenile delinquent shall approximate as nearly as may be that which should be given by his parents and . . . as far as practicable every juvenile delinquent shall be treated, not as a criminal, but as a misguided and misdirected child . . . needing aid, encouragement, help, and assistance."

At least in theory, the juvenile court was to act as a kindly father would towards his child. Accordingly, the JDA allowed for a tremendous amount of discretion to be used in deciding what was in the child's best interests—an amount of discretion that included a tendency to ignore children's legal rights. As Bala (1988) pointed out, there was an absence of legislative guidelines governing judicial sentencing, and indeterminate sentences were common when youths were sent to training schools or reformatories. Release was given only when correctional officials felt that the "rehabilitation" of the youth had occurred. Inasmuch as the court was empowered to act "in the best interests of the child," there was an absence of time-consuming legal safeguards and lawyers rarely represented youths who appeared in juvenile court (where judges frequently lacked any form of legal training). In consequence, "there were occasions when guilt seemed to be presumed so that 'treatment' would not be delayed by unnecessary formalities" (Bala 1988, 12–13).

If the JDA was supposed to focus on the welfare of children, the central philosophy underlying the Young Offenders Act (YOA) is less focused. Its principal aims are to hold young persons who break the law accountable for their actions, to protect society from criminal behaviour, and to protect the legal rights of young offenders. Exactly which of these goals is to take precedence and whether or not the goals are truly compatible with each other are questions that have inspired new debates and arguments since the passage of the YOA. For example, according to the Declaration of Principle of the YOA, "while young persons should not in all instances be held accountable in the same manner or suffer the same consequences for their behaviour as adults," they should "nonetheless bear responsibility for their contraventions" and society must "be afforded the necessary protection from illegal behaviour." Towards that end, the YOA dilutes strict criminal responsibility with the principle of *mitigated accountability*. Thus, the Declaration of Principle also states that young offenders "require supervision, discipline and control but . . . also have special needs and require guidance and assistance" and that "where it is not inconsistent with the protection of society, taking no measures or taking measures other than judicial proceedings under this Act should be considered for dealing with young persons who have committed offences." The YOA similarly outlines that the rights and freedoms of young persons include a right to the "least possible interference" that is consistent with the protection of society, having regard to the needs of young persons and the interests of their families. The Act allows for "alternative measures" in lieu of trial and punishment, prohibits the publication of the names of young offenders (except in exceptional circumstances such as, for example, if a youth is at large and considered by a judge to be "dangerous to others"), and restricts access to juvenile records. It also includes a variety of legal safeguards, for example, guarantees of legal representation, special provisions to ensure there is no improper questioning of a youth by police or other persons in positions of authority, and provisions for the notification of parents or other appropriate adults. All of these safeguards augment the rights extended to all Canadians under the Charter of Rights and Freedoms.

Opinions as to the legal blameworthiness of youths and the best way in which to respond to young offenders have occasioned storms of controversy in recent years. Critics have pointed to home invasions, to swarmings in playgrounds, to youths carrying weapons to school or extorting money from their classmates before the latter are allowed to use the bathroom, to the recruitment of children under age 12 to commit burglaries or to sell drugs, and to the seemingly inexplicable killings of preschool age children by preadolescents, as by-products of a system of juvenile justice that provides for "soft laws, soft jails and a court system in chaos" (Alberta Report, April 15, 1991). If the international media's coverage of the 1993 murder of 2-year-old Jamie Bulger, lured away from a shopping mall in Preston, England, by two 10-year-old boys, who beat the child to death with bricks and a 10-kg metal bar and left his body on railway tracks where it was sliced in two by a passing train, alerted world attention to the potential brutality of preteens, we do not lack for domestic examples. In 1996, for example, Canadians were "treated to the grisly details" of how an 8-year-old Saskatchewan boy helped plan and execute the brutal slaying of a 7-year-old and how, in Toronto, an 11-year-old boy acted as the ringleader of a group of boys who raped a 13-year-old girl and then taunted police, saying, "You got me—so what are you going to do?" (Bergman 1996, 13). A heightened public awareness of crime by young people may result in the police feeling pressure to charge youths or for prosecutors to argue that the case be heard in adult court. Moreover, within large cities, the professionalization of the police and the creation of special "youth units" may, through a change in bureaucratic structure, itself result in a greater likelihood of charges being laid. Accordingly, changes in social tolerance, demands for the police to "do something" about young offenders, and changing law enforcement practices may at least partially explain the increased charging of young offenders.

In an attempt to control youth crime, the Manitoba legislature has considered introducing a Parental Responsibility Act that would make parents liable for damages of up to $5000 upon their child's conviction for a crime involving property damage. With like reasoning, one

Canadian company, Zellers Inc., since the implementation of a loss-recovery program in 1993, has issued "hundreds of letters" demanding restitution from the parents of children caught stealing in their stores and threatening them with legal action if they refuse. In 1996 a Manitoba court heard that a mother had paid Zellers $225 after her son was caught stealing approximately $60 worth of goods. In this case, the judge ruled that the company was not entitled to demand restitution and must return the monies to the woman; however, a Zellers spokesperson noted that the company's program had already collected in excess of $1 million and that they were continuing with the program (Chisholm 1996, 13).

Gender

Hartnagel has noted that in 1992 in Canada "adult males constituted 82 percent of adults charged with Criminal Code offences [and that] [o]ver 80 percent of the young persons appearing in youth courts are male" (101–102). While he points out that from 1968 to 1992 there was a massive 303 percent increase in the arrest rate for all Criminal Code offences committed by females (compared with a 99 percent increase for males), a 328 percent increase in the rate of females charged with property crime (compared with a 74 percent increase for males), and a 585 percent increase in the rate of females charged with violent crime (compared with a 205 percent increase for males), he emphasizes that this is largely due to the small numbers of women charged with committing a criminal act (that is, an increase from two to four persons charged is a 100 percent increase), and that "large absolute differences remain, with the male rates greatly exceeding that of females" (104). He also points to the generally nonviolent nature of female criminality and notes that "82 percent of the increase between 1968 and 1992 in the number of females charged with Criminal Code offences was for nonviolent offences" (104).

Smart (1976, 2) observes that "[i]n the past female criminality has not been thought to constitute a significant threat to the social order and even in the present, criminologists and policy-makers are slow to re-evaluate the notion that female offenders are more than insignificant irritants to the smooth running of law and order." In consequence, theorists (when they troubled themselves to address the issue of female criminality at all) frequently invoked the "good girl/bad girl," "madonna/whore" dichotomy with the suggestion that females are inherently less likely to commit crime than males. Alternatively, the stereotype of the "conniving" female has ostensibly encouraged others to suggest that the statistics on criminality are illusory, that women used their "feminine wiles" to mask their participation in crime and were, in fact, the "brains" behind much criminal activity. Supposedly, female offenders also benefited from the misplaced chivalry of male agents within the criminal justice system (Pollak 1950).

More recently, other theorists have focused on the socially structured differences between men and women and suggested that their different socialization patterns increase the likelihood that women (who are more likely to be strictly supervised and encouraged to be passive, trusting, and helpless) will become the victims of crime, and increases the likelihood that males (who are given greater freedom to explore their environment and encouraged to evidence aggression, independence, and risk-taking behaviour) will become criminal offenders. As Janoff-Bulman and Frieze (1987, 159) observe, "At the same time that the victim role is associated with being female, the assailant role is considered masculine, especially if the victimization involves violence, aggression, or daring." In turn, this *sex role socialization thesis* has encouraged others to suggest that in the statistical increase in female criminality we are witnessing the rise of the "new female criminal" (Adler 1975), another instance of *role convergence* between men and women. That is, as women become more liberated from traditional social roles, the opportunities for them to become "like men" in terms of participation in crime are seen to increase.

Despite the implication that "women's liberation" has resulted in a burgeoning female crime rate, it would appear unlikely that substantial support for the women's movement would be found among delinquent girls and criminal women, "if only because the majority of individuals who become known offenders are recruited from the working classes where there does not appear to be a strong support for the Women's Movement as such" (Smart 1976, 74). It may be noted that, according to a 1990 task force report conducted by Correctional Services Canada, the majority of federally sentenced women are poor, unemployed, and undereducated. Approximately two-thirds of women serving sentences of two years or more have either not completed high school or lacked training or educational qualifications beyond this level. Women who experience the "double handicap" of minority status seemed particularly disadvantaged; many native women were found to be grade school drop-outs, while some had never attended school.

Moreover, as Smart (1976) observes, the suggestion of a direct causal relationship between emancipation and crime may be more accurately seen as testifying to the challenge posed by the women's movement to traditional roles and the "immense fear" (71) of such potential change. She remarks that to attribute the increase in female criminality to a singular variable like the women's movement is logically fallacious. Rather, she suggests that "such explanations, which implicitly serve the purpose of a critique of any change in women's position, have . . . merely succeeded in providing a scientistic legitimation of women's inferior social position" (74, 76).

The question of why men figure so prominently in the commission of crime and, in particular, violent crime, continues to provoke controversy and intellectual debate. Some favour *biological theories* and postulate that men are "naturally" more aggressive than woman. For example, authors such as Morris (1968) and Lorenz (1967) have argued that inasmuch as human beings have descended from what they call "killer apes," the vestiges of our ancestry may still have an effect on *male aggressiveness*. Others, drawing on *frustration-aggression theory*, which postulates that frustration may result in aggression, focus on the masculine role within our society and the stresses that men experience in their challenge to "be a man." These writers argue that cultural definitions of "masculinity" are not merely hazardous to the well-being of individual men but also make being a man hazardous to others.

As feminists have noted, frustration-aggression theory by itself is an inadequate explanation of men's greater use of violence. They note, for example, that a man who is frustrated over not achieving a promotion may desist from attacking his boss but feel it "appropriate" to hit his wife when he returns home. Accordingly, they suggest that to understand why men engage in violent crime more frequently than women, we must focus on the cultural underpinnings of "masculinity" itself.

Race

Griffiths and Yerbury (1996, 386) have observed that "[i]n most jurisdictions in Canada, aboriginal people are overrepresented in the criminal-justice system, from the arrest stage to incarceration in correctional institutions." LaPrairie (1990, 429) has observed that although aboriginal people comprise between 1.5 and 2 percent of the Canadian population, they constitute between 8 and 10 percent of the population within federal correctional institutions and an even greater percentage in provincial and territorial institutions (LaPrairie 1990, 429). In Manitoba, for example, where aboriginal people constitute a mere 6 percent of the total population, they account for over half of the inmates in correctional institutions. Aboriginals accused of committing a criminal offence are more likely to be denied bail, held in pretrial detention, charged with multiple offences, spend less time in consultation with their lawyers, and, upon conviction, be sentenced to a term of incarceration. In Alberta, aboriginal young offenders are less likely than nonaboriginal youths to be referred to alternative measure programs and more likely to be charged, to receive a custodial sentence, and to spend a longer period of time in custody (Griffiths and Yerbury 1996, 386, 389). As Hartnagel (1996, 112) has observed, "[b]y 1991–92, Native offenders accounted for approximately 24 percent of all sentenced admissions to provincial correctional institutions," with native inmates representing "38 percent of the admissions to federal custody in Manitoba, 55 percent in Saskatchewan, 22 percent in Alberta, 17 percent in British Columbia, 50 percent in the Yukon, and 85 percent in the Northwest Territories." In Canada, an aboriginal woman is more likely to go to prison than to university (Kershaw and Lasovich 1991, 227).

Although it is evident that aboriginal people are disproportionately vulnerable to incarceration, there are conflicting views of why this occurs. LaPrairie (1990, 430), for example, suggested that there are three "competing but not mutually exclusive" explanations: "differential treatment by the criminal justice system; differential commission of crime due to non-racial attributes [such as socio-economic marginality, alcohol abuse and so on] which heighten the risk of criminal behaviour; and, differential offence patterns (with Aboriginals more likely to commit crimes that are, for example, more serious or more visible) than non Aboriginal people."

To various degrees, each of these explanations has attracted attention and support. For example, throughout the 1980s and 1990s both media scandal-mongering and the findings of law reform commissions like the Manitoba Aboriginal Justice Inquiry supported the view that racism pervades the Canadian criminal justice system. Nevertheless, some critics considered the formation of such public inquiries to be little more than a stalling tactic or a means to avoid taking action (for example, the establishment of a "parallel" system of justice) that they argued would be more meaningful (Goddard 1991). For others, allegations of widespread racism were simply not convincing.

For example, LaPrairie (1990, 431) argues that although "assumptions about the existence of differential, racist charging practices abound," there is scant empirical work in Canada demonstrating discriminatory actions on the part of the police or the judiciary, and she faults scholarship that would indulge in "the use of rhetoric in the absence of knowledge." Moreover, she suggests that explaining the overrepresentation of aboriginal people "solely in racist terms may be simplistic and misleading with respect to finding real and long-lasting solutions to the over-representation problem" (436).

LaPrairie suggests that an examination of *systemic racism* or "treating unequals equally" might more accurately explain the overrepresentation of aboriginals within Canadian prisons. Thus, she comments that the "deprived socio-economic situation acts against Aboriginal people at sentencing and against communities in the development and maintenance of community-based alternatives." In consequence, she suggests, aboriginals who are unemployed and indigent are more likely to be incarcerated for less serious offences "because [they] do not qualify for probation, and few options but incarceration are available to judges." Moreover, she observes that the remote location of many reserves "makes access to universal sentencing alternatives difficult and often impossible." Accordingly, she says, "[o]ver time, the revolving door syndrome creates a large group of Aboriginal people with long records of incarceration which act against them in subsequent court appearances" (1990, 438).

However, while LaPrairie accepts that "[t]he social and economic marginality of Aboriginal people in Canadian society is the fundamental problem and their involvement in the criminal justice system as offenders is a vivid testimonial to it," she argues that "[t]he criminal justice system is not a vehicle for social restructuring; neither should it be a storage receptacle for social problems" (438). Nevertheless, for others, it would appear that in various ways, the dungeons of corrections have become precisely that.

It has been suggested that the overrepresentation of natives as both offenders and victims may be seen as a consequence of *sociostructural deprivation*. For example, using nationwide Canadian data, Griffiths et al. (1987) note that among the population of registered Indians, accidents, poisonings, and violence account for 35 percent of all deaths, while these three causes account for only 9 percent of the deaths of Canadians as a whole. In Canada, the suicide rate of natives is almost three times the national Canadian rate. Similarly, although natives comprise only 3 percent of the Canadian population, approximately one-quarter of all family-related homicides in Canada from 1974 to 1987 involved native people. "Generally, Natives continue to have a lower average level of education, fewer marketable skills, a higher rate of unemployment, an infant mortality rate twice the national rate, a higher degree of family instability, and a rate of violent death three times the national average" (Hartnagel 1992, 110).

Socioeconomic Status

Analysts of official data have long noted an inverse relationship between socioeconomic status and involvement in crime. Those who are marked by low income, education, and occupational status are more likely than those of higher status to be officially identified as criminal. However, attempts to decode the precise nature of this relationship have been very controversial.

For *strain theorists* such as Robert Merton (1957), the association between socioeconomic status and crime was indirect and could be explained with reference to the concept of *relative deprivation*. Merton noted that in North America the goal of "success" and material wealth is held out as if it were equally attainable by all. He also noted that far less importance is placed on the means through which this success was to be obtained. Merton developed this observation to suggest that criminality may serve to indicate an act of "overconformity" rather than defiance of social values and goals. He stated that if the traditional or conventional means through which people achieve success (ambition, deferred gratification, drive, self-discipline, hard work, intelligence, and education) are unavailable, then "deviant" or illegitimate means would be pursued. Drawing on Emile Durkheim's concept of *anomie* or normlessness, Merton linked deviance or criminality to the norms and values of society (that is, to culturally legitimate goals) and to the differing degrees of access various groups have to these goals through culturally legitimate means. That is, if it is only the *possession* of the mansion, the foreign cars, and the bulging wallet that mark one as "having arrived," then ambitious people may conclude that the end justifies the means, even when the means are criminal. Merton called the person who accepts social goals but pursues illegitimate means of obtaining them an *innovator*. He argued that the typical innovator was not motivated by anything resembling a personal "pathology," but was controlled instead by the structural forces of society.

Similarly, in focusing on the behaviour of gang members in lower-class urban neighbourhoods in the United States, Cohen suggested that delinquency could be viewed as a response to the discrepancy between social goals and the opportunities such youths have to achieve these goals. He argued that lower-class youths were particularly disadvantaged by the "middle class measuring rod" used to evaluate their conduct within school settings. Cohen suggested that nonutilitarian crimes committed by these youths could be viewed as a type of *reaction formation*. Since they were unable or unwilling to achieve status in school by such conventionally recognized strategies as getting high grades, the only way they *could* claim status was through an inversion of goals whereby being a "hell raiser" became a positive achievement rather than a negative one. Moreover, Walter Miller (1958) suggested that due to the *focal concerns* of the lower-class subculture, lower-class youths are more likely than those of a higher socioeconomic status to run afoul of the law. According to Miller, these focal concerns include *trouble, toughness, excitement, autonomy*, and *fate*; youths who embrace these concerns are believed to be particularly susceptible to engaging in delinquent or criminal acts.

In contrast to theorists who contend that youths from deprived backgrounds do in fact commit more crimes, labelling theorists have argued that the association between poverty and crime merely reflects the increased likelihood of police surveillance and court processing of lower-class offenders. For example, Chambliss' (1973) research on two teenage gangs found that the Saints (a middle-class gang) were actually more delinquent than the lower-class Roughnecks. Despite this, Chambliss noted that the behaviour of the Roughnecks was considered more delinquent by the authorities, and argued that that perception was due to the differential visibility of the two groups. Unlike the Saints, who could avoid the public view by cruising off in their families' automobiles, the Roughnecks were readily visible to everyone in the community. Moreover, unlike the middle-class Saints who assumed a courteous, deferential, and penitent demeanour when confronted by a police officer, the lower-class Saints were rude. Accordingly, Chambliss argues that as a result of selective perception and labelling, "visible, poor, nonmobile, outspoken, undiplomatic kids will be noticed, whether their acts are seriously delinquent or not" while others, "who are mobile and monied," will effectively be rendered "invisible" (Robertson 1980, 383).

Moreover, various *self-report studies* (which ask respondents directly about their involvement in crime and delinquency rather than relying on official records of crime) have suggested that there is little relationship between delinquency and social class, except that boys of higher status are somewhat *more* delinquent than lower-class boys (Doleschal and Klapmuts 1973).

Recently it has been argued that researchers' failure to discover an association between socioeconomic status and criminal involvement is due in large part to the inadequacies of self-report surveys as a tool for measuring criminality (Gomme 1993, 191). Despite this, there can be little doubt that there is a gross overrepresentation of the poor and disadvantaged among those who are officially labelled criminal.

CRIME STATISTICS AND THE "DARK FIGURE OF CRIME"

It has become a criminological truism that official statistics drastically understate the *dark figure of crime*, that is, those criminal acts that have gone undetected and therefore unreported. For this reason it is difficult to get an accurate estimate of the incidence and prevalence of any specific type of crime. Similarly, the image of a *crime funnel* has become a pictographic device for noting the attrition rate between the number of people charged with a crime and the number actually tried, convicted, and sentenced (Ericson and Baranek 1982). For example, in their examination of break and enter offences processed through the criminal justice system, Evans and Himelfarb (1996, 63) pointed out that approximately 2 out of 3 break and enters are reported to police and that 1 out of every 10 break and enters reported is regarded as other than an actual crime. For every 8 break and enters, 1 person will be charged; in only 1 out of 20 offences will a defendant be prosecuted. For every 23 break and enters, 1 person will be convicted; for every 43 offences, 1 person will be sentenced to a period of imprisonment.

In Canada, the basic source for crime statistics is the Canadian Uniform Crime Reports compiled by law enforcement agencies and published annually by the Centre for Justice Statistics. These official statistics report only those crimes that have come to the attention of the police; as such, they quite evidently fail to reveal the total amount of crime committed in any given year. For various reasons, including the perception that the incident is a "private matter," that police would be unable or unwilling to assist, fear of retribution, revenge or self-incrimination, embarrassment, or a lack of knowledge that a crime has been committed, individuals may elect not to notify police that they have been victimized by a criminal act.

The Uniform Crime Reports also can contribute to an underestimating of the total number of crimes committed by recording only the "most serious" offence in incidents involving more than one. Moreover, given that the majority of police work is *reactive* (responding to citizen complaints rather than happening upon a crime-in-progress), it is to be expected that statistics on white collar and "victimless" crimes will be inaccurate. In addition, not all reports made to the police are regarded by them as credible or "founded." Especially in the case of alleged sexual assaults, the discretionary judgments made by police officers—which may rely on stereotypes of how victims "should" or "ought" to behave—may contribute to the "unfounding" of the allegations (Rose and Randall 1982). The demeanours of complainants, witnesses, and suspects have been identified as salient influences on police decision-making. Accordingly, police arrest statistics may tell us more about the dynamics of victim-police-offender interactions than provide an absolute measure of criminal activity.

Finally, it should be stressed that although the depiction of the crime funnel as an inverted pyramid might imply that there is a large number of criminals who escape detection and sentencing, it is important to note that the situation may not be quite as bleak as the earlier cited figures suggest. This is partly because one person may be responsible for a dozen or more offences—a situation that is particularly true with burglary and sexual assault. However, the real problem with subscribing too readily to theories such as the *dark figure of crime* and the *crime funnel* is that by suggesting that the majority of criminals go free, they encourage public impatience with what is known in the justice system as *due process*. In recent years there have been a number of cases, both in the United States and Canada, that have highlighted the danger of this sort of impatience.

In Canada, the wrongful murder convictions of Donald Marshall, Guy Paul Morin, and David Milgaard were deeply troubling for many because they showed that false convictions do occur despite our adversarial system of justice. Although our system of criminal justice rests on the assumption of an accused being innocent "until proven guilty," the structure of our court system in a jury trial depends on *groupthink* (Janis 1972) in that a jury that contains dissenters is termed a "hung jury." In similar fashion, the reluctance of police, prosecutors, and Canadian courts of appeal to acknowledge the wrongful conviction in these cases suggest the tenacity with which *groupthink* can operate. In each case, options closed as officials committed themselves to a single course of action, which it became the equivalent of disloyalty to question. Those in power plunged ahead, no longer able to see different perspectives, no longer trying to objectively weigh evidence as it came in, interpreting everything as supporting their one "correct" decision.

Gabor and Roberts (1992, A21) note that "[f]alse convictions can occur for a variety of reasons: 1) Errors by eyewitnesses in identification; 2) perjury; 3) incompetent legal defences; 4) false confessions by the mentally ill or feeble minded . . . ; 5) excessive zeal on the part of the police or prosecutors; 6) community pressure; 7) plea bargaining; and 8) errors by medical examiners or forensic experts." Reportedly, overzealousness by police emerged as the most important of these factors within American-based research.

Although Gabor and Roberts note that "the presence of the death penalty in the U.S. raises the stakes considerably" (in 1991 approximately 2000 inmates were waiting on Death Row), American research indicates that "in about five percent of cases, there was compelling evidence to suggest the wrong person was convicted." Moreover, they predict that in the future wrongful convictions will be more common. In their words, "The increasing levels of fear, exasperation with the justice system, and frequent demands for a 'quick fix' to the problem of crime increase the danger that we will become more intolerant of the presumption of innocence and of erroneous acquittals. When undue pressure is placed on the system to make an arrest and achieve a guilty verdict, wrongful convictions are sure to follow."

ANALYZING THE PROBLEM

The wishful idea that criminals are different from law-abiding people in some readily distinguishable way has long been entrenched in popular theories of crime. In earlier times, criminality was assumed to be evidence of satanic influence. In the nineteenth and early twentieth centuries, theories such as *phrenology*, which focused on physical characteristics supposedly shared by "criminal types," were highly popular. The tacit assumption underlying these theories is, of course, that without the presence of a predisposition such as a maladaptive gene, inferior biological heritage, or some other "pathology," all of us would be law-abiding. Conformity to legal norms becomes the taken-for-granted "natural condition" of human beings.

In the end, it must be admitted that what we recognize to be a "reasonable" explanation of crime and its underpinnings varies over time and place. If placing the responsibility for a criminal act on the presence of "otherworldly forces" or "satanic influences" strikes us as odd, it is nevertheless true that such explanations were viewed as highly credible during earlier times and remain so for at least some members of our society. For example, during the 1980s and 1990s, some social commentators suggested that the rise in violent crimes among young North Americans was attributable to their listening to heavy metal music and thereby being coerced to commit crimes by the "satanic lyrics" such music featured. In a 1990 case in the United States, when 14-year-old Abigail Dartana was charged with killing her father, the prosecutor built his case around Abigail's fascination with the rock group Motley Crue and suggested that this "obsession" had inspired her to kill. He chose to ignore evidence indicating that Abigail's father had subjected her to chronic physical and sexual abuse, as well as her own explanation of the events that immediately preceded her father's death. Abigail testified that her father had, yet again, begun to sexually abuse her and that she had "snapped," unable to endure the attacks any longer. The judge in this case accepted Abigail's account, termed the prosecutor's explanation "specious," and found Abigail not guilty by reason of self-defence (see Mones 1991).

In this respect, it is worth noting that Shaw's (1989) survey of federally sentenced women found a high prevalence of physical and sexual abuse in their backgrounds. She noted that 82 percent of inmates in the federal Prison for Women and 72 percent of women in provincial institutions had at some time experienced physical or sexual abuse. However, there has been a predictable backlash to this sort of finding, with, for example, "dream team" lawyer Alan Dershowitz (1994) suggesting that offenders are now encouraged to offer an "abuse excuse" in justification of their criminal acts. In light of such debates, some would argue that the explanations of crime we in the 1990s deem to be "reasonable" are just as much cultural artifacts as phrenology and demonic possession were in earlier times.

In noting how definitions of crime vary from culture to culture, contemporary criminologists largely reject the notion of a "born criminal" or "criminal type" and the suggestion that there is a single answer to the question of why individuals commit crime. It would be presumptuous to suppose that the actions of the embezzler, the serial killer, the child molester, the shoplifter, and the jaywalker could all be equally well explained by a single theory. In examining the various sociological theories that have been advanced to explain crime, we shall see just how numerous, and at times conflicting, these theories are.

The Functionalist Approach

For functionalists, crime is the result of the social disorganization and erosion of social control that occur as by-products of industrialization and the growth of large urban populations. In contrast to the societies of the past, which were small in size, homogeneous in population, and centred around kinship ties and the church, contemporary Canadian society is characterized by an increasingly heterogeneous, urban population. Accordingly, while the close ties maintained by the traditionalist communities of the past favoured informal sanctions or methods of social control to curb disruptive members, the process of industrialization has made appeals to conformity less meaningful and effective. The functionalist perspective stresses that since the social environment is itself disorganized, societal norms become less binding and various forms of social deviance, including but not limited to crime, ensue. Accordingly, the deviant or criminal is seen to be an "undersocialized" actor, maladapted to the prevailing norms or values of the dominant social group.

For example, among functionalists of the Chicago school writing in the 1920s, a time of massive immigration to the United States, the idea that rapid social change led to social disorganization and crime seemed a fitting description of events. Thus, Shaw and McKay (1931; 1942) argued that delinquency and other social problems were attributable to the clash between Old World and New World cultures. Specifically, they argued that in areas characterized by high delinquency, "the conventional traditions, neighbourhood institutions, public opinion, through which neighbours usually effect a control over the behaviour of the child, were largely disintegrated" (Shaw and McKay 1931, 229). Moreover, they argued that delinquent children grew up "in a social world in which [delinquency] was an accepted and appropriate form of conduct" (Shaw 1938, 356). Schooled from an early age in a delinquent "tradition" wherein the techniques and opportunities to engage in various forms of delinquency (such as stealing automobiles and shoplifting) were readily available, the children drifted naturally into lives of crime. Accordingly, the solution offered by Shaw and McKay was to persuade local communities or sections of a city to adopt prosocial values.

The problem with this solution, as Lowman (1992, 67–68) has noted, is that the concept of "undersocialization" is itself problematic since it implicitly adopts a *consensus* model of society that assumes interchangeable values and social norms. He poses the rhetorical question, "Is it *under*socialization (a consensus model of society) or *different* socialization (a pluralist or class-stratified model of society) that accounts for 'deviance'?" Moreover, he notes that the concept of social disorganization is similarly contentious inasmuch as "[t]he term 'disorganization' is a judgement, not an unproblematic observation, begging the question: Disorganized from whose perspective?"

The Conflict Approach

For conflict theorists, the question of "what is crime" is of crucial importance. It is their contention that the processes involved in the creation of law and the subsequent application of laws by workers in the criminal justice system reflect the varying degrees of power possessed by different groups within a society. Rather than assume that laws arise from a consensually agreed-upon "reality" that recognizes certain behaviours as more "dangerous" than others, conflict theorists argue that laws favour the interests of the "haves" rather than the "have nots" in society.

For example, in his discussion of the "social reality of crime," Richard Quinney (1970, 304) argues that our very conceptions of crime "are constructed with intentions, not merely to satisfy the imagination." Consider, for example, that in Canada, Arthur Ellis probably holds the distinction of killing more people than any other individual. As Canada's official hangman, Ellis is reputed to have hanged approximately 600 people, making him—at least arguably—this country's most prolific serial killer. However, inasmuch as Ellis was paid the fee of $150 plus expenses for a hanging (payable as soon as he got a telegram from the county sheriff asking him to officiate on a specific day and regardless of whether the condemned person was reprieved), we typically do not label Ellis as a "murderer."

Similarly, while we condemn the actions and weapons of "terrorists," we may be relatively sanguine about a superpower's deployment of what are euphemistically referred to as "antipersonnel weaponry." For example, napalm (jellied petroleum heated to 2000 degrees centigrade that, on contacting human flesh, adheres like glue) was specifically developed by private industry for use against human targets and "used with didactic intent against civilian populations" in "free-fire zones" where "killing anything which moves was the order of the day" and in which "pilots were instructed to machine-gun anyone running from an explosion, since these persons, in fleeing, were admitting their guilt" (Griesman 1984). To like effect, if in many countries the numbers of deaths and injuries due to corporate health and safety violations or to the marketing of dangerous products far exceed those due to homicides, assaults, and other violent crimes (Hagan 1987), we may fail to recognize that who and what we view as "criminal" are in themselves socially constructed.

For conflict theorists, our traditional reluctance to view the "white collar" offender as a "criminal" is not an innocuous fact to be ignored. Despite the fact that "the financial losses to society of fraud, embezzlement, tax evasion, and other such economic crimes—the bulk of which are attributable to higher-status white people—may dwarf those accruing from robberies and burglaries" (Roberts and Gabor 1990), our conceptions of crime, Quinney (1970, 25) maintains, are "created and communicated as part of the political process of promoting a particular set of values and interests."

For critical criminologists, "the processes involved in crime-creation are bound up in the final analysis with the material basis of contemporary capitalism and its structures of law" (Taylor et al. 1975, 20). Postulating that "capitalist society is essentially criminogenic, and that only by the total repudiation of the ethic of possessive individualism on which it rests can 'true' equality and 'socialist diversity'—the prerequisites for a 'crime-free' society—be attained" (Downes 1979, 6), the tasks for criminologists are "to argue for a criminology which is normatively committed to the abolition of inequalities of wealth and power" and "to attempt to create the kind of society in which the facts of human diversity are not subject to the power to criminalise" (Taylor et al. 1975, 44). The failure of state socialist societies to create a crime-free Utopia, observes Downes (1979, 6), has in turn generated "a massive apologetic literature concerning the 'wrong road' or whatever taken by the socialist societies in the main. . . . Next time, they say, it will be different" (1979, 7).

Whether one endorses the premise that crime derives from the material facts of life in propertied society, the emphasis placed within the conflict approach on asking "Who benefits?" is particularly helpful in approaching the social problem of crime and in considering the structure of the criminal justice system. What should be regarded as the distinguishing features of a "dangerous" offender? Is there such a thing as a truly victimless crime? Should young offenders be handled in the same way as adult offenders? Are all criminals "insane?" Should we respond to persons who take drugs as "addicts" or "criminals?" Although the different schools of criminological theory would each offer different answers to these questions, critical theorists agree on one point: without radical changes to the structure of society at large and the justice system in particular, we can never hope to ameliorate the social problem of crime.

The Interactionist Approach

The psychiatrist Thomas Szasz once observed that a person who attempted to study slaves without referring to the institution of slavery might find that "such persons are generally brutish, poor and uneducated, and might conclude that slavery is their 'natural' or appropriate social status" (in Vold and Bernard 1986, 249). Similarly, various sociologists have recognized the need for a more critical assessment of whom we label criminals, why we label them so, and what the consequences are of social reactions to deviant or nonconforming behaviour. Szasz's comments direct attention to the social processes involved in learning how deviant or criminal conduct is justified and sustained by both individuals and groups. Similarly, Becker (1964, 3) suggests that we organize our efforts around the following substantive problems: "Who applied the label of deviant to whom? What consequences does the application of a label have for the person so labelled? Under what circumstances is the label of a deviant successfully applied?" By focusing on the *characteristics* of labels, the *sources* of labels, the *conditions* of labels, and the *consequences* of labels, interactionist writers show how criminals are made into a class set apart from the rest of society, a subculture that becomes the natural depository for mainstream society's fears and structures of control.

Some researchers who follow the interactionist tradition emphasize the consequences of deviant labelling, that is, the external restrictions that emerge as a consequence of official labels. For example, a classic study by Schwartz and Skolnick (1962) noted the impact of a deviant label on future economic opportunities. In their study, four résumés were constructed in which the portrait of the candidate (described as a 32-year-old single male with a high school trade education and a satisfactory prior work history) varied in only one respect. One résumé indicated that the applicant had been tried for assault and acquitted; the second indicated that the applicant had been tried for assault and acquitted, and included a letter from the judge attesting to the applicant's innocence; a third indicated that the applicant had been convicted of assault and sentenced; and the fourth made no mention of any criminal record. One hundred potential employers were given one of the four résumés and asked if they would hire the person in question. Not surprisingly perhaps, even the most minimal degree of contact with the criminal justice system as a defendant could be consequential. While 36 percent of employers gave a positive response to the individual described as having no criminal record, the applicant who was described as acquitted and possessing a letter from the presiding judge received positive responses from only 24 percent of the employers; the rate dropped to 12 percent for the applicant who had no such letter, and dropped further to only 4 percent for the applicant who had been convicted and sentenced for assault.

The policy implications of this study would seem clear enough: reduce labelling by decriminalizing certain forms of behaviour. The study also seems to support the practices of *deinstitutionalization* and *diversion*. Instead of recommending incarceration for those who commit crimes, labelling theorists argue that the stigma associated with having been a prison inmate only serves to strengthen a person's self-image as a criminal and therefore promotes recidivism.

Each of the three sociological perspectives opens a window through which we can view the social problem of crime; however, it is doubtful that any one on its own can fully explain *all* types of crime equally well. Nevertheless, confronted with allegations of sexism and racism within the criminal justice system, exhorted of the necessity to "police the police" amidst reports of police misconduct, and reminded by victims-rights advocates of the pain caused by crime's commission, we are challenged to consider and explain the problem posed by crime—its cause, definition, and treatment—in Canada in the 1990s.

AND JUSTICE FOR ALL?
RESPONDING TO OFFENDERS AND VICTIMS

Statistics Canada's General Social Survey noted that many Canadians feel dissatisfied with the way in which their justice system responds to the social problem of crime (Sacco and Johnson 1990). Despite the fact that in 1990–91 approximately $7.79 billion was spent on the combined services of police, courts, and corrections in Canada (Roberge 1992, 5) and that in 1994–95 the total cost of policing alone was $5.78 billion, many have complained that we are still losing the war against crime.

What should we do? Some have suggested that the "obvious" solution is to hire more police and *criminalize* conduct that is increasingly recognized as socially injurious. However, the average per capita cost of municipal and provincial policing during 1994–95 was $155, with Quebec having the highest per capita cost at $171, closely followed by Ontario at $170, while Newfoundland at $104 and P.E.I. at $91 had the lowest (Kong 1997). In a time of fiscal restraint, the possibility of an increased criminal justice budget may simply not be practical. Moreover, it has been repeatedly noted that *saturation policing* merely increases the crime rate by inflating it with petty crimes that would otherwise have gone unnoticed. With many Canadians already critical of the massive time delays between the reporting of an offence and the sentencing of an offender, some would argue that flooding the court system with additional charges is likely to exacerbate rather than resolve the problem in the administration of criminal justice.

Some prefer so-called victim-avoidance strategies, which range from self-defence classes and assertiveness training programs to the purchase of various monitoring and crime-foiling devices. This new technology includes teddy bear video cameras to spy on potentially abusive babysitters, safes designed to resemble soup cans, and inflatable men to place in the passenger seats of cars driven by single women. For others, a focus on community-based measures is thought to be useful; they recommend involvement in programs such as Neighbourhood Watch, Crime Stoppers, and Block Parents. For others still, the formation of vigilante-type groups similar to the Guardian Angels of New York City are thought necessary to balance the scales of justice.

In marked contrast, others Canadians have suggested a policy of *radical nonintervention*, which, drawing support from labelling theory, recommends that whenever possible, we divert offenders away from formal processing in the criminal justice system. They suggest that while Canada's crime rate has grown by 26 percent over the past 20 years and is up almost 150 percent from 30 years ago (Kong 1997, 3), at least part of this increase is attributable to the introduction of new and broadened definitions of criminal conduct. It is suggested that charging and imprisoning offenders are unlikely to help them develop prosocial behaviour and that incarcerating youths, in particular, simply serves to apprentice them to career hoodlums. Accordingly, they advise us to seek out such informal methods as victim-offender reconciliation programs designed to resolve disputes and mediation strategies that allow for a nonofficial forum in which the "offender" and "victim" status of disputants is ignored and agreements are reached through negotiation. In like fashion, proponents of *decarceration* suggest that options such as the fine (the most commonly used penal sanction in Canada), probation, or community service offer alternatives to imprisonment. Similarly, some suggest a more frequent use of the "alternative measures" provisions of the Young Offenders Act, while others call for legislative reform that would *decriminalize* certain categories of conduct currently prohibited under Canadian criminal law. For example, the Alliance for the Safety of Prostitutes (ASP) has lobbied for the decriminalization of adult prostitution, while in the United States the members of the National Organization for the Reform of Marijuana Laws (NORML) suggest, with their acronym, how the use of marijuana should be considered.

Nevertheless, some have suggested that "non-intervention can become a euphemism for benign neglect which in truth is another euphemism for simply doing nothing" (Cohen 1974). It has been suggested that policies that adopt a "do-nothing" approach are often more indicative of a "fiscal crisis of the state" than of a humanitarian measure of reform. Thus, critical criminologists have charged that the increased use of community programs as an alternative measure to imprisonment does not truly reduce the number of individuals subject to imprisonment but simply "widens the net" of the penal system and creates more intensive, intrusive, and prolonged measures of social control. For instance, Lowman, Menzies, and Palys (1987) suggest that "decarceration" may be better identified as *"transcarceration"* or transinstitutionalization.

If critical criminologists have argued that our treatment of offenders is unjust, others have responded that criminologists who champion the rights of offenders have tended to overlook that there are also victims of crime. These people point out that despite the existence of insurance to pay for injury caused by crime, civil awards for damages, or restitution payments ordered by a judge as part of an offender's sentence, few people are truly compensated for being victims of crime. They note that funding for such services as shelters for battered women and sexual assault centres is often in peril and that due to shortages in treatment services for offenders and victims, sexual offenders and their victims may not only find themselves together in institutions and group therapy programs, but sharing bedrooms as well.

The different ways in which individuals respond to criminal victimization depend on such factors as the type of criminal offence experienced, the age and sex of the victim, the presence of prior stressors in the victim's life, and the personality of the victim. However, a common reaction is for the victim to ask a variety of attributional questions—"Why me?"—and to take some responsibility for their victimization. Janoff-Bulman, Timko, and Carli (1985) note that the *hindsight effect* encourages victims to overestimate the extent to which they could have avoided victimization and leads to an increase in self-blame or self-castigation (Fischhoff 1975; Janoff-Bulman, Timko, and Carli 1985). This tendency is also encouraged by our social response, which often assumes a negative view of victims and fails to provide them with any form of social support. As Janoff-Bullman and Frieze (1987, 166) observe, "Victims become stigmatized individuals whom others would rather avoid . . . ; they may be ignored . . . because they are seen as losers . . . or because of fear of guilt by association. . . . Even the closest relationships may be threatened by negative reactions of others to the victims." They suggest that part of our negativity towards victims is due to our desire to believe in a just world in which bad things do not, or more categorically, cannot, happen to good people.

Throughout the 1980s and 1990s, victims-rights groups such as Victims of Violence, We Will Not Forget, and Citizens Concerned With Crimes Against Children have formed to support the often forgotten victims of crime. Their efforts include lobbying the government for changes in laws that are thought to discount, dismiss, or trivialize an offence; advocating special training programs for police and other criminal justice system personnel that emphasize greater empathy and sensitivity to the victim; and promoting special facilities and provisions for child victims and others who may find the response of the criminal justice system threatening. Victims, they remind us, should not be revictimized by our policies and procedures. Nevertheless, some would suggest, to fully reduce the pains of victimization, we must return to our original question of "What causes crime?" and prevent its occurrence. Only in this way, they add, can we hope to truly assist the victims of crime today and in the future.

SUMMARY

1. The popular understanding of crime favours a depiction that suggests it is a unitary phenomenon and the criminal is an easily identifiable type of person. This viewpoint is reinforced by media portrayals and by the individualistic focus of the criminal justice system.

2. Crime is a social construct; although the notion of "harm" underlies our designation of certain behaviours as "criminal," common-sense and legal definitions of crime are not identical. Similarly, our ideas of who and what is "dangerous" may only occasionally mesh with the Criminal Code's designation of a "dangerous offender."

3. The media may be identified as popularizing misleading images of both the criminal offender and the types of crime Canadians most commonly experience. As a consequence, we may develop a fear of crime that is distinct from our actual likelihood of criminal victimization.

4. The seven elements of criminal behaviour—crime as harm, no crime without law, *actus reus, mens rea*, concurrence of conduct and intent, causality, and sanctions—distinguish those behaviours that may be considered conventionally harmful from those that are crimes under Canadian law.

5. Criminologists have noted that age, gender, race, and socioeconomic status are highly correlated with crime; however, causality cannot be inferred and the exact relationship between these variables and crime remains controversial.

6. The question of how we should best respond to the social problem of crime elicits responses that variously direct our attention to the offender, the victim, the criminal justice system, and the criminogenic influence of Canadian society itself. Although surveys have noted that many Canadians agree on the significance of crime as a pressing social problem, there is less unanimity about what must be done to resolve the problem.

INEQUALITY
AND POVERTY

DID YOU KNOW?

- In 1911 Canadian women in full-time employment earned about $0.53 for every $1 earned by a male. By 1967 this figure had risen to $0.58. In 1995 the gender income gap was narrowed to $0.73; single women earned $0.94 of their male counterparts' earnings in 1995, whereas married women earned only $0.69 of what married men earned. According to Statistics Canada, there was almost no difference in the earnings among single, university educated men and women.

- In 1989 an all-party Parliamentary resolution vowed to eliminate poverty among Canadian children by the year 2000. But by 1995 Statistics Canada reported that 21 percent of all children (or nearly 1.5 million) lived below the poverty line—a 58 percent jump since 1989.

- Profits from 200 of Canada's largest companies reached a record $6.9 billion in the first quarter of 1997, up 44 percent from the same period the previous year. In 1996, the average weekly earnings for a CEO in high performing firms was $14 288, up 13.1 percent from 1995, compared to $594 for all Canadian employees, up only 2.8 percent from 1995.

- Highest annual sports salaries by average value: hockey—Joe Sakic, $17.9 million; baseball—Cal Ripkin Jr., $13.2 million; basketball—Michael Jordan, $31.3 million; football—Troy Aikman, $6.5 million. In contrast, upwards of 25 percent of all children in Canada and the United States may live below the federally defined poverty line, a source of embarrassment for countries that routinely rank high on UN developmental indices.

- Many acknowledge the link between poverty and poor health, low educational achievement, and poor career prospects. Yet the face of poverty is changing, afflicting children, young people, and women. The most widely accepted measurement indicates that poverty strikes up to 4.8 million Canadians or 17.8 percent of the population. Of these, about one-half remain rooted in the permanent underclass, while hundreds of thousands of poor bounce in and out of poverty each year, according to Statistics Canada's *Crossing the Low Income Line*, often because of changes in marital status rather than from job losses.

- For a family of four in a large city in 1994, being poor can range in income from a high of $40 560, according to the Toronto Social Planning Council, to a low of $18 709, calculated by Christopher A. Sarlo and updated by National Council of Welfare for Toronto residents. Statistics Canada's low income line is drawn at $30 708 for an urban family of four.

- A quarter of the world continues to live in severe poverty, including 1.3 billion who must live on less than a dollar a day, according to a 1997 UN Development Programme Report. South Asia and sub-Sahara Africa fared worst with 40 percent of their population defined as poor. The poorest 20 percent of the world's population share only 1.1 percent of the global income, down from 2.3 percent in 1960.

- There were no food banks in Canada in 1980; in 1994 there were 463. The number of people relying on food banks has doubled since 1989, from 330 000 to 670 000 according to the Executive Director of the Canadian Association of Food Banks. By contrast, Canada's six major banks grossed a profit of $6.3 billion in 1996 and are on target to hit the $7.5 billion mark in 1997 on the strength of a 19 percent increase from last year's profits.

- By November 1997, nationwide unemployment had fallen to 9.0 percent. The unemployment rate has been stuck at or above 9 percent for 86 consecutive months—the longest span since the Great Depression. National variations remain, with Quebec and the Atlantic provinces hardest hit, while the Prairie provinces have the lowest unemployment rate. Unemployment for young people age 15 to 24 is mired at 17 percent.

- Regional inequalities continue to mar Canada's economic performance. The Atlantic provinces contribute only 6 percent of Canada's output but contain 8 percent of the population. The national employment rate was 59 percent in 1994, but only 41 percent in Newfoundland and 52 percent in New Brunswick.

- According to a major study in 1995, the mean earnings of a Canadian-born white male is $36 563 per year. By contrast, the mean earnings of a foreign-born visible minority male is $28 285—an earning differential of -22.6 percent.

- Since the late 1970s, Atlantic Canada businesses have received more than $1 billion in direct grants and forgivable loans to create jobs in this economically depressed region. Targetted assistance also includes the $1.9 billion Atlantic groundfish strategy to facilitate the transition of 40 000 fishing-related workers to other types of employment through education and retraining programs.

THE PROBLEM

Canadians possess a reputation at home and abroad as a "kind and compassionate" people. In comparison to the United States, with its glaring extremes of conspicuous wealth and abject poverty, Canada strikes many as remarkably egalitarian, with only moderate differences in wealth, in part because of enlightened government intervention. Few Canadians are denied the basic physical necessities of food, clothing, and shelter, even though many may lack creature comforts taken for granted by the comfortable. Evidence of Canada's benevolent nature is bolstered by UN quality of life surveys that consistently rank Canada at or near the top. In 1997 Canada was again ranked as the best country in the world by a UN panel, with the highest standard of living in terms of income, education, and life expectancy. Even Canadians seem pleased with their status; in a survey conducted by Angus Reid for the Royal Bank, 84 percent of Canadians were content or very satisfied with their quality of life, with greatest happiness expressed by those over 55 years of age.

However, not everyone is convinced by this benign portrayal of Canada. On closer inspection, Canada's reputation as egalitarian and tolerant is tarnished by gaping levels of inequality reflected in systems of stratification that support overlapping layers of power, wealth, and status. Those on the bottom layer are more likely to suffer from poor health or to be denied access to proper medical attention, to endure lower educational levels and revolving cycles of poverty, to reside in substandard housing, to relinquish prospects for career advancement, and to be treated more harshly by the justice system. These patterns of inequality are not randomly distributed across society but tend to coalesce around race, ethnicity, gender, class, sexual orientation, age, and region. Women and men who do not fit the mold of success routinely experience prejudice and discrimination. Through little fault of their own, they are confronted with economic dislocation, powerlessness, inadequate levels of service delivery, and threats to a cherished identity.

Most Canadians are only casually acquainted with these harsh realities despite numerous revealing studies, including John Porter's (1965) searing exposé of Canada's social and cultural mosaic. Public ignorance, however, neither excuses nor diminishes the reality of social inequality in Canada. Employment equity initiatives notwithstanding, women in full-time employment continue to earn less than men. The presence of women in the workplace may now be the rule rather than exception, but most women continue to bump into glass ceilings when scaling the corporate ladder of success. The placement of certain racial minorities at the lower end of the socioeconomic scale is beyond dispute (Pendakur and Pendakur 1995). People of colour, such as African-Canadians and Chinese-Canadians, earn considerably less than the mainstream average, and this applies equally to women and men. Aboriginal peoples in Canada are particularly disadvantaged, with a standard of living comparable to Third World levels. The fact that aboriginal incomes hover well below half of the national average is surely a scathing indictment of our priorities and self-delusions (Royal Commission 1996).

Other anomalies are no less a betrayal of our collective positive self-image. The life chances of many Canadians are adversely affected by the centralization of power and resources in the hands of relatively few (a *power elite*) in business or administration (Clement 1998). The power of Canada's capitalist class stems from dense corporate interlocking among top capitalists as well as links with the state (Hiller 1990; Brym 1993). Wealth begets wealth in a spiralling process that consolidates the privileges of the few at the expense of the masses. But a society that condones instant millionaires yet tolerates grinding poverty at some point must confront its contradictions and inconsistencies. How do we reconcile the seemingly inflated salaries of pampered sports stars and entertainment idols with the fact that hundreds of thousands of Canada's children may live below the federally defined poverty line? Can we deplore the impoverishment on many aboriginal reserves in Canada, then turn around and condemn other countries for human rights violations?

Regional disparities are also a problem. A combination of social and historical factors has relegated certain regions in Canada to the status of "have nots" and the situation continues despite federal efforts to reduce the disparities. Equalization payments from federal coffers for 1992 were in excess of $8 billion to the seven poorest provinces (excluding Ontario, British Columbia, and Alberta). Per capita payments varied from $498 in Saskatchewan to $1649 in Newfoundland (The Globe and Mail, January 13, 1992). For every $100 in employment income, Newfoundlanders received $42 of government support, while Ontarians received only $26 (Gherson 1997). These payouts become increasingly difficult to justify during times of fiscal restraint. Even more worrisome is the dearth of realistic prospects for substantial improvement.

Put candidly, Canada is a land of contradiction. It may be one of the luckiest countries in the world, yet it is hardly immune to the harsh realities of inequality (Frizzell and Pammett 1996). The emergence of a capitalist global economy has sharpened disparities between those at the top of the hierarchy and those at its bottom (including the aged, the young, single parents, and minorities), many of whom are losing out because of social, political, and economic changes. Inequality in Canada is not simply the result of market imperfections amenable to resolution through cosmetic reform. Nor can the problem be attributed entirely to earlier solutions that either addressed the wrong issue or incorrectly assessed the situation. Inequities in wealth and power appear to be chronic, firmly embedded, and resistant to quick-fix solutions. Yet various clichés continue to distort the magnitude and scope of inequality in Canada, including the following:

- Canada is a classless society with everyone bunched into the middle.

- People who are poor only have themselves to blame.

- You can make it if you work hard.

- Individuals are rewarded on the basis of merit.

- Canada is an open and socially mobile society.

- Inequality is natural and normal, and there isn't much we can—or should—do about it.

Sociological thought tends to be critical of these assertions. Sociologists are more inclined to depict Canada as a stratified society ruled by a corporate elite and dominated by an affluent class. To be sure, few would go so far as to downgrade Canada to the level of an entrenched oligarchy or a rigid caste-like system. Nevertheless, inequality is deeply entrenched in Canada and its expression in poverty is condemned as unacceptable. This chapter is based on two premises: inequality is a problem, and equality is preferable and attainable. Disagreements over inequality are not about its existence per se, but about the scale of the problem and what, if anything, should be done about it. It is in the self-interest of all Canadians to ensure that inequality is reduced and that social and economic benefits are distributed more equitably among different groups. Failure to do so will increase the likelihood of conflict, with corresponding social and economic costs.

INEQUALITY AS A SOCIAL PROBLEM

"Man is born free, and he is everywhere in chains" (Jean-Jacques Rousseau).

In a prophetic way, this eighteenth century indictment of society strikes at the core of sociology as a discipline (Himmelfarb and Richardson 1991). Despite its glaring lack of gender inclusiveness, Rousseau's assessment captures the ambiguity inherent in society as a moral community. For Rousseau, society had betrayed "man's" natural liberty, equality, and "fraternity." The forces of domination and exploitation had subverted "his" innate goodness by transforming "him" into something sordid and squalid. The legacy of Rousseau continues to persist in Marxist interpretations of inequality as a departure from human "nature."

Not everyone concurred with Rousseau's observations. The English philosopher Thomas Hobbes concluded that social restrictions were unfortunate but necessary in neutralizing our acquisitive and destructive impulses. Society represented a collective agreement (social contract) to protect individuals from the predations of others. Unfettered individualism had to be sacrificed for the safety and survival of the collective whole. This society-as-prior line of thinking eventually culminated in a functionalist perspective. For functionalists, society is most productive when it exists in a state of equilibrium and harmony, with parts both interrelated and collectively attuned to consensus and regulation. Inequality was inevitable in forging a workable and productive society.

These competing views of social inequality furnish the starting point for sociological analysis. Both functionalists and conflict perspectives agree on the universality of inequality, if not on its inevitability or scope. All but the simplest hunting and gathering societies are stratified along age, gender, race, religion, and family affiliation. Disagreement, however, arises over the nature of the chains that historically have shackled women and men. For Rousseau and conflict theorists, these bonds enslaved the human species by crushing natural creativity and inherent freedom. For functionalists from Durkheim onwards, these restrictions are necessary and morally defensible in any complex system, despite costs to certain individuals. By unleashing pent up energy and rewarding skills in short supply, functionalists contend, such inequality was pivotal in generating wealth and spurring evolutionary progress.

The significance of Rousseau's sociological observation should be clear by now. If Rousseau was right, then inequality is an artifice perpetuated by vested interests for self-serving reasons. If functionalists are correct, then inequality and power are integral and inherent to society. Any attempt to tamper with these functional imperatives can only hinder productivity or deter progress. Is there an alternative position? What if both conflict and functionalist perspectives are correct? Is it possible that inequality and power occupy an ambiguous status in society, neither right nor wrong but juxtaposed and interlinked? To what extent can sociology address the issue of inequality in the human experience?

The study of inequality and its relationship to society is inseparable from the sociological enterprise. Sociologists have long been attracted to the study of social inequality. The discipline itself originated at the turn of the century in an attempt to understand shifting patterns of inequality and how best to ameliorate dysfunctional social conditions. Contemporary sociologists remain preoccupied with the concept of inequality, with interests extending to defining inequality, exploring its genesis, evolution, magnitude, and scope, and examining its consequences for society. They want to know what inequality is, why it exists, how it is manifest and maintained, when it is challenged, and what its impact and implications are.

Interest is also focused on who (either as individuals or groups) gets what with respect to power, prestige, and wealth, and why. To a large extent, sociologists have been successful in isolating the concept of inequality for study and analysis, but they have been less successful in concurring on its causes, consequences, or cures. Only recently have they begun to consider how different aspects of inequality—class, race and ethnicity, gender, and regional location— are mutually related and interconnected in ways that intensify human deprivation.

The social categories and lived relations that comprise inequality are constantly changing and contested ("dynamic"). Yet these constructed realities also reveal a sufficient degree of stability and constancy to constitute an enduring framework of social analysis. Societies are orderly but chaotic, behaviour is idiosyncratic yet patterned, and social relations undergo change while retaining continuity. The study of society encompasses both sets of truths, and sociology reveals regular swings between the ascendancy of one perspective over another—from agency to structure, materialism to meaning, stability to fluidity, variability to pattern, and coherence to chaos (Gillespie 1996). One perspective prefers to dwell on the patterned and predictable regularities of social behaviour that persist over time and are manifest in statistical rates. These regularities may be considered as structures in their own right or taken as manifestations of underlying (deep) structures that regulate society or generate behaviour. Another perspective emphasizes the inherently unstable and endlessly changing aspects of social life as individuals define situations and interact accordingly. Postmodern sociology has shifted away from an analysis of social structures to focus on how social meanings are embedded in culture and cultural practices. It remains to be seen if sociologists can incorporate both structure and meaning in analyzing inequality as a social problem (Gillespie 1996).

EXPLAINING INEQUALITY

Problem definition is concerned with how public issues are identified and talked about as a problem for solution (Spector and Kitsuse 1979). Defining social inequality as a social problem encompasses three dimensions: *objective conditions*, *ideological supports*, and *social reforms*. First, an emphasis on the objective conditions invariably leads to questions about the scope of inequality in society, its manifestations, and the reasons behind its existence. Second, attention to ideological supports focuses on the ideas that justify and prop up the realities of inequality regardless of how it is measured or conceived (Curtis et al. 1993). Third, social reforms consist of strategies for reversing inequality, including state-inspired policies such as employment equity. No less relevant is the proliferation of organized resistance and protest groups among the historically disadvantaged—women, racial minorities, homosexuals, the disabled, and the poor.

Social scientists have argued that perfect equality is a contradiction in terms. No human society is "equal" in the sense that everyone has identical access to valued resources. Certain individuals dominate by virtue of achieved skills or ascribed status; others are dominated because of age, gender, race, or birth. Structures of domination are universal—in some cases informal and personal, in other cases formal and institutionalized. The concept of inequality has long captivated the interest and energy of sociologists. Some of the earliest questions they posed centred on inequality: "Why is there inequality in the distribution of wealth and power? Where do its causes lie? Does inequality qualify as a social problem for solution? Can it be reduced, or should inequality be encouraged, within limits?" Inequality per se is not a problem. Inequality becomes a problem when this inequity is relatively enduring and permanent, based on irrelevant criteria such as skin colour rather than on merit, embedded in the institutional structures of society, and seemingly impervious to solutions. That these questions continue to baffle and infuriate sociologists is testimony to their centrality for understanding society and social behaviour. But confusion has also compromised the chance to formulate workable solutions to this most fundamental of social problems.

Inequality can be defined in different ways. Essentially, however, *inequality* reflects a condition and a process in which preferential access to the good things in life is not randomly distributed, but reflects relatively permanent and uneven variations on the basis of individual differences that are socially devalued. For various reasons related to race, class, sexuality, or gender, certain individuals are ranked higher than others in terms of wealth, power, and status. Other individuals by virtue of their skills, expertise, or inheritance are thought of as deserving more rather than less. These differences are socially structured in the sense that access to social rewards is patterned and regular (Grab 1993). Those who are advantaged because of birth or achievement tend to be rewarded and privileged in a cyclical process that "structures and reproduces" the pattern of inequality in time and space (Grab 1993, xi). This allocation of riches leads to questions about patterns of entitlement in society. While responses are difficult to formulate, even the search for answers provides an excellent introduction to the problem of inequality.

That inequality exists is an established fact of life. Inequities are part of a system of social stratification in which society is divided into unequal "strata" such as class, race and ethnicity, gender, age, sexual orientation, or disability on the basis of common attributes and situations (Gillespie 1996). What is less well-established are the reasons behind its tenacity and resistance to reform. Other contradictions are equally glaring. How do we explain that some groups are disadvantaged and unempowered? Why have certain groups overcome critical disadvantages whereas others cower near the bottom of the socioeconomic heap? Who gets preferential treatment and why? Can we account for the existence of poor residential areas? Why is there high unemployment among some groups but not among others? Numerous explanations exist, yet most responses can be sorted into four basic streams: *biological*, *psychological*, *cultural*, and *social*.

Biology

Some prefer to blame individual poverty on inherited genetic characteristics. By invoking Darwinian evolutionary principles, it is argued that certain individuals are better suited for success than others in the competitive struggle for survival (Herrnstein and Murray 1994). Individuals of "superior stock" will prevail and succeed, in keeping with the doctrine of "survival of the fittest." Conversely, those without the "right stuff" will be banished to the edges. For example, those who subscribe to the theory of *biological determinism* label certain racial and ethnic minorities as genetically and intellectually inferior. Such perceptions, if they become sufficiently widespread, can deprive minority women and men of the competitive edge for success in society. Although this sort of theory appeals to some people because of simplicity and self-interest, there is little scientific evidence to support it, and for that reason most sociologists reject biological explanations.

Psychology

Others believe that responsibility rests with the psychological attributes people acquire as they mature. For various reasons, some individuals do not develop normally, but internalize a host of attitudes contrary to commonly accepted definitions of success. This line of thinking holds that victims of poverty and discrimination are responsible for their plights. Under a victim-blame approach, victims are blamed for their sad situations because of poor "moral fibre" or personality flaws for which they alone are responsible. The proposed solution follows from this assessment: With hard work and application to the task at hand, anyone can be successful in a society organized around the virtues of merit, equal opportunity, and open competition.

In addition, members of the mainstream may be responsible for inequality because of *prejudice* towards "others." The solution rests in education and training; that is, improvements in cultural sensitivity and diversity acceptance will reduce hostility and enhance intergroup harmony.

Culture and Socialization

Another perspective focuses on the twin concepts of culture and socialization as an explanation for social inequality. Inequalities continue to arise and are resistant to solutions because the lifestyles of the poor and marginal are self-perpetuating. The emphasis on kinship, sharing, and generosity that one finds in families of the poor or the different may be commendable, but such lifestyles may be an anachronism from the past, at odds with a competitive and consumerist present. Such inadequacy both reflects and reinforces welfare dependency, female-headed households, and lack of ambition and resourcefulness. All of these contribute to perpetuating poverty from generation to generation. Oscar Lewis' (1964) work on the culture of poverty is an example of this school of thought. For Lewis, living in poverty creates a cultural response to marginal conditions. This response is characterized by low levels of organization, resentment towards authority, hostility to mainstream institutions, and feelings of hopelessness and despair. Once immersed in this culture, a self-fulfilling prophecy is set in motion (a belief leads to behaviour that confirms the original belief), which further inhibits mobility and advancement.

Not everyone concedes the validity of a cultural interpretation. Recourse to culture as an explanation is yet another version of the victim-blame approach (Eitzen and Zinn 1992). Social problems are "individualized" by locating their causes within the culture of the victims themselves (Satzewich 1991). Ignored in this type of explanation is the external environment, with its structural constraints and social barriers. Even the ontological status of poverty cultures is debated. What passes for a culture of poverty may be less a coherent lifestyle in the anthropological sense than a strategic response to destitute conditions (Bolaria 1991). Nor is cultural deprivation per se the problem. Cultures themselves are not inferior or deprived; rather non-mainstream cultures are isolated and defined by the powerful as "inferior" and unworthy of equitable treatment.

Social/Structural

There is yet another set of explanations at our disposal. For many sociologists, inequality is not necessarily the fault of individuals, nor is cultural deprivation the culprit. Rather, the inequities of power, wealth, and status are anchored in the structures of society itself. Social structures refer to those aspects of society that involve a discernible and patterned set of interactions. These regularities are seen as structures in themselves or manifestations of deeper structures that produce or regulate behaviour (Gillespie 1996). They include institutional arrangements, economic opportunities, racist/sexist ideologies, discrimination, and the capitalist mode of production. Their expression in roles, institutions, classes, and regions provides social structures with the power to shape people's lives and life chances. As a case in point, studies have shown that educational credentials and hard work are not necessarily the best predictors of employment success. Parental social class is a far more powerful determinant. This fact should alert us to the importance of "ascribed" characteristics, including race, as structural determinants of behaviour or status. In structural perspectives the emphasis is on systemic forces as the underlying causes, rather than on precipitating or immediate factors. Inequality, then, is framed within the context of structure or system, not individual differences or defective genes. It should be noted that postmodernist sociology eschews any structural explanation that crams pluralist experiences into all encompassing ("totalizing") constructs, preferring instead to look at social meanings and their embodiment in cultures or discourses (Gillespie 1996).

Social/structural explanations of inequality often include the broader contexts of domination, exploitation, and exclusion. In the opinion of conflict sociologists, for instance, the root cause of all social problems originates in the capitalist commitment to the systematic pursuit of profit (Bolaria 1991). A capitalist system by its nature is riddled with social contradictions. The owners of the means of production (the *ruling class*) are constantly on guard to reduce labour costs and protect private property. Predictably the *working class* is locked in a struggle to contest this inequity and carve up wealth more equitably. The clash of these competing interests can only encourage intergroup conflicts over scarce resources. Under capitalism, moreover, repressive structures may include those cultural practices that seek domination and control over individuals on the basis of race (racism) and gender (sexism). Clearly, then, inequality constitutes a structural problem in need of social solutions.

How do we evaluate and assess the merits of the respective approaches? Do biopsychological explanations meet the test, or is there validity in social and cultural explanations? As sociologists we have difficulty condoning biological-based arguments, in part because of a reluctance to accept reductionist explanations of social differences and human similarities. Nor is there much enthusiasm for individualistic explanations that magnify a person's problems as her or his responsibility. We tend to agree with Durkheim, who said a century ago that only a social fact can explain another social fact. Similarly, only structural explanations can explain social problems. It is not that individuals as social actors are irrelevant for understanding social life; on the contrary, individual people are ultimately responsible for their actions. But human behaviour is embedded within specific social contexts that are limiting and constraining without being coercive or deterministic. Individuals are free to choose, but only from society-defined alternatives. The institutional structures surrounding individual people are powerful forces that can play havoc—by opening or closing doors—for opportunity and achievement. For these reasons, most sociologists prefer to couch human behaviour in social terms and look for causal explanations within a sociocultural framework. Such an approach recognizes the constraining influence of social structure, but does not deny individual responsibility.

ANALYZING THE PROBLEM

There is no doubt that inequality is amenable to explanation in sociological terms. Yet different sociological perspectives approach the problem of inequality in different ways. On the one hand are those perspectives that suggest inequality is *not* a problem in an open competition, but rather a *solution* to problems that confront modern society. On the other hand are those that portray inequality as a problem associated with profit-driven societies but not societies in general. In this section, we shall emphasize the explanations of two major perspectives—the functionalist and the conflict. Comparing these contrasting points of view furnishes additional insights into the politics of inequality.

The Functionalist Approach

Functionalist theories portray society as the metaphorical equivalent of a biological organism. That is, both society and non-human organisms can be interpreted as integrated systems comprised of interrelated and interdependent parts, each of which contributes to the "needs" of the organism, even if superficially they do not appear to do so. In the case of society, all of these components (such as institutions, values, and practices) are properly understood in terms of their contributions to survival and stability.

For functionalists, then, inequality is integral to a complex society and even necessary to maintain a productive and cohesive social order. A sophisticated division of labour in an urban, postindustrial society demands a high level of skill and training. A system of rewards is required to entice skilled individuals to compete for positions in short supply. Differences in the rates of reward are rationalized as the answer to this societal dilemma. For skilled personnel to occupy key positions, functionalists claim, adequate levels of motivation must be provided as an incentive for recruitment. Failure to do so would eliminate the pool of talent, with disastrous consequences for society as a whole. Reward structures under this model are supported by the "law" of supply and demand. Premier hockey players such as Wayne Gretzky or Eric Lindros are reimbursed more generously than unskilled labourers, not because hockey is more important to society, but because top-notch pucksters—unlike manual labourers—are in short supply compared with the demand. Furthermore, their earning power is enhanced because of an ability to generate more income for team owners. A similar line of reasoning applies between different occupations. Physicians are compensated more for their services than child care workers even though, arguably, both are crucial to our well-being (Davis and Moore 1945). It is also recognized, following Weber, that status (or prestige) at times may be a better inducement than income for filling these positions.

A functionalist perspective interprets inequality as normal and desirable. It is necessary because of the need to fulfil critical positions in society with skilled, but scarce, personnel. Inequality is condoned when the rules of the game are applied fairly and according to market principles. In an open and democratic society, people have a "right" to distribute themselves unequally, provided the competition is based on merit and skills rather than irrelevant factors such as race or ethnicity. To be sure, a minimum degree of government intervention may be required to ensure everyone has a "fair go." "Imperfections" in the system such as unfair trading practices or monopolies may interfere with the proper functioning of the system, making it incumbent on the government to curb these market impediments. But such intervention should be kept to a minimum for maximizing free market expression. Excessive interference also runs the risk of fostering dullness and uniformity, while stifling the creativity and initiative necessary for progress and prosperity. That some individuals suffer more than others in unfettered competition is unfortunate, even regrettable, but necessary as part of the cost of doing business in a free enterprise system.

The Conflict Approach

A radical conflict perspective is opposed to functionalist interpretations of inequality. Endorsed first by Karl Marx in the nineteenth century and subsequently reformulated by legions of followers, inequality for radical conflict theorists is embedded in the capitalist emphasis on the rational and systematic pursuit of profit through private property and commodity production. Inequality is generated and sustained by the contradiction of property relations, with those who own productive property on one side, and those who possess only labour power on the other (see Watkins 1997). In this cutthroat game of winners and losers, individuals are sorted out in a way that polarizes the affluent and the poor. Inequality would seem to be inevitable in this sorting process: Certainly no industrial society could expect to flourish without the exploitation of the working classes.

Is capitalism inevitable in complex societies? Are precapitalist societies "naturally" inclined towards inequality? To what extent is inequality inherent in human nature, or does it reflect social imperatives relative to a particular time and place? The inevitability of inequality—a basic tenet of capitalism and functionalism—is anathema to Marxist conflict theory. Inequality is not inevitable for Marxists because capitalism is not inevitable. Gross inequities occur only in those societies that pit one class against another. For Marx and Engels, primitive societies lived in a "natural" state of equality and cooperation. With few exceptions, formidable economic disparities rarely intruded into primitive cultures, most of which relied on cooperative self-interest for group survival. Such a state of affairs will be reinstituted with the end of capitalism and its replacement by a socialist utopia. Marx predicted proletariat control over the instruments of production, thereby putting an end to alienated labour and the inequality it perpetuated. Once the "dictatorship of the proletariat" was established, all stratification and inequality would cease. It must be emphasized, though, that Marx was speaking of the inequality of social classes rather than its expression in race, age, or gender. Needless to say, no society in the industrialized world has established anything remotely resembling a classless utopia. And so-called socialist experiments to date indicate that inequality based on gender or race do not necessarily vanish even under carefully controlled conditions (Spiro 1975).

Conflict and functionalist theorists differ in their approach to inequality. Functionalists explain it on the basis of differences between individuals with different skills and abilities. Class position and social mobility, they say, are predominantly related to personal achievement. Conflict theorists analyze inequality by looking at group competition involving power and capital. Conflicts that arise are inevitable as each group struggles to preserve its privilege or rearrange these inequities. For functionalists, society exists as an integrated entity inasmuch as value consensus binds social actors into a coherent whole. Inequality is healthy in properly functioning and complex societies, especially if it encourages competition and is based on achieved status, although extremes need to be held in check if society is to survive. For conflict theorists, extremes in inequality are not natural or necessary but relative to a particular place and time. Massive inequities are endemic and entrenched only in those societies organized around the pillars of private property, class relations, and profit-making.

Efforts to justify these gaps as natural and necessary are dismissed as ideological ploys to shore up societal inequities, in part by cushioning the blows of exploitation. Even the ideals of equal opportunity and merit as routes to success are denounced as excuses for perpetuating privilege and inequality. Those who benefit from the system are anxious to support the status quo. Victims and those susceptible to its vagaries tend to be critical. The end result is a constant state of tension and conflict. The rest of this chapter will examine inequality as a social problem at the level of class, race, and region. It will also explore substantive issues related to education and inequality in addition to the politics of poverty.

CLASS

Imagine a society of perfect equality! Individuals would be exempt from extremes of privilege, wealth, or power. What were once scarce resources and unearned privileges would be redistributed in relatively equal fashion. From each according to their ability and to each according to their need. Individuals, of course, would not be clones of each other; rather, differences would be accepted and valued. This egalitarian ethos would apply as well to groups within society. Intergroup conflict would gradually diminish over time with the removal of the reasons for competition.

Does this scenario sound too good to be true? It probably is—at least outside of some utopian fantasy world. There is no historical evidence of a society that maintained perfect equality among its members. Every society is unequal in that all individuals and groups are stratified according to differences in power (privilege), status (prestige), and wealth (resources). These stratifications are dependent on age and gender, as well as race, class, or even region. Societies also differ in degrees of inequality with respect to depth and intensity, permanence and formality, and rationale and solutions. Even the simplest hunting and foraging communities exhibit some degree of stratification. A commitment to egalitarian principles may have ensured relatively open access to the basic necessities for individual survival, but it did little to diminish male privilege. Contemporary attempts to create equal societies—such as the Kibbutz in Israel or the Hutterite communities in North America—have also fallen short of their utopian ideals even if they are more egalitarian in material terms than surrounding communities. Nor is there any evidence that most of us would want to live in a perfectly equal society. For many, it is not the principle of inequality that rankles and disturbs. Rather, objections arise from the magnitude of the extremes between rich and poor, the use of illegal short cuts for attainment of success at all costs, or the inability of certain groups to escape the tyranny of perpetual poverty.

Class Counts

Inequality and patterns of power are expressed in different ways. *Stratification* is but one manifestation of inequality that is virtually universal and widely manifest. All human societies are unequal and stratified into socially significant hierarchies. Both simple and complex societies are stratified by age or gender; only agricultural-industrial societies are stratified by occupation and wealth, class and caste.

Stratification can be defined in different ways. It can refer to the unequal allocation of scarce resources among different groups or households; it can refer also to the unequal distribution of people in relation to scarce resources. This division of society into unequal horizontal layers is known as *strata* (Lundy and Warme 1990). A society is said to be stratified when a group of individuals is ranked along a hierarchy using any convenient criteria such as income (Barrett 1994). Each of these categories of individuals occupies a similar *status* (position) within this strata, based on shared characteristics such as access to scarce resources. The combination of these strata in ascending and descending order create a system of stratification (Boughey 1978).

Different criteria are employed in placing individuals along a stratified system. The most common are *wealth* (or income), *prestige* (privilege), or *power* (education). Access to these scarce resources is not randomly distributed but clusters about the variables of age, gender, race and ethnicity, birth and family connections, and religious affiliation. Sociologists recognize the diverse dimensions of inequality, such as class with its basis in material wealth, as well as race (inequality due to skin colour or culture), status (inequality from symbols), power (inequality as authority), gender (inequality based on perceived sex differences), and region (inequality based on where you live). These intersecting strands also combine to establish patterns of inequality. Inequality, in turn, becomes stratified when institutionalized (that is, supported by norms about what ought to be), embedded within the structure of society, rendered permanent and persistent, and based on membership in a group (rather than person or attitude) (Brinkerhoff et al. 1992).

Debates over inequality initially revolved around social class, even if there was little agreement among sociologists as to its nature and characteristics (Gillespie 1996). Curiously, however, there is a certain taboo about the concept of class among many North Americans (Ehrenreich 1992). The word itself is hushed up in polite company. Any references to class are dismissed as feudalistic remnants, an outdated concept whose only relevance is in relation to countries like Britain with its inherited aristocracy. Many Canadians are uneasy with the very prospect of distinct social classes in this country, let alone that they might have an impact on the way we live or are allowed to live. Several exceptions to this studied reluctance exist nonetheless. For instance, class may be understandable when phrased in terms of material rewards that accrue from having a prestigious occupation. Class may also make sense when used to indicate lifestyle differences as they relate to those who are inordinately wealthy. But for most people the class concept is rarely couched within an economic framework pertaining to ownership and control of productive property (Grab 1993). Many sociologists disagree with this depoliticizing of class. For them, classes in Canada not only are real with a powerful impact, but they "count" as a legitimate field of study involving questions like the following (Grab 1993):

- How many classes are there?

- What criteria should serve as the basis for class typologies?

- Should criteria be based on subjective elements such as self-definition, or should they reflect objective criteria such as income?

- Are classes best restricted to economic grounds or should they take into account productive control over material resources, in addition to political and ideological control?

- Are classes universal or are they intrinsic only to complex, capitalist societies?

- Should classes be thought of as aggregates of individuals who happen to occupy a similar set of positions in society? Or do we conceive of classes as groups of persons who embrace a common membership with a shared set of interests?

Others have begun to challenge the primacy of class as a key explanatory variable. They argue that rapid changes in society and the class structure have rendered the term almost meaningless as a basis for studying inequality, that divisions based on race or gender are not reducible to class even if closely related, and that the diversity of social experiences cannot be explained by references to foundational concepts such as class (Gillespie 1996). Still,

---

CASE 5-1   Caste Versus Class

A caste is defined as a *closed system* of stratification since, for people living in a caste system, social status is ascribed at birth and the hierarchy is absolutely rigid; that is, people can never change their caste (Robertson 1987). This socially ascribed status determines what people can do—what job they can take, who they can socialize with, where they can go, and whom they can marry. Marriage is always *endogamous* (within the caste you were born into) and sexual relations across castes are also forbidden (except when initiated by a superior caste member). Patterns of interaction are strictly regulated; contact with a lower caste is seen as polluting. Should contact occur, often a cleansing ritual is required for removal of the contamination.

The caste concept provides a useful primer on social class. The major distinction between class and caste is in the logic behind social status and social mobility. Caste statuses are ascribed, that is, each individual is conferred a social position at birth. This status remains intact for the duration of that person's life. In class systems, however, status is achieved through competition. Moreover, it is claimed by individuals on the strength of merit, credentials, and personal effort. Even though ascribed status remains important in class-based societies to the extent that much depends on one's family of origin, the ideals of the "self-made" woman and man and of mobility between classes are critical to the functioning of a class-based society.

Castes are not nearly as common as they once were. With the gradual dismantling of South Africa's caste system, only India remains as a classic example. Unlike castes based on race or ethnicity, India's arrangement is anchored in the realities of religion and world view. Four castes dominate in India: priests/scholars, nobles/warriors, merchants/artisans, and common labourers. Beneath them are the outcasts or untouchables. Within each of these castes are thousands of subcastes, each identified with a particular occupation ranging from scavenging to snake-charming.

India's system remains largely intact after 3000 years of existence, despite unremitting efforts on the part of the state to abolish castes as inimical to a sectarian democracy (see Sen 1993). Those who benefit from the system are reluctant to change and have resorted to violence to preserve the status quo (Reuters 1997). So too are those at the bottom who have even more to lose because there is less of a margin for error for them and no government-sponsored safety net. Yet the system is beginning to crumble, in part because of government decree and in part because of the combined forces of urbanization and industrialization.

few would be willing to jettison class as a key variable in analyzing inequality. In general, classes can be defined as groups of individuals who can be categorized in terms of their relationship to scarce and valued resources such as wealth, power, or status. More specifically, a class can be defined as a category of persons who occupy a similar rank with respect to the ownership and means of production. A brief comparison with the concept of caste may shed additional light on what class is not (see Case 5-1).

Counting Classes

How many classes exist in Canada? Is there an absolute number that all sociologists can agree on or does the number vary with the perspectives of the investigator or perceptions of the community at large? Are classes "real" or are they "analytical constructs" established by sociologists to impose order on a system of stratification (Barrett 1994)? What is stratification and how do systems of stratification relate to social class? What is the source of class-based stratification in society? How is it manifest? Why does it exist? What, if anything, should be done about it? Responses to these questions strike at the nexus of sociological debate.

Sociologists continue to spar over the number of classes in society. Consensus is difficult to secure. Sociologically speaking, the number of classes is variable: it reflects both objective criteria (relations to means of production) and a subjective component (how people assess themselves in relation to others). Classes are not real in the tangible sense of the word. Rather, class consists of categories imposed by the investigator or defined by respondents. Any number of criteria, from self-identification to quality of life assessments, can be employed for inclusion. That kind of subjectivity suggests that the possibilities are almost limitless.

Many sociologists define classes as real and objective. The objective dimensions are open to measurement by quantifiable variables such as income or membership in clubs or organizations. The classic example of an objective class system is Marx's division of society into the working class and the capitalist class, each reflecting their relative position vis-à-vis the means of production. The dominant class consists of those who own or control large scale productivity; the working class own only the labour power they must sell to survive. More recent analysis suggests an intermediate (middle) class that includes professionals, technicians, and white collar workers with some degree of training or credentials. There is also a recognizable lower strata known as the underclass. The underclass consists of those without much stake in the system who exist at the margins of society, and represents the homeless, underemployed, and destitute (Grab 1990).

An alternative system exists that combines both objective and subjective features. This typology partitions society into lower, middle, and upper classes, then further subdivides each type into upper, middle, and lower (for example, upper middle class), for a total of nine classes. The criteria employed can vary, but often include self-reported measures of income, education, employment, status, and prestige.

Regardless of the numbers or levels of awareness, society continues to be structured around material relations. The upper (affluent) class in Canada is the smallest in number, yet controls a disproportionate share of societal wealth and property. Members of this class collectively own more, use more, and earn more than the other classes (Helmes-Hayes and Curtis 1998). Twenty percent of the population (the richest quintile) earn a vastly disproportionate amount of the total income in Canada. Likewise, the lowest 20 percent of the population (the poorest quintile) earn a minuscule portion of the total income. In many cases, income distribution has remained relatively constant from year to year. In other instances, disparities between the rich and the poor have accelerated and would be worse if not for transfer payments in the form of tax credits and assistance schemes. In other words, it would be incorrect to infer a societywide shift towards some middle class ground. Rather, it would seem that Canadian society is being polarized into two classes—the "haves" and "have nots" (Bolaria and Wotherspoon 1991; Curtis and Tepperman 1993).

Class Mobility

Are social classes a problem? For many, the central issue is not the existence of class inequities per se, but securing open and equal opportunities for those qualified to move from one class to another. This ability to change one's position in the social hierarchy is called *social mobility*. Four kinds of social mobility can be discerned. Vertical mobility is movement up or down the social hierarchy, with a subsequent change in wealth, status, or power. Horizontal mobility is lateral movement with no appreciable difference in income or prestige. Intragenerational mobility refers to movements within a person's lifetime; conversely, intergenerational mobility consists of household movement over a period of generations.

How much social mobility exists in Canada? To what extent do people move from one class to another? Canada is often perceived to be a relatively open society, a perception honed by constant references to Canada as a land of limitless opportunity. But social mobility is not nearly as extensive as once believed (Hiller 1990; Goyder 1990). As might be expected, rates of mobility can increase during periods of economic expansion and technological growth (Tepperman and Rosenberg 1991). Regardless of the level of expansion or contraction, education remains the single most important factor in overcoming status limitations and moving upwards. To be sure, this is no guarantee that a postsecondary degree will help a graduate snare a lucrative job. Without a degree, however, the chances of employment and promotion are virtually nil in our credential-obsessed economy.

A rags to riches type of mobility is not especially common, but the fact that it happens even occasionally seems sufficient to substantiate people's faith in the virtues of an open system (Lundy and Warme 1990). The reality of social mobility is often overstated. Few societies—Canada included—can afford unrestricted movement up and down the social ladder without obliterating all vestiges of order and stability. In other words, Canadians live in a society where social mobility is highly valued in principle, if not always implemented in practice.

RACE AND ETHNICITY

From afar Canada is seen as a paragon of virtue in the harmonious management of race and ethnic relations. A closer inspection suggests a slightly different picture. The Canada we know is characterized by a high degree of inequality that rewards certain groups and penalizes others because of race or ethnicity. Racial and ethnic minorities do not share equally in the creation or distribution of wealth, power, or social status (Breton 1998). Nor are they highly esteemed for their contributions to Canada. More often than not, minority women and men are scrutinized as "problem people." Instead of an equitable arrangement, racial and ethnocultural groups are sorted out unequally around a "mosaic" of raised (dominant) and lowered (subordinate) tiles (Tepper 1988). So-called white ethnics tend to perform better in terms of income and education than certain visible minorities (Breton et al. 1990; Pendakur and Pendakur 1995). The fact that many minorities occupy the lower rungs of the socioeconomic ladder is not only unfair, but also costly to society as a whole.

Even a cursory inspection of Canada's race relations record is a disturbing experience (Henry et al. 1995; Stasiulis 1997). In the past, immigrants were frequently imported as a source of cheap menial labour, either to assist in the process of society-building (for example, Chinese for the construction of the railway) or to provide manual skills in labour-starved industries such as the garment trade (Bolaria and Li 1988). Once in Canada, many became convenient targets for abuse or exploitation. Immigrants could be fired with impunity, especially during periods of economic stagnation. Promotions, of course, were entirely out of the question. Political or civil rights were routinely trampled on without many channels for redress. Racism and discriminatory barriers proved to be common stumbling blocks, as were the imperatives of a capitalist system. Those on the bottom provided a grim reminder to those in the middle of the fate that awaited anyone who refused to play by the rules.

The situation has improved thanks to human rights and multicultural legislation. Yet both native-born and foreign-born minorities continue to be shunted into marginal employment ghettos with few possibilities for escape or advancement. Immigrant labourers from the Caribbean are brought to Canada on a temporary basis for seasonal employment, primarily in agricultural fields. Domestic workers (nannies) from the Philippines are taken advantage of by middle class families who should know better. African-Canadians are routinely denied equal access to housing and employment (Henry and Ginzberg 1993; Henry 1994). For black youth, relations with the police border on the criminal in certain urban areas (Cryderman, O'Toole and Fleras 1998). Indo-Pakistani Canadians continue to experience widespread dislike and resentment if national attitudes surveys are to be trusted (Berry 1993). In these ways, various ethnic and racial groups are earmarked for the bottom of the socioeconomic heap without much hope for escape or redress.

Few can be surprised by the presence of racial or ethnic inequality in Canada. But not everyone concedes that this is a major problem. Some degree of inequality is seen by many as the price of initial adjustment. Many new Canadians are predictably relegated towards the bottom because of their relative inexperience (Ostow et al. 1991). As is the case elsewhere, new Canadians must contend with poor housing conditions, resistance in the labour market, language problems, inconsistencies in social service delivery, and explicit discrimination from xenophobes. In time, most ethnic Canadians are absorbed into the mainstream without further problems. Problems do arise, however, when this initial inequality becomes permanently entrenched. Further difficulties appear when subsequent generations are disqualified from equal access or equitable outcomes because of characteristics, such as skin colour, that stigmatize most members. The inequities that stem from racial features or ethnocultural lifestyles are in many cases now firmly implanted as a major social problem in Canada, and one that shows no sign of diminishing—with or without government interventions as the next case demonstrates.

CASE 5-2　Canada's Vertical Mosaic: Ethnicity as Inequality

John Porter's seminal study *The Vertical Mosaic* (1965) provides a useful introduction to the concept of racial and ethnic inequality. Identified by at least one sociologist as the most important publication in the history of Canadian sociology (Forcese 1980), the book explores the nature of the relationship between ethnic origin, social class, and power in Canada. For Porter (1965; 1979), Canada's tapestry of cultural differences was stratified vertically along racial and ethnic lines, hence the expression "vertical mosaic." That this term is now thoroughly ensconced in Canada's sociological discourse attests to its power as metaphor and explanation (see Helmes-Hayes and Curtis 1998).

Porter argued that ethnic groups in Canada were arranged hierarchically, with the British and to a lesser extent the French playing a gatekeeper role, regulating who would enter the corridors of power. Based on an analysis of census data between 1931 and 1961, he found that the British and the French (Canada's "charter groups") were in control of privileged positions by an accident of history. The other groups to emigrate to Canada occupied an inferior or "entrance status." For Porter, ethnic inequality and ethnic group solidarity were persistent. This persistence was unfortunate since it violated the principles of liberalism and meritocracy that Porter admired—especially in their purest embodiment in the United States (Brym 1991). Retention of ethnicity also hampered the upward mobility of ethnic minorities, leading to what Porter called an ethnic mobility trap. For immigrant groups, ethnicity and

inequality proved a paradox. If they wanted to achieve social mobility and shed their entrance status, it was necessary to reject their cultural background and assimilate into the mainstream. However, if they severed their ties with their ethnic community, they would stand to lose an invaluable support system. To the extent that racial and ethnic groups became trapped in ghettos and on reserves, Porter claimed, social mobility would be beyond their grasp.

Porter did not think highly of ethnic cultures, seeing them as residues of the past—simultaneously dysfunctional and irrelevant. To Porter, ethnicity was a "problem" in and for society: it put a premium on primordial, nonrational attachments that compelled individuals to sacrifice their personal identities and interests on behalf of the ethnic group rather than to the values of modern society, including rationality, progress, universalism, and equality (see Vallee 1981). Minorities are socialized in a culture that does not adequately prepare them for the demands of a complex and advanced industrial system. This, of course, does not suggest that racial or ethnic minorities are "inferior." Rather, their social and cultural environment is defined as "deficient" in comparison with mainstream values. Rightly or wrongly, according to Porter, most ethnicities would vanish in the face of modernist pressures and global development. Not surprisingly, Porter criticized the Canadian government for its efforts to encourage ethnicity through multiculturalism. Not only would multiculturalism entrench social inequality by relegating

CASE 5-2   **Canada's Vertical Mosaic: Ethnicity as Inequality (continued)**

ethnic minorities to perpetual lower class status, but the promotion of ethnicity would also pre-empt national prosperity.

Since the publication of *The Vertical Mosaic*, there have been many attempts to verify Porter's observations (Helmes-Hayes and Curtis 1998). Many researchers now disagree with his conclusions (see Brym 1991). Some of the key disagreements include:

1) Porter overstated the differences between Canada and the United States in attitudes towards and treatment of minorities (Palmer 1975; Reitz and Breton 1994).

2) Ethnic stratification is not more entrenched than in the past. For example, ethnic differences in occupational status have declined over time for European groups (Breton et al. 1990). However, this flattening process has not necessarily extended to people of colour.

3) Strong ethnic group cohesion does not necessarily restrain mobility (Breton et al. 1990).

4) Ethnicity is not necessarily a strong predictor of socioeconomic status or mobility rates.

5) Ethnic inequality is decreasing, with members of most European ethnic groups experiencing some degree of upward mobility (Levitt 1997).

6) The effect of ethnicity on status attainment decreases with increasing acculturation (deSilva 1992).

In short, many of Porter's key arguments are now being contested. There are growing doubts about the determinacy of ethnicity in shaping Canadian stratification. Many European (or white) ethnics have been incorporated into Canadian society as social equals without having to relinquish affiliation with their traditional pasts. A study by Raymond Breton et al. (1990) found that certain ethnic minorities in Toronto, especially Germans and Ukrainians, had achieved a high level of incorporation into society as measured by economic rewards, job discrimination, and sociopolitical acceptance. Ukrainians were also most protective of their ethnocultural background and ethnic identity; conversely, Germans exhibited the least amount of ethnocultural retention. The status of Jews was ambiguous. Though economically successful and politically incorporated, they were more likely to experience discrimination and social rejection. Their commitment to ethnic retention was highest among the eight groups studied.

For racial and visible minorities, however, considerable stratification continues to exist. Chinese and West Indians remain poorly integrated into the culture and economic structure of Canada. Not only do they rank near the bottom of scales for employment opportunity and social acceptance, but they also score poorly in terms of identity, cultural preferences, residential segregation, social bonds and interaction, and levels of political activity. In short, as Breton et al. (1990) concedes, the vertical mosaic concept needs to be rethought. Certain ethnic groups have little or no trouble with mainstream integration, even when they maintain their ethnocultural

CASE 5-2   Canada's Vertical Mosaic:
Ethnicity as Inequality (continued)

identity. That the same degree of mobility does not apply to all ethnic minorities—especially those who are racially visible—is cause for concern.

National studies support these findings. Earning differentials among ethnic groups in Canada continue to reveal marked disparities, according to 1991 Census data. Pendakur and Pendakur (1995) point to significant earning differences between (a) whites and visible minorities; (b) native-born and foreign-born; (c) women and men; and (d) aboriginal and nonaboriginal populations (see Table 5-1). These differences remain in effect, albeit to a lesser degree, even when controlling for individual characteristics such as age, education level, language knowledge, full-time status, household type, and occupation.

According to Table 5-1 Canadian-born visible minority males earn considerably less than Canadian-born white males. Variation exists within the categories themselves: Canadian-born men of Greek, Portuguese, African, and Chinese background earn between 12 and 16 percent less than males of British origin. Foreign-born visible minorities, in turn, earn around 15 percent less than Canadian-born visible minorities. Aboriginal peoples confront negative earning differentials of between 15 and 19 percent. Earning differentials between men and women proved significant; nevertheless, different earning patterns were observed across genders. Compared with men, there were little income differences between Canadian-born white females and visible minority females. The same applied to foreign-born white females and Canadian-born white and visible minority females. Aboriginal women earned around 7 percent less that white Canadian-born women and 15 percent less than those of British origin.

TABLE 5-1   Mean Earnings by Visible Minority Status

Sex	Immigrant Status	Visible Status	Earnings (Mean)	Earnings (% Difference)
Males	Canadian-born	white	$36 563	–
		visible	$31 653	−13.4
		aboriginal	$28 725	−21.4
	Foreign-born	white	$38 456	+ 5.2
		visible	$28 285	−22.6
Females	Canadian-born	white	$23 173	–
		visible	$23 149	− 0.1
		aboriginal	$19 887	−14.2
	Foreign-born	white	$22 498	− 2.9
		visible	$20 132	−13.1

Note: Adapted from Pendakur and Pendakur (1995). Based on Census Public Use Microdata, Individual File, 3 percent sample of the Canadian population. Population includes permanent residents age 20 to 64 not in school full-time and living in Montreal, Toronto, Hamilton, Edmonton, Calgary, and Vancouver. Does not include persons not reporting an education level, a household type, occupation, or industry, or immigrants arriving after 1989.

Rethinking Ethnic Inequality

A rethinking of racial and ethnic inequality is currently in progress. This is especially apparent at the level of causes and cures. Instead of focusing on the individual or ethnic culture as the source of the problem, theorists now aim at structural factors that encompass class, organization, and systemic barriers (Brym 1991).

The consequences of attributing racial and ethnic stratification to structural causes cannot be underestimated. Focusing on the structures of society as the problem has compelled a rethinking of federal and provincial policy initiatives, most notably those dealing with employment equity programs. These and other changes have also altered the way Canadians approach the dynamics of race, indigenous, and ethnic relations (Fleras and Elliott 1996). Emphasis is on the relational rather than distributional component of diversity, with particular attention on how inequities are created, expressed, maintained, challenged, and transformed at the level of collective action or public policy. The reasons behind this change in thinking are numerous; essentially, however, they reflect both changing demographics and evolving discourses.

Culture as Problem

The concept of racial and ethnic stratification was once most commonly couched within the context of a 1970s-style liberal pluralism (see Agocs and Boyd 1993). At the core of this democratic liberalism was a commitment to individual rights and formal equality as a basis for national unity and prosperity. Canadian society was envisaged as an open and competitive marketplace in which individuals competed as equals and were rewarded because of their skills or production. Institutions would be "multiculturalized" by defining them as public spaces, ensuring equal treatment regardless of race or ethnicity (Breton 1998). Individual success or failure reflected a person's amount of human capital; that is, those people with training, skills, and education succeeded while those without did not.

Imperfections, of course, existed within the system. Ignorance and prejudice on the part of employers hindered a natural sorting-out process. Economic success belonged to those who hired individuals on no other basis than merit. Discrimination in the workforce would vanish once rational employers were shown the irrationality of their ways. Similarly, ethnic minorities had to overcome their ethnicity for success in the marketplace. Ethnic differences had to be suppressed (except at personal or private levels) to circumvent its potential to divide, exclude, incite, or destroy (Breton 1998). The role of the government throughout this adjustment process was essentially passive—to improve access and eliminate discrimination by ensuring a level playing field for all contestants. The introduction of a multicultural policy in 1971 was viewed as a way of eliminating prejudice in the workplace through removal of negative mainstream attitudes (Fleras 1994). It also sought to depoliticize ethnicity by eliminating its salience as a basis for entitlement or engagement in society.

Problematizing Structures

By the early 1980s, thinking about inequality underwent a change in emphasis (Agocs and Boyd 1993). Emphasis shifted from a focus on individuals and attitudes to a preoccupation with systems and structures. The primary catalyst for this change was dramatic increases in immigrants from developing world countries, coupled with a growing chorus of complaints over the lack of progress in mainstreaming diversity. A commitment to *equity* (with its focus on substantive differences and equal outcomes) replaced the principle of formal *equality* as part of this transformation. Similarly the frame of reference shifted from individuals to structures and from ethnicity to race relations.

A new paradigm was proposed to account for institutional resistance to accommodating diversity. According to this perspective, the problem did not rest with individuals or attitudes per se. Rather, the source of the problem was seen to be rooted in the institutional *structures* of society. Inequality and barriers to advancement were derived from structural constraints that were largely systemic and reflected a job market constructed by the "male stream" for self-serving purposes. These barriers to success were subtle but numerous. There was a greater awareness that workplace climates fostered unequal treatment of minorities because of harassment, double standards, and tokenism (see Kanter 1977). In applying the metaphor of a competitive foot race, it was obvious that not all contestants were in a position to compete equally in the labour market. The race was rigged because of characteristics such as skin colour or lifestyle preference that handicapped certain individuals. As barriers, racially ascribed characteristics were just as real and debilitating as those encountered by individuals with disabilities. In both cases, the onus lay on the government to smooth out the playing field through legislation that would ensure at least the appearance of nominal equality.

Even the concept of solution underwent a change of direction. The open marketplace was no longer thought to be the solution to the problem; it was identified instead as contributing to inequality through such entrenched barriers as segmented labour fields, racial division of labour, dual labour markets, and systemic structures of discrimination. Solutions that focused on individual shortcomings to eradicate inequality from the public domain could only touch on the problem. A victim-blame approach could only apply imperfect solutions to fundamental (structural) problems. It was the institutions, not the participants, that required an overhauling for attainment of anything beyond the façade of equality. The focus thus shifted to employment equity as a policy framework not only for removing structural inequalities and systemic barriers but also for engaging race and ethnicity on a more equitable basis (Agocs and Boyd 1993).

Nevertheless, government involvement continues to be fraught with contradiction and concern. On the one hand, Canada is now embarking on a free market experiment within the framework of a free-wheeling global market economy. Evidence suggests the federal government will be forced to abandon many of its interventionist employment policies as the price for improving Canadian competitiveness overseas. On the other hand, central authorities in Canada are increasingly active in managing diversity through more intervention, regulation, and monitoring. Efforts to strengthen the federal Employment Equity Act suggest a still active state; Ontario's decision to rescind its Employment Equity Act indicates an opposing trend. The clash of these competing philosophies should prove provocative as the twentieth century draws to a close.

Re-imagining Equality

That most minorities aspire to social and economic equality is surely beyond dispute. Many Canadians would also agree that equality is to be preferred over inequality. But the concept of equality is subject to diverse interpretations. Mutually opposed definitions may be endorsed by different groups, by different individuals across the spectrum of society, or by competing factions within a group. The situation is further complicated by the possibility of concurrent versions at a given point in time in response to changing circumstances. This proliferation of definitions has led to confusion and misunderstanding over the issue of entitlement, that is, who gets what and why. This element of uncertainty has also complicated the process of solving problems. Without new solutions to the old problem of inequality, the goal of equality will remain lofty but elusive.

Competing Equalities

The concept of equality is employed in three different ways. First, equality is used as equivalent to sameness. Everyone is treated the same regardless of their background or circumstances. No one is accorded special privileges in a system designed around equal opportunity and universal merit. This type of "formal" equality focuses on due process and legal equivalents. Second, equality is used in the sense of numerical or "proportional" equivalence. Under systems of preferential hiring and promotion, each group is allocated positions according to their numbers in society or the workforce. Third, the concept of equality is directed towards the principle of "different but equal." With its emphasis on equal outcomes or conditions rather than opportunities, this position takes into account the unique circumstances of a person or group as a basis for entitlement. People cannot be treated alike because some groups have special needs or unique experiences. They need to be treated differently by making substantive adjustments to the social and cultural components of society.

Consider for example the "special" treatment that extends to individuals with disabilities. Wheelchair ramps, closed caption TV, and designated parking spots are common enough. Yet these concessions can hardly be thought of as special or preferential, but rather as removing barriers to ensure equality of opportunity. Likewise, historically disadvantaged minority women and men encounter barriers that are every bit as real as physical impediments and equally in need of removal for levelling the playing field. In other words, those with social disabilities also require different treatment if only to ensure their right to compete with others on an equal basis.

Each of these perspectives on equality differs from the other in terms of objectives and scope. Formal equality is concerned with mathematical equivalence and a market-driven means for establishing who gets what. It tends to treat individuals as asexual, deracialized, classless, and lacking a history or context (McIntyre 1994). Any measure that rewards individuals on grounds other than merit or competition is criticized as contrary to the natural sorting-out process. This perspective is at odds with more substantive versions of equality known as equity. Under substantive equity, differences are taken into account; after all, identical treatment can produce unequal results and perpetuate group-based inequities when everyone is treated the same without regard to histories of exclusion or restricted opportunities. This makes it doubly important for social policies to consider inequities derived from gender, race, and class (McIntyre 1994) Such a claim also raises a host of questions about which version of equality should prevail. Is one more important than the other, or is it a case of one serving as a necessary precondition for the other?

Equity = Equal Opportunity + Equal Outcomes

The distinction between equal opportunity (competition) and equal outcomes (conditions) is critical. Equal opportunity focuses on the rights of individuals to be free from discrimination when competing for the good things in life. By contrast, equal outcomes concentrates on the rights of individuals for a fair and equitable share of the goods and services in society. A commitment to equal opportunity openly advocates competition, inequality, and hierarchy as natural and inevitable. An equal outcomes perspective is concerned with controlled distribution and egalitarian conditions for members of a disadvantaged group. Rather than mathematical equality, differences are taken into account to ensure substantive equity. This perspective recognizes the need for collective over individual rights when the situation demands it. It also endorses the principle of social intervention for true equality since equal outcomes are unlikely to arise from competitive market forces.

By themselves, equal opportunity structures are insufficient to overcome the debilitating effects of systemic discrimination and institutional racism. Additional treatment is required over and above that available to the general population, since the application of equal standards to unequal situations merely freezes the status quo. Context and consequences are as important as abstract principles of equal opportunity in righting wrongs. Taking *context* into account may mean that in some cases differential treatment will be required to achieve an equality of outcome. Taking *consequences* into account suggests that intent or awareness is less important than effects. The unintended consequences of seemingly neutral practices may lead to the unintentional exclusion of qualified personnel, regardless of motive or consciousness.

To be sure, outcome-oriented equity is not opposed to equal opportunities in defining equality. On the contrary, a commitment to the principle of equal opportunity constitutes a necessary first step in overcoming entrenched racism and discrimination. But ultimately such a commitment cannot achieve a fair and just equality in an unequal competition. Only a dual commitment to equitable outcomes and equal opportunities can free up the playing field for open competition.

REGIONS AND REGIONALISM

Some people have remarked that Canada is a country in search of a reason, while others have declared the absurdity of this country's very existence as a society. These musings can be interpreted in different ways. What each emphasizes, however, is the salience of regional differences to any definition of Canadian society (Economic Council of Canada 1977; Matthews 1983). The existence of regions gives rise to the problem of regionalism in part because of federal commitment to extend the principles of justice and equality to everyone (Wein 1993). According to this line of thought, unchecked market forces create regional deficiencies; only a major redistribution of resources by the government can correct these market failures (but see Corcoran 1996). The different regions of Canada are especially vulnerable to the vicissitudes of global market forces and multinational greed. The reality of regionalism is further encouraged by the logic of a federal system in which provincial governments compete with each other in advancing sectoral interests. Rather than disappearing, the forces of regionalism appear to be gathering momentum in response to Québecois demands and federal attempts to placate pleas for decentralization (Brodie 1997). A series of natural and social "cleavages" have evolved that not only furnish a basis for Canada's regions (Wein 1993), but also expose the dilemmas of building this country along an east-west axis when the natural pull is north-south with eventual absorption into United States (Hiller 1990).

Canada's regional differences are not merely geographic or demographic curiosities. Inequities are also characteristic of regions. Debates over inequality are just as likely to revolve around the "where" of distribution as the "who" or "what" (see Brodie 1997). Regions differ on economic grounds pertaining to housing, health, education, and the resources available to their respective criminal justice systems (Swan and Serjak 1993). Periods of high unemployment and debilitating levels of dependency on government assistance in the poorer provinces are two additional dimensions. Yet regional inequalities have shown a remarkable tenacity despite federal efforts to standardize access to services and goods (Economic Council of Canada 1977). Government intervention has proven a bane rather than a boom (Gherson 1997). According to Fred McMahon (1997), senior policy analyst at the Atlantic Institute of Market Studies, federal transfers to Atlantic Canada (which peaked at about $5000 per person in 1980 (in today's dollars)) have failed to elevate the region out of its "have not" status (see Case 5-3). The transfers may have contributed unwittingly to local economic decline and deterred private sector growth while reinforcing patterns of dependency (see Corcoran 1996). The intractable nature of this inequality has also given rise to regionally based social protests, regional alienation, and separatist movements (Sinclair 1991). Regional parties such as Reform or Bloc Québecois are likely to have an unsettling effect on Canada's political landscape for years to come.

Even consensus over basic concepts such as regions or regionalism seems to elude our grasp (Wein 1993). By a *region* we mean a geographical space occupied by a group of people with (a) similar economic conditions and opportunities, (b) a unique political arrangement vis-à-vis the "centre" of the country, and (c) a relatively distinct subculture that fosters a sense of identity and meaning. For our purposes, regions can be divided into Atlantic Canada, southern Ontario (from Windsor to the Quebec border along the MacDonald-Cartier corridor), Quebec (the southern half), the Prairie provinces, the Pacific Rim in British Columbia, the North (or the rest of Canada outside the Arctic), and the Arctic (the part of Canada beyond the tree line). *Regionalism*, by contrast, is a political concept, and it represents the politicized counterpart of regions as a social or geographical entity. Regionalism is inherently political, Janine Brodie (1997) writes, since economic, social, and cultural interests are defined in territorial terms and articulated around spatial inequalities. In seeking to redefine its relationship with the centre, regionalism begins with the politicization of regional identity because of concern over perceived injustices. This politicizing of regions is followed

---

CASE 5-3   **The Case of Atlantic Canada**

Inequities of wealth and political influence are obvious when conceptualizing Canada as a country of regions. Consider the example of the Atlantic provinces as a "have not" region. By almost any indicator one could choose, there is an enormous disparity in wealth and opportunity between the Atlantic provinces and other regions in Canada. For instance, according to Fred Wein (1993), the 1990 per capita income in Newfoundland stood at $15 846, compared with $25 151 in Ontario—a difference of 63 per cent and a disparity ratio of 1.59 between the highest and lowest incomes in Canada. Variation in the level of unemployment is significant with a rate of 18 percent in Newfoundland in 1991 versus a rate of just over 7 percent

| CASE 5-3 | The Case of Atlantic Canada (continued) |

in Saskatchewan, a disparity ratio of 2.48. In Newfoundland the poverty rate was 15.6 percent in 1990, but was only 11.7 percent in Ontario. Additional markers have been employed, including education levels, where disparities are also significant. The percentage of adults with less than grade 9 education is 11.1 in Alberta but nearly 26.9 in Newfoundland—and the gap has been increasing since 1951 (Sinclair 1991).

Prior to Confederation, the Atlantic provinces were thriving centres of trade, industry, and commerce. The coastal regions were particularly prosperous, unlike their land-locked counterparts in Upper and Lower Canada (Ramcharan 1989). But for the Atlantic region the promise of increased prosperity did not materialize following Confederation. Instead the provinces experienced a gradual economic decline that has persisted to the present. The first National Policy of the Canadian government forged an east-west economic flow, in effect "regionalizing" the country into an industrialized and diversified centre, an export-based western hinterland, and a deindustrialized east (Brodie 1997). A century later, the Atlantic region continues to stagnate. Even the Conservative party's 1993 parliamentary subcommittee on poverty remarked on similarities between the Atlantic region and Third World countries. Nor is there much hope for recovery from the current recession. Prosperity is not likely to materialize with the growing mobility of productivity, company shifts to low-wage

labour countries, the advent of more sophisticated technologies, depletion of scarce resources, and the implementation of "leaner and meaner" corporate philosophies. The recent collapse of the cod fishing industry has also hit hard.

Hiller (1990) and others have tried to account for this turnaround in the fortunes of the Atlantic region. Commonly cited reasons include a drop in the volume and prices of the international fish and timber trades. The decline can be attributed as well to the creation of inland transportation systems that proved disadvantageous to the east coast, the concentration of capital and consolidation of manufacturing in the central regions, and the transfer of political power from the Atlantic provinces to the Prairie provinces. In other words, the enrichment of the central region occurred at the expense of the Atlantic region. Government initiatives to introduce social and economic parity through regional development programs have not had the desired effect. There are few signs of prosperity in store for the vast majority of inhabitants, much less economic diversification for the region as a whole. The tenacity of the problem and its imperviousness to solutions suggests one of two conclusions: the problem is being defined incorrectly or attempted solutions are incapable of dealing with a problem of such magnitude. Alternatively, some problems do not admit of solution when the marketplace defines reality.

by a mobilization of concerned citizens into a protest movement (Hiller 1990). How then do we explain these differences in a federalist system and how should we attempt to rectify them?

Explaining Regional Inequality

There are several explanations that attempt to account for regional inequality and disparities. Predictably, no consensus among sociologists is forthcoming as to which interpretation is more "correct." Some provide a better explanation for the origin of regional imbalances; others are stronger in explaining why these conditions persist. Certain explanations focus on the primacy of "internal" factors (the absence of raw materials or inadequate levels of human capital), while "external" factors (such as market forces) are emphasized by others. Still others argue that the truth lies somewhere in between—in the interplay between internal and external forces (Sinclair 1991). Finally, there are those who would argue that no explanation is sufficient to provide a complete account, that competing explanations are not necessarily incompatible with each other, and that insights can be gleaned from the alternatives (see Sinclair 1991; Wein 1993).

The first explanation is the *staples thesis*. According to the staples thesis, a region's prosperity depends on the availability and marketability of its natural resources. Staples can be a catalyst for growth if capital and labour can be enticed into the region for production purposes. A region will prosper if its valued resources can be profitably marketed as a basis for spin-off growth in manufacturing and services. Conversely, a region will stagnate if appropriate links are not fostered with the broader yet diversified economy. Too heavy a reliance on staples for creating wealth may also be a problem with a prolonged downturn in commodity prices. The region may enter an economic depression from which it will be unable to extricate itself without a new "resource" to jump-start its economy.

The *regional deficiency thesis* argues that regional inequalities stem from inherent shortcomings within the region. Among the key factors for growth and prosperity is location in relationship to markets. Transportation costs and ready access to workers and consumers must be taken into account. Demographic features can play a role in cases where population is sparsely dispersed rather than concentrated in urban areas. The tenacity of traditional cultural values may inhibit an ethic of achievement and an entrepreneurial spirit.

The third explanation is based on *dependency thinking*. Underdevelopment and inequality are generated by the exploitative tendencies of capitalist metropolitan centres. The expansion of one region occurs at the expense of another; development for some is dependency for others. This theory that the ruling elites in Canada's prosperous regions have exploited other regions to procure power, domination, and control has been employed to explain the decline of the Atlantic provinces.

Redressing Regional Imbalances

Regional inequalities are a chronic and complex social problem rarely amenable to solution by rote formula. The challenge for federal government policy is the creation of sustainable regional development. But how does one go about neutralizing the deleterious effects of poor location and resource depletion, the flight of foreign capital, imbalances in free trade created by continentalism, and continued federal cut-backs across the board? Towards that end, government concern has spawned a series of policies and programs since the early 1960s.

The single most active expression of this commitment to regional development lay with the establishment of the Department of Regional Economic Expansion (DREE), which was introduced by Pierre Trudeau in 1972 as part of his "Just Society" initiatives. DREE sought to improve regional imbalances through initiatives directed at investment in infrastructure, including improving human capital through training and education, industrial and relocation assistance, resource development programs, and, most commonly, transfer payments (especially for unemployment and welfare) to individuals and families. The fact that DREE failed to do the job as anticipated speaks volumes about the gravity of the regionalism problem. The problem is manifestly not just one of finances or psychology but of structure; solutions must be devised accordingly (Matthews 1983; Ramcharan 1989).

Nearly 30 years of policy intervention in the field of regional inequality has not achieved the desired result. More accurately, the verdict is mixed. On the one hand, the gap between the richest and poorest provinces is shrinking to some extent. The poorest provinces have improved on per capita income from 50 to 72 percent of the nation's average between 1951 and 1990. As a result, the richest provinces (Ontario, British Columbia, and Alberta) have moved closer to the national average (Wein 1993). Yet even these indices of improvement are deceptive. Much of the improvement is the result of compensatory or transfer payments, such as unemployment insurance from the rich provinces to the poor. Very little equity can be traced to improvements in the productive capacity of poor regions. Nor is there much success in finding and keeping a job—the single most important factor in reinforcing regional inequality (Swan and Serjak 1993). Not surprisingly, the disparity in unemployment rates has scarcely budged since 1971.

The fact that regional inequities remain as entrenched as ever is deplorable given the volume of energy and resources expended. The lack of results confirms the inadequacy of reforms that concentrate on internal changes rather than external forces. Nor is there much hope for substantial change unless the social and structural aspects are taken into account as part of a comprehensive renewal (Sinclair 1991). Failure to confer ownership and control on local communities has hindered the problem-solving process. In contrast with the past when the government sought to buffer regional economies from disruptive international forces, central authorities are now under pressure to curtail spending as a costly luxury while encouraging regional and local economies to compete internationally (Brodie 1997). Not surprisingly, the federal government has hacked away at transfer payments, regional freight subsidies, regional developmental funds, and retraining programs (such as the $1.9 billion Atlantic Groundfish package, which attempted to wean the Atlantic provinces from their dependency on fishing) (Gherson 1997). Political considerations loom large as government initiatives emphasize voter appeal rather than concern with the issue at hand. As Wein (1993) notes, proposed initiatives are as likely to reflect political expediency as economic need. The prognosis for regional equality is even more daunting as governments lose interest in rectifying the spatial distributions of inequality (Cohen 1993).

THE POLITICS OF POVERTY

In the mid-1950s, the average Canadian family of four survived on $4000 per year, or about $26 000 in 1996 dollars. That middle class family of four today would be classified as poor and counted among the 20 percent of Canadians who reportedly live under the poverty line of around $31 000 (Coyne 1996). The Toronto Social Planning Council would label this family as extremely destitute; it has defined any family of four in an urban area earning less than $40 560 as poor in its 1994 income guidelines. By contrast, the Fraser Institute would regard this family as relatively affluent and well beyond its income poverty line of $17 560 (Campbell 1996). Who is right and what is going on here?

Although everyone agrees that poverty exists and is a problem, there is disagreement over its magnitude and scope. What precisely do we mean by poverty? Does being poor mean not having enough to eat or not possessing cable TV? Does poverty mean the same in sub-Sahara Africa as it does in Canada? Where exactly do we draw the line between poverty and inequality? Nor is there any consensus on who is to blame for being poor or what to do about the problem. Is poverty the result of external factors beyond individual control or can it be attributed to internal factors such as laziness or parental neglect? Answers to these questions are important because policy considerations are based on our capacity to propose solutions commensurate with the definition of the problem (Greenspon 1997). Yet a fixation with definitions can be a double-edged sword. Not only are definitional exercises a form of social control in their own right, but they can detract from the spirit of activism and poverty reform (paralysis by analysis). Energy is dissipated in endless debate about the parameters of the problems rather than practical solutions. Worse still, relief may be denied to the truly destitute who for one reason or another do not fall within the accepted definition.

The Scope of Poverty

Readers will approach poverty in Canada in diverse ways. For some, extremes of inequality reflect market imperfections and lackadaisical work habits. Outside of a utopia, they would say, the best we can hope for is a safety net under the deserving poor. For others, intense levels of poverty and alienation are worrisome, especially when some people are disproportionately prosperous. The fact that this poverty is not randomly distributed but increasingly concentrated in female-headed households is also problematic. Children are equally vulnerable: between 20 and 25 percent of children are defined as living in poverty. Chronic levels of poverty among aboriginal peoples and racial minorities is no less aggravating. Regardless of its distribution, poverty appears to be an integral part of Canadian society, and nothing short of wholesale institutional reform can possibly bring it under control.

Still others believe that living standards have improved for all Canadians. Compared with international standards, Canada has virtually no poverty in terms of a destitute underclass living in sprawling ghettos or sordid slums. Many defined as poor in Canada are appreciably better off than even the affluent in some Third World countries. Nobody in Canada needs to starve to death on the streets. Only a handful are forced by circumstances to live out in the open. Few are denied access to health care and welfare services, although specific individuals may fall in between bureaucratic cracks. The poor, it is proclaimed, are better off than before because of the "trickle down" of wealth from an expanding economy. A redistribution of wealth is inevitable as the more affluent assume a larger share of taxes for social security. The UN Human Development Program seems to agree. In conferring on Canada its fifth title this decade as the world's best place to live with the highest quality of life based on income, education, and life expectancies, the UN indicated that poverty was decreasing in Canada but increasing in the United States. When held up to utopian ideals, Canada falls short of its self-appointed benchmark, but it remains a land of opportunity for most. That sociologists continue to dwell on the negative and unflattering despite Canada's lofty standing is puzzling at times. Much of the criticism, however, is not for criticism's sake, but in hopes of improving an already enviable state of affairs.

Unfortunately, there is another side to the story. Evidence in the United States and Canada appears to suggest that the poor are poorer and that the rich are getting richer at the expense of the poor. In the United States, the average per capita income in 1994 has risen to $US 26 397 per year—one of the highest in the world—yet poverty has increased to 19 percent of the population. The Carnegie Corporation reported that nearly one in four American children under the age of three was living in poverty (Gillespie 1996). While Canada basks in the limelight as the best place to live, the proportion of poor increased to 17.8 percent in 1995 from a 20-year stall at about 15 percent. Provincial variations are also acknowledged. While the overall poverty rate in Canada in 1994 was 3.8 percent, Quebec had the lowest rate at 2.5 percent, compared with 3.7 percent in Ontario, 5.6 percent in B.C., and 7 percent in New Brunswick. The disparity may be partially attributable to different cutoff lines; in Quebec the poverty line is $14 524 for a family of four (reflecting the low cost of housing), whereas Ontario's cutoff line is $17 230 and B.C.'s is $18 296 (Watson 1996). Variation by cities is also considerable: 22 percent of people living in Montreal are defined as poor by the Canadian Council of Social Development, with Trois Rivières, Winnipeg, and Sherbrooke right behind at 20 percent. Oshawa has the least number of poor with 9 percent, followed by Kitchener and Thunder Bay at 12 percent (Globe and Mail, June 26, 1996). Intracity variations can be discerned as well: while 33 percent of those who live in inner Montreal fall below the poverty line, the rate falls to only 5 percent in the eastern suburb of Varennes.

Fiddling with Figures

Many acknowledge that women, aboriginal people, persons of colour, people from Atlantic Canada, and individuals with disabilities lag far behind "mainstream" Canadians in terms of power, wealth, and prestige. Moreover, there are few signs that the situation is improving despite a doubling of dual-income families since 1967. The plight of the poor is underlined by the proliferation of soup kitchens and food banks—both solutions once seen as stop-gap measures but now firmly entrenched as part of the Canadian social landscape. That poverty exists—and hurts—is certainly beyond doubt. But it is quite another issue to define the magnitude and scope of the problem.

Take the issue of poverty as a social category. What precisely do we mean by the term poverty? How do we separate poverty from inconvenience in a way that is both respectful of the data and sensitive to the poor? Is the dividing line an absolute measure or is it relative and constantly adjusted in line with social trends and political pressure? The answer lies in how we define poverty (Hunter 1986). The debate over the poverty line is essentially an academic exercise it is alleged. There are no objective measures for quantifying the number of poor and each approach contains its own bias, subjective assumptions, and emotional language. Depending on which measure is employed, the results can lead to high or low measures of poverty.

The basic distinction lies in absolute versus relative measures. Absolute measures look at what it takes to survive in Canada by examining a basket of goods for physical survival (Campbell 1996). The Fraser Institute relies on absolute measures to arrive at its figure of

$17 560 as a base line. Relative measures tend to emphasize the social dimensions of poverty. In a society in which virtually everyone has access to the necessities of life, poverty is measured in terms of social and psychological deprivation (Campbell 1996). Poverty from a relative perspective is defined by comparison with the living standards of society as a whole. The poor are poor because they are impoverished in relation to the rest of society. For example, the Canadian Council of Social Development defines any family that makes less than half the median income of Canadian households as poor. In 1994 its figure for poverty in Canada stood at 22.9 percent; its poverty line was $40 560 (Watson 1996). Included in this figure is an annual one-week vacation, a recreation budget, a tobacco and alcohol allowance, and a VCR. Once this figure is accepted, several related issues come to mind, foremost being whether poverty can ever be completely eliminated since even a doubling of incomes would not disturb the ratio of poor to rich. In other words, the pie may be getting bigger, but the poor are still receiving a disproportionately smaller slice because of across-the-board increases.

Canadian officials have cast about for ways to bypass this definitional dilemma. One compromise has defined poverty by combining relative and absolute standards. According to the "low income cutoff point" employed by Statistics Canada, poverty is defined as present in any household that spends more than 56.2 percent of its income on food, shelter, or clothing. This figure is based on what an average family in 1986 spent on the basic necessities of food, shelter, and clothing (36.2%), plus an additional 20 percent—a largely arbitrary figure that no one can explain (Watson 1996). The low income cutoff line also takes into account the size of the family and distinguishes between rural and urban families. The National Council of Welfare uses Statistics Canada's cutoff line to estimate that 4.8 million Canadians were poor in 1994. Compare this with the Fraser Institute's figure of perhaps 1 million poor households.

Absolute and relative indices of poverty differ in other ways. Absolute definitions of poverty often involve destitution (Valpy 1993). It is what we normally think of as the poor—those who are bedraggled in appearance, perpetually hungry, and homeless. According to this gloomy scenario, poverty-stricken individuals should be given enough basic necessities to ensure they do not sicken and die, become a public nuisance, or impose an unnecessary burden on society. Relative definitions tend to be associated with more progressive welfare systems. The emphasis is not simply on preventing disease or starvation. Reaction is replaced by a proactive commitment to prevention, development, and problem-solving. The focus is on encouraging poor families to invest in themselves as first steps in taking control of their destiny. Relativist definitions also recognize the implicit value of child development as the key to breaking the poverty cycle. Poverty, in other words, is more than insufficient food, clothing, housing, or basic necessities. Rather, as Valpy (1993) notes, an adequate standard of living can mean having enough money to go on school trips or to register for organized sports. What is at stake here is the capacity to participate fully as equals in community life.

The Art of Defining Problems Away

Not unexpectedly, there has been some backlash over this confusing data. In his controversial publication *Poverty in Canada*, Christopher Sarlo disagreed that all those living below the poverty line are actually poor. Poverty lines are arbitrarily constructed and the income cutoffs provide more than what is needed to survive. Much of what passes for official poverty, Sarlo contended, confuses being poor with inequality and lack of access to middle class amenities. For Sarlo, true poverty is rare when measured in terms of "stomach stretching" starvation and lack of fundamental necessities. Others have denied the claim that 3 to 5 million Canadians are living in poverty. This figure, they argue, is an exaggeration concocted for self-serving purposes by welfare advocacy and lobby groups. Moreover, measures such as the low-income cutoff point were designed in such a way that even visible progress would not necessarily lead to any discernible drop in numbers. Still others dispute how the figures for poverty are tabulated. Raw figures are based on pretax incomes and ignore the income-reducing aspects of tax law. Also overlooked is the contribution of income-in-kind, such as free dental care or subsidized housing, that welfare recipients receive. Factoring in parent-supported university students and investment-rich seniors also distorts the picture.

The political nature of these number games should be self-evident. Those whose livelihood depends on the presence of poverty have a vested interest in inflating the numbers of the poor. Other interests would like nothing better than to reduce the number of official poor in Canada for self-serving reasons. The current figures are so grossly inflated, they contend, that they make the government look derelict in meeting its responsibilities—to the detriment of its international reputation. Conversely, a reduction in absolute numbers can be seen as part of a wider government strategy for reducing the deficit through the elimination of social programs. In other words, the government has been accused of trying to define the poor out of existence. The net result is a hardening of public attitudes towards poor people as a social problem, accompanied by cut-backs in government welfare spending and a gradual demonization of the poor as lazy freeloaders and a burden on Canadian taxpayers (Mitchell 1997).

Still, the reality of poverty cannot be brushed off no matter how it is defined. People who lack the necessities of life suffer in obscurity while scholars and statisticians fiddle with measures of poverty that have little bearing on producing positive outcomes. But the poor are people, not just a problem. Up to one child in five faces a higher than average risk of poor physical and mental health, higher infant mortality rates, and higher rates of delinquency and school drop-out. Children's ability to learn is affected by poverty-related hunger, violence, illness, domestic problems, and deprivation (Galt and Cernetig 1997). Children whose parents are on welfare or unemployment lose focus and become easily distracted. They also are subject to substance abuse. Debates about who really qualifies as poor merely divert attention from real needs and the reality of the problem, in effect exacerbating the situation through neglect and default rather than through misdeed and expediency.

Explaining Poverty Sociologically

Initiatives to reduce poverty are thwarted by the popular attitude that the poor are poor because they are idle and prefer hand-outs. The poor are responsible for their own plight, so this line of thinking goes, since individuals are in control of their destiny. This mentality of assigning primacy to personal responsibility is consistent with a conservative, anti-government mindset. Government interventions such as pay equity or employment equity are decried for lowering standards while interfering with the free play of market forces. Welfare, in turn, is accused of perpetuating the very conditions—including irresponsibility and addiction— that it is supposed to eradicate.

Is poverty a cultural response to circumstances in which individuals are located? Proponents of the culture of poverty thesis contend that the poor are poor because of their socialization into a lifestyle. A corresponding set of beliefs and attitudes are internalized, often at odds with mainstream definitions of success and achievement. Those immersed in a culture of poverty are not only hindered by different income levels and cultural resources, but stung by low levels of self-confidence that are conducive to resignation and fatalism. The failure of poor families to resemble their middle class counterparts is also perceived as a contributing factor. As the culture of poverty takes root, moreover, many relinquish any ability to ever escape its restrictions and constraints. A vicious cycle of deprivation is entrenched instead, consolidating what once may have been a temporary adjustment to dire circumstances.

The relevance of poverty cultures as an explanation continues to be hotly debated. Not everyone agrees with the concept because to do so would mean taking a victim-blame approach. Debate on this issue has focused on the culture of poverty either as a permanent lifestyle or as a situational adjustment to exceptional circumstances. There is no definitive answer regarding the overlap between the culture of poverty and mainstream values. Are poverty values fundamentally at odds with the dominant culture or are they simply variations on the mainstream, but incompletely expressed because of diminished confidence or skills to put them into practice?

Above all we must entertain the possibility that poverty stems from social structures. It is a chronic feature of a society in which differences in wealth, power, and status are institutionalized and enforced. The interplay of racism and discriminatory barriers, including systemic bias and pervasive double standards, continues to impoverish members of society. The logic of capitalism, with its creation of winners and losers, also serves as an inhibiting factor. In other words, the loss of jobs and the absence of opportunities are not always the fault of individuals, but implicit in capitalist economies and global market forces. Not unexpectedly, perhaps, the poor are turning their backs on traditional paths towards upward mobility. In part this is because many blue-collar industries are vanishing, and in part it is because of a growing disdain for jobs defined as demeaning (Wrong 1992).

The conclusion is disheartening but inescapable. In a country with such promise and wealth, we cannot be entirely surprised by growing condemnation of Canada for its singular lack of progress in battling poverty. Policy changes in the past decade have further eroded Canada's safety net for the poor. A political commitment to pare away a comprehensive social security system has dulled the political will to improve the position of low-income earners. No less troubling is the obsession with deficit reduction in the name of global competitiveness, even at the expense of long-cherished social programs. At a time when downsizing and plant closures are more the rule than the exception, it becomes increasingly unrealistic to blame the poor for their predicament. Perhaps it is time to hold the affluent and powerful accountable for actions that render Canadians expendable and keep them mired in poverty.

EDUCATION AND SCHOOLING: PROBLEMS AND CHALLENGES

All societies must socialize their children for participation in adult life, yet the means for achieving this goal are varied. Indigenous societies evolved without formal arrangements for education and schooling, relying instead on informal socialization procedures such as parental or peer instruction. Opposed to this are urban-industrial systems whose formal institutions are characterized by a set of norms, values, and practices; a team of specialists both in the class and out; a specific location for systematic induction; and appropriate equipment and apparatus (Robertson 1987). The universality of formal institutions is now the rule rather than the exception, as a literate population is seen as a precondition for progressive development. Three major functions of schooling and education continue to prevail: to impart knowledge and skills, to prepare for the work world, and to develop socially through good citizenship.

Canada spends a significant proportion of its GDP on formal education. At 8 percent per year, it ranks near the top of industrial countries in the amount spent. Canada devotes more of its GDP to higher education (1.7%) than the OECD average of 1.2 percent or the United States with 1 percent (Editorial, October 1, 1997). The cost of educating Canada's 4.9 million primary and secondary students in 1994–95 was $35 billion or $7186 per student, with about 67 percent of the costs devoted to instruction. Spending varies from a low of $5268 per capita in P.E.I. to a high of $7556 in Ontario and Quebec, with no appreciable difference in the quality of high school students (Dare 1996).

Yet the education system as a principle or practice has come under sustained criticism. In a world convulsed by the dizzying pace and deafening scope of social change, schools are faltering under the pressure to be all things to all people—parent, guardian, moral guidance, social worker, and babysitter (Webber 1994). The external world is changing faster than internal mechanisms can cope with in light of rising expectations and shrinking budgets (Orpwood and Lewington 1995). Education systems are experiencing an identity crisis, no longer sure of their roles and responsibilities in contemporary society, yet resigned to plod along as best they can. Controversies and contradictions abound, many of which detract from public confidence of formal schooling.

No level of education is exempt from scrutiny (Keith 1997). At the primary level, there is growing parental concern over declining educational standards, deteriorating pupil performance levels, laxity in discipline, and learning without the "basics." Parents are worried that students are unschooled in basic literacy skills but awash in pedagogical mumbo-jumbo for bolstering self-esteem and personal creativity. That's fine to a point, they might argue, but how does it prepare children to cope with the demands of an intensely competitive global economy? Others are dispirited by the growing secularization of the school system and have responded by establishing private Christian schools as an alternative. The secondary level is no less prone to recrimination, finger-pointing, and second-guessing. High schools are perceived as little more than dens of violence, alcohol and substance abuse, teenage pregnancy, sexual activity and disease dissemination, racism and right wing recruitment, and overt sexism. Equally worrying is the erosion of respect for custom and defiance of convention or authority in response to peer group pressure.

Even postsecondary institutions are subjected to scrutiny or criticism. Universities are depicted as imperious ivory towers, not only out of touch with business realities and globalizing forces but impervious to the demands of diversity and change. Many lament the deteriorating health of the postsecondary system in light of chronic underfunding, dwindling resources, mounting workloads, inadequately prepared students, and impossible teaching conditions. Others pine for the days when a university degree was a mark of distinction—a proof of achievement—rather than just a rite of passage in the maturation process. Widespread belief in a decline in academic standards has done little to allay fears about the future of the university in terms of role and status (see Berger 1993). Talk of a fiscal crisis camouflages a deeper malaise, namely, a crisis of identity as elitist assumptions jostle with the demands of democratization and career concerns supersede a commitment to higher learning (Price 1993).

Education in Crisis

There is little doubt that our education system is in trouble. The shift from old forms of schooling to new ideas about education has created internal turmoil. It also has exposed how ambiguity and paradox are inherent within this increasingly contested system, in effect creating the basis for either paralysis by analysis or creative growth. These paradoxes are shown to reflect and reinforce the mounting crisis over education with respect to identity, roles, objectives, and responsibilities. Many of these dilemmas are neither superficial nor transitory, but chronic and embedded, yet resistant to facile solutions. The magnitude and scope of these contradictions are subject to diverse interpretations, depending on the perspective, context, or vision.

Social equality or class reproduction

Education has long been endorsed as an instrument for social equality. Those with education and credentials were endowed with the resources for social mobility and economic security. Yet the educational system may perpetuate inequities (Sleeter 1991; Giroux 1996). Education and schooling do not resolve or redress inequities; more often than not they intensify patterns of inequality related to class, family expectations, cultural background, language competence, teacher attitudes, and peer group influences (Robertson 1980; Macionis, Clarke, and Gerber 1994). Patterns of inequality may be manifestly obvious, as in the relationship between teachers and students; alternately, they can be rendered invisible because of "hidden agendas" in curricula and classrooms. Inequality can also be reflected in the transmission of mainstream cultural values and social patterns supportive of the status quo. The net effect of this conservative force culminates in the perpetuation rather than elimination of pale male privilege. That alone should remind us that schooling and education do not exist in a vacuum; they prevail within the context of capitalist expansion and bureaucratic welfarism (Bowles and Gintis 1976).

Social mobility or dominant ideology

For the disadvantaged, public education represents the one legitimate hope of escaping poverty and powerlessness (Darder 1990). Yet many minority students continue to underachieve at schools (Giroux 1996). Attempts to answer why often stigmatize minority students as the culprits. Responsibility is "individualized" by laying blame on genetic inferiority or cultural deprivation. Other explanations emphasize social structures as root causes rather than nature or nurture. Inequalities in education are caused by power differences, the pervasiveness of mainstream cultural values, and different opportunity structures. Those pedagogical values and schooling practices related to meritocracy, intelligence testing, teacher expectations, curriculum, and streaming are also seen as structurally suspect. Overtly or systemically, these practices not only condone prevailing power and privilege, but tend to marginalize, silence, and discredit the knowledge of the disprivileged—either by effect or intent (Giroux 1996). Failure to concede the relationship between schooling and society creates a learning environment that is apolitical and unappreciative of how dominant ideology informs minority experiences (Darder 1990).

Emancipation or indoctrination

Education is often touted as the path to liberation. An emphasis on personal growth and social emancipation bestows on education the aura of progress and creative growth. Unfortunately the opposite appears equally true. Too much of what passes for education or schooling is neither creative nor progressive, but a process both inflexible and bureaucratic, at odds with the fast-paced demands of a hyper-technological era (Orpwood and Lewington 1995). As expressed in Robertson (1987, 383), "Not all schooling is educational. Much of it is mere qualification earning . . . ritualistic, tedious, suffused with anxieties, destructive of curiosities, and imagination; in short, anti-educational." In the place of small intimate environments are sprawling bureaucratic organizations where routine and regulation prevail in pursuit of efficiency and standardization. Students, parents, and teachers are expected to abide by ministry decisions even when educational bureaucracies are remote and removed from local concerns and needs (Orpwood and Lewington 1995). Parental involvement is encouraged in theory, but discouraged in practice for fear of disrupting the smooth implementation of board policy. Lip service to the creative and the critical is betrayed by the harsh realities of authority, dogma, routine, conformity, and cost-cutting. Students are sorted into categories for placement from advanced to basic; teachers are increasingly specialized and excessively accredited; curricula reflect philosophies of senior administration or popular pedagogies; administrative convenience supersedes student needs, credentials prevail over learning and have little relation to intelligence or parental concerns; and procedures are standardized to ensure order and predictability. The fact that educational authorities are aware of these flaws, yet appear unwilling to or incapable of addressing the issues in any substantial fashion—notwithstanding constant mantras about empowerment or partnership— attests to the power of inertia in defence of the status quo.

Enlightenment or Western dogma

Education is seen as a repository of everything noble and enlightened about Western society. Schools are expected to transmit core values and beliefs, both implicitly and explicitly, as part of the overall socialization process. Yet something has to give when local schools diversify because of demographic, social, or political changes. Can schools move over and create "cultural space" for minorities with respect to content, styles, and objectives without forsaking internal coherence and operational integrity? Answers are mixed. Educational institutions appear capable of incorporating diversity when superficial or unthreatening. They are much less successful in proposing how we "live together with our differences" when these differences challenge core values and time-honoured practices. That schools have not really addressed the issue of "deep diversity" in any meaningful fashion—and perhaps are unlikely to do so at times of budgetary constraints—does not bode well for the health and survival of the system.

Anti-racist education versus multicultural education

Schools have become demographically diverse as a result of robust immigration. Coping with this diversity has elicited a variety of responses normally associated with the label "multicultural education." While different styles of multicultural education exist, including compensatory, enrichment, and empowerment (Fleras and Elliott 1996), each appears committed to the principle of attitude change through exposure and exchange. This cultural focus has exposed multicultural education to criticism as ultimately self-defeating.

Multicultural education has been criticized as an accommodationist strategy rather than a strategy for change or empowerment. Students are co-opted into the system by defusing their anger over exclusion rather than confronting racism and social inequality (Sleeter 1991). Focusing on the cultural in multicultural education not only circumvents the root cause of minority failures, but hastens the transmission of social knowledge from the powerful to the powerless without any major disruption to the system. In other words, a reliance on "culture" rather than on "structure" as a focal point for change is supportive of the educational status quo.

By contrast, an anti-racist approach looks inwards by analyzing schools as part of the problem rather than the solution. Attention is directed at the pervasiveness of racism at all structural levels. Bias in textbook and curricula are examined, as are deep-seated patterns of discrimination involving students, staff, and administration. The "hidden agenda" is unpacked or "deconstructed" to determine how and why the system discriminates against minorities, either by intent or unconsciously. Unlike multicultural education, anti-racist education downplays cultural difference as a key problem; nor is celebrating diversity perceived as a solution to minority educational problems. It is concerned instead with identifying and removing discriminatory barriers, both systemic and personal, rather than promoting cross-cultural understanding. Direct action is employed for isolating and challenging discriminatory practices and improving minority equality and participation. In short, anti-racist education represents a powerful critique of contemporary schooling. Its very potency, however, creates problems of implementation.

Gendered schooling versus ungendering education

It is commonly assumed that a gender bias exists in schooling and education. Female students were objects of discrimination not only because of personal bias by indifferent teachers and bullying males but because of structural factors related to curriculum and testing procedures. Yet statistics indicate a changing picture: there is no shortage of success when measured by access or graduates. Women comprised nearly 54 percent of all university students in 1992 and in 1991–92 accounted for the majority of students in the disciplines of medicine and health, education, fine and applied arts, humanities, agriculture and biology, and social sciences. Thirty percent of the enrolments in mathematics and physical sciences were women, up from 20 percent in 1972–73. Nearly 20 percent of engineering enrolments were women, compared with only 3 percent as recently as 1972–73. This gender parity becomes more evident if we break it down by age. Thirty-four percent of men over age 45 have a postsecondary degree, compared with only 27 percent of women over age 45. That discrepancy may partly account for the 60 percent wage gap in this age group. By contrast, 21 percent of women under age 25 have postsecondary degrees, while only 16 percent of men under age 25 do. Not surprisingly, there is little or no wage gap for this group.

Process-Oriented Versus Outcome-Oriented

The process of democratization has trickled down to primary schools. The rigidity and regimentation of the past has been replaced by an accommodative system that is more diverse, receptive to freedom of choice, and amenable to reform. Emphasis has shifted from an outcome-oriented, curriculum-driven schooling to a process-oriented, "child-driven" system. Process-oriented schooling aims to bolster individual self-esteem rather than competition for high grades through standardized testing in a concerted effort to improve from within, develop critical thinking skills, cultivate a potential for applied knowledge, and instil a cooperative work ethic through teamwork. Achievement of these goals requires an environment that is nongraded, expands the limits of tolerance, encourages creative play, and is modified to reflect individual progress. In brief, the focus is on the process of personal development of the "whole child" at a noncompetitive pace consistent with a pupil's needs, interests, and capacities.

Not everyone is pleased with this pedagogical shift. For critics, a process-driven approach not only short-changes a student's marketability upon graduation, but can also hinder Canada's global competitiveness by shrinking the pool of qualified personnel. Proposed instead is an overhaul from top to bottom, including a system accountable to parents and community and the use of standardized testing to monitor and evaluate students. Most initiatives involve a commitment to the goals of results, competition, standardization, and accountability. Whatever a child learns must produce a measurable outcome; it must also be (a) subject to objective evaluation in a manner that satisfies parents and business, (b) amenable to monitoring by authorities, and (c) conducted within clear standards that apply to all children. Without such standards of meritocracy, parents argue, there are no assurances that schools and teachers are doing the job expected of them. The issue has come to a head with passage of Bill 160 in early December 1997; the Bill sought to consolidate central authority over educational policy and funding, but not before a two-week, illegal walkout by Ontario's 126 000 teachers.

Democratization or massification

The democratization of education has had its share of success. Universities have become more inclusive by accommodating the historically disadvantaged, including members of the working class, women, and people of colour. Yet success has unleashed many of the problems associated with underfunding and overcrowding (Keith 1997). Expansion and diversification of postsecondary education complicated efforts to meet the educational and training needs of contemporary society. Without a fundamental rethinking, postsecondary education has floundered in its quest for legitimacy and identity in the midst of confusion and uncertainty. Failure of university graduates to find adequate employment is but one of the unintended results of the democratization of postsecondary schooling. The university degree has been devalued by expanding supply at the expense of demand. The devaluation of the moral underpinnings of society has been no less costly: egalitarian democratization is accused of sabotaging deference to authority, esteem for hard-earned accomplishments, reverence for heritage and knowledge of the past, a commitment to rationality and science, and a willingness to assert the superiority of one idea or standard over another (Henry III 1994).

This massification of schooling has had a profound effect on higher education. Pedagogical styles have not kept up with student skills or outlooks (Giroux 1996). Pedagogical techniques that worked well eight centuries ago when the professor owned the only book on campus are hard to justify in multimedia society (McSherry 1993). Overcrowded classes and overworked professors have resulted in a diminished capacity to deduce, integrate, and apply. In its place is a tedious ritual entailing memorized input and scheduled regurgitation, an exercise not dissimilar in consequences to intellectual bulimia. Equally offputting is the fact that there is more knowledge in the community than in schools, yet schools remain devoted to pumping out more information instead of conveying wisdom. This gap between school and society may prove a deterrent for students in the future (Schlechty 1994).

Universities are in crisis not only because of budgets or high enrolments; rather, they are experiencing a crisis of *identity* because they are no longer sure of what is expected of them in confusing and changing times (Price 1993). In trying to be responsive to everything, they may well end up being relevant to nobody. This ambiguity is encapsulated in debates over postsecondary institutions as enlightened sites of *higher learning*, as empowering instruments for *social action*, and as credential mills for *career success*. The *legitimacy* of status and role are under question, in other words, as are conventional rules and relationships both within and in relationship to society at large. For institutions that historically have enjoyed the equivalent of diplomatic immunity from public scrutiny, the call to accountability and adjustment is as disruptive as it is dismaying.

Ivory towers under siege

Universities were once the most pampered and privileged of all institutions (Economist 1993/1994). Ivory towers served to buffer universities from public scrutiny while the ivy-covered walls muted any mutterings of criticism. They were recipients of limitless cash from governments who revered them as engines of economic growth, social equality, cultural sophistication, and political democracy. Intellectuals flocked to them as sites of enlightenment and research. Taxpayers didn't mind the extra taxation; after all, universalizing access to postsecondary education provided avenues of social mobility for their offspring.

Universities are now under siege from various sources: they are distrusted by governments as an expensive luxury in a no-frill economy, lampooned by politicians for perceived excesses in political correctness and pandering to minorities, ignored by decision-makers as irrelevant to intellectual life in a world of think-tanks and information technologies, criticized by the private sector for ignoring the real world, and taken to task for trying to be all things to everybody. Rising costs and declining revenues have led to calls to rethink the postsecondary enterprise. New faculty are not being hired, contract workers are replacing full-time faculty, and students are shouldering an increased burden of operating costs by way of spiralling tuition fees. Students continue to flock to universities (from 8.3 percent of Canadians age 19 to 24 in 1975 to 18.6 percent in 1995), despite tuition fees that rose by 86 percent between 1983 and 1995, while the ratio of government grants received by universities per dollar of student fees dropped from \$5.02 in 1975 to \$2.97 in 1995 (Mitchell 1997). Universities are accused of being "boring" places because of aging faculty whose refusal to move over and make space for "new blood" diminishes the credibility of professors (Carey 1995). Some criticize university faculty and administration as spineless cowards and "cringing conformists" who cave in to multiculturalist cant at the expense of academic freedom (Furedy 1995). Others accuse universities of not being sufficiently diverse and accommodative (Fleras 1995), as factories in which faculty "manage" while student-drones "do." Or as put by David Suzuki (1987, 115–116), contemporary universities are courting disaster by resembling "an assembly line where individuals become ciphers funnelled through the system to justify university budgets" (see also Illich 1971). Still others bemoan the massification of a once elitist institution. Others still are suspicious of growing links between business and the ivory towers.

Business links—boom or bane?

The increasingly close links between business and education are subject to diverse interpretations (Lewington 1997). Debate rages about the mutual benefits of such a "partnership" between boardroom and classroom. For cash-strapped universities, these links provide a much-required dose of relief from relentless government underfunding. Businesses, in turn, look to universities for connections, personnel transfers, and contract work arrangements. Privatization continues to infiltrate universities, ranging from ads in washrooms to corporate donations to foreign buyouts of campus bookstores (Klein 1997). There are lingering fears over loss of academic freedom because of unwarranted interference from business agendas. Faculty in the humanities and social sciences may bristle at perceived favouritism towards revenue-generating, high-tech, skills-oriented programs such as engineering or the "hard" sciences. Still, all signs are pointing to a growing consolidation of industrial-educational links. If business-friendly universities such as the University of Waterloo are any indication, these bonds will continue to flourish and pave the way for redefining the role of universities in a globally competitive society.

Groping for a Solution

The system of schooling and education has come under siege from all quarters. This barrage of criticism indicates a need to rethink the label of "failure." Who says schools are failing, why are they saying this, and on what grounds are these accusations being made (Barlow and Robertson 1993)? The "lets-solve-it-through-schools" mentality tends to inflate the importance of education as an agent of socialization and underestimate the significance of the media and peer groups as forces for change or conformity (Robertson 1984). Such a mindset also allows primary caregivers to wriggle out of responsibilities and schools are scapegoated for failures that rightfully belong to parents. Lastly, education is being blamed for the miscalculations of Canadian business when it fumbles opportunities to compete globally. Rightly or wrongly, only one thing is certain: criticism will continue to escalate because of the impossibly high standards expected of education by a demanding and diverse public. Rising expectations in an era of shrinking resources will keep the heat on schooling.

The education system is praised or criticized in almost sweeping terms. Yet the system is neither homogeneous nor monolithic, but contradictory, ambiguous, and subject to internal dissonance (see Stone 1993). Such a perspective reinforces the notion of education as a "battleground" or "contested site," with progressive and reactionary forces aligned opposite each other. Schools espouse democratic values, yet routinely revoke democracy in everyday practice. They encourage learning but establish structures that inhibit rather than stimulate (Sleeter 1991). Schools are expected to promote equality of access, participation, and outcomes, yet the opposite is likely. Diversity is embraced, but differences are overridden in pursuit of national identity and social integration (Macionis, Clarke, and Gerber 1994). In short, schools are designed for permanence and stability instead of change, for social reproduction of the status quo rather than the reconstruction of social reality. Critics of education must acknowledge this distinction between what is and what ought to be. They should also concede that not every social problem can be corrected by official action, and, in cases where problems are deeply embedded within the educational system, attempted solutions may exacerbate the situation and create new imbalances.

SUMMARY

1. The reality of inequality in Canada cannot be disputed. Inequality can be measured in terms of the following indicators: income, education, occupation, and power. Rather than being randomly distributed across the population, inequality tends to cluster around the poles of class, race and ethnicity, gender, and region.

2. Class, gender, race and ethnicity, and region are interpreted as social constructs that help to explain and justify patterns of inequality in society.

3. Inequality refers to the unequal distribution of scarce resources in society. Preferential access to the good things in life (wealth, status, and power) is often related to a person's race, ethnicity, gender, class, and region. While the different dimensions of inequality (class, race, gender, and region) can be analyzed as mutually exclusive, in reality they are interlinked, thus inflating their cumulative impact on persons or groups.

4. Inequality can be best explained through sociological approaches that emphasize social structure. It is "wired" into the system rather than the fault of individuals or cultural circumstances. Appeals to biology or psychology are not highly regarded as explanatory systems. Nor is there much enthusiasm for a culture of poverty theory that argues that the poor are poor because they are socialized into a lifestyle with a corresponding set of beliefs and attitudes that reinforces their marginal status.

5. Not everyone agrees that inequality is a social problem. According to functionalists, there is nothing inherently "wrong" with a system of unequal entitlement. Inequality under these conditions is legitimate as long as scarce positions are open to everyone on the basis of ability, talent, and unfettered competition. Inequality becomes a problem only when there is outside interference (government) with the natural sorting-out process.

6. Conflict theorists disagree with the functionalist notion that inequalities are necessary and normal in complex, achievement-oriented societies. Not only are gross inequities inconsistent with fundamental principles of justice, but inequality is not normal or necessary to the human condition but intrinsic only to profit motive systems.

7. One of the key dimensions of inequality is social class. The concept of class is given different treatments by Marx and Weber, and these differences provide a basis for various classifications employing criteria of wealth, status, and power.

8. Racial and ethnic difference have long been portrayed as key attributes in systems of inequality. Evidence suggests that some minorities (such as German-Canadians) are not penalized because of their ethnicity. Others, including most visible minorities, suffer from discrimination along different lines.

9. There is a critical distinction between the old and the new vertical mosaic. Under the old mosaic, attaining equality for ethnic groups meant eliminating prejudice and cultural impediments. By contrast, under the new mosaic equality is achieved through institutional accommodation, anti-racism, and the removal of structural barriers.

10. The concept of equality can be examined not only as a solution to an age-old problem, but as a problem in its own right. By comparing the concepts of equal opportunity and equal outcomes, we can develop an entirely new way of looking at equality as a means of dealing with radical diversity. The emphasis on outcome-based equality, with its

focus on consequences, context, and collective rights, is at variance with conventional definitions involving formal, individual equality.

11. Regional inequality in Canada can be analyzed by asking why people in some parts of Canada own more, earn more, and use more than those in other regions. It is important in this respect to understand the origin of regional disparities and the reasons for their persistence, despite government expenditures to achieve parity. It is also important to understand the politicization of regional differences through grievances and protest movements.

12. Regional economic underdevelopment cannot be fixed by sending money. Federal strategy for Atlantic Canada is based on education for jobs in the new communications technology.

13. Poverty exists in Canada. However, there is considerable disagreement about what it is, who is poor, how poverty is to be measured, and what we are to do about it. These debates are important but they also have the effect of creating "paralysis by analysis" if answers are not forthcoming.

14. How we measure poverty is more than a statistical exercise, says Richard Shillington of the Campaign 2000 project, but reflects who we are as a community. For some, only absolute poverty (insufficient food, etc.) is legitimate poverty. For others, any substantial disadvantage relative to the norm constitutes real poverty. Statistics Canada's low-income cut off point, which identifies those who spend 56% of their income on necessities, falls in between absolute and relative poverty.

15. To understand the problem of poverty, it is important to focus on how it is defined and on the politics associated with the definitional process. Relative and absolute definitions of poverty provide different readings on the magnitude and scope of poverty in Canada. No matter how it is defined, efforts to curtail poverty in Canada have relied on government programs, to limited avail.

16. A crisis in education is looming across Canada. Efforts to resolve the crisis have rekindled mounting unease about the "functions" of schooling in a world of change, diversity, and uncertainty. A polarization of opinions solidifies a view of schooling and education as contested and challenged by opposing sectors.

17. Universities are experiencing nothing short of an identity crisis. Part of this crisis can be attributed to a paradigm clash between higher learning and social action on the one hand and career success on the other.

18. A key theme in this chapter is the espousal of sociology as a discipline concerned with studying the social dimensions of inequality, and how this relationship between the social and society is defined, created, manifest, sustained, challenged, or transformed by way of official policy or popular resistance.

C h a p t e r

6

GENDER

DID YOU KNOW?

- In 1992–93, the majority of full-time university students were women: 53 percent of the undergraduate population (up from 43 percent in 1972–73), 46 percent of full-time master's students (up from 27 percent in 1972–73), and 35 percent of full-time doctoral students (up from 19 percent in 1972–73).

- At community colleges, while women accounted for 96 percent of those enrolled full-time in secretarial sciences, 90 percent of those in the educational and counselling service program, and 89 percent of those studying nursing, they accounted for a mere 12 percent of enrolment in engineering and other technological programs, 30 percent of those in mathematics and computer science, and less than a third (32%) of those in natural science and primary industry programs.

- Of all trade apprenticeship programs with over 3000 registered apprentices in 1992, only hairdressing and cooking programs had significant female enrolments.

- In 1993 the average earnings of women university graduates working full-time all year ($40 670) were only 75 percent of those of male graduates.

- According to the National Council of Welfare, 84 percent of women in the 1990s (an increase of 13.5 percent since 1979) can expect to spend a significant period of their adult lives having to independently support themselves and their children.

THE PROBLEM

The June 1993 election of Kim Campbell as Conservative party leader and, shortly after (by ascension), as the first female prime minister of Canada, seemed for some observers evidence of the equality of men and women in our society. Even though newspaper and magazine coverage of the Conservative party leadership campaign had earlier directed attention to Campbell's "mesmerizing" eye colour (green) and "exquisite shoulders" while viewing such trivia as irrelevant in reporting on her male competitors, her election still seemed to suggest that sexism, discrimination against women or men on the basis of their sex, was absent in Canada in all but its vestigial forms.

For this reason, some people found it puzzling that Audrey MacLaughlin, then-leader of the New Democratic party, commented that she would have preferred the election of a man who was concerned with "women's issues" to the election of a woman who was not. Many of us found the identification of "women's issues" (day care, birth control, violence against women) as somehow distinct from important Canadian social issues (the economy, crime, international relations) intelligible but nevertheless vexatious. Why, within our supposedly egalitarian society and *despite* Campbell's election, are issues such as pay equity, poverty, reproductive rights, child care, and the right to protection from physical and sexual violence understood to be "women's issues" rather than fundamental "human rights issues"? And why did Campbell's identification as, variously, "pro-feminist" or "anti-feminist" represent a continuing issue of contention and debate?

Admittedly, we may seem overly concerned with what may simply be the loose usage of terms that can have a technical sense. However, our fascination stems from the fact that we see language as centrally implicated in any discussion of what can be considered socially problematic behaviour. Language, and its proper usage, is important because it allows for the dissemination of a society's ideology on gender roles and stereotypes. Thus, if in the winter of 1991 REAL Women of Canada gleefully reported that 66 percent of women did not consider themselves to be feminists (Reality 1991, 1), we feel compelled to ask how the word "feminist" is defined in the popular imagination. Has it become simply a poorly understood "sneer word" in Canada, with "feminists" assumed to possess, as Salamon and Robinson (1991, 26) suggest, unlovely and unloveable characteristics? In their research, they found that feminists were depicted by undergraduate respondents at the University of Alberta as "arrogant," "masculine," "butch," "men haters," "lesbians," "ugly women," and "sexually frustrated." These terms suggest how gender roles are an outcome of a process of judgment and evaluation that distinguishes certain forms of behaviour as unacceptable or inappropriate (Rowland 1986).

The international research of Williams and Best (1990) has noted the high degree of pancultural generality in stereotypes of men and women. Three qualities were discovered to be female-associated in all of the 25 countries they studied: sentimental, submissive, and superstitious. Six qualities were found to be male-associated in all the countries surveyed: adventurous, dominant, forceful, independent, masculine, and strong. In 24 of 25 countries, additional "female" descriptors were affectionate, dreamy, feminine, and sensitive; additional "male" qualities were aggressive, autocratic, daring, enterprising, robust, and stern (75–76). Overall, "the characteristics associated with men were stronger and more active than the characteristics associated with women" (303).

The content of these stereotypes is noteworthy for several reasons. First, *gender stereotypes*, like other stereotypes, are "belief systems containing generalizations about the characteristics of groups of persons" (Williams and Best 1990, 16). The processes underlying *gender stereotyping* share with other forms of stereotyping three characteristics: "the categorization of persons, a consensus on attributed traits, and a discrepancy between attributed and actual traits" (Secord and Backman 1967, 67). However, as Hawkins and Tiedman (1975, 184) note, "a 'stereotype' commonly implies *incorrect, illegitimate* application of categories and labels." If the content of the stereotype is accepted in an uncritical manner, we may assume incorrectly that all men are, for example, aggressive, and all women are weak, rather than recognize the wide variations possible among persons of both sexes.

Second, if the power of a stereotype rests on little more than the reaffirmation of traditional thought, the stereotype may become an informal source of social control, shaping our attitudes and fashioning motives, perceptions, and reactions. Thus, if the characteristics associated with men and women in the Williams and Best survey support a traditional division of labour with women charged with the primary care of their own and others' children, while men "naturally" assume authority in the workplace, the characteristics associated with men and women may be the *consequence* rather than the *cause* of their disparate social histories. Moreover, as Mackie (1991, 28) notes, "gender stereotype content reflects the fact . . . that every known society esteems males more than females." Accordingly, stereotypes may contain the germinating seeds for a self-fulfilling prophecy whereby the traditional division of labour is justified with reference to what it serves to create.

Within contemporary Canadian society there are numerous illustrations of how, through the unreflective use of language, we characterize many things as gender-related that are not necessarily so. We recognize the terms "good mother" and "unfit mother" as common evaluative descriptors of women who have children and understand "mothering" to encompass a wide range of nurturing behaviour. In contrast, a "good father" may be more narrowly associated with a man's ability to fulfil the role of a "good provider" (Bernard 1981), while the term "unfit father" seems forced and contrived. As David (1985, 22) has pointed out, "Motherhood is a social concept, fatherhood barely recognised. To father a child refers only to the act of procreation." Similarly, indignation over the actions of "sexually irresponsible" unwed mothers or "promiscuous" female "nymphomaniacs" seems to spring trippingly off the tongue. The behaviour of "promiscuous" males, on the other hand, is not evaluated as negatively. Accordingly, what emerges from an examination of contemporary Canadian ideologies of gender may suggest a more limited and limiting view of male and female gender roles than we might like to admit.

The term "role" refers, among other things, to the set of expectations placed on the incumbent of a given position within a society or community. In part, the purpose of roles is to reduce uncertainty and anxiety over what one is "supposed" to do in most situations, thus freeing a person to concentrate on other aspects of living. But this convenience of having a cultural road map to follow can at the same time become a tyranny of constraints in the form of reduced options. As we shall see in this chapter, both women and men have been confined with regard to "acceptable" gender role behaviour. Those who seek to challenge, through word or deed, the legitimacy of the confinements are usually punished in ways that range from mild censure to ostracism to more severe forms of social rebuke.

While modern Canadian law no longer endorses the right of a husband to murder his disobedient or adulterous wife, denies women the right to vote or sit in Parliament, or excludes women from institutions of higher learning on the basis of their sex, it would be presumptuous to suppose that it is only the most violent and exclusionary measures that succeed in enforcing the confines of gender. Informal social controls, such as linguistic commands that cue a woman to "Act like a lady!" or prompt a man to "Be a man!" serve as continual reminders that within our society, norms surrounding gender are both *proscriptive* (telling us what not to do) and *prescriptive* (telling us what we should do).

TWO PERSPECTIVES: THE MAXIMALIST AND MINIMALIST

Are men and women essentially different? For some, the answer is "obviously" yes. According to many Freudian psychoanalysts, conservative Christians, and, somewhat ironically, cultural feminists, men and women have different talents, capabilities, and capacities, and these differences should be recognized, embraced, and rewarded. Although the root cause of these differences may be variously attributed to divine ordination, biology, or social conditioning, common to all is the idea that males and females are *essentially* different. Accordingly, people who favour these approaches forward a *maximalist perspective* (Stimpson 1983), which posits that men and women are unalterably different in their fundamental natures.

For example, resting their arguments on a firm belief in the innate and immutable nature of gender, anti-feminists past and present have argued that the traditional roles are not socially created and maintained but rather biologically and divinely ordained. According to Phyllis Schlafly's *The Power of the Positive Woman,* the superiority of males intellectually and physically "must be recognized as part of the plan of the Divine Architect for the survival of the human race through the centuries" (in Marshall 1989). In like fashion, in *The Inevitability of Patriarchy*, Goldberg (1973) maintains that male dominance is physiologically based (that is, that higher testosterone levels in males give them an aggressive advantage) and that "it is the feminists' folly to believe that new knowledge will render the biological factor any less determinative."

For others, however, the assumption of fundamental differences and dichotomous models of gender is inadequate. Thus, cautioning that "dichotomy is the usual pathway to vulgarization" (Gould 1984), many theorists subscribe to the *minimalist* model as the more accurate way of viewing men and women. According to Epstein (1988, 25), this perspective stresses the essential similarity of the two sexes and "ascribes observed differences in behaviour to a social control system that prescribes and proscribes specific behaviours for women and men."

The positions held on the differences or similarities of men and women are not simply of philosophical interest; as Bourdieu has observed, "[t]he division of reality is a serious struggle" (in Epstein 1988, 5). Because gender is a fundamental *ascribed* status in our society, the postulated differences or similarities are of profound importance. Our understanding of the reality of gender serves as an overarching framework in which we view and evaluate the situation of men and women in society. That is, our understanding of "social problems" in relation to gender is derived from our understanding of the fundamental nature of gender. Gender ideologies serve to fix attention on certain aspects of the social landscape while effectively obscuring others. In this manner, there is a specific connection between what is conceived to be the "reality" of gender, and the ideas and modes of thought that are espoused in relation to the social problems associated with it.

For example, for critics who subscribe to a maximalist perspective, the most pressing social problems associated with gender today stem from women rejecting their "ideal" gender role. Thus, decrying the rise of the "New Age woman" as resulting in a multiplicity of social ills, best-selling Canadian author William Gairdner (1992) describes "family-hating, man-hating, tradition-hating" (118) radical feminists as "the new barbarians of modern society" (302) whose "stock in trade is to lobby for radical changes in our legal, economic, and social/moral systems in order to implement an agenda designed to overturn every aspect of traditional life" (116). Claiming that "all forms of modern feminism rest upon a few simplistic and erroneous notions," Gairdner maintains that "there is a [sic] overwhelming evidence from virtually every field of study that biology is destiny, and that all civilizations, including our own until now, have structured social life accordingly; and it is an accepted fact that we are manifestly a biological species through and through, and that the lives of all biological mammals are species- and gender-specific" (305). Similarly, the comments of Professor Gordon Freeman, in a letter to advice columnist Ann Landers, reiterate this message clearly (see Case 6-1).

In contrast, those who adhere to a minimalist model view the problem of gender within our society in quite different terms. For minimalists, an appeal to resurrect a beatific past in which men and women contentedly engaged in "complementary" rather than equal roles is misguided and suggests only the romantic idealization of some past epoch. Moreover,

---

CASE 6-1   University of Alberta Prof Responds to Student

Dear Ann Landers,
I am a professor of chemistry at the University of Alberta in Edmonton, and have taught about 2000 pre-med students during the last 33 years. I would like to respond to the 20-year-old college student whose life has been wonderfully trouble-free and who now has a secret death wish—wanting to die while she still has "all the chips in her corner."

You are planning to enter medical school where the acceptance process is often arbitrary, and the competition is somewhat cutthroat and unethical. After 20 years of successes, you are afraid of losing face and would rather die before your first failure. Everybody falls down from time to time, and the strong are the ones who always get up again. Our fear of failure is largely a fear that the image other people have of us will be diminished. However, the most important image is the one we have of ourselves, warts and all.

If you have high self-esteem, an occasional failure won't reduce it. So, pick another path. Plan to marry and keep marriage vows "until death do us part." Then be a stay-at-home mom. Your children will not be, as you are, manic about superficial success and wishing to die for fear of failure. Their success will be in valuing themselves because that is what you will have taught them.

Gordon Freeman

***

Dear Professor Freeman,
Thank you for a unique response. Thousands of people wrote about that letter, but your approach was different from all the others . . . .

Source: *The Edmonton Journal*, January 6, 1992: D2.

they might also note that although the concept of "modern" suggests an abrupt discontinuity between present and past forms of socially acceptable "masculine" and "feminine" behaviour, this in itself is highly debatable. They would point out that despite whatever progress has been made in the past 30 years, societies around the world—including Canada—are still in the main patriarchal and women in the main are still oppressed.

In this respect it is worth noting that a 1993 United Nations report concluded that no industrialized country in the world treats women the same as men. Globally, women make up just over 10 percent of the world's parliamentary representatives and less than 4 percent of cabinet ministers or other positions of authority. In the words of the UN report, women are the "world's largest excluded group. Even though they make up half the adult population and often contribute much more than their share to society, inside and outside the home, they are frequently excluded from positions of power" (in Black 1993).

ANALYZING THE PROBLEM

The Biological Background

At the moment of conception, when the male sperm and female egg unite to form a zygote, the process of sexual differentiation begins. Sperm carries either an X or a Y sex chromosome; the egg always has an X sex chromosome. Normally the zygote has a total of 46 chromosomes; 23 from the sperm and 23 from the egg; a 44-plus-XX chromosome pattern is the usual genetic code for a female; a 44-plus-XY pattern is the genetic code for a male. Otherwise, in the initial weeks following conception, male and female embryos are anatomically identical.

During the fifth and sixth weeks of pregnancy, primitive gonads form; depending on future events, they will develop into either testes or ovaries. Male testes and female ovaries are homologous sex organs, meaning that they develop from the same embryonic tissue, known as the primordial gonad. What triggers the differentiation of the primordial gonad into testes remains unclear at present. It was long believed that male differentiation and testes development were dependent on the presence of a chemical substance controlled by the Y chromosome, "H-Y antigen" (Wachtel 1979). However, researchers currently focus on the contribution of the molecule SKY (sex-determining region of the Y), which is activated 35 days following conception and is now believed to trigger a series of events that lead to the masculinization of various tissues, including the transformation of the primordial gonads into testes (McLaren 1990). Based on current understanding, if SKY is not present, the primordial gonad will differentiate into ovaries at a later point in fetal development.

Sexual differentiation then takes place on three levels: in the internal sex structures, in the external genitals, and in the brain; this process is largely controlled by hormonal mechanisms (Money and Ehrhardt 1972). By the eighth week of pregnancy, the male testes begin to secrete two products: the "Mullerian duct inhibiting substance," which causes the Mullerian ducts to virtually disappear rather than form female internal organs, and androgens—particularly testosterone—that stimulate the development of the Wolffian ducts into male reproductive sex features such as the epididymis, vas deferens, seminal vesicles, and prostate gland.

Unlike the process of masculinization, female sexual differentiation is not dependent on the introduction of hormones or a "feminizing agent." Typically, ovaries develop at about the twelfth week of pregnancy; later the Mullerian duct system begins to develop into the uterus, Fallopian tubes, and the inner third of the vagina. Unstimulated by large amounts of testosterone, the Wolffian duct system in the female shrinks into minute fragments. Thus, clear differences in the male and female fetus are observable by the fourteenth week of pregnancy.

Similarly, until the seventh week of development there is little differentiation in external genitals in the male and female fetus. The lack of androgens in the female embryo leads to the development of the clitoris, vulva, and outer portion of the vagina during the seventh to eighth week of pregnancy. During this time, androgen stimulation in the male causes the folds that would develop into the inner vaginal lips of the female to grow together and form the shaft of the penis; the genital tubercle, which in the female develops into the clitoris, becomes the glans of the penis in the male. The labioscrotal swellings differentiate into the scrotum in the male and the outer vaginal lips in the female. Although both the ovaries and the testes first develop within the abdomen of the fetus, the ovaries later move into the pelvis of the female and the testes move into the scrotum of the male.

Research suggests that the presence or absence of androgen "predisposes" or programs the brain to be organized in, respectively, a male or female direction (Plapinger and McEwan 1978; McEwan 1981; MacLusky and Naftolin 1981; Money and Ehrhardt 1972). According to these researchers, this prenatal programming determines the pattern in which the hypothalamus and pituitary glands will function during and after puberty. Thus, women have cyclic sex hormone production, fertility, and menstrual cycles, whereas men have a relatively constant level of sex hormone production. The best-documented structural difference between male and female brains is in the number and location of certain types of nerve cell connections (synapses) in the hypothalamus (Carter and Greenaugh 1979).

The most recent research in this area has directed attention to the fact that the brain is composed of two hemispheres connected by corpus callosum. The separation of the brain into two halves is useful to those who would construct biologically based, dichotomous models of men and women, most especially if it can be established that one hemisphere or the other is more dominant in one sex than in the other. For example, noting that the left hemisphere has been associated with verbal and reasoning ability and the right hemisphere with spatial reasoning and artistic ability, various theorists have suggested that the left and right hemispheres develop differently in males and females. The male brain, they say, is more "lateralized" (that is, more specialized) and the female brain more symmetrical. They also argue that the effect of increased testosterone washing over the male fetus is to somehow produce superior mathematical talents and visual-spatial abilities. However, has the "difference" between men and women now been scientifically established? Not necessarily. Tavris (1992, 48) points out that a parallel exists between nineteenth-century scientists who "kept changing their minds about which *lobe* of the brain accounted for male superiority" and contemporary scientists who evidence similar vacillation over which hemisphere of the brain accounts for male superiority. She notes that when the left hemisphere was considered the "repository of intellect and reason" and the right hemisphere was considered "the sick, bad, crazy side, the side of passion, instincts, criminality and irrationality," men were thought to have left-brain intellectual superiority. However, in the 1960s and 1970s, when scientists began to suspect that the right hemisphere of the brain "was the source of genius and inspiration, creativity and imagination, mysticism and mathematical brilliance," men were thought to possess right-brain specialization.

Scientific inquiries, whether in the natural or social sciences, are not immune to sexist assumptions. Eichler (1984, 20) has noted that, "sexism can enter the research process in at least five ways: i) through the use of sexist language, ii) through the use of sexist concepts, iii) by taking an *androcentric* perspective, iv) through the use of a sexist methodology, and finally, v) through a sexist interpretation of results." In the case of investigations into the biological differences between men and women, we cannot assume a presentation that is necessarily unbiased and nonsexist. Indeed, as Marcel Kinsbourne, a leader in brain hemisphere research, has sombrely remarked, "Under pressure from the gathering momentum of feminism, and perhaps in backlash to it, many investigators seem determined to discover that men and women 'really' are different. It seems that if sex differences (e.g., in lateralization) do not exist, then they have to be invented" (in Tavris 1992, 53).

Theories that posit essential and immutable differences between men and women have obvious implications for the way in which men and women are regarded by themselves and others, the opportunities and social roles considered "fitting" or "inappropriate" for members of one or the other sex, and the extent to which interventionist strategies are thought necessary or desirable. For illustration, let us consider one fairly recent attempt to explain the differing behaviour expected of men and women as well as the implications of this approach.

Sociobiology

First proposed by biologist E.O. Wilson in *Sociobiology: The New Synthesis* (1975), "Sociobiology is the application of evolutionary theory to understanding the social behaviour of animals, including humans" (Barash 1982). Sociobiologists hold that at some point in human evolutionary history, certain forms of behaviour (territoriality, aggressiveness, sexual selection, the double standard, and so on) maximized the reproductive success of the individuals who exhibited them and that such forms became universal in the species by the operation of Darwinian natural selection. Thus, certain social behaviour became coded into the human genotype.

Drawing on numerous examples from insect life, sociobiologists suggest that the fact that women in most societies care for children can be explained using the concept of *parental investment*. Parental investment refers to actions or investments the parent makes with respect to the child that increase the child's chance of survival but cost the parent something. Theoretically, a woman has the greatest investment in the survival of the child because, from the moment of conception, she contributes something that is more precious than the contribution made by the man. Whereas male sperm are "cheap" small cells (there are 300 million sperm in the average male ejaculate, and this number can be replicated in 24 to 48 hours), female eggs are "precious" because a woman produces only one egg per month and the egg is a large cell. Moreover, because a woman invests nine months and her bodily resources in the gestation of the child, it would be "evolutionary insanity" (Shibley-Hyde 1985, 68) for her to relinquish primary responsibility to another after her child is born.

The argument of the "cheap" sperm and the "precious" egg is used to explain, as well as legitimate, the double standard of sexuality; it is evolutionarily adaptive for a man to attempt to impregnate as many women as possible because it increases the likelihood that his genes will contribute to the next generation. However, a woman's promiscuity is discouraged; she must be careful and selective with regard to "mating" if she wants to find the best partner with whom to intermix her genes. With similar logic, the monogamous mating system is touted as producing the greatest likelihood of infant survival. Given that a child is particularly helpless, the presence of two individuals who are pledged to each other is considered genetically adaptive and desirable if the child is to survive. The female orgasm has similarly evolved to hold this dyad together because it sustains the woman's interest in sex during non-ovulation times. Her continuous interest in sex during all phases of the menstrual cycle has ostensibly evolved to solidify the monogamous bond that is favoured for infant survival.

Critics have charged that sociobiology's tenets are less than truly scientific and simply convenient rationalizations for perpetuating the status quo. Thus, Shibley-Hyde (1982) has noted that both the examples given and the theory itself are blatantly androcentric; studies that confirm the masculine superior position are stressed, while those that contradict it are ignored. For example, the female chimpanzee (the chimpanzee is our nearest evolutionary relative) is indiscriminately promiscuous when in estrous, mating with many males. But by and large, sociobiologists, who are otherwise fascinated by questions of evolution, ignore the behaviour of the chimpanzee. Moreover, as Kamin (1985, 78) has remarked, "By restating age-old claims that human nature is fixed and unchangeable, and that efforts to ameliorate social woes by changing the social environment are doomed to fail, sociobiology gives aid and comfort to supporters of the status quo."

Psychoanalytic Theory: "Anatomy Is Destiny"

Psychoanalytic theory, as formulated by Sigmund Freud, relies heavily on anatomy to explain the differences between men and women. Freud's views on the origins of these differences, and on the nature of female personality, are derived almost exclusively from his work with patients who sought therapy.

To understand Freud's theory of the development of personality, it is necessary to consider the basic tenets of psychoanalysis. Freud stated that in human beings there are different levels of awareness of feeling, of thought, and of experience, and he hypothesized three mental structures: the *id*, which represents biological influences or drives governed by the *pleasure principle*, the *ego*, which seeks to impose limits on the id and is reality-oriented; and the *superego*, which represents the individual's conscience. Although the id is present from birth, the individual must pass through a series of five developmental stages—the oral, anal, phallic, latency, and genital stages—to achieve an ego and a superego, that is, to acquire a mature adult personality and behaviour.

For Freud, human beings are dominated by instincts, and the sex drive, or *libido*, an instinctual craving for sensual pleasure, is one of the key forces motivating behaviour. During each of the five stages, which Freud postulated as occurring in a fixed chronological sequence, the libido is centred on one particular *erogenous zone*, an area sensitive to sensual stimulation. During the *oral stage* in the first year of life, the infant's mouth acts as the major focus of sexual energy and gratification. During the *anal stage*, from ages one to three, sensual pleasure is derived from the anal region; being able to allow or restrict bowel movements gives the child physical and psychological pleasure as well as the first opportunity for freedom from parental control.

According to Freud's theory, both boys and girls pass through the oral and anal stages of psychosexual development in similar fashion, and at this time, the mother is their chief love object. However, during the *phallic stage*, from approximately ages three to five, the genders diverge, and boys and girls follow separate developmental pathways.

During the phallic stage, erotic interest focuses on the genitals, and masturbation is the primary source of sexual gratification. The small boy becomes fascinated with his penis and develops the fantasy of possessing his mother sexually. This fantasy leads to the *Oedipal complex*, named for the Greek myth of Oedipus, who unwittingly killed his father and married his mother. During the phase of the Oedipal complex, the boy becomes intensely attached to his mother, and he resents the presence of his father, whom he perceives as a rival for his mother's affection. The boy considers his father to be a formidable opponent and fears that his father will retaliate and punish him by castration. Thus, *castration anxiety* develops in the boy.

Freud considered castration anxiety essential to the development of a masculine gender identity. The young boy, fearful of his father, is thought to repress his sexual desire for his mother and come to identify with his father. In doing so, he assumes the values and ideas represented by his father as his own and develops a conscience or superego. In seeking to become as much like his father as possible so that he too will some day be able to satisfy his sexual cravings, the young boy takes on the qualities that his father supposedly possesses—strength, power, and so on—and thus acquires a masculine gender identity.

According to Freud, the female experience of the phallic stage is the *Electra complex*, named after the Greek legend of the princess who helped kill her mother. For the young girl, the first critical event during the phallic stage is her realization that she does not possess a penis; she then feels envious and inferior as a result of this realization. Freud writes, "[Girls] notice the penis of a brother or playmate, strikingly visible and of large proportions, at once recognize it as the superior counterpart of their own small and inconspicuous organ, and from that time forward fall a victim to envy for the penis." This so-called *penis envy*, coupled with the girl's belief that her mother has mutilated her (she thus rejects her mother), is transformed into a desire to be impregnated by her father.

Freud hypothesized that the girl can never fully resolve the Electra complex because she remains "that mutilated creature" and can never possess a penis. Whereas the boy's powerful fear of castration can be resolved by the critical process of identification with his father, the girl has already "lost her penis." The girl's unsuccessful resolution of the Electra complex leads her to lifelong feelings of inferiority, a predisposition to jealousy, intense maternal desires, and a less mature sense of conscience or morality ("an immature superego"). Supposedly, because penis envy persists throughout her life, a woman remains dependent on others for her values and is less mature psychologically than a man.

According to Freud's theory, the Oedipus or Electra complex is generally resolved by age six; the child then enters the *latency stage*, in which sexual impulses recede in importance and the child becomes focused on nonsexual interests. In puberty, the *genital stage* is precipitated by internal biological factors, and the adolescent learns to direct his or her sexual interest towards heterosexuality and mature genital sexuality.

Although our treatment of Freudian theory must be cursory, we do wish to present a few of the many criticisms that have been made of it. First, feminists have noted that there is a profound "phallocentricism" in Freud's theory. As Greenglass (1982, 49–50) notes, "Empirical work on many of Freud's assumptions about women has not given support to such ideas as penis envy and the Oedipus complex. For example, little evidence exists that girls and women envy male anatomy, while there is considerable evidence that women and girls envy the masculine role for its greater power and privilege—its greater socio-cultural advantages."

Second, Freud's heavy reliance on biological determinants of human behaviour effectively negates the consideration of sociocultural and environmental influences on the development of differences between girls and boys. By proclaiming that "anatomy is destiny," Freudian theory has encouraged a polarized depiction of men and women. Within this framework, women are seen as "weak, inferior, passive, fragile, soft, vacillating, dependent, unreliable, intuitive rather than rational, castrated and handicapped" while men are depicted as "aggressive, controlling, strong, superior, proud, independent, venturesome, competitive, hard and athletic" (Miller 1974, 367).

Third, from an empirical viewpoint, a major problem with psychoanalytic theory is that its concepts cannot be scientifically evaluated; they are simply assumed to exist. In stressing the importance of unconscious forces in human behaviour, Freud's concepts do not lend themselves to testing; consequently, they must, like a secular religion, be accepted on the basis of faith.

Finally, in the last decade several authors have challenged the very foundation on which, according to Freudian theory, gender differentiation "inexorably" rests, that is, on Freud's formulation of the Oedipus and Electra complexes. For example, Jeffrey Moussaieff Masson (1985) observes that in April 1896 Freud presented a paper to the Society for Psychiatry and Neurology in Vienna in which he discussed findings of an alarming prevalence of childhood rape and incest and of its pathogenic effects on adult women. Although his professional peers advised him never to publish this paper, he defied them, and "The Aetiology of Hysteria" appeared that year. However, from his review of Freud's personal documents, including letters to his colleagues, Masson concludes that Freud experienced such severe professional censure that he retracted his views on the etiology of hysteria in women (that is, the belief that actual childhood sexual traumas formed the basis of hysteria) and reformulated them into the Electra complex. Masson asserts that this decision was simply the result of professional expedience and notes that, in a letter written to his friend Wilhelm Fliess, Freud acknowledged, "My own father was one of these perverts and is responsible for the hysteria of my brother . . . and those of several younger sisters." According to Masson, the Electra theory, which suggests that allegations of childhood sexual abuse are simply the manifestation of unfulfilled longings, universally experienced during the phallic stage of psychosexual development, gave "intellectual sophistication to a wrong view [that women invent rape] for the perpetuation of a view that is comforting to male society" (xxi).

While Masson attributes Freud's reversal of position to a lack of moral courage in the face of professional censure, Miller (1988) suggests that Freud suppressed his theory out of a desire to protect himself and his friends from the pains of self-examination. Thus, she states that Fliess's son discovered decades after the event that "at the age of two, he [Fliess's son] had been sexually abused by his father and that this incident coincided with Freud's renunciation of the truth." If Masson and Miller are correct, the entirety of Freudian theory, especially that regarding the phallic stage of psychosexual development in women, requires careful re-examination.

Although psychoanalytic theory may be contentious, there can be no doubt about its importance in psychology, law (Edwards 1981), and the popular imagination. Especially in discussions of violence towards women, theories of the "masochistic" woman who seeks out an abusive lover are still depressingly popular (Clark and Lewis 1977). For feminists, an attempt to understand issues such as violence against women solely through concepts like "feminine masochism" and "penis envy" is to mask the questions that lie beneath gender role oppression. They point out that in psychoanalytic theory social forces and the structure of society are treated as if innocuous while the "dysfunctional qualities" of the "patient" are stressed and validated. Feminists argue that even if individual women may appear "masochistic," it would be presumptuous to assume that all women are inherently so. Rather than assuming that women who appear masochistic are responding to a deeply anchored and biologically impelled force within them, feminist writers urge us to consider the social forces that impel women to behave in ways that appear to be "masochistic" or in other ways that are considered stereotypically "feminine."

FEMINIST THEORY AND THE STUDY OF GENDER

What is generally referred to as feminist theory was formulated in large part in reaction to the perceived limitations of traditional or mainstream social science theories (and related methodologies and empirical findings). Traditional theories have focused primarily on subjects of interest to men. To the extent that theory informs research that, in turn, reflects back on theory, feminist writers have claimed that most, if not all, sociological theorizing has treated women as if they are invisible. The only notable exception to this has occurred in the area of marriage and the family, where, until the past decade, research focused on women almost to the exclusion of men.

Traditional theory, particularly that of the *structural functionalist genre*, has developed the concepts of *instrumental* and *expressive* roles and linked them with men and women, respectively. As McDaniel (1988, 2) has noted, "[W]omen are seen to serve the economy as mothers by not only perpetuating the species and the labour force, but by moulding their children into the contributing workers of tomorrow. Should this process not be entirely effective, however, the responsibility is placed squarely on the shoulders of mothers who are seen to have failed to provide adequate maternal care." Directly and indirectly, functionalists have suggested that a specialized division of labour, whereby men perform mainly instrumental roles within the public sphere and women practise mainly expressive roles within the private sphere, produces an efficient and complementary social and family life. Researchers were thus directed to treat men and women differently, the assumption being that they were, in essence, different but equal. By compartmentalizing the domestic and extra-domestic worlds, traditional theories largely ignored issues of significant sex differences in power, property, and prestige or, if they acknowledged them, implied that they were necessary for the efficient functioning of the social world. Similarly, it was assumed that the process of *sex-typing*, defined by Williams as "the prescription of different qualities, activities, and behaviours to females and males in the interest of socializing them for adult roles" (in Mackie 1991, 77), was of vital necessity for both the psychological adjustment of individual men and women and for the optimal functioning of society.

Feminist sociological theories challenge the mainstream assertions that such a division of labour is necessarily sex-linked, functional, and complementary. Moreover, they argue that the "myth of separate worlds" (Kanter 1976) denies the interlinkages between roles played within the family and within the labour market and renders invisible the work of women. As Lopata (1993, 170) argues, "The invisibility of women's work camouflaged the very simple fact that such a neat division of the world into two spheres never really existed, except as an ideological tool for trying to keep women out of areas defined by the homosocial dominant group as its own." Furthermore, they challenge the theorizing and researching enterprise within sociology by questioning the traditional prescription that social science should be value-neutral and should be kept separate and distinct from policy applications at either the individual or social level (Eichler 1984; Wilson 1986). However, although all theories start with the premise that men and women are not evaluated similarly in a society such as Canada, and therefore that women live under conditions of oppression that are neither natural nor inevitable, each type of feminist theory identifies and examines what it considers to be the primary causes of that oppression and provides guidelines for eliminating the inequality.

Liberal Feminism

Liberal feminism is the most moderate of all the feminist theories and identifies its goal as "a just and compassionate society in which freedom flourishes" (Wendell in Tong 1989, 13). Like other liberal discourses on equality, it is grounded on the assumption that society is organized as a *meritocracy* in which inequality and hierarchy are both inevitable and acceptable. "[F]ramed by the twin axes of individualism and rationality . . . [t]he . . . individual would seek to realize his [sic] own satisfaction on the basis of his [sic] work" receiving rewards for the demonstration of effort, energy, and initiative (Bell 1972, 58). According to liberal theory, "Society was to make no judgments between men [sic]—only to set the procedural rules."

Liberal feminism maintains that women are valued less in societies such as Canada in terms of social rewards because of their unequal participation in institutions outside the family and domestic sphere—in particular, the economic institution. This theory is described as moderate because it does not propose to radically restructure the nature of basic institutions in Canadian society, but rather stresses the need to restructure the distribution of individuals within these institutions. Thus, as Wendell observes, "Liberal feminists usually are . . . committed to major economic re-organization and considerable redistribution of wealth, since one of the modern political goals most closely associated with liberal feminism is equality of opportunity, which would undoubtedly require and lead to both" (in Tong 1989, 12).

According to liberal feminists, women are unequally distributed within the economic institution because of a combination of discrimination based on sex and a lack of equal-quality education. The solution to women's oppression requires that such obstacles be eliminated and equality of opportunity for both women and men be assured. Within this framework, *equality* is defined as equal opportunity. Liberation from oppression is thus based on equality of opportunity to develop as a human being. Men and women would, as a result, rise or fall within the existing system of social stratification based solely on their talents. The reader will note, however, that liberal feminists accept a reality in which inequalities of power, prestige, and property are still found among individuals of the same sex. This approach focuses, therefore, on eliminating sexual, but not other, forms of oppression, such as those stemming from class distinctions.

Liberal feminism is sometimes derisively referred to as "assimilationism" (Williams 1991, 95), both for its focus on providing opportunities for women in areas that were traditionally reserved for men and for its focus on "sameness"—that is, on how women are like men. Some critics have argued that by focusing attention on sameness and advocating *for* "gender-neutral" categories that do not rely on stereotypes of men and women, and *against* differential treatment, liberal feminists ignore how women as a group differ from men as a group. By advocating gender blindness, they point out, liberal feminists ignore the gendered structure of wage labour and the family. Thus, these critics suggest that because of liberal feminism's focus on "gender-neutrality," women have been exposed to increased economic and social vulnerability.

The "feminism of difference" has emerged to counter the stance of liberal feminism and to argue that a focus on gender-neutrality is myopic and neglects, to the peril of women, the fact that men and women do differ as groups. For "difference feminists," works such as Carol Gilligan's *In A Different Voice* (1982) are highly influential in countering a view that suggests that women's "difference" from men be judged, through male norms, as if it provided evidence of their "inferiority." Gilligan contends that women speak "in a different voice" from men and that while women are nurturers, contextual thinkers, and defined by their relationships, men are abstract thinkers and defined by their individual achievements. It is the woman's voice, Gilligan argues, that is potentially transformative, offering a society based on "womanly values" of responsibility, connection, community, negotiation, altruism, and nurture, rather than on "male values," which emphasize separation, self-interest, combat, autonomy, and hierarchy. While Gilligan does not explicitly state that women's morality is of a higher order than that of men, there is a certain likeness between her arguments and those of anti-feminists who extol women's "natural role" as "guardian" against male vice and chaperone of children's spiritual development (Lebsock 1984).

Perhaps more important, however, are the practical consequences of any perspective that would posit inherent and immutable "differences" between men and women. For example, in the famous American case of *Equal Employment Opportunities Commission* (EEOC) *vs. Sears*, Sears argued successfully that women's underrepresentation within its relatively high-paid, commissioned sales staff stemmed from women's "lack of interest" in these positions rather than from the company actively discriminating against them. To argue this effectively, Sears largely adopted the language of *relational feminists* (as adherents to Gilligan's position have been termed) and argued that women have less interest in the high-powered, competitive area of commission sales. According to Sears' lawyers, women prefer to forfeit work advancement and profitable employment in favour of congenial working environments and increased hours to devote to their families. They buttressed their case by calling on, among others, historian Rosalind Rosenberg, who cited the work of Gilligan and other relational feminists to endorse her testimony that the EEOC's "assumption that women and men have identical interests and aspirations regarding work is incorrect. Historically, men and women have had different interests, goals and aspirations regarding work" (in Williams 1991, 103). Although a second professor of history, Dr. Alice Kessler-Harris, was called on to challenge Rosenberg's interpretation of working women and argued that "[f]ailure to find women in so-called nontraditional jobs can . . . only be interpreted as a consequence of employers' unexamined attitudes or preferences, which phenomenon is the essence of discrimination" (Cooper 1986, 779), the presiding judge ruled that the EEOC had not proven its charges against Sears.

The ongoing debates within feminism as to "sameness" or "difference" of men and women mirror in many ways those that exist beyond its borders. However, for liberal feminists, an insistence on "difference" only serves to reinforce the inequality of men and women in both a symbolic and practical way. Thus, if a return to "maternal preference" would, on one level, favour women who attempt to gain custody of a child in contested cases, it would also reinforce the notion that women are to be defined in terms of their relationships to others—be it as daughter, wife, or mother. Moreover, they argue that a "maternal preference" would simply reflect the traditional assumption that the role of primary caretaker is best assumed by the person who possesses a uterus. Nevertheless, because in our society the current gender system does assign to women the role of primary caregiver, encourages them to "stay at home" with children, and slots them into economically disadvantageous occupations (for example, nurse versus doctor, teacher versus engineer, secretary versus accountant), "gender-neutrality" may be less than fully effective. The aftermath of the *canalization* process that encourages males and females to engage in traditionally "masculine" and "feminine" roles both within the labour market and the family may be to increase the difficulty for women of attaining real equality within Canadian society.

Marxist Feminism

In contrast to the liberal viewpoint, Marxist feminism insists that the entire structure of our society must be changed before true gender equality can be attained. The Marxist feminist approach argues that the economic institution, as it is organized in a particular society, determines the nature of all other institutions, and that one's place within the economic institution determines one's relationship to all other aspects of social life. Therefore, the capitalist economic institution is the source of female oppression in Canada, as it is in many other countries. The capitalist system, organized as it is around the principles of private property and the pursuit of profit, ensures the existence of unequal distributions of property. The Marxist approach focuses on the public world of the formal economic production process. Accordingly, the best way of eliminating female oppression is to change the economic institution from one based on capitalism to one based on communism. The economic production process will thereafter belong to society as a whole; every individual will have the same relationship to the process and will thus receive the same economic rewards. Once the fundamental economic oppression inherent in capitalism is eliminated, the oppression of women will necessarily disappear.

We should note that from the Marxist perspective, the unequal status of women is analogous to that of any other disadvantaged group in our country, such as aboriginal people and the poor. Sexual, racial, and class inequalities are all believed to be by-products of the same underlying cause—the capitalist economic system. The situation of women is not a special case requiring a separate explanation or solution, but simply another example of how the capitalist system works. As Tong (1989, 51) observes, because of its basis in Marxist theory, Marxist feminism has focused attention on women's work-related concerns: "how the institution of the family is related to capitalism; how women's domestic work is trivialized as not real work; and, finally, how women are generally given the most boring and low-paying jobs." Similarly, although issues such as wages for housework and pay equity for work of comparable worth are not regarded in the same way by all Marxist feminists, discussion of these issues is seen in itself as valuable inasmuch as it provides for "an opportunity to challenge the market basis of wages—that is, to force us to reconsider why we pay some people so much and others so little" (Tong 1989, 59).

Radical Feminism

Radical feminism, which originated in the 1960s, does not share the same point of view as Marxist feminism. Radical feminists do not identify the capitalist economic system of production as the source of gender inequality. Rather, they suggest that women live under conditions of inequality in most systems of economic production, whether they be capitalist, socialist, or communist. The most fundamental oppression, in terms of temporal priority, near universality, and pervasiveness, is the oppression of women by men. That oppression is ultimately based on a system of ideas that promotes the belief in male superiority and therefore supports and justifies the domination of women by men (see Caputi 1989; Cottle, Searles, Berger, and Pierce 1989; Roberts 1990). This system of ideas is referred to as *patriarchy*. According to radical feminists, patriarchy pervades not only the public world of the formal economic production process but also, perhaps more oppressively, the private world of family or domestic relations and processes. Solutions must be sought that will apply equally to the public and private domains. Thus, patriarchal ideology must be eliminated before any meaningful change in women's oppression can occur. This means that the central belief that men and women are different and can be evaluated differently must be eliminated.

Both implicitly and explicitly, radical feminists argue that most apparent differences between men and women are the product of a socialization process that is predicated on patriarchy. If patriarchy were eliminated, major changes in both the content and processes of socialization would occur, and existing social differences would also eventually disappear.

According to some proponents of the radical feminist perspective, women must also be liberated from the limitations of their bodies, which form the foundation of patriarchy. As long as women's roles and rewards are tied to reproductive differences and the beliefs associated with them, true gender equality cannot be realized. Technologies have been developed to provide for extra-uterine gestation of a fetus and for alternative forms of child care so that the child bearer does not need to be the child rearer. It is not unreasonable to suppose that a technology could be developed in the future to allow for the possibility of artificially impregnating men as well as women. In this regard, the radical feminist perspective is more "radical" than the Marxist feminist perspective, which generally forgoes consideration of reproductive differences because they are fundamentally problematic. The ultimate goal of radical feminism is to eliminate one's biological sex as a basis for any social action and social response.

Socialist Feminism

The socialist feminist analysis combines those of the Marxist and radical feminists. In part, socialist feminism attempts to extend and enrich Marxist analysis by including radical feminist insights. As we have seen, Marxist feminism seeks to eliminate class oppression, while radical feminism seeks to eliminate sexual oppression. These different solutions are predicated on the identification of different root causes of female oppression. Socialist feminists seek to eliminate both class and sexual oppression, that is, both capitalism and patriarchy. From the socialist feminist viewpoint, it is the historical combination of the capitalist economic and political system and the patriarchal ideology that leads to the oppression of women in so many ways. Not only must the organized system of producing goods and services be restructured to promote a truly egalitarian outcome for women and men, but also the systems of sexuality, child bearing, and child rearing.

Cultural Feminism

Although it evolved in the mid-1970s from radical feminism, because it focuses primarily on the substantive area of sexuality, cultural feminism warrants its own label (Echols 1984). According to Echols, radical feminism desires to suppress and eventually eliminate not only gender differences, but gender as a social category. She suggests that a number of former radical feminists are now identifying the cause of women's oppression as the repression of female experiences and values. Accordingly, their solution is the nurture and rehabilitation of these values so that they will ultimately supersede the dominant patriarchal value system. Their goal is thus not to eliminate male-female differences, but to build on the ways in which women differ from men and create an "alternative female consciousness" (53).

For example, Russell (1987) has described what she terms "the nuclear mentality" as "a perverted outgrowth of this culture's notion of masculinity" (10). It is Russell's contention that "[t]he development of these lethal [nuclear] arms has been the culmination of a long history of male-dominated governments for whom military superiority over other nations justified the expenditure of enormous resources—even while people living in these countries starved for lack of basic human needs" (12). She argues that while ruling class white males are responsible for the development of nuclear weapons, the violence and threat of violence posed by nuclear warfare may be seen as simply an extension of patriarchal thinking and male violence. Thus, while nuclear warfare "has considerably more evil and destructive consequences," Russell argues that "there is no reason to believe that most lower class men would behave differently . . . if they had the power that upper class men have. . . . [C]rime statistics . . . indicate that men in powerless positions are even more prone than men in powerful positions to commit murder, rape, robbery with violence and aggravated assault" (12). Accordingly, she contends, "Nuclear war is a feminist issue because the threat of nuclear obliteration is a consequence of the distorted values, psyches, and institutions that sexist arrangements have bred. . . . We must face the fact that at this point in history the nuclear mentality and the masculine mentality are one and the same. To rid ourselves of one, we must rid ourselves of the other" (15).

The etiology of sex differences (biological, psychological, or cultural) does not appear to be a focal issue for the majority of cultural feminists, although they seem to favour a biological basis. Echols notes (1984, 51) that "eco-feminists" and "pacifist feminists" claim that women's "bond with the natural order" makes them uniquely qualified to resolve the threats of nuclear holocaust and ecological disaster. For example, Helen Caldicott (1984) has argued that "[o]ne of the reasons women are so allied to the life processes is their hormonal constitution" (294). It is Caldicott's thesis that males are *naturally* more fascinated by killing (296). These claims, along with certain cultural feminist anti-pornography proposals, stem from the belief that women's experiences are quantitatively and qualitatively different from men's and must be nurtured, not eradicated. Short-term and long-term goals for cultural feminists are difficult to determine. For some, lesbianism and the establishment of lesbian communities is the solution; for others, the immediate goal is simply to provide support for what has been systematically devalued under patriarchy.

Inclusive Feminism

While MacKinnon (1991, 85, 87) stresses that "the sexes are not socially equal . . . [g]ender is . . . a question of power, specifically of male supremacy and female subordination;"

others, who may be termed inclusive feminists, such as Marlee Kline (1989), Enakshi Dua (1992), and Sharene Razack (1993) have contradicted the notion of the "universal woman" and argued "that although the oppression of women *is* universal, if you isolate gender from race and class (among other things) . . . you will miss some very important insights into how gender is constructed in specific context" (Razack 1993, 39). They suggest a need to extend analysis to challenge "traditional race-class-sexuality-power arrangements," which not only favour men over women but, as well, "whites over non-whites . . . able-bodiedness over non-able-bodiedness . . . and the employed over the non-employed" (Elliot and Mandell 1995, 4–5). Rejecting the notion that "the women's movement is a homogeneous group experiencing the same forms and degree of oppression," it has been argued that white feminists have neglected the concerns of aboriginal women, women of colour, and the differently abled (Lucas et al. 1991/1995, 534).

Maintaining that "gender studied in isolation is an abstraction, a rhetorical device that enables us to confine women's daily experiences to a frame in which race and class privilege and many other norms go unexamined," Razack (44) advocates the expanded task of uncovering and addressing not only the domination and oppression of women, but also the examination of all types of related oppressions. For inclusive feminists, "gender is clearly not one identity but a set of relations" (Razack 1993, 47).

Anti-Feminist Feminism

In marked contrast to other feminist theories, a variety of "anti-feminist feminists" have emerged in the 1990s to combat what they identify as the "failure of feminism." For example, Camille Paglia achieved best-selling status with her book *Sexual Personae* (1990), a work peppered with such provocative comments as, "If civilization had been left in female hands, we would still be living in grass huts." In her second book, *Sex, Art and American Culture* (1992), Paglia reiterates her view of "masculinity" and "femininity" as analogous to the colours of black and white and claims that "[n]o legislation or grievance committee can change these eternal facts" (108). Extolling the singer Madonna as "the true feminist . . . [who] exposes the puritanism and suffocating ideology of . . . feminism, which is stuck in an adolescent whining mode" (4), and rhapsodizing about actress Elizabeth Taylor as a "pre-feminist woman . . . [who] wields the sexual power that feminism cannot explain and has tried to destroy" (15), Paglia's approach often suggests a fusing of biological determinism and *The National Enquirer*.

In the case of feminist theories on gender, as with other theories of gender, we witness a plurality of ideologies and posited utopias. Each focuses on some areas while ignoring others. Each theoretical framework involves thought, belief, and action. It has become commonplace in the study of gender for the norms and truths that were once assumed to be absolute to be questioned and discarded. However, since the nature of sex and gender roles seems so irrefutable, so rooted in the natural order, it is perhaps not surprising that arguments over whether men and women are the same or different (and accordingly, which gender is superior or inferior) remain as strident in the 1990s as in earlier times.

In large ways and small, the "second wave" of the women's movement that took shape in the 1960s continues to sensitize us to the subtle and blatant discrimination women have experienced because of gender. Feminist scholars, gay liberation theorists, and other critical analysts have also enabled us to sharpen our understanding of selected aspects of the male gender role. We are slowly beginning to understand how ironic it is that while the confinements of gender were created by males, the outcome has often been just as detrimental to them as it has been to females.

Men's Liberation

Safilios-Rothschild (1974) has defined the goal of women's and men's liberation as empowering both sexes to "act according to their wishes, inclinations, potentials, abilities and needs, rather than according to the prevailing stereotypes about sex roles and sex-appropriate modes of thought and behaviour" (7). However, the term "men's movement," like the term "women's movement," is actually composed of numerous groups that begin with different assumptions, work towards different goals, and conceptualize the "problem" of gender in different manners. For example, those in the *profeminist men's movement* adopt the "minimalist" position of gender and agree that the differences that exist between men and women in contemporary society are the consequences of social and structural arrangements— not the by-products of biological imperatives. Accordingly, profeminist men's movement writers such as John Stoltenberg (1990) and Harry Brod (1987) are highly sympathetic to feminist concerns and stress the need for an outright rejection of dominating masculinity. They also call for a new definition of success for men that will "humanize" them, champion high paternal involvement in child rearing, and stress as an ideal a society that is nonviolent and characterized by egalitarian beliefs and generally similar gender roles.

In contrast, others such as Robert Bly's "mythopoetic men's movement" conceptualize the issue to be confronted quite differently. Although Bly advocated in the 1970s that men should embrace their "feminine principle," in the 1980s and 1990s his message changed quite markedly as he adopted a more obviously "maximalist" position on gender. Thus, in *Iron John* he disparages "soft males" who, in seeking to please women, have become women-defined men, and stresses the need for men to be "independent" and "manly." According to Bly, women-defined men are unhappy because they have stopped short in "their path towards wholeness" by failing to connect with "the instinctive, the sexual, the primitive"—the "Wildman"—inside them (1991, 19).

Maintaining that "the possessiveness that some mothers exercise on sons . . . cannot be overestimated" (1991, 23), Bly advocates that men distance themselves from their mothers (to avoid contamination by "too much feminine energy"), recapture age-old rites of male initiation, and assuage the effects of the "absent father syndrome" (caused by the structuring of industrial society, which removed fathers from the home) by finding a surrogate father figure or "male mother." "Even the best-intentioned woman cannot give [her son] what is needed. . . . When a father and a son spend long hours together . . . we could say that a substance almost like food passes from the older body to the younger. . . . A physical exchange takes place. . . . The younger body learns at what frequency the masculine body vibrates" (1990, 93). Not only individual men but our whole culture, Bly suggests, is yearning for "the King."

Despite such notable differences, those active in the "men's movement," like those involved both historically and currently in the woman's movement, have often suffered from a process of stereotyping that depicts them as "weak," "whining," and potentially "dangerous." Similarly, just as "feminists" have been derided by some as being "masculine," those men who would challenge the confines of the traditional masculine role have often been pilloried as "effeminate." In this way, the men's movement is reduced to a cartoon of weepy guys engaged in a group hug, hen-pecked househusbands with frilly aprons, and more recently, a ridiculous gathering of "Wild Men" or "Warriors" (Bly 1990) with "fire in their bellies" (Keen 1991) who meet in the wilderness to beat drums and search for the "deep masculine."

The Confusion of the Individual

In the midst of this multiplicity of theoretical positions and evaluations of "appropriate" and "inappropriate" behaviour stands the lonely individual, the confused man or woman who can no longer quite make out how they are expected to behave or if there is any difference any longer between masculine and feminine behaviour. This confusion is not only a challenge for the individual, but for society as well.

For example, recent research suggests that while some males still adhere to the traditional notions of wanting their "ideal" female partner to possess only homemaking and people-nurturing skills, most males now seem to want a female who can do it all—a sort of cuddly Superwoman who can not only take care of business but still channel considerable energies into making and sustaining relationships (see Doherty 1992). On the other side of the coin, journalist Wendy Dennis has suggested that men are now being directed to transform themselves "from dull but dutiful breadwinner, in the Ozzie Nelson mold, to androgynous danger-boy, in the Mick Jagger mold, to caring-sharing-and-relating soul-mate, in the Phil Donahue mold, to risk-taker with a vulnerable heart, in the Bruce Willis mold, to sensitive but sexy man-boy, in the Kevin Costner mold" (1992, 61)—in other words, a cuddly Superman who takes care of business but also sustains a relationship with his partner in all of the desired dimensions.

However, the challenge posed by gender is not confined to negotiating acceptable arrangements within individual intimate relationships. The challenge to become free from sex-role stereotypes is multifaceted. Posluns and Tough (1987) identified nine areas of change in individual attempts to become freer from gender-role stereotypes: job/study, self-image, personal behaviour and lifestyle, relationships with women, attitudes towards the situation of women, relationships with children, assertiveness/independence, relationships with men, and participation in social action. Their research noted that in their sample of 60 women and 20 men who had been freeing themselves from sex-role stereotyping, the largest number of women identified the area of self-image as their most important area of change, followed by changes in job or study and changes in relationships. While positive consequences were noted, such as feeling better about themselves and leading happier, richer lives, negative consequences were also noted, including "feelings of pain and confusion, marital separation, alienation from men and society, loss of friends, distancing from family and friends, and interacting mainly with women."

As Posluns and Tough observed, the process of change is often difficult and involves confronting both internal and external obstacles, as well as the negative consequences of the change process itself. It is evidently difficult for persons to proceed with the presupposition that men and women should be treated equally, when so much of our society reminds us that, continuing into the 1990s, they are not.

GENDER SOCIALIZATION: LEARNING TO BE UNEQUAL

Gender socialization, the process through which individuals acquire a gender identity as well as ways of acting, feeling, and thinking that are appropriate to the gender expectations of their society, is of fundamental importance in maintaining gender stratification within Canadian society. Indeed, the task of learning how to be a "male" or "female" has been described as "[t]he most complex, demanding and all-involving role that a member of society must learn to play" (Eitzen and Zinn 1992, 229).

Learning to be masculine or feminine involves the acquisition of role knowledge and the application of this knowledge to oneself. Obviously, the content of these male and female "scripts" (Laws 1977) may vary from the extremely sex-typed to the androgynous. However, the tenacity of "masculine" and "feminine" scripts is in itself sociologically intriguing. While the specific content of these "blueprints" of gender may be modified somewhat by class, race, religion, ethnicity, and even by the region of the country one lives in, socialization into specific gender roles must nevertheless be recognized as significantly uniform.

Through interaction with the family, the peer group, and the school, males and females receive differing messages that instruct them how they should act. Reinforced by the subtle but nevertheless influential cues provided by religion, language, and the media, "masculinity" and "femininity" may be seen as socially created by-products of a society.

The Family

Cregheur and Devereaux (1991, 3) have commented that "[b]y world standards . . . Canadian children are among the fortunate few. Child mortality rates are low and have fallen significantly in the past decade. Virtually all children attend school, and most live in homes with an array of modern conveniences and entertainment equipment." Yet, despite the advantages that many Canadian children enjoy in the 1990s, the gender socialization that they receive within the family may nevertheless be considered a negative influence to the extent that it often perpetuates and reinforces gender stereotypes.

The child's earliest socialization occurs within the family. Even prior to birth, there is evidence that girls and boys are perceived differently. Thus, folk wisdom informs us that the prenatal position of the fetus indicates its sex, with boys supposedly carried high and wide and girls carried low and neatly positioned in front. Similarly, Lewis (1972) reported that parents frequently speculate on the sex of their unborn child by the amount of activity the fetus engages in; the greater the amount of activity, such as kicking, the greater the tendency to assume that the fetus is a boy. As Richardson (1981) has noted, in North America and in the majority of other countries, most couples acknowledge a preference for a son as their first-born child, a preference at any time for sons rather than daughters, and a greater likelihood of "trying again" for another child if only daughters have been born into the family.

During the first year of life, meaningful interaction between parents and children occurs primarily on a nonverbal level, with parents reacting to the actions of their newborn. Research indicates that parents as well as others differentially interpret the actions of their infants, depending on the child's sex. For example, Rubin et al. (1974) reported that when parents were interviewed within 24 hours following the birth of their child, their descriptions of their infants followed stereotypical sex lines: daughters were described as delicate, weak, beautiful, and cute, while sons were described as strong, alert, and well-coordinated. These depictions are especially interesting in that the infants did not differ in average length, weight, or Apgar scores (which reflect muscle tone, respiratory function, reflexes, and heart rate). It would seem that infant actions are selectively perceived through the filter of their gender.

In their review of the literature of parental interaction, Sidorowicz and Lunney (1980) note that research has consistently found that parents treat girls as more physically fragile than boys. For example, during the first six months of life, boys receive more physical contact and less nonphysical contact (being looked at, being talked to) than girls. Accordingly, it is not surprising that boys are allowed more independence and freedom to explore their physical environment. Similarly, beyond the age of six months, boys are more likely to receive physical punishment and other forms of negative feedback from their parents than girls; however, they also receive more positive feedback, such as praise (Richardson 1981).

In general, it would seem that while both parents are concerned about gender-inappropriate behaviour, the behaviour of boys in this respect especially concerns parents and, in particular, fathers (Huston 1983, 430). Indeed, the "sissy" boy is particularly likely to receive reprimands and punishment. Boys are more likely to receive more proscriptive responses ("Boys don't do that.") than prescriptive ones ("Boys should do this."), and proscriptions are customarily aimed at eliminating inappropriate "feminine" behaviour. When reinforced by the peer group, where "unmasculine" behaviour is greeted with the labels "sissy," "cry-baby," "fag," or "queer," the implicit message is that "feminine" behaviour in males is linked to homosexuality and that both "femininity" and "homosexuality" are to be disparaged.

In addition to actively reinforcing conformity to normative gender roles in boys and girls, parental actions also provide for the transmission of more subtle messages about gender in the types of books, toys, and clothing they provide for their offspring. For example, Basow (1986, 132) has observed that by the time boys and girls are four years old, they show a strong preference for quite different sets of toys, toys that conform to gender-appropriate stereotypes. In general, toys considered gender-appropriate for boys emphasize creativity, visual and spatial manipulations, and actions oriented towards the world outside the home. Gender-appropriate toys for girls are significantly more oriented towards the world inside the home. If toys are the building blocks for the future, the future suggested for females is one circumscribed by the boundaries of the home and consisting of rearing children and providing domestic services. Similarly, various critics have commented on the ramifications of the "Barbie culture" for females; the finding that some four-year-old girls are now complaining that they are "too fat" (Wolf 1991) means that the high rates of eating disorders such as anorexia nervosa and bulimia will continue (Orbach 1980; Szekeley 1988a; 1988b).

Formal and Informal Education

In Canada, compulsory education laws and the wide availability of kindergarten have resulted in school attendance by the vast majority of children age 5 to 14. As in other industrialized nations, the school is of fundamental importance in the socialization process. As Parsons (1959) observed, the educational system performs the functions of channelling individuals through occupational programs into positions within society's socioeconomic structure and reaffirming children's commitment to society's values. Feminists argue, however, that the socialization provided is not gender-neutral. Rather, as Abbott and Wallace (1990, 49–50) point out, females are disadvantaged in the educational system in that they are socialized into subordinate roles, encouraged to accept dominant ideologies of "masculinity" and "femininity," channelled into gender-appropriate subjects (English and history instead of mathematics and science), and, in consequence, face restricted opportunities in the labour market.

Increasingly in Canada, children spend some portion of their preschool years in child care settings—day care, preschool, or junior and senior kindergarten—with teachers or child care workers assuming the role of surrogate parents. However, within these nontraditional settings, as within the home, there is evidence to suggest encouragement of stereotypical gendered behaviour. The predominance of female workers within such settings may symbolically suggest that caring for children is a woman's role rather than one that can be filled equally well by a man.

Challenging sexism within the school system is increasingly recognized as being of fundamental importance in Canada. In 1970 the Royal Commission on the Status of Women made the following recommendations: "adoption of textbooks that portray both sexes in diversified roles and occupations; provision of career information about the broad field of occupational choice for girls; improved availability of sport programs for both sexes; development of educational programs to meet the special needs of rural and immigrant women and of Indian and Inuit girls and young women; and the continuing education of women with family responsibilities" (as noted in Mackie 1991, 158). Gaskell, McLaren and Novogrodsky (1989) note a trend since the 1970s towards a more integrated curriculum in which boys and girls learn, for example, both auto mechanics and cooking. However, it would be presumptuous to suppose that the process of education provides identical messages to young women and men. To paraphrase Mark Twain, school may continue to interfere with a person's ability to get an education.

For example, based on the findings of a three-year study conducted in more than 100 fourth, sixth, and eighth grade classes in four U.S. states, Sadker and Sadker (1987) suggested that there exist a variety of subtle but salient differences in the way that teachers respond to their male and female students. They reported that "[t]eachers praise boys more than girls, give boys more academic help and are more likely to accept boys' comments during classroom discussions" (43). They noted that while teachers tended to give boys detailed information on how to accomplish a task on their own, they would perform the task for girls rather than give them directions. Similarly, they found that teacher feedback offered to male students was more precise and encouraging than feedback offered to girls. They suggested that the enforcement of girls' passivity in the classroom not only detracted from their learning experiences but also resulted in lower SAT scores later in their educational career.

Contrary to teachers' perceptions, Sadker and Sadker reported that it is boys, not girls, who vocally dominate the classroom, whether the subject is mathematics, science, or language arts. They reported that boys were eight times more likely to call out answers than girls, and that teachers were far more likely to accept and condone this behaviour in boys than in girls. Moreover, they described a behaviour they termed "mind sex;" that is, once a teacher called on a student of one sex, there was a tendency to continue calling on children of that same sex. Since boys tended to be called on more in the first place and were more apt to call out answers without being called on, they received a disproportionate amount of teacher attention and dominated class discussion. Sadker and Sadker's research documents the tenacity of gender differentiation in the process of education and suggests that, in various ways, teachers' behaviour fosters dependence in girls and independence in boys.

About a century ago, leading educators claimed that a female's womb dominated her mind. Because females are equipped for childbirth, education was considered dangerous for them, and educators urged young women to study only one-third as hard as young men—and not to study at all during menstruation. Clearly we've made considerable progress since that time. Consider that in 1991 young women age 20 to 24 were more likely than young men to have a university degree (10% versus 8%) or to possess a postsecondary certificate or diploma (21% versus 14%). In 1992–93, the majority of full-time university students were women: 53 percent of the undergraduate population (up from 43 percent in 1972–73), 46 percent of full-time master's students (up from 27 percent in 1972–73) and 35 percent of full-time doctoral students (up from 19 percent in 1972–73). However, what men and women study reinforces male-female distinctions. Women remain underrepresented in mathematics, the physical sciences, engineering, and the applied sciences at university. At community colleges, while women account for 96 percent of those enrolled full-time in secretarial sciences, 90 percent of those enrolled in the educational and counselling service program, and 89 percent of those studying nursing, they account for a mere 12 percent of enrolment in engineering and other technological programs, 30 percent of those in mathematics and computer science, and less than a third (32%) of those enrolled in natural science and primary industry programs. Of all trade apprenticeship programs with over 3000 registered apprentices in 1992, only hairdressing and cooking programs had significant female enrolments (Normand 1995).

If we follow students into graduate school, we see that with each passing year the proportion of females decreases and that accomplishments are gender-linked. For example, of doctoral degrees awarded in 1993, women received 54.5 percent of those awarded in education, 44.5 percent of those awarded in social services, and 38.4 percent of those awarded in the humanities, but only 11.2 of those awarded in engineering and applied sciences, 16.8 percent of those awarded in mathematics and the physical sciences, and 28.4 percent of those awarded in agriculture and biological science (Normand 1995). If we follow those who earn doctoral degrees back into colleges and universities, we find gender stratification in rank and pay. Throughout Canada, women are less likely to be full professors, the highest rank. As well, female full professors earn less on average than male full professors; also, on average, women academics earn 82 percent of the salary of male academics of comparable rank (CAUT Bulletin 1995).

GENDER AND WORK

The booming economy of the 1960s and 1970s, coupled with an expansion of the female gender role, contributed to an increase in female labour force participation. During the 1980s and continuing into the 1990s, the ravages of recession and inflation added impetus to the necessity of female employment. In 1991 Canadian women constituted 45 percent of the Canadian workforce, almost one-half of all employed Canadians. Indeed, the massive increase in the number of Canadian women in the workforce has been one of the most notable social changes in Canada during the past 50 years. Between 1975 and 1991, the participation of women age 15 and over in the Canadian workforce accounted for 72 percent of the rise in employment (Ghalam 1993, 3). Nevertheless, it would be presumptuous to assume that the working experiences of Canadian men and women are now interchangeable or that women have usurped men's former position of advantage. In 1991 the majority of

Canadian women remained clustered in traditionally female-dominated occupations: 71 percent were employed within five occupational groups—teaching (6%), nursing or related health occupations (9%), clerical (29%), sales (10%) and service (17%). In marked contrast, these occupational groups accounted for approximately 30 percent of employed Canadian men.

Despite the fact that the number of Canadian women within the 20 highest-paid occupations quadrupled between 1971 and 1981, women constituted only 27 percent of all doctors, dentists, and other health-diagnosing and -treating professionals in 1991. Consistent with the stereotypic image of female as subordinate-helper, women accounted for 87 percent of nurses, therapists, and other medical assistants during those years. Although the proportion of women employed in management and administration increased from 27 percent in 1981 to 40 percent in 1991, it has been noted that "[m]uch of this increase is attributable to changes in occupational definitions, such as some clerical jobs being reclassified into the management/administrative category" (Ghalam 1993, 4). According to a 1993 survey by *The Financial Post*, less than 1 percent of the top executives in Canada's largest companies are women (Maclean's 1993). Women remain marginalized within the natural sciences, engineering, and mathematics, increasing only slightly from 16 percent of professionals within these fields in 1981 to 18 percent in 1991. In the majority of the traditionally male-dominated goods-producing occupations, female participation remains slight; as Ghalam (1993, 5) points out, "[W]omen accounted for 15 percent of employment in primary, manufacturing, construction, transportation, and materials handling jobs in 1991, ranging from 22 percent in the primary industries to only 2 percent in construction." Moreover, women in Canada are less likely than men to be self-employed. Women accounted for only 29 percent of all self-employed workers in 1991. Only 9 percent of female workers (compared with 19 percent of Canadian workers) worked for themselves in 1991.

Despite the dramatic growth in the number of women in the Canadian workforce, employed Canadian women continue to earn substantially less than male workers. In 1991 the average earnings of female managers/administrators were 63 percent of those of their male counterparts. Among health technicians and other related workers, women's earnings were on average 58 percent of the earnings of male workers. Among medical and health professionals, the female-to-male earnings ratio was very low (49%) and would seem to reflect the concentration of women in the lower-paying fields such as nursing, and the greater likelihood of men occupying the higher-paying fields of medicine and dentistry. Within some of the nonprofessional occupations, such as clerical work, the female-to-male earnings ratio was above the national average at 72 percent. However, it should be noted that within these occupational groups, salaries are generally low, and that within other nonprofessional occupations female-to-male earnings ratios were below the national average. Logan and Belliveau (1995, 33) point out that in 1993 the average earnings of women university graduates working full-time all year ($40 670) were only 75 percent of those of male graduates. Table 6-1 is instructive; in 1993, regardless of age or education, employed women still earned considerably less than employed men.

In contrast to male patterns of employment, much of women's employment in Canada is part-time. Since the 1980s, women have constituted at least 70 percent of all part-time employees, and in 1991 slightly over one-quarter (26%) of all Canadian women were employed part-time, compared with 9 percent of employed men. While many (36%) Canadian women work part-time by "choice," Canada's 1991 Labour Force Survey noted that almost 400 000 Canadian women reported that they desired full-time employment but were only able

TABLE 6-1	Average Earnings of Women Working Full-Time as a Percentage of Those of Men, by Education and Age, 1993					
Age group	**25–34**		**35–44**		**45–54**	
Level of Education	**Earnings**	**As a % of men's**	**Earnings**	**As a % of men's**	**Earnings**	**As a % of men's**
Some secondary	$20 380	63	$21 810	62	$21 890	60
Graduated high school	$23 860	74	$25 270	68	$27 100	67
Some postsecondary	$23 060	65	$26 090	67	$27 250	51
Postsecondary diploma	$26 490	75	$30 030	76	$31 120	73
University degree	$36 450	84	$43 910	77	$43 950	72
Total	$27 200	76	$30 260	72	$30 400	67

Source: Logan and Belliveau 1995, 33.

to obtain part-time positions. An additional 187 000 women (13%) indicated that they elected to work part-time because of "personal or family responsibilities;" 24 percent of female part-time workers age 25 to 44 cited personal or family responsibilities as their reason for working part-time. This finding suggests that despite increases in the labour force participation of married women and women with children, attempts to juggle work and family roles may result in qualitatively different experiences for male and female employees.

In 1981 47 percent of Canadian married women were employed; in 1991 this figure had increased to 56 percent. As a consequence, dual-income families increased in Canada from 32 percent in 1967 to just over 71 percent in 1991. For women who are married, their contributions to a dual-income family most typically represent an attempt to provide an adequate standard of living that is otherwise unachievable on a single provider's salary. The income of wives accounted for 29 percent of family income in 1990 (an increase of 3 percent since 1967), while the contributions of husbands declined from 63 percent in 1967 to 56 percent in 1990.

Similarly, there has been a rapid growth in the employment of women with children. In 1981 half of Canadian mothers with children under the age of 16 were employed; in 1991 this figure had increased to 63 percent. Moreover, the most dramatic increase in the proportion of employed mothers occurred in relation to women with children under the age of 6, rising from 42 percent to 57 percent over this same 10-year period. Yet, as Ghalam (1993, 4) observes, "[T]hese mothers were less likely than mothers whose youngest child was school-aged (6 to 15 years) to be in the work force (69 percent) in 1991." Inasmuch as the division of labour in the home continues to be gender-stratified, with females assigned primary responsibility for indoor housework and for the nurture and care of children, the consequences of this *second shift* of female labour (Hochschild 1989) must be recognized as salient.

Pleck (1979; 1980; 1985) has directed attention to the "differential permeability of work and family boundaries" for men and women that still exists within contemporary society (Mortimer and London 1984, 28). It is women, Pleck notes, who are expected to disrupt their careers to accommodate their families. Obversely, it is considered acceptable for men to disrupt their families (for example, through job transfers, commuter lifestyles, or long hours spent away from home) to accommodate their careers. Because women are commonly assigned the task of primary caregiver in Canadian society, those who seek to combine a career with motherhood must often address the issue of motherhood in a way that is qualitatively dissimilar from the issue of fatherhood for men. As Akyeampong (1992, 27) remarks, "Due to cultural traditions, many women carry a dual role as both a member of the paid labour force and the adult with the primary responsibility for the care and maintenance of the home and family. Also, among husband-wife families, the paid worker with the lower wage, usually the wife, may assume more family obligations during working hours, especially if meeting such responsibilities results in a loss of wages."

Akyeampong (1992, 26) has also noted that between 1977 and 1990, "the percentage of Canadian workers missing scheduled work time for personal reasons, excluding vacations, has increased as has the length of such absences . . . in almost all industries, occupations and provinces." However, he notes that much of the increase in absenteeism is the result of family-related leave taken by female workers and "linked to both improvements in employment contract entitlement for personal leave, including maternity leave, and to the increasing number of mothers participating in the paid labour force" (26). In 1991 women were more than twice as likely as men to be absent from work because of personal or family responsibilities. Thus, during an average week 3 percent of all employed women (but only 1.2 percent of employed men) were absent from work for these reasons. Similarly, Ghalam (1993, 6) observes, "In 1991, 11 percent of women in two-parent families with at least one child under age six, and 6 percent of comparable lone mothers, missed time from work each week because of family responsibilities. Absentee rates dropped to around 2 percent for both lone mothers and mothers in dual-parent families whose youngest child was aged 6–15. In contrast, the presence of young children had little effect on the work absences of fathers. Only two percent of fathers in two-parent families with preschool-age children and one percent of those whose youngest child was aged 6–15 lost time from work."

In 1990 there were more than 1.3 million preschoolers (under the age of 6) and 1.7 million school-aged children (ages 6 to 12) whose mothers were in the labour force. However, while the number of children who required an alternative to the "stay-at-home mother" form of child care increased from 1.4 million in 1971 to about 3 million in 1990, in 1990 there were only 321 000 licensed spaces for Canadian children. In 1990 less than one in five preschool children (18%) whose mothers were in the labour force were in licensed family or day care centres full-time (Burke, Crompton, Jones, and Nessner 1991). While unlicensed child care services may form part of the "underground economy" and provide parents with a less expensive form of child care, the lack of regulations governing such arrangements as well as the variable quality of caregiver training provided, may prove disconcerting and dangerous. It is not surprising that research has shown that professional women without children tend to be more successful in their career pursuits than those women who have children (see Anderson 1988).

In the late 1980s, there were increasing media claims that relative lack of career mobility was not particularly troublesome for the women involved. Schwartz (1989) proposed that two "streams" of career mobility could be pursued: a *fast track* for men and those women who would not allow their children to interfere with their career pursuits, and a separate "mommy track," a lower-paid, lower-pressure career path into which other women (whom Schwartz termed *career-and-family women*) would be placed. How corporations were to distinguish between these two "types" of women did not seem to trouble Schwartz to any marked degree. Rather, she seemed more concerned with the "inconvenience" that women posed to organizations by their being mothers and the need for companies to find an efficient way to deal with the problem that "career-and-family women" posed. Thus, the "problem" of women's professional marginalization supposedly lay in women, not in the structure of organizations or the structural arrangements in wider society.

If some saw the "mommy track" as furnishing an admirable and sensible solution that allowed women to "have it all," others were less enthusiastic in their response. Thus, Ehrenreich and English (as cited in Mackie 1991, 214) suggested that "[b]umping women —or just fertile women . . . or whomever—off the fast track may sound smart . . . [but] it is the corporate culture itself that needs to slow down to a human pace. . . . Work loads that are incompatible with family life are . . . a kind of toxin—to men as well as women, and . . . to businesses as well as families." Accordingly, alternative strategies, such as *flex-time* (where employees are allowed to manipulate daily work hours, within limits, to accommodate other demands, as long as the weekly work hours remain constant) and/or home-based *telecommuting* or *teleworking*, are believed to offer workers greater flexibility in twinning work and household-related demands.

For example, it has been argued that *job-sharing* "let[s] women enjoy [the] best of both worlds" (KW Record 1997d). According to Statistics Canada, which released its first national data on job-sharing in 1997, although job-sharing "is still not a widely practiced work arrangement . . . [it] is becoming an increasingly important work option." In 1996 approximately 8 percent (or 171 000 Canadians) shared a job; the vast majority of job-sharers were professional women over the age of 35 with college or university degrees who had children at home. Approximately one-quarter of job-sharers were teachers and nurses and one-fifth had worked in their job for over 10 years. The average hourly pay of job-sharers was $13.51, a figure that is $3 an hour more than that earned by regular part-time workers. According to the report, the number of Canadian collective agreements with provisions for job-sharing increased from 3 percent in 1986 to 12 percent in 1993; the Royal Bank of Canada, with 1100 employees sharing jobs as part of its work-family program, has the largest program of any Canadian corporation. Job-sharers identified the strategy as allowing them to attain a better balance between work and family demands, reduce stress, and increase their energy and job satisfaction. Employers reported that the strategy increased worker productivity, efficiency, job commitment, and enthusiasm and decreased absenteeism. However, the report notes that among the drawbacks of job-sharing are, for the worker, a lesser likelihood of career advancement and, for the employer, an increase in paperwork (KW Record 1997d).

In summary, it would seem difficult to sustain the image of the "modern" working woman suggested by alarmist critics in responding to women's expanding role within Canadian society. Indeed, if for conservative maximalists statistics on women's growing labour force participation are used to sound alarm about the "crisis," "decline," "decay," or "death" of society as we know it, minimalists might suggest that it is testament only to the enormity of work that remains to be done before men and women are truly equal in Canadian society. The necessity of women's economic self-sufficiency would seem of paramount importance. According to the National Council of Welfare's 1990 report, *Women and Poverty Revisited*, 84 percent of women in the 1990s (an increase of 13.5 percent since 1979) can expect to spend a significant period of their adult lives having to independently support themselves and their children.

THE FEMINIZATION OF POVERTY

Cartoonist Nicole Hollander once described what she felt a world without men would be like. "There would be no crime," she commented, "and lots of happy, fat women" (Tavris 1992, 29). While Hollander's statement offers an amusing commentary on the gendered nature of both crime (which is disproportionately male (see Hartnagel 1991)) and eating disorders (which are disproportionately female (see Orbach 1984; 1986; Szekely 1988a)), the more obvious and immediate reality for Canadian women of life without a man is poverty. As Harman (1992, 6) observes, "Simply put . . . [the feminization of poverty] means that without the support of a man, a woman is likely to be poor."

In Canada, the demographic fact that after age 40 women are less likely than men to be married is important inasmuch as marital status significantly affects the likelihood of poverty during old age (The National Council of Welfare 1990). While the rate of poverty among the Canadian elderly declined from approximately 22 percent in 1980 to 9 percent in 1991, married seniors have a much lower poverty rate than seniors living alone or with non-relatives (Poverty Profile Update for 1991, 1993). Part of the answer to why this occurs lies in the fact that while federal income security programs are effective in protecting most senior couples from poverty, they are less effective in safeguarding seniors who live alone.

At present, Canada's retirement income system is composed of three tiers: government benefits (e.g., Old Age Security (OAS) and the Guaranteed Income Supplement (GIS)) designed to forestall the likelihood of poverty by furnishing all seniors with a taxable, flat rate benefit (adjusted every three months as the Consumer Price Index increases) that is paid monthly, regardless of their work histories or life circumstances; government-sponsored Canada (CPP) and Quebec (QPP) pensions plans designed to provide workers with a retirement income that is based on their pre-retirement earnings from ages 18 to 65; and private savings, which include employer-sponsored private pensions plans, private investments, and Registered Retirement Savings Plans (RRSPs) (Townson 1995, 27). While both men and women become eligible to receive OAS benefits at age 65, there are some exemptions to this. For example, immigrants who have lived in Canada for less than 10 years are ineligible for benefits. Since July 1977, eligibility requirements stipulate that, since age 18, an individual must have lived in Canada for a period not less than 40 years. As well, since 1989, Canadian seniors whose annual net incomes are in excess of $50 000 are required to repay some or all of their OAS benefits.

Townson (1995, 31) notes that inasmuch as the CPP/QPP is designed to replace pre-retirement income, "to the extent that women have low earnings, an income replacement pension plan will give them low benefits." She notes that in many ways the CPP is "an ideal pension plan for women" (31) and points out, for example, that it accommodates women's often-interrupted work careers with a "child-rearing drop-out provision" that allows women to exclude from their calculation of earnings those years when they had a child under age seven if it is in their advantage to do so. In addition, in that the CPP/QPP does not discriminate between full-time and part-time workers, the plan is thought to be "ideally suited to women, who are much more likely than men to be employed part-time" (Townson 1995, 33). However, in general the level of benefits available from the CPP/QPP is low relative to earnings, with the retired worker receiving simply 25 percent of his or her average annual lifetime earnings, up to a maximum that is adjusted yearly with increases in the Consumer Price Index. Moreover, women, on average, receive a monthly retirement benefit that is much lower than that paid to men. Townson (1995, 33) reports that while women who retired in 1993 received an average monthly CPP benefit of $263, men received an average monthly CPP benefit of $478. As we shall see, it is evident that the CPP only indirectly recognizes women's unpaid work within the home (through drop-out provisions for family responsibilities, credit splitting, derivative benefits, etc.) and that these benefits are based on a woman's relationship to a wage earner rather than on her own individual need or contribution.

Women may receive additional CPP benefits through a spouse in three ways: a sharing of benefits at retirement; a division of credits upon divorce; or, upon death, through benefits for surviving spouses of contributors. While sharing benefits at retirement is not available to members of the QPP, it can provide a woman who has been a full-time homemaker and who has not contributed to the CPP with an independent form of income. However, as Townson (1995, 34) points out, "pension assignment" only occurs on a voluntary basis and, since the inception of this program in 1987, only 50 000 couples have applied for credit-sharing at retirement.

The division of credits may also occur at marital breakdown, and since early 1991, pension credits earned during the course of a marriage are equally divided between spouses upon divorce (except in the provinces of Saskatchewan and Quebec, where provincial family law allows couples to waive credit-splitting in the event of a divorce). Couples who have lived common-law may also apply for credit-splitting in the event that their relationship breaks down, but are required to do so after they have resided separately for a minimum period of one year and a maximum period of three years. However, Townson (1995, 35) reports that a lack of awareness of this provision leads many eligible, formerly married women to forfeit this opportunity to gain CPP credits; in addition, she notes that others "traded" this benefit for other, perhaps more immediately tangible, assets. In consequence, she reports, "[t]he data indicate that, unless their divorce took place within the past year or two . . . divorced women who are now 45–54 are unlikely to have benefitted from a share in a husband's CPP/QPP credits," (1995, 35) with divorced women in Quebec more likely than women in other parts of Canada to have benefited from this option.

Survivor benefits are available to the spouses of contributors to the CPP/QPP provided that the deceased contributed to the plan for at least 10 years or one-third of his or her "eligible years." Under this provision, the term "spouses" applies only to persons within heterosexual relationships; currently, about 90 percent of those receiving survivor benefits are women. The benefit to the spouse is calculated as 60 percent of the amount that would have been payable had the deceased turned 65 on the date of his/her death. In 1994 the benefit had a ceiling of $416.66 per month for a surviving spouse age 65 and older and $384.59 per month for a surviving spouse who was less than 65 years of age. This benefit is payable even if the surviving spouse remarries. In Quebec, the amounts paid to survivors are considerably more generous than in the rest of Canada (see Townson 1995, 35).

The GIS is designed to assist those seniors whose incomes (excluding the OAS) fall below a specified level and provides benefits that are graduated by income and marital status. As of 1994, the maximum GIS benefit available for a single elderly person was $458.50 monthly; a single person who had an income in excess of $917 a month from other sources was not eligible for this supplement. For married couples, eligibility was determined by a ceiling of family income, excluding OAS, that was less than $1194 a month. For those who qualified, the maximum monthly benefit available in 1994 was $597.30 per couple (or $298.65 per person). Unlike the OAS, GIS benefits are not taxable and, over the years, have been increased on an ad hoc basis (Townson 1995, 29). Taken together, in 1994 these benefits furnish single individuals with a maximum guaranteed annual income of $10 132, and couples with a maximum annual income of $16 427 (Townson 1995, 30). Consider, however, that in 1993 the low-income cutoff line for a single person living in an urban area with a population of 500 000 or more was $16 482; for a two-person family in an urban area of that size it was $20 603 (Columbo 1996, 83).

While, to a certain degree, CPP/QPP and GIS provisions forestall the likelihood of individuals falling into poverty during their retirement years, it has been noted that the risk of poverty for elderly women remains significant in that relatively few have access to private pensions or those pension plans provided to employees by employers. Based on statistics derived from Statistics Canada's Labour Market Activity Survey and prepared specifically for a Canadian Advisory Council on the Status of Women report (Townson 1995), approximately half (53%) of Canadian women versus 77 percent of men in the 45 to 54 age group were covered by private pensions in at least one of the jobs they had held between 1988 to 1990. Moreover, certain groups of women, such as aboriginal women and disabled women, were noted to be particularly unlikely to be covered by a private pension plan. These groups were also characterized by lower levels of education and incomes than non-disabled women and part-time employees.

For example, while the disabled in general face a heightened risk of poverty (with a 1991 post-Census survey reporting that 42.7 percent of those persons age 15 to 64 with a disability earned less than $10 000 in 1990 versus 34.9 percent of other Canadians), the likelihood of poverty is particularly pronounced among elderly women with disabilities (Ross et al. 1992, 41; DAWN 1986). Noting that disabled women are more likely to be unemployed than disabled men, less likely to be college-educated, earn substantially less when vocationally rehabilitated than vocationally rehabilitated men, are less likely to find a job post-disability, are more likely to absorb a cut in pay, and are more likely to live in families at or below the poverty line, Fine and Asch (1981) have referred to the experience of disabled women as "sexism without the pedestal." Moreover, women with disabilities are also twice as likely to be separated or divorced than non-disabled persons (Barile 1992, 32).

According to Statistics Canada, in 1992 slightly over one-third (35.3%) of women versus 41 percent of men in the Canadian labour force were covered by private pension plans; when the unemployed are excluded, 42.5 percent of women versus 51.8 percent of men in paid employment were covered by private pension plans (in Townson 1995, 37). To a large degree, women's lack of pension coverage reflects their relative absence from work in sectors such as manufacturing, construction, transportation and communication, and government services, where pension coverage is quite high, and their overrepresentation in the areas of retail trade and "community, business and personal service," where coverage is low. A woman employed as a secretary or as a salesperson for a small business is unlikely to receive a benefits package and, if she does, it is unlikely to be as comprehensive as those provided to workers whose pension plans are negotiated by trade unions on their behalf. Accordingly, the low percentage of women workers who are unionized (28 percent of women versus 36 percent of men) becomes significant (Townson 1995, 39). Moreover, Boyd (1989/1995, 217) reports that substantial numbers of Asian, Caribbean, and South European women immigrants are self-employed as seamstresses, domestics, or other marginally paid roles within the "invisible economy" and that these women are likely to receive no benefits for their years of underground employment.

While having any type of pension is advantageous, differences in pensions plans undoubtedly influence an individual's financial future. "Defined contribution plans" or "money purchase plans," typical of many small businesses, refer to a type of pension plan in which both employer and employee make contributions to a fund, but in which only the contribution—and not the benefit—is guaranteed. Rather than providing a benefit linked to earnings or years of employment, the monies received by a worker at retirement simply reflect the investment performance of the fund. "Defined benefit" pension plans, which provide benefits at retirement that are linked to a worker's salary and years of service, may or may not require contributions by the worker. Townson (1995, 43) notes, however, that employers who provide such plans are more likely to be in the public sector, or to be large businesses or institutions. Although only Ontario currently has provisions that guarantee that pensions will be paid (up to $1000 monthly) in the event that a company undergoes bankruptcy, various reforms have been made in the past decade to protect workers covered under this system of benefits, including "vesting" or the decrease in the number of years of employment required before an employee is guaranteed the right to retirement benefits. In addition, persons who change jobs may now transfer the benefits accumulated under an old employer to a new pension plan or place the funds accrued into a locked-in RRSP. However, while such provisions allow employees a greater range of options than was previously available to them, they are not retroactive. In consequence, as Townson (1995, 43) points out, Canadian women who are now 45 to 54 may find their financial future based on an admixture of systems and old and new rules. Given that, up until the late 1970s and early 1980s, pension plans often contained discriminatory provisions that stipulated, for example, that women were required to retire at an earlier age than men or were ineligible to join an employer-sponsored plan until they reached an older age than that stipulated for men, "there are undoubtedly women in the age group 45–54 today whose financial future will be affected by this kind of past discrimination in their employer's pension plan" (Townson 1995, 44).

Although women born between 1937 and 1946 are participating in the Canadian paid labour force in record numbers, their financial security at retirement will be hampered by both their typically low earnings and their shorter length of service. Statistics Canada's 1991 Survey of Aging and Independence reported that workers age 45 to 54 with incomes less than $20 000 annually were the most likely to face financial hardship during retirement. The survey additionally noted that 44 percent of women in this age group had incomes below this level. While women who possessed a university education in this age group earned, on average, an annual income of $45 000 (compared to $19 000 among those with less than a high school education), "only about 11% of employed women over age 45, compared with 16% of men in the same age group, have a university degree" (Townson 1995, 51). In that "housework brings no work-related benefits, no disability or unemployment insurance, no health benefits, and, most importantly, no pension coverage" (Wilson 1996, 54), women will continue to be penalized for their interrupted labour-force participation rates and patterns.

For example, although the term "mandatory retirement" is, in itself, somewhat misleading in that Canadian law does not specify an age at which all Canadians must retire, involuntary or mandatory retirement must be recognized as particularly disadvantageous to women. The Supreme Court of Canada has ruled that although forcing a worker to retire at a specific age is discrimination, it is legal under the Canadian Charter of Rights and Freedoms. However, as dissenting justices noted in the case of *Dickason vs. University of Alberta* (September 24, 1992: 67):

Women are penalized, in particular, because they tend to have lower paying jobs which are less likely to offer pension coverage and they often interrupt their careers to raise families. These socio-economic patterns combined with private and government pension plans which are calculated on years of participation in the workforce, in some ways make mandatory retirement at age 65 an issue of gender as of age discrimination.

The majority of women today who are 65 and over did not anticipate that it would be their financial responsibility to provide for their children or themselves. Rather, they likely accepted the traditional model that suggested women invest in a marriage rather than in a RRSP and optimistically forecast that husbands would always provide. Despite this assumption, many of these women are now finding that their husbands did not or could not provide. In 1990 elderly Canadian women age 65 and over had a median income of approximately $11 000, suggesting that a majority of these women lived below the poverty line (Crompton 1993). Moreover, while 35 percent of elderly, unattached Canadian men were poor, 53.1 percent of elderly, unattached Canadian women were living in poverty (Ross et al. 1994, 119). Although women's traditional roles within the family may increase their likelihood of poverty in their later years, it is evident that traditional ideologies continue to hold considerable sway. Lowe (1992) notes that although Canadian women are less likely than men to have an employer pension plan, they are more likely than men to opt for early retirement. Lowe additionally notes that while health-related reasons were identified by both men and women as important factors that influenced their decisions to retire, women were more likely than men to identify marriage and/or family responsibilities as important in their decisions to retire early. Canada's 1989 General Social Survey also reported that women were more likely than men to retire before age 65 (65 percent of women compared to 61 percent of men) or before age 60 (43 percent of women compared to 28 percent of men). As Townson (1995, 7) suggests, "[g]iven that women generally marry men who are older than they are, it seems reasonable to assume that many women left the paid work force because they wanted to retire at the same time as a spouse or because they had to care for older spouses." Moreover, while being married *may* provide a protective buffer against poverty, "the need to depend on a spouse for support in retirement raises issues of women's financial autonomy. And married women may experience serious financial hardship if the relationship ends" (Townson 1995, 2).

The National Council of Welfare (1990/1995, 214) suggests that encroaching poverty may force widows to sell their family homes and move to rental or institutional settings because they lack the money to live and keep up with the inexhaustible expenses that home ownership entails (roofs, furnaces, and windows that need replacement, property taxes, driveways that require repaving, etc.). Inasmuch as individuals are likely to identify someone from their own generation as the "family comforter" (Rosenthal 1987/1995, 348) who provides emotional support and advice, this move might entail an increase in social isolation. Nett (1993) suggests that the isolation of elderly women may explain research findings that suggest that the mental health of older women is less than that of older men. Moreover, while most older men "have built-in housekeepers and nurses—their wives" (National Council of Welfare 1990/1995, 214), the future for incapacitated elderly women may be especially bleak. If older individuals are apt to identify living independently as an important measure of personal autonomy (Mutchler 1992), the financial ability to do so would seem as important here as physical health per se. In 1991 approximately one in five older, senior women, compared with one in ten older, senior men, lived in institutions such as special care homes and hospitals (Priest 1993).

For many Canadians, including the near-elderly, the issue of financial security during retirement seems remote and of only distant concern. Moreover, as Townson (1995, 6) has remarked, "[s]urveys indicate a wide gap between the optimistic expectations of Canadians for retirement and the reality of inadequate final resources that most will face." She observes that, according to a 1992 Canadian survey, while three-quarters of the respondents recognized that they will be personally responsible for a significant portion of their retirement income, "three-quarters are also doing little or no planning for retirement" (6). Although an annual retirement income of $50 000 requires a lump sum deposit of $500 000 (or for a person with 20 years remaining until retirement, annual deposits of $11 000 at a 7 percent rate of return), the savings of most Canadians are far more modest. Including contributions made to an employer's pension plan, 50 percent of Canadians in the paid workforce save less than $2000 annually (Townson 1995, 6).

In addition, it has been increasingly recognized that the aftermath of divorce often places women and their children in a financially disadvantaged position. Since the mid-1960s, divorce rates have increased significantly in Canada and currently hover around 40 percent. The 1968 Divorce Act distinguished between orders made for support payments for spouses and those made for children. Amendments to the Act made in 1985 recognized that both spouses have a joint financial obligation to maintain their children and that this obligation should be proportioned between the spouses according to their relative abilities to contribute. Amendments to the Divorce Act also state that the financial ties between the former spouses should be limited as far as possible; accordingly, there has been an increase in the number of support orders for fixed time periods and cases in which no order of support has been granted. Galarneau (1993) observes that the movement towards favouring financial self-sufficiency of former spouses has had negative consequences particularly among middle-aged women who were not in the workforce prior to divorce and women in their thirties and forties who are given custody of the children. It is argued that fixed-period support does not necessarily allow women, especially those with child custody, sufficient time to acquire the job skills or education necessary to become self-supporting.

Following from the March 1996 federal budget, changes in the tax rules for child support were announced to become effective May 1, 1997. Previously, the payer could deduct child support payments where there was a written agreement or a court order in effect and the recipient was taxed on these payments. However, for child support agreements or court orders established after May 1, 1997, the payer receives no tax deduction and the recipient pays no income tax on the monies paid. The taxation of spousal support payments is unaffected by these new rules. While child support agreements made prior to March 1996 are unaffected by the new rules (unless both parties agree to have the new rules apply or one party receives a court order to that effect), agreements or court orders made between March 1996 and May 1, 1997, could specify that the new rules would apply. Under these new rules, it is increasingly necessary to specify which payments are made for spousal support and which are made for child support; if doubt exists about the recipient of the payment, the assumption is made that it is for child support. In the event that only a portion of the total required spousal and child support payments are made, monies for child support payments are considered to be paid first.

In addition to these changes, the federal government has attempted to introduce guidelines, based on the income of the payee, for use in establishing the amount of child support payment that will be mandatory for child support orders made from April 30, 1997, under the Divorce

Act. The court may adjust the amount in consideration of child care expenses for preschool children, medical expenses not covered by provincial health care plans, educational expenses, "extraordinary" expenses (e.g., extracurricular activities), or evidence of demonstrated hardship (to any party).

Despite such changes, a support order, in and of itself, does not guarantee that payments will be made. For example, according to a 1991 estimate, in Ontario alone there are 90 000 unpaid support orders, representing $470 million in delinquent payments (cited in Galarneau 1993, 9). Ontario's Bill 17, which became effective on March 1, 1992, implemented stricter support payment enforcement measures that required employers to withhold alimony payments from the wages of employees who were delinquent in their payments. Like deductions required for Unemployment Insurance or the CPP, such deductions are obligatory. However, such provisions are not uniform throughout all provinces nor enforceable in the United States should the delinquent payer elect to seek employment across the border to escape payments. Similarly, while Alberta, Nova Scotia, and Saskatchewan have legislation to revoke the driver's licences of people not making payments, Ontario, Quebec, New Brunswick, and Newfoundland do not have similar laws on the books.

For anti-feminists, the solution proposed to this problem is to restore the nuclear family wherever possible by making divorce more difficult (thus forcing the man to take responsibility for his family) and to force women on welfare to name the fathers of their children so the men can be forced to pay support (Ehrenreich and Stallard 1982). For liberal feminists, the customary demand has been that fathers be forced through child-support legislation to take responsibility for their children. For socialist feminists, however, both approaches are misguided. Thus, Brenner (1987, 455) maintains, "The claim that women's poverty is caused by deadbeat fathers, similar to the claim that Black poverty is caused by teenage mothers, is not only factually incorrect but looks to the restoration of the nuclear family as the solution to the problem of dependent care." This construction of women's poverty, she suggests, simply reinforces the role of the male breadwinner as well as the "imagery of female victimization" (451–452).

It is Brenner's contention that

> [p]ortraying poor women as innocent victims of men's irresponsibility may win sympathy for the plight of poor women but at the cost of failing to challenge deeply held notions about feminine dependence on a male breadwinner and distinctions between the deserving and the nondeserving poor, in particular between the "good" woman who is poor because her husband refuses support and the "bad" woman who is poor because she has had a child outside of marriage or has married a poor man who cannot provide (452).

Brenner also takes issue with feminization-of-poverty literature that fails to explore the differing experiences of women of different races and classes following divorce or widowhood. She stresses that "[w]hile many white women are 'only a husband away from poverty,' many minority women *with* a husband are poor" (453, emphasis in original). Moreover, she notes that this same literature often denies the poverty of men, especially minority men. Citing Malvaux (1985), who argued that the slogan, "by the year 2000 all the poor will be women and children" is accurate only if genocide or full employment should be the fate of all minority men, Brenner emphasizes that "women make up an increasing proportion of the poor because more women are falling into poverty, not because more men are getting out" (453). Finally, she maintains that women's greater life expectancy is an additional reason why the numbers of poor men are fewer than those of poor women. "For the underclass," Brenner maintains, "minority or white, poverty is not simply a problem of women without men—it includes their sons, husbands and ex-husbands, and fathers" (454).

For these reasons, Brenner stresses that "[t]he familistic ideology and state policy that denies collective responsibility for dependent individuals, forces women to take on the burdens of caring, and assumes that only men have a claim to economic independence and citizenship, must be transformed." She suggests a need to reframe the "feminization of poverty" issue in a way "that connects it to the movements of working-class people and people of colour" and comments that "[i]n the longer run, a living wage, quality child care, and good work are necessary for everyone, but especially for women who choose not to share child care with a man." (454).

As a final note, inasmuch as one social problem is indelibly linked to others, we may observe that although the increased availability of divorce has theoretically allowed women to end abusive or unsatisfactory relationships, the financial consequences of divorce effectively penalize women, and their children, for doing so. Accordingly, it is ironic that we still ask of the battered woman who remains in an abusive relationship, "Why does she stay?" Her unwillingness or inability to leave may simply reflect a particularly keen understanding of the social and economic hardships entailed by her leaving.

SUMMARY

1. In Canada, the "problem" of gender is conceived differently by various groups. Some argue that deviations from traditional gender roles cause problems in society; others view a strict adherence to traditional gender stereotypes as thwarting the actualization of men's and women's full potential as human beings.

2. Theoretical models of gender have often adopted a taken-for-granted "reality" about the nature of gender and the ensuing division of labour. In contrast, feminist theorists challenge the mainstream assumptions that contemporary gender roles are "natural" or "equitable."

3. "Feminism" must be understood as offering a multivocal approach to addressing the social problems associated with gender. Feminism is not a monolithic philosophy; rather, divisions within feminism mirror the varying ways the problems associated with gender may be framed and solutions may be proposed.

4. The tendency to view deviations from or discomfort with traditional gender roles as an individual "dysfunction" or an intensely personal trouble has been marked and continues into the 1990s, both within the popular press and within the flourishing inventory of "syndromes" that pathologize anyone who would challenge the confines of traditional gender roles.

5. The confinements of gender are supported through both gender-role socialization and the social structure of Canadian society.

6. Analysis of where women work and the "second shift" of work assigned within the home suggests the legacy and continuance of labour market segmentation.

7. The phenomenon of the "feminization of poverty" suggests that structural changes in society may be necessary to combat both sexism and poverty.

RACE,
ETHNICITY, AND
ABORIGINALITY

DID YOU KNOW?

- Canada can claim many "firsts" in the management of race, ethnic, and aboriginal relations. Canada remains the first and only official multicultural country in the world. It is also the first and only country to recognize and constitutionally entrench aboriginal rights. For its efforts in international refugee work, Canada was awarded the Nansen medal by the United Nations in 1986—the first and only country to be honoured in this way.

- Canada's mistreatment of aboriginal peoples is widely condemned both nationally and internationally. On some reserves, unemployment rates are up to 95 percent of the employable population, suicide rates for young people are six times the national rate, three times as many suffer from diabetes as the national average, and deaths by accidents or violence are four times that for the country as a whole.

- To those who thought that segregation of African-Americans happened only in the American South, think again! Blacks in Canada were routinely barred from access to services, entry to public venues, and employment in all but the most menial jobs until the 1950s and 1960s. Even the Ku Klux Klan flourished in parts of Canada, especially during the 1920s.

- As recently as 1989, Canada's acceptance rate for refugees stood at about 80 percent. By the end of 1993, it dropped to 48 percent. Most European countries, including the Scandinavian states, are in the 10 to 20 percent range. In terms of sheer volume, few can match Germany with nearly 6.4 million asylum seekers since 1980, compared to Canada's

400 000, but in Germany refugees, including children born on German soil, are rarely allowed German citizenship.

- A small percentage of Canadians (perhaps 10 to 15 percent) appear to be generally free of prejudice towards others. By the same token, the number of outright racists in Canada is relatively small (about 10 to 15 percent) according to most national surveys. The overwhelming majority fall somewhere in the middle between tolerance and bigotry.

- The racial mix in Canada's population is rapidly expanding. With between 200 000 and 220 000 new Canadians per year, Canada's immigration rate on a per capita basis far surpasses that of Australia and the United States. Only New Zealand is showing comparable rates. Nearly 75 percent of new Canadians come from Third World countries; as a result, the proportion of Canadians with some degree of non-British or non-French ancestry now stands at about 40 percent. People of colour comprise just over 9 percent of the total population, with the vast majority preferring to live in major urban centres.

- Race and class can play an important role in shaping outcomes. A study conducted by York University's Institute for Social Research found that graduates from lower income and visible minority families had a tougher time finding full-time work after graduation. While 58 percent of graduates of European origin quickly found work, only 40 percent of black students and 35 percent of students with Chinese background were successful.

- Nearly 90 percent of Quebeckers outside of Montreal do not speak English. Conversely, around 90 percent of English-speaking Canadians outside of Ontario's bilingual belts cannot speak French. Is it any wonder that Canada's two charter groups are accused of failing to communicate?

THE PROBLEM

Canada is internationally renowned for many qualities, but two are uppermost. First, people overseas marvel at Canada's ability to withstand the pressures of absorption as the fifty-first state of the world's most powerful society. How, they ask, can Canada keep the juggernaut to the south at bay while pursuing a relatively independent course of action? Former Prime Minister Pierre Elliott Trudeau captured the enigma in a Washington speech in 1969 when he said, "Living next to you is in some ways like sleeping with an elephant; no matter how friendly and even-tempered is the beast, one is affected by every twitch and grunt. Even a friendly nuzzle can sometimes lead to frightening consequences." That Canadians have managed to keep their distance in a spirit of friendship and cooperation, without succumbing to the lure of American cultural industries or jingoistic nationalism, is a testimony to the resilience of its people.

Second, many are amazed by our ability to forge a remarkably prosperous and coherent society from the challenges of diversity. How, indeed, has Canada managed to avoid the racial violence that periodically engulfs the United States, as it did in Los Angeles in May 1992? How do Canadians manage to keep a lid on interethnic strife, with its potential to dismember societies into warring factions? Admittedly, the forces for rending Canada asunder are never far from the surface. Nowhere is this more evident than in cobbling together the competing demands of a three-nations state (including aboriginal peoples, Québécois, and English-speaking Canadians) within a framework of official multiculturalism. Nevertheless, while other countries seem to be groping in the dark for solutions, Canada has managed not only to address the challenge of diversity, but also to survive as one of the world's oldest federal systems. Do these achievements stand up to scrutiny?

Canada the Good

There is little doubt that Canada ranks as one of the most desirable countries in the world in which to live (Levitt 1997). That much is obvious when comparing Canada with countries whose regimes routinely imprison and torture dissidents who dare to question the status quo. Canada possesses an enviable reputation for its enlightened management of race, ethnic, and aboriginal relations—often praised, occasionally copied. To be sure, our reputation shows a bit of tarnish on closer examination. Still, Canada holds up well in any comparison and evaluation, as the next points indicate:

1) Canada remains the world's first and only official multicultural society. Not only was it the first to pass a Multiculturalism Act (1988), but a federal department of state was later instituted (since disbanded) for the implementation of multicultural policies and programs. In keeping with demographic, political, and social changes, official multiculturalism has shifted in style and substance since its inception in 1971—from an initial focus on "cultural sharing" to a later emphasis on "managing diversity." Current commitments include the notions of "belonging" and "citizenship" as part of a civic multiculturalism (Fleras 1994; Annual Report 1997). Canada's experiment with the multicultural management of race and ethnic relations continues to evoke worldwide admiration despite shortcomings in design and implementation (see Lewycky 1992).

2) Canada is the first (and only) country to constitutionally entrench aboriginal and treaty rights. The Constitution Act of 1981–82 acknowledged the primacy of existing aboriginal and treaty rights as a basis for managing the federal government's aboriginal policy. Recent government moves to constitutionally restore the *inherent* self-governing rights of aboriginal peoples as *peoples* continue to make Canada a pace-setter. To date, tangible results have been relatively modest, except perhaps for the Nunavut agreement in the eastern Arctic. As well, government expenditures by the Department of Indian Affairs continue to rise while conditions on many reserves resemble those of the Third World (Fleras 1996). Still, Canada remains active in exploring channels for decolonizing aboriginal–state relations, without shattering territorial sovereignty or emptying the public purse in the process.

3) Canada's immigration and refugee policies and practices are in a class by themselves. With about 215 000 immigrants each year (in addition to about 20 000 to 25 000 refugee claimants), Canada outranks both Australia and the United States as a world leader in immigrant entries on a per capita basis. A refugee acceptance rate of just under 50 percent further consolidates Canada's progressive status. Its receipt of the Nansen medal in 1986 for its humanitarian response to the global refugee problem—the first and only country ever to be awarded that honour by the United Nations—confirmed what many had suspected: Few can match Canada's international commitments when it comes to helping the less fortunate.

4) Canada has garnered a well-deserved reputation for initiatives in facilitating the settlement and integration of immigrants. A variety of programs are available for improving education and employment skills. Training in one of the two official languages is also

actively encouraged. With few exceptions, moreover, the social climate is generally receptive to race and ethnic minorities (Berry 1993; Berry and Kalin 1995). Levels of intolerance towards visible minorities appear to be decreasing in response to government initiatives that prohibit prejudice and discrimination. Even the gradual increase in the number of race-related incidents is not necessarily indicative of social breakdown. Instead, it may reflect greater public awareness of hate crimes, coupled with a greater willingness by minority members to report racial slurs and other acts of discrimination.

The Bad and the Ugly

There is no question of Canada's lofty reputation for the astute management of racial, ethnic, and aboriginal relations (Kurthen 1997). In a world where minority rights are routinely sacrificed on the altar of expediency, Canada is a leader in advancing diversity—at least in principle if not always in practice. Some of this praise is deserved; some of it, unfortunately, is not. Closer scrutiny suggests that although Canada's race relations record is better than most, it is still far from being perfect. Perhaps this comes as a shock to those enamoured of visions of Canada as the true north, strong and free. Canada has had its share of shameful episodes in the mistreatment of racial, ethnic, and aboriginal minorities. Slavery and race riots, along with the segregation of minorities and suspension of civil rights, were commonly practised. The fact that racial, ethnic, and indigenous peoples continue to be denied or excluded, albeit more politely than before and by consequence rather than intent, is no reason to gloat. A partial list of Canada's less flattering "underside" would include:

1) Many aboriginal communities can only be described as downtrodden and impoverished. High rates of unemployment and imprisonment, coupled with low rates of educational and career attainment, attest to that (Royal Commission 1996). The cumulative effects of dependency and underdevelopment have left many aboriginal communities no better off than some of their counterparts in the developing world. The material poverty is gruelling enough. Worse still are the dispiriting effects from the disempowering erosion of language, culture, and identity. Their combined impact has accelerated the demise of aboriginal communities, leaving many of them vulnerable to incidents of social, psychological, and physical abuse (Shkilnyk 1985).

2) Outright racism towards racial and ethnic minorities has been common (McKague 1991; Henry et al. 1995). Highly restrictive immigration policies were endorsed at the turn of the century, including the notorious head tax, the continuous journey laws, and the exclusion acts. Chinese and East Indian immigrants were particularly hard hit during the nineteenth and early twentieth centuries (Stasiulis 1997). Asian populations were allowed entry to Canada for nation-building purposes, but once the work was completed, most were severely restricted in their movements, subjected to harassment and discrimination, exposed to bullying racists, and stripped of basic human and civil rights. Rights for Asians (including the right to migrate to Canada or to vote) were not restored until after 1947 when Canadians resolved the paradox of fighting for freedom overseas while reneging on minority human rights at home.

3) African-Canadians in Nova Scotia and Ontario were segregated. Despite Canada's reputation as the land of the free, many slaves who fled oppressive conditions in the United States simply exchanged one system of oppression for another. African-Canadians

were routinely excluded from restaurants and other public venues by laws as discriminatory as those in the southern United States. Segregated schools, for example, were not taken off the books in Ontario or Nova Scotia until the early 1960s. This exclusion from equal access has not diminished in some cases, notwithstanding formal equality before the law. Whether by default or intent, African-Canadian youths continue to be excluded from full societal participation because of stereotyping and systemic biases.

4) Japanese-Canadians were interned during the Second World War after coming under suspicion immediately after the bombing of Pearl Harbor on December 7, 1941. In British Columbia, thousands of Japanese-Canadians were stripped of property and citizenship, then relocated in what essentially were concentration camps across Canada. They remained there for the duration of the war, despite no proof of disloyalty, and were encouraged to leave Canada following the war. A formal apology and compensation package in 1988 furnished partial atonement. At least four other minority groups, including Chinese, Ukrainians, Italians, and Sikhs, are currently seeking reparations for similar violations.

5) A pervasive anti-Semitism in the 1920s and 1930s had the effect of denying even the most basic human rights for Jews in Canada. Landing rights were denied to Jewish refugees from Nazi genocide on the grounds that "none was too much" (Abella and Troper 1982). Jews (as well as Catholics) were automatically excluded from employment in major institutions such as the police. Even at universities, signs were posted that frankly reminded applicants that "Jews need not apply." Signs warning "Jews and dogs not allowed" were posted along Toronto's lake fronts. Rather than disappearing, however, anti-Semitism continues to fester as evidenced in outright acts of vandalism and hate graffiti. Denials of the Holocaust are yet another example of hostility towards Jews.

6) No less disconcerting is the proliferation of racial supremacist groups. These relatively organized groups have long been engaged in activities to dehumanize and deny minorities full and equal participation in society (Li 1995). They first appeared in B.C. during the late nineteenth century as anti-Asian hate groups, flourished as Ku Klux Klan in the 1920s, and currently exist as white supremacists who condone the superiority of Caucasians as the basis for social and political order. Ranging in style from urban skinheads to neo-Nazi offshoots (Barrett 1987), splinters of the far right are capitalizing on Canadian fears by targeting minorities as scapegoats for the country's economic woes. These hate groups also endorse "white pride" and racial purity as a quick-fix solution to complex problems.

7) People of colour continue to experience widespread discrimination in the fields of housing, employment, and education (Henry and Ginzberg 1993). In some cases, this discrimination is palpable but polite; in others, it is systemic and difficult to detect except at the level of consequences and outcomes. The law may apply equally to all, but its equal application favours some, disfavours others, and perpetuates inequality in the guise of ostensibly neutral rules (Jakubowski 1997).

8) The looming crisis in police–minority relations is worrying (Cryderman, O'Toole and Fleras 1998). Police shootings of African-Canadians in Montreal and Toronto have sparked accusations of police brutality and insensitivity. Worse still, police initiatives to

establish closer cooperation through community-based, culturally sensitive policing have not had the desired effect.

9) There is growing resentment in the country towards immigrants and refugees. For the past decade, nearly three-quarters of all new Canadians have arrived from non-European and non-American sources. This expanding diversity has precipitated a backlash against immigrants and racial minorities, with increasing demands to review policy and practice. The stoking of dormant prejudices not only subjects new Canadians to verbal abuse or physical attacks, but also undermines Canada's reputation abroad. While many are genuinely concerned about immigration to Canada in terms of numbers, sources, and categories, others are hiding behind the rhetoric of "national interests" to mask their prejudice and bigotry.

The "In Between"

It may be argued that little can be gained by pointing a finger (either glowingly or accusingly) at Canada's efforts in the management of race, ethnic, and indigenous relations. The best approach is one that straddles the inbetween. Canada is neither the model of virtue when it comes to managing diversity nor is it paragon of all evils, but probably falls between these extremes. Compared with the race relations record of other societies, Canada is light years ahead. Compared with the lofty aspirations that Canadians have set for themselves, we still have a long way to go in approximating these ideals. In contrast with our historical track record, Canada has progressed smartly in shedding its openly racist and exclusionist past. Put simply, our assessment of Canada lies somewhere between the poles of good or bad. Initiatives for managing race, ethnicity, and indigeneity are enlightened at times, but callously expedient at others as Canadians attempt to balance "national interests" with the emergent rights of minorities. To couch the analysis in terms of good or bad is simply to prejudge the issue. That kind of prejudgment may well complicate the challenge of analyzing race, ethnic, and indigenous relations as a social problem.

Sociologists are interested in the social dimensions of race, ethnicity, and aboriginality, particularly how minorities have been labelled as social problems and mistreated accordingly. Defining the problem of diversity may entail a fourfold process: identifying public issues; framing an appropriate discourse; incorporating the discourse into the agenda; and formulating a response (Rochefort and Cobb 1994). But establishing the parameters of this problem is itself problematic. For example, minorities are routinely regarded as a social problem. Yet minority women and men are not the problem per se. More accurately, minorities have been *defined* as a problem by those with a vested interest in preserving power and privilege. That, in turn, raises the questions of why people define minorities as a problem and how social arrangements have evolved to confirm their problematic status. After all, in a globalizing world of diversity and change, it is *conformity* rather than diversity that is a problem. Those who would deny the validity and value of diversity are jeopardizing Canada's competitiveness and coherence at home and abroad. In short, reaction to diversity can be problematic if it (a) undermines Canada's vision of itself as a progressive and egalitarian society; (b) inflicts social, cultural, or psychological harm on targeted minorities; (c) extracts costs that outweigh benefits; (d) culminates in conflict and the possible dismemberment of society; and (e) violates both national laws and international agreements to which Canada is a signatory.

Problematizing race, ethnic, and aboriginal relations as relationships of inequality makes it doubly important to understand how these inequities are created, expressed, maintained, challenged, and transformed at the level of policy and practice (Fleras and Elliott 1996). The following type of questions are commonly raised: What are the structural factors underlying racial discrimination? Under what social circumstances are patterns of inequality likely to arise, persist, or decline? In what ways do government policies solve problems or create new ones? How is ethnicity manipulated in the competition for scarce resources? Sociologists like to look for answers beyond the immediate or precipitating causes. They prefer to concentrate instead on root causes related to power, structure, and values. The structural and situational are emphasized rather than the personal and attitudinal as a basis for analysis and reform. This chapter makes no promises of delivering ready answers and finely honed solutions to seemingly tenacious problems. The field is littered with divergent and competing interpretations with respect to causes, cures, and consequences. Perhaps the best we can hope for in this volatile field are informed questions and plausible answers that reflect a "sociological imagination."

RACE MATTERS: A PROBLEM IN SEARCH OF SUBSTANCE

The significance of race in shaping intergroup dynamics cannot be underestimated. Race continues to matter in shaping people's lives and life chances, for better or for worse (see D'Souza 1996). Racism and racist groups will continue to exist as long as people use the concept of race to explain the existence of social problems or as an excuse to deny or exclude others. Many are baffled by how a biological concept of essentially limited worth exerts a profound influence over the course of human history—in effect confirming the sociological aphorism that "Phenomena do not have to be real, to be real in their consequences." The race concept originated and evolved in an attempt to explain intergroup relations, to legitimize conquest and condone exploitation, and to account for human diversity as parsimoniously as possible in a modernist world (Goldberg 1993). The construction of race types and racial typologies not only facilitated European colonialization in the eighteenth and nineteenth century, but imparted a pseudo-scientific sheen to actions involving domination and control. Current references to race are dismissed by many as poor science and bad politics. Nevertheless, the race concept continues to attract public support as a means of (a) explaining group differences, (b) justifying differential treatment, and (c) condoning a lack of concerted action. Then as now, the problem of race must be confronted squarely if we are to appreciate its role in generating group dynamics and social inequality.

Race as Social Construct

Human beings belong to a single biological species (*homo sapiens*) within a larger grouping or genus (*homo*). Biologically speaking, the human species resembles other floral and faunal species because of population clusters with varying gene frequencies across spatial dimensions. Discussions about plant and animal species are conducted around internal diversity as responses to evolutionary forces, with little interest in subspecies variation known as race. By contrast, talk of human diversity is often couched in terms of race. There has been no dearth of initiatives to (a) classify people into racial categories on the basis of fixed and arbitrary characteristics such as skin colour, (b) attribute certain physical, social, psychological, and moral properties to these categories, and (c) evaluate and rank these categories in ascending and descending order of inferiority and superiority. For our purposes, we can define the concept of race as the arbitrary classification of population groups into categories (types) on the basis of perceived physical characteristics. This definition clearly acknowledges the concept of race as a social construction—that is, a hypothetical construct, without any basis in biology or scientific validity.

Race Types and Typologies

Early explanation of human variation drew inspiration from the race concept. This preoccupation reflected a nineteenth century quest for unitary schemes to explain the totality of human experience in conjunction with European exploration and exploitation (Goldberg 1994; West 1996). The race concept sorted human groups into a finite number of permanent types, each with a fixed and distinctive set of characteristics, to which all individuals belonged (Banton 1987). Designated groups were subsequently slotted into predetermined categories (racial typologies) that reflected a hierarchy of superiority and inferiority. Europeans were not the first or only group to mistreat others; however, they were among the first to "normalize" the race concept as a scientifically grounded rationalization for exploitation and control. The aura and authority of these pseudo-scientific classifications accentuated group differences by making them appear more comprehensive, more permanent and unchangeable, more scientifically valid, and more devastating in impact and consequences (Stocking Jr. 1968; Stepan 1982).

A variety of classificatory schemes (or typologies) were launched during the nineteenth century. However, the most common and widely known system originated during the last century. It endorsed a threefold division of humanity into Caucasoid (white), Negroid (black), and Mongoloid (Asian) (Rushton 1995). All human populations could be classified into one of these three categories by virtue of common physical features such as skin colour (black, white, yellow, or red), hair type (fuzzy, wavy, or straight), eyelid shape (wide, narrow, or slanted), and so on. The distinctive attributes of each "type" had evolved (or were created) independently. Only physical commingling with other "stocks" could undermine the permanency of these types (Biddiss 1979). Also implicit within this typology was the proposed linking of physical characteristics and behavioural attributes, followed by a ranking of these "types" into ascending and descending orders of progress or moral worth.

Many social scientists are resolutely opposed to the race concept when applied to human affairs (Miles 1982; Spoonley et al. 1996). They have discarded the validity of race as germane to the understanding of human diversity. Racial types and typologies have been discredited as pseudo-science and dangerous politics, without any redeeming explanatory value or empirical merit, except to preserve privilege or exert control. Discrete and distinct categories of racially pure people—the cornerstone of racial classification—do not exist because of migration, social exchanges, and intermarriage. Proposals that rank human diversity along cascading lines of superiority are suspect when deprived of any biological justification for such evaluation. Equally criticized is the largely unwarranted correlation of select physical characteristics (biology) with certain behavioural, moral, or cognitive properties (culture). Yet theories of race and doctrines of racial supremacy continue to flourish.

The following case study deals with one effort to revive race-related typologies for sorting people into categories of superior or inferior. Recent controversies over racial determinism are indicative of the fallacies associated with the race concept. However fallacious this line of thinking, the assertion that one race is superior to another historically has exerted a powerful influence on the lives and life chances of certain minorities. Equally worrying is the fact that such pronouncements continue to attract the attention of those with the power to put misguided thinking into practice.

CASE 7-1   Debunking Race

Biological theories of race and evolution have come and gone, and in all probability will continue to elicit pockets of support in the foreseeable future. From the nineteenth century doctrines of Social Darwinism to the 1960s' "Scientific" Racism of Jensen and Schockley to the contemporary proposals of Charles Murray and Richard Herrnstein, a variety of claims have purportedly linked biology and intelligence or morality in an evolutionary hierarchy that asserts the superiority of one race over another. Publication of *The Bell Curve: Intelligence and Class Structure in American Life* has reincarnated debates on biology and behaviour. The authors, Charles Murray and Richard J. Herrnstein, argue that intelligence (as measured by IQ) is inherited. Innately low levels of intelligence are responsible for a host of social pathologies such as poverty, lawlessness, and dysfunctional families, none of which is expected to respond to remedial measures. If this trend is allowed to continue, the authors contend, the eclipse of the United States as a superpower is assured. The following are key planks in their position (see also Browne 1994):

- Intelligence is real and measurable.
- Intelligence can be quantified through IQ tests.
- Intelligence is partly inherited, which makes it resistant to reform.

- Intelligence has a predictive value, that is, it correlates with positive (success) and negative (welfare or crime) achievement; those with more intelligence are successful while those with less are destined to fail.
- Intelligence varies across ethnic and racial groups; some races have high levels of intelligence while others don't. Whites, for example, are smarter than Blacks, and these intellectual differences are innate.
- The proliferation of intellectually impoverished ethnic and racial groups (by migration or natural birth) will diminish a country's ability to produce, compete, or prosper.
- Innate differences in intelligence should serve as a basis for social policy. Why throw good money after bad when compensatory or affirmative-type programs are destined to fail?

In short, patterns of inequality and class (who is rich and who is poor) are not randomly distributed. According to Murray and Herrnstein, these patterns are dependent on inherited measures of intelligence. Those with intelligence are successful; those without it are dysfunctional. Social problems will proliferate unless something is done to minimize the presence and impact of the intellectually impoverished underclass. Yet another interpretation that falls squarely into the sociological camp is plausible.

CASE 7-1	Debunking Race (continued)

Levels of intelligence do not generate social dysfunction; rather, dysfunctional social contexts are more likely to produce low intellectual levels. This inversion is not meant to be playful or humorous, but to accentuate the social dimensions of human problems.

The United States provides a fertile source for racist diatribes, yet Canada is not exempt from this hate-mongering. Philippe Rushton, a professor of psychology at the University of Western Ontario, unleashed a maelstrom of controversy regarding the genetic determinants of human behaviour. In his publication *Race, Evolution, and Behavior: A Life History Perspective* (1995), Rushton posits a theory of evolution to account for racial differences across a broad and hierarchical spectrum of physical, social, mental, and moral domains. Rushton argues that separate races, namely Mongoloid, Caucasoid, and Negroid, evolved a distinctive package of physical, social, and mental characteristics because of different reproductive strategies in coping with diverse environments. High reproductive strategies (many offspring, low nurturing) evolved in tropical climates; low reproductive strategies (few offspring, intense nurturing) evolved in temperate climates. A racial pecking order can be observed on the basis of this evolutionary adaptation by way of careful measurement of physical, social, and mental attributes for the respective races. According to Rushton, Mongoloids are superior to Caucasoids who, in turn, supersede Negroids because of measurements involving skull size, intelligence, strength of sex drive and genital size, industriousness, sociability, and rule-following. Mongoloids are more intelligent, more family-focused, more law-abiding, but less sexually promiscuous than Negroids. Caucasoids happily occupy the terrain in between—neither too hot nor too cold but just right. Table 7-1 compares the three major racial categories employed by Rushton in his typology.

How valid is Rushton's proposed hierarchy of racial groups? Many social scientists would deny the validity of such claims on scientific and political grounds, yet concede his right to speak on contentious issues. While there is no reason to deny the existence of individual variation, there are good reasons to reject a racial interpretation of human behaviour and achievement. The concept of human races has long been discarded as scientifically valid or biologically real. No evidence can support the existence of discrete and well-defined categories of humans with unique sets of homogeneous and fixed properties. References to the concept of human races have no explanatory value since social and cultural explanations can often account for differences or similarities. Why, then, biologize human behaviour when alternative explanations exist? Perhaps simplistic and bioreductionist explanations have become increasingly acceptable in an era in which cut-backs in social spending are the rule rather than exception.

TABLE 7-1	Rushton's Race Typology		
	Mongoloid	**Caucasoid**	**Negroid**
Cranial Capacity	1415 cc	1408 cc	1330 cc
IQ Score	106	100	85
Sexual Activity	Low	Moderate	High
Temperament	Calm/Cautious	Moderate	Aggressive/Excitable
Marital Stability	Secure	Moderate	Brittle
Social Organization			
(A) Law-Abiding	Conformist	Moderate	Deviance
(B) Crime Rate	Low	Moderate	High

Note: The terms Mongoloid, Caucasoid and Negroid reflect Rushton's terminology. Adapted in part from Rushton 1995, 5.

RACIAL DISCRIMINATION: A SOCIAL PROBLEM

There is ample evidence that discrimination is a pervasive and persistent feature of Canadian society, despite our collective self-image as a tolerant and generous people. Questions arise that, because of the enormity of the problem, deserve careful thought and consideration, including:

- Why we do we discriminate against others?
- Under what social circumstances is discrimination likely to arise?
- What is the relationship of discrimination to racism? Of prejudice to discrimination?
- How is racial discrimination manifest in society?
- Who or what is responsible for discrimination?
- What can be done about it?

These questions may appear deceptively simple. Responses, however, are complex and elusive; they rarely admit of consensus. Perhaps the battle against racial discrimination is unwinnable, and the best we can hope for is a stalemate between competing forces. After all, not all problems are amenable to solutions that are definitive or long-lasting (Dickey 1997). That we appear no closer to a solution in this area reveals the complexities in grappling with a moving target. Yet neither widespread disagreement nor disillusionment can diminish the urgency for appropriate responses.

It is obvious that Canada is not nearly as free of discrimination as it was once thought to be. In fact, discrimination may be as inherently Canadian as a professed support for the virtues of diversity and equality. Discrimination persists because it nurtures white esteem and deep-seated values pertaining to who gets what, and why, in society (Powell 1992). People discriminate, whether consciously or unconsciously, because it is in their best interests to do so. White, male managers like to hire their "own kind" on the conviction that this practice reduces uncertainty, enhances loyalty and trust, and improves productivity. Friendship circles become exclusive because members prefer their "own kind." Capitalism itself is a fertile ground for discrimination, with winners and losers consigned to a perpetual struggle for power, wealth, and status. Its role as a system of social control in capitalist societies has been widely documented (Bolaria and Li 1988). Rather than being a deviation from the norm, in other words, discrimination in Canada may be the rule rather than the exception.

The presence of racism and discrimination is widely regarded as a personal problem. For minorities, racial discrimination is not an abstraction for analysis but an aspect of everyday reality that shapes their lives and life chances. Coping with discrimination induces personal anguish by precluding full and equal participation in society. On too many occasions, pent-up energy is dissipated in a protracted but ultimately unproductive effort to surmount irrelevance, marginality, and powerlessness. Yet racial discrimination is a social problem: it originates within the structures of society, is expressed through social interaction, and has consequences for society at large. Its costs to society may be staggering; one only needs to consider the loss of productivity that ensues from workplace harassment to appreciate how discrimination squanders potential assets. The extent to which discrimination is a social problem for minorities in particular, in addition to society as a whole, puts a different spin on a proposed solution.

The pervasiveness of racial discrimination does not simplify its analysis. Analysis must begin by distinguishing racism and discrimination from prejudice, while keeping in mind that what qualifies as racial or discriminatory for some is not for others. Different expressions of racial discrimination can be discerned for analytical purposes, each varying in terms of scope, intensity, duration, and level of intent. That fact alone makes it necessary to formulate diverse strategies for solutions. Proper understanding also respects a distinction between precipitating factors (immediate factors such as drunkenness or emotional distress) and root causes (with their focus on deeper structures and wider contexts). Finally, it is important to separate psychological and sociological approaches. The former concentrate on the individual mental states behind racial discrimination, the latter on structures and situations.

Prejudice

For our purposes, prejudice literally refers to prejudgments we make about others on the basis of incomplete and stereotyped information. Stereotypes themselves consist of unfounded preconceptions about all members of a defined group (for example, Germans are thought to be industrious and Blacks are perceived as natural athletes). Prejudice begins by clouding our perceptions of others in a haze of half-truths. It concludes by reinforcing a set of preconceived notions of how things are and a rigid set of expectations about how they should be.

There is nothing inherently wrong with prejudging the world around us; hastily contrived prejudgments are inescapable in the fast-paced world in which we live. Nor should prejudice be confused with preferences. Prejudice becomes a problem only when it interferes with making accurate assessments of the objective world. It also becomes problematic when others are judged on the basis of either gross generalizations (stereotypes) or culturally unfamiliar standards (ethnocentrism). Problems thus arise from a refusal to (a) recognize the relativity of cultural values, (b) acknowledge the logic inherent in other cultural systems, and (c) overlook the centrality of social and structural forces in human behaviour. Prejudice also is problematic when prejudgments give rise to discriminatory treatment that interferes with the rights of others in a multicultural society.

Discrimination

Discrimination is often defined as prejudice "in practice." Whereas prejudice refers to personal attitudes or individual beliefs, discrimination entails the behavioural component of these thoughts and emotions. For example, to think someone inferior because of her skin colour is regressive but inevitable in a democratic society in which it is impossible to regulate what people think or believe. But to put this belief into practice by denying or excluding on the basis of skin colour is discriminatory and wrong. Under discrimination, minorities are deprived of access to employment or promotions for reasons unrelated to merit, ability, or credentials. Denying someone the right to equal treatment because of their race, ethnicity, or gender is illegal in Canada; it is also a recipe for social chaos if left unchecked.

Prejudice does not necessarily lead to discrimination. Conversely, discrimination can exist without prejudicial attitudes. In the first case, most individuals are socialized to conceal their negative attitudes from the public. Even strongly prejudiced individuals may be reluctant to put their beliefs into practice for fear of incurring negative sanctions, both formal (through the courts) or informal (ridicule or ostracism). In the second case, individuals may engage in discriminatory practices without expressing malice or prejudicial intent. Defending traditional institutional arrangements against minority challenges is one such case. No prejudice is intended by protecting the status quo against minority demands for change. Nevertheless, the logical consequence of criticizing minorities as wanting too much too quickly may be discriminatory in reinforcing a racialized social order. Such thinly veiled discrimination is no less destructive of minority aspirations than incidents of open bigotry.

In short, prejudice and discrimination may exist independently. Intent or deliberation is not necessarily a precondition for discrimination. Rather, discrimination may be embedded within institutional structures and be condoned by accepted values and routine procedures. With this distinction in mind, we can define discrimination as *any action either by intent or consequence that adversely excludes or denies others from equitable treatment on the basis of membership in a devalued group*. Power is implicit in all forms of discrimination. Power is employed to manipulate arrangements for the benefit of some at the expense of others. Those in positions of power can enact laws and implement policies that keep minorities powerless and in their place. The conflation of power and discrimination may lead to racism.

Racism

The concept of racism is no less difficult to define. This term has been employed indiscriminately across various contexts that may not have involved a racist (or racial) dimension in the strict sense of the term. This, of course, creates the potential for abuse. For example, white police officers have been accused of racism in dealing with minority community members. But how do police actions compare with the openly racist doctrines of neo-Nazi groups who explicitly extol white supremacist doctrines that link inferiority and skin colour? Can both of these scenarios be regarded as expressions of racism without fear of trivializing the term? After all, if every action that criticizes minorities is defined as racist, then nothing is racist since the capacity to make distinctions is lost. Employing this line of reasoning, it is doubtful that police in Los Angeles or Toronto are racist in the doctrinaire sense. Nevertheless, there is little doubt that much of what passes for policing may be discriminatory—at least in consequence, if not in intent. The consequences of such discriminatory policing may in fact reinforce racism against minorities.

Racism can be defined as a system of beliefs and a corresponding set of discriminatory practices that target certain groups as inferior and deprive them of equal treatment. There are two components of racism: hate and power (Fleras and Elliott 1996). Racism as *hate* entails a level of dislike towards groups perceived as racially different and inferior. Racism as *power* refers to the power that some have to put these negative beliefs into practice in a way that denies or excludes others on the basis of their membership in a devalued group. At one level, racism refers to beliefs about race that associate biology with thought and behaviour. Minority women and men are diminished, deprived, excluded, or exploited primarily on account of their race. At another level, racism can be construed as any form of domination— either explicit or implied, at personal or institutional levels—that has the intent or effect of preserving prevailing distributions of power and resources. In other words, racism is not a tangible thing or a fixed object. Nor does racism have to be deliberate or display intent. Rather racism can be defined as an attribute associated with any action or inaction that has the intent or consequence of perpetuating an unequal status quo. Its status as a "moving target" makes it doubly difficult to isolate, let alone to challenge and eradicate.

Racism is not a problem with minorities, but a majority problem. It reflects the actions of those in positions of power who are anxious to keep minorities in their place and preferably out of sight. It also reflects an unwillingness on the part of the privileged to move over and make space for fear of losing their powerful status. Racism is not necessarily about individuals with regressive beliefs or dormant prejudices; rather, it prevails in structures, both deep and intractable (Bonilla-Silva 1996). Racism as a justifying ideology and practice exists in societies where the political, economic, social, and cultural domains are structured around the placement of minorities in categories of race (racialized social systems). The idea of racism as a structural problem is also acknowledged by critics of capitalism (Bolaria and Li 1988). Racism inheres in a capitalist society because of its need to regulate the labour supply, to assign certain groups of people to a particular site in the production process, and to ensure divisions within the workforce (Satzewich 1991). This is not to suggest that racism is derivative of class relations or the result of irrational ideology (false consciousness). Rather, racism provides a rationalization for group interaction in racialized social systems (racially structured societies) (Bonilla-Silva 1996).

Racism is inseparable from social control. Its existence as social control in unequal contexts makes the concept of power critical to racism. Thus, many prefer to see racism as an interplay of prejudice and discrimination within a context of power (prejudice + discrimination + power = racism). This relationship can be phrased in another way: in contexts of ethnic inequality and racial domination, racism provides the theory, discrimination is the practice, and prejudice (when applicable) serves as the catalyst.

Types of Racial Discrimination

Racial discrimination does not come in neatly wrapped packages with a singular frame of reference. As practice or discourse, it spans the spectrum from the personal and deliberate to the systemic and inadvertent, with countless variations and shades in between. The content of racial discrimination can vary in response to altered circumstances. For example, treating others negatively because of skin colour may not have been seen as racist a generation ago. At present, it may be racist to ignore a person's difference by failing to take into account the context and consequences of action that have an adverse yet unintended effect. This variation makes it difficult to agree on a common definition, let alone to propose a solution, despite emphasizing racial discrimination as a form of social control in the competition for scarce resources.

Five types of racial discrimination can be discerned, each of which is distinctive from the others despite some degree of overlap (Fleras and Elliott 1996). These levels may be compared in terms of style, expression, intention, intensity, and scope. In no way do we imply that the levels are mutually exclusive. Nor do we suggest that only one type exists to the exclusion of others at a particular time or place. Reality is much too messy for such easy classifications.

Redneck

This is the kind of racial discrimination with which most people are familiar. Redneck racial discrimination is a highly personal action, involves a combination of ignorance and fear, and is both conscious and deliberate. It can consist of malicious actions by one or more persons against others, as in the case of anti-Semitic slurs, the defacing of Jewish synagogues, or the espousal of Zionist conspiracy theories. It can also be expressed by the actions of shopkeepers who may refuse service on the grounds that "we don't like your type around here." This form of discrimination is generally marked by intense personal animosity; it may also involve a deliberate intent to harm another person. There is no question that redneck discrimination is less visible at present than in the past, when minorities were openly persecuted. This decline may be attributable to the passage of anti-discriminatory laws, to the enactment of the Charter of Rights and Freedoms, and more generally to changes in the social climate.

Institutional

Institutional discrimination is similar to its redneck counterpart, since both forms are concerned with blatant and conscious efforts to deny or control people who are considered different. Unlike the redneck form, though, this type of discrimination prevails at organizational rather than personal levels. It is reflected in the corporate practice of not hiring people of a certain skin colour, or hiring them only for menial jobs. These actions are then legitimized and excused by reference to organizational values, rules, and procedures. Institutional discrimination also occurs less frequently than in the past. South Africa's apartheid regime once exemplified institutional discrimination. Blacks and "coloureds" were kept in their place (literally and figuratively) by a convoluted set of colour-coded laws that separated the races from normal interaction. A comparable if somewhat less codified situation also existed in Canada; racial minorities were long denied entry to Canada, or were segregated and persecuted once they settled here. Modern day examples of institutional discrimination include the discriminatory practices of employment agencies in selectively placing workers of colour. Both the Denny's restaurant chain in the U.S. and Texaco U.S.A. have been found guilty of infractions that discriminated against African-Americans.

Polite

Polite racial discrimination is a toned-down version of its redneck cousin. Unlike the deliberate and explicit intent of other versions, polite discrimination denies and excludes others in a discreet and subtle manner, with only moderate levels of intensity. Polite discrimination is muted in expression. For example, while it may be illegal to deny employment on the basis of certain irrelevant characteristics such as skin colour, an employer can circumvent the law by falsely telling a prospective employee that a position has already been filled. Other employers may rely on employment agencies to screen out unwelcome applicants. Rather than telling a person of colour that he or she is unwanted, a polite racist simply says the apartment is already rented. Individual hostility to employment equity may be another example. Opponents of equity initiatives are likely to camouflage their antipathy in euphemistic language such as reverse discrimination, diluted standards, and violation of values such as merit or ability. Finally, polite discrimination can also be present when a minority person is "praised" for not being like the rest of "them," thus denying the person their ethnicity as well as revealing some unresolved ambivalence towards that particular minority group. This quintessentially Canadian expression of racial discrimination may cushion the blow, but the outcome remains the same.

Subliminal

Polite discrimination can also be present at an unconscious level. In this sense, it may not be expressed directly, but "subliminally" through opposition to policies or practices of benefit to minorities (Fleras and Elliott 1996; Henry et al. 1995). A degree of ambivalence lies at the core of subliminal racism. On the one hand, many will support minority grievances; on the other hand, they may resent proposed solutions to address these concerns. Proposals for reform may be criticized for asking too much, proceeding too quickly, or being too out of character with Canadian society. Thus, someone who endorses the principle of diversity may be less enthusiastic about putting this principle into practice when factoring in costs. Individuals may support progressive legislation as a matter of principle yet disapprove when asked to move over and make space or share power. This class of person may abhor openly discriminatory treatment, yet seem reluctant to get involved (walk the talk) if personal sacrifice is involved.

This ambiguity appears to reflect an inescapable dichotomy in our core values (see Myrdal 1944). On the one hand, we place a value on the public good, with its emphasis on collective rights, special treatment, equality of outcomes, and fair play. On the other hand, there remains a powerful commitment to competitive individualism, with its focus on personal freedom, self-reliance, meritocracy, and competition. Subliminal racism arises from the interplay of these oppositional values. It consists of a way of thinking that enables individuals to maintain two apparently conflicting values—one rooted in the egalitarian virtues of justice and fairness and the other in a competitive free-for-all with everybody for him- or herself. The contradictions are reformulated around democratic principles. The very principles that define a democratic right to compete can be inverted to erect barriers to competition (Henry et al. 1995). Even those who profess egalitarian attitudes and a commitment to racial equality are unwilling to—or incapable of—"grappling" with the contradiction.

Systemic

Systemic discrimination is an impersonal form of discrimination based on the belief that, although people themselves may not be openly prejudiced, discrimination may be built into systems (from organizational policies to reward structures). Even though systemic discrimination does not spring from a specific intent to discriminate, its consequences can be devastating. And systemic discrimination can be difficult to identify because its expression is so diffuse, so much a part of organizational daily routine, that most employees never notice it.

The essence of systemic discrimination is summed up in the expression, "We treat everybody the same here." Yet it is precisely this practice of treating everyone the same that is inherently discriminatory. Treating unequals equally in a unequal world is tantamount to freezing the status quo since advantages belong to those with a head start. Applying identical standards may be systemically discriminatory since the different needs, concerns, and experiences of disadvantaged minorities are ignored yet need to be taken account in a colour-conscious world. In other words, systemic discrimination reflects the consequences of seemingly neutral rules whose cumulative impact is exclusionary or exploitative. Even well-intentioned actions may be systemically biased if they exert a negative consequence on disadvantaged minorities.

What does systemic discrimination look like? In the past, qualifications pertaining to weight, height, and education were routinely enforced for certain types of employment. This was especially the case for applicants to police and fire departments. These qualifications may not have had much bearing on job performance, yet they effectively barred certain groups from careers in these fields. Immigration laws that excluded those who were defined as unassimilable also represented a form of systemic bias. So did the demand for "Canadian experience" for some jobs, in effect blocking most immigrants and refugees from entry into certain forms of employment. As well, the continued reliance on seniority as a basis for entitlement within institutions is systemically discriminatory, regardless of the original good intentions of this practice. Under the principle of seniority, minority sectors such as women or people of colour are most vulnerable to the last-hired, first-fired syndrome. No malice or intent is evident. Nevertheless, the consequences of these impersonal rules and universal procedures are just as punishing in the long run for minorities.

Solutions to Racism: Anti-Racism

As sociologists, we are interested in how unequal relations are created and supported. Racial discrimination constitutes one of the pillars that serve to bolster patterns of inequality and it is inextricably linked with the process of social control for preserving the status quo. Yet we also are concerned with challenges to these unequal relations. Initiatives in recent years have attacked the racist dimensions of Canadian society. Collectively, they fall under the category of anti-racism, and anti-racism has emerged as a major force in transforming social institutions (James 1996; Fleras and Elliott 1996).

Anti-racism can be defined as the process that isolates and challenges racism through *direct action* at personal and institutional levels. The scope of anti-racism is expansive:

> Anti-racism questions White power and privilege and the accompanying rationality for dominance in the schooling process . . . problematizes the marginalization and delegitimatization of subordinate groups, and their voices, knowledge, and experience in the education system . . . critically examines the role of the educational system in producing and reproducing inequalities in society, linking issues of identity with schooling, and particularly with the processes of producing knowledge (Sefa Dei 1996/97, 59).

Unlike non-racism, which disagrees with racism in principle rather than in practice, anti-racism openly challenges and rejects racism as an individual right of choice. Two styles of anti-racist strategy can be discerned. One is concerned with modifying individual behaviour through education or sanctions; the other is concerned with the removal of discriminatory structural barriers through institutional reform. This distinction corresponds to some extent with the concept of racism as *hate* versus racism as *power*. It also reflects an analytical division between personal and institutional anti-racism.

Taken at its most obvious level, racism is normally envisaged as a personal problem involving hatred of others. It constitutes a visceral dislike of others because of who they are or what they represent. Defining racism as a personal problem calls forth strategies for containment or control that focus on modifying individual behaviour. Four strategies are normally included in the anti-racist package: interaction, education, law, and language. Racism may be reduced if people have an opportunity to equitably interact with others. Education about racism in the past and at present may also be useful in sensitizing individuals to inequities. The threat of legal sanctions may be effective in deterring people from engaging in discriminatory actions. Understanding how language can be discriminatory (e.g., references to "those people") may be useful as well.

Anti-racist initiatives at individual levels have elicited some guarded optimism. But are these initiatives of sufficient strength to purge racism at its roots? Racism may be expressed in and through people, but individuals are products of their social environment. Put bluntly, the structures of society are difficult to reform through personal transformation. Rather, anti-racism must focus on the institutional structures in defence of a capitalist society. Personal solutions such as multicultural education are useful but ultimately comparable to applying a bandage to a cancerous growth—compassionate and humane to be sure, yet ultimately self-defeating given the severity of the disease. The problem of racism cannot be eliminated except within the wider confines of political domination and economic control.

Institutional anti-racism consist of measures and mechanisms for dismantling the structures of discrimination. Any institutional enterprise will foster racism intentionally or unintentionally when it perpetuates mandates that are exclusionary, refuses to share power or decision-making, promulgates a monocultural set of values and beliefs as normal and necessary, maintains an inflexible or unresponsive set of structure and operations, and endorses unequal distributions of resources (Fleras 1996). Systemic biases are most likely to occur at the level of mission statement, culture and subculture, power and decision-making, structures (including rules, roles, and relationships), and distribution of physical, financial, and human assets. The removal of discriminatory barriers is central; selection and recruitment procedures as well as rules for promotion and reward are scrutinized for hidden bias in the interests of equitable treatment. These multipronged anti-racist initiatives sound plausible in theory, but their implementation may be another story.

It's relatively easy to dismiss racism as a personal problem. It is equally tempting to situate racism within a system of vast and impersonal forces that are largely beyond individual responsibility and outside the bounds of human agency. Individuals may not be the root cause of racism, yet racism is precipitated by people in everyday situations that link agency with structure (Essed 1991). When applied to the realm of racism and proposed solutions, the personal is indeed the political. The political in turn defines the personal. That is, changing the system invariably alters people's attitudes; altering people's attitudes may correspond with changes to behaviour and culminate in revisions to society. Thus, anti-racist strategies must take into account the interplay of social forces and intersubjective experiences of individuals. Only a comprehensive anti-racist approach can deliver the goods with any hope of success. But recent moves in disbanding the anti-racism initiatives of Ontario's Ministry of Citizenship and Ministry of Education and Training do not bode well for the future (Tator 1997).

OFFICIAL MULTICULTURALISM:
PROBLEM OR SOLUTION?

Multiculturalism has established itself as a major framework for analyzing race and ethnic relations (Gordon and Newfield 1996). It is widely regarded as a uniquely Canadian way of coping with the problem of racial discrimination (Cardozo 1996). Its inception as official government policy in 1971 has resulted in widespread international praise of multiculturalism as a tool for the harmonious management of race and ethnic relations in an increasingly diverse and changing society (Berry and Kalin 1995). Multiculturalism not only furnishes Canadians with a practical alternative to America's melting pot mentality, it also empowers minorities to pursue the dual goals of ethnicity and equality (Esses and Gardner 1996).

Public reaction to multiculturalism is extremely varied, ranging from acceptance to rejection, from indifference to ambivalence (Abu-Laban and Stasiulis 1992; Berry and Kalin 1993; Vasta and Castles 1996). Most agree that multiculturalism has lived up to its billing as an instrument of change—to the approval of some and disapproval of others—without inflicting serious damage to Canada's institutional structure (see also Woodley 1997). For some, multiculturalism is as much a problem as a solution to Canada's woes. There is mounting resentment, for instance, towards multiculturalism in matters of law and government policy. Many people resent government expenditures in areas that others regard as essentially personal or private (see Bissoondath 1993/1994). For others, however, multiculturalism symbolizes the solution to many of the problems associated with pluralism in a democratic society. The protective canopy of multiculturalism alleviates some of the inequities confronting minorities. It also is capable of defusing the threat of society-destroying interethnic strife. For still others, it is uncertain whether multiculturalism constitutes a problem or a solution. They prefer instead to acknowledge its ambiguous nature. On the one hand, multiculturalism can be conceived as social glue for bonding together Canadians; on the other hand, it can be viewed as a pair of scissors for shearing apart Canada's social fabric. For yet still others, there is nothing to be gained from talking about multiculturalism in judgmental terms. Rather, they prefer to discuss multiculturalism within the framework of doing what is workable, necessary, and fair (Fleras 1994).

Such a cacophony of voices is not altogether surprising. The politics of diversity complicate the very process of Canadian society-building. Endorsement of multiculturalism has proven a boon to some, a detriment to others, and a source of confusion to still others. Such an assessment provides two insights into the construction of social problems. First, debate over the pros and cons of multiculturalism reveals how contemporary social problems are "contested sites." Competing groups with different priorities and unequal resources struggle to gain control of the agenda in hopes of defining the problem and solutions. Second, the definition of a social problem does not remain constant. Rather, as we saw in Chapter 1, Introduction, it involves a process that reflects a natural history. That is, the nature of the problem changes over time, with corresponding pressure to revise definitions and solutions. There is a second variation on this theme. Solutions to social problems often trigger unanticipated consequences. Solving one problem may uncover additional but previously unmentioned grievances; alternatively, solutions may upset certain groups who previously were content with the status quo. Focusing on this dimension reinforces an awareness that the distinction between problem and solution is only an interpretation apart.

Putting Multiculturalism to the Critical Test

Those who argue that multiculturalism is a problem rather than a solution often resort to a host of criticisms. For the sake of analysis, adverse reactions can be classified into four categories (Fleras and Elliott 1991): 1) multiculturalism as "divisive" since it undermines Canadian society; 2) multiculturalism as "regressive" since it defuses minority aspirations and needs; 3) multiculturalism as "ornamental" since it manipulates symbols to foster the illusion of change; and 4) multiculturalism as "irrelevant" since cultural solutions are inappropriate for structural problems. Each of these criticisms will be put to the critical test to determine its validity as problem or solution. In this way multiculturalism will be revealed for what it is: an imperfect but modest social experiment for accommodating diversity in a changing and diverse society (Abu-Laban and Stasiulis 1992; Fleras 1994).

Is Multiculturalism Divisive?

Multiculturalism is denounced as an irritant to social unity and national identity. The promotion of multiculturalism runs the risk of "Balkanizing" Canada by fomenting conflict between ethnic groups. Construction of a national identity is next to impossible, according to these critics, when minorities are encouraged to pursue ethnic "tribalisms" at the expense of their duties as citizens (Bissoondath 1994). Gina Mallet (1997, D2) captures this sense of doom when she writes, "Although the drive to honour diversity through official multiculturalism was originally undertaken in order to promote tolerance, it is accomplishing the opposite. By setting Canadians against one another and emphasizing our differences rather than the many things we have in common, diversity has, in fact, gone too far." A close analysis of these arguments suggests an alternative view.

Multiculturalism originated and continues to exist as a pragmatic instrument for cementing Canadians into a "distinct society." Multiculturalism is not concerned with the promotion of diversity per se, as demonstrated in a careful reading of the Multiculturalism Act of 1988 (or of Trudeau's multiculturalism speech in 1971). It is even less concerned with the promotion of minority cultures. Rather, the goals of multiculturalism are firmly fixed in building a united society through adjustments that depoliticize ethnicity as a potential threat. Multiculturalism seeks to create a cohesive and prosperous Canada in which diversity is incorporated as an integral and legitimate component of society without undermining either the interconnectedness of the whole or distinctiveness of the parts in the process (Fleras and Elliott 1996). In lieu of self-sufficient ethnic groups, multiculturalism emphasizes the right of individuals to identify and affiliate with the ethnocultural tradition of their choice. Nor does multiculturalism encourage an "anything goes" mentality. Tolerance of diversity is accepted only to the extent that its practice does not violate the laws of the land, interfere with the rights of others, or discredit fundamental political and economic institutions. Put bluntly, everyone has the right to be different, but they must be different in the same kind of way, in effect neutralizing any potentially disruptive tendancies (Eisenstein 1996). In other words, multiculturalism is not about ethnic separatism or divided loyalties, but about the promotion of secular tolerance for minorities as a basis for Canadian nationalism and society-building.

To be sure, there is always an element of risk associated with any policy that promotes diversity as a conflict-resolution device. At times, minorities may be singled out because of special needs; yet this preferential treatment is not intended to encourage social conflict as much as to achieve positive social goals. Even the notion of multiculturalism as "celebrating differences" is directed towards intercultural sharing as a means of demolishing barriers. Similarly, the conferral of hyphenated citizenship (for example, Lithuanian-Canadian) should not be feared as divisive. A hyphenated identity can be thought of as two strands of a single Canadian citizenship. The primary strand involves a commitment to core Canadian values and institutions, while the secondary strand allows an optional identification with the cultural values and symbols of a person's choice. In short, multiculturalism serves as the buffer that makes Canada safe "for," but also safe "from," ethnicity (Moynihan 1993).

What about Canadian identity? Does multiculturalism foster a "visionless coexistence" through the mindless promotion of endless diversity, as lamented by Reginald Bibby in his acclaimed text *Mosaic Madness*? Perhaps this is sometimes so in practice, but an adherence to multiculturalism does not necessarily detract from a coherent Canadian identity. To the contrary, multiculturalism enhances a perception of ourselves as a community that is tolerant of diversity. In fact, one could argue that a commitment to multiculturalism (within a bilingual framework) is one of the definitive characteristics that distinguishes Canadians from Americans. Rather than undermining a sense of Canadianness, in other words, multiculturalism encourages a shared identity by furnishing a set of myths or symbols for binding Canadians into a moral community (Jamieson 1993). The fact that immigrants continue to become naturalized citizens at rates that supersede those in Britain or the United States (neither of which are officially multicultural) would suggest a positive role for multiculturalism in forging Canadian unity and identity (Ungerleider 1997).

In summary, it is not multiculturalism that divides Canadian society and excludes certain groups from full participation in it. More to the point, a commitment to "monoculturalism" is the problem (Mitchell-Powell 1992). Under official multiculturalism, the expression of ethnicity is encouraged, but only to the extent that it conforms with core cultural values at the heart of Canada's society-building project. Nor is multiculturalism divisive in the same sense as the cultural politics of Quebec or First Nations. Most voluntary migrants are not anxious to dismantle Canada, but want to strengthen the country of their choice. The divisiveness within multiculturalism—where it does exist—arises from its manipulation by some opportunistic politicians and minority leaders who have sabotaged pluralist principles for ulterior motives.

Is Multiculturalism Regressive?

Multiculturalism has been discredited by some critics as a regressive tool that distracts minorities from the business at hand, that is, from abolishing class lines and gaining access to the corridors of power and resources. This notion of multiculturalism as the crucible for a "vertical mosaic" does not always stand up to scrutiny (Fleras 1994).

First, racial and ethnic minorities are not uniformly marginalized in Canadian society. Certain ethnic groups earn more income than "mainstream" Canadians, while foreign-born Canadians often outperform native-born Canadians in areas such as education (Agocs and Boyd 1993; Pendakur and Pendakur 1995). Other Canadians, such as African-Canadians and aboriginal peoples, of course are less fortunate, but their exclusion and exploitation long predated the appearance of official multiculturalism. Second, the explicit intent of multiculturalism is the removal of discriminatory barriers to equality. Since 1971, multicultural policies have sought to dismantle the cultural fences that block ethnic involvement in

Canadian society. The current anti-racist thrust of contemporary multiculturalism focuses on structural rather than cultural blockages to minority participation. Consequently, programs and initiatives for righting past wrongs have been directed towards removing institutional barriers and expanding opportunity structures. Official multiculturalism continues to focus on the 1988 directive for federal departments and agencies to integrate diversity into their mandate (Annual Report 1997).

It should be obvious, then, that multicultural objectives are concerned with assisting minorities to gain a rightful place in society. The concept of institutional accommodation looms heavily in this platform. In the past, immigrants and minorities were expected to fit into the existing institutional framework as part of the adjustment process. Now, however, institutions also are expected to move over and make space (Annual Report 1997). Reforms are focused on rooting out systemic biases related to recruitment, hiring, promotion, and training. Admittedly, there has been little proof of dramatic shifts in minority socioeconomic status because of multiculturalism. The strength of this policy resides instead with the creation of a society that fosters acceptance of diversity as normal, necessary, and valuable (McLeod 1987). Its strength also lies in creating a supportive social climate in which proactive measures for managing diversity can be implemented without public backlash. Finally, multiculturalism equips minorities with an official platform through which they can articulate their grievances and hold the government accountable for actions at odds with multicultural principles.

Is Multiculturalism Ornamental?

Manoly Lupul (1983) once remarked that multiculturalism is not taken seriously by anyone who is a somebody. There is some element of truth in this observation (Jaworski 1979). Multiculturalism has appeared at times to be little more than a frivolous political diversion whose currency is symbolic rather than substantial. Here the critics get it right—albeit for the wrong reason. There is no question that multiculturalism embraces a restricted, often symbolic endorsement of ethnoculture. Yet multiculturalism is not interested in preserving the substance of ethnic lifestyles. The entrenchment of relatively autonomous minority groups—complete with parallel institutions and separate power bases—would pose a threat to national sovereignty. Instead, multiculturalism endorses a commitment to ethnicity that is symbolic and situational, rather than political. In this way, minorities are entitled to identify and affiliate themselves with the cultural tradition of their choice without incurring a social penalty or provoking a state clampdown.

Even dismissing the symbolic value of multiculturalism may be premature. Symbols have the power to move mountains and the symbol of Canada as a fair and tolerant society provides multiculturalism with the moral authority to demand social changes. Official endorsement of multiculturalism accords the highest level of recognition to racial and ethnic diversity (Seiler 1996). By relativizing the powerful, multiculturalism has exposed the constructed character (rather than the normalcy) of the dominant culture, in effect advancing shared understandings while helping to make sense of our actions in a changing and diverse world (Eller 1997). The symbolic value of multiculturalism also extends to the creation of a social climate in which diversity can flourish without penalizing its proponents. Besides, many Canadians prefer the limited responsibilities of a symbolic ethnicity over the rigours of full-time ethnicity. Critics may scold multiculturalism for focusing on the symbols of diversity rather than its substance, but their criticism simply chides multiculturalism for something it is neither equipped nor prepared to do within the framework of a liberal pluralism.

Is Multiculturalism Irrelevant?

The final criticism of multiculturalism is perhaps the most difficult to refute. It has often been denounced as impractical or irrelevant in a society organized around the principles of profit, private property, competitive individualism, and insatiable consumerism. There is some doubt whether cultural solutions can be applied to structural problems like systemic discrimination (Agocs and Boyd 1993; Satzewich 1993). Can a policy directed at reforming society possibly address root problems, or is it yet another case of applying a bandage to a gaping wound?

There are two ways of countering this criticism. First, multiculturalism was never intended to do what international communism proved incapable of accomplishing, that is, to bring capitalism to its knees. Multiculturalism was devised to work within the existing system by softening its harshest blows for its weakest members. A morally authoritative framework was established in which minority inequality could be addressed, debated, challenged, and transformed by holding governments accountable for actions inconsistent with multicultural ideals (Vasta and Castles 1996). Second, it could be argued that multiculturalism "lends its weight to the social transformation of capitalism" by establishing the primacy of "equality rights" over "inequality wrongs" (Fleras 1994). The reinvention of multiculturalism from a focus on culture to structure indicates a willingness to apply a human face to capitalism. And as the globalization of capitalist market economies continues to expand, multiculturalism provides the mindset to confront the challenge of a shifting and increasingly borderless life that is likely to be our lot in the twenty-first century (see also Woodley 1997).

The Good, the Bad, and the Necessary

There is little doubt that multiculturalism originated as a political program to achieve political goals in a politically astute way (Peter 1978). Yet by now multiculturalism has assumed a life of its own beyond that specifically promoted by the state. It has evolved in directions never envisaged by its originators: a framework is currently in place that legitimates the normalcy of diversity at cultural and institutional levels. What originated as a policy for "European ethnics" has secured a Canada that is relatively comfortable with the presence of new Canadians from all parts of the world.

Has it been worth it? On balance, yes. Multiculturalism has resulted in the establishment of a policy and a corresponding set of initiatives for advancing minority interests that strike many as necessary, fair, and workable within Canada's liberal-democratic framework. That may not sound like a lot to those with unrealistically high expectations, but the contributions of multiculturalism should not be diminished by unfair comparison with utopian standards. A sense of proportion and perspective is required: just as multiculturalism cannot be blamed for everything that has gone wrong, so too should we avoid excessive praise; the nature of its influence exists somewhere between the poles of unblemished good and absolute evil. Multiculturalism is neither the root of all Canada's social evils, nor the all-encompassing solution to problems that rightfully belong to political or economic domains. It is but one component—however imperfect—for engaging social diversity, while at the same time seeking to balance the competing demands of individuals, minority groups, and the state.

Multiculturalism remains the policy of choice for a changing and diverse Canada. As philosophy, policy, or practice, it symbolizes an innovative if imperfect social experiment for managing diversity without compromising our collective self-image as a free, open, and tolerant country. Multiculturalism has done much to revamp Canada from an Anglocentric outpost to its much ballyhooed status as a trailblazer in the enlightened management of race and ethnic relations (Kurthen 1997). Under the circumstances, it is not a question of whether Canada can afford multiculturalism. More to the point, Canada cannot afford not to embrace multiculturalism in its search for political unity, social coherence, economic prosperity, and cultural enrichment.

THE QUEBEC QUESTION

"I've never met an English-speaking Canadian, but I'm sure they're as nice as any other foreigner" (Alice Simard, mother of Lucien Bouchard, premier of Quebec, quoted in *Report on Business*, January 1996).

Dueling Discourses

Canada is widely regarded as the world's best place to live if judged by a UN quality of life ranking that combines tangible measures related to traditional income and less quantifiable dimensions such as political freedom, environmental sustainability, and racial and gender equality (Editorial, *Report on Business*, January 1996). Yet for all its resources and resourcefulness Canada is in danger of splintering along ethnic faultlines. Canada is not alone in this predicament: the forces of ethnicity (as well as language, region, or religion) in this modern age pose a greater threat to the sovereign integrity of states than the threat of invasion by outsiders (Simpson 1996). Traditional cross-border wars, in the conventional sense of using force to capture coveted territory, have been replaced by threats "from within" because of aggrieved minorities. Quebec's threat to Canadian unity is but one expression of a global drive for national affirmation, according to Anthony Smith in his book *The Ethnic Origins of Nations* (1996). The search for collective touchstones of identity, including race or ethnicity, may be the defining challenge to the stability of our impersonal and homogeneous world. Yet existing states seem incapable of dealing with these nationalisms because of structural constraints or constitutional limitations (Qadeer 1997).

French–English relations have coexisted uneasily since 1841 when Upper and Lower Canada combined into an incipient nation-state, a situation aptly described by Lord Durham as the equivalent of "two nations warring in the bosom of a single state." Interaction has vacillated from stretches of sullen isolation (two solitudes), to periods of convulsive social change (the Quiet Revolution), with occasional flashes of violence in between (two scorpions in a bottle). Points of conflict are varied and numerous, from interminable language rights battles to provincial–federal squabbling, but tend to focus around Quebec sovereign aspirations as a "distinct society" within a vastly revamped federalist framework. The Québecois constitute a powerful political community of people who claim some degree of sovereignty (autonomy) by virtue of a shared history, a collective vision, a set of grievances, and collective goals, and whose distinctiveness as a nationality is derived from common ancestry (see Juteau 1994). In contrast to a deep emotional attachment to their homeland of last resort, Quebeckers see English-speaking Canada as a remote, even unfriendly, place with its own set of priorities and preoccupations, few of which concern or apply to Quebec (Gagnon 1996; Conlogue 1997). The clash of these "founding societies" has intensified pressure for reshaping the political contours of Canadian society. The lack of satisfactory resolution has also propelled Canada perilously close to the brink (see also Burgess 1996; Boismenu 1996; Jenson 1996).

The potential for misunderstanding is complicated by the politics of language. Debates over bilingualism have infuriated and divided the country as few other issues have. Quebeckers dismiss bilingualism as an act of appeasement bereft of any moral legitimacy; English-speaking Canadians bristle at the inconvenience associated with bilingualism. Francophones throughout Canada have depicted English-speaking Canadians as insensitive not only to language aspirations, but to Quebec's legitimate interests as a cultural homeland of last resort. Anglophones, in turn, have dismissed the Québécois as rabid nationalists, with little or no respect for liberal values or individual rights, much less any concern over "national interests" in treating Canada as a treasure trove for plunder rather than as a community to nourish. The often passionate zeal of Quebec's language police has continued to provoke derisive howls from English-speaking Canada (White 1997). Sensitivities are further inflamed when the English-speaking media pounce on minority issues to portray Quebec as harsh and intolerant (Sniderman et al. 1993), in effect contributing to a siege mentality and the need for Quebeckers to be perpetually on the defensive.

In short, both sectors are locked into seemingly unflattering images of the other. Each regards its counterpart as the "problem." English-speaking Canadians tend to support a Trudeau vision of Canada as having a strong central government, multiculturalism, no special status for Quebec, official bilingualism, individual rights, and equality of provinces. This vision has less currency in Quebec where the commitment lies in strengthening Quebec, enhancing the French language, assimilating immigrants, and seeking special arrangements for Quebec within a renewed federalism (McRoberts 1997). Quebec has made some important gains as part of a restructuring within Canada, yet it continues to chaff under federal containment and anglophone insensitivity (Gagnon 1993). English-speaking Canadians appear increasingly opposed to fundamental concessions, preferring a status-quo federalism of formally equal provinces (McRoberts 1993). Failure to foster a rapprochement between these two founding nations strikes at the very core of Canada's survival. Yet even the close referendum decision in October 1995 (50.6 percent for federalism, 49.4 percent for sovereignty) does not appear to have stimulated any new vision of—or urgency about—how Quebec and Ottawa can get their act together (Honderich 1996; Cohen 1996). What, then, is the problem? Where do we begin when polls elicit conflicting messages? Quebeckers believe that separation is inevitable, yet many sovereigntists prefer a renewed deal within Canada. Up to 85 percent of Quebeckers think Canada is a good place to live, yet 54 percent would vote yes to separation in a future referendum (Globe and Mail, February 24, 1996). In other words, Quebeckers are attached to Canada but their attachment is conditional (Stewart 1997). Similarly, English-speaking Canadians may be positively predisposed to Quebec but not if special deals are involved (Winsor 1996).

Forging a workable accommodation between Ottawa and Quebec is unlikely without a major rethinking of Canadian society. The fundamental question is whether two communities with such divergent interests can share a common cultural space (Salee 1995; Salee and

Coleman 1997). Flag-waving or finger-pointing may not solve what increasingly is perceived as a structural problem rather than a simple case of mutual pigheadedness. Unless the social, political, and cultural context is taken into account, there is not much hope in isolating the problem for analysis, let alone in working towards a solution. The Quebec question appears inseparable from flaws in Canadian federalism. Put simply, just as the idea of provinces may be antiquated and irrelevant (Diamond 1997), so too is a federal system based on a parliamentary process designed for a small, agricultural, unitary state (Gillies 1997). Continued recourse to a nineteenth century political framework for solving contemporary problems may be misguided or counterproductive in a late twentieth century world of global realignment and national retrenchment. Engin Isan of York University writes of the need to reconsider the Quebec question within the rapidly changing and shifting identities in the new world order:

> [P]olitical boundaries no longer represent the social and economic realities facing Canadian provinces today. Loyalties of Canadian citizens and their sense of belonging are divided along other lines than the nineteenth century territorial boundaries represented by the provinces. There are many other territorial identities and regions that are articulated into the different spheres of the global economy, rendering provincial loyalties and identities increasingly not only banal but counter-productive (1996, 6).

In other words, the Quebec question is really a Canada problem. Federalism as a system for co-opting Quebec may have worked in the past for reconciling conflicting diversities, but its effectiveness in addressing ethnonationalisms as a basis for society-building may be inappropriate at present (Burgess 1996; Balthazar 1996). The words of Sir John A. Macdonald in 1872 are prophetic, but perhaps not in the way they were originally intended: "Confederation is only yet in the gristle, and it will require five years more before it hardens into bone" (quoted in Olive 1996, 13).

The Problem with Federalism: Province or People?

Quebec is part of Canada's federalist system. The political compromises that culminated in the 1867 Constitution Act (BNA Act) established a centralized system; it also incorporated Quebec's linguistic, legal, and social distinctions as part of the constitutional fabric, in effect confirming Quebec's special place in Confederation (Burgess 1996). Yet federalism as a system of political compromise invites diverse interpretations. These interpretations or visions include federalism as a "contract" and federalism as a "compact." A third vision, Canada as a "three-nations" state, is slowly gaining acceptance. The coexistence of these competing visions generates much of the dynamic underlying French–English relations.

Canada as a Contract

According to this first interpretation, Canada constitutes a federalist system of 10 provinces under a central authority in Ottawa. A contract exists between the provinces (including Quebec) and the federal government. The provinces (including Quebec), as well as the federal system, are sovereign within their own jurisdiction as set out in the Constitution; neither can usurp the authority or powers of the other. In 1867 the BNA Act specified the limits and scope of provincial versus federal powers. Competition over these powers is such that Canadian history can be interpreted as a struggle by provinces and federalist forces over who has control over what jurisdictions.

Two variations of the contract thesis exist. First, provinces (including Quebec) are equal to each other, but subordinate in status and power compared with central governing structures. Conferral of federal priority is justified because of its responsibility for advancing Canada's national interests both at home (comprehensive social programs) and abroad (diplomatic or military initiatives). Second, federalism is defined as a network of relatively autonomous provinces that have freely entered into accord with the federal government. Under the terms of the agreement, Ottawa has assumed those duties and responsibilities that the provinces were unable—or unwilling—to discharge. As a result of this freely agreed-upon division of power, all 11 players are equal in status, with a corresponding division of jurisdiction as outlined by constitutional decree. Demands for greater decentralization with attendant powers and levels of autonomy are consistent with this perspective. Quebec is perceived as equivalent to the other provinces in legal status; nevertheless, some concessions may be allowed for Quebec to pursue its language and culture objectives, even if these should regrettably interfere with fundamental Charter rights (Chodak 1994).

Canada as a Compact

A second vision interprets Canada as a compact between English-speaking and French-speaking Canadians. This vision is strongly endorsed by the Québecois, who reject definitions of themselves as ethnic minorities or Canadians who happen to speak French or live in Quebec. Even the notion of Quebec as a province in the conventional sense is dismissed. Canada is not a union of one central authority with 10 equal provinces, of which Quebec is but one province, but a compact between the French (Quebec) and English (Ottawa). There is a fundamental dualism in Canada that is rooted in constitutional law and long-standing political agreement. The BNA Act recognized the right of Quebec to promote its distinctive culture and language without undue interference from Ottawa, except in cases involving national concerns. The notion of Canada as a "covenant" between two founding nations dominated political discourses prior to the appearance of Trudeau in 1968. But the dynamics shifted from compact to contract because of Trudeau's commitment to a centralized Canada, strict equality between provinces, individual rights, official bilingualism, and multicultural equalities (McRoberts 1997).

A compact perspective endorses a vision of Quebec as a "nation within" the Canadian state whose self-governing powers are equivalent to those of Ottawa. Quebec does not like to be viewed as just another province with equal rights and privileges. Nor does it want to be treated as an ethnic group with a need for solutions through government intervention or assistance. It is a nation not only deserving of recognition of its differences, but entitled to those powers for securing its distinctiveness against outside intrusion (McRoberts 1997). Quebeckers are a "people" with a shared language and culture occupying a homeland of last resort. Quebec entered into Confederation with assurances that it would retain its status as a nation and, as founding people, its entitlement and special citizenship into perpetuity. These self-governing powers include the right to establish immigration policies, conduct foreign policy, and initiate bilateral agreements that fall under provincial jurisdiction.

Interpreting French–English relations as a compact casts light on the logic behind Quebec's aspirations, concerns, and political moves. It also points to potential sources of conflict. Quebeckers perceive English-speaking Canadians as politically and economically powerful agents for assimilation whose agenda reflects a commitment to a unitary federal state by centralizing its powers at the expense of other provinces. Moves to strengthen federalism are frequently interpreted as assimilationist in consequence if not in intent. Not surprisingly, Quebec's leaders have sought to secure the gap between Ottawa and Quebec. They have looked for ways to transfer power and resources from Ottawa for fulfilment of Quebec's ambitions. Public support has been galvanized to legitimate their nationalist policies as well as to strengthen Quebec's hand in dealing with Ottawa. Québecois leaders have capitalized on the public's inclination to equate language issues with the status of French–English relations. Widespread public support for language issues is thus manipulated as leverage for extracting various concessions from the federal government.

Canada as a Three-Nations State

A new and equally provocative vision of Canada is slowly gaining ground. Canada is neither a contract between a centre and the provinces nor an exclusive compact between Ottawa and the French. Canada is leaning towards a three-nations state model, that is, it comprises three separate founding nations with overlapping citizenships, each of which possesses rights and jurisdictions within their sphere (Kaplan 1993; Webber 1994). The survival of Canada will hinge on our ability to acknowledge and incorporate a plurality of ways of belonging because of deep diversities (Taylor 1993). Belated recognition of First Nations as a nation within Canada and a distinct society will complicate an already complex relation that exists between the two charter groups (Whitaker 1996).

The nationalism of Quebec's nationhood is instructive. As Salee and Coleman (1997) point out, Quebec provides a social laboratory by which to analyze the transformations in democratic social formations since World War II. Moves to affirm themselves as *maîtres chez nous* and to redress the political and economic imbalances resulted in a pronounced shift to democratize their political, social, and educational institutions during the 1960s, in the process repositioning Quebec from a defensive inward-looking community to an active and open society. These initiatives have created the contours of a nation-state, together with viable state institutions to support developments in the political economy without forsaking a French-dominated framework for conducting public affairs within the province. To some extent, Quebec's nationalism is essentially liberal and couched in universalistic value-neutral terms. Yet Quebec's attitude towards ethnic others is riddled with the ambivalence of a society with an uncertain future because of its minority status within a wider, global, socioeconomic context. As a result, developments in Quebec oscillate between democratic impulses for inclusiveness and enlarged citizenship and concerns over losing its distinctiveness, historically determined identity, and political powers. Quebeckers continue to grapple with addressing the concerns of particular identities without endangering the foundations of hitherto homogeneous societies. In short, Quebec stands as an interesting test case for democracy in an age of heightened identity politics and recognition of difference. For unless Quebec concedes the necessity for public space on the basis of difference rather than the priority of a single cultural system, its nation-building revolution may be aborted (Salee and Coleman 1997).

Sovereignty without Secession

"Le Quebec, ma patrie, Le Canada, mon pays" ("Quebec is my homeland, Canada is my country," Lysiane Gagnon, *Globe and Mail*, April 4, 1992).

French–English relations remain as fraught with tension as they were immediately before the 1995 referendum. There has been a lot of talk between the two sides, but little dialogue, or a *dialogue des sourds* (dialogue of the deaf), as both sides continue to talk past each other in the spirit of mounting animosity (McRoberts 1997; Conlogue 1997). The unthinkable—Quebec separating from Canada—is now actively entertained in the aftermath of the referendum that nearly brought Canada to the brink. Polls conducted since the early 1990s point to a similar conclusion: a majority of Quebeckers are attracted to some form of renewal within the present federalist system and fewer appear to be inclined towards any outright separation. These polls reveal a contradiction: a sizeable majority want Quebec to be sovereign while an overwhelming majority want Quebec to remain in Canada (Gagnon 1996). Even that most conservative of constituencies, the business sector, approves of Quebec's dissociation from the rest of Canada in light of that province's economic strength, abundance of human and natural resources, and the need to stabilize an uncertain political and investment climate.

A healthy skepticism towards polls and statistics is called for, yet no one should dismiss the significance of these projections for the viability and future of Canadian society. Three scenarios are possible. First, we are presiding over a turbulent period of intensive social change from which Canada will emerge a strengthened and restructured union. Second, we are currently witnessing the breakup of Canadian society into a "swiss cheese" federalism of relatively autonomous political entities along the lines of the European common market bloc. Third, it will be business as usual once all the sabre-rattling and politics of brinkmanship subside. We cannot predict which scenario is the most feasible, but we can ask, What then do the Québecois want, and what is being done to address the demands of Quebec's ethnic nationalism? In another context, we could just as easily ask, What do English-speaking Canadians want from Quebec, and what are the Québecois doing to accommodate these demands?

What Does Quebec Want?

It is unfair to imply that the Québecois have a uniform set of expectations and aspirations. Responses range from those who prefer only moderate changes to those who wish to radically restructure Quebec's relationship with Canadian society at large, even if outright secession is the only alternative. Responses to the "Quebec question" do not always reflect a perfect consistency; ambiguities often prevail that reflect situational circumstances. For example, the prospect of cultural security and political determination may be appealing, but the economic disadvantages of severing ties with Canada are no less powerful and provide a huge incentive to stick with the status quo. In other words, the Québecois want the best of both worlds, or as quipped by Yvon Deschamps, a French Canadian comedian: "They want an independent Quebec inside a united Canada" (Globe and Mail, June 18, 1994).

Even terms such as sovereignty or separation are fuzzy or misleading, with meanings that vary with context and person. The distinction between separation and sovereignty is subtle but valid. Sovereignty is what the Québécois already possess, as far as many Quebeckers are concerned, because of its charter group status and evolution as a distinct society. It is the supreme power from which all other powers are derived and expressed (see Kickingbird 1984). Separation, by contrast, is something that perhaps only a small percentage of Québécois are willing to entertain. Thus, sovereignty is not merely a softer version of separation, much less a sign of confusion in the minds of the electorate, but a nuanced reading of the Canadian federal system and Quebec's place in a globalizing and interdependent world (Editorial, Globe and Mail, March 11, 1994). Quebeckers may not want to quit Canada, in other words, but neither do they want to appear weak or vacillating or capitulate to the demands of English-speaking Canadians.

Generally speaking, all Quebeckers are anxious to maintain the French character of their society. They want to create conditions, both political and economic, with which they can protect and preserve the distinctiveness of Quebec as their homeland of last resort in North America. As long as Quebec remains in Canada, it needs the capacity (power, recognition, and space) for self-determination as a majority culture in a wider context where its minority status is a foregone conclusion (Burgess 1996). Quebec's nationalism is rooted ultimately in the desire of the Québécois to exist collectively and to have this collective existence recognized at political levels (Balthazar 1993). But agreement over goals does not always translate into consensus over means (Fournier 1994).

On the one side are the moderates, who generally prefer accommodation within Canada by strengthening Quebec's position within the federalist system, in large part by reinforcing Quebec's presence in Ottawa and expanding Quebec's access to power and resources. A new constitutional division of powers is also anticipated to ensure that each level of government controls what it does best (Johnson 1995). Moderates may define themselves as sovereigntist yet disagree with the principle of separation, preferring instead a kind of flexible federalism with sovereign control over internal jurisdictions of relevance. In short, the moderates can be described as federalists who endorse affiliation with Canada as their country, yet continue to identify first and foremost with Quebec as their homeland.

Radical perspectives entail some degree of separation from Canada. Many *independantistes* are tired of being labelled a minority group that English-speaking Canadians define as a costly problem people. They prefer a space that Quebeckers can call their own, where they are the majority and they call the shots. Quebeckers want to be in the "big leagues"—a state within a state—not just an administrative subunit of Canada (Latouche 1995). Or as put by Louise Beaudoin of the Parti Québécois, "I want to be a majority in my own country" (Editorial, *Globe and Mail*, March 1, 1995). The high risk of being permanently outmaneuvered (tyranny of the majority) is sufficient to justify a fundamental shift of power from federal to provincial levels, as confirmed by a *Globe and Mail*/Leger poll (*Globe and Mail*, May 20, 1994). The transfer is as critical as it is radical, and was recognized a generation ago by a Canadian national-unity commission:

> Quebec is distinctive and should, within a viable Canada, have the powers necessary to protect and develop its distinctive character. Any political solution short of this would lead to the rupture of Canada (Task Force on National Unity (Pepin-Roberts Report), 1977–79).

Many Quebeckers are also weary of those English-speaking Canadians who appear unwilling to accept even minimal concessions to confirm Quebec's distinctiveness. English-speaking insensitivity is seen as stemming from failure to discard a conquest mentality.

This insensitivity is also attributed to a lack of distinct anglophone cultural identity. While Québecois know who they are, English-speaking Canadians are perceived as bereft of common vision or grand design, except in opposition to something else, thus inhibiting their capacity to accept Quebec for its differences and history. Others argue that the federal system is no longer viable and that Quebec cannot possibly associate itself with a system that is incapable of dealing with its own problems (Castonguay 1994). Federalism does not pay; rather, staying in Canada extracts a heavy economic cost because of extra layers of government and the perpetual gridlock between Quebec and Ottawa (Fournier 1994).

Separatists believe that Quebec is poised to make a move: it has a broad industrial base, a healthy government financial structure, a reduced dependency on federal government, and autonomous sources of revenue. Only procedural questions remain: Can Quebec secede only with public opinion and international law on its side or must it abide by constitutional law and provincial consent? Secessionist moves come in different packages, from outright separation to sovereignty association, but most proposals entail some degree of political independence (including control over culture and language), without loss of close economic ties such as free trade and common currency (J. Laxer 1994). To be sure, sovereignty will come with economic and social costs, but ethnicities everywhere have shown a willingness to make sacrifices for heroic ideals, and Quebeckers appear ready to engage in such a trade-off as part of a sacred duty (Olive 1996). Sovereignty will not solve all of Quebec's problems, concedes Jacques Parizeau (1996), but it will create a more normal situation and reduce overlap by sharpening the lines of jurisdictions.

A Regrettable Necessity

> What is wanted is a larger bed (more space for each partner) maybe even twin beds. But there is definitely a desire to continue sharing the bedroom. This is a marriage not of passion but of reason and convenience—a fine arrangement based on common history, shared interests, and mutual respect (Lysiane Gagnon, *The Globe and Mail*, July 27, 1996).

The picture at present is transitional. Yet there is room for guarded optimism. Canada's federal system is remarkably flexible in its capacity to endlessly tinker with the balance of power between Ottawa and the provinces. De facto (informal) arrangements have been worked out that recognize the distinctiveness and relative autonomy of certain provinces. Quebec, for example, has its own pension plan, has its own system of private law, levies its own income tax, and exercises a degree of control over immigration that is unprecedented in any federal system (McRoberts 1996). As well, according to Stephane Dion, the Inter-governmental Affairs minister and the key constitutional adviser to the federal Liberal government, Quebec resembles a quasi-state in control of the powers for setting provincial priorities and controlling jurisdictions (Steward 1994). With or without constitutional guarantees, Quebec is acting as if it were a distinct society by exercising powers of a relatively sovereign nation. Ad hoc arrangements, in other words, do not appear to be the problem. The stumbling block resides in moves to legally recognize Quebec's distinct society status. As Charles Taylor (1993) notes, English-speaking Canadians may be willing to accept negotiated and pragmatic arrangements, but many balk at the idea of formalizing those concessions at odds with conventional views of Canada (as a social contract) that violate certain values related to formal equality (the principle of equal provinces) and create imbalances within Canada's federal system because of preferential treatment. There may be an additional barrier: formal recognition may restructure Quebec–Canada relations in a way that complicates that quintessential Canadian question, "What is a country for?" (Taylor 1993, 83).

THE FIRST NATIONS

Canada's treatment of First Nations is generally considered a national tragedy and an international disgrace (Royal Commission 1996; Canadian Human Rights Commission 1997). There is no dearth of examples of the federal government's neglect and oppression of aboriginal communities. Historically Canada's First Nations have been either pitied or condemned by mainstream society. From the nineteenth century on, aboriginal peoples were dismissed as a "problem people" whose refusal to discard the past and assimilate into the future only exacerbated the problem. They have also been castigated as problem-makers involving costly reparations at odds with national interests. This assessment raises several questions. First, what exactly is meant by the expression "Indian problem?" Second, how is this problem manifest with respect to social and cultural indices? Third, why does the "Indian problem" still exist? Fourth, what has been done about the problem in terms of government policy? And fifth, what can be done from an aboriginal perspective? We approach this section of First Nations as a so-called social problem involving certain conditions that provide the basis for claims to change through collective action or public policy (see also Best 1995; Gusfield 1996). After all, social problems refer to more than conditions "out there." Social problems also include what people define as social problems and responses to these definitional aspects of social reality that are perceived as troublesome or disruptive of normalcy and in need of collective repair.

From Problem to Peoples

Aboriginal peoples constitute the indigenous occupants of modern nation-states. In Canada, the Constitution defines aboriginal peoples as belonging to four major groups—status Indians (who are registered as Indians for the purpose of special entitlements), non-status Indians (whose Indian status has been extinguished for various reasons), the Métis (offspring of Indian and non-Indian unions), and the Inuit (formerly the Eskimo). Currently just over one million persons identify themselves as aboriginal, with about one-half now residing off reserves and away from band jurisdiction. Despite legal, historical, and developmental differences, aboriginal societies in Canada and abroad share much in common with each other. They see themselves as descendants of the original occupants whose collective and inherent rights to self-determination over jurisdictions pertaining to land, identity, and political voice have never been extinguished but remain intact as a basis for entitlement and engagement (Fleras 1996; 1997). Many, including American Native Indians (Cornell 1988), Australian Aborigines (Lippman 1996), New Zealand Maori (Walker 1995; Durie 1995), and the Saami of Scandinavia (Eidham 1985; Paine 1985), have long struggled to (a) retain control over the development of traditional lands and resources, (b) cope with government intervention in their lives, (c) survive as a culturally distinct population, and (d) sever the bonds of dependency and underdevelopment inherent within a system of internal colonization (Stea and Wisner 1984).

Aboriginal struggles once revolved around the goals of socioeconomic equality and cultural preservation. Though important still, these concerns have been replaced by a focus on decolonizing their relations with the state along the lines of the "nations within" (Fleras and Elliott 1992; Royal Commission 1996). Attainment of formal equality before the law or in the marketplace is of relatively marginal concern (Kelsey 1986). They are less willing to accept a token acknowledgment of their cultural heritage as an anachronistic novelty at odds with contemporary existence. Rather, we are witnessing a reconceptualization of aboriginal peoples as a distinct "social type," with a common set of aspirations and a corresponding package of claims against the state. Aboriginal peoples do not regard themselves as immigrants or minorities. They prefer instead to see themselves as relatively independent peoples of the Fourth World (the nations within) with customary rights to self-determination over land, political voice, and identity (Maaka and Fleras 1997).

Politicians and the public have reacted adversely to this reconceptualization. Many officials have attempted to address aboriginal concerns, but only from within the central policy structure of a liberal-democratic state (Fleras 1989). As a result, conflicts and contradictions continue to pervade the interaction between political and aboriginal sectors. Some Canadians are confused or frustrated by what they consider to be the highly unorthodox nature of aboriginal demands. Others refute the validity of these demands altogether, preferring to maintain the status quo. Still others are in general agreement with aboriginal aspirations but remain concerned about the long-term implications of the more radical proposals (Fleras 1992).

At one level, Canadian politicians appear willing in theory to acknowledge the plausibility of aboriginal demands as a policy item, if only to avert a crisis of legitimacy and restore some semblance of political tranquillity. Such an endorsement can be attributed in part to a desire to maintain credibility in the face of potential embarrassment and ridicule (Dyck 1985). But this support also feeds on a fear of international censure and the threat of reprisals. Few politicians can afford to dismiss the existence of aboriginal rights or the validity of special status and preferential treatment. What is debated instead are answers over defining their limits, and how best to concede these rights without destroying the social fabric of society in the process. Also evident is political willingness to negotiate issues related to self-determination, even self-government if necessary, although not to the extent of condoning territorial secession and dismemberment of the state.

At another level, however, there are widespread misgivings about the concept of aboriginality and the corresponding assumptions underlying the distribution of power and resources in society. The principles behind aboriginality and aboriginal rights continue to confound and confuse Canadian politicians. National interests must take precedence over aboriginal interests, they say (Boldt 1993). For them, aboriginal self-government should represent a political concession rather than an inherent right derived from natural or spiritual law. Rather than endorsing radical change from within, political concessions are geared towards control, predictability, and reliability, and this is accomplished primarily by reinforcing the rules of bureaucracy. Finally, there are irrevocable perceptual gaps. Aboriginal claims—with their focus on indigenous status and non-negotiable collective rights—are often in conflict with the individualistic and universal values embedded within liberal-democratic contexts (Weaver 1984; Boldt and Long 1984). Not unexpectedly, both politicians and the Canadian public have been slow to acknowledge aboriginality as a guiding principle for redefining aboriginal–government relationships.

The Problem with Problems

After nearly 400 years of sustained contact and interaction, the relational status of Canada's First Nations continues to reflect the strains of domination, control, and exploitation (Long and Dickason 1996). The imposition of a colonialistic relationship has exerted a powerful but negative effect on aboriginal peoples (Bienvenue 1985). In some cases, government policies deliberately undermined the economic and social viability of aboriginal communities as a means of keeping them under control. Of particular note was the government's policy of assimilation and relocation and its practice of denying basic rights to aboriginals, both on and off reserves. In other cases, however, this decline came about through the unobtrusive, yet equally powerful, educational efforts of Catholic and Anglican missionaries. The end result? Aboriginal peoples confront massive disarray in their own communities, where regulatory systems have collapsed and social problems are rife (Royal Commission 1996)

Socioeconomic Status

Aboriginal people continue to perform poorly in Canadian society despite growing public concern and increased government spending that amounts to billions of dollars annually. No matter how they are evaluated or assessed, aboriginal peoples have problems. They remain at the bottom of the socioeconomic ladder in terms of education, income, employment, and health. Housing is inadequate on many reserves, failing to meet even the most basic structural standards. Fewer than 50 percent of reserve homes possess sewer or water hook-ups, and 50 percent can be described as overcrowded (Frideres 1993). Unemployment rates are three times the average of those for nonaboriginal Canadians. On certain reserves, virtually the entire population subsists on welfare or unemployment benefits. Income levels are well below average both on and off reserves. Only about 20 percent of aboriginal students finish secondary schooling, despite some noticeable improvements in recent years. Few ever make it to university, a situation likely to worsen with recent government restrictions on spending for postsecondary schools. Of course, not all aboriginal people are destined to fail according to mainstream standards. There are individuals who possess secure and satisfying jobs with comfortable homes and exceptionally enriched lifestyles. As a group, however, most live under conditions that evoke images of grinding Third World poverty.

The deterioration of aboriginal culture has compounded the difficulties of identity and adjustment. As well, numerous aboriginal languages are currently under threat because of pressure from the schools and mass media (Fleras 1987). Equally detrimental has been the psychological effects derived from a sense of powerlessness, alienation, and irrelevance (Shkilnyk 1985). Young aboriginals are angry, defiant, or bored; they crave urban excitement. Too many suffer from a self-loathing that culminates in suicide, violence, and substance abuse. Whether through accident or disease, aboriginal death rates (including infant mortality) are four times the national average. Violent deaths and suicides are also out of proportion when compared to the general population. In fact, with a suicide rate six times the national average for certain age groups, Canada's aboriginal peoples represent one of the most self-destructive groups in the world at present. Aboriginal involvement with the criminal justice system is also out of proportion with national averages (LaPrairie 1997). Nearly 70 percent of status Indians have been incarcerated in a correctional centre by the age of 25. Nearly 40 percent of the inmates in western Canada's prisons are aboriginal, even though they comprise only about 12 percent of that region's population. The combination of these constraints and experiences has robbed many aboriginal peoples of any positive self-concept, in turn leading to self-fulfilling cycles of despair and decay. Nor can we disregard the sometimes disastrous consequences of often well-intentioned but misguided government policies and programs (Shkilnyk 1985).

Whose Problem Is It?

It is obvious the First Nations have problems. But whose problem is it? Defining aboriginal peoples as "the Indian problem" is not as straightforward as appearances suggest. Consider only the following questions from a social-problem perspective. What precisely do we mean by the so-called "Indian problem?" How did the label come about? Why? By whom? Is the labelling an accurate reflection of reality? Or are there different ways of talking about this problem? Answers to these questions are not merely academic. Inasmuch as government policy continues to be predicated on solving "the Indian problem," the issue is relevant for all Canadians.

References to "the Indian problem" imply that aboriginal peoples bear full responsibility for their plight. First Nations have problems that many see as of their own making, compounded by refusal to do something about it by assimilating (see Waldram 1994). "By blaming the victim" for the predicament, some critics suggest that only eliminating aboriginal culture and society can possibly solve "the Indian problem." The federal government has at times subscribed to this view, and it has employed several strategies to remove social and cultural "obstructions" to Western-style economic development and growth. Band members were encouraged to renounce their Indian status by moving to cities from reserves, and both aboriginal culture and reserves were dismissed as nothing more than breeding grounds for violence, apathy, and alienation. Exposure to modern values and institutional involvement was thought to be the key to a brighter future. Alternatively, the government has been anxious to modernize reserves by upgrading facilities and infrastructures with federal funding and expertise. If this transformation was successful, the hypothesis held, the so-called "Indian problem" would simply melt away.

But one could plausibly argue that "the Indian problem" is not an aboriginal problem per se. Is it essentially a "Canada problem" created by European expansion and settlement and perpetuated through systems of domination, control, and exploitation (Waldram 1994). Many of the problems that exist today did not happen until European "refugees" decided to transform Turtle Island into a colonized settlement by dispossessing the First Nations of their land and cultural traditions. Logic suggests that solutions to this problem must reside in destroying colonialist domination, especially the bonds of dependency and underdevelopment that have curtailed aboriginal growth. What we have, in other words, is a "white–aboriginal problem" that originated in the interplay and competition between different systems within a capitalist context. The so-called "Indian problem" must be placed squarely within a political-economy perspective and analyzed within a capitalist framework of domination, control, and exploitation (Wotherspoon and Satzewitch 1993). The problematic nature of aboriginal–white relations stems from the competitive struggle between a dominant sector and a subordinate one over power, resources, and status. Tensions arose from the interplay of culturally different lifestyles—one based on the principles of consumerism, competition, and progress, the other based on a commitment to spiritual values, community, and consensus. Redefining "the Indian problem" as a "white problem" casts a different light on how the problem arose and what can be done to solve it.

Policy as Problem

From its inception, the Canadian state confronted a quandary common to most colonizing powers: what to do with indigenous people it had dispossessed (see Behrendt 1996). Policies were formulated to deal with this conundrum in the hope that the indigenes would die out—physically or culturally—and thus solve the problem of their own accord. For the past 125 years, government policy and its administration by the Department of Indian Affairs have operated on the principle that aboriginal peoples are a social problem in need of a solution (Ponting and Gibbins 1980). In keeping with a commitment to assimilate and civilize, departmental policy labelled aboriginals as people whose lack of "culture" interfered with a smooth settlement of Canada. As a result, aboriginal peoples were victimized by a system of internal colonialism that was imposed on them by central authorities (Bienvenue 1985). Four consequences resulted (see Blauner 1972):

1) Aboriginal peoples were directly exploited for land, resources, and labour power. Indirectly they were disadvantaged because of restricted opportunities for economic self-development inherent in the Indian Act and through government interference. Thus, aboriginal communities comprise the underdeveloped component of Canadian society, reflecting in part their dependency on the government and in part economic stagnation on reserves.

2) The government consciously and unconsciously attempted to undermine and destroy aboriginal cultures and lifestyle. Foremost in terms of tactics were the assimilationist pressures inherent within the education system imposed on aboriginal children. Equally devastating was the modernization philosophy that guided government actions for improvement of aboriginal economic status. Even the best-intentioned policy can go wrong when based on erroneous premises.

3) Aboriginal cultures were disparaged for being primitive, irrelevant to modern society, and counter-productive to social and economic progress. It was thought that only adherence to the modern values of the dominant sector (a belief in progress, competition, and individualism) would extricate aboriginal peoples from the quagmire of the past.

4) Aboriginal lives were controlled and constrained by government bureaucrats. Although government policies were ostensibly intended to assist and protect aboriginal peoples, the latent functions (or unintended consequences) of government involvement were the continued domination, control, and exploitation of the target population.

Federal policy towards aboriginal peoples has evolved over the last century. An initial period of cooperation and accommodation gave way to the principles of assimilation and wardship as set out under the Indian Act (Tobias 1976). Segregation involved the concentration of aboriginal residents on reserves for assimilation into the mainstream as independent and hardworking Christian farmers. By the late 1940s, there was evidence of a shift towards integration and the formal rights of ordinary citizenship. Integrationist policies and programs sought to "normalize" relations with aboriginal peoples by severing their ties with federal authorities. Yet aboriginal reaction to the termination of federal responsibility was sharp and succinct. By the early 1970s, policy discourse shifted towards a greater tolerance of aboriginal languages and culture as well as proposals for granting them institutional control over health and education. At present, federal government and aboriginal leaders have continued to explore the logical consequences of aboriginal self-government models. The government's recent acceptance of the inherent right to aboriginal self-government within a Canadian framework promises to further alter the relational status of aboriginal peoples as the "nations within" (Fleras 1996).

Aboriginal Solutions

In their misguided arrogance and trenchant ethnocentrism, Canadian policymakers have long advocated certain solutions for eliminating "the Indian problem." These solutions have varied over time, but are best embodied in government polices of assimilation, integration, and limited autonomy. What is common to each of these (besides their built-in failure factor) is a refusal to formulate the issue except in terms with which members of the dominant society feel comfortable. In recent years, aboriginal peoples have finally succeeded in taking ownership of solutions to "the Indian problem," in part by redefining the terms of the debate. In place of a white agenda, aboriginal leaders have proposed a series of solutions they feel are consistent with their peoples' needs, concerns, and aspirations. Three themes recur throughout this redefinition process: first, conferral of "indigenous-plus status" on all aboriginal peoples; second, restoration of inherent rights to self-determination through self-government; and third, recognition of aboriginal and treaty rights. In each case, a common thread can be detected; namely, a belief in the inappropriateness of structures that once were used to colonize the First Nations. Proposed instead are indigenous models of self-determination that sharply curtail state jurisdiction while bolstering aboriginal empowerment (Alfred 1995).

Indigenous-Plus Status

In response to the question of what aboriginal peoples want, the most direct answer is, "the same things as all Canadian citizens." Aboriginal peoples are anxious to live in a just and equal society in which (a) their cultural lifestyles and languages are protected from unnecessary assimilationist pressure, (b) select elements of their culture can be preserved and interpreted within the framework of contemporary realities, (c) bureaucratic interference in their lives is kept to a minimum, (d) discrimination and racism is eliminated from their contacts with politicians, bureaucrats, state agents, and the general public, and (e) collective access to power, resources, status, and meaningful involvement in decision-making is within their grasp. Most of us would agree that these objectives and aspirations are not altogether dissimilar to what we expect as citizens of a multicultural society (Fleras and Elliott 1992).

Aboriginal peoples have also expressed a desire to be different. They want to transcend the constraints of formal citizen status and explore novel ways of redefining Canadian citizenship and belonging. The concept of "indigenous-plus status" means a recognition of pre-existing rights that have never been extinguished. These rights include

1) the right to control land and resources;

2) the right to protect and promote language, culture, and identity;

3) the right to conduct their affairs on a nation-to-nation basis; and

4) the right to establish indigenous models of self-government.

For aboriginal peoples, the recognition of indigeneity is paramount. Equal opportunity or equality before the law is necessary but insufficient. On the premise that equal standards cannot be applied to unequal situations without perpetuating inequality, aboriginal leaders have demanded special status and preferential treatment as a basis for restructuring their relationship with the rest of Canada.

In other words, aboriginal peoples have claimed the right to be different as well as the right to be the same (hence the expression, "indigenous-plus status"). They want equality of treatment (formal equality), yet demand unique concessions (equality of outcomes), such as a third tier of government with control over internal jurisdictions. They feel they are owed this, in part because of their unique legal status as original occupants and in part because aboriginal problems cannot be solved in a conventional manner. They are anxious to receive the benefits and privileges of Canadian citizens, but not at the expense of their rights as founding members of Canadian society. Nor do they see any contradiction in making these demands. As far as they are concerned, aboriginal peoples paid for these concessions with the loss of land, lives, livelihood, and cultural lifestyles. Canadian politicians and policymakers rarely dispute the validity of aboriginal arguments for unique status and preferential treatment. The entrenchment of aboriginal rights in the Constitution and the proposed recognition of the inherent right to aboriginal self-government are proof of that. Debate still exists, however, over the best way of defining the nature and scope of aboriginality.

Self-Determination Through Self-Government

A second step in the redefinition process consists of winning government recognition of the inherent right to aboriginal self-government by entrenching this right in the Constitution. The rationale for this argument is based on several points, including (a) the belief that all aboriginal peoples have the right to control their destiny; (b) the fact that international law stipulates the right to aboriginal self-determination; (c) the fact that the Royal Proclamation of 1763 affirmed and protected aboriginal nationhood, and (d) faith in the notion of inherent self-government to avert the further erosion of aboriginal life and culture (see also Royal Commission 1996). Aboriginal leaders have endorsed self-determination as essential in severing the cycle of deprivation, dependency, and underachievement that afflicts so many of their communities. While acknowledging various models of self-determination (for example, guaranteed parliamentary representation (Fleras 1992)), current appeals focus around the concept of inherent self-government powers, a proposal of such elusiveness and potency that most calls for clarification have generated more heat than light.

Even though the attainment of political self-determination through inherent self-government is touted as a key aboriginal plank (Penner 1983; Little Bear et al. 1984; Boldt 1993; Royal Commission 1996), the concept of self-government is proving difficult to define. There is no consensus among aboriginal leaders regarding an ideal self-governing model, and major differences are evident between models proposed by some aboriginal leaders and those favoured by government officials. Probably no single model is adequate for realizing the goal of autonomy and control. Some models will involve a reinterpretation and revival of traditional structures, others will involve the creation of new structures, and still others only advocate greater control in the provision of government services (Royal Commission 1993). Despite this diversity, general patterns can be detected. First, self-governing structures are envisaged as genuine political units, encompassing a distinct order of government at federal and provincial (occasionally at municipal) levels. Second, self-governing structures are not delegated by federal authority or Canadian law, but rooted in the reality of aboriginal nationhood, which has never been extinguished. This right to self-government is inherent in the sense that it has always existed (but was usurped by European settlement) and will continue to exist because aboriginal peoples did not voluntarily relinquish these rights by conquest or through treaties. Third, initiatives for self-government must originate with the aboriginal peoples themselves, must be conducted in cooperation with federal and provincial authorities, must ensure a degree of structural flexibility in design and implementation, and must provide a sound economic and resource basis for survival (Royal Commission 1996).

At the core of these wrangles are debates over who will control what (Royal Commission 1995; Fleras 1996). Jurisdictional matters are expected to vary from band to band. In all likelihood, they will include (a) control over the delivery of social services such as policing, education, and health and welfare; (b) ownership of resources and use of the land for economic regeneration; (c) the means to protect and promote distinct cultural values and language systems; (d) a final say over band membership and entitlements; and (e) input into the federal budget expenditures according to aboriginal rather than white priorities. Also anticipated are political structures that reflect local decision-making or consensual styles as well as a workable division of labour between the different levels of government. Lastly, strategies to sustain the legitimacy of self-governing doctrines will need to be devised.

The concept of self-government can also be discussed in terms of what it is not. Contrary to popular belief, most aboriginal peoples are not interested in seceding from Canadian society. Sovereignty is not identical to political independence or territorial autonomy except in the rhetoric of a few activists. Aboriginal leaders are hardly eager to incur the costs associated with autonomy and sovereign status. Many retain a vested interest in remaining within Canada, albeit on aboriginal terms. What is promoted instead is the concept of functional sovereignty with relatively autonomous powers over political, economic, cultural, and social domains. The right to self-determination is paramount; whether aboriginal groups choose to exercise that right will depend on a host of circumstances (Fleras 1998).

The adjustment process is driven by aboriginal endorsement of a "nations within" status (Fleras and Elliott 1992). By this means, aboriginal leaders categorically reject the view of themselves as a collection of Canadian citizens who happen to live on reserves. They see themselves instead as sovereign and self-governing nations that have a distinct political status within the Canadian nation-state. Certain inalienable rights follow from this fundamental recognition. As a "nation within," they are anxious to deal with federal authorities on a government-to-government basis. Yet their failure to date to achieve these self-governing rights—despite constitutional guarantees to this effect—indicates that further struggles are in store throughout the restructuring process.

Aboriginal Title and Treaty Rights

Recognition of aboriginal title and treaty rights comprises the third component in the process of redefining "the Indian problem." Under the Charter of Rights and Freedoms, many public issues have been framed as rights issues for resolution. Consider aboriginality. Aboriginal peoples have spurned being labelled as another ethnic or disadvantaged minority. They prefer instead to define themselves as a sovereign entity whose collective and customary rights are guaranteed by virtue of their ancestral occupation of their land. Nor are they anxious to be integrated as an ethnic component of a Canadian multicultural mosaic, partly because they feel this would involve a corresponding diminishment of their claims. What they have proposed instead is a recognition of their sovereign status as the aboriginal inhabitants of Canada. Claims to sovereignty are defended either by an appeal to natural law or by reference to spiritual grounds (Ahenakew 1985). As the original occupants whose inalienable rights have never been extinguished by treaty or conquest, aboriginal peoples defend their claims against the state as intrinsic and basic rather than contingent on government largesse. In short, aboriginality refers to a political statement involving aboriginal claims against the state and to the rights and powers associated with this unique relationship (Weaver 1984). It also involves the politicization of aboriginal grievances as claims against the state over a proposed redistribution of power and resources.

Equally important to aboriginal aspirations is an enforcement of federal treaty obligations. They regard treaties as ongoing and organic agreements that specify the special legal status of aboriginal nations. By formally establishing aboriginality as a legal status, the treaties also serve as a basis for meaningful political interaction with the federal government. Aboriginal spokespersons have long upheld treaties as semi-sacred and binding documents. Land and resources were exchanged for treaty rights guaranteeing access to goods and services in perpetuity. As far as aboriginal leadership is concerned, the government remains bound to honour the contractual obligations of these treaties. Access to benefits and services (such as free education and tax exemptions) is not a charitable hand-out. Nor should it be regarded as a benevolent gesture on the part of a munificent authority. Rather, treaty benefits derive from a legally binding exchange that the aboriginal peoples have paid for over and over again, not only by the expropriation of land and resources, but also through the loss of their lives and lifestyle.

Aboriginal leaders also feel that recognition of land claims settlements is of utmost importance. Aboriginal ownership and control of land and resources is imperative for securing a solid economic base as a basis for further prosperity and development. Economic benefits can be derived from renting out lands and resources at rates that are favourable to aboriginal interests. Advantages also can be achieved through local development (in tandem with public or private interests) at a pace that reflects community priorities and developmental levels. Recourse to a secure economic foundation is important. Indeed, any fundamental changes in the status of aboriginal people can only be achieved by negotiating from a position of economic strength and the political power that sustains it.

In summary, aboriginal demands are consistent with their claim for inherent self-determining rights as a unique nation within a Canadian framework. Aboriginal peoples are not seeking to separate from Canada. They do not want to impose their vanishing lifestyles on the non-native component. Instead, they are looking to find a middle way—to strike a balance between extremes. This search for balance and consensus is evident in several points of agreement among aboriginal leaders.

First, while there is little inclination to separate from Canada in the territorial sense, any move towards assimilation is categorically rejected. A commitment to the inherent right of self-government is endorsed instead as a compromise between the poles of separatism and absorption. Second, although aboriginal peoples don't want to preserve their cultural lifestyle in amber for the edification of purists or tourists, they also refuse to abandon their language, culture, and identity in exchange for an alien and incompatible package of nonaboriginal values and beliefs. As a compromise, they want to take relevant elements of the past and apply them selectively to the realities of the present. They want to be modern, in other words, but not at the expense of what makes them unique. Third, aboriginal peoples are pragmatists who wish to achieve a working balance between tradition and progress. Balancing the cultural and spiritual values of the past with the technological benefits of modern society remains a pressing priority. Fourth, achievement of political and economic power is viewed as critical to restoring aboriginal communities as flourishing centres of meaningful activity. Yet these goals are unacceptable if attained at the cost of undermining their spirituality, collective and community rights, and cultural values. Whether aboriginal peoples can use the resources available to forge a "golden mean" between seemingly unworkable extremes cannot be answered as yet. Nevertheless, the healing process has begun, even though the journey promises to be a long and arduous one (Mercredi and Turpel 1993).

SUMMARY

1. The dynamics and conditions associated with race, ethnicity, and aboriginality continue to be defined as a social problem, with the potential to unravel the social fabric of Canadian society. Failure to define the problem accurately—as has long been the case with aboriginal peoples in Canada—can only lead to flawed solutions and unsatisfactory outcomes

2. Canada's overall record for treatment of racial, ethnic, and aboriginal minorities is inconsistent. There is much to be proud of in the progressive management of diversity, yet marked hostilities towards minorities existed in the past and continue into the present.

3. Discrimination in one form or another (including prejudice and racism) is still pervasive in Canadian society; it varies in magnitude and scope, and is best approached by sociological rather than psychological explanations. Proposed solutions to the problem of discrimination are complex and vary according to how it is defined, that is, as redneck, polite, institutional, systemic, or subliminal.

4. The notion of discrimination is interpreted within the context of intergroup activity. Employed in this sense, discrimination consists of a "rational" solution by the privileged to consolidate their advantage in the competitive struggle over scarce resources. The emphasis on discrimination as group dynamics within unequal contexts also confirms its essentially social (rather than psychological) dimensions.

5. Official multiculturalism can be interpreted as a problem or a solution. On the one hand, it serves as an innovative, if imperfect, device for engaging Canada's diversity, especially in the fields of discrimination and racism. On the other hand, it can be viewed as yet another government-imposed problem that diminishes social unity and national identity.

6. Multiculturalism has been criticized for being divisive, regressive, irrelevant, and impractical. These same criticisms can be turned on their head to show how multiculturalism represents a workable and necessary way of dealing with the realities of change and diversity.

7. Multiculturalism is neither the source of nor the solution to all of Canada's intergroup problems. It represents a flawed experiment for managing diversity consistent with Canada's society-building aspirations.

8. A central issue in this chapter asks the question: "What is really going on in terms of Quebec–Ottawa relations?" Answers to this question suggest the necessity to see Canada

from a variety of diverse perspectives, including Canada as a contract, a compact, or a three-nations state.

9. What do the Québecois want? While answers are varied and reflect a certain ambiguity, consensus points to a need to protect, preserve, and promote the conditions that will enhance the distinct and sovereign character of Quebec's identity, language, and culture. Ambiguities in response may reflect the diverse means employed to achieve these goals, with moderates who are willing to work within the federalist system on one side and radicals who want to scrap federalism in exchange for some degree of separation on the other. Recent debates have focused on whether Canada's and/or Quebec's borders are divisible.

10. Despite considerable expenditure and public goodwill, Canada's relationship with its aboriginal peoples has left everything to be desired, at least judging by the social, cultural, economic, and political status of most aboriginal communities. Initiatives to eliminate "the Indian problem" revolve around the politics of aboriginality, and First Nations' efforts to implement inherent self-governing arrangements have shown some promise. Whether central authorities will concede such powers of self-determination is open to debate at present.

11. Aboriginal concerns focus primarily on decolonizing their relationship with government authorities, in large part through promotion of objectives pertaining to indigenous-plus status, self-determination, and aboriginal and treaty rights.

P a r t

3

INSTITUTIONAL
PROBLEMS

THE FAMILY

DID YOU KNOW?

- During 1974 to 1992, a married women was nine times more likely to be killed by her spouse than by a stranger. Of 164 women murdered in Canada in 1993, 77 were killed by a current or past partner. In Ontario alone, 64 women were murdered in 1993 with over half (35) killed by a partner or former partner.

- According to the Violence Against Women Survey, 3 out of every 10 Canadian women (29%) currently or previously married, or living in a common-law relationship, have experienced at least one incident of physical or sexual abuse at the hands of an intimate partner.

- According to the 1991 Census, 13 percent of all families (almost 1 million families) were single-parent families with never-married children of all ages. Approximately 60 percent of single mothers live in low-income situations.

- The first gay marriage to be widely publicized in Canada occurred when two homosexual men were married by a Unitarian-Universalist minister in Winnipeg in 1977.

- In a 1990 survey of 1200 randomly selected adults who were asked to define the word "family," only 22 percent selected the definition "a group of people related by blood, marriage, or adoption." Almost three-quarters of the sample surveyed chose a more expansive definition that defined the family as simply "a group of people who love and care for each other."

THE PROBLEM

For most of us, the question "What is a family?" would not seem to pose a very formidable challenge. Regardless of what type of family we grew up in or what type of relationship we are currently involved in, the image of the prototypical "ideal family" comes to mind readily enough. As anthropologist Edmund Leach (1967) has observed, we are daily inundated with images of what he terms "the cereal-packet norm family:" the father as head of the household, the smiling mother whose duties remain centred solely around the home, and, of course, their two or more cherubic-faced children. This imagery is especially potent because it is sheathed in the "charm of hominess" (Gottlieb 1993, 270), or a vision of Home Sweet Home in which the family is portrayed as offering a safe harbour from a sometimes heartless world. The scene suggested is reminiscent of a Norman Rockwell painting—the white picket fence, the gingham-clad daughter and denim-clad son playing happily with the frolicking puppy, mom's chocolate chip cookies cooling on the window sill, dad cutting the festive turkey—and creates an enticing portrait of comfort, cosiness, and security.

Extolled by the Republican party during the U.S. presidential elections, by the Conservative party (the "party of the family") in England since the late 1970s (Abbott and Wallace 1990, 73), and within Canada by the Family Coalition party (Conway 1990, xi), the Reform party, and the Christian Heritage party, the traditional patriarchal nuclear family, "that immemorial unit of married man and woman and their dependent children living together in the same house" (Gairdner 1992, 3) is championed as universal, idyllic, and sacred. However, as Abbott and Wallace (1990, 73) have observed, one of the subtle consequences of heralding this image of the family is that it constructs an evaluative framework by which all relational forms are to be judged. Thus, a particular type of family, characterized by a gendered division of labour (that is, the male "breadwinner" and the female "housewife") is depicted "as the normal, natural, and inevitable family form." Implicitly, forms of relationships that contradict or challenge this imagery are viewed as "deviating" from, or inferior to, this posited ideal. In consequence, even though the reality of Canadian life suggests that the "cereal-packet norm family" is becoming increasingly challenged by other definitions, the image of this "ideal" may still be heralded as the most desirable, the standard by which all other forms of relationships are to be judged. While the emergence of other forms may be dismissed as "faddish," heralding the patriarchal nuclear family as *the traditional family* suggests that this form is time-tested, ever-enduring, and representative of a higher stage of civilized social life. Moreover, inasmuch as "good people" enter into "good (that is, conventional) relationships," this ideal suggests that persons who would turn their backs on the traditional family are to be regarded at best as suspect, and at worst as inferior.

As Gottlieb (1993, 7) notes, in its origins the word "family" stems from *famulus*, the Latin word for "servant." The word *familia* was used in Classical times originally to refer to the live-in staff of a household, and from there it came to mean the household itself or the members of it. The term *pater familias* was so commonly used to refer to a "householder" that it took on the connotation of "an ordinary citizen." *Mater familias* was also commonly used to refer to the "woman of the house" in the sense of the person who directed its domestic affairs. Already the gendered division of household responsibilities (man's realm was public, woman's was private) was evident in the common terminology. Nevertheless, as Gottlieb observes, "By now the [original] meaning [of family as domestic staff] is not only obsolete but very strange indeed to modern ears."

The sense of strangeness occasioned by the original meaning of the word "family" is important, for it serves to remind us of the taken-for-granted nature of social forms and institutions, including that of the family. Our ideas of what is and is not a family are products of our society, reflecting dominant ideologies about the social roles of men and women, about their sexuality and sexual behaviour, about fertility and procreation, and about the care and socialization of children. Given that these issues intersect within discussions of the family, it is evident that the topic will often summon passionate engagement and intense debate.

For example, the issue of whether homosexual relationships can constitute a family has considerably agitated those people who would categorize homosexuality as a "sexual perversion" and view homosexuals as a threat to the normative social order. Thus, some maintain that the family must, by the definition they would employ, include "adults of *both* sexes, at least two of whom maintain a socially approved sexual relationship, and one or more children of their own, or adopted of the sexually cohabiting adults" (Murdock 1949, 1, emphasis added). Although the first gay "marriage" to be widely publicized in Canada took place in 1977, when two gay men were married by a Unitarian-Universalist minister in Winnipeg (Jackson and Persky 1982), until relatively recently, Canada has not been guided by a concept of "different, but equal" when it comes to sexual orientation. For example, a recent Gallup poll reported that fewer than half (49%) of Canadians believe that homosexual couples should be entitled to the same benefits (e.g., dental, health, survivor) as heterosexual couples, and fewer than one-third (31%) of Canadians feel that gay or lesbian couples should be permitted to adopt children (Schaefer et al. 1996, 254). Similarly, although Katherine Arnup (1995, vii) observes that "a recent study has estimated that there are between 3 and 8 million gay and lesbian parents in the United States, raising between 6 and 14 million children," and suggests that "we can assume that, proportionately, the numbers of lesbian mothers [in Canada] is equally high," those studying families have typically ignored or viewed these alternative family forms as deviant or pathological. Although in recent years there has been a knowledge explosion in this area (e.g., Benkov 1994; Stone 1990; Weston 1991), Karen Williams (1995) notes a variety of reasons why, for example, writings on gay and lesbian parents remain sparse. She observes that for many lesbian parents, "the prospect of losing custody is never far from view" and that for all, "the threat of exposing our children to the profound homophobia that still permeates our society hovers over us as we write" (ix).

For many Canadians, homosexual behaviour deviates from the "taken-for-granted" nature of sociosexual reality and accordingly is viewed as "deviant." Homosexuality challenges the common-sense assumption that human beings have a heterosexual destiny and that the ways in which most of us conduct our sexual affairs are both natural and morally right. It challenges classification systems surrounding the family and marriage, gender, and love and sexual experiences. The "protective cocoon" (Scott 1972, 20) of the natural order is threatened by homosexuality's assertions that human beings need not live in family units, need not have children, need not "fall in love" with an opposite-sex partner, indeed, need not "fall in love" at all to engage in sexual activities.

In other words, the existence of homosexuals suggests that the world may not be quite so simple as those who believe in a natural order suggest. Even though same-sex couples throughout Canada have made much progress over the past few years in winning rights and benefits that were previously denied them, it would be presumptuous to assume that homosexuality itself and the homosexual marriage are positively endorsed by the majority of Canadians (Salamon 1989). Indeed, the obverse would seem to be true.

Human rights, sometimes referred to as civil rights, are essentially extended in both Canada and the United States as guarantees of equal rights protection to individuals who could be singled out for prejudicial and discriminatory treatment based solely on their possession of a quality over which they have no control. Prior to 1986, the Quebec Charter of Rights and Freedoms established Quebec as the only jurisdiction in Canada to include "sexual orientation" as a prohibited ground of discrimination under statute law (Yogis, Duplak and Trainor 1996, 1). Although on May 9, 1996, the passage of Bill C-33 by a 153–76 free vote in the House of Commons paved the way for the Canadian Human Rights Act to include "sexual orientation" as a prohibited ground of discrimination, an amendment to the federal human rights legislation cannot eradicate stereotypes or militate an end to prejudice. Both before and after the debate in the House of Commons, various Canadian MPs voiced concerns that evidenced intolerance towards homosexuals and 28 Liberals voted against their own party's policy (Toronto Star 1996).

All of us are likely to seek the form of family life that will meet our needs. Some therapists refer to this as "scripting," that is, that people attempt to find someone who fits the "script" they have concocted for their love interest—the right qualities, attributes, or characters that define a partner as desirable. The "needs" typically identified within these scripts have shifted over the course of history from the simple desire for a sexual partner, to a preoccupation with continuing a family lineage, to a focus on financial support, to a focus on love and emotional intimacy. At the same time, popular ideas of how best to achieve these needs have also changed. In addition, there are open disagreements between different segments of the population over whether the "new" family and relationship forms are desirable for individual family members and even society itself.

Seligman (1992, 177) observed that in a 1990 study of 1200 randomly selected adults who were asked to define the word "family," only 22 percent selected the definition "a group of people related by blood, marriage, or adoption." Almost three-quarters of the sample surveyed chose a more expansive definition that defined the family as "a group of people who love and care for each other." However, for others, departures from the so-called traditional family are viewed as symptomatic of a society in decline. For example, for members of the New Right or Moral Right, and their intellectual advocates such as George Gilder (1973; 1974; 1978; 1982; 1985; 1986) and Charles Murray (1977; 1984; 1988; 1990), the "war against the family" (Gairdner 1992) is the favourite metaphor for a supposed assault on a way of life in which a stable, patriarchal nuclear family is viewed as central. For these social critics, state intervention in family life (for example, through legalizing abortion or subsidizing day care), feminism as a sociopolitical force, divorce, and "sexual deviancy" (that is, homosexuality, nonmarital sex, and contraception) are considered threats that must be vanquished if society is to remain stable.

As an example of this genre of writing, in his "no nonsense, tell-it-like-it-is . . . frankly offensive" (xiii) *The War Against the Family: A Parent Speaks Out*, Canadian author William Gairdner (1992) is eager to point out the sources of the social malaise that ails Canada. To wit,

> the antifamily ideology and arguments of radical feminism . . . [which] hamper the efficiency of the military and distort the truth about daycare and domestic violence . . . the radical homosexual movement, with its strident effort to destroy the concept of the traditional family and its widespread campaign of AIDS disinformation . . . the liberalism of the mainstream churches . . . [and] the antifamily role of the law. (xii)

Gairdner maintains that anyone who would argue with him is "brain dead" (ix) or has been "brainwashed" by "left-liberal" "academic and political demagoguery" (57) written by sociologists with "ideological axes to grind" (56). According to him, sociologists, like "social workers, therapists, and thousands of government employees . . . *have a vested interest in family breakdown*" (56, emphasis in original) in that it supposedly provides them with boundless opportunities for professional advancement and financial recompense. Like vultures swooping down to prey on the wounded, these money-hungry sociologists are supposedly ill-disposed towards the "natural family" (56) as they greedily "soak up tax dollars trying to bring it down" (56). Encouraged in their efforts "through a large variety of censorship devices, such as the Social Sciences and Humanities Research Council, various governmental and academic 'ethics' committees and local government or university granting mechanisms which ensure that only 'politically correct' research proposals will be approved and funded" (57), "left liberal radicals" have "cornered the academic market" (57). "Canadians," writes Gairdner, "should be good and mad about this situation. What it boils down to is that we are financing our own brainwashing" (57).

The New Right's image of the family has an undeniably popular appeal. For example, in a study of 700 elementary school children across Canada, the researchers found "that almost without exception, the girls expected to marry, to have children, and to assume there would be a husband to provide for the family" (in Mackie 1991, 84). "There do not seem to be any unmarried mothers, deserted wives, widows or divorcees among the imaginary women Canadian schoolgirls expect to become" (as cited in Mackie 1991, 84). Similarly, Baker's research on Canadian adolescents reported that three in four adolescent females expected to get married and have children; "few expected divorce, or if they saw divorce as a possibility, thought that it would not have much of an impact on their lives. Most saw marriage in highly romantic terms: relaxed evenings with their husbands while untroublesome children slept contentedly" (Conway 1990, 98). In like fashion, Spade and Reese (1991) report that in their random sample of 320 undergraduate students, "both men and women expect that women will play a more prominent role in the family and men a stronger role in the workplace" and that "the orientation and plans of these college students do not anticipate symmetrical relationships in which both men and women share household and work responsibilities" (309). Nevertheless, despite the popularity among adolescents of the "ideal family" as a wished-for future, Canadian demographic trends suggest that very few of them will actually participate in this type of lifestyle.

THE CHANGING DEMOGRAPHICS OF THE CANADIAN FAMILY

There can be little doubt, as Wilson (1991, 28) has observed, that "demographic, economic and attitudinal changes of the last decades have profoundly altered family life" in Canada. She notes that although approximately 90 percent of Canadians will eventually marry, "at any point in time about 40 per cent of adult women are unmarried" and that despite the media image of the affluent single woman, "the reality is that most are older widowed women, most of whom are poor." Moreover, she observes that according to statistics provided in 1990 by the National Council of Welfare, "based on current patterns of marriage, divorce, and life expectancy, 84 per cent of Canadian women" will spend a significant portion of their adult lives in households without a husband where they will be responsible for the support of their children and themselves (28). For these women, their family will be markedly unlike that of the prototypical ideal.

In Canada, marriage rates evidenced a slow decline from the mid-1970s so that by 1980 the *crude marriage rate* (i.e., the rate of marriages per 1000 population) was 7.8. It then continued a very slow but steady decline throughout the 1980s, falling to 6.8 by 1990, and evidenced a sharper decline in the early 1990s: in 1991 the crude marriage rate was 6.1 and in 1992 it was 5.8. The figures for 1993, 1994, and 1995 were constant at 5.5 per 1000 (Noult 1996, 47; Statistics Canada 1996). The decline in the crude marriage rate would undoubtedly be considered most significant by those who posit the "traditional family" as an ideal.

A 1995 survey conducted by Statistics Canada on approximately 11 000 people across Canada suggests that, as a consequence of increases in separation, divorce, remarriage, and cohabitation on the one hand and drops in mortality, fertility, and marriage on the other hand, the so-called "alternate families" now outweigh the so-called "traditional families." Indeed, the newest portrait of the Canadian family is no longer a single representation but one of increasing diversity. Married couples with children at home made up simply 45 percent of all families in 1995, down from 64 percent in 1961; almost one in three married couples had either no children or children who had left home. The tendency away from large families is also marked. In 1953 there were 10 636 children born into families with 9 or more children; by 1992 this figure had declined by 98 percent. In 1991 only 1 percent of families with children at home had 5 or more children; in 1971 10 percent of families with children at home had 5 or more children (Columbo 1996, 66). The decline in family size also reflects an overall trend in the total fertility rate. Although we are witnessing an *echo boom* as the last of the "baby boomers" have their children, there is a marked tendency away from the large families of the past.

During the last 20 years, the most radical change with regard to families has been the increase in lone-parent families; in the last 10 years, it has been the increase in common-law families. Consider that Statistics Canada only began recording common-law families as a separate category in 1981, and that the number of common-law relationships has almost tripled in the past 15 years from 355 000 to 997 000. It would seem that common-law unions are not simply envisaged as a prelude to marriage but as an increasingly viable alternative to marriage and remarriage. In 1991 the provinces with the highest percentage of married-couple families were Newfoundland and Saskatchewan. The province with the highest percentage of common-law families was Quebec with 16.3 percent of all families—a figure that is close to double the Canadian average—living common law. The high proportion of common-law and lone-parent families in Quebec would seem to reflect the continuing legacy of the "Quiet Revolution" during the 1950s and 1960s, Quebec's increasing urbanization, and in particular, the significant changes in female gender roles.

As the combined result of increases in separation, divorce, and illegitimate births, many Canadian children grow up in one-parent families, the majority of which are female-headed. While in 1941 the percentage of lone-parent families also reached a high level, the principal explanation then was the death of a partner. Between 1941 and the 1960s, the proportion of lone-parent families declined and did not begin to increase until the introduction of the Divorce Act in 1968. By 1991 the principal explanation had shifted significantly to divorce. By 1995 the number of single parents—80 percent of them women—raising children represented 22 percent of all Canadian families with children. Over half (55%) of these single-parent families were the result of separation and divorce.

According to Statistics Canada estimates, 45 percent of Canadian children will experience the separation or divorce of their parents before reaching age 18. While widows and widowers raising children alone represented two-thirds of all single parents in the 1950s, this type of single-parent family dropped to just 16 per cent of all single-parent families in 1995. In marked contrast, the number of single parents who have never married (although they may have been in a common-law relationship that ended) has increased markedly; while never-married lone parents accounted for merely 10 percent of all lone parents 15 years ago, they now represent 1 in 4 of all single parents.

Because three-quarters of divorced men and two-thirds of divorced women eventually remarry, and because half of all remarriages include dependent children, the children of divorced or never-married parents are likely to find themselves within reconstituted families. In 1995 questions on remarriage were asked for the first time by Statistics Canada; the results note that Canada's 430 000 step-families currently account for approximately 10 percent of our 4165 million families. Moreover, even step-families are becoming far more diverse than they were previously. While in the past step-families were typically the result of one spouse dying and the survivor remarrying, in 1995 slightly more than half of all Canadian step-families consisted of a mother, her children, and a stepfather, 10 percent were composed of a father, his children, and a stepmother, and more than a third were blended or reconstituted families (involving a mixture of children brought by both parents from previous unions or a mix of children from previous marriages plus others from the current union).

HOME SWEET HOME OR THE TIES THAT BIND?

Increasingly, commentators have suggested that the image of Home Sweet Home is in itself a colossal unreality founded on a collective pretence. Specifically, recognition of the myriad forms of family violence such as spousal abuse, child maltreatment, and elder abuse—all of which went largely ignored as an area of academic attention until the 1960s and early 1970s—has focused attention on the horrors that may be concealed by drawing lacy curtains over the topic of the family and depicting it as a "haven in a heartless world" (Lasch 1977). Since the "discovery" of child abuse (Pfohl 1977) in the 1960s, attention and social concern directed towards it has "laid the groundwork for the study of other problems under the rubric of family violence" (Leroux and Petrunik 1990, 653–54).

According to Straus and Forward (1979), these three factors had particular importance for the "discovery" of family violence as a social problem: 1) a greater professional and public sensitivity to the issue of violence in the 1960s and 1970s in the aftermath of social protest, political assassinations, and the rising rates of violent crime; 2) the rise of the second wave of the women's movement; and 3) conflict theory's challenge to the consensus model of society. Additionally, the implementation of child abuse laws, the establishment of battered women shelters, and increasing recognition of the pervasiveness of family violence combined to "challenge the ideal of the family as a cohesive social unit" (Leroux and Petrunik 1990, 654).

It would be fair to say that over the past two decades there has been a "knowledge explosion" in the area of family violence, with academic studies, generalist books, and autobiographies of the victims of family violence appearing at an exponential rate (Bell 1984). Consider that from 1939 to 1969, the premier journal for the sociological study of the family, the *Journal of Marriage and the Family*, did not contain a single article with the word "violence" in its title (Nuefeld 1993) nor a single article on violence against wives. In marked contrast, in 1983 alone, three academic journals were launched that focused on family violence (Hotaling and Sugerman 1986, 101). Similarly, Sullivan (1992) observes that since 1965, when the *Indexus Medicus* first listed "child abuse" as a "new medical category," the growth of information has been little less than astounding. "In 1965 there were no books on this specific topic . . . there are now many thousands of entries and . . . more than 70 books have been published since 1980. There is a corresponding growth in the literature in each of several specialty areas as well" (32–33). The analyses undertaken have not led to a single interpretation but rather to controversy and disparate claims as to ownership of "the problem" as it is variously conceived. However, there is little doubt that for some the experience of the family is both horrific and devastating (Fraser 1987; Armstrong 1986).

In 1984 the *Report of the Committee on Sexual Offenses Against Children and Youths* (the Badgley Report) and in 1985 *The Report of the Special Committee on Pornography and Prostitution* (the Fraser Report) reported a startlingly high incidence of child abuse in Canada: one in two females and one in three males had experienced one or more unwanted sexual acts at some time during their lifetime; four in five first offenses occurred when the victim was under the age of 21. The assailant was most commonly a family member or someone the child knew well and who was in a position of trust over him or her. Despite the image of the "child abuser" as a stranger who frequents playgrounds, children are more likely to be the victims of sexual or physical violence at the hands of their caregivers than at those of a stranger. More recently, in what is considered the largest study of the physical and sexual abuse of children, a team of researchers from McMaster University interviewed nearly 10 000 Ontarians age 15 and over in 1990 and 1991 and found that 11 percent of their male respondents and 9 percent of their female respondents reported being kicked, bitten, punched, hit, choked, burned, scaled, or physically attacked as children. Severe physical abuse was most often perpetrated by natural fathers, followed by natural mothers. The authors also reported that nearly one in three males (31.2%) and more than one in five females (21.1%) reported less severe forms of physical abuse while growing up. Rates of physical abuse reported by men were higher in families where the breadwinner had not finished high school, although this finding did not hold among female respondents. For women, rates of physical abuse were higher for those raised in rural areas, a finding that did not hold among male respondents. Sexual abuse was reported by 4.3 percent of the males and 12.8 percent of the females. Unlike physical abuse, sexual abuse among males and females was not linked to a parent's educational level or the size of the community in which the child grew up (KW Record 1997c). Mones (1991) has suggested that *parricide*, the murder of a mother or father by their children, is not infrequently the final desperate act of a youth with a history of chronic sexual, physical, or emotional abuse.

In part, the historical and continuing "invisibility" of family violence stems from the fact that the behaviour occurs within the private sphere of the home. In addition to social injunctions that direct us not to meddle in family matters, our society promotes an ethos of "non-intervention" in various other ways. Accordingly, the incidence and prevalence of family violence is difficult to determine. While actions that result in obvious, tangible forms of injury may result in intervention, the quiet desperation of some people who experience more subtle forms of injury may never result in official notification. At the same time, as we noted in an earlier chapter, our definitions of abusive conduct within the family are themselves somewhat problematic. Some, for example, have argued that in using broad definitions of "child abuse" or "spousal abuse," we have condemned our responding agencies to failure. For example, Bush (1988) has suggested that child welfare legislation that mandates intervention in all cases of suspected child abuse, which it broadly defines as physical, sexual, emotional abuse or neglect, poses insurmountable obstacles for the professionals charged with responding to and preventing child abuse. In contrast, if we formulate too narrow a definition, we may only succeed in courting a type of myopia in which the "dysfunctional family" becomes a metaphorical snake-pit while the functional family is presumed to be a veritable paradise.

DeKeseredy and Hinch (1991) have argued that despite attempts by researchers to gauge the incidence of family violence, the most common measure used, the Conflict Tactics Scale, is too crude a measure to capture the plurality of ways in which families can be abusive. This measurement tool, which asks respondents to indicate the number of times they have engaged in a range of "violent" behaviour (from shoving to attempted murder and rape), is considered problematic for a number of reasons. For example, some critics have noted that women tend to overestimate their abusive conduct while men tend to underestimate theirs. What further muddies the waters is that within our society women and men may perceive differing degrees of support for reporting personal victimization. Thus, the man who reports being assaulted by his female partner may be chided for being "less than a real man;" first, because he let her get away with it and second, because he would "whine" about it. However, it is just as true that women are reluctant at times to report abuse because of the tenacity of traditional female role expectations, which remain anchored to images of the "good wife" who, like such historical heroines as patient Griselda and Penelope, is loyal, faithful, and self-sacrificing no matter how ignominiously treated.

Analysis of data obtained from 15 Canadian police departments for the year 1991 points out that women were more likely to be victims of assault at the hands of their husbands or ex-husbands (52%) while men were more likely to be assaulted by strangers (44%). While women in Canada tended to be killed by husbands or ex-husbands (48%), men were more likely to be killed by acquaintances (53%), rather than by a wife or ex-wife, another family member, a friend, a business relation, or a stranger (Trevethan and Samagh 1993). Using a nationally representative sample of 12 300 adult (18 years of age and older) women only (Rodgers 1994), the Violence Against Women Survey reported that 3 out of every 10 Canadian women (29%) currently or previously married, or living in a common-law relationship, had experienced at least one incident of physical or sexual violence at the hands of an intimate partner. Counting each victim only once, the survey found that 29 percent of ever-married women had experienced wife assault; 16 percent had been kicked, hit, beaten, or choked, had had a gun or knife used against them, or had been sexually assaulted; and 11 percent had been pushed, grabbed, shoved, or slapped. Two percent had experienced nonphysical assaults, such as being threatened or having something thrown at them. Women of partners who witnessed marital violence in their youths endured more severe and chronic violence than women whose partners were not exposed to marital violence in their youths. Children witnessed violence against their mothers in about 40 percent of violent marriages, including over 50 percent of the cases in which the women feared for their lives and 62 percent of the marriages in which women had been injured.

The 1992–93 Transition Home Survey, which obtained information from 332 of the 371 shelters for abused women in Canada found that "children witnessing violence in the home appeared to have been a factor in women's decision to go to a shelter" (Rodgers and MacDonald 1994, 13): three-quarters of women who sought refuge in one of the transition homes that participated in this survey were admitted with their children. Shelters provide abused women with a wide array of services including general information and crisis counselling, court accompaniment, crisis telephone lines, referrals to mental health–related services, addiction programs, and legal and medical services. Among the shelters that participated in this survey, over 40 percent reported that they could accommodate women with special needs, 25 percent reported the ability to accommodate women with either a serious mental disorder or a history of personal violence, 44 percent reported wheelchair access, 16 percent had audiotapes and Braille material, and 11 percent had telephone devices. In addition, 4 out of 10 facilities noted that they liaise with groups representing the differently abled. Although only 20 percent of the shelters primarily serve aboriginal women, 44 percent reported that they offer culturally sensitive services to aboriginal women and 41 percent provide ethnocultural and visible minority women with culturally sensitive services. However, at the same time, the survey's findings indicated that for 1 in 10 women who used a shelter during the period under review, accessing the shelter required that the woman travel over 100 kilometres from her principal residence.

Although not all sociologists agree that it is necessarily women who are more likely than men to be abused in an intimate relationship (Brinkerhoff and Lupri 1988; Straus and Gelles 1990, 118), any notion of gender equality vanishes when it comes to the effects of violence. As Straus (1992) emphasizes, even though she may throw the coffeepot first, it is generally he who lands the last and most damaging blow. Many more wives than husbands need medical attention as a consequence of marital violence (Dobash and Dobash 1995), and women are more likely to become the victims of spousal homicides. Between 1974 and 1992 the annual rates of spousal homicide in Canada remained relatively constant, with an average of 13 wives and 4 husbands killed per 1 million couples per year. The ratio of wives killed by their husbands to husbands killed by their wives was 3.2 to 1. During this time period, a married woman was nine times more likely to be killed by her spouse than by a stranger (Wilson and Daly 1994). Of 164 women murdered in Canada in 1993, 77 were killed by a current or past partner; in Ontario alone, 64 women were murdered in 1993 with over half (35) killed by a partner or former partner (Toronto Star, December 6, 1994: A12).

Growing attention to the phenomenon of "elder abuse" is an additional reminder that abusive treatment within the family is widespread and assumes a number of forms. Some writers have suggested that much of "elder abuse" is simply "family violence that has grown old" (that is, spousal violence rather than children assaulting their parents). Others, however, have argued that within our society, and particularly within the patriarchal nuclear family, those who are financially, emotionally, or physically dependent are especially liable to abusive treatment because of the structured inequality peculiar to the traditional family form. As Propper (1990, 272–73) has observed, "[t]he targets of serious intrafamily violence are not randomly selected. . . . Husbands direct their violence at wives, and parents direct their violence at children, in part because the offenders have greater economic and physical power. Historical and contemporary cultural and legal forces support these power differentials."

Feminists have charged that "the ties that bind" (Smart 1984) the patriarchal nuclear family "legitimise the preconditions which create an unequal power structure" (xi–xii) both inside the family and within larger society. That is, the nuclear family contains elements of a tradition wherein male power over women and children, including the prerogative of violent control, has been sanctified and legitimated. Thus, in their work *Violence Against Wives: A Case Against the Patriarchy* (1981), R. Emerson Dobash and Russell Dobash pointedly note that "history is littered with references to, and formulas for, beating, clubbing, and kicking [women] into submission. Women's place in history often has been at the receiving end of a blow." It has been suggested that physical and sexual abuses of power may be particularly promoted within the patriarchal nuclear family because of the heightened dependence of women and children on the male "head of household." Thus, according to research conducted in the United States by Straus, Gelles, and Steinmetz (1980), wife assault was about 20 times more likely to occur in male dominant households than in egalitarian families wherein husbands and wives shared the decision-making equally. Similarly, the Calgary-based research of Brinkerhoff and Lupri (1988) reported that women who worked full-time were less likely to be beaten than those who worked part-time or not at all outside of the home. Accordingly, feminists argue that even though the right of a man to "physically chasten" his wife is no longer formally enshrined within law (see Case 8-1), the structure of the traditional family may in itself provide the scaffolding for family violence by conceding too much authority to the male head of household.

CASE 8-1   A History of Control

For centuries, male violence against women was viewed as something completely normal, often necessary. . . . The actions of men were sanctified, while women were blamed for the smallest step beyond the acceptable and narrowly prescribed boundaries. . . .

- One of the first marriage laws was proclaimed by Romulus, the legendary founder of Rome (753 BC). While outlining that the woman would share in the man's possessions and rights, it also "obliged the married women, as having no other refuge, to conform themselves entirely to the temper of their husbands and the husbands to rule their wives as necessary and inseparable possessions."

- Roman husbands had the legal right to chastise, divorce, or kill their wives for engaging in behaviour that they

themselves engaged in daily. But it did not take something as extreme as marital infidelity to rouse the man of the house to raise club and boot—or sandal—to the erring wife. If she were caught tippling in the family wine cellar, attending public games without his permission, or walking outdoors with her face uncovered, she could be beaten. . . .

- Throughout the medieval period, women were important commodities in the pursuit of building alliances or buying peace with other large households or political entities. With this shift, the concern over a woman's chastity increased significantly. For women, adultery was viewed as a grave property offence committed against the husband, or owner, and was severely punished. For example, in 1240, a Spanish

---

CASE 8-1 **A History of Control (continued)**

woman who committed adultery could be killed with impunity by a husband or fiancé. It was legal for a Frenchman to beat his wife when she wronged him by committing adultery, or by preparing to do so, or by refusing to obey him. The English husband was enjoined not to inflict bodily damage other than that which "pertains to the office of a husband for lawful and reasonable correction."

- In the city of Sienna, Italy, men were cautioned not to beat their wives without good reason. "You should beat her . . . only when she commits a serious wrong; for example, if she blasphemes against God or a saint, if she mutters the devil's name, if she likes being at the window and lends ready ear to dishonest young men, or if she has taken to bad habits or bad company, or commits some other wrong that is a mortal sin. Then readily beat her, not in rage but out of

charity and concern for her soul, so that the beatings will rebound to your merit and good."

- A popular 16th-century adage from Gloucestershire, England, affirmed that "a woman, a spaniel and a walnut tree, the more they are beaten, the better they will be."

- One of the most famous laws allowing violence against women was Britain's "rule of thumb," which allowed men to beat their wives with a stick no thicker than their thumbs.

In each of the above examples, the woman was judged to have violated a moral or political code; male violence was viewed as a necessary sanction to maintain control over women's behaviour.

From Ron Thorne-Finch, *Ending the Silence: The Origins and Treatment of Male Violence Against Women* (Toronto, 1993), 110–12, by permission of University of Toronto Press.

POWER WITHIN INTIMATE RELATIONSHIPS

All interpersonal relationships, regardless of the degree of intimacy involved, contain a dimension of power, that is, the ability of one person to influence the behaviour of another person, regardless of that other person's wishes. It also implies the corresponding ability to resist the influence of other people. Relationships can vary in terms of how explicit or obvious the power dimension is. Accordingly, power can be exerted in ways that range from subtle reminders that one person's wishes are held to be more important than another's to coercive and violent acts of control. It would appear that even in the most egalitarian relationship, the power dimension is to some extent present.

Power, within or outside of relationships, does not exist within a vacuum. The sociocultural context influences not only what will be considered valuable resources but who will have greater access to those resources. Western patriarchal societies have traditionally granted greater power to males. In the past, power in the family was based on the ownership of socially valuable resources, which in turn was directly linked to one's gender, and this remains the case today.

Due to the higher status of men in society, they enjoy a positional advantage over women in terms of "legitimate" power, that is, power based on rank and position. Similarly, in chapter 6, Gender, we noted that within the labour market, *job segmentation* exists, with women typically concentrated in fewer and less prestigious occupations than men are. Accordingly, men are more likely than women to possess concrete resources and positions of authority in which knowledge and expertise are assumed. This concentration of power is significant inasmuch as *dependence* and *power* are inversely related. That is, the lesser one's dependence on another, the greater one's power over that person.

In 1938 the sociologist Willard Waller enunciated what has come to be known as *the principle of least interest*, which states that the person who has the least interest in maintaining a relationship has the most power within that relationship. Having the "least" interest comes from having a greater choice, be it real or perceived, of alternative sources of gratification. If your needs are not being met in your current relationship, and you believe that those needs could be met in another relationship, then you will be less willing to make major sacrifices to maintain the current relationship. Conversely, the more you want or feel you need a current partner—for what they are, or what they have, or what they can do—and the fewer your alternatives, the more dependent and the less powerful you are in that relationship. Whether we wish to acknowledge it publicly or not, the stage is thus set for an inequitable position for men and women to negotiate from, both within society and within intimate partnerships.

Throughout Western history, men have *generally* controlled the resources of money and social status while women have *generally* controlled the resources of love and sexuality. As Westoff (1983, 102) observes, "Women have traditionally offered childbearing and domestic services in exchange for the protection, security and status deriving from men's economic position." Women not only face a generally more restricted economic opportunity system, they also have received a socialization that places greater emphasis on and preparation for love and intimacy. Not only do men and women have differential access to different resources but the *mating gradient* further promotes the pairing of two basically unequal partners, despite the current existence of an egalitarian ideal.

As Bernard has remarked:

> Take a young woman who has been trained for feminine dependencies, who wants to "look up" to the man she marries. Put her at a disadvantage in the labor market. Then marry her to a man who has a slightly initial advantage over her in age, income, and education, shored up by an ideology with the male bias. . . . Then expect an egalitarian relationship? (cited in Peplau and Gordon 1985, 273–74).

In Canada today, women are slowly increasing their share of economic power and, in the process, becoming less economically dependent on men. As that dependency lessens, women's share of relationship power increases and, as a consequence, relationships move towards a more egalitarian arrangement. However, as Armstrong (1990, 75) observes, "while women's access to any wage does mean some increase in power . . . [t]he combination of higher male wages, female segregation, and traditional attitudes towards men's labour force work means that men's jobs in the market take precedence over those of women." The *Superwoman syndrome* (Wilson 1991; Ferree 1987) is a well-known phrase used to describe the woman who "has it all"—that is, all of the major responsibilities inside the home and an equal share of responsibilities outside the home. Thus, despite the expansion of the female role to include paid labour and despite the fact that the dual-provider marriage and family are a statistical majority, women in Canada today are still saddled with primary responsibility for the "second shift" (Hochschild 1989) of household, family life, and relationship maintenance (Jackson 1996). Although progress has been made, women still have less economic power and do more housework and child care. It is this continuing inequality that is largely responsible for the lack of a true egalitarianism within intimate relationships.

The Blumstein and Schwartz (1983) research on American couples and their relationships noted that power within a relationship was a direct reflection of economic power for heterosexual married and cohabiting couples and for gay male couples, but not for lesbian couples. They note, "These patterns have led us to conclude that it is men—who for generations have learned in the work place the equation that money equals power—who have recreated this experience in the home. Wives and cohabiting women fall prey to the logic that money talks" (55–56). Since women in general do not earn an income equal to men, trying to maintain an egalitarian economic arrangement is fraught with difficulties for heterosexual cohabiters. In the instance of unequal economic contributions, male dominance is still the statistical norm within these heterosexual cohabiting unions. Moreover, the forces of convention are still powerful, even when women earn more than their male partners. For example, Steil and Weltman (1991, 175, 177) observed that among their sample of 60 dual-earner couples, "wives who earned significantly more than their husbands were very concerned about arousing competitive feelings but this was not the case for husbands who earned more than their wives. . . . Both partners seem inclined to collude to protect the husband's breadwinner status." Similarly, Hochschild (1989) has noted that couples will go to great lengths to conceal a high-earning wife's income.

Women's increased share of economic resources has, arguably, even greater implications for the future of intimate relationships between husbands and wives. We have already noted that increased economic power reduces female dependence and thereby increases their alternatives. It appears that as women increase their economic independence, the likelihood of divorce also increases. Thus, according to research summarized by Ambert (1990, 194),

1) "employed married women consider divorce as an option more often than unemployed married women,"

2) "women who can be independent financially initiate the decision to separate more often than women who depend on their husbands' financial support," and

3) "women's divorce rates increase with each additional thousand dollars they earn."

In addition, not only has the incidence of divorce increased, but rates of first marriage and of remarriage have decreased. In this case as well, reluctance to remarry may be more common among high-income than low-income women. Thus, Ambert (1983) reports that while her sample of high-income women desired to remarry as frequently as did her low-income sample of women, the high-income women felt less social and financial pressure to do so. While low-income women saw themselves as *gaining* from remarrying, high-income women were more cautious about entering into marriage again. As one of Ambert's respondents, a 38-year-old executive, remarked, "[I am] very cautious because I have so much to lose" (in Ambert 1990, 20). Similarly, Baker (1990c, 7) observes that, "since the mid-1970s . . . the average age of first marriages has risen slightly, reflecting the greater independence of women, more non-legal unions, economic uncertainty, and some disillusionment with traditional marriage. Furthermore, as more women attain post-secondary education and become self-supporting, an increasing number delay or decide against legal marriage."

Although it would be misleading to suggest that all of these changes are due to the one simple cause of increasing female economic independence, the evidence does suggest that there is an increasing reluctance on the part of women to either enter into or remain in relationships that do not offer them sufficient gratification in every sense of the word. The options for women seeking changes in their lifestyles appear to have increased. As Macklin (1987, 342) has observed, "Although most persons still marry, have children, live in single-family households, prefer heterosexuality, and wish for permanence and sexual exclusivity, increasing numbers choose other lifestyles at some point in their lives, and even more acknowledge the rights of others do so." More and more Canadians are "voting with their feet" by forsaking the traditional family and seeking satisfaction in alternative arrangements.

In addition, both love and sex have become increasingly independent of the traditional form of marriage. They can now be obtained among a growing plurality of forms of intimate relationships, ranging from cohabitation to casual dating. Despite the AIDS scare, available evidence indicates that sexual encounters are common outside the confines of a legal marital relationship. Just as economic autonomy can be negotiated independently, so too can love or sexual intimacy. In other words, the exchange no longer involves one resource for another (such as money for love), but an exchange of amounts of the same resources. The resources are not completely independent of one another and "trade-offs" are still possible, especially since heterosexual partners within an intimate relationship are still unlikely to have achieved the position of "equal" bargainers.

Within contemporary Canadian society, then, there is a plurality of alternative arrangements that challenge the norm of a patriarchal nuclear family as the ideal form of a family. These arrangements include legal marriage, common-law families, one-career or dual-career families, two-parent or one-parent families, first marriages, reconstituted families, and gay marriages. However, some critics have argued that rather than speak of the "death" of the traditional family or employ other such emotive terms, we can simply view the emerging alternatives as "evolving" families (Eichler 1988). There is little doubt that Canadian family life is changing; however, the assessment of whether these changes are beneficial, detrimental, or innocuous is dependent on one's point of view.

ANALYZING THE PROBLEM: PATRIARCHY AND THE FAMILY

The Functionalist Approach

For functionalists, the family as an institution is of vital importance to the maintenance of social order for several reasons. These include the replenishing of the population in a regulated and orderly fashion, the regulation of sexual behaviour, the care and socialization of the helpless young, the provision of emotional support and companionship, and the economic and physical protection of family members (Goode 1971). However, since functionalists favour social stability and view disruptions to it as "dysfunctional" or "pathological" in some way, they have been rather uncritical of existing social arrangements. They assume, in circular fashion, that the existence of the traditional family attests to its functionality and that its functionality is "proven" by its existence. Accordingly, for functionalist theorists, many of the social problems we witness in relation to the family attest to the enormity of changes that have occurred in contemporary Canadian society and that have placed substantial strain on the family system. To the extent that the family has failed to adapt to these changes, "social disorganization" is said to have occurred.

For theorists such as Talcott Parsons (1942; 1949; 1955), the *nuclear family* (defined as a family unit consisting exclusively of a husband and wife and their offspring) was the cultural ideal for industrialized societies. Indeed, Parsons went so far as to state that any significant departure from this arrangement would result in a "reduction in the productivity of our economy and drastic limitation on the realizability of our democratic values. . . . " (1955, 23). However, it can hardly be doubted that the nuclear family does contain certain defects that make it dysfunctional in certain circumstances. For example, because of such factors as improved living standards, nutrition, sanitation, health care, and standards of occupational health and safety, Canadians, particularly Canadian women, are living longer. Accordingly, the issues of mortality and survivorship are increasingly salient when discussing the family. Available data indicates that women born in Canada in 1991 have a life expectancy of almost 81 years, while men born in 1991 can expect to live 74.56 years (Columbo 1996, 65). If the typical age difference at first marriage in Canada (which has consistently been from one to three years) holds for these newborns, and if this first marriage lasts until the death of one of the partners, we would expect these females to be widows for approximately nine years (a difference in age at marriage of two years plus the difference in life expectancy of almost seven years). Currently, 60-year-old women in Canada can expect to live for another 24 years (average life expectancy increases the longer one has lived, up to a certain limit), while 60-year-old men can expect to live another 19 years. This *life expectancy gap* creates problems for wives who outlive their husbands.

Because of the *double standard of aging* that women face in our society in relation to evaluations of their attractiveness (that is, men are thought to become "distinguished" with the passage of time while women merely become "older" [Banner 1992; Sontag 1972; Brecher 1984]), the chances that women will remarry grow smaller as they grow older. Accordingly, if in times past women could expect to spend the majority of their adult lives within "wife/mother" roles, the increase in longevity, the rise in the divorce rate, and the declining birth rate has made it likely that in the future these roles will occupy a considerably shorter period of women's lives.

In Canada, the birth rate has gradually declined from 31 births per 1000 population in 1901 to 1911, to 26.1 in 1961, to 14.7 in 1986, and to 13.4 in 1994 (Columbo 1996, 64). Increases in urbanization, the use of contraception, the costs of raising children, personal expectations of affluence and mobility, and participation rates of women in the labour force all account for this decline in the birth rate. However, if traditionally the majority of women's adult lives were occupied with the rearing of dependent children, "[t]oday . . . a couple might spend two-thirds of their married life free of the responsibility for young children, and a third without any children at home" (Robertson 1980, 269). Although some have described this as causing the *empty nest syndrome*—a sense that one's life is empty and meaningless (see Faludi 1991 for a critique of this concept)—a newer phenomenon, the not-so-empty nest, may cause both financial and emotional strain. With prolonged education, an uncertain labour market, and the growing cost of establishing a household, North American children are leaving home later (Goldscheider and Goldscheider 1994). In addition, many children who struck out on their own have found the cost or responsibility too great and are returning to the home nest. In Canada in 1991, the number of single (never-married) children between the ages of 22 and 24 living in their parental home was 1 515 130, and the number of children age 25 and over still living at home was 645 720, a figure that does not include *boomerang children* whose return home was precipitated by their becoming separated, divorced, or widowed (Statistics Canada 1992, Cat. 93-312). Similarly, reports on *skip-generation parents* (Seligman 1992, 80) indicate that "an increasing number of grandparents are finding themselves recycled as parents—to their children's children" (Larsen 1991, 32)—due to such factors as death, abandonment, incarceration, mental illness, physical or sexual abuse, and in particular drug or alcohol addiction. This phenomenon additionally suggests that the traditional nuclear family is undergoing substantial change and redefinition.

It is obvious that the traditional nuclear family was never truly designed to accommodate many of the changes that have occurred in contemporary Canadian society. Accordingly, these changes have resulted in imbalances between what the family is able to provide and what changing cultural values suggest is desirable, permissible, and acceptable. Indeed, the issue of reproduction in contemporary Canada poses at least three challenges to the traditional notion of a family. First, if children were thought to be the defining feature of a family, the declining birth rate may suggest an erosion of the family's status.

Childlessness, for example, has become increasingly common. Grindstaff (1995, 16) points out that among women who had ever been married, the proportion age 35 to 39 who had never given birth grew from 7 percent in 1971 to 13 percent in 1991, while among ever-married women age 25 to 29, the proportion who were childless tripled from 14 percent in 1961 to 38 percent in 1991. Although the tendency to delay child bearing may result in a sizeable proportion of these childless women opting for children later in life, the delay in child bearing has obvious implications for Canada's fertility rate.

Grindstaff (1995, 14) notes that in marked contrast to the 1950s and 1960s, when only 10 percent of children born to mothers age 30 to 34 were first-born children and half of all children born to these mothers had 3 or more already-born siblings, in the 1990s 1 in 3 children born to mothers age 30 to 34 are first-born children and the likelihood of 3 or more already-born siblings has dropped to 1 in 10. Similarly, Grindstaff (1995, 14) points out that "[i]n the 1950s and 1960s, about 5 percent of children born to women aged 40 to 44 were first-born children and over 75% were a fourth child or higher. By the 1990s, however, just over one-half of all children born to women that age were a first or second child" (Grindstaff 1995, 14).

Second, the increase in illegitimate births or out-of-wedlock pregnancies poses a challenge because an increasing number of women are deliberately electing *not* to get married rather than to "do the right thing." That is, increasing numbers of pregnant women, whether they are in their teens, twenties, or thirties, are deliberately choosing parenting without a parenting relationship (see Conway 1990, 26–27). Third, the new reproductive technologies offer a formidable challenge to the family by facilitating the possibility of children within same-sex relationships that formerly would have been childless. For those who desire children, an increasing number of aids and arrangements are possible, including artificial insemination, surrogate mothering, embryo transfers, prenatal sex selection techniques, and artificial wombs. The option of having children, with or without a partner, through a medically facilitated pregnancy or a "rent-a-womb" arrangement, is becoming increasingly available. In consequence of this "reproductive revolution" (Eichler 1989), new questions are being posed. For example, "what does parenthood mean when artificial wombs are being developed by which men can be pregnant through the implantation of an embryo in the male abdomen? When women are impregnated from semen which combines donations from their husbands and strangers? When babies conceived through artificial insemination from the husband are carried by surrogate mothers?" (Mackie 1991, 118).

Nevertheless, the nostalgic conservatism of functionalism has often served to influence judgments as to what is "functional" or "dysfunctional" about the family. Moreover, because they have traditionally focused their attention on the relationship *between* the family and society while largely ignoring relationships *within* the family (Abbott and Wallace 1990, 74), functionalists have stood accused by feminists of promoting *familialism* and a strongly conservative agenda. Familialism refers to an ideology that maintains that the patriarchal nuclear family is natural and universal. However, feminists challenge both of these assumptions and argue that "familialism is an ideology that serves to subordinate women to the needs of men and capitalism" (Abbott and Wallace 1992, 25). They point out that although *functionalists* may regard the co-resident nuclear family with its gendered division of labour as particularly well-suited to the needs of an industrial society, this evaluation implicitly supports the premise that a woman's place is in the home and, preferably, pregnant.

The Feminist Challenge: The Conflict Approach

For feminists, there are two principle reasons why "the family is a site of inequality where women are subordinated and women's roles perpetuated" (Abbott and Wallace 1990, 75). First, a woman's position as wife and mother in the typical traditional family renders her vulnerable to exploitation and abuse. As Okin (1989, 4) observes, "an equal sharing between the sexes of family responsibilities, especially child care, is 'the great revolution that never happened.'"

Some feminists have argued that in a materialist culture in which social worth is linked to earning capacity, the unpaid labour of "women's work" within the home perpetuates their low status and social invisibility. They point out that it is only recently that government agencies have begun to recognize the value of unpaid work. For example, the 1996 Census was the first Canadian census to measure the amount of time Canadians spent in such unpaid work as housework and child and elder care. Moreover, the results of Canada's 1992 General Social Survey indicated that Canadian women continue do about two-thirds of the unpaid work spending, on average, "78% more time in 1992 on unpaid work than men . . . (1,482 hours per year compared with 800 hours)" (Jackson 1996, 29). In 1992 the average time spent by married fathers employed full-time was 3.2 hours per day; for married mothers employed full-time the respective figure was 4.8 hours and for married mothers who were not employed, it was 7.9 hours a day. When the value of unpaid work is calculated using the "generalist replacement cost method" (which values unpaid activity using the wage rate of domestic employees), the value of unpaid work in Canada in 1992 was $235 billion or almost $11 000 per adult; among unemployed married women with children, the value of their unpaid work was $24 400 each (Jackson 1996, 29).

Second, male domination and female subordination are perpetuated in the socialization processes within the family, and children internalize and reproduce these patterns when they, in turn, become parents (see Thorne 1982). These processes are seen as multifaceted and pervasive. For feminists, analysis of the forces that promote the assumption of gendered roles within and outside the family is necessary to challenge conventional views that posit women's roles as natural, inevitable, or biologically impelled. Moreover, they dispute the vision of the family promoted by the New Right, maintaining that "[t]he lost society is not a 'golden age' but one that secured the interests of capitalism and patriarchy at the expense of the working class, of women, and of children" (Abbott and Wallace 1992, 6).

Feminists stress the need to recognize that experiences within the family cannot be *assumed* to be symmetrical or functional. As Abbott and Wallace (1990, 76) note, "women's experiences of motherhood and family life have demonstrated that families embody power relationships that can and do result in conflict, violence, and the inequitable distribution of work and resources." Finally, feminists stress that viewing the family as a "private sphere" promotes the marginalization and trivialization of the experiences of women and children and encourages a dichotomized construction between issues that are considered "private troubles" or "women's issues" and those that are considered "public issues" in need of social consideration, intervention, and redress. For feminists, the family and, in particular, the patriarchal nuclear family are viewed as functional only because sociologists and others have been eager to record a male-defined history while disattending to *herstory* (Wells 1982). For feminists, discussion of the *power imbalance* within the family is of critical importance.

The Evolving Family

In addition to the challenge feminists have posed to the conventional sociology of the family, other conflict theorists have focused attention on the conflict of values that exists among various groups and is evidenced by their contrasting and competing definitions of what is to be either desired or deplored within Canadian society. It is evident from our earlier discussions that opinions vary greatly, with some viewing the "traditional family" as an ideal to be strengthened, some maintaining that it should be modified, and others arguing that a radical change and redefinition is needed. Moreover, the conflict approach reminds us again of the problem-solution-problem conundrum; obviously, solutions proposed by feminists are likely to be viewed as problematic by members of the New Right, while the reverse is also true. Indeed, conflicts over the definition of what is and is not a family and over the specific form a family should take are likely to continue to galvanize debate in Canada as the "family" continues to experience change as well as "politicization." That is, for groups such as the Moral Majority, the traditional family is an important and strategic symbol of conservatism and social stability, but for feminists, an appeal to return to the way things were in the past is obviously not very tempting.

It is important to note that although we have been using the term "traditional family" to refer to the patriarchal nuclear family, the use of the term "traditional family" is somewhat misleading. It suggests that the family form depicted in television programs of the 1950s and 1960s—the "good provider" husband, loving and contented housewife mom, and dutiful children—was the only model of the family until relatively recently. This, in fact, is not the case. In many ways, our society offers a curious amalgam of arrangements, which attests to the probability of conflicting notions about the most desirable form the family should take.

As Nelson and Robinson (1995) observe, for much of recorded history in western Europe, the *institutional family*, as sociologists generally refer to it, was essentially a sociopolitical-economic arrangement, and marriage was basically a functional partnership rather than a romantic relationship. Marital partners were usually selected by parents, with or without some socially acceptable intermediary. The institutional family was organized around economic production by the members of the family unit to ensure physical survival, close ties with an extended kinship network, and a male-dominated authority structure that gave the husband control of family members and of the family's goods and services. Indeed, Nelson and Robinson have argued that the concept of an "intimate relationship" could not be appropriately applied to this family form in that feelings of affection for family members were not considered to be essential, or even important, for effective family functioning. That is, within the institutional family system, family duty, or what the individual could do for his or her family, was expected to be paramount. As they observe, the notion of a family as a "romantic intimate *partnership*" did not become meaningful until much later in history.

In chronicling the changing conceptions about the family, Nelson and Robinson point out that the next major shift occurred as a result of the Industrial Revolution. Thus, as muscle power was replaced by machine power, the place for working with machines was made separate and distinct from the home. In that industrialization required the establishment of a centralized workplace, the "family" and "work" became separate and distinct. In addition, with the introduction of a cash economy, work itself became equated with the concept of paid labour. Labour that did not receive monetary payment came to be socially defined as being of lesser value, and this was most notably the case with labour that took place in the home. The home itself slowly became equated with the family and family activities only, and became increasingly privatized—something that was to be shielded from public eyes. Over time, as well, work and the family became gendered. The social truisms developed that a woman's place "was in the home," while a man's place was "at work." Accordingly, almost all activities having to do with the home (such as housework), the family (such as child rearing), and private relationships (such as love) were eventually considered to be part of a woman's sphere or domain. The only exception to this division was sex, which, although private, was held to be an area of masculine expertise.

These transformations resulted in the creation of what Bernard (1981/1995) has termed the *provider* role for men. Social conventions developed that required a man to leave home each day, go to a centralized work location, engage in paid labour, and then bring money home to be spent on necessary provisions for his family. While both women and children did engage in paid labour, most notably during the early stages of industrial development, pressures mounted for men to be the one family member to perform the "good provider" role. This notion soon spread throughout all social classes in all Western societies and became entrenched as a central defining element of ideal masculinity. Thus, as Bernard (1981/1995, 180) observes, "[s]uccess in the good-provider role came in time to define masculinity itself. The good provider had to achieve, to win, to succeed, to dominate. He was a bread*winner*" (emphasis in original). In contrast, the wife came to be measured by her performance in housewife and mother roles, roles that, it was argued, could not be evaluated by, or denigrated by association with, a dollar sign. Accordingly, what historians term the *cult of true womanhood* developed. Women were to be the spiritual guardians of their family and, through their gentle touch, act as mitigating forces against the harshness of urban industrial life. Their role was to be "pure, pious and submissive, but also capable of effective nurturing and efficient household management" (Gaffield 1990, 37). For a woman to enter the workforce was seen as effectively "co-opting the man's passport to masculinity" (Gould as cited in Bernard 1981/1995, 180). As Bernard (1981/1995, 180) has observed, "If a married woman had to enter the labor force at all, that was bad enough. If she was making a good salary, however . . . [her husband] was effectively castrated." Obviously, this ideal of woman as domestic nurturer was never equally tenable for women of all socioeconomic classes.

Over time, the "institutional" family gradually gave way to a new ideal, fashioned during the 1920s, that sociologists term the *companionate* family. Changes in the nature of the industrial economy along with the widespread use of such inventions as the telephone and the automobile produced increasing social and geographic mobility. These changes led to significant alterations in the nature of the ties within the extended kinship network. Increasing emphasis was placed on the nuclear family unit, specifically on companionship relations between husbands and wives (still, however, within the framework of male domination), and between parents and their immediate in-home children. Family life became even more private, and the expectation developed that the family was to be a source of personal satisfaction and individual fulfilment. Marriage in particular was to be based on continued companionship, love, and affection, and not just on the satisfaction of economic survival needs. To enable men and women to find their "companion," a new institution evolved—*dating*. Beginning late in the previous century, and essentially completed by the 1920s, the power over mate selection shifted from parents to the prospective mates themselves. Whether they wanted to or not, parents and parent substitutes gradually lessened their supervisory control over the activities of the young as more single men and women spent more years in schools and universities and various work settings. Modern inventions such as the automobile, the telephone, and the public-private, conveniently dark cinema provided for greater independence of single people and more opportunities for getting acquainted without having to run the gauntlet of family intermediaries and the old, stiff formalities of proper introductions. The increasingly powerful mass media of radio, magazines, and the movies promoted images and models of the new romantic ideals. It was during the transition from the institutional to the companionate family that love and romance became socially defined as essential ingredients for the formation and continuance of intimate relationships.

The social changes of the 1960s and 1970s, referred to by Lillian Rubin (1990) as the *sexual, gender*, and *therapeutic* or *human potential* revolutions, altered many aspects of the companionate family and gave rise to a third new set of family and relationship standards. An emerging emphasis on the values of gender equality and personal freedom supported the right of men and women to seek out relationships that would meet their personal needs and, if a given relationship did not satisfactorily meet those needs, to seek out alternatives. By emphasizing self-fulfilment, the modern man or woman asks what the family in general, and intimate partnerships in particular, can do for them, and not the other way around. Self-realization through intimacy with another person has come to be defined as one of the most important criteria for initiating or maintaining a relationship.

This new set of ideals does not promote the existence of only one legitimate family or intimate relationship form to the exclusion of all others, but, both explicitly and implicitly, suggests that satisfaction of individual needs may be found in any number of alternate arrangements to legal marriage. In other words, the *pluralistic* family ideal has come, to varying degrees, to be accepted within most modern Western societies. But this acceptance has been hard won, and the debates it has engendered among social critics, philosophers, and legal scholars have helped to define the terms of those relationship forms that are regarded as legitimate today.

As we have seen, though, the "new" family forms do not enjoy complete support from other social institutions, particularly business, the courts, and the political institution. Moreover, even within subgroups of the population, no homogeneity of opinion should be assumed. For example, Salholz et al. report that "many in the [gay] community oppose quasi-straight unions, on the ground that they are too imitative and not uniquely gay." If "sex is a good thing" has traditionally been the ethos of the male homosexual community (Blachford 1981), homosexual cruising and promiscuity are argued to be worthy pursuits inasmuch as they challenge the "straight" idea that sex should be procreational rather than recreational. Accordingly, for some gays the slogan for the 1990s is a "Just Say Yes" pro-sex campaign that advocates safe sex but also a *militant eroticism* (Salhotz et al. 1992).

Similarly, feminists are divided among themselves over whether the new reproductive technologies are, as radical feminists had originally hoped, a liberating force or simply a Trojan Horse. Since the 1978 birth of test-tube baby Louise Brown, the first child to be conceived from *in vitro* fertilization techniques, it has become increasingly common to engage in methods of conception that are not, by necessity, limited to heterosexual intercourse. The growth of fertility clinics and sperm banks may strike some as offering the possibility of reproductive choice to women who desire to become pregnant and otherwise would be unable to do so. However, others are less sanguine about the potential uses and abuses of the new reproductive technologies.

Spallone's (1989) *Beyond Conception: The New Politics of Reproduction* views reproductive technologies as simply presenting a new opportunity for the patriarchy to devalue women. Similarly, Hamner and Allen (1980) suggest that the increasing availability of artificial reproduction is "the ushering in of the female apocalypse" that may promote *femicide* with reproductive engineering serving as the "final solution" to the "woman problem." Accordingly, feminists are exhorted "to infiltrate the key laboratories and governmental agencies where reproductive research and policy are being created . . . [and] masquerading as secretaries and cleaners, to transform themselves into saboteurs as a way of averting the universal misogynist conspiracy" (St. Peter 1989, 257). In contrast, Shalev's (1989) *Birth Power: The Case for Surrogacy*, while noting the history of women's reproductive and sexual oppression, views female autonomy within the field of surrogacy as crucial to women's liberation.

In addition, it has been noted that the costs of the new reproductive technologies are high and, in consequence, are unlikely to be an equally viable option for all women. As Mackie notes, "In Canada, an *in vitro* fertilization costs $30,000 to $40,000." In consequence, some feminist critics have voiced concern that arrangements such as *surrogate mothering* may be classist and result in poor women effectively serving as "baby farms" for those who are well-off and being exploited by those who would seek to become well-off. Thus, French (1992, 149) observes that "[t]he mothers . . . are paid a small fee; the lawyers, doctors, and middlemen who arrange the implantation are paid a large fee."

In Canada, the issues of artificial insemination and surrogate mothering have also been the subject of inquiry and concern. Legal questions have been raised, such as "Who is liable for birth defects? Is it ethical for doctors to be involved with surrogate mothering? What is the legal status of the child?" (Marshall 1987, 80). Marshall additionally notes that all Canadian provinces have legislation prohibiting payment for a child; will surrogate motherhood, then, provide the underpinnings for a black market in babies? Moreover, ethical questions remain troubling. For example, Thom's 1988 research documented cases in which women undergoing hysterectomies were not told that their eggs were being removed for implantation in other women (in Mackie 1991, 119). In addition, the long incubation period of the HIV virus and variable screening measures used in acquiring sperm may increase the likelihood of pediatric AIDS in children who have been conceived through unknown-donor insemination. Finally, although in theory artificial reproduction may facilitate the expansion of homosexual and, in particular, lesbian families, some recent decisions by doctors over who is to be regarded as a "suitable patient" for the new reproductive technologies suggest that, here again, questions and controversy may arise.

For example, in 1993 a lesbian couple sought and were refused artificial insemination in Vancouver, British Columbia, by the only doctor whose practice made available artificial insemination by frozen sperm. In consequence, the couple, who were a lawyer and a doctor, complained to the British Columbia College of Physicians and Surgeons. Their appeal was rejected and they received a letter that stated that since "the service you sought was not urgent nor emergent" the doctor's refusal to take them as patients was justified. In drawing media attention to their experience, the couple stated that they sought to publicize discrimination against lesbians as potential users of the new reproductive technologies. Their claims would seem valid. As the federal Royal Commission on New Reproductive Technologies reported in 1991, "being a lesbian was probable or possible grounds for being refused artificial insemination in 28 out of 49 Canadian fertility programs" (Vancouver Sun 1993). It is likely that many of the debates surrounding reproductive technologies will continue to perplex and preoccupy Canadians for some time in the future.

In general, Canadians are far from unanimous in their opinions of how men and women should live their lives and organize their families. Mackie (1991) has noted that although we are becoming more egalitarian, "Canadians' attitudes concerning gender arrangements in the domestic sphere are more traditional than their public sphere attitudes" (for example, 64 percent believe that a mother with young children belongs in the home and 40 percent believe a wife should accord her husband's career a higher priority than her own). As Boyd (1984, 23) observes, Canadian attitudes evidence the enormity of changes that have occurred but "also reveal a residue of earlier norms and practices."

CANADIAN FAMILIES AND INTIMATE RELATIONSHIPS TODAY

There are obvious problems and difficulties intrinsic to the establishment of intimacy with any other person—be they man or woman, heterosexual, homosexual, lesbian, or bisexual. In a social environment in which fear of AIDS has led to an increase in both homophobia and publicity about the dangers of casual sex, the "exclusivity" offered by an intimate partner may be appealing to both heterosexual and homosexual couples. In this section we shall examine some of the dominant family forms that exist in Canada in the 1990s: the dual-earner family, the single-parent family, the common-law family, the transitional family, the blended family, and gay and lesbian families. In each case, we shall attempt to point out some of the strains that these relationships face and to note some of the interlinkages between various family arrangements and their participants' work roles.

The Husband/Wife Dual-Earner Family

In Canada, as the result of a combination of social forces that include economic pressures, changing gender ideologies, liberalized divorce legislation, improved contraception, increased life expectancy, and the marked trend towards smaller families, the *dual-earner* family has become the most prevalent form. Indeed, Moore (1990, 24) has referred to the dual-earner family as "the new norm" in Canada.

We can distinguish two subtypes within the dual-earner family: the *dual-provider* family and the *dual-career* family. Each form demonstrates different links between family and work. Within the dual-provider family, women's labour force participation has often been prompted by the rising unemployment rate of men as well as the decline in real wages. Thus, Moore (1989, 25) notes that "staying out of debt" and the necessity of a second income has often impelled women to enter the labour force: "only four percent of dual-earner families, compared with 13 percent of traditional families, had incomes below Statistics Canada's low-income cut-offs. Without wives' earnings, however, about the same proportion of dual-earner (14 percent) families would have been classified as having low incomes." The 1995 Poverty Profile compiled by the National Council of Welfare (1997, 85–86) reports that while in 1995 the poverty rate for all husband-wife families under age 65 was 10.8 percent, and a total of 627 000 were living in poverty, "[w]ith the earnings of wives removed and everything else remaining the same, the poverty rate would have jumped from 21.9 percent, and the number of families living in poverty would have more than doubled to 1,268,000."

As we noted earlier in this chapter, power within relationships tends to follow economic resources; accordingly, this *power of the purse theory* (Baker 1990b, 53) predicts what many have noted about both the *single male provider family* (that is, the "traditional family") and the dual-provider family. Within such relationships, the "decks are stacked" (Baker 1990b, 53) against women. If women typically earn less than their male partners, contributing on average approximately one-third of the family income (Baker 1990b, 54), the forces of the traditional gendered division of labour are unlikely to be dislodged. In support of this, numerous studies have documented that when husbands of homemakers and husbands of employed women are compared, the difference in the amount of time they spend in family work is negligible—approximately 15 minutes per week (see Pleck and Rustad 1980; Mortimer and London 1984). Particularly within the working class family, beliefs about "men's work" and "women's work" are likely to be tenacious. In consequence, women within dual-provider families may find themselves heavily reliant on the assistance of relatives and friends and on their own ingenuity to "make do" with a limited amount of time, energy, and provisions.

Within the dual-career family, some, but not all, of these limitations are abated because of the increased amount of disposable income that such couples possess. In Canada, younger and better educated married women are particularly likely to work; however, professional women, most notably those with children, may face severe obstacles in their attempts to integrate their family and work roles.

It is obvious that if the traditional gendered division of family responsibilities remains unaltered, the dual-career family will result in extreme role overload for women as they attempt to juggle two competing sets of demands. As Mortimer and London (1984, 31) observe, "Excessive work time—the need to work nights and weekends, the travel requirements, the mobility expectations and opportunities, and the intrinsically rewarding characters of careers all represent 'centrifugal forces' . . . pulling each spouse away from the family." Moreover, inasmuch as women, by convention, are expected to be the nurturers of their children, there is a social inducement to feel guilt over the amount of time spent away from home in pursuit of careers. While the adage states that "it's not the quantity but the quality of time that one spends with one's family that is important," day-to-day constraints may make time itself a commodity in short supply. Presuming that parents will work until 5:00 p.m. and that elementary school-aged children will have a bedtime in the vicinity of 8:00 to 9:00 p.m., the mundane but necessary tasks of preparing and eating supper, washing up dishes, running baths, and ensuring that teeth are brushed and hair is washed may occupy a fair proportion of this "quality time." Although the very wealthy may be allowed to dispense with these pursuits by hiring nannies, cooks, and housekeepers, for others the stress of their responsibilities within the dual-career family is not insignificant.

For both dual-provider and particularly dual-career families, the fact that both spouses work means that each will be somewhat less likely to act as a "buffer" for the other. That is, inasmuch as each spouse is likely to experience job dissatisfaction, career pressure, and variable work schedules, the other spouse cannot be presumed to be always available or sympathetic to these work-based demands. If both spouses have deadlines for the following morning, tensions may mount as each insists that it is the other's job to keep the children quiet and occupied, prepare the coffee, and murmur encouraging words. Claims that the other "doesn't appreciate" their work, is "selfish," or is trying to "sabotage" their efforts to "get ahead" may result if the sharing of family tasks is not perceived to be equitable. Finally, as we have earlier noted, the increasing longevity of Canada's population poses challenges to the traditional nuclear family. In particular, the phenomenon of "parenting one's parents" suggests that "the stresses on this 'sandwich generation'—those with children and parents to provide for" (Mason 1993, 36) may be considerable.

The Husband/Wife Single-Provider Family

Although the husband/wife single-provider family remains celebrated by the New Right as the traditional and ideal family form, it is increasingly becoming the exception rather than the rule among Canadian families. While predominant during the 1940s and 1950s, this family form now accounts for only 22 percent of all husband/wife families (Conway 1990, 24). For the majority of Canadians, it is simply not financially viable; those involved in single-provider families typically have lower incomes and experience a higher risk of poverty than those in families in which both spouses work. According to Conway (1990, 24), spouses within husband/wife single-provider families "tend to be older than the spouses of dual-earner families and less well-educated . . . tend to have more children, and wives in such families tend to have had children at a younger age than their dual-earner counterparts."

Throughout this chapter we have noted numerous difficulties that confront the traditional family, including the economic dependence of women within it, the pressures placed on men to define themselves in relation to the family by being a good provider, and so on. We have also noted that for some, it remains the ideal form of intimate relationships. At this time we shall simply note that for a small minority of Canadian men and women, a new option—the husband/wife family with only the wife working—is becoming viable as well.

In the majority of cases, the lifestyles of the female breadwinner and male househusband are hardly those glamorized renditions that appear within the pages of best-selling novels. The reality of these relationships, which constitute 4 percent of husband/wife families in Canada (Conway 1990, 25), is that their lifestyles are anything but lavish. That the wife works and the husband does not is largely accounted for by the husband's retirement from the workforce. As we have seen, in the majority of marriages the male is older than the female; because of the decline in the employment of men age 55 to 64 (due to early retirement or corporate "rationalizing"), some Canadian families will find themselves in a role reversal of the "traditional family."

The Single-Parent Family

According to the 1991 Census, 13 percent of all families (almost 1 million families) were lone-parent families with never-married children of all ages. The number of single parents raising children increased from 712 000 in 1981 to over 1.1 million in 1995 (Toronto Star 1996). According to the Survey of Consumer Finances, during the late 1980s almost two-thirds of all lone-parent families (65%) had at least one child under the age of 18 living at home; female lone parents were more likely to have young children. Over two-thirds of lone mothers (68%) had children under age 18, while approximately half of lone fathers had children under the age of 18. Moreover, 29 percent of lone mothers had children under the age of 7; the corresponding figure for men was 11 percent (Oderkirk and Lochhead 1992). According to their research, although the major source of income for the majority of lone-parent families was wages and salaries (followed by income transfers from the government such as Social Assistance or Unemployment Insurance), more lone fathers (71%) than lone mothers (57%) had salaries or wages as their major source of income. About one-half (52%) of all male lone parents earned $30 000 or more from wages, salaries, and self-employment income, compared with 21 percent of female lone parents. Female lone parents (33%) were more likely than male lone parents (25%) to earn between $10 000 and $29 000. About 22 percent of female lone parents and 9 percent of male lone parents had no income from these sources. Fifty-six percent of lone mothers and 20 percent of lone fathers with children under age 18 were living with incomes below Statistics Canada's low income cut-offs (LICOs).

According to the National Longitudinal Survey of Children and Youths (NLSCY), in 1994 "the overwhelmingly majority" (Canadian Social Trends 1997) of single-parent families remained headed by women; in that year, one in six children under the age of 12 lived in lone-mother families and, when compared to children from two-parent families, evidenced considerable disadvantage. Fifteen percent of 4- to 11-year-old children from lone-mother families versus slightly under 8 percent of children with two parents suffered an emotional disorder. Among children 6 to 11 years of age, children from lone-mother families were twice as likely to have repeated a grade (11% versus 5%) or to have had academic difficulties at school (6% versus 3%). The difficulties experienced by the children of lone mothers are often linked to the fact that these families are likely to have low incomes; the study reported that 7 out of 10 children (71%) living in single-mother families lived at or below Statistics Canada's LICO (compared with 15 percent of children living in two-parent families). Moreover, data from the NLSCY also suggest that, regardless of the family's income, children from lone-mother families are more likely to experience emotional and behavioural problems. For example, while 1 in 10 children in low-income two-parent families were hyperactive, the comparable figure for children in low-income lone-mother families was 17 percent; in lone-mother families where the family income was above the LICO, the figure was 14 percent. Canadian Social Trends (1997, 8) observe that "[t]he likelihood that a child with a lone mother will have one or more behaviour problems was 1.8 times higher than that of a child with two parents, even when controlling for income differences between families."

Let us briefly examine the changing conditions that have resulted in the increase in Canada's single-parent families.

Single by Choice

Beginning in the 1970s and continuing throughout the 1980s, more and more women elected to have and keep babies conceived out of wedlock; Conway (1990, 26) notes that "in the 1980s . . . over 86 per cent of unmarried mothers in Alberta and over 88 per cent in Ontario" kept their babies. As we have already noted, the new reproductive technologies have allowed women to become mothers without being wives, girlfriends, or even carnally intimate with a male partner. However, if the new artificial technologies and an increasingly liberal attitude towards unwed pregnancy facilitate the *prospect* of parenting, the *problems* of parenting do not end with getting pregnant. All the trials associated with combining child rearing and work will be compounded for those who attempt to raise a child alone.

Moreover, if feminists support the premise that women should have the *choice* as to whether they wish to become mothers, it should not be supposed that they are unanimous in their enthusiasm for the variety of means and strategies through which women today can become pregnant. In particular, some see the new developments as suggesting how fully the ideal of motherhood may shape certain women's lives. That is, the *ideology of motherhood* is seen to encourage women in the belief that they are "incomplete" until they give birth and raise a child. However, there is a wide gap between motherhood as an ideal and the experience of mothering, which, as Abbott and Wallace (1990, 89) point out, is "hard *work*" (emphasis added).

Research has noted the isolation, loneliness, and drudgery that is experienced by housewives in general (see Oakley 1974; Luxton 1983/1995). These feelings are redoubled for the single parent who is unemployed. Indeed, various authors have suggested that addictions to cigarettes and alcohol represent the aftermath of attempts to cope with the stresses involved in caring for preschool-aged children. For example, Graham (1987) has argued that for working class women, the time spent sitting down to smoke a cigarette may be "the one peaceful time they have" (Abbott and Wallace 1990, 91). Similarly, the description of gin as "mother's helper" has a long history. In addition, Conway (1990, 28) points out that "single parent mothers face more sexual harassment, at work and socially, since many men view single parent women as 'fair game.'"

As we suggested in Chapter 6, Gender, in our discussion of the *feminization of poverty*, the assumption of parental duties in a society in which women's earnings are less than men's and in which women of colour and disabled women are doubly disadvantaged makes the issue of single parenting for women one that must be considered in a broader context than that of the family. It is not simply an issue of the "family" or "reproduction" per se. Rather, it is linked to debates about welfare and welfare states and must be considered in the context of social, economic, and political changes within the larger society.

Divorce

Prior to 1968 adultery was the only grounds for divorce in Canada, except in Nova Scotia, where cruelty was sufficient grounds even prior to Confederation (Morrison 1987). The 1968 Divorce Act expanded the "fault grounds" under which a divorce could be granted. In addition to adultery, proof that one's partner had engaged in prohibited activities such as mental or physical cruelty, gross addiction to alcohol or other drugs, sodomy, bestiality, and homosexual acts, entitled the petitioner to an immediate divorce. Moreover, the 1968 Divorce Act introduced what are often termed "no fault" grounds that allowed couples to divorce without requiring them to stipulate their specific reason for doing so. In these cases of "marital breakdown," couples were required to live apart for a three-year period before applying for a divorce and jointly consent to being divorced. In the event that one party did not wish to be divorced, the court required that five years pass from the time of separation before applying for a divorce. In addition, Morton (1990, 213) notes that "[a]s an added protection for the economically dependent spouse in cases of unilateral separation, courts were given the discretion to refuse a divorce if a 'granting of the decree would be unduly harsh or unjust or would affect the making of reasonable arrangements for the maintenance [financial support] of the spouse.'"

The 1968 Divorce Act represented a compromise that sought to satisfy those who felt that marriage should not be regarded as a terminal condition and those who felt that divorce was unacceptable on moral or religious grounds. In seeking to satisfy everyone, the act satisfied virtually no one. First, the act placed a strong emphasis on the virtues of reconciliation, with the lawyers for each spouse legally obliged to discuss reconciliation with their clients. Similarly, divorce trial judges were required to determine whether the couple's reconciliation was possible. However, criticisms of these provisions soon emerged. As Morton (1990, 213) notes, many felt it neither practical nor desirable for the courts to act as pseudo–marriage counsellors, and critics charged that "divorce legislation should not be used to aggravate already existing tensions between the spouses by reviving an unhappy marriage and providing them with a public forum in which to continue their quarrel" (Morton 1990, 213). Second, for those who felt that the law should support marriage, the availability of "no fault" provisions for divorce were seen as unduly liberal. In contrast, others charged that the fault grounds were too narrow. Third, it was noted that the disparate degrees of access to divorce provided by fault cases and no-fault cases promoted a degree of connivance and duplicity among those who did not wish to wait for three years before they were legally divorced. Thus, Morton (1990, 213) observed that "most fault divorces were adultery cases and . . . these cases were really consent divorces disguised to allow the spouses to avoid the three-year waiting period."

In 1985 a new Divorce Act became law. It was drafted in response to many of the criticisms outlined above, but again has not proven immune to controversy. Under the new act, there is only one ground available for divorce—marital breakdown—but this is defined in three ways:

1) the spouses have lived apart for one year;

2) one of the spouses has committed an act of adultery; or

3) one spouse has treated the other with mental or physical cruelty.

While proof of fault entitles couples to an immediate divorce, those opting for a one-year separation "may apply for a divorce any time after separation to ensure that their case is heard soon after the year is up" (Morton 1990, 214). Although lawyers are still required to advise their clients of mediation services, the new act attempts to avoid the adversarial implications of the 1968 act.

In the past, it was common for social problems texts that broached the topic of divorce to contain an obligatory section on "divorce-prone families," as if there were some readily identifiable traits that distinguished people who divorced from those who remained married. In a society in which around 40 percent of marriages end in divorce, it seems somewhat nonsensical to provide such a discussion. As Ambert (1990, 196) observes, "Many unhappy people stay together while some happily married persons eventually divorce." We are all likely to be aware of an unhappily married couple in which the spouses stay together "for the sake of the children," or because of the economic hardships separation could bring, or because of religious prohibitions against divorce. The process of uncoupling, which Vaughan (1985) has termed the *long goodbye*, may have its roots in a variety of reasons; however, it would seem that for many Canadians, divorce has become an option that is increasingly viable.

Child Custody

It is important to bear in mind that the law only becomes involved in custody decisions when a dispute arises between divorcing partners. Judges can overturn or disregard the private arrangements that parents have made if they believe that such arrangements would be harmful to the child. However, judges seldom intervene, although no official statistics are kept in this regard.

In general, it is safe to conclude that the law is less clear with regard to the issue of child custody than it is with regard to the division of other material assets at the time of a divorce. However, it should also be noted that, in the event of a separation order, where it can be obtained, or an interim order prior to divorce, the following guidelines are applicable.

Prior to the mid-1800s, custody decisions were based on British common law decisions that had established the precedent of *paternal preference*. Children were held to be the "natural property" of their fathers, a position reflecting the facts that women did not have rights as independent persons before the law and that fathers needed the labour of their children (especially older children) for family survival. Also, since fathers were stereotyped as strong and mothers as weak, it was believed that a father's hand was required to turn young people into mature adults.

Towards the end of the nineteenth century, the influence of the newly developing psychoanalytic theory and the increasing recognition of women's and children's rights led to a gradual replacement of the paternal preference doctrine with the *tender years* doctrine. As child development theories evolved that recognized emotional development as being of equal or greater importance than physical development in children, judicial opinion shifted towards a belief that, all things being equal, children during their tender years should be raised by their mothers. Thus, the *tender years* doctrine became a euphemism for "maternal preference." The "tender years" themselves were never precisely defined, but usually ranged from birth to ages 7 to 12.

The tender years doctrine has supposedly been supplanted in the Divorce Act of 1985 with a new principle known as the *best interests of the child*. Section 16, subsection 8, of the act states that "[i]n making an order under this section, the court shall take into consideration only the best interests of the child of the marriage as determined by reference to the condition, means, needs, and other circumstances of the child." While the "tender years" doctrine does not appear in the wording of the Divorce Act of 1985, it appears to have been subsumed under the definition of what constitutes the "best interests" of a child. While the letter of the law is gender-neutral, actual custody awards appear to favour "maternal preference" consistent with the theme of the "tender years." If it is the judgment of the court that a child's best interests are to be met in emotional nurturance, then males will be stereotypically conceived as less capable of parenting. Not only will such a popular stereotype influence judicial decisions, but it may also influence the presentation of custody petitions themselves. The result may be that significantly fewer petitions are initiated by fathers, and that fewer are contested by fathers when they are initiated by mothers. Moreover, in that the subsection does not define what actually *are* the best interests of a child, considerable discretion is permitted to the judiciary. Richardson (1987) suggests that, based on various judgments, the principle appears to include such factors as the wishes of the parents, the child's relationship to the parents, the child's current state of adjustment, the length of time the child has lived with one parent, and the relative emotional and financial ability of each parent to raise the child. Although, theoretically, the expressed wishes or preferences of the child could be taken into account, they apparently rarely are.

In addition to the above-mentioned factors, the conduct of a parent is considered to be an important influencing factor if that conduct is believed to be directly relevant to the best interests of the child. In this regard, adultery would not be important, but substance addiction and particularly child abuse would be important. In the case of spousal assault, however, the courts have held that a husband's beating of his wife does not invalidate his application for custody or his claim to be a "good father." In contrast, although "nothing in Canadian law stops a homosexual parent from applying for custody . . . the courts will often only take judicial notice (that is, recognize that it could easily be proved) of the fact that some harm might arise from living with a homosexual parent" (Yogis, Duplak and Trainor 1996, 56). In general, Canadian case law suggests that only "discreet, non-militant homosexual parents who do not flaunt their sexual orientation" are successful in obtaining child custody (Yogis, Duplak and Trainor 1996).

The "friendly parent rule," created in the Divorce Act of 1985, additionally requires the court to take into consideration which parent would be most likely to provide the other with "liberal and generous" access to the children. Based on the belief that children benefit from as much contact with both parents as possible, a judge is required to consider the willingness or likelihood of each parent to facilitate the potential noncustodial parent with access. If one partner is hypothesized to be relatively unwilling or "uncooperative" to provide such access, it is unlikely that he or she would be granted custody.

In general, the alternatives available to the courts appear to be those of sole custody to one parent, joint custody, or split custody. Of these three, the most common is sole custody awarded to the mother; in 1991, for example, mothers received sole custody in 73.6 percent of cases, fathers received sole custody in 11.8 percent of cases, and joint custody was awarded in 14.3 percent of cases (The Globe and Mail 1995). These decisions, of course, reflect only the actual judicial decision and do not necessarily reflect the actual living relationships that exist between the two parents and the child. It is possible that a mother with sole custody may still involve the father in all or almost all dimensions of the child's life, and therefore parenting is, in fact, shared. Similarly, joint custody may not really mean equal parenting participation by both mother and father.

A situation often exists wherein there is joint "legal" custody (the decision of record), but sole "physical" custody of a child. In other words, the child lives with one parent only, but all major decisions pertaining to the child's education, health, religious upbringing, and so forth may be made between the parents jointly. In contrast, the "joint" custody may be realized both physically—with the child having two residences and dividing time between them more or less equally—and legally—with all life decisions made jointly by both parents. *Split* custody, which would appear to be very rare, involves cases where there is more than one child and the children are apportioned between the parents, usually with the father taking the boys and the mother taking the girls. The term "split" could also theoretically be used to refer to a distinction between legal and physical custody and would be even rarer still.

Increasingly, the concern has been raised that judgments based on the "best interests of a child" may exhibit a subtle bias against women and reinforce the ideology of motherhood. Thus, Boyd (1987, 172) argues, "The ideology is a double-edged sword for women in custody battles because the bias it creates in favour of mothers only operates where the mother's conduct or life-style accords with the assumptions and expectations of the ideology of motherhood. If they do not, the chances are good for a father who wishes to challenge the 'unfit' mother for custody." In this vein, Phyllis Chesler's *Mothers on Trial* offers numerous illustrations, based on U.S. custody cases, in which women lost custody because they worked (too ambitious), did not work (lazy), were involved with a man (immoral), a woman (immoral), or not involved with a partner (did not offer the child a stable family), and so on. However, others have charged that the assumption that men cannot care for their children and that women are "wronged" by the court's decision to award custody of a child to the father is also based on sexist and stereotypic assumptions. With the rise of mothers' and fathers' rights groups in Canada, one may expect that the issue of child custody will become increasingly controversial in the decades ahead.

Despite the ineffectual Mr. Mom stereotype, Conway observes that "studies of single parent fathers suggest they are quite successful at parenting, and they express more satisfaction than single parent mothers" (29). As he notes, this finding may reflect the fact that in comparison with single mothers, single fathers tend to be older, better off financially, and, because of the vestiges of the "tender years" doctrine, more likely to be parenting older children than younger children.

The Common-Law Family

For a growing number of Canadians, particularly the young, entrance into a common-law marriage will precede entrance into a legal marriage. Occasionally termed a "trial marriage" or simply "living together," the common-law marriage is often a prelude to or an interim phase before marriage. Thus, Conway (1990, 30) notes that "[c]ommon-law marriages are most typically a one-time event; 63 percent end in legal marriage after a duration of 2.3 years." Because the couple is not married, there may be the perception that the relationship offers the prospect of sustained intimacy without the relative obstacles to severing a union posed by a legal marriage. Similarly, it may be assumed that this relationship allows them the possibility to "get to know each other" without the artificiality found within a dating relationship, where each attempts to dazzle the other with their best behaviour. However, this family form is not immune to the burdens that befall legally married couples such as violence, adultery, child abuse, and poverty. Indeed, because of the relative impermanence of the union, individuals may perceive themselves to be less bound by restrictions against actions like adultery. However, this very opportunity to "test" a partner's long-term desirability may be precisely what gives common-law relationships at least part of their appeal.

The Transitional Family

The term *transitional family* refers to a work-family pattern in which women attempt to stagger the demands of work and family through a sequential patterning of "motherhood" and "paid labour." According to Daniels and Weingarten (1984, 211), this type of accommodation pattern is also termed an *employment brackets motherhood sequence*. It occurs when a woman interrupts her education or employment to devote herself to motherhood for a period of time and then returns to continue her role as student or employee. In this way, "some period of parenthood is cordoned off, as it were, insulated and protected from the competing demands of other work" (Daniels and Weingarten 1984, 211). However, the period of time that can be devoted exclusively to the mothering role has become shorter and shorter.

As we pointed out earlier, the majority of Canadians would seem to believe that a mother's place is in the home when her children are very young. However, increasingly it has become less financially feasible for mothers to take extended periods of absence from the workplace. Particularly among dual-provider families, the financial necessity of the wife's contribution to the family income often necessitates that only a brief absence be taken from the labour force; for some, the time spent as a "transitional family" may be restricted to that period allowed for under provisions of maternity leave. It may also be noted that although unemployment insurance allows women 15 weeks (the first 2 of which are nonpayable) of pregnancy benefits, it requires that they have worked at least 700 hours during the previous year and provides them with only a percentage of their weekly pay. For those earning in excess of $375 a week, benefits are calculated at 55 percent of the individual's gross earnings over the past 26 weeks; for those earning less, benefits are calculated at 60 percent. Although either parent may apply for parental benefits following the birth of a baby for an additional 10-week period, this provision would seem to encourage mothers rather than fathers to pursue primary parenting. That is, should the husband decide to seek the 10-week parental benefits, he would not receive benefits for the first 2 of the 10 weeks. Similarly, if the couple decided to split the parental benefits, two of the five weeks during which the father assumed primary care of the child would not result in payable benefits. In contrast, if the mother cared for the child continuously following its birth, she would receive payment for the entirety of the 10 weeks since she had already satisfied the 2-week nonpayable period.

Whether women attempt to overlap their family and career roles in a *simultaneous* pattern of motherhood or engage in a sequential pattern of roles, the consequences of motherhood for careers and earning capacity in Canadian society remain high. For those who attempt to simultaneously juggle the demands of work and motherhood, the result may be an extreme role overload. Those who attempt to stagger the two demands may forfeit their seniority, salary, and potentially their position themselves by taking time out of the workplace. In that the standard for "success" within a profession is typically predicated on a *male model of work*, which presumes a worker will have a work life uninterrupted by absences due to child bearing and other family demands, women may be evaluated as "less committed" to work and thus as less desirable employees, simply because their career path departs from the standard by which it is judged.

The Blended Family

Variously termed the "reconstituted," "melded," or "remarriage" family (Conway 1990, 33), the *blended family* is becoming increasingly common because "three-quarters of divorced men and two-thirds of divorced women eventually remarry" (Ambert 1990, 206). Thus, the death of one family often results in the formation of another within Canadian society. However, while research on this type of family is still in an embryonic stage, some have raised concerns that various forms of child abuse are more likely to occur in this type of family due to the lack of early bonding between children and step-parents (particularly stepfathers) and to the perception that the child is other than one's own "flesh and blood."

For example, Finkelhor (1979) has reported that father-daughter incest is almost five times greater in families with stepfathers than those with natural fathers. Similarly, Russell (1984) observed that in her random survey of American women, 17 percent (1 in 6 women) who had a stepfather as a principal figure in their childhood years were sexually abused by him. In comparison, 2 percent of women (1 in 50) who had a biological father present during their childhood years were sexually abused by him. Moreover, when Russell distinguished between the types of sexual abuse her sample of women experienced, it was noted that 47 percent of stepfathers versus 26 percent of biological fathers had engaged in very serious forms of abuse (for example, forced penile-vaginal penetration, anal intercourse, and so on). While it can be noted that there is truly no form of sexual abuse that is "nonserious," Russell suggests that stepfathers are more likely to engage in actions that involve penetration, force, and the physical invasion of a child's body and may feel less bound by the normative disapproval of incest.

Similarly, Herman (1991) has argued that due to their absence during the early years of their stepchildren's lives, stepfathers may be less likely to see their stepdaughters as "children" and more likely to be sexually abusive towards them. For Herman, the enormous discrepancy that exists between mothers and fathers as sexual abusers of children is explained by the fact that women as principal nurturers are less likely to view their children as sexual beings. That is, after months or years spent diapering bottoms or assisting in wiping them, it may be hard to envisage the child's genitals as either alluring or sexual. She argues that if fathers and stepfathers shared with their wives the task of nurturing their children, they would be less likely to engage in sexually abusive acts with children.

In general, blended families with adolescent children are likely to pose more difficulties than those with younger children. However, the presence of a "ready-made family" or "add-ons" to each spouse's own family may pose various difficulties whatever the age of the children, including hostility between stepsiblings, animosity towards the new mother or father, unresolved feelings of guilt, hostility, or anxiety left over from the experience of divorce, and financial strain due to the presence or absence of child-support payments. Moreover, there is typically a larger age difference between women and their second or subsequent partners than that which existed during their first marriage. Accordingly, Ambert (1990, 207) notes that each partner may be at a different stage in their life cycle, with each wishing to pursue activities that the other might view as ill-conceived or uninteresting. For all these reasons, second and subsequent marriages have an increased likelihood of ending in divorce.

The NLSCY reports that in 1994 approximately 9 percent of Canadian children under the age of 12 were living in step-families, with approximately half of the children being stepchildren and the other half being children who had been born or adopted into these families. In that stepfathers outnumbered stepmothers by five to one, it should not be surprising that the most common step-parenting relationship was that of stepfather–stepdaughter. Based on their interviews with children age 10 to 11, the NLSCY reports that children in step-families have more difficulties with their parents and a less favourable view of their interactions with their parents than children from intact families: 33 percent of stepchildren versus 27 percent of children from intact homes reported lacking emotional support from their parents, 44 percent versus 28 percent reported difficulties getting along with parents and siblings in the six months prior to the interview, and 43 percent versus 33 percent reported erratic punishment (Canadian Social Trends 1997). As well, adult children from blended families are also especially likely to leave home early. Boyd and Norris (1996, 15–16) note that young adults age 18 to 29 are much more likely to live at home when neither of their divorced parents has remarried; among those with only one remarried parent, a "higher proportion of young adults lived with a parent if the father had remarried (56%) than if the mother had (47%)." Due to the family conflict that blended families often experience, "when remarriage occurs for one parent and not for the other, a young adult living at home is more likely to be with the unmarried parent, regardless of whether it is the father or the mother" (16).

CONFRONTING THE PROBLEM

As we have seen, the "problem" of intimacy within contemporary Canadian society is not really one specific problem per se. Rather, what emerges is a series of competing visions as to what is considered the ideal context for intimacy and the directions that Canadians should pursue to achieve it. In many ways, discussions of intimacy bring together our dreams and fears of what the future will hold.

Gottlieb (1993, 249) has observed that "[t]he word 'home' packs such an emotional punch today that sellers of real estate use it to refer to empty buildings." Similarly, companies that would emphasize their congenial and supportive "teamwork" often adopt the term "family" to express the type of relationships they offer in their office environment. Both of these terms are potent and powerful; however, we are increasingly challenged to understand what a family is and confront many of our taken-for-granted assumptions about its definitive features.

If individuals within an intimate relationship can "create a world within a world," it is apparent that they cannot simply ignore the one around them. For this reason, as we have seen, the social problems associated with intimacy must be seen as inextricably bound with other social problems confronting Canadians in the 1990s.

SUMMARY

1. Images and ideologies of the "family" underlay conceptions of the problems posed by intimate relationships in Canada in the 1990s.

2. Increasingly, the patriarchal nuclear family, in which a provider-husband, his homemaker wife, and their dependent children reside together within the home, is being challenged by alternative definitions and forms of the family.

3. The issue of reproduction has traditionally been the *sine qua non* of the family. Accordingly, our understanding of the family is increasingly challenged by the advent

of the new reproductive technologies, the rise in use of contraception, and the decision of some women to remain childless or to bear children without being married.

4. Understandings of the "ideal" marriage and family have varied through time from the institutional family to what now is termed the pluralistic family. Simultaneously, the functions served by the family, such as reproduction, sexual intimacy, and the socialization of children, are becoming available outside of legal marriage.

5. Despite movement towards an egalitarian ideal, gender remains a salient issue in discussions of power within intimate relationships, sexuality, and the division of labour in the contemporary Canadian family.

6. The mythology surrounding intimacy suggests that it is within intimate relationships that we will achieve our desires for love and respect. However, it may be precisely within this realm that inequalities, particularly between men and women, become most troublesome.

THE MEDIA

DID YOU KNOW?

- A national poll of over 1000 American adults identified media products, namely, MTV, movies, television, and popular music, as four of the most negative influences on children. The fifth? Politicians.

- It is estimated that many children will have seen 8000 made-for-TV murders by the end of elementary school. This total may rise to 25 000 by the time they graduate from university. The number of violent acts per hour on prime time TV is 4; for children's programming (notably cartoons) it stands at 34!

- The average Canadian watches about 23 hours of TV per week. Young adults consume the least (at about 19 hours), whereas seniors are the heaviest viewers at 35 hours. Yet which group is more likely to engage in violent activity?

- More than 3000 studies in the past half century have explored the relationship between TV violence and violence in society. Most conclude that television is a contributing factor, although there is still no consensus regarding the precise nature of this relationship.

- Twenty-four journalists were murdered in 1995 (73 in 1994). At least 180 journalists remain imprisoned in 22 countries.

- The merger of Time Inc. and Warner Brothers in 1989 (combined assets of U.S. $18 billion) created the world's largest direct marketer of information and entertainment.

In 1994 Canada had its own version of media concentration when Rogers, Canada's leading cable operator, completed a takeover of Maclean-Hunter, Canada's third-largest media empire.

- Nearly 90 percent of the newspapers in Canada are owned by Hollinger or the Thomson chain. Coupled with Torstar (*The Toronto Star*), these monopolies account for 72 percent of the daily circulation, up from 45 percent in 1970 when a Special Senate Committee on Mass Media raised a warning about media concentration. Conrad Black is now the Western world's third-largest newspaper magnate, behind Rupert Murdoch and the Gannett chain in the U.S.

- Since 1991 jobs in Canadian media companies from movie making to television programming have almost doubled from 15 000 to 28 000. Indirect employment has also grown to 44 000, up from 24 000 in 1991. Federal policies that foster the conditions that allow these firms to flourish may account for this growth.

- Women and men, young and old, tend to use television in different ways. According to a study of TV viewers in major Canadian cities, men are more likely than women to channel surf (28% versus 19%), men are more likely than women to report that they control the remote (49% versus 30%), and those between 18 and 25 are more likely than older viewers to watch two channels simultaneously.

- Most media exist as outlets for advertising. Advertising in the U.S. is a $183 billion industry. Advertising revenues are escalating annually: a 30-second clip during the Super Bowl can command over U.S. $1.3 million, while *Seinfeld* and *ER* routinely pull in $500 000 per 30-second slot. No wonder Jerry Seinfeld can command $1 million per episode while his three co-stars earn "only" $600 000 per episode.

- A report by the American Association of Advertising Agencies found that the average prime time hour in November 1996 contained 15 minutes and 21 seconds of commercials and promotions. Daytime viewing may consume 20 minutes and 5 seconds of each hour with non-program fare.

- Coverage of religious events is almost nonexistent. From 1993 to 1996, ABC, CBS, NBC, CNN, and PBS presented 72 000 evening news programs and 104 000 morning show segments. Just 1.3 percent of evening news and only 0.8 percent of morning coverage was devoted to stories on religion.

THE PROBLEM

Is there any Canadian who has not capitulated to the lure of the media or succumbed to the persuasiveness of their message? Probably not. For if there is a common denominator in Canadian society, it is our absorption into a media culture, either as producers or consumers. Contemporary lives are awash in the media; their pervasiveness is such that media intrude in our lives without awareness or resistance. The events that matter are media events; the media, in turn, are defined as eventful by association. Reality is not lived per se except through images and representations that mold the reality of lived experiences (Gray 1995). For those saturated with television since childhood, personal identities are inextricably linked with and defined by media images (Owen 1997). The end result is a growing inability to distinguish reality from its representation by the media whose activities reformulate the very realities under observation (Fiske 1994; Abercrombie 1995).

Concern over the media and their impact on society continues to escalate. At the heart of the debate is the notion that the media not only construct realities by shaping our perceptions of the outside world but constitute a constructed reality in their own right, with specific agendas and priorities that are often at odds with the needs or interests of the audiences. In a strict sense, the media are not a problem in their own right. Problems arise with what we do to the media and what the media purportedly do to us. Problems also arise because of discrepancies between what we expect of the media and what the media can deliver. Failure of the media to contribute to a particular vision of society is seen as problematic as well. To their credit, many Canadians generally seem aware of the media as a powerful social force, with the capacity to distort, conceal, or evade reality. Few, however, possess the critical skills necessary to delve into media dynamics and to analyze the techniques behind mass persuasion. Even fewer are equipped to put these skills into practice on a daily basis.

It is obvious that the social world we inhabit is profoundly influenced by the media and by the information circulated by mass-produced communication. In fact, the influence of the media is so pervasive that many people have described the twentieth century as the age of mass communication. Mainstream media may provide a major source of information that shapes our view of the world and establishes agendas for political and economic priorities (CAFCA 1996). Yet much of the information we consume is increasingly "morselized" into entertaining bits whose one-sidedness renders a public disservice (see Atkinson 1994). Fierce commercialization ensures that all media are increasingly driven by ratings and audiences rather than providing a service. The gradual transformation of the world into a computer-mediated "electronic bulletin board" has further underscored the media's prowess as an agent of change. In advancing the shift to digital culture from the linearity of a print culture, computer-mediated technologies have cultivated the potential to (a) dismantle traditional hierarchies of status and power, (b) shatter shared perceptions and modes of thought rooted in reason and causation, (c) democratize knowledge by making it more accessible and interchangeable, and (d) redefine how society organizes that knowledge in the very act of reconstituting itself (Chambers 1997). In short, the media have the potential to empower or enlighten as well as to alienate or disempower, and this interpenetration of "good" and "bad" raises a raft of issues.

Reaction to the ubiquitous presence of the media has been mixed. Some people defend the expansion of the media as a positive force for the advancement of human progress. The media are touted as indispensable in the construction of an open and cosmopolitan society, firmly rooted in the principles of free enterprise and liberal democracy. Others are less sanguine about their effects. They deplore the media as an insult to the human spirit, an instrument for promoting mediocrity or stifling creativity while encouraging antisocial or passive behaviour, a device for reinforcing racism and sexism in a changing and increasingly diverse society, a cultural frame of reference inconsistent with widely accepted goals or national interests, and a discourse in defence of privilege (Fleras 1998). To be sure, the media cannot be blamed for all the social problems in society; nor can they be expected to provide all solutions (Peart and Macnamara 1996). Yet media-bashing has become a favourite pastime among those looking for a quick fix to society's problems. Scapegoating the media may have the virtue of simplifying the problem for analysis, but it does little to advance our insight or offer a solution.

Between these two extremes are those who are inclined to dismiss such debates as puerile and unproductive. Rather than pigeonholing the media into slots of good or evil, the media are portrayed as a complex social construction, with contradictory roles, ambiguous messages, multifaceted functions, and diverse impacts (see Stone 1993). The media are neither good nor bad but simultaneously good *and* bad. Media processes and their outcomes appear to be sufficiently complex and contradictory that they often blur the distinction between positive and negative. To one side, the media are known to embrace a largely conservative and commercial agenda; to the other side, a combination of investigative journalists and ethnic/alternative presses possess the capacity to criticize those in power, raise awareness, mobilize the masses, and spark social change. This ambiguity is expressed in the love–hate relationship people have with the media; that is, they buy, consume, and condone as they ban, block, and condemn (Katz 1997). Moreover, as the media continue to be blamed for the shortcomings of society and its youth, developments in communications technology have enlarged people's accessibility—and enjoyment—of the media (Davies 1996). The enigmatic character of media–society relations is nicely captured in this quote from Raymond A. Morrow (1994, 189), who reminds us that even pleasurable activities such as media entertainment have consequences that resonate with danger:

> How can "having fun" be a social problem? Without falling back on any puritanical moralizing about the sinful nature of pleasure, the response is easy enough: my having fun or your having fun can be destructive to you or me or the community now or in the long run. . . . Having sex without birth control or protection in risky situations can be great fun, but it is also a potential threat to the unborn or oneself or future partners. . . .

In short, contemporary media exist as "contested sites" filled with contradictions and animated by diversity and dissent. Clearly, then, we must go beyond the notion of "media as bad" without necessarily ignoring their potential for negativity. The pervasiveness of the media ensures that virtually no part of our society or culture is untouched as a continual point of reference (Davies 1996). In their ability to redefine normal conduct and shape new standards of desirable behaviour, popular media not only change our notion of what is accepted but alter our idea of what is expected (Medved 1996). This formidable power reinforces the absurdity of reducing the media to simply a mechanical transmission of information on a massive scale. The media are this and more, with consequences as disturbing as they are revealing.

This chapter examines select aspects of the media, namely, newscasting, advertising, and TV programming, from a social problem perspective. It focuses on the social dimensions of the media, rather than on technology per se, by exploring the contested relationship between media and society. We look at the concept of media as "enlightened propaganda" by discussing the nature of media–minority relations at the level of representations. The postmodern paradoxes of computer-mediated communication provide a fitting conclusion to the chapter. Three themes prevail in problematizing the media: First, the media are interpreted as being problematic in their own right. Many contradictions within society are reflected in the internal conflicts evident in various media at the level of newscasting, advertising, and programming. Yet posing cultural solutions to social problems does not solve anything, Rick Salutin (1997) writes, but may add to the problem by *appearing* to do something. Second, the media are known to generate social problems by perpetuating patterns of social inequality within contexts of power. Their status as agents of social persuasion reinforces— for better or for worse—how we think and act, the dynamics of group interaction, and the kind of society we have. That knowledge makes it doubly imperative to explore media from a social problem perspective by discussing how media messages are created, expressed, maintained, challenged, and transformed. Third, the Janus-faced nature of media-saturated society leads to a raft of questions: What do we mean by defining media as a social problem? Who says they are a problem and why? If the media are a problem, how is the problem manifest? In what ways do the media create problems, yet provide solutions? And what, if anything, can be done to minimize media damage? Before we begin to answer some of these questions, we take a brief look at recent changes to media in terms of structure and study.

ANALYZING THE PROBLEM

Defining the media is more enigmatic than should be the case for something so popular and pervasive. In a text devoted to the social dimensions of contemporary media, it would be inappropriate to define the media solely in terms of technology for information transmission. Definitions such as Joseph Turow's (1992, 9), "Mass media are the technological vehicles through which mass communication takes place," are correct to a point but insufficient. We also regard it simplistic to refer to media as simply messages created by a dominant elite through rapid transmission for consumption by a large and heterogeneous audience. Most definitions point to mass media communication as a one-way system of communication with a largely singular message through mechanical devices for accessing a large number of people in a short period of time. But we may need to reassess the media as a technology-driven process of persuasion by which standardized "information" is beamed at a broad audience in light of evolving changes to media technology.

"Mass" Media

Mass media communication once encompassed a transaction between sender and mass audience involving a technologically mediated exchange of standardized information. It entailed a process in which the few manipulated the many in pursuit of vested interests or national concerns. The linearity of this model is illustrated by the following list of attributes. At the core of traditional media was the notion of mass. The concept of mass was applied to different levels of the communication process, including standardized message, mechanized transmission, a large and undifferentiated target, impersonal contact, and linear, one-way flow of information. Of particular relevance was the concept of "mass" audience. Audiences were defined as large and amorphous aggregates, both passive and disorganized, as well as widely dispersed and subject to manipulation. Mass audiences were also perceived as uniform in their needs and wants; as a result, media messages could be pitched accordingly. However erroneous, that kind of mindset may have simplified the task of marketing media products, from advertising to programming. It certainly did not reflect the reality of consumer audiences who were much more discerning—and differentiated—than given credit.

The concept of "mass" gave rise to a host of invidious distinctions (Grabe 1997). One of these lay in the contrast between mass culture and high culture, popular culture and elite culture. Mass culture was mass-produced, driven by profit, consumed by a largely gullible audience. Not only was "popular" culture condemned as dangerous and decivilizing, the content of "lowbrow" media culture was perceived as subjective, its tone as sensational, its audience as working class, and its main goal to excite or distract audiences. By contrast, "highbrow" media culture was individual crafted, driven by aesthetics, consumed by elites, and provided a refining effect on a discerning audience. It was also praised as objective, sophisticated in its approach and tone, and influential in informing the educated elite classes. That kind of distinction made it very difficult to generate scholarly interest in media and popular culture as serious subjects for analysis (Bassett 1995b).

The "New" Media

With advances in user-friendly technology, the concept of media has undergone a change in structure, function, and process. It is now possible to create, store, and manipulate vast amounts of information at dizzying speeds (Madger 1997). The different ways in which large bundles of diverse information may travel have had the effect of inverting meanings and bending rules (Katz 1997). Young people in particular are deserting in droves the "old" media (best symbolized by the television as a piece of furniture in the corner of a home) and flocking instead to manipulate vast communication empires with links to every corner of the planet (Zerbisias 1997). The very idea that a "mass" mediated society may vanish is fundamental in appreciating Canada's evolving mediascape (see also Hutchison and Lealand 1997).

Technology has taken the "mass" out of mass communication, in effect imparting a new dynamic with respect to media–society relations. The notion of the mass audience as passive and uninvolved in processing media information is now discredited. Interactive technologies from the Internet to interactive TV, from zapper to VCR, have taken the passivity out of audience–media relations. Information is no longer the preserve of linear, fixed, and authoritative accounts by remote authors, but consists of ideas that are readily accessible in digital form (hypertext) to be cut and pasted, interpreted, or dispersed at will in a nonlinear and interactive fashion (Chambers 1997). Creative control has shifted from producers to consumers. Consumers can control what they see, provide instantaneous feedback, and interact with others through networked connections. The emergence of interactive technologies is also dissolving the structures that promote monopolies of knowledge as a basis for social control (Madger 1997). Finally, references to mass audiences have been discarded because of demassification technologies that define demographics on the basis of lifestyle, concerns, and buying patterns. Instead of comprising a single mass market, society is viewed as fragmented along race, class, gender, sexual orientation, and age (Rothenberg 1997). The advent of market niches and target marketing strategies has compelled a more customized view of an increasingly segmented audience, with particular attention to the needs of individualized consumers.

Even the way we talk about the media is changing in response to technological innovations and intellectual trends. Media are no longer portrayed as monolithic institutions with dictatorial powers to dominate, but as a "contested and contradictory site" in which opposing interests (from owners to audiences) engage in a competitive struggle for control or resistance. Audiences are portrayed as actively involved in creating or "negotiating" meanings according to special needs and situational circumstances, rather than from a vantage point of atomized individuals susceptible to persuasion and harmful effects (Gillespie 1996). From a focus on outputs (impacts and effects), debate is shifting to how people use the media instead of how media use people (uses and gratification) and from a concern with the ideological role of the media to the goal of exploring audience interpretations within a specific context. A preoccupation with media structures is being replaced by an interest in social meanings and their embeddedness in cultures. Meanings are neither fixed nor focused on predetermined readings according to this new line of thinking, but constructed and reconstructed through interaction between text and the socially located discourse of diverse audiences (Ang and Hermes 1994; Fiske 1994; Thomas 1995). Totalizing models of media–society relations such as Marxism or mass society theory are gradually losing lustre in response to a postmodernist turn in social science thinking (Curran and Gurevitch 1994). In place of foundational explanations are approaches that emphasize text, intersubjectivity, and interpretation. A critical perspective has displaced behaviourist approaches to the study of media, with their emphasis on measuring audiences and behavioural effects through surveys or controlled experiments. By focusing on the media as a creative human accomplishment, a critical perspective is broadly culture-centred because of its preoccupation with social constructions, cultural meanings, and aesthetic appreciation. Table 9-1 provides a capsule summary of the "new" versus "mass" media as competing models of explanation with respect to underlying assumptions and open assertions.

TABLE 9-1 "Mass" Media versus the "New" Media	
Mass Media Model	**Postmodern Media Model**
grand narrative/totalizing theory	competing discourses
media as "social control", i.e., as agent of class, gender, race domination	media as "contested site," i.e., as struggle between opposing groups for ascendancy
media as "hegemony" for social/thought central	media as "negotiated" reality
media make people	people make media
audience = passive, victimized, cultural dopes	audience = active, creative, cultural brokers
mass media = monolithic institution	demassified media = contradictory and fragmented
media structure = solid, enduring, closed, and and determining	media structure = dynamic, constructed, evolving formation. Determining only in the first instance
media and reality = separate	media *are* reality = fused and inseparable since media not only record reality but encode and frame it

Adapted in part from Curran and Gurevitch 1994.

Unscrambling the Media

What do we need to know about the "new" media if we are to understand underlying logic and contemporary dynamics? The media constitute a socially constructed system of technologically driven communication that are anything but neutral or passive in delivery. Media are actively involved in shaping messages and circulating meanings. As a social construction the media encapsulate within themselves a number of hidden agendas and dominant ideologies that serve vested rather than common interests. The constructed character of the media is rarely conveyed to audiences, many of whom are often unaware of the production process behind the apparent "naturalness" of media products (Abercrombie 1995). Not only are the media constructed through human agency, they also construct realities by "naturalizing" our perception of the world as necessary and normal rather than conventional and constructed. Cultural frames of reference are imposed that define some aspects of reality as acceptable and others as unacceptable. Of those ideas and ideals that pervade media content or process, few are as pervasive as the commercial imperative and the perpetuation of values consistent with conspicuous consumerism. The media do not exist to inform or to entertain or even to persuade. As a rule they are not interested in solving social problems or fostering progressive social change unless consumer goods are directly involved. The media are first and foremost business ventures whose bottom lines are organized around the need to maximize advertising revenues by attracting the largest possible audience.

Yet the ideological components of the media cannot be discounted. The media are loaded with ideological assumptions that not only reflect the ideas and ideals of a dominant discourse, but preclude the values and views of those that might contest an unequal order (Abel 1997). As discourses in defence of ideology, the media are effective because they can encode particular values by pretending to be something they are not (see also Abercrombie 1995). Media messages combine to "naturalize" contemporary social arrangements as normal, necessary, and inevitable rather than as self-serving social constructs (Supermedia 1995). For example, media messages (a) represent dominant interests as universal and progressive rather than particular and parochial, (b) deny contradictions such as those related to capitalist production and distribution, and (c) naturalize the present as "common sense." Media are hegemonic; in other words, they win consensus through consent rather than coercion (Apple 1996). Defining the media as agents of thought control by effect rather than intent suggests a process of "enlightened propaganda"—not in the overt, brainwashing sense of the word, but in terms of systemic consequences. To the extent that social inequality is invariably portrayed by the media as a matter of individual choice rather than structured experience— not as social and constructed by way of power differences but natural and normal—the media may be interpreted as propaganda. The fact that minorities are invariably stereotyped as problem people may be seen as an exercise in propaganda. That every ad and all TV programming (and its conflation in "commercialtainment" (Andersen 1996)) say it's better to buy than not to buy also constitutes propaganda. In short, the media define situations and impose "frames" of interpretation that "normalize" media priorities or corporate imperatives rather than consumer needs.

There is little question that the media are powerful agencies with the capacity to dominate and control. In some cases, the exercise of power is blatant; in others, media power is sustained by an aura of impartiality, objectivity, and balance. An ability to frame issues and set agendas in ways that bolster the status quo contributes to media potency. Yet the media are not monolithic structures with conspiratorial designs on the general population. Media represent a contested site, a kind of ideological battleground where different interests struggle for control over media agendas (Wilcox 1996). The constructed nature of media reality is amenable to analysis. Just as books are thought of as constructed texts for analysis, so too do media qualify as texts for deconstruction in that both convey meaning by authors who use language and conventions to tap into shared understandings and underlying assumptions. Television, radio, and newspapers are organized around tacit codes and implicit meanings that permit communication to occur. To be sure, texts cannot be divorced from the material world of industrial production (Jakubowicz et al. 1994). It is their very "constructedness" in a material reality that enable a "deconstructing" for "preferred readings," most of which are "structured in dominance" along all points of the communication process (Messner et al. 1996). Nevertheless, learning how to unscramble these largely hidden and often unspoken codes is no longer a "soft" option in a world where reality and representation are inescapably fused and hopelessly entangled. The acquisition of media-proofing skills has become a "hard" necessity in securing an intellectual self-defence for the *fin de siècle* (Fleras 1998).

MEDIA AS PROBLEM: NEWSCASTING

What images come to mind when you think of news? This is not as trivial a question as it may seem. If you are like many other Canadians, preliminary thoughts turn to television news, with its sense of immediacy, arresting visual clips, and fast-paced action. A smaller but still significant number might associate news with newspapers or weekly news magazines such as *Maclean's*. Though lacking in television's visual appeal and sense of immediacy, print news is preferred by many because of its depth of coverage, broader scope, and more leisurely style. Then there are those who would not even bother with a distinction between print and electronic news. Stylistic differences exist, they admit, but television news is little more than newspapers with moving pictures.

On further reflection, a number of you may describe news as a product that is both objective and relatively accurate. News items are collected by reporters who disinterestedly relay the facts about various events for public consumption. Media bias exists to be sure, and is amply demonstrated in a number of conservative, urban tabloids, but we like to think of ourselves as sufficiently perceptive to correct for any inserted bias by critically reading "between the lines." Others may dispute this largely benign view of impartiality, preferring to see the news as a manufactured commodity along all phases of the newscasting process. Huge resources are expended in manipulating a perception of the world that reflects the interests of the affluent and the influential (CAFCA 1996). The effects of these distortions cannot be discounted: what is conveyed to the audience is not necessarily news in the sense of an accurate depiction of important developments in the world. News is ultimately condensed into what is defined as "newsworthy" by the industry.

The question "What should be news?" may entail a variety of responses. Are you, for example, inclined to see news as possessing a conservative bent, thanks to cosy links with big business, collusion with government, and commitment to the status quo? Or do you prefer to condemn the news as "too radical," with an overwhelming bias against government and business, not to mention an unhealthy identification with left-wing causes and protest movements? Or is news too "neutral" for your tastes? That is, in its obsessive yearning for neutrality and balance, news items are framed in a detached and noncommittal sense, with the tragic and significant juxtaposed with the trivial and comedic—without any sense of outrage, context, or history. Finally, do you have a preference for a "middle" position, one in which the news media are seen as striving for accuracy and balance, but pulling up well short of the mark because of organizational barriers?

This list of responses could go on, but the point should be apparent by now. What we call news is an enormously complex and multifaceted problem that is subject to varying interpretations and diverse points of view depending on one's political sympathies, economic status, and social circumstances. What is defined as news represents the "distilled" outcome of institutional practices, commercial commitments, and consumer demands. The notion of news as a professionally defined set of news values may not be a problem, but its potential to be problematic cannot be discounted. News becomes a social problem when it detracts from fostering a democratic society of critically informed citizens. News is a problem when (a) it provides a largely one-sided point of view rather than balanced coverage, (b) it is driven exclusively by commercial interests rather than the interests of service, and (c) it is framed exclusively as entertainment rather than a source of information within a context. News that fails to conform to its standards and expectations is also problematic, and its resolution provides a starting point for framing news as a social problem of concern to many Canadians.

What's News?

Quickly now! Define news. Isn't it astonishing that something so simple and routine can pose such difficulties in definition? Problems of consensus result because people define news in different terms. It can be considered in terms of functions (the role news plays in society), by way of structure (its nature and properties), or at the level of processes (that is, whatever it is the news media do). With respect to functions, for example, news can be viewed as a system of communication that facilitates dialogue and interaction. News, as Eamon (1987) notes, can also be viewed as a body of knowledge for expanding our understanding of the world as it unfolds in time and space. In some cases, this knowledge is not necessarily consistent with official doctrines and dominant ideologies; in many cases, it is.

At the level of structure, what passes for news is normally associated with a property called newsworthiness (Abel 1997). Generally speaking, news in North America is regarded as an "event" with one or more of the following characteristics: it must be immediate; be proximate (events further away are less likely to be reported); feature prominent individuals or flamboyant personalities; employ direct quotes and authoritative (although often unnamed) sources; involve magnitude in terms of cost or loss of life; embrace the unusual or odd; be obsessed with conflict, anguish, and tragedy; and be easily labelled and condensed for quick reference and recall (Fuller 1996). Unexpected events that constitute a break from norms and the routine also qualify as news values (Madger 1997). Not surprisingly, coups and earthquakes get top billing, as do crimes, clashes, and crises (McGregor 1996).

This list of characteristics that ideally comprise a news item is expansive, and this raises the question of which criteria prevail in selecting stories for prominent exposure on nightly newscasts. Situational factors may account for why one item takes priority over another. Time and budgetary constraints may intrude (Abel 1997). An item of local interest may take precedent over a global issue in a regional paper; conversely, a large urban daily may ignore regional interests. On balance, however, conflicts involving Hollywood celebrities are more newsworthy than mass killings in Africa. A frenzy of cameras followed Princess Diana's every move, yet there are yawns at the prospect of doing another piece on environmental degradation. The media appeared mesmerized by the killing of a fashion designer rather than analyzing why such an incident should consume so much space. Items for inclusion also depend on their "presentability," and this is determined by the media's access to visuals, the availability of quotable reactions, and the novelty of the sound bites. Adversity and adversarial situations are preferred over the cooperative; so too are angles involving the unusual, kinky, quirky, or kooky. In other words, what passes for news is not simply a formulaic process; it consists of a series of judgment calls within the framework of tacitly accepted ground rules for linking advertisers with audience without abdicating a commitment to news values.

Case Study 9-1 is both timely and topical. It examines the somewhat uneasy relationship between fame and media by focusing on the life and death of the world's most photographed woman, Diana, Princess of Wales. Press reaction to Diana both before and after the Paris car crash provides a valuable insight into how the media define newsworthiness as it pertains to the cult of celebrity. Debate over press coverage also serves as a starting point for a profound self-examination of what the media are for, and why.

CASE 9-1	Media and Fame: Spontaneous Combustion or Lethal Mixture?

The English government is about to pass a law that abolishes the upper class sport of foxhunting. Hunting animals to the point where they drop from exhaustion or are ripped apart by dogs is increasingly condemned as cruel and regressive in a civilized society. But hunting royalty remains a popular pastime, according to Wellington columnist Rosemary McLeod (1997), even though the chase can be every bit as vicious and fatal. In statements made to *Le Monde* a week before her death, Diana, Princess of Wales, complained bitterly of a predatory press: "The press is ferocious, it never forgives anything. It is only interested in mistakes. Every good intention is diverted, every gesture is criticized." Photographs of Diana reveal the look of a hunted animal, cornered by the enormity of fame but too petrified to flee her stalkers. Such is the price of fame, or so it would seem.

But with death comes respect for those who live hard and die young. In a stunning reversal from their usual dismissal of Diana as "flawed," the media engaged in a virtually unprecedented binge of sanctimonious hyperbole that left nothing tarnished and everything forgiven. Even Diana's past mistakes were reformulated as strengths to be emulated rather than criticized. The same media that only days before the fatal Paris car crash had unceremoniously dubbed Diana a "few diamonds short of a tiara" (*Daily Telegraph*) read the public mood correctly and redeemed themselves just in time to lionize the "Queen of Hearts" who was now beyond blemish and above reproach. Put bluntly, the media dusted off yet another reincarna-tion of Diana while discarding earlier images of her as flaky or manipulative. Having contributed to the tragedy, moreover, they then wallowed in the collective catharsis, aware that even the slightest criticism of the "people's princess" would invoke the equivalent of a public lynching.

The massive outpouring of glowing media affection serves to problematize the relationship between media and fame. The connection is relatively straight-forward, at least on the surface. Media and fame are an indissoluble pair, as one editor of a Spanish magazine aptly phrased it. Each leans on the other in ways that are mutually reinforcing yet oddly contradictory. News media crave celebrities to "sell copy" and celebrities cater to the media to sell themselves. Celebrities pump the lifeblood of a fiercely competitive commercial enterprise; media are the oxygen that fans fame. Fame is a media invention; certain media are a function of fame. Media court fame, then play the famous for fools; celebrities seek publicity, then despise its intrusiveness when held accountable to media criticism. Commercial media bask in infamy; fame shrivels without media voyeurism, a metaphorical equivalent to the silence of a falling tree in a forest when no one is around to hear it. Such co-dependency is career enhancing. As Nicole Kidman proclaimed in the film *To Die For*: "You're not anybody in America unless you're on TV. Because what's the point of doing anything unless people are watching? And if people are watching, it makes you a better person."

Yet the relationship between media and fame is eminently ambivalent—a positive or negative force, both symbiotic and parasitical, depending on who is asking the question and why. Sadly, it took the death of Diana to propel the media into the spotlight. Diana was astutely conscious of the power of the media; she knew how to deftly pamper the press when it suited her purpose in creating an image and identity or in channelling media obsession into her favourite causes. To her dismay, however, Diana discovered that even the media could not control what she had unleashed by accident or design; what flattered and idolized proved demeaning and ultimately destructive. Still, the media appear discriminating in how they go about conferring fame or undressing infamy. Public moods and possible audience reactions are carefully monitored before taking a position. For example, the media had no compunction whatsoever about publishing unflattering pictures of Sarah Ferguson's sexual romps, in part because there was little public sympathy for her. In contrast, pictures of a topless Diana have never been published, but remain secured in a Spanish vault, with apparently little demand to be released for fear of unleashing public backlash among those deeply enamoured of Diana. Just as Diana loved and loathed the press, so too were the media of two minds in cozying up with the world's most photographed woman—attracted by that rarest of human qualities, a photogenic nature that never quit, but repelled by fears of being duped or looking foolish. You can't win with the media, Madonna once said, cooperate and you are accused of being manipulative, refuse to cooperate and prepare to be criticized as evasive or arrogant. Rosemary McLeod (1997) captured the fickleness of the media in her scathing attack on its remorseless capacity for building up only to take pleasure in tearing down:

> Di tried, like so many do, to reach an accord with it. She was obliging, so the beast wanted more. And when it got more, it wanted more. Remember her shyness? It got bored with that: when it christened her "Shy Di" it wasn't being kind.
>
> With better clothes and grooming, she learned to look up when she smiled. Then she was too *confident*. She might be vain, and she was certainly too skinny, the beast sniffed.
>
> Yes, she finally admitted. She had been bulimic. She had been miserably unhappy, hated herself, felt valueless—as who mightn't whose essence was being robbed daily? Whose marriage was being exposed as a disaster?
>
> The beast gloated. It had pretended she was perfect, that her life was a fairytale romance, only to have the pleasure of revealing its own lies. Now it began to smell blood. That was exciting.
>
> She had foolish love affairs—as who doesn't who is unloved in their marriage. . . . Women journalists in the British press were especially ruthless, mocking whatever seemed sincere about her, rejoicing in what caused her pain, reading vanity into her most selfless acts.

| CASE 9-1 | Media and Fame: Spontaneous Combustion or Lethal Mixture? (continued) |

Visiting the dying? Comforting the sick? How ludicrous! She must be deranged.

Now the beast is smelling the images of immanent death in her eyes. Of course it is. There's a fortune to be made

At a deeper level, the relationship between media and fame is somewhat more enigmatic. Who deserves fame and why? When is saturated coverage a function of fame, or vice versa? Do the media create fame or are they merely attracted to the famous, or is the answer a bit of both? Why do the media lavish attention on select celebrities, but not others, even if this notoriety is seemingly undeserved? Elizabeth Hurley comes to mind as a person who is famous for *being famous* rather than for any accomplishment, unless, of course, wearing a revealing dress in the company of Hugh Grant counts as an achievement. Is fame fickle, or is media fickleness the cause of fleeting fame? Does anyone remember or care about Tonya Harding or Loreena Bobbit? How do the media decide whose fame merits attention? Compare the relatively limited amount of media exposure accorded to Mother Teresa in relation to the convulsive outpouring over Diana, even though the "the saint of the gutter" was arguably more deserving of attention for a lifetime of compassionate sacrifice. Why do celebrities attain only in death what eludes them in life? Fashion designer Versace represents a person who achieved posthumous fame beyond a narrow circle of glitterati, but only after his murder. A host of departed pop and rock stars from Buddy Holly to Selena can attest to becoming larger than life after death.

No less interesting is how fame and infamy are defined, constructed, conferred, or withdrawn. Some can do no wrong yet others are incapable of right no matter what they do. Eventually nothing went right for Sarah Ferguson, the Duchess of York, with a corresponding lapse in press attention, whereas media interest never dimmed for Diana, regardless of how much she orchestrated her media moves in hopes of coming to grips with personal demons. Yet even Diana could do no right when the press chose to dislodge her from the very pedestal it had created, judging her at various times as "neurotic," "flighty," "unbalanced," "frivolous," and "in sway to fame and frocks." The fact that few noticed how the media giveth, yet taketh away, Christopher Hutchens (1997) explained, was proof of their power to have *people's actions judged by their reputation, instead of reputations by their actions*. Nowhere is this more evident than with Prince Charles, whose star dipped below the horizon. What is wrong with him, the media subtext asks, that he could not love someone as adorable as Diana—even if her life was hyped in headlines and captured through snapshots. And the myth-making process cranked into overdrive with the media raking over the most minute details of Diana's past in iconizing her martyrdom—in effect, continuing to engage in precisely the kind of media overkill that Diana allegedly deplored.

CASE 9-1	Media and Fame: Spontaneous Combustion or Lethal Mixture? (continued)

The ironies are inescapable. The media appear to be blissfully unaware in running one sanctimonious tribute after another—and invading the private grief of mourners in the process—of their very role in recreating the kind of hyperbole that precipitated press harassment in the first place. Empty pontifications about taking the moral high road in their coverage of celebrity are betrayed by postmortem hysteria that is every bit as intrusive as before, judging by the volume of posthumous publications about Diana in print, telecast, and music. Irony also awaits those who listen to public caterwauling over the media from the very people whose voracious appetites for the lurid indiscretions on the celebrity circuit brought about the very intrusiveness they now righteously discredit. There is yet further irony in watching the very media who once hounded Diana and mocked her femininity, figure, and fragility now trip over themselves to beatify her. Any semblance of truth is all but forgotten in the resulting feeding frenzy, says Jonathan Dimbleby (1997), the official biographer of Prince Charles: "As in war, so in grief: truth is the first casualty. In their desolation, those millions of people who have been bereaved by the death of the Princess of Wales cannot bear their entranced visions of her life to be doubted or disturbed."

Responses to these issues and paradox can be hotly debated. Yet there is one issue that seems to supersede the others: What is it about fame that makes it such an eagerly sought commodity by the media? Perhaps one answer is a growing media preference for "fluff" over substance, morselization over meaningful dialogue. As the tabloidization of the media continues apace in a fiercely competitive environment, the press will stop at nothing to get the scoop, regardless of the costs or consequences. The journalist Sandra Coney (1997) captured this quest for simplification when she claimed:

> Television vampirises people—it consumes them then tosses them aside. The subtleties and complexities of human personalities are beyond the capabilities of commercial television. Instead people are reduced to stereotypes and labels. The medium creates a crude identity for the person, more of a caricature than the real thing. So people are saints or sinners, heroes or failures, victorious or disgraced, somebodies or nobodies. There is no middle ground. People are shifted from one category to another in the blink of an eye.

Greed and profit provide another set of related answers. Magazine editors will readily concede that any cover issue dealing with high-profile celebrities (but especially Diana) is like money in the bank. Readers revealed an insatiable appetite for prying into the lives of those whose values or accomplishments reflect the commodification of contemporary culture, however disproportionate their impact or importance to society.

The pull of Diana was understandable: Part soap opera, part fairy tale, part Greek tragedy, Diana became an icon of our time, symbolizing the chaos and confusion of a postmodernist era with its preoccupation with image yet yearning for meaning in a world of pastiche. She proved to be one of those rare individuals whose star qualities resonated with a certain *je ne sais quoi*, often by way of (and precisely because of) conflicting messages. Diana was glamorous and remote yet seemingly ordinary with a common touch; she was modern and cosmopolitan yet remarkably traditional in her work and love of family; she was liberated yet her emancipation was contingent on the most antiquated of institutions, the Royal Family; she was capable of profound change in both her personal and public life yet proved a pillar of constancy for those around her; she was of privilege and aristocracy yet cared for the outcasts of society. Diana's appeal was such that people insisted on seeing her as an underdog—a Cinderella-like working class waif with whom the lowly masses could identity—despite being one of Britain's richest women who hobnobbed with millionaires and dined in private suites at the Ritz. The "people's princess" was an intriguing mixture of "everywoman," from Mother Teresa and Jackie O to Marilyn and Madonna, and many women saw in her joys and unhappiness a reflection of themselves and their lives. Elizabeth Kastor (1997) of the *Washington Post* put it best when suggesting that celebrities like Diana do more than distract, but provide a "screen onto which we project the movies of our most intimate thoughts."

There is yet another possibility in explaining the appeal of fame. It resides in a media ability to transmute celebrities into appealing melodrama, then to melodramatize celebrities as newsworthy, a point made by Ted Fishman in a recent issue of *Harper's*. People may say they prefer news that deals with substantial issues in a thoughtful manner, but most vote with their hearts by switching to the fables and foibles of the rich or infamous, where every story must reflect a morality tale in which good is rewarded and evil is punished. We know it and moneymakers know it, and that makes media obsession with fame tantamount to an "us" problem. Earl Charles Spencer, Diana's brother, was only partly right when he accused the press of killing his sister by sneering at her intentions and hounding her to death. The man who himself had sold family stories to weekly magazines should have prodded further in rethinking the politics of blame. Was Diana's death the fault of the paparazzi who shoot pictures for a living? Who can blame these "pictorial bounty hunters" for titillating shots that can fetch half a million dollars from eager buyers? (The photos of "The Kiss" between Dodi al-Fayed and Diana at St. Tropez were parlayed into a tidy $2.3 million for the lucky photographer.) Do we blame the tabloids or magazine editors who buy salacious pictures to bolster corporate profit, in the process unleashing a culture of greed that provokes irresponsible behaviour to slake this unquenchable thirst for "dirt"? Or should we point fingers at the public, whose compulsive demand for invasive photography knows no bounds and has yet to be sated as a way of making important lives that are not.

The sociologist in us would look for a structural relationship between media and fame. Maybe the real culprit is the "system," with its espousal of superficial images that privilege the cult of appearance at the expense of inner freedom, even if the beauty myth can kill in its remorseless quest for perfection. Let's face it, Dr. Cathie Dunsford (1997) writes: Diana was not stalked or driven to distraction because of her work with victims of landmines or AIDS—Princess Anne would surely have been a better candidate for her tireless efforts—but because she was perceived as a person of glamour and grace whose fashion sense and extraordinary beauty conformed with media definitions of what it takes to get noticed. Diana may have played into the superficiality of the media, but in massaging the media for unfashionable causes through her "heart politics" she may yet prove that it is possible to change the world. Inasmuch as Diana proved a photo opportunity, a media headline, and a ratings winner, Sandra Coney (1997) concludes, her commodity value was subjected to the discipline of the market—and the market won.

Bias in Newscasting

In purporting to present only the facts, mainstream media have long endorsed the goals of objectivity in terms of fairness, accuracy, balance, and impartiality. However admirable such objectives may be, they ignore the numerous factors that interfere with their attainment. Objectivity itself is a human impossibility since no one is so utterly disinterested as to be transparent (Fuller 1997). News is not something out there waiting to be plucked for placement as newsworthy. Rather, news is a constructed reality and, as a human accomplishment, is susceptible to various demands and pressures, both intentional and inadvertent. Collectively, these constraints blunt the media's capacity for balanced and accurate coverage. Many of the difficulties arise from the corporatization of the news media, the selectivity inherent in the news collection process, and the politics of news presentation. Each of these factors—business-driven coverage, selective collection, and packaging and presentation—reinforces the problem with news.

Coverage: News as Big Business

Contemporary news (both print and broadcast) originates from several large corporate sources (Winter 1994). This is certainly the case in Canada, where independent news sources are a vanishing breed. In lieu of independents are chains such as Hollinger or Thomson. Often transnational in scope, these corporations approach the news sector as nothing more than a profit-making business venture. Even publicly owned networks such as the CBC appear to be increasingly market-oriented.

A commercial imperative exerts a considerable strain on the integrity of the news media. It sharpens the potential for a conflict of interest between corporate needs and consumer concerns. A preoccupation with profit can lead to erratic (or non-existent) coverage of issues that require exhaustive investigative journalism. This "bottom line" mentality ensures a version of the news that is anything but impartial or detached. More to the point, news becomes whatever the industry defines as news, especially if it is consistent with the interests of the affluent and conservative. The cumulative effect of this implicit "collusion" between news and big business (and the government) is not necessarily "conspiratorial" in intent, but rather a disquieting convergence of interests. Nor should we ever lose sight of the self-censorship at play in the news media. For in the final analysis, mainstream news is as conservative as any other big business—with one eye cocked to audience ratings, the other to corporate revenues.

Consider the situation in Canada. As recently as late 1995, Hollinger Inc. a Vancouver-based mining consortium owned by Conrad Black was a relatively minor player in the newspaper business. That all changed in the space of several months in the mid-1990s when Black went on an unprecedented buying spree that secured majority ownership of Canada's daily newspaper circulation while transforming the mediascape in ways that rankled or dismayed. By 1996, Hollinger Inc. had emerged as a major player in Canada's newspaper sweepstakes with ownership or control of 58 papers from a total of 104 nationwide and 42 percent of this country's readership. Hollinger's average total copies per week of 14 164 097 nearly doubled the weekly sales total of all other papers combined (currently at 20 204 797).

In addition to Canadian holdings, Hollinger Inc. has been active on the international front with a slew of newspaper buy-outs, ranging in profile from London's *Daily Telegraph, The Jerusalem Post, The Chicago Sun-Times*, and *Sydney Morning Herald* to *Punxsutawney Spirit* in Pennsylvania. With worldwide daily circulation of over 5 million, Hollinger now ranks only behind News Corp Ltd. of Australia, the global communications empire owned by Rupert Murdoch (7 million) and the Gannett Co. Inc. of Arlington, Virginia (6.6 million).

Is media monopoly a problem? Canada's 1970 Special Senate Committee on Mass Media lamented that control of the media was passing into fewer hands, with a corresponding conflict of interest. It also predicted that this trend was likely to continue. Twenty-five years later this observation appears extremely astute. Corporate groups account for about 93 percent of all copies of daily newspapers sold in Canada, up from 77 percent in 1970. Canada's three largest dailies in 1958 controlled around 25 percent of the daily newspaper total; in 1996 the figure had risen to 66 percent (Winter 1997). While 41.5 percent of the daily newspapers in Canada were independently owned in 1970, the figure had fallen to 17 percent by the mid-1990s. Of Ontario's 42 dailies, only 3 independents exist: *Stratford Beacon Herald*, Brockville's *Recorder and Times*, and *London Free Press* (Saunders and Mahood 1996). Corporate concentration has reached the point where four provinces are without English-language daily newspaper competition, three of which are under control of a single owner (Saunders and Mahood 1996). The Irving estate continues to control the English-speaking dailies in New Brunswick, while Conrad Black's Hollinger Inc. owns both of Newfoundland's and P.E.I.'s dailies, in addition to the four dailies in Saskatchewan. Such interlinkage with Canada's biggest circulation newspaper, *The Globe and Mail*, creates the potential for a conflict of interest.

Collecting the News

There is a lot going on in the world at any particular point in time. How do the news media decide what is worthy of being reported? The news industry is nominally committed to the principle of reporting only what is newsworthy. In reality, the industry is equally bound to making a profit by "selling" as much copy as possible through advertising and subscription rates. This dual commitment puts a premium on bolstering audience size and network ratings by appealing to the broadest possible audience. The news collection process is driven by a focus on the dramatic and spectacular, with particular emphasis on conflict, calamity, and confrontation. Newsworthiness is enhanced by the presence of flamboyant, preferably corrupt personalities with a knack for the outrageous or titillating. The noncontroversial and cooperative are often ignored because they lack intrinsic appeal for an audience with a short attention span and an "action" mentality.

The "jolts" and "jiggles" mentality inherent in the news process has been widely criticized. Tabloid-style journalism is taken to task for fixating on the spectacular, such as the Bernardo/Homolka trials or murdered child beauty queen JonBenet Ramsay. Mundane but important topics are pushed aside, in the process denying the realities of the everyday world. The lack of context is especially disturbing. It not only imparts a sheen of superficiality to news, but also robs events and developments of any meaningful reality. Minorities in Canada and abroad have complained about news portrayal of them as belligerent, ruthless, or indifferent towards human life. No less flattering is their depiction as victims, vulnerable to social decay and societal disorder, enmeshed in graft and corruption, and without much capacity for cooperative, productive activity. Stereotypes, prejudice, and discrimination become easily entrenched under these circumstances.

A second source of bias is readily discernible in the news collection process itself. The investigative journalist with a nose for news may also be an unwitting agent in relaying bias. Social and professional assumptions create particular frames of reference that do not reflect a neutral view of reality (Abel 1997). Even a fierce commitment to objectivity and neutrality does not preclude the possibility of bias in news collection and packaging. All human beings, including those in the news industry, are embedded in social contexts that shape perceptions and interpretations. Neutrality can be difficult to achieve, according to Roger Landry, publisher of *La Presse* (Globe and Mail, March 4, 1997), especially since journalists cannot help but be influenced by personal interests or aversions. Words may be manipulated (unconsciously in many cases) when drawing attention to certain aspects of reality and away from other dimensions that are deemed less significant. The camera lens or tape recorder may not "lie" in the conventional sense of the term; however, each instrument only records a minute portion of what occurs around us. The ubiquity and pervasiveness of this bias undermines any pretext of objectivity and value-neutrality. For that reason alone, members of the public must cautiously approach what they are told to see, hear, or read—especially if they lack firsthand knowledge of the situation in question.

Bias also arises from news sources. Reporters are heavily dependent for their livelihood on official sources in the government, bureaucracies, police forces, and corporate sectors. Collectively these sources are difficult to access and prone to secrecy. Yet they are highly sought after because they lend credibility to stories and sometimes offer the promise of a "scoop." Not surprisingly, many organizations employ professional public relations and media consultants whose job description rarely includes telling the truth. They appear more interested in impression management than in providing the facts (Peart and Macnamara

1996). What emerge from these news "scrums" are highly selective bits of information that make the organizations look good at the expense of balance and accuracy.

Even unofficial sources of information can be suspect. On-site reporting seeks to conjure up an image of painstaking and meticulous objectivity. Reality is reported as it unfolds before our eyes without the filter of interpretation. In fact, however, what passes for reality may be as contrived and manufactured as official reports. Demonstrations and protest marches may be staged and managed for the benefit of the evening news slot. The rhetoric produced by these telegenic displays is concerned with manipulating sympathy or extorting public funds, not with accurate reflections of the facts.

Packaging the News

Bias in newscasting is compounded by problems in presentation. Distortions can be attributed to a variety of reasons. Problems arise from the very act of squeezing a complex and fluid reality into the straitjacket of visual images and sound bites, with a beginning and end, separated by a climax. An adversarial format is frequently superimposed to convey some "bite" to the presentation. Isolated and intermittent events may be spliced together in a story, in the process accentuating a magnitude of crisis or urgency where none actually existed. Media hype and public concern may not coincide. For example, the media portrayed the 1995 Quebec referendum as being of grave import to Canada. But the rapid disappearance of constitutional concerns from Canadian politics immediately after Quebeckers voted narrowly to stay in Canada implied a media out of step with the people. The presentation can be twisted in other ways. According to David Taras (1991), for each edition of CBC's *The National* up to 1 million words and 40 hours of videotape are collected. This volume needs to be distilled into 20 minutes of news and enough verbiage to fill about one-third of a newspaper page. This example shows why it is so important that we understand the grounds for editorial decisions: What is kept and what is discarded? Who decides and why? Answers to these questions are central in understanding the packaging process.

What finally appears as news hinges on decisions by editorial "gatekeepers." Editors are influenced by personal bias and political considerations. Editors and editorial decisions are likely to identify with corporate goals or media industry values. The increased commercialization of mainstream media puts an onus on revenues and ratings, in the process reinforcing the shared outlook of editors and owners. A highly conservative agenda is not explicitly spelled out. It may reflect instead a convergence of assumptions over what should appear as news. After all, it's hard to imagine anyone moving into management without absorbing corporate values along the way. As a result of this socialization, editors are prone to winnow out the subversive or irritating, leaving behind the filtered residue they call news.

The way in which a story is framed for presentation, particularly through headlines or positioning, can dramatically affect its interpretation (Abel 1997). Consider the placement of visuals and words. The location of a news item may influence the audience's perception of that particular incident. Yet its placement (or exclusion) reveals more about operational biases than about reality. A highly publicized trial in the United States featuring celebrities is likely to capture more space or time than an isolated tragedy in the Third World. Likewise, the nature, wording, and size of a headline may also affect a reader's reaction to a story. Priorities become very clear in a headline that declares: "Two Americans injured as thousands die in quakes." No less interesting is the division of reality into the categories of news, sports, opinion, entertainment, business, and lifestyle, and the filing of each event into its appropriate slot. The 1980s rape trial involving Mike Tyson appeared in the news and sports pages, as well as in entertainment columns. Tyson's assault in biting the ear of his opponent in a title match was also splashed across the media—even if editors waffled over whether to treat it as news, sports, entertainment, or lifestyle.

It should be clear, then, that the news is not an objective exercise in reality transmission. What eventually becomes the news is not something intrinsic to reality, with clearly marked and widely agreed-upon labels. Neither an impartial slice of reality reported by trained professionals nor a random reaction to disparate events, news as "invented" reality is shaped by organizational values and commercial concerns (Parenti 1992). This constructed character would appear particularly evident during election campaigns (Taras 1991; Levine 1997). A preference for image and angles rather than editorial analysis of party platforms exposes weakness in journalism—namely, biased reporting, quick judgments, fascination with the trivial, obsession with the horse race (who's winning), lack of historical perspective, and deep cynicism (McKie 1997). The necessity to compete for advertising dollars ensures a news package that not only sugar-coats reality with a dollop of entertainment but also reinforces media priorities.

In short, what eventually is "distilled" as news is expected to run a "reality" gauntlet in which the truth is the victim. The news process is subject to numerous biases and hidden agendas. It is formatted to attract audiences and secure advertisers, then filtered through selective mechanisms that only serve to enlarge the reality gap. News becomes a manufactured commodity where any semblance of reality is accidental. In place of objectivity, there is an "invented" reality that embraces media priorities rather than any commitment to consumer needs or an honest appraisal of what actually exists. This notion of news being subject to a reality gap applies particularly to its presentation on TV.

Television no less than newspapers is selective in coverage or presentation. Reality is beamed into our homes, not in the sense of an exact replica, but a form of realism purged of its sordid and messy elements lest it rattle nervous advertisers. This ambivalence has turned the news into an electronic equivalent of Orwellian doublespeak, a process whereby two opposing thoughts (entertainment and information) are accepted simultaneously without contradiction. In effect, then, TV news is packaged to meet audience demands and advertising priorities. In an age of zappers and satellite transmission, what is passed off as news are visual bites for fun and profit. Without visuals, a story is unlikely to get on the air, while complicated ongoing issues with unclear protagonists are likely to be shunned (Madger 1997). There is nothing wrong with having news packaged in an entertaining fashion. But, when all subject matter is presented as entertainment, as Neil Postman (1985) writes in his biting commentary on television, it makes it increasingly difficult for people to distinguish fact from fantasy. What are the consequences of this unreflective emphasis on bitability and action? Perhaps the greatest cost is a diminished capacity for genuine outrage and committed activism.

MEDIA AS PROBLEM: TELEVISION PROGRAMMING

Some issues defined as social problems may catch the reader by surprise. For those not versed in media literacy, for example, the concept of newscasting as a social problem may have caught them off guard. Even those suspicious of the news industry may not have appreciated the magnitude of the disservice rendered to the viewing public. Others issues, however, are almost too obvious to mention as social problems. Television (and the programs it offers) falls into this category, even if the occasional study exonerates it as a positive or relatively benign force in society.

For many, television is a major social headache. Commercials are denounced as irritants while programming is slammed for insulting the viewer's intelligence. Some are disturbed by the prodigious amount of television (23 hours per week) consumed by the average Canadian, excluding the VCR and video games. Time spent watching TV, so the refrain goes, is time away from constructive activities. This loss of interconnectedness with the real world invariably leads to indifference and desensitivity (see Tate and McConnell 1991). A kind of "dumbing down" occurs by dissolving the boundaries between adulthood and childhood to the point of meaninglessness as television makes the content of an adult world available to everyone (Meyrowitz 1986). Adulthood has lost much of its aura and appeal as a result, with a corresponding decline in deference to authority or hierarchy that once existed simply because of age differences. Other critics are bothered by the effects of television on otherwise normal individuals. They say that viewers are transformed into a variety of unsavoury types from "couch potatoes" to violent aggressors. Still others flinch from the amount of sex and violence on television, not only during prime time, where it is supposed to be carefully monitored, but on children's shows, newscasts, sporting events, and music videos. Strictly speaking, there is no conclusive evidence linking television with violence, either on the street or in the home. Still, the negative conclusions from more than 3000 studies cannot be discounted. With that kind of negative publicity and community concern, it is not surprising that pressure is mounting to censor television violence.

Television is arguably the most powerful yet enigmatic of contemporary social forces (Andersen 1996). For some it is a "revolution in a box" with a capacity to enlighten and reform; for others it is a "tyranny of the trivial" with few redeeming qualities. Once a device for creating consumerism as an acceptable lifestyle after the Second World War, television continues to provide a pipeline for promulgating the essence of the consumer lifestyle. It also furnishes an outlet for those in search of convenient babysitting, companionship, solace, a sense of community, and escapism. No less worrying for many is television's role as a nemesis of democracy. Instead of substance and stance, the art of politics now revolves around telegenic candidates, stage-managed platforms, and eight-second visual bites. Television tends to portray a nasty and dangerous world, according to noted communications theorist George Gerbner (Stossel 1997), further undermining the cohesion and interaction required of a democracy. With such multiple functions at its disposal, television has replaced religion as an important arbiter of who we are, what we want to do, and where we want to go. Its impact as an opiate of the masses is even more pronounced for those without access to alternate sources of information. That being the case, a knack for "unscrambling" the codes of television—its content, agenda, and style—is hardly a luxury in these times but a primary survival skill.

The Holy Codes

Television programs have come and gone in the last half century. To the casual observer, television appears blessed with an endless array of plots and storylines. Despite this illusion of diversity, however, television programming is locked into a remarkably formulaic process.

The dire need to bolster audience ratings leads to an endless cycle of "tried and true" formats, copycat programs, spin-offs, and repeats (Madger 1997). The faces may change and props may evolve to reflect the times and technology, but essential themes and underlying messages are circulated over and over again. This uniformity reflects the presence of a set of implicit codes and tacit assumptions that govern program selection. Foremost among these is the injunction to keep it "safe, simple, and familiar." Under this formula, TV content is sanitized and bleached of any controversy for fear of disturbing the public (Jhally and Lewis 1992). Television characters are typecast in roles that cater to the expectations of the lowest common denominator. Complex and sensitive issues are largely ignored or superficially addressed to bolster the undisturbed flow of advertising messages. Plots and characters are organized around simplistic morality tales of good triumphing over evil. Context is all but forgotten as TV adjusts its distinctive glasses for interpreting the world. The formula is so routinely applied that exceptions only confirm the rule. Defiance against this conventionality is the rarest of all qualities, and may help to explain the popularity of shows such as *The Simpsons* or *Rosanne*, with their reversal of well-worn clichés and "political correctness."

Is the banality of TV programming a deliberate attempt to insult the audience? Are audiences perceived as incapable of complicated plot lines or complex characterizations? Is there a creative void in programming decisions? Is it part of an elaborate hoax to fool all of the people all of the time? We would argue that the content of TV programming is driven by commercial imperatives rather than audience concerns. Put bluntly, TV programming (and media in general) constitutes a vehicle to make money through advertising (Fleras 1998). Programming is created to please advertisers who prefer programs that create the right atmosphere for product amplification. To the extent that audiences are important to programmers, they are seen as products (or commodities) for sale to advertisers. The bigger the audience, the merrier the profits (Tehranian 1996). If this line of argument is true, and evidence supports these assertions (Andersen 1996), we need to playfully invert our understanding of the relationship between advertising and programming (see Ellul 1965). Programming is not the normal function of television, with advertising as an interruption to the norm. Rather programming is an interruption to television's normal function of advertising. Programming is the filler between commercials. Television itself is one long commercial, interrupted by programming breaks, for connecting advertisers with the right kind of audience. Even the distinction between programming and advertising has blurred ("commercialtainment") with the proliferation of placement ads, programming environments (certain products will advertise only on certain types of programs), MTV (music videos are ads), and tie-ins (especially on children's shows). In short, the quality of programming is aimed at pleasing advertisers, who are its main consumers, rather than audiences. And those who pay the piper get to select the tune.

Reality Programming?

How does television programming line up with reality? Answers to this question are open to diverse interpretations and exemplified by the proliferation of metaphors that purportedly capture the essence of the relationship between media and social reality. The media are variously seen as a "window" on the world, a "filter" for selectively screening reality, a "frame" for imposing structure on reality, a "mirror" that reflects social reality, a "signpost" for guidance in constructing reality, a "trick mirror" that distorts our perception of the world, and a "black hole" that sucks up everything in sight. Inaccuracies result from squeezing programs into the formula of safe, simple, and familiar. TV reality is "boxed in" to conform to the rectangular constraints of a 26-inch screen, a half-hour time slot for plot resolution, and a storyline filled with characters of implausible virtue and unremitting consumer habits. Yet TV programming is not completely impervious to the intrusions of reality. Plots and characters must be recognizable to ensure audience identification and consumer connection. The spate of affliction-of-the month specials can also testify to such a relation. Still, TV reality is constrained by rating demands and revenue coffers to produce inoffensive programming for the broadest common denominator. Reality is further hemmed in by media perceptions of the audience as unwilling or unable to comprehend complex or socially sensitive issues.

Television is a product of culture and the production of this culture is not evenly distributed. TV programming is incapable of reflecting reality in all its diversity, even if efforts are made to be realistic (by disguising production values) and to feature realism in characters and setting (Cairns and Martin 1996). Television programming remains for the most part a male preserve, controlled by a handful of white, middle-aged, Los Angeles–based writers and producers, with scripts that invariably depict reality from a "pale male" perspective. Even the expanding profile and commercialization of gay and lesbian cultures (culminating in Ellen DeGeneres's much ballyhooed "coming out" on April 30, 1997) is less a reflection of emancipation than an embrace of an identifiable market niche with loads of disposable income (Israelson 1997). Few issues over reality programming have garnered as much attention as the relationship between television and violence in society. Equally controversial is reliance on censorship as a solution to violent programming.

CASE 9-2   TV Violence, Violent Society?

The statistics have been trotted out before, but they continue to disgust and concern. Judging by the incidents of violence reported by the police and covered by the media, Canadian society has grown increasingly violent over the last 10 years. Beatings and shootings are perceived as relatively routine, even outside major urban centres. There is another set of statistics that can trigger shock and indignation, and it relates to the disturbing amount of violence displayed on television. The average Canadian watches about 23 hours of television a week, that is, we spend about 20 percent of our waking hours glued to the TV. Programs designed for adults are violent enough, but the violence in children's programs is even more prevalent. Some researchers estimate they contain as much as 10 times the violence in prime time programming.

Portraying TV Violence

In addition to the numbers, concerns are raised about how violence is portrayed and its acceptability as a problem-solving device. Graphic portrayals of violence as pathological are one thing; depictions of random and explicit violence as a joke in itself (think *Pulp Fiction*) no longer have shock value but simply allow people to see more but feel less (see Giroux 1996). The degree to which this

CASE 9-2   TV Violence, Violent Society? (continued)

violence is "sugar-coated" is also disconcerting. Violent encounters are portrayed as humorous, exciting, and glamorous—in part to suit the entertainment demands of prime time audiences. TV routinely takes what is harrowing about reality and sanitizes it into something cosy and reassuring for the benefit of audience ratings and advertising revenue. Thus, what would by all accounts be a sordid and grisly event is transformed into something relatively painless or harmless, even ennobling. As well, this preoccupation with violence condones its usefulness for solving interpersonal problems. Negotiation and compromise tend to be time-consuming and inconclusive; by contrast, violent solutions are clear-cut and unambiguous.

Relation or Correlation?

How do we interpret the increasingly violent behaviour among youth and the proliferation of violent images on television? Is there a causal relationship? Will increased exposure to violence on TV activate aggressive behaviour in the viewer, as many are prone to believe? If so, what precisely is the nature of this cause–effect relationship? Does TV provide the cues, establish the models, serve as reinforcement, or stimulate the learning of violence patterns? Or does the causality work in reverse? That is, it is possible that more aggressive individuals are drawn to violent fare on television; if TV violence has any real effect on these people, it is merely to reinforce a pre-existing disposition. Even more intriguing is the possible absence of any direct relationship between TV

and violence. TV violence does not exist in a social vacuum. In a violence-saturated society such as ours, violence becomes the norm from which there is no escape. To isolate TV as the prime culprit while ignoring other sources is sociologically irresponsible and socially dangerous.

Additional questions come to mind when analyzing this relationship. Does TV exert a similar influence on everyone who watches it, or is its impact dependent on personal differences and social circumstances? For example, the amount of television that people watch varies by region (those in Atlantic Canada watch the most), by gender (women watch more than men), and by age (older people watch more than younger people). Other important variations pertain to socioeconomic status and levels of education. Finally, the entertainment industry has defended its depiction of violent excess by (a) denying conclusive proof of any relationship, (b) claiming only to be reflecting society, (c) giving the public what it wants, and (d) reminding people of alternatives such as switching channels if they dislike brutality (Medved 1996).

Rethinking the Relationship

These are some of the questions that confront sociologists when addressing the link between television and violence. Foremost is the question of whether prolonged exposure detracts from civility in society. Most published results in this area—more than 3000 since the 1940s—support a positive correlation between media violence and violent behaviour (Mietkiewitz 1993). Prolonged exposure

CASE 9-2　TV Violence, Violent Society? (continued)

to TV violence may generate several negative side-effects, including callousness, indifference to the suffering of others, and an inability to feel outraged by even the most depraved atrocities. Common sense tells us that such conclusions are reasonable. Not all sociologists would agree with them, however, and the basis for this disagreement may well reside in the different research strategies of different disciplines.

Most experimental and survey research arrives at the same conclusion: there is a positive link between TV violence and violence in society. But this relationship is not as direct or as predictable as frequently implied. Many of the studies in this area have lacked what researchers call external validity. That is, the studies were conducted in artificial contexts where social significance and sanctions did not apply, and for this reason the individuals being tested lacked any incentive to act normally. In other words, these studies, which often involved university students or preschool children, looked good on paper, but they failed to replicate external realities because of investigator bias. A natural environment that allowed observation in an undisturbed setting would have been preferable (Williams 1991).

Common sense convinces us that prolonged exposure to explicit violence leads to aggressive behaviour, especially among young males. Yet a causal relationship is not nearly as certain as many people would believe. A number of variables must be taken into account since the influence of TV varies from person to person and reflects

characteristics such as age, gender, education, socioeconomic status, and family life. Even more important is the reason for watching TV. Older people may watch it for entertainment and presumably are less affected by it. Younger people may turn to television as a source of information about how they should act; thus, they would be more impressionable. In other words, people may only see what they want to see; they may absorb only what they are predisposed to accept.

We must guard against too mechanical an interpretation of cause-and-effect relations. Perhaps the media only create a social climate, with a corresponding cultural frame of reference that defines some things as acceptable, others as unacceptable. Whether a person chooses to accept one option rather than another depends on a complex array of factors. In a society saturated with violent images and symbols, it is difficult to separate out one component as the causal factor. In fact, the media–violence relationship may be correlational simply because of the difficulties in isolating causes (TV violence) from effects (violent behaviour) in a society where competition and aggression are the norm rather than the exception. Finally, protracted exposure to media violence may influence people's attitudes or beliefs. What is open to debate is whether negative attitudes inevitably lead to antisocial behaviour. The perception that attitudes and behaviour are necessarily linked is questionable at best. Both the literature and our everyday experiences confirm that actions do not necessarily correspond with attitudes. The ability to

---

CASE 9-2   TV Violence, Violent Society? (continued)

compartmentalize attitudes from behaviour (what psychologists call cognitive dissonance) applies equally to other areas such as prejudice and discrimination.

In short, research on the causal relationship between TV violence and violent behaviour can best be described as inconclusive. A relationship may well exist, but a causal connection may be difficult to prove or disprove. Despite advances in statistical analysis and qualitative research, Davies (1996) points out, there are difficulties in "isolating" media effects within the context of a complex environment. Perhaps all we can conclude at this point is that those who are heavy consumers of television violence are more likely to think and act aggressively. This suggests that we should rephrase our original question. Instead of asking whether TV violence creates violent behaviour, it might be more advantageous to inquire, "Under what circumstances and for what group of people is prolonged TV exposure a contributing factor to violent behaviour?"

Censorship as Solution?

In times of convulsive social change, people frequently turn to quick-fix solutions to complex problems. But superficial responses are not the answer, if only because they so often ignore the context of the problem or the consequences to society at large of the proposed solution. A similar line of reasoning (but on a grander scale) pertains to issues of censorship and televised violence. Censoring the bad and the ugly on television has a certain appeal: It is reasonably simple to introduce through rating systems or technological devices, monitoring is relatively easy, and public acceptance can be counted on. But for many, censorship in a free and democratic society is as much of a problem as a solution. The right to "freedom of opinion and expression" as enshrined in Article 19 of the United Nations' Declaration of Human Rights is regarded by many as the cornerstone of democracy. Grave doubts are raised about our ability to limit censorship once it is in place and about the chilling effect such restrictions can have on freedom of expression. For others, censorship is a minor but necessary irritant. Its restrictions as reasonable limitations that are justifiably demonstrable are a small price to pay to protect society from its own worst inclinations.

For our purposes, censorship can be defined as a deliberate interruption in the flow of information from a sender to a receiver. Censorship is endorsed by people with a particular view of society and a desire to muzzle those whose visions do not coincide with their own. This definition is admittedly broad, but it reinforces the notion of censorship as a process applicable to a wide range of human activities. If we accept the terms of this definition, we can draw several conclusions. First, censorship is going on all the time. To be human and live in society implies entanglement in a web of restrictions. Interruptions in the flow of information are a routine and necessary component of social life. Thus, the issue is not one of censorship per se, which is unavoidable, but of where to draw the line in its application.

| CASE 9-2 | TV Violence, Violent Society? (continued) |

Second, there is no such thing as absolute freedom of speech. Nobody, nowhere, has ever had the right to do and say exactly as they pleased. Rather, the right to free expression is relative to time and place. What is permissible in one era is not in another, especially in times of uncertainty, change, and diversity. Context is also important. Yelling "theatre" in a crowded firehall is not likely to get you arrested, although it could get you "committed." Shouting "fire" in a crowded theatre is an entirely different matter. Context is important in another way. Almost everyone except the people who use it agree on banning child pornography, but there is less agreement on what to do about "explicitness" involving consenting adults. However repulsive blatant sexual exploitation may be, not everyone agrees that scuttling free expression is the solution. In other words, some degree of censorship is necessary, but the question of drawing the line is still open to debate.

Third, there is no agreement on how effective censorship is in curbing the flow of unacceptable information. Is censorship a solution to problems or simply a knee-jerk reaction that dodges key issues and costly commitments? Does censorship accomplish what it sets out to do? What proof do we have of this, either for or against? Are restrictions on media brutality an effective way of improving attitudes, modifying behaviour, empowering women and minorities, and changing social structures? Will censorship deter or will it create the right kind of noise and a million dollars' worth of free publicity. For example, advertising a program that carries a warning of violence is likely to attract rather than repel young audiences; they are also more likely to express positive attitudes towards the products being advertised during that program (Strauss 1997). The lack of consensus on many of these questions and paradox does not auger well for censorship as a solution to the problem.

MEDIA AS PROBLEM: ADVERTISING

Many of us have a love–hate relationship with the world of advertising. We enjoy being massaged by the message of more, yet bristle at the banality and superficiality that this implies. Much of our uneasiness stems from the sheer volume of advertising we are exposed to: most of us will see millions of ads that cumulatively squander months of our life. It may not be immediately obvious, but whether we think of advertising as a blessing or a curse really depends on our view of society.

Public reaction to advertising is mixed—it is a problem for some, a benefit for others. Many endorse advertising as part of the cost of doing business in a capitalist society. As the link between mass production and mass consumption, advertising is itself big business—the propaganda of capitalism as it is sometimes called. Others are less sanguine about advertising as an industry, holding it responsible for everything from the decline of the west to intellectual dwarfism. Advertising is accused of fostering discontent and creating insecurity by exploiting our fears, hopes, and anxieties. By harnessing these emotions to the purchase of a product, advertising not only exploits an obsession with our self-image, but also encourages weakness and dependency because relief is defined as a purchase away. Worse still, advertising encourages waste, contributes to the disfigurement of the environment, and creates an imbalance in human values. Even so-called green advertising is no solution since the underlying message is the same, that is, use more, not less. An environmentally friendly car, after all, is still a gas-guzzling, steel-bending commodity at odds with the idea of public transit. Even the widely acclaimed slogan "reduce, reuse, and recycle" has been co-opted by big business. Finally, many ads are under criticism for their treatment of minorities. This is a serious enough charge in its own right, but even more ominous in a country that aspires to multicultural ideals.

Advertising in Society: "Generating Discontent"

Sociologists are interested in the social dimensions of advertising. Their interest extends to exploring not only the relationship between society and advertising but the social consequences beyond the commercial aspects. Advertising encompasses a number of functions. Foremost is the need to generate profits by selling products, generating brand name recognition, and fostering corporate legitimacy (Williamson 1978). Central to all advertising is a simple message: For every so-called need, there is a product solution (Andersen 1996). Widely regarded strategies are employed to ensure product amplification in solving this problem, including targeting a market, capturing attention, arousing interest, fostering images, neutralizing doubts, and creating conviction (Fleras 1998).

A distinction between manifest (articulated) and latent (unintended) functions may be useful in understanding what's beneath advertising. A manifest function is to sell a product by symbolically linking consumers with a commodity or service. A social value component is added to the product by glamorizing it through images and messages that purportedly strike a responsive chord. A latent function entails the selling of fantasies. As recently as the mid-twentieth century, ads sold a product by touting its virtues and practical applications. But contemporary advertising sells fantasies by employing images that promise more of everything. By buying into fantasies, people are transported by images into a world of glamour and popularity by way of consumer goods. Advertising is also associated with selling a lifestyle anchored around the pursuit of conspicuous consumption. This association makes it difficult to separate advertising from discourses embedded in capitalist ideology (McAllister 1995). Advertising is ideological in that it represents ideas and ideals that protect and preserve the existing social order while excluding values and views that threaten dominant groups (Andersen 1996). Equating advertising with dominant ideology reinforces its links as enlightened propaganda on behalf of capitalism and confirms the hegemonic properties of advertising. By normalizing consumption within the framework of a capitalist society (McAllister 1995), audiences are actively involved in perpetuating patterns of control.

In short, advertising is much more than a process of moving goods off a shelf. It goes beyond a fact sheet about the product in question. Advertising in the final analysis upholds a philosophy of life commensurate with core societal values about the good life. As propaganda for capitalism, advertising refers to those socially constructed ways of making sense of the world that appear natural and normal. To the extent that every ad says it's better to buy than not to buy, advertising is propaganda; in that every ad reinforces the social ideals of consumerism as inevitable, advertising is propaganda; insofar as advertising teaches us to take pride in our external appearances and the way we present ourselves to others, it is propaganda; and by equating consumerism as a matter of individual choice rather than a socially structured process, advertising is propaganda (see also Jhally 1989).

The cumulative effect of this enlightened propaganda is overwhelming. Consumer advertising exploits audiences by preying on gaps in their self-esteem by way of seductive images and fantasies (popularity, sex appeal, intelligence) that remind us that we are never good enough. These impressions concentrate on distinguishing between who we are and who we would like to be or how we would like others to see us. To be sure, meanings are never imposed unilaterally by an omnipotent authority through an absolute code that gullible audiences absorb (Goldman 1992). Nevertheless the foundational codes of advertising and our absorption into an advertising culture make it increasingly difficult to escape the clutches of a preferred reading. On their own and taken out of context, each ad may not make much difference. Collectively, however, their impact cannot be discounted. For in the final analysis, advertising instils the essential cultural nightmare in our society: the fear of failure and envy of success. Only through conspicuous consumption can we escape this recurrent dilemma by buying into contentment and happiness—at least until the next consumer product comes along to foster further discontent. How then do we explain the thinking behind the Benetton campaign as it sought to violate nearly every rule in the book for effective advertising?

CASE 9-3 Benetton: The Politics of Images

How would you respond to an advertising campaign whose images included a newborn baby covered in blood and still connected by an umbilical cord, a black woman breast-feeding a white baby, a nun and priest kissing, the bloodstained T-shirt and pants of Nicaraguan freedom fighter, flying condoms, copulating horses, and a human torso with "HIV Positive" tattooed on it? Many will recognize these references as ads for Benetton, the enormously successful Italian clothing giant with sales of U.S. $2 billion and 7000 retail outlets on six continents. In spite of (or because of) the controversy generated by these ads, Benetton has become an international household name primarily on the strength of an issue-oriented advertising campaign

based on selling the image of social consciousness (Hume 1994).

There is no question that the graphic images associated with the Benetton campaign violate the fundamental rules of advertising. Most ads operate on the principle of creating needs that can be satisfied only with the purchase of product X (Hume 1994). Audiences are "narcotized" through promulgation of feel-good content into acceptance of a fantasy-filled status quo. Advertising claims for product X have nothing to do with truth but everything to do with deception in the same way that cavorting in a crystal clear stream has nothing to do with the purity of cigarettes but everything to do with positive associations. By contrast, Benetton specializes in

CASE 9-3   Benetton: The Politics of Images (continued)

pricking people's conscience through images that startle or provoke. Oliviero Toscani, the catalyst behind these ads, defends marketing the downbeat or risqué as an effective tool for raising public awareness of social issues (Vivian 1997).

Reactions to this prickly advertising campaign have varied. Some applaud Benetton's boldness and welcome the idea of making the masses more aware of contemporary issues through the medium of advertising. Others recognize that Benetton is selling an image based on attitude rather than anything to do with the product. The ads may convey the message of concern and willingness to be connected with the world at large, yet Benetton is not doing anything different from other ads in terms of pitching colourful images to attract the interest of a specific market. Its "edge" lies in a willingness to make virtue out of vice by capitalizing on the unpredictability of a market that ostensibly eschews conventional ads. Still others are critical of Benetton for capitalizing on the suffering of others as a basis for generating profit (for example, their use of a dying AIDS patient). After all, Benetton exists to make money, and the radical assumption that corporate awareness and risk-taking can be selling points in their own right (Hume 1994) is simply a marketing ploy of sinister value.

Benetton fully appreciates that many are repulsed by these hard-hitting images. That is precisely the point; these ads are not meant for everyone. Benetton has written off the part of market that is

unlikely to buy into these ads, let alone to purchase Benetton products. Benetton ads are aimed at the relatively affluent youth market that responds to unorthodox pitches by putting its principles into spending. For young people who are tired of "fake" ads, Benetton provides a level of anti-advertising that encourages sceptical individuals to feel clever through creation of their own messages about social consciousness. It draws the blasé and sceptical consumer through promotions that simultaneously pander to and smirk at the product in a subversive kind of way. Eager consumers, in turn, are reassured about buying without forsaking principles. And as every leading-edge company recognizes, jumping aboard the youthful bandwagon is like money in the bank. Such an approach is likely to pay dividends by appealing to those markets that are still at an impressionable age, not yet locked into name brands or crippling debts, and experimenting with future buying habits (Strauss 1995).

This focus on customer needs rather than product specifications confirms that advertising is not about selling products. Ads ultimately are about buying an image. Benetton capitalizes on the desire of people in social settings to say something about themselves by the brands they choose (MacDonald 1996). "Badge goods" say something about the user above and beyond the functionality of the product. Such a marketing approach would suggests that green remains the preferred colour for the United Colors of Benetton.

Problems in Advertising

Many of the social problems associated with advertising reflect issues of perennial concern within the industry (Singer 1986). First, there are debates about what should be allowed in advertising. Should the industry tolerate the advertising of products that are legal but at the same time contrary to our concept of the common good? Both the tobacco and alcohol industries depend on advertising, in part because sales are directly related to transforming dubious products into desirable social commodities. However, many regard it as irresponsible to advertise products that are anything but healthy when used as prescribed. In addition to a virtual ban on tobacco advertising through broadcast media in Canada, restrictions have been implemented to reduce the amount of advertising that is overtly sexist or racist. Such ads create an environment inconsistent with the needs of minorities and at odds with an egalitarian society.

Second, questions have been raised about who should be given access to advertising. Corporate sponsorship has been singled out as a questionable style of advertising. In the case of tobacco companies, event marketing ads represent one of the few outlets currently available in Canada. Underwriting symphonies, sports tournaments, and rock tours is a favourite way of reaching out to audiences, while bolstering an image as a good corporate citizen. Corporate sponsorship of "high-brow" events may provide access to a sophisticated market that otherwise would shun conventional advertising. Yet a positive association with an ethically dubious product through corporate links is widely criticized. Even political advertising is frowned on since techniques perfected to sell consumer goods are applied to political candidates, in effect transforming elections into market exercises and voting into consumer options. Still, politicians have little choice except to play along; as Preston Manning, the leader of the Reform party, said in response to questions about his makeover during the 1997 election: "If your teeth are crooked or your voice is strange or your clothes are out of sync, or if you stand out with your old hairdo or the wrong suit, people will not hear what you are saying. I'm interested in getting my message out" (Wong 1997).

Third, there are moves to regulate specific techniques and target groups. Product placements and promotional tie-ins are directed at children and families by subliminally manipulating the subconscious (Madger 1997). For example, many critics are concerned about the use of children's shows—from *G.I. Joe* and *Mighty Morphin Power Rangers* to *Strawberry Shortcake* and *Sailor Moon*—as a carefully orchestrated market strategy involving an imaginary world of consumer goods (Kline 1995). Interestingly, marketers now focus directly on children to take advantage of guilt-ridden, anxious parents. Of special concern has been the use of prepubescent girls to sell perfumes or sunscreens. In a society where child abuse is of worrying proportions, the inclusion of youthful seductresses in ads sends out a mixed message about what is socially acceptable.

The use of women in advertising has long been subject to criticism for its tastelessness and the way in which it perpetuates sexist stereotypes (Lindsay 1997). Women are portrayed in ways that have nothing to do with the product except to confirm that sex sells. They are depicted as obsessed with their appearances (thin, youthful, beautiful, fit, and white) or preoccupied with domestic-maternal activities (cleaner, brighter, and whiter). Not surprisingly, women tend to be defined in terms of their relationships with men (be it husband, father, or brother) or in terms of who they are or how they look rather than what they do. To be sure, women in ads are appearing in a broader range of roles. They no longer are cast only in domestic-maternal situations, but now appear as movers and shakers who need only consumer goods to make a point or stay in style. This concession conceals more than it reveals. Put simply, advertisers have simply expanded the number of products they are pitching at working women. In addition to conventional consumer goods, women now require additional products for coping with the demands of paid employment. The challenge of "having it all" demands a look that is both traditionally feminine yet consistent with all the "right stuff" for career satisfaction and advancement. Women also require more labour-saving devices for unpaid domestic work. When these new developments are coupled with women's guilt and worry about their children, the potential for the female market has expanded, paradoxically, by capitalizing on trends critical of the industry.

Fourth, there are problems with how goods can be advertised. Questions of good taste and community standards come into play. Shock tactics are increasingly employed not only to cut through the commercial clutter of 2000 to 3000 daily messages, but to appeal to hard-to-please audiences. Offending some people through outrageous images is a small price to pay for making the right noises to capture the attention of a lucrative yet difficult teenage market (Saunders 1997). This issue has come to the forefront with one of the more controversial yet successful ad campaigns in recent years. Benetton ads proved a resounding success partly because of their aversion to conventional images that glamorize consumption.

MEDIA AS (ENLIGHTENED) PROPAGANDA

Few would dispute the ability of the media to shape the way we look at the world, how we understand it, and the manner in which we relate to it (see MacLean 1981; Eamon 1987; McQuail 1987). A media-dominated society such as ours elevates electronic and print media to the position of an arbiter in deciding what is right or wrong, acceptable or unacceptable (Troyna 1984). Those in control of the media to a large extent define the beliefs, values, and myths by which we live and organize our lives. They impose a cultural context for framing our experiences of social reality, in the process sending out a clear message about who is normal and what is desirable and important in society (Abel 1997). Our dependence on the media for reality construction assumes even greater relevance in the absence of direct experience. For instance, what we know about Oka has been filtered through several interpretive layers. Without necessarily impugning the integrity of the media, how do we know what really happened during that 78-day stand-off? Whose interpretation made it onto the screen or into print? For many, the whiff of propaganda was real, and perhaps reflected a bias integral to (rather than peripheral to) the media process.

News in totalitarian regimes stands accused of foisting propaganda on the hapless masses. It becomes an arm of the state to promote specific values and doctrines. In contrast, news in Canada is defended as open, free, and exempt from the taint of propaganda. How accurate is this assessment? Is it true that news in fascist societies may be an excuse for brainwashing the masses? Often no attempt is made to dodge this allegation. The former Soviet news agency TASS openly admitted that the role of the press was explicitly pro-Soviet and anti-West. However, a moment's reflection suggests that the press in Canada and the United States is equally one-sided, except that the bias was anti-communist and pro-capitalist. Throughout the Cold War, Soviet moves were interpreted by the Western press as part of a sinister plot for world supremacy. Soviet actions were duly dismissed as aggressive and imperialist, while American military actions were defended as saving the world for democracy. The U.S. invasion of Grenada struck a blow for freedom and democracy; Soviet intervention in Afghanistan was imperialist and self-serving. The "home team" bias is also reflected in reporting on Third World countries. Those sympathetic to Western interests are favourably judged, regardless of their human rights records. Those with ties to unfriendly regimes (such as militant Islamic countries) are exposed to intense scrutiny. The conclusion seems inescapable. News organizations in Canada and the United States appear to endorse the unrestricted exchange of information, but are just as susceptible to being used as a tool for propaganda as the press in a socialist state.

The concept of enlightened propaganda may be helpful in explaining the nature of media–society relations. Propaganda can be defined as a process of persuasion by which the few influence the many. Symbols are manipulated in an organized and one-sided fashion to modify attitudes or behaviour (Qualter 1991). In taking this perspective, we do not equate propaganda with blatant brainwashing or crude displays of totalitarian censorship. Nor do we label propaganda as deliberate lying. Propaganda, we argue, is not necessarily something deliberately inserted into the media. Rather, it is inherent in media rules and operations, in the same way that systemic discrimination reflects the negative but unintended consequences of even well-intentioned rules or procedures (Fleras and Elliott 1991). The net result is the same in both cases: a one-sided interpretation of reality that is of benefit to some, but not to others.

Media objectives are directed towards the goals of "manufacturing consent" and "generating compliance" (Herman and Chomsky 1988). Their very unobtrusiveness in achieving these goals transforms the media into a powerful agent of domination and control. Media images about what is desirable or acceptable are absorbed without much awareness of the indoctrination process. The media fix the premises of discourse by circumscribing the outer limits of what is permissible for discussion. This is accomplished in many ways: by suppressing information at odds with powerful interests and through the perpetuation of stereotypes and ethnocentric value judgments. As Herman and Chomsky (1988) remind us (a) powerful interests can fix the parameters of debate and narrow the range of information; (b) government and the corporate elite have monopolized access to what eventually is defined as news; (c) large advertisers can dictate the terms of newscasting; and (d) media owners can influence what will or will not appear. A similar effect can be attained by the placement of articles and their tone, context, and fullness of treatment. Admittedly, the media do not act in collusion when presenting a monolithic front. Nor are media biases driven by a cabal of conspirators. They disagree with each other, criticize powerful interests for actions inimical to the best interests of society, expose government corruption and corporate greed, and rail against measures to restrict free speech and other rights.

However, internal conflicts of this sort are more apparent than real, suggest Herman and Chomsky (1988). There is disagreement to be sure, but this generally splinters over the means by which to achieve commonly agreed-upon goals. Thus, the illusion of diversity and debate is fostered. Yet few bother to disagree over the underlying agenda, with the result that debates are limited to niggling over details, not substance. Spirited discussion and lively dissension may be encouraged, but only within the framework of assumptions that constitute an elite consensus. The fundamental premises driving our society—the virtues of materialistic progress and competitive individualism—are generally off limits. For example, the media provide a venue for debating the pros and cons of free trade or global competitiveness, but what is conspicuously absent from these discussions are questions about the desirability of capitalism as a system that destroys as it enriches. Also unexamined are the tacit assumptions underlying the interpretation of reality from a predominantly white, male, middle-class, and able-bodied orientation. The dynamics of propaganda, in other words, provide a vantage point for analyzing the media's treatment of reality. This is especially noticeable in their treatment of the news, but no less so when applied to other media outlets such as TV programming or advertising. Under these conditions, the necessity for media literacy becomes even more pressing.

Even though consequences are unintentional, they are not inconsequential. Propaganda can lead to the exclusion of alternate points of view, a reduction in dissent and disagreement, the creation of consensus and compliance with dominant ideologies, and the restriction of free debate. For these reasons, we prefer to see the media as a system of propaganda for securing majority interests without explicitly violating the principles of a free and open press. The cumulative effect of such newscasting is a one-sided view of what is normal, acceptable, and necessary. Redefining the media as propaganda may not be flattering to the industry, but that is how we see the media—especially when applied to media representation of minority women and men in Canada.

CASE 9-4   Media and Minorities: Couched in Compromise

Canada is universally proclaimed as a multicultural society whose commitment to managing diversity at institutional levels is admired and occasionally copied. But these accolades gloss over certain contradictions that obscure discrepancies between the reality and the rhetoric of Canada's multicultural aspirations (Cummins and Danesi 1990). Criticism by academics (Bibby 1990) and authors (Bissoondath 1993/1994) has proliferated, often charging that multiculturalism is irrelevant, wasteful, divisive, counter-productive, expedient, naive, decorative, and misplaced (Fleras and Elliott 1991). Failure by major institutions to incorporate ethnoracial minorities into the institutional mainstream has made them particularly attractive targets. Few institutions, however, with the possible exception of urban police services, have attracted as much criticism and concern as the media for short-changing minority aspirations and needs.

The media have been singled out as being negligent in responding positively to Canada's racial diversity (Siddiqui 1996). As repeatedly observed in sociological literature and research (Fleras 1994), the media have produced a biased and inaccurate coverage of aboriginal peoples and racial minorities, many of whom continue to be insulted, stereotyped, and caricatured. This criticism applies across the board, from employment opportunities for minorities in the media on the one hand to media portrayals of minorities on the other. The media tend to focus on the symptoms of problems, not the causes, thus robbing audiences of any sense of context or rationale (Maracle 1996; Abel 1997). The cumulative impact of such discriminatory behaviour is unmistakably clear. Unless improvements are forthcoming, the media will ruin Canada's potential to rank as a truly multicultural society.

CASE 9-4   Media and Minorities: Couched in Compromise (continued)

What precisely is the nature and scope of this relationship? Certain patterns can be discerned if we look closely at media themes and trends. Put bluntly, people of colour and aboriginal peoples tend to be portrayed as 1) invisible, 2) stereotypes, 3) problem people, or 4) adornments. This interpretation holds up to scrutiny for the most part, whether applied to print or electronic media and at the levels of news, advertising, and television programming.

Minorities as Invisible

Numerous studies have confirmed what many regard as obvious. Canada's racial diversity is poorly reflected in the advertising, programming, and newscasting sectors of the popular media (Fleras 1994). Racial minorities are reduced to an invisible status through "underrepresentation" in programming, staffing, and decision-making. In 1989 Robert MacGregor concluded that women of colour remained largely invisible in Canada's national news magazine *(Maclean's)* when measured by the number and quality of their appearances in ads and articles during a 30-year span. His findings were subsequently reaffirmed by a recent study (Kunz and Fleras 1998). Or consider the case of African-Americans on television: Most TV sitcoms continue to be segregated, there is not a single drama built around black actors (in the belief that there is no sizeable demographic audience for this kind of material), and black-themed programs are demeaning or stereotyped (Braxton 1997). With the

possible exception of *North of 60*, a similar situation applies to Canada with regards to aboriginal peoples.

In general, then, minorities are ignored or rendered irrelevant by the mainstream media. Otherwise coverage is guided by the context of crisis or calamity, involving natural catastrophes, civil wars, and colourful insurgents. While such events do occur, the absence of balanced coverage results in distorted perceptions of minority needs, concerns, or aspirations. This distortion may not be deliberately engineered. Rather, the misrepresentation is systemic in light of media preoccupation with readership and advertising revenues. The flamboyant and sensational are highlighted to satisfy audience needs and sell copy, without much regard to the effects of sensationalism on racial minorities. The media may shun responsibility for their discriminatory impact, arguing that they are reporting only what is news. Nevertheless, the outcome paints an unflattering portrayal of minorities as "subhuman" and hardly worthy of our sympathy or assistance (Steward and Fleras n.d.).

No less disturbing than media "whitewashing" is the absence of diversity in creative positions in the industry. Despite some improvement, minorities are largely excluded from roles as producers, directors, editors, and screenwriters. Fewer still are destined to attain the upper levels of management where key decision-making occurs. One consequence of such exclusion is that minority realities are inevitably refracted through the prism of white-controlled

**CASE 9-4   Media and Minorities:
Couched in Compromise (continued)**

media. For women of colour, the situation is even more perilous. They are doubly jeopardized by "pale male" ideologies that devalue their contributions, distort their experiences, limit their options, and undermine their self-confidence and identity as Canadians. In this type of situation, one might conclude, what is not included by the media is just as significant as what is.

Minorities as Stereotypes

Minorities have long complained of stereotyping by the mainstream media (Gray 1995). Historically, people of colour were portrayed in a manner that did not offend prevailing prejudices. Liberties taken with minority depictions in consumer advertising were especially flagrant. In an industry geared towards image and appeal, the rule of homogeneity and conservatism prevailed. Advertisers wanted their products sanitized and bleached of colour for fear of lost revenue. Images of racial minorities were steeped in unfounded generalizations that emphasized the comical or grotesque. Media stereotyping of minorities tended to fall into a pattern. For example, media stereotypes of aboriginal peoples dwelt on three recurrent themes: "Indians" as *primitive savages* (bloodthirsty barbarians, feisty radicals, or "Indians" with attitude); "Indians" as *primitive pastoralists* (victims of progress, romantic warriors, trusty sidekicks, mystics, ecological trustees); and "Indians" as *problem people* (have "problems" or create "problems"). People from the Middle East were portrayed as sleazy fanatics or

tyrannical patriarchs, while Asians were typecast either as sly and cunning or as mathematical whizzes. Blacks in prime time shows, for the most part, remain stuck as superheroes/athletes or sex-obsessed buffoons surrounded by a host of secondary characters such as hipsters, outlaws, and working class blokes (Cuff 1997).

The cumulative effect is stereotyping of the worst sort. Through stereotypes minorities are put down, put in their place, or put up as props for the edification of the mass audience. Why stereotyping? It simplifies the media process by tapping into a pool of images and ideas as a kind of convenient shorthand. Reliance on preselected images based on fantasies or fears creates readily identifiable frames (tropes) that may impose a thematic coherence to people or events to which audiences can relate (Taylor 1993). Nor should we ignore the wider context of stereotyping. Rather than an error in perception, stereotyping constitutes a system of social control through the internalization of negative images. Stereotypes, for example, are employed to keep aboriginal peoples in their place and out of sight, while massaging white guilt over exploitation (Churchill 1994). With stereotypes, it becomes progressively easier to disregard their humanity and status as a distinct people. Such stereotyping may also contribute to white identities. Imaginary aboriginals are constructed around European prejudice and preconceptions, in the process projecting Euro-Canadian fears and fantasies by defining themselves in relation to others. Insofar as images of the "other" provide a basis for collectively defining mainstream identities, stereotypes may say more about "us" than about "them."

Minorities as Problem People

Persons of colour are frequently singled out by the media as a "social problem," that is, as "having problems" or "creating problems" in need of political attention or scarce national resources. As problem people, they are taken to task by the media for making demands that may imperil Canada's unity or national prosperity. Consider the case of Canada's aboriginal peoples when they are depicted as 1) a threat to Canada's territorial integrity (the Lubicon blockade in 1988 or the Oka confrontations in the summer of 1990) or to national interests (the Innu protest of NATO presence in Labrador), 2) a risk to Canada's social order (the violence between factions at the Akwesasne Reserve or the occupation at Gustafsen Lake, B.C.), 3) an economic liability (the costs associated with massive land claim settlements or recent proposals to constitutionally entrench inherent self-governing rights), and 4) a problem for the criminal justice system (ranging from the Donald Marshall case to police shootings of aboriginal peoples, including the killing of Dudley George at Ipperwash, Ontario) or an unfair player (cigarette smuggling or rum-running across borders).

The combined impact of this negative reporting paints a villainous picture of Canada's first peoples. Time and again they come across as "troublesome constituents" whose demands for self-determination and the right to inherent self-government are inimical to Canada's liberal-democratic tradition. Elsewhere, racial minorities, both foreign- and native-born, are targets of negative reporting. This negativity stems in part from content, as well as from the positioning and layout of the story, length of article and size of type, content of headlines and kickers (phrases that appear immediately after headlines), use of newspeak or inflammatory language, and use of quotes, statistics, and racial origins. Media reporting of refugees usually refers to illegal entries and the associated costs of settlement into Canada. Immigrants are routinely cast as potential troublemakers who steal jobs from Canadians, engage in illegal activities such as drugs or smuggling, and imperil Canada's unity and identity.

Minorities as Adornment

The media tend to portray minorities as mere adornments to society at large. This decorative aspect is achieved by casting minorities in roles that are meant only to amuse or divert the audience. Minorities are paired with exotic and tropical areas, portrayed as famine victims (usually children) in underdeveloped countries, enlisted as congenial boosters for athletics and sporting goods, or ghettoized in certain marketing segments related to rap or hip hop music. Blacks on television are locked into roles as villains or victims or, alternately, as buffoons or folksy sitcom types (Cuff 1991). Rarely is there any emphasis on intellectual or professional prowess,

CASE 9-4   Media and Minorities: Couched in Compromise (continued)

much less recourse to positive role models to which youth can aspire outside of athletics (Cuff 1997). Their impact on society is diffused—and depoliticized—by casting them as children or as subservient adults. They may be viewed only as part of the crowd, or as "walking away from the camera," as jazz pianist Oscar Peterson remarked in describing the presence of black musicians in beer commercials. The typecasting of minorities as decorative elements is distortive. It also has the potential to desensitize the audience by making it more callous and indifferent towards minority experiences in a predominantly white society.

Consider how media have historically portrayed Canada's First Nations as the "other"—a people removed in time and remote in space. This image of aboriginal peoples as the "other" has been filtered through Eurocentric lenses and has ranged in scope, from their eulogization as "noble savages" and "primitive romantics" to their debasement as "villains" or "victims," with the stigma of "problem people" sandwiched in between (see also Blythe 1994). Most portrayals embraced a mythical image of an imaginary warrior who occupied the Plains between 1825 and 1880 (Francis 1992). The standard for generic North American "Indian" could be packaged with ingredients in a so-called "Indian Identity Kit" (Berton 1975) that consisted of the following items, few of which were indigenous to the First Nations prior to European settlement: wig with hair parted in the middle into

hanging plaits; feathered war bonnet; headband (a white invention to keep actors' wigs from slipping off; buckskin leggings; moccasins; painted skin tepee; and tomahawks and bows and arrows. This "one size fits all" image applied to all First Nations, regardless of whether they were Cree, Salish, Ojibwa, or Blackfoot. These images could be further broken down into series of recurrent stereotypes, in effect reinforcing a "seen one Indian, seen 'em all" mentality. Collectively, these images reinforce the notion of First Nations as a people from a different time and place, whose histories began with the arrival of the white man and whose reality only makes sense in terms of interaction with Whites. Collective resistance to their colonization is rarely depicted, although individual acts of protest may be, in effect depoliticizing the concerns and contributions of First Nations to Canada. The net effect is an image of First Nations as "safe, exotic, and somewhere else," as Philip Hayward writes with respect to music industry co-optation of aboriginal artists.

Negative portraits inflict a degree of symbolic and psychological violence on the lives of First Nations people. Their identity as a people is distorted by socially constructed images. Their sense of self-worth plunges through images that remind them of their status as a devalued "other." To be sure, media have begun to invert conventional stereotypes between Whites and First Nations, with much greater emphasis on the beauty and nobility of the indigenous people of the land versus the rapacious greed of white

CASE 9-4 Media and Minorities: Couched in Compromise (continued)

settler colonization (think *Dances with Wolves*). Nevertheless, there is a long way to go, as Maurice Switzer, a member of the Elders' Council of the Mississaugas of Rice Lake First Nations at Alderville, Ontario writes (1997, 21–22):

> The country's large newspapers, TV and radio news shows often contain misinformation, sweeping gener-alizations and galling stereotypes about natives and native affairs. Their stories are usually presented by journalists with little background knowledge or understanding of aboriginals and their communities. . . . As well very few so-called main-stream media consider aboriginal

affairs to be a subject worthy of regular attention.

We live in a world that is pervaded and transformed by images. The control of knowledge and its dissemination through media images is fundamental to the exercise of power in society. This is especially true for minorities, where images provide a window on the historical process by which they have been isolated and marginalized (see Maracle 1996). With images as powerful as they are, it makes it even more imperative for the First Nations to wrest control of representations about who they are and what they want to be.

Why, then, in such a seemingly progressive society have the media lagged behind in offering a fair deal to Canada's minorities? In many ways a no-win situation prevails. Federal and provincial initiatives for inclusiveness in government advertising are criticized as tokenistic. Inclusion of minorities in television programming is shrugged off as little more than a cynical publicity ploy that oversimplifies complex problems. Critics pounce on the media for focusing on the negative and the confrontational, yet are equally critical of excessively upbeat reports. The combination of unrealistic role models and unattainable expectations, it is claimed, may foster resentment and feelings of inadequacy among those who are less fortunate. Bewildered and taken aback by criticism of their efforts, or lack thereof, the media have moved cautiously—much too cautiously, in many eyes—in engaging diversity.

THE NETWORKED SOCIETY

A truism of contemporary society is the pervasive influence of computer-mediated communications in advancing the much touted information age. Emergence of information as basis for wealth creation and reality construction is heralded as one of the more radical innovations in recent times, comparable in social impact with the invention of the wheel or the domestication of plants and animals. The information revolution may have an even more powerful effect on society, given the combination of the speed of its innovations, global scope, direct impact on individuals, and capacity to deal with corresponding problems (Editorial 1996). Contemporary societies appear to be in the throes of a transition from an industrial society to a postindustrial (or information) era. Statistics support this observation. In 1880 50 percent of the American workforce was engaged in agriculture; by the year 2000 the projected total will have dwindled to 2 percent. Manufacturing and commerce, which occupied 36 percent of the workforce in 1880, will have shrunk to 22 percent. Information-related industries (including education) will have escalated from 2 percent in 1880 to an anticipated 66 percent in 2000 (Cleveland 1985). In short, increased reliance on computer-mediated communications has accelerated this shift from an economy rooted in manufacture and industry to one animated by the production and distribution of information as a primary source for creating wealth (Cordell 1991).

The future has begun to reformulate into what many call a "networked" society (Time 1997; Webster 1995). We live in a "wired world" in which human social existence is inseparable from the instantaneous exchange of information across vast distances. Commentators increasingly refer to the "informatisation of social life" (Webster 1995, 1) as a definitive component of the modern world. Financial markets will rarely rely on paper, business will tap into global markets, hackers are poised to defraud computerized accounts, and bureaucrats will cast for ways to balance information with freedom. This global interconnectivity heralds an information revolution whose consequences are transforming how we go about our business in society. Increasing computerization and the power of networked communication is reformulating how society functions through changes in the workplace, family life, and social relations (Johnston 1997).

Those who dismiss the potential of the digital revolution do so at their own peril. Computer-mediated communications are more than a quick-fix solution in search of a problem. They are not simply a machine for doing what print does, only more quickly and less expensively (Max 1994). Nor can they be dismissed as a more efficient instrument for data retrieval or distribution—despite public perception of digital technology as just another labour-saving device for simplifying repetitive tasks. What we have instead is a fundamental shift in how we relate to the world "out there," as radically different in laying the foundations of a new society as the urban industrial system from the feudal agricultural order. Many believe the microchip revolution will do to print culture what the car did to the horse and buggy. Even conventional understandings of mass media communication are recast into sharper relief, in effect confirming McLuhan's observation that the advent of a new medium tends to expose the premises and practices of traditional media (McLuhan 1960; Morris and Ogan 1996). It will also reinforce the view that creation of new media themselves (not just the content) will profoundly reshape individuals and society (Kerckhove 1995). The possibilities are so limitless, in other words, that reducing the discourse about computer-mediated communication to a level of good or bad, progressive or regressive, has the effect of trivializing both process and impact.

The Good: Anarchy Rules

Much has been said in praise—and condemnation—of computer link-ups (Internet), satellite transmission, and microchip technology. Who cannot be impressed by a medium that compresses large amounts of data for rapid transmission via fibre optic cables; according to John Vivian (1997), a total of 50 medium-sized novels per second can be transmitted at nearly the speed of light. Supporters of the information age tout its virtues in enhancing democracy and freedom through delivery of information power to people without prescreening by central authorities.Through this "anarchic" dissemination of information, modern communication systems are able to strip large organizations of their monopolitistic access to information, thereby eroding the hierarchies around which institutions are created and maintained. The potential for broader participation in political and policymaking decisions is also enhanced through two-way flows of information—without the censorious intervention of teachers or controllers of information. This digital era of free-flowing electronic communication will spell doom for the forces of censorship (Barlow 1997)—even as the forces of repression are learning to fight back (Wise 1996). Rather than killing jobs through jobless economies and robotic automation, computer-mediated communications may enhance opportunities at home and abroad by virtue of their ability to harness untapped potential. Finally, in a world where people are losing faith in traditional institutions (from government to religion), computer-mediated communications provide a sense of empowerment that bridges the social gap between ourselves and the world at large (Roberts 1996).

The Bad: Electronic Alienation

Yet detractors remain sceptical. It is one thing to advance the free flow of information; it is quite another to conclude that much of this information is subject to manipulation by elites with hidden agendas who prefer to preserve prevailing patterns of power and privilege while fostering the illusion of power-sharing with the masses. A computer-driven information society may accentuate social fissures that already exist, in effect relegating the computer illiterate and disconnected to the margins (Editorial 1996). Anarchy is not the same as freedom; what is online for some is offside for others. That is, the rich, educated, and English-speaking will monopolize access to the Internet, while freedom from government censorship may pave the way for everything from harassment to disinformation (Wise 1996). Equally worrisome are the commercial implications. The hype behind computer-mediated communications is one thing, reality may be another (Interrogating the Internet 1996). The democratizing of information may play a secondary role to the creation of a vast medium for advertising. In the same way that "TV programming really is just baling wire strung up to exhibit the commercials," (Turner 1997, 63) so also is the Internet a medium for linking audiences with advertisers. Theodore Roszak (1996, 12) writes:

> In contrast, the Web is a creation of the entrepreneurial worldview. It favors high tech effects and attention-grabbing tricks. The key forces behind it are seeking desperately to transform the medium into the new television, the new movies. Their objective is to get millions to look at their site so that they can make a lot of money. This is no secret: The main, ongoing story about the Web is how much profit its backers are (or are not) making. What passes through the medium is bound to be shaped by those values, not by any significant regard for quality, truth, or taste.

In addition, there are problems of access, interaction, privacy, regulation, and copyright. Damage that hackers can do to Web sites (from corporate secrets to national security systems) is widely known and feared (Ward 1997). The unfettered flow of digital information complicates the preservation of cultural borders—to the detriment of national decision-making (see Shields 1996). The proliferation of hate sites with their espousal of neo-Nazi white supremacist dogmas is proving no less disturbing (Visanta 1996). Computer-mediated communications can also lead to loss of freedom, individual surveillance, invasion of privacy, centralization and control of power, and reduction of human contact. Computer technologies may be the most powerful forces at work today, in other words, but they are also among the most isolating for a species that is social by nature and has evolved through interaction in primary communities. The hidden costs of deepening inequality, social alienation, and community dissolution cannot be taken lightly (New Internationalist 1996).

The Banal: "Information Is Not Knowledge"

Not everyone agrees with this assessment of good or bad. In arguing that both positions are overstated, they tend to define computer-mediated communications as trivializing to the point of banality. Of particular note are doubts about the content that accompanies digitalized information. Neil Postman (1995) points to our movement from a society with an information deficiency to one mired in a glut of decontextualized data untied to human needs.The end result is more and more information, but less and less knowledge (Webster 1993). Yet knowledge without context equals noise (Interrogating the Internet 1996). Without a coherent or meaningful framework, we may become more informed about economic indicators but less knowledgeable about assumptions that underlie the economy, particularly about work, wealth creation, and human dignity (Roszak 1994). Worse still, the information produced by multimedia may constitute a kind of "garbage" (GIGO—garbage in/garbage out) by virtue of its sheer volume, lack of context, incoherence, and meaninglessness. The dissociation between information and ideas, between data and knowledge, is likely to widen further as computer-savvy children equate research with little more than a point and click. Even more distressing is the loss of learning through firsthand experience, as lamented by Stephen Talbot in *The Future Does Not Compute*:

> The most critical element in the classroom is the immediate presence and vision of the teacher, his [her] ability to inspire, his devotion to truth and reverence for beauty, his moral dignity—all of which the child observes and absorbs in a way impossible through electronic experience. Combine this with the excitement of a discovery shared among peers in the presence of the actual phenomenon occasioning the discovery (a caterpillar transforming itself into a butterfly . . .) and you have the priceless matrix of human growth and learning.

How do we reconcile the paradox of increased information while acknowledging how this glut of "raw" data may diminish rather than enhance independent creative thinking (King 1995)?

The In Between

In between these extremes are those who dispute some of the overhyped excesses of digital media, without necessarily disclaiming the social benefits of modem technology. This intermediate position acknowledges the inherent ambiguities in computer-driven information. Computer-mediated media are increasingly the norm in our society; yet this technology is useful when informative, user-friendly and interactive, but regressive when intensifying existing patterns of one-way, top-down interaction (Gooderham 1997). Like any technology, the Internet possesses contradictory impulses towards liberation and domination, colonization or emancipation, oppression or resistance (Interrogating the Internet 1996). The same digital forces that compress data may coerce people; they may control yet provide a catalyst for resistance. In other words, every new link to the Internet in a plugged-in world has the potential for good or evil. Perception is key: Those who fear the government denounce the Internet as yet another arrow in the quiver of Big

Brother; those who fret about anarchy are concerned by the potential of Internet to attract everyone from mild eccentrics to cold-blooded terrorists (Stephenson 1997). Case 9-5 puts these issues to the test by examining how computer-mediated technologies hold both promise and peril for developing countries.

CASE 9-5   **Globalizing the Internet**

Communication is central to the development of any society. Control of the media constitutes an essential first step in managing the public in a way that bolsters national interests, however narrowly these may be defined. This is especially true of Canada, where media communication has been routinely employed as a basis for society-building. In Third World countries, the impact and contribution of the media have been mixed at best, destructive at worst. The introduction of digital technology and computer-mediated communications is likely to intensify existing social cleavages thanks to differential access, controlling content, and cultural vulnerabilities.

If computer-mediated technologies constitute tools of empowerment to maximize participation, consensus, information distribution, and self-directed development, it stands to reason that developing countries must have some say in the content or process. Yet the transfer of information technology from north to south has not been universal or equitable. A pattern of dependency has been re-established along traditional colonialist lines (Searle and Lilley 1995). In cases where such systems are imposed without much local input or control, the effects have been disruptive to say the least. Encouraging societies to employ computer-mediated technologies often reinforces their dependency and reliance on the north. Once on line, local cultures often have little choice except to adapt to this globalizing force through creation of more opportunities for Western business, in the same way that television reinforces unnecessary needs and assimilation of cultures. Unforeseen intrusions by the media wreak havoc on the stability and integrity of traditional cultures and social patterns—a concern not necessarily shared by change-oriented and technologically driven societies in the West with decades of experience or historical precedents.

As well, the dominance of English is problematic. With the sudden explosion of worldwide interest in the Internet, English is rapidly emerging as the *lingua franca* of the online set. That may be a problem for the vast majority who do not speak English but who want to tap into the resources and potential of the information age (Pollack 1995). Computer link-ups outside of English-speaking countries encounter difficulties because non-Latin alphabets are rarely translated into software. Africa in particular finds itself under extreme duress; poorly developed infrastructures may account for the gap, while the large number of languages and alphabets complicate the process of electronic communication. Additional fears exist that an English-dominated computer technology will inundate national states since few protections exist to defend sovereign borders. While few are bold enough to predict the collapse of the nation-state, it remains to be seen what effect information technology will have on the bundle of sovereignties that comprise unitary states (Drohan 1996). With entrenchment of English as the international language of business and science, other languages may decline as preferred systems of communication, while cultures will be further eroded by the dominance of English-driven cyberspace. Equally certain is the inevitability of confrontation between those who believe in the sanctity of the sovereign state and advocates of cyberspace who endorse free-wheeling realities beyond law or regulation.

Not all is doom and gloom. The Developing World is not immune to the benefits of computer technology. An ability to communicate local grievances to the outside world may (a) increase international support for their cause, (b) improve mobilization of local resources, and (c) diminish the capacity of the central authorities to act in a unilateral or hostile fashion (Alam 1996). Increasingly, conflicts are being conducted through the Internet, in effect changing the contours of guerrilla action and civic protest. Where once freedom fighters lugged around AK-47s and delivered battlefield news in rolled pieces of paper carried by runners across treacherous mountain passes, the postmodern revolutionary carries a laptop to plug into the Internet (Vincent 1996). Rebel groups from the IRA to Peru's Shining Path have discovered the information highway as a cost-effective way to promote their cause, disseminate information about their side without state interference, raise funds, and sway public opinion.

For example, Ya Basta is the Internet homepage of the Zapatista National Liberation Army that rose up in arms in the state of Chiapas on New Year's Day 1994. Ya Basta serves as a Web site that articulates insurgent demands for greater democracy and indigenous rights. Despite a cessation of open confrontation, the information war between the government and the Zapatistas is escalating, with the Internet as a key theatre of conflict. The "netwar" has enabled disparate opponents of the Mexican government to communicate and plan strategy with the Chiapas. Even more importantly it is has enabled Zapatista supporters to rally around the flag while preventing the Mexican army from openly crushing the rebels (Globe and Mail, July 9, 1995). To date, the government has stumbled in the war of words because of hesitancy in articulating their version of events on the Internet. That may change shortly as the government awakens to the power of the Internet as an axe that can swing both ways.

Towards a New (Cyber)World Order

What will happen to societies because of this revolution in communication? In theory, computer-mediated technologies imply an infrastructural potential for a distinct global culture that transcends the concept of the nation-state. It also promises an intensely democratized society in which information is readily accessible and interchangeable. Yet freedom for individuals may pose problems for the integrity of nation-states as claimed by John Perry Barlow (1996, 43), ex–Grateful Dead lyricist and co-founder of the Electronic Frontier Foundation for the protection of civil liberties in cyberspace:

> The real issue is control. The Internet is too widespread to be easily silenced by any single government. By creating a seamless global-economic zone, borderless and unregulatable, the Internet calls into question the very idea of a nation-state. No wonder nation-states are rushing to get their levers of control into cyberspace while less than 1% of the world's population is on-line.
>
> What the Net offers is the promise of a new social space, global and antisovereign, within which anybody, anywhere can express to the rest of humanity whatever he or she believes without fear. There is in these new media a foreshadowing of the intellectual and economic liberty that might undo all the authoritarian powers on earth.

The new world order is organized instead around the computer-mediated principle of "unfettered exchange of information on a worldwide basis" (McKie 1991, 473). The declining significance of borders may be a problem for countries such as Canada, with their concern for control over communication and broadcasting (Pike 1995). But controlling information is increasingly difficult in the borderless world of multimedia. The Karla Homolka trial in 1993 revealed as much. Despite a gag order, details of the trial were widely circulated on the Internet, in effect raising the question not only of what to control but how to control it when millions are surfing the Internet unimpeded (McKie 1991). The fluidity of such information flow poses a peril for national sovereignty.

Yet these very threats to its existence may provide a clue to national survival. Creation of digital cultural environment may prove beneficial for societies when flexibility is key to the future (McLuhan and Powers 1989). The rigidity associated with a strong identity and equally strong commitments and goals may prove a downfall in a world of diversity and change. Social systems that insist on rules from above are likely to experience such intense internal and external pressures that the dismemberment of society is a possible outcome. The collapse of the Berlin Wall and the demise of the Soviet Union are but two examples of how modern media can assault the sovereignty of the state and the sanctity of its borders.

Conversely, societies that encourage rules from below (anarchy) are more likely to flourish when challenged by the "bottom up" demands of a computer-mediated technology. That kind of resiliency comes with a cost; the promise of power-sharing and discourse with a spirited electorate can become extremely unwieldy in societies with a carefully contrived system of checks and balances for protection from unruly masses (Grossman 1995). But in a rapidly changing world, what once were strengths can become weaknesses, and weaknesses can become strengths. As a country with many border lines, Canada may well possess the resources and the resourcefulness to withstand the stresses and strains inherent in a networked reality.

SUMMARY

1. The media are a powerful, socially constructed force with the potential to destroy or enhance, promote or retard. To appreciate the magnitude and scope of the media as a social problem, it is important to become literate about what the media are, what they are doing to us, and what their societal implications are. Without a knowledge of the media's operations and logic, we shall not be able to judge whether there is a net benefit or detriment to Canadian society in the way the media conduct their business.

2. Reactions to media are mixed. Some regard the media as the cornerstone of an open, sophisticated, and democratic society. Others see the media as a diabolical plot to pulverize the moral basis of society. In consequence or by intent, the media are thought to stifle, destroy, alienate, and narcotize through constant exposure. Those in between argue that media are both good and bad, given their complex and contradictory characters, depending on the circumstances and criteria. Finally, a few are willing to dismiss the media as neither good nor bad but as an inevitability for getting on with the reality of life.

3. From a social problem perspective, the media can be interpreted as a form of propaganda with respect to process and outcome. This is especially true when analyzing the logic behind the dynamics of newsmaking, advertising, and television programming.

4. The concept of newscasting is examined from a social problem perspective. What eventually becomes the news does not arrive at a particular media outlet with clearly marked labels that everybody can agree on. Nor is news a random reaction to disparate events by detached professionals. News is properly interpreted as a socially constructed reality that reveals more about the industry and its operations, values, and audience than about what is going on in the world. There is a bias inherent in all news that results from commercial demands, and there are some important differences between the way news is handled on TV and in print.

5. With print news emulating the visually oriented bias of TV news, accusations of news as little more than mere infotainment (information + entertainment) are increasingly difficult to refute or dispel. It is also evident that news is used for propaganda purposes, even in Western democratic countries with a supposedly free press.

6. The logic behind television programming revolves around the code of restricting program material to that which is simple, safe, and familiar. Media distortions of reality are particularly evident because of this formulaic process.

7. There is a growing concern in Canadian society over explicit sex and gratuitous violence in the media. Research to date suggests a "probable" link between TV and violence, although the relationship may be indirect rather than causal, entail social rather than psychological variables, and encompass attitudes rather than behaviour.

8. The issue of censorship, especially in respect to pornography and the right to free expression, may rank among the most contentious of all issues in a liberal and multicultural society. But censorship is a routine and common practice in society, and this means that restrictions on free speech are relative rather than absolute. The politics of censorship invoke struggles by competing groups to define where the line will ultimately be drawn.

9. In a consumer-oriented society, media dynamics are driven by the demands of advertising. A reliance on fantasies and images as primary selling tools underscores the subliminality at the core of all advertising.

10. By their very nature, the media invent a reality that not only distorts the world around us, but reflects the priorities of vested interests. The media create a climate (a cultural frame of reference) in which certain lines of action are defined as acceptable or desirable. Media portrayals of women and minorities, both past and present, are indicative of this socially constructed character.

11. Canada's racial minorities and aboriginal peoples have been misrepresented, underrepresented, and overrepresented by mainstream media. The depiction of minorities is focused around four basic patterns: they are rendered invisible, treated as problem people, defined as stereotypes, or dismissed as adornments. Efforts to "mainstream" minorities into the media tend to gloss over some very real barriers to solutions.

12. The digital revolution created by computer-mediated technologies has elicited a variety of responses. Those who look at the bright side are opposed to those who prefer to dwell on the less positive. In between are those who are not sure or who appreciate both benefits and drawbacks.

13. Computer media provide exciting new possibilities in the processing of information that is relatively free and open. They may also deepen the patterns of alienation in society while destroying our capacity to think and analyze with a deluge of facts.

14. The developing world may be falling behind the English-speaking world in its capacity to harness computer mediated technologies as a basis for communication.

WORK AND WORKPLACES

DID YOU KNOW?

- Canada's official unemployment rate dropped to 9.1 percent in mid-1997. But the true unemployment figure may be closer to 20 percent if we take into account part-time workers who want full-time work, young adults who are staying in school because of lack of job prospects, older workers who have "voluntarily" retired, and people who have stopped looking for work altogether. That one in five want to work but are unable to do so is a serious social problem.

- Canada's total revenue sources for 1997–98 amount to $137.8 billion. Personal income tax contributes to just under half of the total ($66.5 billion) whereas corporate tax contributions (at a time of record-breaking profits) amount to around 11.5 percent ($16.2 billion).

- About one quarter of Canada's labour force are working 9 hours a week overtime; meanwhile, at least 20 percent of the labour force are either unemployed or working part-time and would like full-time work.

- The International Federation of Robotics says the world's robot population now numbers 630 000. On the assumption that each robot replaces 4 jobs, over 2.5 million people are out of work because of robotic automation.

- The unemployment rate for young adults age 15 to 24 is nearly 17 percent, or twice the rate for adults. In the past decade, adult employment has risen by 2.1 million jobs but youth employment has fallen by 600 000 jobs. If youth were participating in the labour force at the same rate as in 1986 (rather than staying in school or dropping out of the labour market altogether), the youth unemployment rate would be closer to 26.7 percent.

- Is "downsizing" a move to improve global competition or an excuse to cut costs and bolster profits by shedding excess labour. Wall Street tends to reward companies that announce large-scale layoffs, according to the October 1996 issue of *Report on Business*. Xerox Corporation's announced 10 000 job cut in 1995 resulted in a stock price surge of 7 percent. Shares of Moulinex SA soared 21 percent when it announced a workforce reduction of 20 percent.

- From 1990 to 1992 men accounted for 90 percent of the 325 000 predominantly construction/manufacturing jobs that were lost. Between 1992 and 1996 men gained 54 percent of the 835 000 net employment. For the period as a whole, women picked up 69 percent of the 510 000 net employment. Yet nearly 70 percent of these jobs were part-time (less than 30 hours per week) and 75 percent fell into the self-employed category.

- Despite talk of "breaking the glass ceiling," women continue to be concentrated in traditional fields of clerical work, nursing, and teaching. Overall, 85 percent of employed women in 1991 were in the service sector, with more than 3 in 10 in the lower tiers of retail and consumer services. Women occupied 81 percent of clerical jobs, which consumed 29 percent of the female labour force.

- The economy continues to emit mixed signals. While a record-shattering 14.4 million Canadians reported employment income in 1995, median income dropped to $20 600, or $1000 less in real income since 1990. Additional job trends for 1997 include the following reversals: (a) increases in full-time employment compared to part-time jobs (in June 1997 94 000 full-time jobs were created but 42 000 part-time jobs were lost), (b) private sector increases at the expense of the self-employed, (c) large increases in manufacturing jobs (at $2.18 billion, manufacturing payrolls are at their highest since February 1990), and (d) half of new job increases in Quebec and the Atlantic provinces (see *Toronto Star*, July 12, 1997).

THE PROBLEM

"The 20th century shall be the century of Canada and Canadian development" (Sir Wilfrid Laurier, 1904).

"Some are lucky, some are unlucky. That's life" (Prime Minister Jean Chrétien, offering "solace" to young unemployed, 1996).

To participate in contemporary society is to be surrounded by large-scale organizations from cradle to grave. We are born into the complex organization of a hospital, educated in a series of institutions, often take a job in a large corporation, pursue political or leisure activities in organized settings, engage in government bureaucracies, and are laid to rest according to the regulations of a religious institution. Often our identity and self-esteem are constructed around the strength of our involvement with institutions of one sort or another.

This observation should surprise no one. Everything we do and use is somehow connected with organizational structures, with the result that our lives and life chances are intimately bound up in what Robert Presthus (1978) calls an "organizational society." Institutions and organizations exert a powerful impact on society because of their size, complexity, and pervasiveness. Many of the goods and services that we normally associate with the good life are produced and distributed by organizations. Organizations impart a degree of permanence and durability in a world of change and uncertainty, yet their costs can be exorbitant when measured in personal or social terms. Organizations and workplaces have a way of separating us from what we do and who we are. Bureaucratic organizations are known to stifle democracy and freedom at a time when these fragile commodities are most needed.

Overestimating the power and autonomy of organizations is as foolhardy as underestimating their impact. The power of organizations can never be in doubt in light of the resources at their disposal for setting agendas and establishing control. Yet many organizations are as vulnerable as individuals to the forces of change. They find themselves continually subjected to a barrage of demands, regulations, pressures, and trends. Internal pressures for change stem from increasingly alienated workers in search of empowerment to harried CEOs under the gun to maximize profit. External pressures arise from equally disgruntled clients who are unhappy with the quality of goods or services. Radical shifts in the business environment because of globalization have also prompted changes. The moorings that secured convention and prediction have been cast adrift. The search for simple solutions to complex problems is tempting, but misguided and dangerous. Reliance on outdated forms of thinking—with their emphasis on linearity, oppositions, individualism, and hierarchy—also impedes our ability to solve problems in a world of confusion and contradiction (Rothenberg 1992). In coping with these challenges as expeditiously as possibly, organizations have responded with a package of concessions for renewal and reform. Three dimensions reinforce this perception of organizations as sites of social problems: transforming organizations, diversifying the workplace, and rethinking work.

Transforming Organizations

For organizations, the winds of change constitute a menacing and disruptive component of institutional life. These forces exert a powerful impact both internally at the level of group dynamics and externally through institutional links and customer relations. In the midst of a free market revolution, organizations and workplaces are under protracted pressure to change—in part because of intense global competition, in part because of global movements of capital and labour. Rules and priorities that once anchored the organization while securing a blueprint for success are increasingly irrelevant in an era of uncertainty. A restructuring of the workplace has flattened out the organizational pyramid. Layers of management have been peeled away, thus paving the way for more horizontal forms of decision-making and power-sharing. The combination of worker demands and consumer dissatisfaction has compelled companies to debureaucratize from within or lose flexibility in coping with changes.

New ways of thinking about organizations have also evolved (Chorn 1991; Capon et al. 1991). Revisions are apparent in how we think and talk about organizational entities with respect to structure, functions, and process. At one time complex organizations were dominated by simple physical tasks that entailed mechanistic mindsets for maximizing productivity (Chorn 1991). Decision-making and problem-solving were defined by pattern and predictability. A managerial perspective prevailed, with its commitment to rationality, goal pursuit, and causality. Management–labour relations were organized around the principle that managers managed and workers worked. Such a clearly defined pecking order may not have been perfect, but it did simplify organizational relations. The external world was intrinsically ordered as well. Stable markets and reliable suppliers made it relatively easy for each organization to carve out its own niche.

Organizations in the 1990s are no longer characterized by the illusion of stability or order. Complex and contradictory forces have exerted a profound impact on organizational design and workplace practices. The era of paternalistic management–worker relations is drawing to an end. So too is the notion of lifelong employment and corporate loyalty because of downsizing, restructuring, and delayering. Reliable suppliers and predictable markets are virtually a thing of the past. Instead of patterned and predictable environments, there are fluid and dynamic contexts that seldom lend themselves to regulation or control. Direct cause–effect relations are now viewed as naively simplistic compared with the principles of multiple causation and complicated feedback loops. Nor is there an end in sight: The mantra of economic rationalism—competition cures everything—has emerged as an all-embracing ideology that justifies any market-friendly transformation, however disruptive it may prove. As cryptically put by one author, if it moves, regulate it; if it generates losses, sell it; if you can't tell what it is doing, contract out or convert to user-pays (Stewart 1997).

Diversifying the Workplace

In addition to pervasive social change, organizations are also coping with the challenges of diversity both inside and outside the workplace. The movement of women into the labour force, as well as into the corridors of power, is one dimension of this surging diversity. Another sign of the times is the expanding presence of visible minorities. People of colour now comprise over 9 percent of Canada's population, with the majority concentrated in the largest urban areas. More importantly, as a group they are no longer content to linger by the sidelines. They too want recognition and participation, even if demanding equality means getting "uppity." Workplace inclusion of people with disabilities and aboriginal peoples has further diversified the organizational mosaic, and brought pressure for formulating innovative ways of engaging this diversity.

The focus on diversity goes beyond the simple "celebration" of workplace differences. Rules for *entitlement* (who gets what, and why) are being revised in response to minority demands for a bigger slice of the corporate pie. The concept of institutional accommodation is not limited only to maximizing productivity by capitalizing on international contacts. Nor does it simply entail providing services that are culturally sensitive and community-based. Rather, the crux of the challenge rests with incorporating diversity as a legitimate and integral component of the multicultural workplace by meshing it into institutional structures and corporate bottom lines. Central to this commitment is the removal of discriminatory barriers that distort the processes of recruitment, promotion, training, and compensation. Moves towards increased inclusiveness through employment equity initiatives for improving minority access, representation, and equitable treatment are widely acclaimed yet bitterly resented.

As well-intentioned as these initiatives might be, moves to engage diversity pose a challenge for existing structures and vested interests. Women and minorities want to be seriously appraised as productive and vital members of the workforce. They are anxious to be taken seriously for what they do rather than for what they are or how they look. Yet the process of transforming workplace structures along minority and gender lines is fraught with ambiguity, tension, and hostility. A diversified workforce sounds good in theory, but differences are just as likely to divide and frustrate as they are to empower and engage. Entrenched interests have not taken kindly to proposals for institutional reform. The largely unintended consequences of seemingly neutral structures and procedures have a way of penalizing those who fall outside the "inner circle." Many companies balk at implementing the spirit of "mainstreaming diversity" and content themselves with implementing just enough of the letter of the law to avoid court actions or human rights complaints. Still, the capacity for engaging with diversity will no longer be seen as a luxury or an option but as a necessity in terms of career enhancement and organizational survival.

Rethinking Work

Organizations and workplaces are undergoing change with respect to what they look like (structure), what they are supposed to do (function), and what they really do (process). The corporate air is filled with slogans about the "new economy," "the information highway," "total quality," "empowerment," "total quality management," "quality circles," "downsizing," "restructuring," and "delayering." In contrast, more traditional bromides such as "seniority," "job security," "company loyalty," and "benefits" and "pensions" are rapidly fading from memory. Historically, people's lives have revolved around work, but human labour is gradually being purged from the economic process because of computer-mediated automation and corporate reorganization (Rifkin 1995). For those with skills and connections, work is not necessarily a process for pay as much as an opportunity for challenge or for taking control of a project (Chiose 1997). For others, work will remain a dreary dead end activity— from fast food floor to white collar factory workers (for example, telephone operators who handle customer calls)—with few rewards and fewer opportunities (Clement 1997). Others still will be lucky to get a job. Lifetime working patterns may entail a combination of contract work for a variety of companies, interspersed with periods of unemployment. A split-labour force is truly in place: some have so much work that personal and family life suffers, while others have so little work that they also experience deprivation at personal and social levels (Gwyn 1996). Nor is there the prospect of much improvement, given the realities of a deficit-cutting government and a restructuring corporate sector. A corporate reluctance to risk quarterly earnings by investing in long-term growth is also an inhibiting factor. The reality for most, as the Canadian Council of Social Development reminds us, is temporary jobs (short-term or contract), most of which promise low wages, little security, and few benefits (Kennedy 1996).

The combination of workplace diversity and organizational flux has redefined the notion of work and workplace (Lerner 1997). Organizations are rapidly being transformed from structures organized around jobs to fields of work needing to be done (Lynch 1997). In some cases, the rules have changed so much as to invert conventional wisdom; as a result, what once were virtues are now vices, and vice versa. Much of the uncertainty can be attributed to changes in the rules that formerly governed "how work was done around here." Work is rapidly disappearing in certain quarters as automation kicks in and corporations kick out. Changes are also evident in the nature of working. The prospect of *job permanence* is vanishing in reaction to organizational restructuring, managerial delayering, and workforce downsizing. The days of lifetime job security are numbered. Once cherished as a mark of virtue, corporate loyalty is now likely to caricatured as a sign of weakness, lack of ambition, or a stalled career. The interplay of mechanization and predatory corporate philosophies make mockery of any plans for steady and secure employment. That in its own right is not a problem. Problems are created when such arrangements fail to capitalize on the full potential of each individual. It also becomes problematic when society at large is robbed of contributions by all its members.

This chapter addresses the topic of work and organizations from a social problem perspective. The chapter is organized around four major themes.

1) Workplaces and organizations are social problems in their own right because of the way they are designed and defined. Workplaces are particularly problematic sites for those who are exposed to dangerous or demeaning jobs.

2) Organizations are responsible for creating social problems because of their negative impact on contemporary workplaces. Consider changes in the style of labour–management relations. While promising in some cases, these participatory models of decision-making have yet to prove that they can thrive within traditionally restrictive workplace environments.

3) Organizations and workplaces are themselves sites of social problems. They are especially vulnerable to external forces. Organizations are under pressure to democratize labour–management relations, improve productivity, reduce the rigidity and hierarchy of internal structures, empower workers and satisfy clients, forge cooperative relations with other organizations, and enhance global competitiveness without forsaking their image as good corporate citizens. Juggling these competing demands poses a problem in its own right.

4) Solutions to the problems of work and organizations often generate conditions that create more problems. This neverending spiral of problem-solution-problem may be typical of the social problem field in general, but is particularly typical in the workplace, where solutions for some (in the form of labour-saving automation) often create problems for others (labour-shedding practices and unemployment).

In keeping with earlier themes, our interests lie in the social dimensions of work and organizations, with special emphasis on the evolving relationship between the workplace and society. Towards that end, organizations are not interpreted as concrete "things" in their own right, but as "sites" of "contestation" where things happen in response to internal forces and external pressures. Much can be gleaned by approaching workplaces as an ideological battleground involving competitively different groups in a constant struggle for control of the agenda. Diverse forces, such as labour and management, with varying amounts of power and resources, are locked in perpetual combat—competing when pushed, but cooperating when necessary. Since each group seeks ascendancy by imposing its own agenda and solutions, organizational realities are seen as lying somewhere between the poles of chaos and regulation, between structure and agency, between continuity and change, and between resistance and control. Such an interpretation may not yield elegant models of organizations and neat workplace flowcharts, but it does capture the essence of organizational dynamics during periods of change, diversity, and uncertainty.

FROM CRISIS TO CHALLENGE

> Work is about daily meaning as well as daily bread. For recognition as well as cash; for astonishment rather than torpor; in short, for a sort of life rather than a Monday through Friday sort of dying... (Studs Turkel, *Utne Reader,* May/June 1995).

Work has been around since the beginning of time. It remains the most essential of human activities in providing both physical sustenance and the basis for personal identity and self-esteem (Krahn and Lowe 1994). But until the nineteenth century, people did not have jobs; more accurately, they *did* work (Keegan 1996). As pointed out by William Bridge (1995), author of *Job Shift,* work was not something that a factory provided in exchange for pay. Rather, work was an activity that had to be done at a certain time and place. It often was difficult to disentangle work from the rest of a person's life. But organized work (having a job) evolved with the Industrial Revolution and the mechanization of the productive process. Even then, barely 50 percent of the workers in the industrialized world belonged to a company by the turn of this century. Workplaces were small, family-owned, and rudimentary in organization (Campbell 1996). It was not until the early 1970s that labour-intensive industrialization raised the job figure to 90 percent of the workforce.

But the concept of work has continued to evolve. No sooner had the culture of full-time work begun to take hold—including the notion of a full-time job for life, career paths, and corporate loyalty in exchange for job security—than countervailing forces combined to dismantle the very nature of work and working (Keegan 1996). Both companies and government embarked on a labour-shedding process that eliminated jobs in response to automation and digital technology, particularly those that entailed repetitive aspects of production. In a market-oriented climate that defined greed as good, General Motors Ltd. may have posted the largest profit of any private company in the history of Canada, but that did not deter it from slashing thousands of jobs in the process (Hargrove 1996). The end result of this corporate downsizing is a bifurcated workforce; on the one hand, there is a core of a permanent employees (if stressed out and demoralized by pressures to produce or else), and on the other hand, there is an outer perimeter of part-time or contract workers with little opportunity for security or success. The "work-rich" have secure jobs with continuous, high-value employment as a function of their skills; the "work-poor" are relegated to semi-employment status with generally lower wages and few benefits (Gwyn 1996).

A World without Work

Jobs have become an endangered species with the onslaught of the information age, the robotic economy, and new technologies. To be sure, not all jobs will disappear. A knowledge-based economy will produce jobs for scientists, engineers, software analysts, and biotechnology researchers (Rifkin 1995). Those in the caring sector (from teachers to caregivers for the elderly) should manage to hold on. But there is little hope for the masses or the drop-outs. No amount of retooling or upgrading will help the millions who are let go as automation penetrates every aspect of the productive process. Blue collar workers may become obsolete in a workerless world, with massive unemployment of a magnitude never yet seen as computer-guided machines replace most workers from shoe clerks to surgeons (Rifkin 1995).

The creation of a two-tiered economy has very serious repercussions for society at large. Companies that downsize ("dumbsize") rarely perform better, except on the stock market, but may suffer from absenteeism, cynicism, creative blockage, demoralization, passive resistance, open sabotage, and risk-taking aversion (Robertson 1997). Those employees clever enough to seize the opportunity will prosper at the expense of the less fortunate, while rupturing the sense of community at the core of a sustainable society (Stewart 1997). A large reservoir of underemployed (or never employed) not only intensifies the gaps between rich (skilled) and poor (unskilled), but the balance of decision-making powers is tilted towards owners and employers. A recipe for social disaster is created as well, insofar as the disenfranchised (many of whom are young males) may see few options except crime and violence for no other reason than having nothing to lose when nothing is at stake (Keegan 1996). As Jeremy Rifkin says, "If the talent, energy, and resourcefulness of hundreds and millions of men and women are not redirected into constructive ends, civilization will continue to disintegrate into a state of increased lawlessness from which there may be no easy return" (quoted in Goar 1996). Finally, the very existence of capitalism may be threatened when nobody can buy what workerless factories produce. What indeed will happen when we don't want what they have, and they can't buy what we sell (see Rifkin 1995)?

The need to rethink work and working stems from a variety of factors. The gradual decline of smokestack industries may be attributed to the internationalization of capital and labour as profit-hungry companies seek offshore locations to reduce production costs. Introduction of a computer-driven microelectronic revolution has put the onus on information processing as a source of wealth creation. Computers may be creating more jobs than they have destroyed, but this technology is undermining unskilled workers in repetitive jobs (Little 1997). Even new skills or retraining may not help if there is a dearth of jobs. The forces of automation and digital technology have also undermined the availability of repetitive work, that is, work that can be done by a machine without coffee breaks or costly dental plans. Conventional wisdom advocates getting rid of costly workers in the rush to improve productivity and profits. As Michael Dunkerley writes in his book *The Jobless Economy*, "People are now the most expensive optional component of the production process. . . . People are now targetted for replacement as soon as the relevant technology is developed to replace them" (quoted in Gwyn 1996, F3). Yet no new sector appears to be emerging to soak up excess labour from the three conventional engines of economy—manufacturing, service, and agricultural. In contrast with the Industrial Revolution, which may have eliminated the need for certain kinds of labour, the introduction of computer automation is removing the need for either brain or brawn power (Keegan 1996).

A Solutionless Problem?

> Part of the problem is the very American mind-set that there's a solution to every problem, and then an end to it (Bruce Hoffman, American Director of the Centre for the Study of Terrorism and Political Violence, St. Andrews University, Scotland. Quoted in Dickey (1997)).

Are we at the end of work or just at the end of particular kinds of jobs? A globally based, knowledge-driven economy cannot possibly provide work for everyone, yet one should never underestimate the resiliency of a free enterprise system. Is there a solution to this problem? Murray Campbell (1996) observes that, notwithstanding the time and effort expended in freeing people from the drudgery of work, we still have no idea of how to deal with additional leisure time. We have even less idea of what to do with the thousands of workers who have been cut adrift from the rhythms of the world, unsure of how to make their contribution. Some have suggested there is no problem. Because policymakers believe that full employment is neither attainable nor desirable, they propose a "natural" rate of unemployment of around 8 to 9 percent—in effect implying that Canada's 9.1 percent unemployment rate is acceptable. Others suggest that the demise of work is greatly exaggerated (Matas 1996). Both the government and economists cite the creation of 671 000 new jobs since 1993, with the result that employment now stands at 13.7 million, up from 12.8 million at the low point in 1992 (Campbell 1996). Each new technological advance has the potential to create new products, new needs, and new employment patterns. In other words, the introduction of microelectronic technology is not the end of work as much as the end of work as we know it.

The rules of the new economy have altered the nature of work, how work is organized, and how wealth is generated by workers. The government is no longer convinced of a Keynesian need for investing in the economy to stave off depression or stimulate economic activity. Employment patterns that once reflected boom–bust cycles are drawing to a close. Job recovery does not automatically follow a recession; labour shedding continues even with economic recovery in the headlong rush to downsize regardless of the bottom line. Thirteen million white and blue collar jobs were lost in corporate United States between 1991 and 1993, including 40 000 at AT&T, a high tech colossus in the vanguard of creating new jobs. Petro Canada, which employed 6200 workers in 1990, had scaled back its workforce to 4800 by 1995, with promises of more cutbacks, *despite healthy profits*. Other blue chip companies such as GM slashed 2500 jobs yet recorded record profits of $1.39 billion, citing fears of another recession and competitive pressures from free trade and deregulation (Ip 1996). Even the service sector (from banks to retail) is beginning to automate in hopes of replacing managerial layers with highly skilled professional teams, outsourcing for specific needs and sophisticated technology (Rifkin 1996). Young Canadians have been hit especially hard by this kind of mindset; with unemployment rates for Canadians under age 25 at 17 percent in December 1995 (closer to 30 percent, according to a survey by the Bank of Nova Scotia, if we include drop-outs, part-timers, and school returners), many young people are barred from even entry-level jobs (McHutchion and Crane 1996).

Both pessimists and optimists concede the lack of simple answers to the complex problem of work, workplace, and employment in a knowledge-based, market-driven economy. A raft of solutions have been proposed, including reducing the work week to spread around the supply of jobs (Rifkin 1995), a redistribution of profits from the private sector to underwrite community service and voluntary sector jobs, and a commitment on the part of government and the affluent to convert excess wealth into job creation. A fundamental rethinking may be required to ensure a balance. Most would agree that Canada must remain internationally competitive. But is the goal that of economic competitiveness regardless of cost, or would most Canadians prefer a better quality of life through reasonable standards of living, employment security, and opportunities for meaningful work (Krahn and Lowe 1994)? To what extent should the discipline of the market provide the model for the public sector or the running of government as a business (Mintzberg 1996; Stewart 1997)? Solutions that rely on "letting the market decide" may need to be rethought. The balancing of profit with civic responsibilities through work policies not only protects citizens from uncertainties and dismissals, but ensures a decent life for the many, not just for the elites (see Krahn and Lowe 1994).

Rethinking Work: Workerless Factories and Virtual Workplaces

Canada's workplaces are changing with unnerving rapidity, and since the world of work casts a long shadow on the rest of life, many Canadians are anxious about the future. The continued presence of high unemployment and the rarity of employer commitments to job security have contributed to a pervasive feeling of economic insecurity in Canadian society (*Collective Reflection on the Changing Workplace*, Federal Report. Quoted in Vienneau 1997, A4).

Work and workplaces are currently being swept along by the tides of change, diversity, and uncertainty. A globalizing free market revolution has exerted bewildering pressure on organizations and workplaces, in part because of intense global competition and movements of labour and capital and in part because of automation and technological innovations. Manufacturing jobs are disappearing and white collar workers are no less vulnerable, according to Jeremy Rifkin (1996). Many are being replaced by highly skilled professionals employing state of the art computer technology and just-in-time support personnel as one way of squeezing labour costs. One dimension of contemporary work can be best described as temporary in duration, part-time in nature, contingent in orientation, and contractual in obligation. A restructuring of the workplace has flattened out the organizational pyramid, with layers of management pared away for democratizing more horizontal forms of decision-making and power-sharing. The era of paternalistic management–worker relations is waning; even the distinction between management and labour is increasingly fuzzy as human resources paradigms supersede the principles of scientific management in certain occupations. The prospect of a more inclusive and democratic workplace is showing signs of modest improvement under equity directives. Yet appearances may be deceiving. No one should underestimate the autocracy that remains entrenched, sometimes discreetly, other times openly. Nor can we ignore the human costs and squandered potential in this obsession with leaner and meaner.

Rules that apply to work, workers, working, work environment, and workplace are rapidly changing. Marked differences reflect major shifts in the production process—from *Fordism* to *post-Fordism*. A mode of production named after Henry Ford and the practices he brought to car manufacturing, Fordism included the mobilization of masses of labour into huge factories to produce large batches of standardized goods for mass consumption (Holly 1996). Fordist means of production dovetailed with Taylorist principles of scientific management, including a carefully calibrated division of labour and authority. Fordism became associated with rigidity, mass production, standardized products, large inventories, labour de-skilling, vertical integration, and global firms. Fordist models of production are vanishing except in select service industries. Post-Fordist models of production have shifted to production processes that incorporate more flexible means of wealth creation with respect to product types, amount of production, degree of mass labour, reliance on outsourcing (contracting out), and networking. According to Brian Holly (1996), emphasis is on small batch production, differentiated production, inventories, skills upgrading, vertical disintegration, and industrial districts. To be sure, Holly (1996) reminds us, a dualistic framework between Fordism and post-Fordism always distorts by oversimplifying; nevertheless, such a distinction provides a basis for analyzing differences and similarities.

How then does the new (postmodern) workplace compare with the old (modern) workplace with respect to work environment, work skills, worker status, working style, nature of work, workplace, work site, work philosophy, and worker–management relations?

The Old (Fordist) Workplace

The old work environment sought to regulate and control both the internal and external environment by eliminating uncertainties from all facets of production or distribution. Fordist models were based on an integrated assembly line, rationalization of production and labour, product standardization, economies of scale, and principles of scientific management (Perry et al. 1995). The work environment was rigidly stratified and regimented, with managers who managed on top and workers who worked at the bottom. The conventional workplace could be described as autocratic in that it was organized around the bureaucratic principles of an authoritarian hierarchy where everything was in its place and done in a proper sequence ("just in place"). Work skills relied heavily on the physical strength or manual dexterity normally associated with smokestack industries. The mind, for all intents and purposes, could be parked at the factory gate. Workers were seen as cogs in the machine of industry. A specialized division of labour placed emphasis on workers with specialized training. It was assumed that workers were motivated primarily by extrinsic rewards (money) rather than job satisfaction. Work itself was seen as a full-time, lifetime activity. Company loyalty and commitment to its goals over the long haul (seniority) provided the stepping stone to career success. The work site constituted a large cohort of males rooted in one place and compartmentalized into cubicles or conveyor belts who produced something in exchange for rewards and promotion. The rigidity and regimentation of traditional work could be symbolized by the expression "nine to five." At the management level, work success was measured by how big the company grew in size. Proof of success was inclusion in the Forbes 500 survey of the biggest and the best.

The New (Post-Fordist) Workplace

The certitudes of the "old" work environment have been abandoned by the flux of uncertainty. New ways of organizing work are characteristic of the post-Fordist workplace, including reduced tiers of management, greater worker discretion, just-in-time production, and new approaches to industrial relations (Perry et al. 1995). Reliable suppliers and predictable markets are virtually a thing of the past. Instead of pattern and predictions, fluid and competitive environments prevail that seldom lend themselves to regulation or control but entail risk-taking. The creation of wealth is based in postindustrial employment patterns rooted in knowledge and services rather than in manufacturing (Castells 1993). While the old work is organized around mass labour, the new work is advanced by knowledge elites. This transformation from a focus on brawn to brain has created a two-tier system. On the one hand are the "knows" with high-paying, relatively secure jobs who are expected to serve as catalysts in generating wealth; on the other hand are the poorly paid and underemployed "knows-not," in the phrasing of *Globe and Mail* columnist William Thorsell (February 2, 1996), whose service jobs have been de-skilled by automation. Accompanying these changes are transformations in the workforce with the entry of women and minorities. Diversifying the workplace has allowed management to tap into a broader pool of talent and expertise; it also meant adjustments in corporate rules and procedures to ensure equity in treatment. Equally noticeable is the disappearance of a large, permanent workforce. Companies are looking for ways to prune costs by eliminating those layers of "fat" that do not actively contribute to the bottom line. CEOs prefer a workforce that can meet fluctuations in the business cycle: just-in-time labourers can be hired quickly during business upturns and dismissed promptly when profits shrink (Lerner 1997).

The concept of work is also undergoing radical change. Teamwork and reliance on outside expertise are increasingly commonplace and widely touted. The shift from lifetime employment and career aspirations to just-in-time employment (part-time) puts the onus on personal "reskilling" and lifetime learning. Workplaces are no longer characterized by a rigid pecking order, with the lowly worker at the bottom and a maze of management on top. What we have instead is a flattened hierarchy that demands decentralized and participatory decision-making. Even the concept of a work site is losing its sense of physical locale. Corporate offices are being replaced by virtual offices/virtual corporations that exist only in name and modem address, in effect releasing contemporary work sites from the constraints of time or space (Arnault 1995). Without the constancy of a physical location, the new workplace redefines traditional relationships by forcing people to reorganize their lives and relationships accordingly. Not surprisingly, corporate bigness for the sheer sake of being big is losing lustre in an era of flexible specialization. Table 10-1 provides a brief synopsis of the differences that ideally distinguish the new work from the old.

Table 10-1 can only make sense as an opposition between ideal types. Reality suggests that modern work is riddled with ambiguity since it combines aspects of Fordism and post-Fordism. Perhaps it's more accurate to say that the new work is superimposed on the old without

TABLE 10-1 Comparison of Old Work and New Work		
	Old (Fordist) Work	**New (Post-Fordist) Work**
Work Environment	Control, Order, Certainty	Chaos, Uncertainty
Work Skills	Brawn "McDonaldization of Work"	Brain The Information Highway Computer Literate
Worker Status	Cog "Another Brick in the Wall"	Catalyst Two-Tier = Creativity + Deskilled
Working Style	Nose to the Grindstone Career-Oriented	Empowerment, Teamwork Reskilling/Lifelong Learning
Workplace	The Bureaucratic Pyramid Autocratic	Delayered Democratic
Work Site	"The Firm" 9 to 5	Virtual Reality ("Hotelling") Anytime/Anywhere
Management Philosophy	Full Employment Contract for Life	Downsizing = Leaner and Meaner Contract for a Job
Management–Labour Relations	Scientific Management	Human Resources
Workforce	Homogeneous	Diverse and Accommodative
Work Ethos	In Its Place	Just-in-Time

dislodging the latter. Since neither model is powerful enough to dislodge the other, the workplace may reflect a contested site involving competitive struggles between the new and the old. Contradictions or inconsistencies also pervade the workplace: it is ostensibly more democratic and inclusive yet remains as autocratic as in the past because of its competitive pressures. There is much greater emphasis on being more accommodative, inclusive, flexible (less rigid, participatory, and discretionary), and worker-friendly (less harassment), yet demands continue to escalate in terms of productivity and output. Employees are touted as a company's greatest asset, but remarkably little is done to foster this resource. Loyalty is disposable since bottom line considerations are not averse to slashing these valued "assets" to cut costs and bolster profits. The introduction of modern technology is no less ambivalent. Labour-saving devices may reduce much of the drudgery associated with traditional tasks (friend), but they also have a tendency to be labour-shedding (foe). It remains to be seen whether the corporation can continue to be lean without necessarily becoming mean in the process.

HUMANIZING THE WORKPLACE

The traditional workplace was authoritarian by nature. Not only did most workers exert little control over the production process, but the work itself was often alienating or exploitative, if not openly dangerous. Stress factors contributed to high rates of staff turnover and absenteeism, while mind-numbing routines could lead to anything from thoughtless complacency to sabotage. Managerial interests took top priority at the expense of workers who were relegated to the background (Olive 1992).

Many have criticized the traditional workplace. Labour unions and worker advocates have denounced workplace horrors as befitting machines rather than humans. Academics have pounced on organizational workplaces as inhumane and counter-productive and have sought to expose the logic behind the process of exploitation and control. Proposals have been put forward for transforming the workplace into a worker-friendly environment that is still capable of functioning under budgetary limits. The introduction of a human resources approach to shop-floor dynamics is but one solution to the challenge of a productive yet humane workplace. First we need to look at what created the problem.

Scientific Management: Workplace as Machine

The emergence of big business during the nineteenth century posed a series of logistical problems. Through mergers and vertical monopolies, organizations grew in size and complexity. Such expansion exerted additional pressure to develop the means for taking control of sprawling operations and far-flung empires. This, in turn, entailed a need for reducing the uncertainty created by expansion, enhancing the coordination of disparate parts into a smooth functioning whole, and maximizing productivity and profits during an era of financial expansion. Equally important was the need to keep control of potentially disruptive workers. For the managerial class, the principles of scientific management proved to be a godsend in furnishing the formula for maximizing production while controlling labour.

Scientific management as principle and practice is associated with Frederick Winslow Taylor. His ideas were introduced in the 1890s, quickly found their way into American industry, and were firmly entrenched in Canada by the First World War (Campbell 1996). Taylorism sought to make complex organizations more efficient and productive by shifting control of operations from family ownership to a professional class who relied on the principles of rationality (including intervention, regulation, precision, calculation, and coordination) as a basis for generating wealth. It recommended a new approach for managing the workplace that relied on machine-like regulation and precision. The drive for efficiency transformed the workplace into a glorified machine with every part in place. The workplace was also based on the notion that (a) workers did not require a skill to do a job, (b) workers didn't need to start and finish a job, (c) management could monitor and control what workers did on the job, and (d) the secret of efficiency lay in controlling costs (Campbell 1996). The following procedures were thought to be elemental:

1) A simple division of labour, best summarized in the aphorism, "Managers think, workers do." Managers assumed responsibility for all aspects of the planning and design of activities. By definition, they were best positioned to monitor and manipulate the organization at large. For managers, primary functions revolved around command, control, and coordination; workers were expected to demur and passively obey.

2) The use of carefully calibrated methods to determine the most efficient work procedures. Through precise measurement and reliance on time-and-motion studies, scientific management sought to reduce waste or expenditure of superfluous energy. An optimum level of performance could be devised, in large measure by dividing a job into its smallest constituent units for assignment to trained workers.

3) Select and train the best person for each job. Each worker would possess the training for a particular job, and no other. Productivity was optimal when the right person could perform a specialized task without waste or loss of energy. Yet individual workers were expendable; through training, each cog could be replaced with a component of comparable value, without destroying the balance.

4) Encourage productivity by increasing monetary rewards as the central incentive for hard work. Workers were perceived essentially as economic animals whose motivations were purely material self-interest. Payment in high wages provided an incentive to work harder and reduced the threat of strikes or subversion. A new social contract evolved: namely, company loyalty in exchange for secure, well-paid employment.

5) Depersonalize work. "Craftsmen" who took a manufactured product from start to completion were discarded and replaced with workers (robots) who knew how to do one job and did it repeatedly for the entire shift. Workers and the machines they tended became cogs in the conveyor belt. Isolating workers from each other also minimized opportunities for waste or shop-floor sabotage.

The consequences of scientific management have been immense. Taylor's decidedly undemocratic principles gave rise to the moving assembly line that Henry Ford incorporated in 1913 for his Model T. Even today these principles serve as a model for workplace relations, despite altered circumstances and competing perspectives. The current mania for measurement and management (Mintzberg 1996) is providing a rationale for improving productivity and profit by controlling costs through greater efficiencies. Nowhere is this mindset more enthusiastically embraced than in the fast food industry, which continues to extol the virtues of a conveyor belt mentality in dealing with customers and employees (Morgan 1986; Reitzer 1996; Ritzer 1993). Case 10-1 deals with the mechanization of this industry and the corresponding de-skilling of work in such a regulated environment. This portrayal of work experiences at a Toronto-based Burger King restaurant demonstrates how the preoccupation with standardization applies not only to food preparation but to customer relations and workplace dynamics. The fact that everyone is treated as little more than a cog in the fast food machine suggests that the principles of scientific management are alive and well.

CASE 10-1	**Conveyor Belt Burgers**

"Any trained monkey could do the job" (Reiter 1992, 167).

The principles of scientific management reflect a mechanistic image of organizations. The primary focus is on reducing production into the smallest parts that can be modified and rearranged to increase efficiency and improve productivity. Workers are not treated as individuals, but essentially as replaceable cogs in the work machine. Work is subdivided into minimal units, allocated to trained workers, supervised carefully, folded into an explicit chain of command and hierarchical control, and rewarded generously for maximum impact. The end result is work conditions that can best be described as extolling the virtues of efficiency, routine, reliability, and predictability.

The contemporary fast food industry in Canada and the United States is organized precisely around the principles of scientific management. Central to this philosophy is the dehumanization of the workplace. Rigid operational procedures and standardization are adopted not to improve food quality but to eliminate the key obstruction to *fast* food service, namely, the human element. Or as one of the original McDonald brothers once said about his golden arches: "If we gave people a choice, there would be chaos" (Love 1995, 15). Attainment of this dehumani-

zation process is organized around the pursuit of *quality* (the ideal of standardization and predictability in the preparation of food), *service* (speed in the delivery of food to each customer), and *cleanliness* (associated with "order" and consumer "appeal" rather than healthfulness). Each outlet combines unskilled machine operators and auxiliary staff and sophisticated technology to produce a highly polished product through painstaking attention to design and planning (Reiter 1992, 75). To the extent that these goals are achieved, each fast food outlet conforms with the ideals of scientific management. Many of the examples below are taken from Ester Reiter's (1992/1996) book on a Burger King franchise in Toronto, *Making Fast Food: From the Frying Pan into the Fryer*.

A Burger King franchise is regulated to the most minute detail. Pots and pans, as well as chefs and dishwashers, have been replaced by automated routine and a crew of undifferentiated machine-tenders. With the aid of computer technology, Burger King can slot almost any crew person into any food processing function at the outlet by simply cross-training workers to conduct a number of simplified tasks. Both worker movements and emotions are considered to be at the disposal of the franchise. Those who work at counters and take customer

CASE 10-1   Conveyor Belt Burgers (continued)

orders are expected to display a ready smile, a cheerful yet energetic disposition, and clichéd lines in promoting the sale of meals. Kitchen workers are no less programmed in terms of appearance and lines of interaction.

Consider the preparation of food. All food enters the store in its final cooking stages: hamburgers arrive as frozen precooked patties while buns are precooked and caramelized to ensure an appealing image. French fries, chicken, and fish are precooked to ensure a standardized product. Condiments such as onions or pickles (with the exception of tomatoes) are presliced or preshredded. The instore preparation of these foods is essentially that of machine-tending—the incorporation of assembly line technology in the food service industry. For example, hamburgers are placed on a conveyor belt that transports the frozen meat patty through a gas broiler in a space of 94 seconds. A worker at the other end of the broiler picks up the cooked patty with tongs and transfers it to the bottom half of the bun. The ungarnished hamburger is then placed in a steamer where it can remain for up to 10 minutes before being discarded. Workers at the burger board "assemble" the burger by adding the condiments (cheese slices, pickles, onions, mayonnaise, lettuce, tomatoes, ketchup, and mustard). Pickle slices are spread evenly over the meat or cheese (no overlapping is allowed). Ketchup is applied by spreading it in a spiral circular motion over the pickles. Mayonnaise is applied to the top of the bun in a single stroke while three-quarters of an ounce of shredded lettuce is sprinkled over the

mayonnaise. Two slices of tomato (three is permissible, but only with management's permission) are then put on top of the lettuce. The assembly process itself should take no longer than 23 seconds for a Whopper. The finished burger is placed in a box or wrapper, reheated in a microwave for 14 seconds, and put in a chute.

Service without a Snarl

Numerous tasks are associated with food assembly. Jobs are divided and arranged in a way that is easy to master and measure for the sake of efficiency. Workers are treated as little better than commodities along a conveyor belt. A worker at Burger King is expected to place her or his responsibility to the franchise above family or friends. Each worker is asked to work as hard as possible, to come to work at short notice, or to put in irregular hours. The self-discipline and control required of workers contrasts sharply with the image of self-indulgence and convenience offered to customers. Customers are thus shielded from the exploitative work situation that confronts Burger King workers; they only see the benign image of benevolence and wholesomeness.

The fast food industry employs work processes and labour–management relations in an unusually restrictive environment that reduces labour and work to its simplest components. The principle of formal rationality strikes at the core of this process and relationship (Ritzer 1993). Rationality is characterized by a commitment to efficiency, predictability, and calculability, the substitution of nonhuman technology for human

CASE 10-1	Conveyor Belt Burgers (continued)

labour, and control over uncertainty. Applied to fast food, there is little question that the operation is predictable (consistent when it comes to taste, appearance, and speed of delivery) and calculable since quantity is emphasized over quality (the bottom line is not in the taste of the food but in the number of customers processed, the speed with which they are processed, and the profits produced); that workers are expected to act in robot-like fashion (people are trained to work in an automatic, unthinking way whether in preparing food or serving customers); and that control over the product is secured by managing the behaviour of workers. Customers are no less controlled into accepting such standardized fare as food. With nearly 60 percent of the restaurant market captured by fast food establishments (*Globe and Mail*, July 5, 1997), few anticipate any major changes to the culinary tract.

Human Resources: Working in Circles

The 1980s heralded a new wave of management thinking in redesigning manager–worker relations. Impetus for this shift stemmed from the success of Japanese management techniques and the influx of women into the workforce. Managerial concern over worker productivity, cost-cutting, and offshore competition were also contributing factors. The human resources perspective repudiated the principles of scientific management by turning them on their head. Job enrichment and enlargement replaced the notion of simplification and excessive specialization. Workplaces were seen as a collection of competencies rather than a hierarchy, particularly once layers of management had been eliminated (Schellhardt 1997). Instead of defining workers as purely economic animals to be pushed or prodded, they were seen as whole persons who craved psychological satisfaction and creative outlets within the workplace. Metaphorically, the focus shifted from the conveyor belt to a quality circle with a holistic and democratic environment of active and concerned participants.

Human resources objectives sought to reduce alienation and meaninglessness from the workplace by empowering workers as individuals and group members. In contrast with the past when workers were thought to resemble wheelbarrows, since the best way to make them work was to load them up and push them around (Nisbet 1994), employees were now seen as enjoying work and being productive, provided they were given the right conditions to flourish. Workers were expected to assume responsibility and control over the production process rather than park their brains at home. In perhaps the most significant shift of all, workers (and customers) were redefined as assets and resources, not simply a problem for solution or replacement. The vaunted chasm between management and labour was displaced by a cooperative philosophy, with workers (and customers) as the most important asset for success. Paradoxically, management was increasingly labelled as a problem in need of pruning or renewal. Excessive management stood in the way of achieving institutional potential by foreclosing patterns of communication and channels for creativity (Adams 1996).

Of the many initiatives encouraged by the human resources model, few have proven as alluring or as contentious as those that fell under the umbrella of "participatory management." Once organizations represented tall hierarchies that divided into a complex division of labour among individuals. Workers were expected to be obedient and do as they were told in discharging their obligations. By contrast, worker participation is now defined as the cure for organizations that need to become more flexible (and profitable) in the face of rapid environmental change (Jackson and Ruderman 1995). The goal of participatory management entails a reworking of the factory floor into work teams. The concepts of work teams and participatory management reflect a shift in assumptions about the natural inclination of individuals for creating groups and establishing standards of conduct. Self-managing teams (quality circles) of 6 to 20 workers assumed direct responsibility for immediate matters pertaining to their sphere of productivity and working conditions (Southerst 1994). Inside these work teams, individuals could rotate jobs to stave off boredom or acquire multiple skills. Each worker has the option of attending after-hours meetings with other quality circles to discuss plant problems and quality improvements. Work teams from different departments then convened to plot strategy, improve productivity, and consult with senior management over a broad range of relevant issues. Everyone allegedly benefited from this arrangement since, collectively, it is in their best interests to increase productivity, reduce costs, enhance quality control, and improve customer service and satisfaction. Case 10-2 examines community policing as a response to a particular type of human resources approach. Case 10-3 will again focus on community policing to determine why organizational response is slow in coming.

CASE 10-2   Community Policing: Humanizing the Service

One of the more innovative approaches within the human resources circle is known as total quality as principle or practice. Total quality seeks a wholesale transformation of organizations that goes beyond the superficial or cosmetic. The organizational structure and culture are redesigned to ensure the primacy of the clients (in terms of entitlement to services, equity, and impartiality); to maximize employee satisfaction and rewards (through partnership and meaningful consultation); and to secure the involvement of both the community and management in spearheading a service culture that prioritizes consumer concerns without losing sight of the bottom line (Perry et al. 1995). Several factors have been singled out as integral in distinguishing between bureaucratic control and service orientation (Seguin 1991).

Meaningful Consultation

In contrast with impersonal and bureaucratic structures that routinely impose decisions without client involvement—alienating many who recoil from a process they cannot hope to influence—total quality seeks meaningful consultation with clients and workers that goes beyond mere rubber-stamping. Steps are taken to engage the public in the general problem-solving process. Communication is concentrated

CASE 10-2   Community Policing (continued)

around the removal of disincentives that deter participation. Feedback and monitoring mechanisms are secured to ensure a customer-friendly service (Rawson 1991).

Worker Participation

Worker participation is now defined as a cure for top-heavy organizations. There is a commitment to delayer management and delegate decision-making powers to workers, thus empowering the workforce with a say in those aspects of productivity pertaining to schedules, outputs, service delivery, working conditions, and shop-floor waste. Workers are seen not as "functionaries" but as resource personnel who desire participation in decisions and engagement with colleagues.

Worker Satisfaction

A commitment to worker satisfaction has assumed a higher profile with the emergence of workers who are less subservient or deferential. With improved levels of education, both employees and clients are increasingly informed, critical, and demanding of better treatment (by way of rewards, recognition, or service). Many are less tolerant of corporate inefficiencies at a time when more has to be done with less as resources dwindle and competition intensifies. The empowerment of employees can come about through improved consultation, increased authority, and enhanced discretion (balanced by the requirement of accountability to the community and employers alike (Rawson 1991)). Failure to address personal and career needs of frontline workers can derail even modest organizational reforms.

Risk-Taking

The system of employee placement and promotion needs to be restructured in a manner that brings out the best in each worker. Once, individuals were singled out for praise if they followed guidelines, avoided risks, minimized mistakes, justified action (or inaction) according to the book, and slavishly carried out what was expected of them. Under total quality, however, the shift from command and control to employee empowerment has rendered these virtues increasingly obsolete and counter-productive. What is required are self-starting individuals anxious to embrace organizational visions and client needs, even if this involves some degree of risk-taking.

Community Sensitivity

Operation style must change from inward-looking (law unto themselves) to an outward focus (client needs), from bureaucratic rigidity to organizational flexibility (Rawson 1991). Relationships with the community are also changing as the organizational mindset that once isolated service from the community is about to erode. In place of stonewalling or indifference are citizens' demands for involvement in the design and delivery of community-based social services. Related to this is the greater demand for public servants to be accountable for their actions and outcomes. But will the bureaucrats listen? Will the police as a paramilitary organization make the commitment to redesign their relationship with an increasingly diverse public along the lines of total quality?

CASE 10-2 **Community Policing (continued)**

Community Policing: Principles and Practices

Interest in community policing has expanded to the point where it no longer symbolizes only a promising experiment in redesigning police–community relations (see Cryderman, O'Toole and Fleras 1998). The principles of community policing have catapulted to the forefront of contemporary Canadian policing, even if rhetoric may outstrip reality. Its appeal may reflect an ability to evoke powerful emotional symbols that pluck at contemporary cultural concerns, including "democracy," "power to the people," or "small-town morality" (Seagrave 1997). Acceptance of community policing is consistent with trends elsewhere in view of commitments to the principles of decentralization, human resources management, and customer satisfaction. This commitment to community policing has focused on transforming the police from a technically driven, bureaucratic, and professional crime-fighting force to a customer-inspired service that is community-responsive, culturally sensitive, problem-oriented, and "user-friendly." Such lofty ideals raise the question of what exactly is meant by community policing? How does it differ from conventional police styles? In what ways does community policing differ from traditional police work while endorsing the principles of total quality?

Professional Crime-Fighting Force

Police in Canada are a component of the criminal justice system (McDougall 1988). In 1991 there were 56 774 police officers in just over 420 police

jurisdictions across Canada at a national cost of $5.3 billion (Leighton 1994). About one-quarter (27%) of the total number of officers work for the RCMP, 16 percent belong to the three provincial police services (Ontario, Quebec, and Newfoundland), and the remainder are members of regional or municipal departments. Canada's five largest police jurisdictions—RCMP, Ontario Provincial Police, Sûreté du Québec, Metropolitan Toronto Police, and Montreal Police—account for 60 percent of all officers. Policing roles at all levels tend to revolve around protection of life and property, prevention of crime, law enforcement, apprehension of criminals, and public-order maintenance (Seagrave 1997). Police are empowered to use deadly force in discharging their obligations, but only to the extent that its use is reasonable and demonstrably justified in light of Canada's democratic and legal traditions. This monopoly of coercive force on behalf of the state "politicizes" police work in the sense that policing is perceived as beneficial to some sectors and detrimental to others.

"Taking the police out of the public"

Canada's police at federal, provincial, and municipal levels have relied for the most part on a "professional crime-fighting" model as a blueprint for appointed duties (Walker 1987). Acceptance of this model drew its inspiration from developments in the United States. American police reformers adopted a professional ethic as one way of circumventing widespread corruption, questionable service, and political interference within local precincts. A

CASE 10-2   Community Policing (continued)

commitment to professionalism defined the police as a highly trained force with a shared identity and code of ethics for crime control and law enforcement. Police effectiveness was measured by way of (a) random patrol as a deterrent to criminal activities, (b) rapid response to calls for all services, (c) arrest, conviction, and clearance rates, and (d) citizen satisfaction surveys. An "incident-driven," "complaint-reactive" approach was bolstered by administrators who sought to bureaucratize policing by linking organizational procedures with technique and the latest technology. Structurally, the police were organized into a paramilitaristic model of bureaucracy involving a top-down chain of command and control, law enforcement by the book, a compulsion with internal rules and regulations, and an explicit system of checks and balances to deter corruption, enhance control, monitor activities, and maintain surveillance. Rewards and promotions were allocated to some extent on the basis of the "big catch," in addition to loyal and long-standing service to the "force."

Certain assumptions about the community prevailed under a professional crime-fighting model. The police envisaged themselves as a "thin blue line" between the community and chaos; their job was to keep disorder at bay. Community involvement was kept to a minimum; citizens were expected to report crime to the police by way of the 911 system, to provide information on possible criminal activities, and to cooperate in the apprehension and conviction of lawbreakers (Tomovich and Loree 1989). Beyond that, however, police interaction with the community was brief and to the point, idealized by the immortal words of Sergeant Friday of the TV series *Dragnet*: "Nothing but the facts, ma'am." Oettmeier and Brown (1988, 15) explain the rationale behind this "fortress mentality:"

> Officers are not expected to look beyond an incident to attempt to define and resolve a particular problem. Once dispatched to handle calls, the patrol officers are encouraged to return to service as quickly as possible to resume random, preventive patrol. Because of the emphasis to have patrol officers handle their calls as quickly as possible and return to service to continue performing preventive patrol to suppress crime, little attention was directed toward the service needs of citizens that had become victims of crimes.

Put bluntly, community participation was dismissed as irrelevant to the social control process. Crime control was viewed as the prerogative of a professional and distanced bureaucracy. Just as too much community involvement had once compromised the principle of impartial policing, so now an arm's-length distance would provide police with the latitude to professionally discharge appointed duties. Confronted by this indifference, the police and community drifted apart. Such a rift did not imply that all police departments embraced the perspective of "two solitudes." Not all police officers subscribed to a detached and impersonal style of policing (consider, for example, those with roots in small-town environments). Rather,

CASE 10-2 **Community Policing (continued)**

conventional policing may be interpreted as a specific style that flourished at a particular time and place in the evolution of modern urban policing. The professional crime-fighting model has prevailed to the present as a cornerstone of policing. For better or worse, its values and visions continue to frame police experiences on a daily basis.

Crisis in crime-busting

The introduction and popularity of community policing reflects an increased disillusionment with conventional police styles, many of which are perceived as inefficient, ineffective, and inequitable (Rosenbaum 1994). Critics have raised questions over the value of a "cops, courts, and corrections" approach to curb crime, fear of crime, urban disorder, incivilities, and social decay. Consider the statistics for Canada: In 1995 a total of 2.9 million crimes were committed, an increase of 300 000 in the past 6 years, or about 12 percent. Public sector costs of police, courts, and prisons topped $10 billion, with an additional $2 billion spent on private security, an increase of 34 percent in the past 6 years (Howard 1996). With costs continuing to escalate despite a slowdown in offending, the time is ripe for rethinking crime control. Of foremost concern are the following:

1) Increases in police numbers, technology and resources, and patrol strength have had minimal impact on the overall volume of crime, clearance rates, or levels of citizen satisfaction (Bayley 1994).

2) Random preventative patrol has little substantive effect on deterrence or the apprehension of offenders.

Motorized car patrols are rarely effective since the crimes that people fear or that directly affect them are never encountered in progress. Nor will the prospect of having police drive around in squad cars and respond to radio calls have much impact in alleviating persistent community problems (Rosenbaum 1994).

3) Except in certain life-threatening situations, reduced response times to calls from the public do not result in increased apprehension of criminal suspects. Offenders are rarely caught in the act, largely because of citizen delay in reporting incidents. Studies indicate citizens prefer a predetermined response time according to the gravity of the situation.

4) Numerous studies indicate that police on their own have a limited capacity to solve crime (Robinson et al. 1989). Instead, effective policing is contingent on access to information from the general public. When police are provided with information from witnesses or victims of reported crime, they clear up to 90 percent of the cases. The success rate drops to less than 1 in 10 without local input.

5) Criminal investigation techniques are not as successful as once thought. Investigations rarely make an impact on overall levels of apprehension. Fewer than 3 percent of all cleared cases are solved using specialized investigative skills and sophisticated forensic techniques of detection (Robinson et al. 1989).

CASE 10-2   Community Policing (continued)

6) The most likely determinant of solving crime is the information supplied by the victim or witness. Establishing two-way communication is the easiest way of ensuring open lines of interaction for crime prevention or detection.

7) Complaint-reactive, incident-driven styles of policing are largely incapable of dealing with the precipitating causes of crime. They rarely are in a position to prevent crime at the source or foster cooperative relations with minority communities. The remoteness of bureaucratic policing is also thought to breed passive and unresponsive communities that further depress police effectiveness.

8) Time-honoured strategies are not only ineffective and limited, but often irrelevant to citizen concerns for safety, reduction of fear or danger, and accessibility. Police preferences for "big busts" continue to be at odds with community concerns of safety and local order. Police cannot prevent crime as long as workers are deployed around the need to be available and criminal investigations are geared towards the clearing of cases (Bayley 1994).

From Force to Service

The concept of community policing eludes simple definition despite its widespread use and popularity. The concept is used interchangeably and indiscriminately to include everything from "neighbourhood watch" programs and "bobbies on bikes" to a major revamping of police operational style and institutional structure. References to community policing may denote a set of programs grafted onto existing police work. Conversely, community policing may refer to a paradigm shift that entails nothing less than a total redesign of police philosophy and operations. Or it may signify nothing of substance or permanence. Definitions tend to revolve around common attributes: Community policing represents a reaction to reactive-incident law enforcement styles. It consists of a hybrid of enforcement and community service for crime prevention. Objectives include a framework for assisting police to help communities to help themselves by way of citizen-defined community problems (Seagrave 1997). It envisions a demilitarization of police departments—a downshifting of authority through management ranks—to enhance discretionary powers for police on the street in hopes they go beyond arrests and focus on analyzing problems through community cooperation. Its most optimistic supporters envisage a new age of policing where critical thinking and problem-solving skills prevail over playing by the book. Successful implementation of community policing entails fundamental changes not only to police functions but to community expectations of police activities and responsibilities for public safety.

Community policing can be broadly defined as a clearly articulated philosophy about the nature of police work and the place of police in society. It consists of a strategy (including a set of principles, policies, and programs) by which police are engaged with

CASE 10-2 **Community Policing (continued)**

community members in the joint pursuit of local crime prevention. This definition is consistent with Lee Brown's (1988, 78) reference to community policing as an "interactive process between the police and community to mutually identify and resolve community problems" (also Royal Commission on Aboriginal Peoples 1995, 91). Five recurrent themes distinguish community policing from conventional policing: partnership perspectives, proactive/preventative policing, problem-solving orientation, power-sharing, and pluralism. This list partially coincides with David Bayley's (1994) observation that serious community policing is associated with four operational elements: consultation, adaptability (devolve resources and decision-making to local levels), mobilization of citizens, and problem-solving for remedying conditions that generate crime and insecurity.

Partnership perspective

It is widely acknowledged that policing is impossible without community cooperation. Police power and effectiveness as agents of control are derived in part from public approval and support. Yet the police have been criticized as too remote; the community has been criticized as too removed. Community policing is concerned, paradoxically, with making the police less of a community (insular, defensive, and protective of their own), while mobilizing inchoate masses into active communities. It is also concerned with arrangements that remove the police from the isolation of motorized patrol, and replace this estrangement with

consultative dialogue and meaningful co-production of crime-prevention strategies. Mutual benefits are anticipated: the community sees policing in a positive light and the police are less likely to see the community only as a problem.

A partnership status entails certain modifications in police perception of the community. A working partnership rejects a view of the police as experts with exclusive credentials for crime control. In its place is an image of police as "facilitators" and "resource personnel" who cooperate with interested citizens to solve problems. This collaborative arrangement may span different levels of intensity and scope. At times, police involvement with the community is relatively minor (Neighbourhood Watch or Crime Stoppers). At other times, participation may encompass a sustained relationship to root out the precipitating cause of local problems. Constant throughout these approaches is the collaboration of the police with the community as partners in crime prevention

Preventative/proactive

Community policing is inseparable from preventative or proactive policing. Arguably, all policing is concerned with crime prevention. Whereas conventional policing sees law enforcement as the main deterrent to criminal offending, community policing endorses prevention through community partnership as the preferred alternative. Proactive approaches attempt to deal with problems before they arise rather than after the fact—better a net at the top than an ambulance on the bottom, as the slogan

CASE 10-2   Community Policing (continued)

goes. Prevention is sought through proactive mechanisms designed by the community in consultation with the police. As "diagnosticians" and "catalysts," the police are strategically positioned to (a) analyze community strengths and weaknesses, (b) jointly recommend solutions for preventing future occurrences, (c) mobilize the community in their fight against crime, and (d) galvanize whatever resources are available to deal with the problem at hand. Examples of proactive policing include school-liaison programs that sensitize youths to police work. Proactive innovations such as juvenile diversion are also widely acclaimed. The consequence of this proactivity is limitless: inasmuch as preventative and proactive procedures address the precipitating causes of problems, community-development policing is well positioned to reduce the caseloads that are overwhelming the courts and social service agencies.

Problem-solving

Problem-solving is central to the notion of community policing. Many have criticized the futility of continuous responses to recurrent incidents in the same area by a small number of repeat offenders. Repeated calls for service are seen as losing propositions that squander scarce resources and foster frustration. Proposed instead is a style that diagnoses the underlying causes rather than just responding to symptoms (Saville and Rossmo 1995). A problem-solving strategy seeks to (a) isolate and identify the underlying causes of recurrent problems, (b) evaluate alternate solutions,

(c) respond by applying one or more solutions, (d) monitor the impact, and (e) redesign solutions if feedback is negative.

A problem-solving approach is not necessarily synonymous with community policing. Even conventional styles of policing can incorporate problem-solving techniques without any degree of community involvement. Practice suggests that community policing and problem-solving are mutually dependent. Community policing provides an ideological framework in which problem-solving techniques can flourish; conversely, problem-solving styles bolster the legitimacy of community policing. To be truly effective, in other words, policing must work in close cooperation with the community to solve mutually defined problems (Roberg 1994). Admittedly, even a problem-solving mentality cannot hope to address the root causes of community problems (such as poverty). It is unrealistic to expect the police to protect the community from the consequences of its own neglect or indifference (Bayley 1994). But problem-solving has the potential to confront the immediate (or precipitating) causes, for example, derelict properties or abandoned cars.

Power-sharing

A commitment to power-sharing with the community is essential to community policing (Doone 1989). Without a sharing of power, community policing is simply tokenism or a publicity stunt. Police are under pressure to share power by loosening organizational structures, transferring authority and resources to communities, and implementing mutually

CASE 10-2 **Community Policing (continued)**

agreed-upon goals. The ability to identify, prioritize, and apply creative solutions to problems is also predicated to some degree on a sharing of power. As well, power must be redistributed throughout all levels of the police hierarchy. Community policing officers require discretionary power if they are to be flexibly equipped for stamping out crime before it begins. A certain latitude is indispensable for front-line officers to take advantage of latent community resources and local resourcefulness. As Wilson and Kelling (1989, 49–50) claim in defence of empowering community policing officers:

> Authority over at least some patrol officers must be decentralized, so that they have a good deal of freedom to manage their time (including their paid overtime). This implies freeing them at least partly from the tyranny of the radio call. It means giving them a broad range of responsibilities: to find and understand the problems that create disorder and crime, and to deal with other public and private agencies than can help cope with these problems. It means assigning them to a neighbourhood and leaving them there for an extended period of time. It means backing them up with department support and resources.

What does a sharing of power involve? First, police organizational structures need to be decentralized. The decentralizing process is likely to enhance community access to police services through storefront offices or mini-stations. Second, central authorities must be persuaded to devolve power to the local community. Power-sharing must not only entail additional responsibilities for carrying out activities that police find burdensome, but also must allow for meaningful input in the design and implementation of local programs. Third, a commitment to power-sharing implies that the police are accountable to the community for police actions (Doone 1989). Such an assertion casts new light on the perennial debate over to whom the police are accountable—the community or the law. It also reminds us that power is rarely relinquished without a struggle.

Pluralism

Community policing is increasingly directed at culturally diverse constituencies. A commitment to cultural diversity cannot be taken lightly. With Canada in the midst of a demographic revolution, it is only a matter of time before mandatory measures are imposed to improve effective cross-cultural encounters and eliminate racism at all levels. Policing from top to bottom must become better acquainted with the multicultural community in terms of its varied needs, entitlements, demands, and expectations. A commitment to diversity also compels the police to view cultural differences as a resource of potential value in preventing crime. Attempts to multiculturalize the police have incorporated several organizational adjustments, including looser weight and height restrictions (which traditionally discriminated against minority applicants). Appearance regulations have also been modified in light of recent decisions by the RCMP to allow turbans as head covering, by the Peel Regional Police to permit kirpans (Sikh ceremonial swords), and by the Calgary police (and the RCMP) to accept braided hair among First Nations officers. These modifications, however symbolic, do signify a growing willingness to make adjustments that reflect minority rather than organizational priorities.

Comparison: From React to Reduce

Efforts to compare community and conventional styles of policing yield interesting results. In theory, community and conventional policing are diametrically opposed at the level of assumptions, objectives, philosophy, inner logic, content, operational style, and anticipated outcomes in the same way that the principles of total quality are at variance with those of scientific management. In reality, the distinction is blurred and complex. Table 10-2 provides a basis for such a comparison over a comprehensive range of dimensions. This comparison is not intended to be exhaustive, nor should it imply that all policing can be mechanically slotted into either column. Police practices continue to combine both crime-fighting and service elements, often switching back and forth as the situation demands or individual preferences dictate. In fact, much of the tension underlying contemporary police work derives from this uneasy juxtaposition of oppositional readings regarding police work. It should also be noted that the community-policing column does not automatically exclude aspects of conventional policing. Community policing often incorporates

aspects of the latter, but in a way that embraces the priority of community service over law enforcement.

The fact that neither model of policing has taken charge as the preferred approach suggests that police are in the midst of a paradigm shift of yet uncharted proportions. The professional crime-fighting model remains popular, but it no longer commands the respect, widespread appeal, and legitimacy it once had. Community-policing models are drawing interest and are conceded as overdue, yet remain poorly understood and widely resented as an unwarranted intrusion on police autonomy, mandate, and self-image. Crime-busting styles are not always applicable or effective, but a community-policing orientation is not readily available or relevant. Role conflicts are painfully evident: most officers do not want to appear heavy-handed or indifferent to community concerns, but neither do they want to be seen as capitulating to outside interests, much less as weak and vacillating on crime. What we have instead of a paradigm shift is a paradigm muddle as Canadian policing hovers between models. The clash of these competing paradigms has focused attention on those most fundamental of questions: What are police for? What can a society expect? It also raises the question of whether it is possible—let alone desirable—to transform an enforcement-oriented paramilitary bureaucracy into a public service agency on behalf of the community. Case Study 10-3 will return to this question.

TABLE 10-2 Comparison of Values, Strategies, and Operations		
	Conventional	**Community-Based**
Police Mission	Professional Crime-Fighting	Community-Oriented Service
Police Mandate	Enforcement	Service
Police Work	Reduce Crime	Prevent Crime
Police Roles	By the Book	Creativity
Primary Tactics	Random Car Control	Community Engagement
Training Skills	Technical Aspects	Human Relations
Priorities	Complaint-Reactive	Problem-Solving
Evaluation Criteria	Police Standards	Community Standards
Measurement of Success	Arrests and Citations for Bravery	Quality of Service to Community
Style of Policing	Law Unto Themselves	Public Servants
Police–Community Relations	Remote/Detached	Partnership
Police Accountability	Law	Community
Sources of Authority/Legitimacy	Legal	Moral (from within Community)
Level of Communication	Central Dispatch/Dictate	Dialogue
Decision-Making	Unilateral	Bilateral
Organizational Design	Bureaucracy	Human Resources Model
Organizational Structure	Centralized	Decentralized
Status of Power	Autonomy	Power-Sharing
Outlook on Diversity	Treat Everyone the Same	Cultural Sensitivity
Operational Strategies	Reactive	Proactive
Key Metaphor	The Thin Blue Line	Police Are the Public; The Public Are the Police

Human Resources: Revolution or Hegemony?

The concept of human resources is widely regarded as a solution to the problems created by a scientific management approach to doing business. Yet solving one problem by way of innovative solutions often creates conditions for a raft of new problems. Neither organized labour nor management are enthralled with human resources initiatives. Labour is worried about increased competition between worker teams, the prospect of the intensification of work itself, consolidation of managerial power and centralized control, and new peer pressures to perform (Slotnick 1989). Not all levels of management are coping. Many managers have been trained to manage, that is, to take control and produce results, but they are less adept at catering to the emotional well-being and security of workers. They are even less capable of playing the role of symphony conductors who must coax maximum output of the ensemble.

Even the concept of participation is being contested. The principle itself sounds good in theory, but participation can represent a lot of unpaid overtime and personal commitment. Company time can be particularly demanding on women who are torn between home and work. Nevertheless, refusal to participate may well have long-term consequences in terms of promotion and retirement benefits. Refusal may also be interpreted as letting down your team. Work teams can be problematic in other ways. They may exist to enhance flexibility, creativity, and productivity, yet the heightened level of diversity may preclude the possibility of working together effectively (Jackson and Ruderman 1995). Nor is there any proof that participation involves a real say in decision-making or power-sharing. Appeals to the virtues of empowerment, partnership, participatory management, and quality circles may be interpreted as window-dressing. Illusions of meaningful involvement are fostered without actually relinquishing any of the levers of power. Substantial decisions regarding relocation or hiring remain firmly in the grasp of management. The irony is inescapable: that thousands of workers are losing their jobs in the midst of a human resources revolution makes references to worker empowerment an especially cruel hoax.

ORGANIZATIONAL CHANGE/WORKPLACE RESISTANCE

Organizations are under pressure to change, yet organizational change is notoriously difficult to understand and infuriating to implement. Even a cursory glance over material in this section reveals the magnitude of the challenges confronting organizational structures and workplace dynamics. Management–labour relations have evolved from a scientific management mentality to a human resources mindset with its Japanese shop-floor styles and total quality commitments. Changes in the workplace have altered the very nature of work and working in response to the demands of the new (post-Fordist) economy. No less challenging have been developments at the level of gender and minority relations. Initiatives to manage diversity by way of employment equity and racial/sexual harassment policies are indicative of major transformations within the workplace—even if there is still concern about resistance to reforms by entrenched interests and systemic barriers.

Organizational ground rules are changing in other ways. Only recently, the corporate world was organized around a relatively stable and coherent reality where everybody knew their place in the overall scheme (Gay 1992). Organizational dynamics operated according to a number of tacit, yet widely accepted assumptions about who did what and why. Simply put, managers managed and workers worked. The reciprocal nature of the social contract was unmistakable. Management offered the prospect of long-term employment and job security in return for deference, increased productivity, and shop-floor harmony. For management, the key to corporate excellence was most clearly articulated in a list by Tom Peters and Bob Waterman (1982), with its emphasis on the virtues of "bias for action," "staying close to the customer," "autonomy and entrepreneurship," "productivity through people," "sticking to the knitting," and "simple form/lean staff." These qualities admittedly were difficult to implement but sensible enough to aspire to. Employees, in turn, demurred to authorities not only because they knew their place in the organizational pecking order, but because promises of a weekly paycheque and an ever-shortening work week were too tempting to rock the boat.

Organizations in Crisis

These rules barely apply any longer. Many corporations have had little choice but to rethink the rules for survival in a rapidly changing world. The controlled reality of management–labour relations has begun to unravel as the competition for profit intensifies.

Once-reassuring patterns of interaction are now subject to revision and reform, and openly contested in some cases by those at the margins. Instead of clockwork obedience, Marti Symes (1994) warns, employers now want workers who are not threatened by change or diversity, but thrive on risk-taking and multiple tasks. Thousands of employees have been made redundant, despite rhetoric about corporate missions and shop-floor democracies, in effect sapping worker morale and making a mockery of any pretext to loyalty or participatory democracy. Instead of lifelong employment, job-hopping has become a reality for many. The commitment to leaner and meaner may turn around corporate fortunes in the short run, but it does little to put food on an unemployed worker's table.

Organizational change has occurred because of a growing awareness that things don't work like they used to. It is a topic both timely and relevant. Not only does a study of organizational change reveal important features about society and social behaviour, it has practical significance, since organizations are keen to improve productivity, enhance labour–management relations, and cope with the challenges of change and diversity. Yet numerous barriers interfere with organizational renewal and reform. Environments are seldom controlled, individuals cannot be preprogrammed in a predictable way, and ground rules cannot be formulated in a way that will please all parties concerned. The most common of these obstacles are mistaken notions about organizations themselves, namely, the role of organizational culture and subcultural systems, questionable insights into human "nature," and naiveté about the process of planned change. The implementation of progressive programs can be sabotaged because of workplace resistance to changes that threaten individual livelihoods. But change is inevitable, and corporations that refuse to bend will find that they can no longer compete.

The Challenge of Change

It is one thing to contemplate the concept of organizational change. It is another thing to put these principles into practice in a way that makes an appreciable difference. Perils and pitfalls await those who underestimate the complexity and uncertainties associated with deliberate organizational transformation. The concept of organizational change nominally entails a process by which the demands of change, diversity, and uncertainty are incorporated at the level of structure, function, and process but without undermining either profitability or cohesiveness in the process. Five components would appear uppermost in specifying the parameters of organizational change, including representation, institutional rules and operations, workplace climate, service delivery and community relations.

Changing the Workplace

First, an institution's workforce should be representative; that is, the composition and distribution of its workers should be relatively proportional to that of the regional labour force—taking into account both social and cultural factors as extenuating circumstances. Such numerical representation applies not only to entry-level jobs, but to all levels of management, access to training, and entitlement to rewards. Second, institutional rules and operations cannot deny or exclude anyone from the process of job recruitment, selection, training, and promotion. This commitment to root out discriminatory barriers, both systemic and personal, demands a careful scrutiny of company policy and procedures. Third, the institution must foster a working climate conducive to the health and productivity of all workers. At minimum, such a climate cannot tolerate harassment of any form; at best, differences are accepted as normal and necessary to effective functioning and creative growth. Fourth, an accommodative institution ensures that delivery of its services is community-based and culturally sensitive. Such a commitment requires both a varied workforce and a sense of partnership with the community at large. Fifth and finally, institutions do not operate in a social or political vacuum. They are part of a community and cannot hope to remain outside of it in terms of accountability and responsibility if success is anticipated. Institutions must establish meaningful relations with all community members to ensure productive lines of communication and full community involvement in the decision-making process.

Barriers to Change

An array of personal and social barriers interfere with the process of institutional change. Debate in this field is polarized by those who advocate change without much thought to the costs and difficulties versus those who are resolutely opposed and resist change at all costs. Theories of organizational change are known to operate on the 30-50-20 principle (Laab 1996): 30 percent of workers will willingly accept imposed changes, 50 percent will resist initially but can be converted to the cause with arguments or threats, and 20 percent will resolutely oppose any change and nothing can dissuade them. Such divergences are to be expected, as implementing institutional changes is not like installing a new computer technology. Institutions are complex, often-baffling landscapes of domination and control as well as resistance and rebellion. Conservatives and progressives are locked in a struggle for power and privilege. Conventional views remain firmly entrenched as vested interests balk at discarding the tried and true. Newer visions are compelling, yet many lack the singularity of purpose or resources to scuttle traditional paradigms. The interplay of these juxtapositions can be disruptive or disorienting as the institution is transformed into a "contested site" involving competing world views and opposing agendas.

Numerous barriers exist that interfere with the process of directed institutional change. Stumbling blocks include people, hierarchy, bureaucracy, corporate culture, and occupational subcultures. People themselves are a prime obstruction. Institutional actors are likely to resist any appeal to move over and make space when they misunderstand what is going on and why. This should come as no surprise, as few individuals are inclined to relinquish power or privilege without a struggle. The dimension of hierarchy will also inhibit accommodative adjustments. Those in higher echelons may be highly supportive of institutional change for a variety of reasons, ranging from genuine concern to economic expediency, with an eye towards public relations in between. Yet publicly articulated positions in defence of internal reform may be long-winded on platitudes but short-minded on practice or implementation. Middle and lower management may be less enthusiastic about changes, preferring to cling to traditional authority patterns for fear of rocking the boat through institutional adjustments. Even more disruptive to organizational change are occupational subcultures. The subcultural values of frontline workers may differ from those of the higher echelons because of differences in experiences or expectations. This slippage may prove fatal to the transformation process, especially if resistance turns to open sabotage (see Gillmor 1996). Bureaucratic structures can also inhibit institutional engagement with diversity or change. Larger systems operate on bureaucratic principles of rational and hierarchical control. Such an imperative is not conducive to adjustment and accommodation in a structure known for its inherent conservatism.

Bureaucracy as Barrier

Of the many impediments to organizational change, few are as daunting as the presence of bureaucracy. The concept of bureaucracy is often associated with certain structures and sets of rules that are found within large-scale, complex organizations. All complex organizations are systematically organized by means of formal rules, with departments of trained experts coordinated around a hierarchical chain of command. They are also distinguished from informal groups by a centralization of authority, an emphasis on impersonal procedures, and a reliance on written documents (Weber 1947; Blau 1963). Bureaucracy can also be defined as a principle of organization. Organizationally, bureaucracies are imbued with an explicit commitment to maximize efficiency and achieve coordination and control through creation of a strict division of task, a supervisory hierarchy, and attachment to rules and regulations (Morgan 1986; Hummel 1987).

Two themes prevail: first, bureaucracies resemble machinelike instruments designed for rational goal achievement or crisp efficiency in service delivery. Bureaucratic work can be partitioned into a coordinated set of specific tasks; each task is then assigned to trained specialists who are responsible for dealing with particular cases or issues. In this sense bureaucracies are the epitome of scientific management principles. The second feature entails a commitment to the routine, the standardized, and the predictable as the preferred way of doing things in the organization. Not only do bureaucratic principles conflict with the elements of improvisation and the unexpected, the essence of bureaucracy revolves around reducing all human affairs to the rule of reason. Bureaucracies are in the business of stamping out the informal or discretionary aspects of reality at odds with efficiency or control. In their place are appeals to universality and professionalism, coupled with the application of uniform standards and formal procedures. This universality simplifies the administration of a large number of individuals (both workers and customers) without getting bogged down with paralyzing detail. Adherence to the virtues of rationality and standardization is critical. Rationality attempts to reduce human affairs to the rule of reason within the framework of formal regulations, clearly defined roles, and prescribed relations. It also justifies any course of action on the grounds of rationalizing workplace efficiency, organizational productivity, or corporate profits (Hale 1990).

At the core of all bureaucracies is the logic of rational control (Hummel 1987). In contrast with the world of everyday social interaction, which expects meaningful engagement with people as unique and complex individuals, the bureaucratic world is more attuned to control through cases, efficiency and calculation, functionaries, bureaucratese, and the status quo. Bureaucracies are not interested in people as complex and personal entities. As a rule, they are concerned with imposing formal procedures as one way of reducing all complexity to a single dimension known as a "case." Any situation that falls into a particular category will be treated just like all others in the same category. This reliance on cases and standard procedures provides a veneer of fairness and equality to the delivery of services. It also ensures some degree of control through the imposition of order and conformity. "Functionaries," as frontline workers are known, are expected to work according to a standard blueprint. This allows them to deal with a variety of situations through rote formula and technical rules. Failure to abide by these procedures by taking exceptions into account can lead to reprisals—from demotion to dismissal—in effect applying additional pressure to play it safe and go by the book. Such commitment to uniformity and common standards enables bureaucracy to strip organizations of all individuality and emotion, in the process transforming (routinizing) the world of diversity into uniformity, heterogeneity into homogeneity, and flexibility into rigidity. There is some question whether a bureaucracy can respond to a change model that (a) delegates responsibility and power to clients and employers, (b) encourages creativity and risk-taking, (c) establishes participatory decision-making and open lines of communication, (d) fosters a group-oriented climate involving trust and cooperation, (e) recognizes employee performance and promotes professional growth, and (f) monitors organizatonal performance to ensure commitment to mission and values (Report 1991).

Workplace Change: Give a Little, Take a Little

Directed organizational change and institutional accommodation are all about compromise. Even the most enthusiastic organizations are not concerned with promoting change for its own sake. Rather they are receptive to change as legitimate and integral only insofar as it does not interfere with the corporate bottom line or shareholder interests. Changes are acceptable, but not at the expense of institutional coherence and interconnectedness. A dual focus is required in creating an institution both representative of and accessible to all community members, as well as equitable in treatment and culturally sensitive. The adjustment process must occur at the level of institutional structure as well as within individual mindsets. It must also concentrate on the relationships within (the workplace environment) in addition to relationships without (clients). That alone should confirm the magnitude of the challenges that await institutional reform.

Workplace accommodation through organizational change is no longer an option or luxury, but necessary and overdue. The diversification of Canada's population demands a rethinking of traditional ways of doing things—if not for social justice, then for institutional effectiveness. Yet institutional inertia and resistance are equally powerful forces. A business-as-usual mentality is difficult to dislodge unless the impediments to adjustment and change are isolated and challenged through direct action. Institutions and the people who inhabit them may not be rigid and unbending by definition. Nevertheless, compromises and adjustments will materialize only if a promise of a payoff is forthcoming. Case 10-3 explores this concept of organizational change by examining the challenges of institutional accommodation within the police services. It points out that even the seemingly most progressive policies are likely to founder if certain precautions are not taken. Both subcultures and bureaucratic structures appear to be major impediments to institutionalizing the principles and practices of community policing. The fact that community policing continues to flourish more in theory than in practice, despite the crisis in police legitimacy, should forever dispel glib references about the inevitability of organizational change.

CASE 10-3   "Unbending Granite"

Police in Canada have come under pressure to change from different quarters. They are accused of losing the fight against crime because of outdated workplace styles. Allegations of harassment, brutality, double standards, intimidation, abuse, corruption, and racism have fuelled the fires of criticism towards police. Additional questions arise over police effectiveness and efficiency in a society that is increasingly diverse, ever changing, and more uncertain. This growing loss of public confidence raises certain questions: Is police misconduct an isolated act, or should we regard it as pervasive and structurally based? Is policing marred by a few "bad apples" or is it rotten to the core? What is it about policing that creates "bad" officers—is it the recruitment and selection process, the nature of the work, the organizational framework in which work is conducted, or negative experiences with the public at large? The concept of community policing is widely endorsed as one way of warding off this potential crisis in police legitimacy and restoring public confidence. The popularity of community policing is not under dispute: virtually every police service in Canada is officially committed to community policing principles (Leighton 1994). Parts of its popularity reflects a capacity to strike a responsive chord without imposing any substantial changes. Its appeal is further enhanced by the fact that community policing can mean many things to different people. Yet community policing appears stronger on paper than in reality. Why?

Community Policing

Broadly speaking, community policing is about redefining the nature of police work by rethinking the position of policing in society. More specifically, it can be seen as a reaction to limitations in conventional styles of policing (Bayley 1994). Professional crime-fighting models defined police as a highly trained and mechanized force for crime control and law enforcement. Police work could be described as incident-driven and complaint-reactive, and its effectiveness was measured by random car patrols, rapid response rates, and high conviction and clearance rates. Structurally, police were organized into a paramilitary model of bureaucracy involving a top down chain of command and control. Rewards and promotions were allocated on the basis of the big catch or long-standing loyalty to the force.

Community policing is about transforming the police from a "force" to a "service." It can be defined as a strategy that is adopted by the police to achieve the objectives of crime prevention by successfully engaging the public (see Moir and Moir 1993). Community policing is anchored around five principles: partnership, prevention, proactive, problem-solving, and pluralism (Fleras 1992). Community policing is about establishing a closer and meaningful partnership with the local community as part of a coherent strategy to prevent crime through proactive efforts in problem-solving. The community emerges as an active participant in crime prevention rather than as a passive

CASE 10-3   *"Unbending Granite" (continued)*

bystander, with the potential to deal with problems before they criminalize. The police in turn are expected to shed their "crime-buster" image in exchange for proactive styles that embody a willingness to work more closely with increasingly diverse communities through establishment of liaison and communication (see Shusta et al. 1995).

Debates about community policing are not about whether to implement it, but how much and at what pace (Leighton 1994). Yet not everyone is supportive of this shift in priorities from crime-fighting and law enforcement to public service in consultation with the community. For example, the Metropolitan Toronto Police Association has gone on record as being totally opposed to community policing, despite (or in spite of) wholesale endorsement by senior management (Gillmor 1996). Resistance is to be expected: community policing principles appear to be at loggerheads with conventional police work. Many perceive community policing as inconsistent with long-standing police practices, a threat to cherished values and images, an impediment to career enhancement, and an attack on police powers and relative autonomy. Implementation of community policing will invariably challenge vested interests; community policing principles also appear diametrically opposed to occupational subcultural values and bureaucratic structures (Chan 1997).

Barriers to Change: Occupational Subcultures

People who occupy a similar occupation may develop distinctive ways of perceiving and responding to their social environment (Chan 1996). They also are likely to endorse a common system of norms and values related to work. The police are no exception. They belong to a type of occupational subculture defined by the demands of the job and the constraints of public expectations (Desroches 1992). A distinctive set of norms, values, and beliefs has evolved and become entrenched through shared experiences, similar training, common interests, and continual interaction.

The grounds for this police occupational subculture are not difficult to uncover. Most police officers in Canada are male, white, able-bodied, French- or English-speaking, and of working class origins. This homogeneity in sex, social class, and ethnicity is reinforced by similar socialization pressures related to common training and peer group influence. The resultant solidarity is reinforced by the sense of isolation from the community (us versus them), by police perception of the public as ignorant and unsupportive of law enforcement activities, and by the nature of police work, which encourages a degree of caution or defensiveness. Suspicion towards those outside the profession compounds the pressures of isolation, mutual distrust, and alienation. Adding to the divisiveness is the need to appear efficient and in control at all times as part of doing police work (James and Warren 1995). Not surprisingly, police deeply resent those segments of the community that defy police authority or violate concepts of order and stability. Police solidarity and estrangement from the community are further reinforced by

CASE 10-3 **"Unbending Granite" (continued)**

the requirements of the job, including shift work and mutual support in times of crisis and danger.

The values and priorities underlying the police occupational subculture are inconsistent with those of community policing (Seagrave 1997). These differences can be summarized by way of contrasting outlooks (see Seitzinger and Sabino 1988, 45–46):

- Officers see themselves as crime-fighters, not as social workers.

- Officers are law enforcement agents, not community workers, facilitators or problem-solvers.

- Officers define police work as "man's work" in that they condone aggressiveness and a take-charge mentality as a means of conflict resolution and path to career success (Worden 1993).

- Officers feel comfortable reacting to crimes, but many are uncomfortable dealing with community organizations.

- Crime control continues to be defined as "real" police work and everything else as a "soft option" or "luxury" for public relations reasons (Robinson et al. 1989).

- Officers have been trained to believe in rapid response and random patrol as key crime-fighting tools. Walking the beat, by contrast, is often perceived as a punishment, the preserve of misfits or those about to retire, or a sign of a "stalled" career.

- Community police officers tend to be isolated from their peers, in some cases actively disparaged as "traitors"

or "phoneys" who jeopardize the lives of fellow officers by not pulling their weight (Chan 1996).

- The lack of career structure for community policing makes it a questionable measurement of success and stepping stone for advancement.

This lists confirms the lack of enthusiasm for a community policing option. The police openly resist those aspects of community service at odds with the reassuring confines of the traditional policing subculture. Evidence indicates that many police officers do not want to be seen as "facilitators," "resource personnel," or "peacekeepers." They see themselves as law enforcement agents who define success by the number of arrests and citations. Many resent a "social welfare" tag, preferring a "take-charge" identity that reinforces their self-perception as professional crime-fighters. Again, we turn to Oettmeier and Brown (1988, 15):

> The organizational culture of municipal policing has, in general, continued to condition police officers to think of themselves primarily as "crime-fighters." Traditionally, police departments have attempted to identify and recruit individuals into policing that have displayed bravado. Organizational incentives have also been designed to favour self-conceptions of *machismo*, conceptions that are reinforced through pop art (e.g., detective novels, "police stories," "Dirty Harry" movies, etc.). Many, if not most, of the approximately 500,000 law enforcement officers in policing in America today have strong

CASE 10-3   "Unbending Granite" (continued)

opinions about what constitutes "*real police work*" (emphasis added).

With its focus on service, community policing does not coincide with popular perceptions of police as professional crime-fighters. Community police officers may experience isolation and alienation even from colleagues as allegiances shift from professional crime-fighting to service on behalf of the community (Asbury 1989). The following passage from Wilson and Kelling (1989, 52) speaks eloquently of the potential anguish:

> In every department we visited, some of the incident-oriented officers spoke disparaging of the problem-oriented officers as "social workers," and some of the latter responded by calling the former "ghetto blasters." If a community-service officer seems to get too close to the community, he or she may be accused of "going native."

The gap between policing and community policing, between police and community, could not be more striking (see Eck and Rosenbaum 1994). Community policing culture endorses the virtues of trust, familiarity, cooperation, and respect. The community is viewed not as a problem but as a "resource" with unlimited potential for dealing with local issues. Opposing this is the occupational subculture of the police with its detachment from the community. The community is dismissed as disinterested in social control work, indifferent and passive (waiting to be policed), incompetent to carry out even simple tasks, disorganized to act in unison, and

misinformed about the pressures and demands placed on the police. In short, the community is perceived as irrelevant to the point of an impediment for effective policing except in the most passive way of providing information (Gillmor 1996). This clash of visions makes it difficult to imagine a situation more conducive to misunderstanding and distrust. Even the influx of women into policing is not likely to foster a more receptive climate for community policing. To be sure, women are known to see police work differently than men, seek out different relations with the community, employ different concepts of morality and justice, prefer community service to law enforcement, and engage in communication rather than control through aggression (Worden 1993). Yet these community-oriented qualities may be for naught in the face of pressures to join the "brotherhood" or "get out."

Barriers to Change: Bureaucracy

No less inhibiting of organizational change is the pervasiveness of police bureaucracy. The police as an institution are organized around bureaucratic principles. Police personnel from top to bottom play roles as bureaucrats whose primary obligation rests with anyone but the community. These bureaucratic dimensions serve as barriers at odds with community-based initiatives.

The police are widely regarded as a bureaucratic organization with paramilitary overtones. They are governed by a central command and control structure, with a ranked hierarchy, complex division of labour, impersonal enforcement of formal rules, carefully stipulated procedures, and the provision

CASE 10-3   *"Unbending Granite"* (continued)

of a rationally based service. Police bureaucracies exist to control a large number of persons (both internally and externally) without prejudice or explicit favouritism. This control function is attained through rational control procedures, standardization, conformity through rule-following, and accountability to the organizational chain of command. A commitment to control would appear consistent with a traditional professional crime-fighting model yet complicate efforts to respond to community demands or to initiate positive changes in police–community relations (Clairmont 1988).

The principles of bureaucracy and community policing appear mutually opposed. The partnership ethos and the reciprocity inherent in community policing is strikingly at odds with an entrenched bureaucracy and occupational subculture. Community policing emphasizes collaboration, creativity, joint problem-solving, accountability to clients, and co-responsibility for crime control and order maintenance (Normandeau and Leighton 1990). Bureaucracies by contrast are destined to be remote, isolated, and case-oriented. They are also bound by rules, organizational procedures, and hierarchy. One model is programmed for control and routinization, the other for cooperation and consultation.

The police have their work cut out for them if they are serious about community policing. A fundamental reorientation is called for that entails a debureaucratization of role, status, functions, reward structures, operational styles, training programs, and objectives.

Yet fundamental questions remain: How can creative problem-solving techniques flourish under organizational conditions that expect obedience and compliance while discouraging questioning, self-motivation, and innovation (Tomovich and Loree 1989)? Can innovative—even risk-taking—solutions be reconciled with a mindset based on "not rocking the boat" or "shut up, and do as you're told"? Who can be surprised that community policing initiatives have withered under such intimidating conditions?

Rethinking the Thin Blue Line

Even the brightest proposals for change will not take hold without an adequate analysis of barriers and constraints. The introduction of new ideas is likely to encounter resistance from entrenched interests or established values, especially in a conservative bureaucracy renowned for its reluctance to move over and make space. The introduction of community policing principles represents such a threat. Community policing provides a conceptual framework for initiating changes to transform the police organization in a way that improves community involvement in the design and implementation of programs for crime prevention. But reference to community policing rarely acknowledges the barriers that stand in the way of successful implementation. It is likely to meet with resistance and resentment unless management finds a way to (a) break down the barriers to social change, (b) educate all police officials about its benefits and advantages, (c) address manageable problems before embarking on widespread reforms, (d) convey that

CASE 10-3   *"Unbending Granite" (continued)*

community policing is a natural outgrowth of developments within the department, (e) demonstrate the merits of community policing to the general public and elected officials, (f) give clear indications of changes in training, reward structures, and career enhancement, (g) indicate willingness to experiment with innovative ideas and structures, (h) reveal how administrative styles and management techniques will be redesigned to meet new concerns, and (i) clear up misunderstanding and misconception regarding the goals, content, and scope of community policing (Brown 1989).

Community policing will not make its mark until police are convinced of its application to the "real world" (see Chan 1997). This is not likely to happen as long as senior administration are perceived to be out of touch with reality and beholden to political rather than police interests (Gillmor 1996). Much of what passes for community policing

deals with appearances, not substance. It may comprise little more than an expedient repackaging of small-town policing to placate the public, to curry political favour, to extract additional resources from the government, or as public relations exercises for damage control, conflict resolution, and impression management. Nor will it make much of an impact until the goals of community policing are shown to be attainable, realistic, and rewarding—especially for those officers who stand to benefit or lose from its introduction. As long as individual officers believe they have nothing to gain from community policing, and that rewards lie with "kick-ass policing," the prospect of attitudinal change is remote. In the final analysis, the success and failure of community policing rides on its capacity to bring frontline officers around to a vision of a "new blue line."

SUMMARY

1. Problems associated with organizations and the workplace are best examined from a social problem perspective. In this way, organizations and workplaces are perceived as 1) problems in their own right, 2) creating problems for clients and employees, and 3) subject to external pressures that generate further problems. The realities of change, diversity, and uncertainty have intensified many of the problems associated with organizational workplaces.

2. The crisis in work cannot be underestimated. Technology and ideology have combined to reshape the nature of work, the availability of work, the concept of the workplace, and the very notion of wealth creation. The combination of radical technologies and a rapidly globalizing economy continues to (a) eliminate access to adequately waged jobs; (b) reduce manufacturing work by outsourcing to lower-paid workers in less-developed

countries; (c) displace workers by "smart" machines and "slash and cut" management philosophies; (d) transfer public sector responsibilities to the private sector, with a corresponding shredding of the safety net; and (e) transform both public and private sectors into bottom-line enterprises in pursuit of efficiency, user-pays arrangements, and zero-deficit goals (see Lerner 1997).

3. While generally regarded as an improvement over ad hoc methods of organization, bureaucracies are routinely denounced as major social problems because of their rigidity and inflexibility, resistance to change, and inability to cope with uncertainties—qualities of utmost importance in a changing and diverse society.

4. Bureaucracies constitute a separate reality, with a distinctive psychology, language, and political structure and their own set of norms and behaviours. The need to control vast numbers of people (both internally and externally) without undue privilege or prejudgment is central to the logic of any bureaucracy.

5. The principles of scientific management reflected and reinforced a bureaucratic approach to the workplace. Rather than disappearing, as many had anticipated, these principles appear to be flourishing in the fast food industry.

6. Recent initiatives for addressing workplace problems have endorsed a human resources model of management–labour relations. The shift from scientific management to human resources management is consistent with a sharpened focus on improved worker participation, consensual decision-making, and workplace democracy.

7. The introduction of a human resources model of management may sound good in theory. In reality, the proposed changes are likely to generate additional problems because of the lack of "fit" between Japanese corporate cultures and those of North America.

8. Community policing represents an example of a human resources approach to work known as total quality. With its commitment to crime prevention through community-based service, community policing seeks to displace a professional crime-fighting model with one that emphasizes partnership, proactivity, and problem-solving.

9. There may be a general shift away from a mechanized model of workplace towards a model that uses the principles of the human resources approach. The metaphorical switch from conveyor belt to quality circles may symbolize this shift. Yet in a world of slash and burn downsizing and leaner and meaner management, talk of worker empowerment is decidedly contradictory.

10. Organizational change sounds good in theory but is difficult to implement. Numerous barriers exist—from the individual to the structural—that impede the implementation of change.

11. A commitment to community policing has not worked out as many had hoped because of interference from bureaucratic structures and police occupational subcultures.

GLOBAL
PROBLEMS

GLOBALIZATION AND GLOBAL PROBLEMS

DID YOU KNOW?

- One percent of the world's population owns 60 percent of its resources; the bottom 80 percent are forced to scramble for 15 percent of the resources.

- Among the G-7 countries, Canada is the most trade dependent with 40 percent of its total economic output based on exports. In 1995 79.7 percent of Canada's exports went to the United States, with the European Union next at 6.3 percent. Such dependency exposes Canada to swings in the American economy.

- Foreign firms control two-thirds of book sales in Canada, 80 percent of educational publishing, 80 percent of the market for English-speaking magazines, 64 percent of the programs aired on TV, and 95 percent of the screen time in Canadian movie theatres. By 1994, David Crane (1997) points out, Canada had accumulated a $4 billion deficit in cultural products.

- There are an estimated 37 000 multinationals in the world at present. Together, they control about one-third of all private sector capital and generate annual sales valued at U.S. $8.4 trillion in 1994. The leading multinationals in terms of foreign assets continue to be auto-related. The top four are: Royal Dutch/Shell, Ford, General Motors, and Exxon. BP is sixth according to UN figures for 1990.

- Nike increased its profits by 700 percent between 1987 and 1992, in part by moving its factories to countries with low wages and lax working conditions. A pair of Nikes that sell for U.S. $70 can be produced in Indonesia for U.S. $1.66 on wages that average less than U.S. $2 a day.

- For the fifth time in this decade, Canada has been judged the world's best place to live by the UN Development Programme on the basis of income, education, and life expectancy. France, Norway, United States, and Japan were close behind. Yet problems lurk behind this glossy exterior. Canada's environment continues to deteriorate rapidly according to a study by the National Centre for Economic Alternatives. Canada ranked second to last among nine industrial nations for long-term environmental degradation.

- Foreign aid from the 21 OECD countries continues to shrivel up, down to $82 billion or 0.25 percent of GNP in 1996. Northern European countries remain the most generous donors with contributions of between 0.86 percent and 1.16 percent of their GNP. The United States donates only 0.18 percent of its GNP although its total of $9.9 billion is second only to Japan's $13.2 billion; Canada's commitment has dwindled as well, from $3.2 billion in 1991 to a projected $1.9 billion in 1998, or 0.24 percent of its GNP—its lowest rate since 1965 and well below the UN target of 0.7 percent of GNP.

- The world population stands at 5.8 billion; it is expected to increase to 6.1 billion by the year 2000, with about 95 percent of the increase in developing countries that already claim 83 percent of the global population. Thirty-one percent of the population is under 15 years of age.

- Half of the world now lives in cities. In 1996 the UN acknowledged that a third of the urban population lived in 270 cities of 1 million people or more, including 20 megacities of over 8 million. Heading this list of urban conglomerates is Tokyo (26.8 million), Sao Paulo (16.4 million), and New York (16.3 million). By 2015, the list will be headed by Tokyo (28.7 million), Bombay (27.4 million), Lagos (24.3 million), and Shanghai (23.4 million).

- By 1996, there were 447 billionaires worldwide whose net worth matched the combined income of half the world's population. As well, the income gap between the top 20 percent of the world's population and the bottom 20 percent has doubled since 1961. By the same token, Gwynne Dyer (1996) argues, the gap between the top 20 percent and the middle 60 percent is closing.

- The Developing World continues to be wracked by ethnic conflicts. Of the 82 wars that have broken out since 1990, only 3 involved conflicts between governments (Handelman 1996). The rest took place in "collapsed" states or "paralyzed" economies where the loss of central authority created a power vacuum for ethnic confrontation and cleansing.

- The demise of the nation-state because of globalization and free market dynamics is greatly exaggerated. State expenditure as a proportion of the GNP rose from 27.6 percent to 35.3 percent in the United States between 1960 and 1995, and from 21.1 percent to 34.6 percent in Japan between 1970 and 1994 (Livingstone 1996).

- In 1992, Canada pledged to reduce its emission levels by the year 2000. Since then the output of greenhouse gases has risen by 13%—making Canada one of the world's most profligate energy users.

- On any given day, Erik Swyngedouw (1996) observes, a staggering U.S. $1 trillion will be exchanged around the globe. About 10 percent is used for settling international trade transactions. The rest is taken up with finance speculation (stock markets, futures, derivatives, securities, commodities) in search of security or gains. No wonder Jacques Chirac has condemned speculative movements in the international finance markets as the scourge of national economies.

- The British economist Adrian Wood has calculated a transfer of 9 million jobs from the north to the south. Manufacturing labour costs may have had much to do with this shift: in 1993 average labour costs in the United States were $16.90 per hour but only $4.90 in South Korea and $0.50 in China.

THE PROBLEM

The world is full of contradictions, conflict, and change. Whether we approve or disapprove, broad historical forces are establishing innovative scenarios for the next century. Not only are the ground rules changing, but so too is the game itself as players and strategies reposition themselves in redefining outcomes. Issues that engulf the world at present resonate with ambiguity and tension at a time in which traditional realities are reversed so rapidly that new expectations cannot take shape (Kanter 1995). Past privileges and earlier priorities have been revoked or swept aside in a way scarcely imaginable a generation ago. What once were seen as vices are now accepted as virtues, and vice versa. The net results are as disruptive as they are demoralizing. Governments and economies are reeling before the onslaught of forces seemingly beyond comprehension. People, too, are becoming increasingly edgy over (a) the pace of change, which appears out of control; (b) unemployment rates that show no signs of easing; (c) politicians that no longer inspire confidence in political systems that seem hopelessly archaic; and (d) the loss of community that the discipline of market forces cannot recover (Aitken 1997).

Reaction to this upheaval and restructuring has been mixed. People around the world breathed a collective sigh of relief when the Cold War ended at the turn of this decade. Many assumed the collapse of superpower hegemony would usher in prosperity and peace among nation-states, but the euphoria turned out to be short-lived. Nearly a decade after the dismantling of the Berlin Wall and the demise of the Soviet Union, the world remains transfixed by depression and despair in the wake of violence so stunning in its savagery as to question the "nature" of human nature (Ignatieff 1993). Instead of a brave new global order, a dreary and demoralizing round of random violence has culminated in ethnic cleansing, smart bombs, final solutions, and racial purity. Haunting images of emaciated refugees cowering in makeshift camps without food or medicine yet victims of pillage or rape have become so commonplace as to have lost all shock value. Instead of peaceful and cooperative coexistence, the primacy of financial markets has displaced the threat of mutual deterrence as a unifying power (Attali 1990). The new global disorder is collapsing into an ideologically homogeneous market where the slogan, "greed is good," is the prevailing mantra for justifying even the most callous of actions. Evidence points to growing inequities between the "haves" and the "have nots," in spite of trade liberalization and developmental assistance (Vidal 1996). Any hopes of progress in the poorer developing countries are derailed by population explosions, urbanization, poverty, environmental degradation, and the revival of racial and ethnic rivalries (Jackson 1992). Each of these threats carries the potential to terminate planetary existence if left unchecked (Kaplan 1994).

Equally disruptive are global changes in the economy. Just as the Industrial Revolution signified a radical break with its feudal predecessors, so too has contemporary post-industrialism created a fundamentally different way of generating and distributing wealth. The new economic order is not simply a reorganization around a knowledge-driven, microelectronic economy; a revolutionary shift in ways of "doing business" is now taking place (Daniels and Lever 1996). Perhaps for the first time since the birth of capitalism, the economy is becoming truly global with the internalization of investment capital and the relatively free movement of goods and financial services across increasingly porous borders (Horsman 1993). Of particular note is the worldwide penetration of free market principles in all parts of the world in the relentless quest for profits and expansion (Robinson 1996). The triumph of global capitalism has culminated in an integrated global system in which all societies are differentially incorporated into a vast productive loop as cost-effective "links." Yet the globalization of capitalist economies has not been without costs. In such an intensely competitive environment, international capital and multinational corporations have shown they can shun countries that dare to maintain protective trade barriers or deter investment through taxation, labour and environmental laws, and costly social programs (Laxer 1996). The welfare state and Keynesian economics have withered under relentless assaults by advocates of an unfettered free market (Kelsey 1997). Getting lean and mean in a global economy may be good for economic elites; after all, stock markets are soaring, corporate profits are escalating, inflation is dead, and shareholders are clutching hefty returns on investments. Yet leaner and meaner is tough on workers who feel betrayed by government repudiation of its postwar commitment to full employment and comprehensive social welfare (Kapstein 1996). To be sure, the forces of globalization are capable of generating new freedoms and material affluence by unlocking dormant potential. Yet global integration is inseparable from local disintegration, with benefits directed at shareholders rather than shared with stakeholders at large (Crane 1997).

To say that we are living in interesting times is something of an understatement. Nowhere is this aphorism more applicable than in the contradictions that concurrently connect yet divide the world (Kanter 1995). The basic units of geopolitics, the nation-state, have become less dominant, less self-sufficient, less independent, and less separate than in the past because of technology that has the power to move everything from products to money from one part of the globe to another without permission if necessary (Economist 1995/96). The legitimacy and autonomy of the traditional nation-state are being contested by outward-leaning multinationals and inward-looking ethnic nationalisms. Powerful forces are simultaneously drawing us closer together into a global-economy yet pulling us further apart because of competition. Governments and nation-states are criticized as too large to solve the small problems of the world, but too small to tackle the larger problems. How, then, do we interpret the current global disarray? Are we on the brink of a precipitous decline because of ruinous competition for scarce resources, the polarization of the world into rich and poor, or confrontations between "tribal" forces? Or is this disarray merely symptomatic of a transition from one social era to another? Perhaps the problems confronting societies are not "pathological" in the sense of being unhealthy, but better seen as normal "growing pains" in the unfolding of new realities.

Canada is no less immune than other countries to the clash of contradictory forces. The crises that confront Canada can only be comprehended against a backdrop of a world in the throes of transformation and disruption (Griffiths 1996). Canada's economic prosperity once rested on a commodity-based export sector in conjunction with a heavily protected domestic manufacturing industry and an extensive social welfare system (see Robinson 1996). But major structural shifts in the global economy exerted pressure for a fundamental reordering of the economy, dismantling of protectionist frameworks such as import-substitution industrial strategy, the deregulation of economic life, and calls for new international competitiveness. For better or worse, Canada is increasingly enmeshed in a globalizing world of free trade agreements, exposed to the harsh realities of a competitive marketplace and made vulnerable to outside forces for its very livelihood. Incorporation of Canada into a multinationally driven, global marketplace demands a national economy bereft of unnecessary barriers and institutions that interfere with international competitiveness. Governments are increasingly compelled to measure the success of their activities in terms of how world money markets respond to the merits of cost-cutting initiatives (Rizvi 1996). As a trading nation with 40 percent of its wealth created through foreign trade, the prospect of freer trade in goods and investment is of potential advantage; yet each arrangement and accord runs the risk of imperilling Canada's culture and sovereignty (Ford 1996). Canada wants to derive benefit from a free-wheeling global economy without abdicating a commitment to a fair and just society (Barlow and Clark 1996; Goar 1997). The Canadian state is dismantling itself in terms of redistribution policies such as health and welfare, but strengthening its capacity to regulate in favour of market priorities (Albo and Jenson 1996). Yet the ambiguities of globalization are not the only corrosive element eroding the fabric of Canadian society. The forces of ethnicity—from aboriginal peoples to the Québecois—may still undermine the concept of a sovereign Canada, despite widely acclaimed initiatives for engaging diversity, from official multiculturalism to inherent aboriginal self-government rights (Fleras and Elliott 1996).

The challenge for a globalizing Canada is straightforward enough: how to transform a resource-based economy into an aggressive global competitor without dissolving either its social conscience or integrity of the constituent units that shape its distinctiveness. On the assumption that world systems are a force to be reckoned with in shaping Canada's destiny, this chapter will examine globalization as a problem for some and a solution for others. The fact that potential drawbacks coexist with apparent benefits seems typical of social problems in general. This is particularly evident when discussing global problems, and the role of Canada in creating and solving the problems that confront developing countries. No less revealing is how previous solutions are now defined as problems to be replaced by a new set of solutions that already show signs of being problematic.

GLOBALIZATION: PROBLEM OR SOLUTION?

The term globalization has leapt into ordinary discourse with a vengeance. Many would concur that globalization can be hailed as the defining historical moment of our times, despite suffering from overuse and lack of definitional clarity (Editorial 1996). With the potential to transform structures and influence outcomes, globalization constitutes a fundamental dynamic that is animating all the major referent points of human society through the internationalization of economic, social, political, and cultural processes (Robinson 1996). At the same time globalization is generating gaping inequities as regions and states compete for corporate investment, in the process lowering wages, environmental standards, and human rights protections (Mander 1996). Hype notwithstanding, there is nothing especially new about its constituent features. References to globalization include some or all of the following historical trends: multinational corporations, economic interdependence, capitalist penetration, export trade, intensified competition, international division of labour, integrated markets, regional integration, mobile money, convergence through compression of time and space, rapid communication, permeable borders, and microchip technologies. These components are organized into ideological principles, including unregulated free market dynamics, free trade as a catalyst for growth, elimination of import substitution economies that foster economic self-sufficiency, privatization of public enterprises, and an aggressive consumerism (Mander 1996). What is new about globalization is the striking speed, scope, and intensity of this transformation. What also is new is not the importance of international trade to the economy, which has been going on since the seventeenth century, but the incorporation of the national economy as a unit at the global level in real time and space (Castells 1993).

Perceptions of Globalization

Public reaction to globalization tends to be varied, welcomed by some and lamented by others. In its effects, globalization is dialectical, both a problem *and* solution as well as a problem *or* solution. The worldwide reorganization of markets *has* dismantled trade barriers, but it has also meant "rationalizing" domestic markets in the scramble for global advantage. Trade liberalization has been a bonus to some nation-states, but disruptive for those whose goods and services incur a "value-added tax" because of higher environmental, social, and labour costs. A more competitive money market has increased the number of BMWs on city streets, yet the pressure for profit amplification has complicated employment access for recent graduates, minorities, and older workers in "smokestack" industries. For some, globalization is viewed as a catalyst for national prosperity through the elimination of artificial barriers to free enterprise. The future lies in the creation of a borderless world of boundless prosperity, anchored in the promotion of global consumerism and demise of market-meddling state institutions (see Capling 1997). Freeing up global economies through the discipline of the market is thought to increase choice, reward risk, unleash creativity, and eliminate wastes. But market-motivated philosophies can throw people out of work and dissolve social service access—in effect foreclosing choices, widening disparities, diminishing diversity, and eroding national identity (Editorial 1996). Women, particularly in dependent countries, have suffered because of austerity measures associated with structural adjustments that reduce national deficits but intensify local deprivation (Duggan and Dashner 1994).

For others, globalization is scorned as a thinly veiled evil for crushing the world under capitalist hegemony. In a strongly worded critique, William Robinson (1996) couches globalization in highly apocalyptic terms as a *world war* between the global rich and the global poor from which no economy can escape involvement and whose human and environmental impact is comparable in scale to nineteenth century colonial predations. Erosion of a civil society is but one cost of this neo-colonialism; environmental destruction is yet another in an era in which short-term profits take priority over long-term sustainable growth. Such short-sightedness makes the global economy inherently unjust, unstable, and unsustainable. Still others are unsure of how to respond. For them, just defining the concept—let alone sorting out the mélange of pros and cons—is puzzling and infuriating.

Defining Globalization

The term globalization can be defined in different ways. This plurality reflects the multitextured strands of globalization, including that of the political, social, and cultural. Globalization involves the supplanting of modernity (and its quintessential expression in the nation-state) with the postmodern (and its expression in the local or the global) as a common frame of reference for human organization, wealth creation, and social action (see Albrow 1996). Globalization can be seen as a process of change involving the interplay of increased cross-border activity with information technology and instantaneous communication (Kanter 1995). It entails a process by which the local and the national are amalgamated with the global to make a single integrated world system by the geographical expansion of capitalist market relations into new realms of production, from the commercialization of agriculture to the commodification of social life (Barlow and Clarke 1996; Bromley 1996). Globalization is inseparable from increasing interdependence and global enmeshment as everything from money and markets to people and ideas move swiftly and smoothly across national boundaries (Hurrell and Woods 1995). Four broad processes are mutually interlinked: mobility (rapid movement of capital, labour, and ideas); simultaneity (everywhere at once with rapid acceptance of new ideas); bypass (multiple choices that circumvent conventional channels); and pluralism (decentralization of structures and devolution of power, especially to consumers) (Kanter 1995).

Most definitions equate globalization with new forms of wealth creation by way of economic restructuring on a global scale (Laux 1990/91). There is growing faith in worldwide markets and unrestricted competition as a means of sorting out "who gets what." Under globalization, national economies are reorganized around an integrated system of production for the express purpose of maximizing profit and minimizing risk (Robinson 1996). This reorganization of production into global loops of cost-effective sites compels economies to specialize or perish in the unremitting competition for markets, investments, and jobs (Laxer 1991). In global trade parlance, this specialization conforms to the law of *comparative advantage*; that is, prosperity is best achieved when each economy specializes in what it does best (Clegg 1996). The production process itself is transformed under globalization. Fordist models of production, with their emphasis on mass and standardized production, vertical integration, economies of scale, and de-skilled labour, have given way to more flexible systems for producing more varied and specialized goods and services (Holly 1996). Production is geared primarily for export rather than for domestic consumption. Inefficient industries are abandoned while foreign investment and onshore jobs are vigorously pursued through the creation of "business-friendly" environments. Finally, trading in financial services (from currency speculation to commodity futures) vastly supersedes trade in material goods (Swyngedouw 1996). Money no longer exists only as a means for buying something but as a valued commodity and an exchange value in its own right (Daniels and Lever 1996).

Two implications follow from this spectrum of meanings. First, globalization goes beyond a simple economic shift created by the combination of high technology, instantaneous communication, borderless investment, reduced subsidies, and free trade. The globalization of business has prompted a reorganization of products, markets, and finances of unprecedented magnitude and scope, in effect creating interdependencies that could not have existed in the past. No economy is left untouched in the ruthless competition to displace precapitalist economies with a capitalist market economy (Robinson 1996). The resulting interdependency is uneven and fragmented, with gross disparities in the control of power, resources, and status. Second, the interplay of world economic markets and globalization has undermined conventional thinking about national sovereignty. Borders have become increasingly porous with the advent of microchip technologies, while the salience of the nation-state as a relatively autonomous unit of political economy is challenged by the unimpeded flow of capital and investment. The integrity of the sovereign state is diminished further still when stateless corporations known as multinational conglomerates replace domestic production as the engine for growth.

CASE 11-1   Multinationals: Engines of Globalization

The term globalization was coined relatively recently, but there has been a comparable trend in existence for several centuries, known as colonialism. Since the end of the Second World War, neo-colonialist pressures have further intensified the concept of international trading links within a capitalist framework. The cumulative effect of this capitalist expansion is a global system in which the world is partitioned into unequal sectors of "haves" and "have nots." All countries are now absorbed into a capitalist world system to the extent that production and distribution of goods and services are conducted along free market principles. National economies are inextricably linked with a free-flowing international division of labour. Competition for markets, jobs, and resources is increasingly conducted without much interference from the regulatory mechanisms of national boundaries. The end result? Affluent countries enrich themselves at the expense of the poor by taking unfair advantage through the control of investment, bank loans, trade and tariffs, and industrial dependency. The catalysts behind this uneven development and imbalanced international division of labour are multinationals (or trans-nationals).

Few will dispute the impact of multinational enterprises in transforming the world along global lines (Clegg 1996). Once reviled in capitalist and communist countries alike, multinationals are now endorsed as the embodiment of modernity and progress, with governments around the world lining up to attract these money-making machines (Emmott 1993). They are the foremost actors on the global stage, straddling national boundaries and generating sales in automobiles, oil, electronics, computers, and banking that often exceed the aggregate (GNP) output of most countries (Carnoy 1996). Their spectacular growth in recent years can be attributed to different factors, including failure to regulate national barriers against overseas investment, rapid telecommunication and transport systems, and the freeing up of domestic markets for foreign activity. Multi-nationals have taken advantage of largely American-driven moves to integrate the world market by exploiting wage and cost differentials for labour and commodities among different regimes in the world (Palat 1996). In rationalizing the production of goods and services for maximizing profits, multinational business is rapidly becoming a global affair as reflected in largely expedient decisions regarding plant location, resource extraction, and market or investment futures. The ultimate goal is an integrated global production system in which individual countries constitute but one link in a vast production chain of multinationally controlled "stateless corporations" (UN World Development Report 1993 in Crane 1993).

Multinational corporations can be defined as multitiered networks that include parent companies, foreign affiliates, alliances with other companies, and contractual agreements that enhance control over the entire production process. This control extends from

CASE 11-1   Multinationals: Engines of Globalization (continued)

research and development to transport, assembly, marketing, and finance. The magnitude and scope of multinationals are undeniable. The world's biggest multinationals—most of which are located in the United States, Europe (primarily Germany and Switzerland), and Japan—own about one-third of the world's private-sector assets (Clegg 1996). The stock of foreign investment controlled by multinationals has tripled from U.S. $488.2 billion in 1980 to U.S. $1496 billion in 1992. Canada is a primary target for multinational investment. Total foreign investment in Canada stands at $108 billion—greater than all of Latin America and just slightly less than Asian Pacific Rim countries. This ratio could change shortly. Foreign investment doubled in Canada during the 1980s, but tripled in Latin America and quadrupled in Pacific Rim countries. This increase is typical of developing countries in general. As Crane (1993) notes, developing countries now consume 20 percent of foreign investment, but this is expected to rise to 50 percent by the year 2020. Even the type of investment has shifted in recent years, according to the *UN Report on Development* (1993). In 1970 resources attracted 22.7 percent of all foreign investment, 45.2 percent went to branch plant manufacturing, and 31.4 percent went to services (telecommunications, transportation, and real estate). By 1990, the figures reflected the following: 11.2 percent in resources, 38.7 percent in manufacturing, and 50.1 percent in services. This trend is likely to continue in the future (Daniels 1996).

Few would dispute the global economic power harnessed by the transnational mobility of these stateless conglomerates. Unfettered as they are by national boundaries or loyalties, multinationals can move to whatever part of the globe that promises the best return on their investment. Such transnational mobility creates the basis for redesigning the means of production. Global systems of production are created involving components and assembly in different countries, with a new international division of labour on the basis of job location (Crane 1996). Manufactured goods are no longer what they appear to be. Consider a Mazda Miata: The financial package was negotiated in New York, the car design originated in California, the first prototype was built in Britain, and components were manufactured in Japan and then assembled in Mexico and Michigan (Valaskas 1992). Not surprisingly, Chrysler cars have more Japanese than American parts; conversely, Honda has more American than Japanese components. Elsewhere, Sony televisions destined for the American market are assembled in Mexico from parts built in Japan. The transformation of the world into a global loop of cost-effective sites of production makes a mockery of the expression, "Made in country X."

The role of multinationals in advancing global systems is self-evident. Yet the integrity of the sovereign states is being eroded by precisely this process. Thanks to the power of economies of scales, these stateless corporations now

CASE 11-1 **Multinationals:**
Engines of Globalization (continued)

wield more economic and political clout than many national governments. Multinationals can shift production from one location to another when profits dictate because of increased capital mobility. In this way, they can play one country off against another by moving labour-intensive operations offshore to take advantage of cheaper labour and more favourable tax incentives (Marchak 1991). After all, there is not much point in staying in a country in which average *hourly* industrial wages are about $15 in contrast with countries in which wages are $15 a *day*, with few worker benefits and even fewer workplace protections. Both rich and poor countries have little choice except to bargain with powerful capitalists who thereby gain leverage for controlling future investments. Impoverished countries are even more susceptible; in order to maintain reserves of foreign or "hard" currency for servicing its debts, the host country will often sacrifice subsistence agriculture for cash crop production, with a concurrent loss of livelihood for its people and a diminishing of its own self-sufficiency (Goldenberg 1997). Multinational investment in resource industries leads to a profusion in capital-intensive resource extraction at the expense of a sustainable subsistence base.

Put bluntly, multinationals are in the economic driver's seat because they 1) dictate terms of investment and plant location, 2) define prices, wages, and returns on investment, 3) deter growth by channelling profits outside of the host country with only modest trickle down for local economies, and 4) determine whether new technologies will be used to upgrade existing industries (Drache and Gertler 1991). With no loyalty but to themselves, Zillah Eisenstein (1996) argues, multinational global capital can flow anywhere, in the process creating its rules and escaping accountability and blame behind the cover of the global economy. With this kind of power at their disposal, it is little wonder that the concept of sovereignty is being put to the test by these multinationals who continue to dominate their former colonies, but this time through corporate protocol and trade agreements (Khor 1996). It remains to be seen if a growing backlash will compel greater accountability among multinationals in terms of responsibility to communities and employees (Crane 1997).

GLOBALIZATION: THINK LOCALLY, ACT GLOBALLY

There is little doubt that capitalist globalization has redefined the notion of how "business is done around here." Advances in telecommunications and transportation have compressed the world into a globally integrated production loop of cost-effective sites. On paper, the economic benefits of globalization are too tempting to dismiss. Who would argue with a logic that correlates national wealth with the removal of pesky tariffs for international trade, improving productivity through competition, enhancing the climate for jobs and investment, and reducing unwarranted government intervention and social spending. A fundamental restructuring in the relationship between society and the economy has taken place under globalization, and many have been rewarded in the process. Yet the structural adjustments associated with globalization have not developed as many had hoped, succeeding in the political realm to be sure, but not socially in terms of equality or safety, leaving behind a citizenry who feel increasingly betrayed or disillusioned (New Zealand Herald, August 7, 1997). The ascendancy of globalization has also compelled a rethinking of "what society is for." Not only is the concept of a sovereign society under attack, but globalization has sharpened the debate over the role of the market versus the state as a mechanism for society-building.

From State to Market

For more than 50 years, Western democracies clung to interventionist philosophies as a means of managing the economy. The limitations and inhumanity of an unbridled market-riveted economy was starkly exposed by the Depression in the 1930s. The crudely competitive capitalism of the nineteenth century gave way to Keynesian policies of government intervention and state regulation through welfare and social security. Since then, the state has been actively involved in stimulating the economy. Throughout the many succeeding cycles of boom and bust, its duties have included controlling employment levels, distributing incomes, encouraging consumption, protecting local industry, and furnishing social programs as a safety net. Strategies of state management have varied, of course, but often incorporated social investment, consumer subsidies, trade and tariff regulations, monitoring domestic growth and prosperity, and supervising collective bargaining sessions (Laux 1990/91; Drache and Gertler 1991).

A new social contract eventually shaped the postwar economy. A nationalist-inspired industrial strategy took root, with an activist state at the helm to stimulate the economy and generate wealth through domestically controlled capitalist accumulation (Shields and McBride 1994). The principle of collective bargaining took precedence over the practice of wages freely determined by a supply-side market. Linking wages with productivity and growth contributed to the material well-being of workers; as a result, consumerism and economic growth spiralled upwards. A second key policy initiative focused on servicing the domestic market. Export trade was not spurned outright, but served primarily as an extension of the domestic market rather than as an industrial strategy. Capital had to be kept at home rather than pursue overseas investment to ensure jobs for Canadians (see Daniels and Lever 1996). Interventionist strategies involved protection (through tariffs) and procurement (by government purchasing) as well as state ownership of key industries as a basis for generating national wealth (Laux 1990/91). To be sure, the shift from competitive to regulated capitalism did not profoundly alter the balance of power between labour and capital; capitalist ownership remained firmly in place. Nor did it question the fundamental premise of capitalism, namely, the rational pursuit of profit through private property. Nevertheless, a relatively high degree of security and prosperity evolved under this reciprocating arrangement.

The concept of an interventionist state is losing its lustre. The flow of international capital had already escaped national borders by the mid-1970s, followed shortly after by the mobility of production in search of cheap labour (Trotter 1995). By the early 1990s, international trade had reached a point where multinationals sought to eliminate most remaining manifestations of national sovereignty. A new industrial strategy for wealth creation has evolved in response to the multinationalization of global economies (Shields and McBride 1994). The national agenda is now firmly planted in the narrow pursuit of commercial interests through foreign markets, unfettered trade, global competitiveness, and a deregulated state. In lieu of state intervention for stimulating the economy, an open market is endorsed instead for conducting business—a scenario that pleases certain sectors and disappoints others.

> [B]usiness elites have welcomed the prospects of unleashing the market on a world scale. They want new rights to invest and divest with minimal restriction and establish their businesses without regard to borders. Where existing programs are perceived as barriers to business, they have to be modified. . . . If present standards stand in the way of harmonization and competitiveness, new standards have to be imposed (Drache and Gertler 1991, 3).

In this new world order of triumphant transnational capitalism, the government's role has shifted from a public agenda to a takeover by business interests, from a protector of society against market excesses to a defender of corporate interests from public demands—to the detriment of our integrity as a just society (Barlow and Campbell 1996).

In a globalizing marketplace, the government must find ways of paring down the costs it imposes on the business sector to ensure international competitiveness. Key elements in this structural readjustment process include a raft of austerity measures, ranging from the sale of state assets and elimination of protective tariffs to the elimination of agricultural subsidies and a cap on welfare spending (Kelsey 1997). References pertaining to sovereignty, cultural identity, social progress, and the common good are dismissed as market impediments. As a result, interventionist states have little role in a global economy except to create conditions that facilitate the flow of capital, labour, and investment.

Adoption of a free-wheeling global strategy is endorsed by neo-conservatism as a springboard for prosperity. Yet this endorsement strikes at the heart of political debate over the primacy of state versus market in regulating society. On one hand, governments are anxious to improve the competitiveness of domestic production in a globalizing market. On the other hand, they must impose limits on the movement of capital within their borders. On yet another hand, they must ensure some level of social spending for those likely to be victimized by the ruthlessness of the competition. For central authorities, the challenge is clear: they must reconcile the forces of market competitiveness with state concerns for protection of political sovereignty, at least for as long as the boundaries of political legitimacy coincide with the realities of a territorially based nation-state. In other words, an economic strategy must be devised that enhances state security yet attracts international investment while improving Canadian competitiveness abroad without shredding the social safety net. All this must be accomplished without the support of now-discarded ground rules of "doing business." As a result of these competing pressures, governments are caught in a bind as they juggle the opposing demands of the free market with those of national economic security, social conscience, and territorial sovereignty. How is this possible, and why has it happened?

From Local Production to Productive Loop

Canada is heavily implicated in these globalizing changes—by choice and by chance. Between 1984 and 1993 the Conservative government endorsed the principle of free market trade—despite public resentment and social costs—as the solution to all of Canada's economic problems (Drache and Gertler 1991). A business strategy was devised for managing society and the national economy around private-sector models (Barlow and Campbell 1996). The objective was to improve competitiveness by cutting back costs, in part through eliminating social costs, in part through job attrition, labour shedding, and plant closures. Also on the chopping block were inefficient industries once coddled from outside competition. Slash and burn industrial strategies were introduced that stripped protection from uncompetitive workplaces. Workers were unceremoniously dumped in the ensuing downsizing.

Exposure to the logic and discipline of the global market economy constitutes a radical departure from the past. In the old system of branch economies, a foreign corporation would establish a branch plant (subsidiary) for the express purpose of manufacturing a product primarily for the Canadian market. For example, the 1965 Canada–U.S. Auto Pact stipulated that for every American car sold in Canada, one had to be built here (Laver 1994). The big three auto makers, General Motors, Ford, and Chrysler, invested billions of dollars in Canadian plants to meet Canadian content rules. Later, when Toyota and Honda began Canadian production, they were assessed a 9.2 percent duty because of failure to meet the Auto Pact targets for Canadian production. Until recently, most car production was geared towards the domestic market, and Canada erected tariffs and duties to protect its domestic industry (Hiller 1990). Higher Canadian prices reflected the costs of doing business in a country where smaller economies of scale prevailed. This protectionist mentality resulted in the manufacture of the same product in several different provinces to supply the needs of local markets. Such an arrangement may have ensured "full" employment and a measure of control over national decision-making, but it also encouraged inefficiency and duplication.

The rules of the game have changed in the wake of globalizing waves. With a new global division of labour and rapidly expanding foreign markets, a manufacturing strategy has emerged that focuses on export productivity rather than on protecting domestic industry. The branch plant mentality has vanished because of advances in technology and communication, followed by the disappearance of trade tariffs and investment barriers. On January 1, 1994, for example, the Canadian government slashed or eliminated duties on a wide range of auto parts, in effect burying the 1965 Auto Pact (Laver 1994). The production process has also been revamped. From a branch plant economy both regulated and protected, each country such as Canada is now expected to become part of the production loop in which labour (jobs) and capital (in the form of goods, services, investment, and markets) are integrated under intense pressure to compete in a global market. Instead of making a product only for domestic use, a Canadian plant might make a component for export around the world; another foreign plant would make a different component. Outputs from these plants would be linked together in a worldwide operation. Borders count for little under such an arrangement.

Canada's industrial strategy is now centred on market-driven export trade rather than state-controlled expansion of domestic markets. The role of the state in advancing national interests has shifted accordingly. Instead of bolstering domestic growth, the state is concerned with reducing barriers for investment and trade while forging a social climate hospitable to international trade. Social spending as a percentage of the GDP has declined from historic highs in the pre–free trade era (Drache and Gertler 1991). With few exceptions, social programs from health to education have suffered cutbacks and budgetary restrictions under budget-pruning, social contract arrangements. Universities have been particularly hard hit, with many continuing to shoulder a disproportionately smaller slice of the economic pie, despite oft-quoted platitudes about advanced education as a prerequisite for economic prosperity.

There is nothing inherently "bad" about such an economic process. Problems arise from the loss of self-determination when corporate functions can be located anywhere. Canada can be banished from the production loop if it fails to comply with a paring of costs related to skilled labour, infrastructure, social welfare, and taxation. Multinationals will avoid locating in countries where barriers to investment or trade are maintained. What emerges from this competitive free-for-all is a global division of labour largely determined by corporate agendas rather than national interests. The costs of intense competition are tough on a socially progressive country such as Canada. The disappearance of branch plants is bad enough; loss of national autonomy and control over business decisions is tougher still in the face of growing competition from developing countries over investment, jobs, and markets. As bluntly stated by Adam Zimmerman, chairman of Noranda, "If you are in a business that can move, why bother with the hassles of staying in Canada?" (as quoted in Hurtig 1991). Why, indeed, when employees at the Bata plant near Trenton, Ontario, earn up to $10.50 per hour while Bata workers in Pacific Rim countries earn $2.20 for an entire *day*. The debate over free trade captures the dilemmas of globalization and its impact on Canada, as Case 11-2 shows.

CASE 11-2   Free Trade: Bonus or Bogus?

The principle of open competition as a catalyst for Canada's industrial strategy is reflected in policy initiatives both market-based and trade-oriented. A substantial portion of Canada's wealth continues to depend on exports and international trade. Currently, two trends in trade are noteworthy. On the one hand are agreements for loosening restrictions on the movement of goods and services across all borders. Negotiations over a General Agreement on Trade and Tariffs (GATT) since 1947 have been aimed at opening international trade by dismantling protective barriers and punishing tariffs. The principle behind free global trade rests on a belief in comparative advantage, namely, that prosperity follows those countries that maximize what they produce best because of history or geography. Free trade among these countries is the key to prosperity especially when products of one country are matched with those of another without the distortion of tariffs or regulations.

On the other hand, there is the trend towards restricting trade to regions. Examples of this are regional trading blocks such as the European Economic Community (EEC) as well as regional blocks in Southeast Asia and South and Central America. Regional trading blocks are justified on the grounds of improving economies of scale by unfettering the movement of goods and services among "natural" trading partners. The economic benefits of many regional arrangements are plausible. The creation of these regional blocks has compelled companies to set up plants in these regional markets to circumvent the tariff barriers they have surrounded themselves with, in effect making companies more multinational

CASE 11-2   Free Trade: Bonus or Bogus? (continued)

(Daniels and Lever 1996). But social costs related to government assistance programs and local industries invariably raise debate about the desirability of free trade agreements in North America.

For Canada the dilemma is obvious. Since the mid-1970s it has lost preferential access to the European Union, with a corresponding loss of trade to Britain. Canada has had little choice but to explore alternate trading arrangements for its products and exports, particularly in North America. What could be more attractive than the prospect of trading with a regional block of 360 million consumers, with the potential for more as agreements are negotiated? But the opening of American and Mexican markets to Canadian exports has threatened to eliminate some programs and regulations that historically have bolstered the costs of doing business in Canada. For instance, certain environmental regulations and collective bargaining agreements that involve employment protection could well be scuttled in the interests of making Canadian businesses more competitive. Protection of Canada's cultural industries and social programs is likely to be challenged by American-style private enterprise models. Such concessions may appeal to those whose who live and die by the bottom line, but they may look a lot less appealing for those whose lives and life chances are negatively affected by pure economic calculation.

Canada and Free Trade

How does Canada stack up in the free trade stakes? The Free Trade Agreement (FTA), which was signed in 1988 by Canada and the United States, advocated the gradual abolition of trade tariffs as impediments to markets. Supporters argued that free trade would bring about national and regional prosperity; detractors feared the absorption of Canada into the U.S., with a corresponding threat to social programs and sovereignty (Conway 1996). A continental free trade agreement secured American access to Canadian resources, while smoothing the path for increased American investment in Canada. It also enhanced the export of Canadian goods to the world's richest and largest market. As well, the FTA compelled the Canadian economy to harmonize its policies with the practices of a business-friendly U.S. by curbing unwanted government intervention, regulation, and social spending. A similar commitment—to bolster Canadian economic prosperity by liberalizing trade through open markets—characterized the North American Free Trade Agreement (NAFTA), signed in 1994 by Canada, the U.S., and Mexico. Under NAFTA, U.S. and Mexican investors must be treated no less favourably than Canadian investors, with a host of prohibitions on minimum levels of Canadian ownership or purchase from local suppliers (Shields and McBride 1994; Barlow and Clark 1996). In 1996 the intercontinentalization process was further extended when Canada and Chile signed a bilateral agreement for expansion of trade entry into Latin American markets (Ford 1996).

As yet there is no consensus regarding the final outcome of NAFTA. One report indicated that Canadians to date have been the prime beneficiaries of NAFTA in terms of jobs and a predominance of Canadian exports over American imports (Beltrame 1997). Yet critics of free trade point to the loss of control over foreign investment in Canada, the growing privatization of key public services such as health and education, and the erosion of minimal protection for workers and the environment. Others are worried by the disappearance of jobs that comes with exposing inefficient industries to the cold winds of competition. Both Canadian and American industries have closed shop and shifted operations to more profitable locations because of lower wages and social security payments and poorer working conditions. Estimates suggest a loss of 461 000 manufacturing jobs since the signing of the FTA, constituting nearly 23.1 percent of the total jobs in the smokestack industries. This figure compares with the totals during the Great Depression at a 29.7 percent loss between 1929 and 1933 (The Globe and Mail, January 30, 1992). Across Canada, over 2 million people now receive some form of social assistance—at a time of government cutbacks in social spending—and perhaps 600 000 are reliant on food banks at some point. Even the continued flow of investments into Canada is no cause for celebration. According to Mel Hurtig (1991), much of this investment is funnelled into company takeovers that provide few jobs. Yet profits and dividends continue to be siphoned from the country at alarming rates. Finally, the FTA may not actually create a level playing field. Increased exports are not generating new jobs; nor are increases in production of much help

to workers who find corporations driving down wage demands and working conditions (Anderson et al. 1996). With its colossal resource base, the United States can advance its interests by falling back on the courts or trade legislation to punish Canadian protectionist measures (Hurtig 1991). The ability of the Canadian government to control its destiny as a sovereign society is left in doubt.

Further integration into an intercontinental economy comes with a hefty price tag. Canadians have yet to work out the political, cultural, and social ramifications of NAFTA, even if North American regional economic integration was already advanced at the time of the signing (Thompson 1996). The costs of closer economic ties could culminate in political union, according to James Laxer (1993), at the expense of social programs and an activist state. Nor are the costs of dependency and underdevelopment evenly distributed. The richer provinces have suffered, but poorer regions such as Atlantic Canada have suffered even more, with the result that local and regional economies remain even more dependent on government grants as traditional jobs dry up in fishing, forestry, resource extraction, manufacturing, and defence. In this restructuring from a resource-based to a service-oriented economy, many Atlantic Canadians have been consigned to seasonal or makeshift work, supplemented by social assistance or unemployment. The prosperity that was supposed to follow the signing of NAFTA never materialized. Instead of jobs, there is an economic ideology that valorizes the market even as stagnation prevails, that demonizes and underfunds government intervention, and that diminishes humans to little more than widgets in a continental shopping mall (Anderson et al. 1996).

More or Less Trade?

Many believe that free trade is natural and normal in a global economy. It is perceived and defended as the only solution to the problem of inefficient economies (Saul 1995). Yet the underlying assumptions of this stance are rarely examined. People need to be convinced that the ambiguous effects of globalization are not a historical inevitability that we are powerless to challenge or resist, but the result of conscious policies by vested interests—in the same way that high unemployment is not a regrettable necessity of the economy, but a ruthless decision that suits monied interests rather than the general public (Editorial 1996; Sandbrook 1997). In many cases, the appropriate questions have yet to be asked (Smith 1993):

1) Is free trade the best and only option for Canada? Some would argue that free trade is workable only when all parties to the agreement are relatively equal in terms of resources and full employment is the norm (Smith 1993). Others would endorse free trade, yet concede that there is no assurance that market-driven trade will stimulate economic growth or enhance living standards for everyone (Corcoran 1993).

2) Will free trade work as outlined? Nobody can be sure because nothing approaching unrestricted free trade has ever been attempted. Without the luxury of hindsight or precedent, conventional wisdom simply dictates that trade barriers have a negative impact on consumers and on manufacturers who wish to export their products. But how then can one explain the postwar success of Japan, which succeeded in spite of punishing barriers to foreign markets?

3) What kind of jobs will be affected by free trade? Again, conventional wisdom holds that Mexico will capitalize on unskilled labour and labour-intensive sweatshops, while Canada and the United State will secure managerial jobs and capital-intensive industry. This sounds plausible, but underestimates the vast reservoir of skilled personnel in Mexico willing to work for a fraction of the wages paid to Canadians (Matthews 1993).

4) Is free trade really a viable proposition? Consider the reality in Mexico. NAFTA has the potential to create a trading block of 360 million persons, with $6 trillion gross in consumer products. This is likely to grow even further into a hemispheric trading block with the addition of other Central and South American countries over time. But what is the point of having such a huge market if there is no corresponding increase in consumption from an increasingly impoverished population?

5) To what extent is self-interest disguised as public good in the debate over free trade? It is argued that an interlocking cabal of political and economic elites are calling the

CASE 11-2   Free Trade: Bonus or Bogus? (continued)

shots in arguing that freer trade is necessary, normal, inevitable, and profitable all round. But is there only one way of thinking about the problem and only one set of solutions? To what extent should other concerns and public interests play a role in decision-making in a democratic society (Saul 1995)?

6) Is free trade a death knell for an interventionist state? Free trade ideologues believe that political units such as the nation-state are irrelevant or counter-productive when the economy functions internationally and is subjected to the liberating discipline of a competitive market. The government is rebuked as a meddlesome hindrance rather than a help in creating a corporate society. Evidence, however, suggests otherwise. An interventionist state may underpin global economic activity and has done so successfully in the boom economies of Japan and Southeast Asia (Livingstone 1996), but evidence also suggests that economic and social development may not be secured without some degree of government involvement, particularly in the field of social programs (Crane 1997).

The debate over free trade versus protectionism will never be resolved to everyone's satisfaction. This lack of resolution stems in part from radically different perceptions of the economy, coupled with the government's role in generating wealth. Free traders believe that wealth is generated when the economy is driven by prices freely and competitively set according to the laws of supply and demand. The government is seen as an impediment to the free play of unfettered market forces. Jobs, investments, and plant locations will materialize only in those countries whose national outlooks are business-friendly. A country's attractiveness is bolstered by lowering taxes, paring production costs, pruning government programs and spending, loosening government regulations, reducing the debt load, dismantling the welfare apparatus, dropping wage rates and related costs to competitive levels, and making trade as free as possible by cutting tariffs and artificial barriers (see Francis 1993).

Protectionists disagree with the definition of the problem; consequently, they propose different solutions. For protectionists, the unfettered market is not a solution, but a problem for control by an interventionist government. Free trade is viewed as contrary to a caring and compassionate society. Proposed instead is protection for Canadian industry and trading arrangements consistent with national interests, not just those of the wealthy elite. Such intrusion is costly, of course. Costs include raising taxes and security payments to ensure a level playing field, expanding capital projects for make-work activities, increasing government regulation in defence of worker rights, and establishing equity initiatives for inclusion of the marginal. Maximizing export trade is important in this equation. Equally significant, however, is Canada's survival as a humane and egalitarian society. And Canadians appear to be rebelling against the onslaught of government cutbacks

CASE 11-2   **Free Trade: Bonus or Bogus? (continued)**

and looking to the government to protect their interests through job creation and social security (Walkom 1997). Even the epitome of economic restructuring, New Zealand, has come under criticism for its decision to exchange its vaunted egalitarianism for a culture of greed that benefits a few at the expense of many (New Zealand Herald, August 7, 1997).

How do we assess free trade in terms of its impact on Canada? To what extent does globalizing provide benefits exclusively for big business rather than for the workers who bear the brunt of cost-cutting, profit-bolstering moves? Can we safely assume that what is good for the Canadian economy is equally healthy for Canada's cultural and social agenda? The era of an interventionist welfare state is being replaced by a globally diffused, individualized, and unregulated system of power and a selectively residual state whose prime functions are to create the conditions for successful private enterprise and the internationalization of labour, capital, and investment (see Kelsey 1997). Accompanying this change is the shift from a heavily protected and highly regulated economy to an open economy

dominated by international money markets and financial speculators. The restructuring process has been attended by personal costs. Just as Canada does not possess full control over economic decisions, so too are there many private citizens helpless in the face of economic decisions that render them disposable. It makes little sense to blame a worker for loss of employment when the local plant has moved to Mexico where labour is cheaper and social costs are nonexistent. Instead of blaming the victims of economic restructuring, it is time to examine the social context for answers. Is technology a cause of unemployment, or do technological advances enhance productivity and wealth, thus stimulating consumer demand and creating more jobs? Is the problem one of political will and expediency, or is it based purely on economic calculation and the laws of supply and demand? Do high wages and expensive social benefits price Canadian goods out of the market while diminishing worker incentive? What is the point, in other words, of improving Canada's global competitiveness if this culminates in the impoverishment of many Canadians?

Whither Now Canada? Between Free Trade and a Free Society

"Canada is a solution looking for a problem" (Comment attributed to a former Mexican ambassador to Canada (Barlow and Clark 1996)).

Canada is often described as a semi-periphery country. It is relatively rich (core) compared to most Third World countries, but it is also "poor" (periphery) because of its colonial past, dependence on exports and branch plants, and control by high levels of foreign investment. Canada is rich when measured by conventional standards of GNP and manufacturing productivity but poor since the value of finished goods is low compared with that of exported raw materials. Canada is neither powerful enough to dominate the world's economic stage, nor so inconsequential a player that it is completely at the mercy of other nations. Two factors have shaped Canada's core-periphery status: its roles as a supplier of raw materials such as timber or minerals and as a buyer of finished, manufactured products. Initially Canadian wealth depended on the export of largely unprocessed staple products. Extraction of these raw materials required little in the way of permanent settlement or local development. Only with Confederation did manufacturing concerns assume a priority. A flourishing manufacturing sector emerged, aided by protective tariffs and subsidies. But most plants were foreign-owned—partly because of local reluctance to invest in manufacturing—with the result that industrial decision-making slipped through Canadian hands (Hiller 1990; but see Laxer 1990).

At present, aspects of the Canadian economy remain in the hands of American and other multinational corporations. They continue to be shaped and truncated by a high reliance on resource-based export trade and a branch plant industrial production (Watkins 1997). The combination of foreign ownership and internationalization of production has enabled Canadian capitalists to collude with American capitalists to gain hegemony over a continental trade block (Clements 1997). Lack of economic independence makes it difficult for Canadians to cooperate with Americans as equal partners in bilateral trading arrangements. The subsequent outflow of capital and profits jeopardizes domestic investment and local job creation. Foreign investors have erected a network of branch plants with restrictions on what they can do (often the assembly of goods from parts made outside the country) or to whom they can sell. Collaboration with Canadian elites has been critical in securing this downward spiral. The net impact has been a stunted industrial sector that has arrested Canadian development (Zeitlin and Brym 1991).

Canada is currently exposed to the chilly blasts of globalization in the competition for scarce resources. The seeming lack of viable alternatives to capitalism following the demise of the Soviet Union has reinforced the remorseless march of globalization and free-market principles. The globalization of Canada's economy has intensified competition with wealthy industrial giants such as Germany and Japan. Canada's ability to attract jobs and markets has been further blunted by inroads from aggressive newcomers such as the Asian "tigers" of Singapore and South Korea. Its social and political priorities will be altered even further as competition and export-led trade impose their own economic agendas on the Canadian state. A new set of challenges now exist. Canada must devise an industrial strategy that maximizes its global advantages, insulates it from the worst effects of pure competition, ensures a decent standard of living for everyone, and enhances its capacity as a sovereign and "distinct" society. The challenge, in other words, requires a tricky balancing act among the conflicting demands of economic restructuring, a reorganization of the labour market, incorporation of different production technologies, and retention of Canada's vaunted social programs. It remains to be seen whether these dynamics and demands can be reconciled to mutual advantage in sorting out the competing forces of global competitiveness, state sovereignty, and social compassion.

GLOBAL PROBLEMS

The world we live in is in a shambles, or at least this would appear to be the case judging by media sensationalism and the accompanying howls of public anguish. Too many people exist, according to the headlines, and too many of them live in all the wrong places, with too many problems and not enough resources to address those problems. Perceptions of contradictions abound. The Developing World desires the material trappings of a modern society, with a standard of living comparable to that enjoyed by First World nations, yet it appears incapable of paying the price for economic progress. TV news "bites" convey the impression of a collapse into tribalism, tradition, and ethnic chauvinism instead of pulling together for national unity and the common good. Many developing countries are recipients of Western generosity through foreign aid or favourable trade arrangements, yet opportunities for development are squandered because of corruption or gross incompetence, without even a murmur of gratitude to their hosts. Lip service to the ideals of democracy means nothing in light of the authoritarian rule of despots, military juntas, and religious fanatics. The sheer volume and intensity of this pending anarchy is disturbing, as the social fabric of human societies is being shredded by a scarcity of resources, crime, disease, tribalism, and overpopulation (Kaplan 1994). Human life is depicted by the media as cheap and disposable, and easily extinguished by interclan killings or natural disasters. The cumulative result of these ungovernable forces cannot be underestimated. Developing countries appear to be hopelessly mired in an endless cycle of crisis, conflict, corruption, and catastrophe, with no solution in sight (Kaplan 1994).

Africa is an especially tragic example of what can happen in the aftermath of colonialism, even if many of the countries have achieved a nominal political independence (Kaplan 1994). Statistics can only hint at the enormity of the problems. African countries occupy 9 of the bottom 10 positions in the United Nations' Human Development Index (which uses criteria of education, living standards, and so on), despite high levels of foreign aid, which in 1993 amounted to $38 per person compared to $8 per person in Latin America (Chege 1997). Economic successes in certain countries are counterbalanced by deteriorating levels of public health and education (Stackhouse 1996). Resources continue to be depleted at alarming rates, giving rise to further cycles of starvation, disease, or pestilence. Economically, the situation as a whole continues to be grim. Since 1970, according to Attali (1990), African productivity for the global market has shrunk by 50 percent; its debt is now equivalent to its GNP, having multiplied twentyfold in recent years; percentage of food production in the sub-Sahara is about 15 percent lower than in the late 1970s; and per capita income has plunged by 25 percent from 1987 (Parris 1997). Despite savage interethnic killings and death in refugee camps, the population continues to escalate, with estimates of 750 million at present and projections of 1.5 billion by 2025. Perhaps half of the population lives in abject poverty, with women representing two-thirds of new poverty victims (Toporizis 1990). The feminization of poverty in Africa is rooted partly in patriarchal traditions and partly in the difficulty in accessing development programs. Finally, a combination of droughts, ethnic and clan killings, and armed conflicts under military juntas has created a refugee pool of between 5 and 10 million people. The plight of Africa could well emerge as the world's single most important social problem in the twenty-first century.

How valid are these perceptions of reality? Human diversity being what it is, there are dimensions of truth to these observations. Who could deny the intrusiveness of poverty, despotic rule, crowded living conditions, interethnic and religious rivalries, and the threat of natural catastrophes in the Developing World? This is not the entire story, however, and a critical perspective provides a sense of proportion. First, not all Developing Countries in Africa are economic basket cases. Economic growth is substantial in certain areas, life expectancies are inching upwards as are school enrolments, and democratic institutions are gradually displacing authoritarian regimes (d'Aquino 1997). Second, poverty, crowding, despotism, conflict, and disasters may be pervasive, but neither Canada nor the United States is exempt from such patterns. Consider only First Nations reserves in Canada, whose living conditions are comparable to those in some developing countries. Besides, any "civilization" that spawned two world wars and continues to supply arms and land mines for ongoing conflicts can hardly afford to hug the moral high ground. Third, too much of our understanding of life in the Third World as "nasty, brutish, and short" reflects a media preoccupation with "triggers" such as India (religious conflicts), Bangladesh (natural disasters), Somalia (clan killings), and South Africa (tribal hostilities). But not all Third World countries are patterned after these media hot spots. Many are relatively peaceful and reasonably well-adjusted to the surrounding environment. Moreover, fixation on the sensational tends to overlook the routines of daily life—the cooperation, consensus, and regulation—that must surely exist in most cases. Fourth, the media are largely responsible for negative perceptions of the Third World, not only because of racist personnel, but because of media preference for the flamboyant and telegenic as newsworthy (Steward and Fleras n.d.). Cooperation and consensus do not sell copy or create compelling visuals for the six o'clock news. This selectivity reinforces a predominantly one-sided view of the Developing World as hell-bent on destruction and demise.

The Developing World is not necessarily at fault for the difficulties in which it finds itself. Centuries of exploitation under colonialism and multinationals have stripped many Third World countries of resources and resourcefulness, leaving behind a bulging residue of poverty and violence. Superpower hegemony during the Cold War did much to distort patterns of dependency and underdevelopment. Western aggression and global "greed" must share the blame for Third World problems. To do otherwise, by holding the victims entirely accountable for forces beyond their control, is ultimately an abdication of Western responsibility. This suggests that the Western world is as much a part of global problems as it is a part of the overall solution.

This section will emphasize the problems of overpopulation, sprawling urbanization, deepening poverty, ethnic nationalism, and ecological destruction. Discussion of these major problems will provide a penetrating glimpse into the kind of pressures engulfing the planet at present. Placement of global problems in this section is not meant to suggest that the Developing World is the architect of its own misfortunes. As we make clear throughout, there is no compelling reason to blame the Developing World for global problems, much less to expect it to make more sacrifices for solution. To the contrary, Developing World problems are arguably First World problems in light of past history and current events. Convenience, however, dictates that we discuss global problems where they are most graphically manifest and where solutions are more desperately needed (Kaplan 1994).

CASE 11-3   *Bon Appétit*: A Recipe for Bungled Development

Many have remarked on the need to think globally but act locally. To do so, it is argued, is to appreciate how local problems can have global implications in terms of causes and cures. Few, however, would be prepared to see how their food preferences may contribute to the impoverishment of developing countries. Take, for instance, our seemingly insatiable taste for prawn and shrimp and its detrimental effect on the ecosystems of the Developing World. An article by Suzanne Goldenberg (1997) points out how hundreds and thousands of acres of coastal land in countries such as Bangladesh have been transformed into crustacean farms to take advantage of a $9 billion trade in prawns. A few have benefited from the transformation, but many farmers have lost their ability for self-sustenance in exchange for increased dependence on outside subsistence. The ecological disaster is equally dismaying. In the process of flooding their lands with brackish sea water, farmers have destroyed rich mangrove stands that have been designated as national treasures. To add insult to injury, this type of aquaculture is a shifting cultivation, with the result that flooded lands are unfit for human or animal use after five years. Economic loss occurs through environmental degradation involving a host of outcomes from desertification to deforestation, with water pollution and erosion in between (see Khor 1996). As one Indian environmental activist says about this "rape and run" industry, "I have spent twenty years of my life in environmental work and fought horrible disasters, and there is nothing so

devastating of such rich ecosystems and of systems that lend themselves to sustainable life" (quoted in Goldenberg 1997, 24).

It is obvious that local farmers have not shared in the wealth. The crustacean industry has been hijacked by a few powerful land barons who think nothing of ruthless intimidation to expand their empires. Paradoxically, however, it was precisely benefits for rural farmers that prompted the World Bank and associated agencies to invest heavily in aquatic farming as an alternative source of income for a chronically impoverished region. The trickle down effects have been disappointing; the national index may have grown, as well as the income of a few local land magnates, but little was added to the local economy. Instead, farmers have watched in despair as their once arable land has lapsed into a saline desert unfit for rice paddies or jute fields. What can we conclude? Think-big and quick-rich schemes are unlike to work as solutions to developing world problems. More often than not they create unhealthy patterns of dependency that foster further underdevelopment and inequality (Pelto 1990). A few become enriched at the expense of others, thus increasing the gap between rich and poor. Grandiose plans are less likely to work when imposed from the outside without local consultation. There is an additional lesson: Third World poverty is often the consequence of external decisions. No one is suggesting that we stop eating prawns or shrimp. However, we might think about the repercussions of pleasing our increasingly demanding palates.

Overpopulation

There is a saying among sociologists: "The rich get richer, the poor get children." Despite its mocking tone, the expression latches on to a popular perception of the Third World as teeming with people who have neither the resources nor the space to support their own children. There is some truth to this perception. The world is experiencing a population explosion that is unprecedented in human history. In 1987 the world population reached 5 billion, an increase of more than 2 billion in 27 years. By 1996, the total had climbed to about 5.8 billion, with projections of 6.1 billion by the end of this century and 8 billion by 2020. Virtually all of the growth is occurring in the poorest of developing countries; even in countries such as Rwanda, large families of 8 to 9 children are the norm. Many people are alarmed and for good reason. As far back as 1968, Paul Erlich had already published dire predictions about the world's population capacity—at a time when the world's population stood at 3.5 billion.

Why this demographic explosion? Longer life spans are the obvious answer. Life expectancies have increased substantially while infant mortality rates have declined in response to improved medical care, the eradication of certain fatal diseases, and advances in technology. The growing impoverishment of the poor may also be a contributing factor. Family sizes continue to expand in reaction to mounting poverty. The inability of many Third World governments to provide even rudimentary social programs is also a factor. Larger families provide a margin of safety for survival in environments of grinding poverty, economic emergencies, and an absence of any safety net for the aged or unemployed. That fact serves to remind us that what we define as a global problem (that is, large families) may serve as a solution for survival among those without the luxury of alternatives.

Other repercussions become apparent on closer scrutiny. Increases in population through control of diseases and death rates is a positive goal. Yet this creates additional pressure on dwindling resources and existing social services. Local environments are especially vulnerable to escalating demands. The depletion of basic necessities coupled with the proliferation of waste is worrying in its own right. Satisfying the food needs of 100 million additional persons each year will pose new challenges as the worldwide recession diminishes outputs from grains, grasslands, and marine sources (Brown 1993). The effects of overpopulation are not restricted to the Developing World. Rich countries are also effected. Yet the spillover from demographic pressures has precipitated a host of reactions, ranging from terrorist attacks to mass emigration.

Urbanization

Half of the world's population of 5.8 billion people is estimated to live in cities (Clarke 1996). In the Third World, the figure stands at about 23 percent of the population, up from 13 percent in 1950 (Bowring 1993). Africa and East Asia have the lowest rates, while 71 percent of the Latin American population is urban (including 86 percent in Argentina). The rates in Canada and the United States are about 80 percent at present. Singapore and Hong Kong are almost entirely urban. Yet even in areas with low urban to rural ratios, the presence of sprawling urban agglomerations is the rule, not the exception—from Sao Paulo at 17.4 million and Shanghai at 13 million down to Manila at 7 million and Bangkok at 6 million. Elsewhere the figures are equally formidable, with a projected 30 million in Mexico City by 2020.

Despite obvious drawbacks for most newcomers, many people are attracted to the city by a process often referred to as "push and pull." Migrants are pushed out of rural communities because of unemployment, limited land resources, lack of opportunity and employment, boredom, and dislike of social patterns such as crowding. Migrants are pulled into cities for precisely opposite reasons. For some, economic survival for themselves and their children is a compelling reason; for others, the lure is that of glamour, excitement, and sophistication. The decision to uproot is not always productive. Newcomers may exchange intermittent agricultural jobs for low-paying urban jobs, often supplemented by proceeds from scavenging and the invisible economy. For many, however, perceived benefits do outweigh the costs.

In theory, most countries profess to discourage urban migration, citing problems related to employment, sanitation, limited transportation and traffic snarls, pollution, access to services, and crime. The fact that most of these cities were not built for the numbers in their midst exacerbates these problems. Even more daunting is the prospect of newly evolving but "infrastructureless" cities such as Surat, India, whose 1.5 million people must survive without garbage collection and waste-water treatment, and with the threat of bubonic plague. Despite difficulties, it's business as usual. Many countries gear public policy towards urban residents in an effort to keep them distracted and subservient. Only lip service is paid to bolstering rural economies and social services. National pride is often at stake as well. Cities are viewed as symbols of progress as well as centres of industry and wealth, even though much of the city is captured by slums and derelict housing projects.

In short, Developing World urbanism would appear to qualify as a bona fide social problem. Potential damage to society and the environment is such that attention must focus on consequences. Yet many in these cities may not see it that way. They do not see much point in returning to resource-depleted and socially stifling environments. Even the inconveniences and dangers of city life are a small price to pay for its opportunities and excitement. Solutions to the problem of global urbanization must reflect these differences in perspective.

Poverty

Many are aware of poverty as a major social problem in the Developing World. What most do not recognize is the real magnitude of this problem, the reasons why it exists, and why eradication is a formidable, if not impossible, task. The globalization of world economies does not automatically confer equal access to the benefits of commercial success. Even media portrayals of the Third World as generally poor gloss over the presence of affluent classes, with remarkable disparities in wealth, power, and status. Still, poverty remains the rule rather than exception, with the poor comprising the bulk of the population in many areas.

Defining Third World poverty can be a problem. Many are absolutely poor when compared with North American standards of consumerism or measured by GNP per person. In emphasizing economic factors, however, such criteria overlook improvements in the general standard of living related to health or education. They also ignore how costs of living are considerably less because of reduced needs and diminished expectations. Also overlooked are how community networks and an informal economy can bolster standards of living, although this may not show up in the national figures.

Why does Developing World poverty exist? Many regard overpopulation as the main cause of Third World poverty. Conversely, the reverse may be an equally valid interpretation. It may be argued, for example, that poverty increases the population by necessitating large families as a survival tactic (Brown 1993). The fact that the poorest countries continue to be the fastest growing suggests there may be some merit to this argument. But no less important as contributing factors are unequal economic distribution, the lack of political will to correct this, and the legacy of colonialism with its reinforcement of dependency and underdevelopment (Skinner 1988).

Expressions and causes of poverty vary from rural to urban regions. For urbanites, poverty is directly related to lack of jobs. It is most graphically expressed in squalor and derelict housing, a lack of sanitation or waste disposal, and the constant danger of violence. For farmers and peasants, poverty stems from inadequate prices for goods produced for export. International prices fluctuate wildly, or the demand for agricultural products or raw materials may collapse in the face of synthetics and substitutes. The presence of poverty in the midst of high expectations can create problems. The terminally impoverished, as Jacques Attali (1990) calls them, may rebel, and this rebellion can be channelled into religious movements at odds with secular rule. Others prefer to protest via terrorism or mass insurrection. These options may not strike us as valid or viable, yet what other choices are there for those with nothing to lose?

Ethnic Nationalism and Ethnic Conflict

The integration of human societies into a global system is counterbalanced by an equally powerful surge of separatist-leaning ethnic nationalisms (Guibernau 1996; Breton 1995; Balthazar 1996). Ethnic nationalist groups are also competing for control of the hearts and minds of their people, with equally disruptive threats to an orderly society. The potential of radical ethnicity to create a kind of global mosaic of mutually antagonistic entities spells disaster for conventional state sovereignties (Ignatieff 1994). The invocation of "ethnic cleansing" in what was once a multiethnic Yugoslavia reminds us all too depressingly of the dangers implicit in this sort of jingoism. The imploding effect created by ethnicity threatens to divide even established democracies into squabbling factions. Some observers predict that its impact will intensify in the future. As the traditional nation-state recoils from the challenges of capital mobility and international trade, ethnic nationalisms may rush to fill the political void created by the eclipse of sovereign states. Under the influence of ethnicity, in other words, the nation-state may relinquish its legitimacy to act on behalf of its citizens, and concede ground to ethnic conflict every bit as demoralizing as that in Bosnia or Rwanda.

Ethnicity itself is not a social problem. Those who embrace ethnicity see it as a solution to many contemporary problems, both social and personal (Solomos and Black 1996). Ethnicity is endorsed as a means of survival on a changing and diverse planet. A commitment to ethnicity allows an escape from feelings of irrelevance, powerlessness, alienation, and impersonality. Appeals to ethnicity foster a sense of continuity, belonging, and security— especially for those at the margins of society without alternate channels for coping with societal stress. It constitutes an oasis for meaning and commitment—even relaxation and enjoyment—in a rapidly changing and complex urban-technological environment. At other times, it has furnished the impetus for mobilizing people into goal-directed action (Rex and Drury 1996). The pooling of combined resources allows ethnic minorities to compete more effectively. Under the banner of ethnicity, members of a group seek to maximize their social and economic advantages in a rational and calculated manner (Olson 1965).

What some see as a solution, others define as a problem. Critics have denounced the surge in ethnocultural pride or identity as divisive, backwards-looking, and counter-productive (Porter 1965). With the onset of modernization and forces of globalization, ethnic attachments are rebuked as atavistic survival mechanisms and repudiated for being inconsistent with cultural rationality and national integration (Connor 1972). Ethnically based nationalisms have been singled out as major contributors to international conflicts as well as a threat to the cohesion and integrity of states around the world (Brown 1989). Ethnicity is condemned as an inexcusable reversion to "tribalism" in which blind conformity to the collective and an obsession to avenge past wrongs may degrade all that is noble in human progress. It runs counter to the liberal values that underpin globalization; that is, a belief that what we have in common is more important than what divides; that what we do as individuals is more important than what group we belong to; that the content of character is more important than the colour of skin; and that reason prevails over emotion as a basis for thinking and doing. Instead of a shared humanity and common values, radical ethnicity emphasizes a dislike of others and a refusal to cooperate in a state of ethnic coexistence.

For still others, the question goes beyond the notion of good or bad. Like it or not, they say, ethnicity is here to stay as a formidable presence in human affairs. The very forces of globalization are likely to intensify rather than defuse demands for more local attachments (Paz et al. 1996). The tendency towards homogenization is being countered by opposing tendencies towards pluralization (Gillespie 1996). Indigenous peoples are demanding levels of political autonomy that reflect their status as the original occupants whose collective rights to self-determination over jurisdictions from political voice to land and identity have never been extinguished, but remain intact as a basis for rethinking who gets what in society (Fleras 1997). Instead of the nation-states we now know, boundary lines will be redrawn to reflect loose confederations of ethnic and indigenous communities tied together into regional or global trading blocks. In short, if the twentieth century was heralded as the age of ideological nationalism, the twenty-first century may well belong to ethnic nationalism. The challenge of making society not only safe *for* ethnicity, but also safe *from* ethnicity may well emerge as the key global problem (Schlesinger 1992).

The Environment

The natural environment plays a prominent role in shaping each country's global agenda (Jackson 1992). Consider the ways in which the following environmental problems could influence government policy or public perceptions: a shortage of raw materials, drought and crop failure, deforestation in the tropics, and pollution ranging from waste mismanagement and noxious emissions to global warming and ozone depletion. Efforts to do something about this crisis in global fragility are often lost in a haze of platitudes, rarely leading to concerted or coordinated cooperation. In 1992, for example, 150 heads of state gathered in Rio, Brazil, and raised righteous concern over the deteriorating environment. The Rio Declaration promised that "[s]tates shall cooperate in a spirit of global partnership to conserve, protect, and restore the health and integrity of the Earth's ecosystem." Five years later a follow-up summit of more than 60 leaders will learn that, lofty rhetoric notwithstanding, the global environmental crisis has deepened in terms of forest destruction, fresh water shortages, worldwide overfishing, and mass extinction of species (Schoon 1997). The gap between the rich and poor nations has increased, as has the division between rich and poor within societies, with predictable effects on the environment as the poor of the world strip forests for warmth and cooking while the rich want more air travel and more air conditioning. Emissions of fossil fuels by rich nations have risen to the point where artificially contrived climatic shifts are a real possibility with the build-up of greenhouse gases. That the Rio Declaration was a failure is regrettable but understandable in light of political grandstanding. Public posturing in 1992 was cheap, especially since pronouncements of global partnership were not legally binding. That heads of state have reconvened in hopes of re-enacting their own version of gaseous emissions (reinforcing the problem in the process) without acknowledging their hypocrisy is unforgivable.

The world now confronts a global ecocrisis of frightening proportions. Even Canada's image as squeaky clean does not stand up to scrutiny (Wallace and Shields 1997). Canadians put a premium on protecting the environment over promoting economic growth; 73 percent of Canadians support putting the environment before the economy, second only to New Zealanders (McArthur 1997). Yet the political will is absent, together with public fears that thinking green may interfere with economic growth (Knox 1997). Nor is a growing reliance on global free trade likely to enhance environmental concerns as competition at all costs takes hold (Abley 1997). Not surprisingly, the Canadian Institute for Business and the Environment has pinned a C- on Canada for its lack of progress since the Rio Declaration. The institute cites federal budget cutbacks in environmental protection as one problem; the other is provincial refusal to do more in the face of slashing costs (Gallon 1997). According to another study, Canada's environment has deteriorated dramatically in terms of air and water pollution, loss of wetlands, waste and nuclear disposal, and chemical poisons in soil and the food-chain (Kitchener Waterloo Record 1995). These assaults on Canada's environment are the result of global warming, automobile traffic, nitrates in rivers, reliance on pesticides, deforestation, toxic substances, and depletion of otherwise sustainable resources. The virtual collapse of the ground fishing industry in the Atlantic provinces, coupled with widespread layoffs in west coast fishing, attests to the damage that can be inflicted by greed and carelessness. Despite these threats to the environment, politicians in Canada continue to prattle on about jobs and deficits, as if sensible and somehow painless solutions to these problems can be discovered in a world shorn of its natural resources (Suzuki 1993). This suggests a need to reconsider whether the economy is the primary issue. Instead of seeing a booming economy as the solution to all of Canada's problems, Suzuki contends, we should question whether the profit-motivated private sector can possibly protect the "ecological capital" that sustains all planetary life. A political obsession with the economy may pose more of a problem than a realistic solution.

Proposals to address environmental issues must be couched as global social problems. We are all in this together, and together we have to make changes, with the rich helping the poor (Schoon 1997). First, the natural world does not exist in isolation from human communities. One billion people live in unprecedented prosperity; another billion live in abject destitution. According to Durning (1991), both rich and poor engage in consumption patterns (one from greed, the other from need) that exert pressure on existing resources such as water, land, forests, and atmospheres. Recognizing the relationship of people to the environment helps to "frame" many of the global problems in play at present. Second, political decisions rather than the forces of nature are overwhelmingly responsible for defining the basis of this relationship. Much of the decision-making originates in the north rather than the south, and this observation puts the blame where it rightfully belongs (Jackson

CASE 11-4   The Politics of Environmental Economics: Clayoquot or Clearcut?

Many environmental issues have come and gone since publication of Rachel Carson's *Silent Spring* in 1962. Few issues have possessed as much staying power as the debates and protests over the preservation of existing forests. Some of the more controversial developments have taken place in British Columbia, where protests over logging in the Clayoquot Sound region have led to numerous arrests and convictions, with no end in sight to the hostilities between those who champion the "economy" and those who favour the "environment." The issues have become even more convoluted with recent recognition of aboriginal land claims in British Columbia. The Clayoquot is the homeland and the traditional hunting grounds of First Nations peoples who have not relinquished their right to ownership on the basis of original occupancy. Once again, Canada has been thrust into the international spotlight and criticized for its indifference to environmental and aboriginal issues. This criticism does not square well with Canada's image as a pace-setter in progressive issues. It also makes those Canadians who castigate others for violations of indigenous rights and environmental abuse sound like hypocrites.

The forests in British Columbia's Clayoquot region on the west coast of Vancouver Island represent one of the largest and only tracts of virgin temperate rain forest in the world. Nearly 90 percent of the world's temperate rain forest may be already denuded, but one-quarter of the remaining rain forest stands in British

Columbia. Old-growth forests, some of which may be 2000 years old, provide an econiche for a dazzling diversity of wildlife. The Crown, which owns about 95 percent of the forest, has allocated timber rights to a few multinational conglomerates (Rowell 1996). Since the mid-1950s, companies such as MacMillan Bloedel and B.C. Forest Products have negotiated exclusive logging rights with the government, but without either public consultation or resolution of outstanding aboriginal land claims (Dobson and Jackson 1993). With the takeover of small timber companies, conglomerates such as MacMillan Bloedel have turned to large-scale clearcutting of old-growth forests, claiming that the indiscriminate felling of trees is less labour-intensive and more profitable. By the early 1970s, the corrosive effect of clearcutting had become a public issue. Environmentalists proposed sustainable, selective cutting of old-growth forest that was more labour-intensive and less profitable—a solution that did not appeal to a profit-maximizing, damage-minimizing multinational conglomerate (Rowell 1996). Finger-pointing pitted environmentalists against loggers against corporate profits against First Nations claims, and against government interests. A relentless spiral of events led to accelerated clearcutting, blockades and protests, arrests and removals, task forces on sustainable development, and a quasi-moratorium on logging prior to public recommendations on land use.

In 1993 the British Columbia government proposed a compromise

CASE 11-4   The Politics of Environmental Economics: Clayoquot or Clearcut? (continued)

between the economy (the legitimate concerns of the logging company and local loggers) and the environment (the equally legitimate aspirations of local environmentalists and aboriginal peoples). Clayoquot Sound was divided into lands designated for full logging (45 percent), lands for special management logging (17 percent), and lands under protection (33 percent). Economic interests were relatively pleased with the arrangement; after all, it meant business as usual. Environmentalists, however, were outraged. The issue was not about logging per se, but about the nature and intensity of how to exploit the forests. They criticized the terms of the division (much of the land slated for protection was of marginal quality or already under protection as provincial parks); failure to protect old-growth forest and a diverse ecosystem; lack of monitoring and enforcement provisions, as well as inadequate penalties for transgressions; and tolerance for a logging system (clearcutting) that is highly destructive in terms of soil erosion, river and lake siltation, wildlife survival, and loss of biodiversity. Especially galling was a decision to destroy a rapidly vanishing natural resource by moonscaping the environment. The government was singled out for condemnation: Not only did it own the largest single interest in MacMillan Bloedel, implying a conflict of interest, but the government was putting its faith in a company already convicted in Ontario and British Columbia of pollution and other flagrant violations.

The aboriginal peoples were no less angry, especially the Nuu-cha-nult. The

Nuu-cha-nult First Nations had occupied the area for thousands of years, without ever explicitly extinguishing their rights to ownership on the basis of original occupancy. Upon entry into Confederation, the British Columbia government unilaterally extinguished aboriginal rights over land that had been guaranteed in the Proclamation Act of 1763 and declared, instead, wholesale ownership of the territory under terms of conquest and discovery. It was not until 1992 that the provincial government decided to reopen the issue of aboriginal rights to unceded land. Despite promising to compensate aboriginal tribes prior to any logging development, the government gave the go-ahead to MacMillan Bloedel, in effect leaving the Nuu-cha-nult in a dilemma. Ongoing development will either hinder their case in court or render a hollow victory over a decimated land (Dobson and Jackson 1993). Promises to consult local aboriginal groups are no longer taken seriously in light of increased development of aboriginal land by large corporations.

In reaction to public protest and acts of civil disobedience, the B.C. government put together a panel of scientists and aboriginal leaders. In mid-1995, the Clayoquot Sound Scientific Panel recommended an end to clearcutting and its replacement by more selective means of timber cutting. The government agreed and put a stop to the practice to ensure the character of old-growth forests. Shortly thereafter, environmentalists again accused the government and MacMillan Bloedel of

CASE 11-4   The Politics of Environmental Economics: Clayoquot or Clearcut? (continued)

backtracking on their commitments and urged a complete moratorium (Rowell 1996). The battlelines are drawn: In the long-standing struggle between the economy (profit, exports, and jobs) and ecology (preservation, survival, and human rights), the "tree cutters" are pitted against the "tree huggers" in a scenario in which neither side seems able to see the "forest for the trees." Logging companies accuse environmentalists of destroying much-needed employment (they rarely mention the need for profit). An emergent anti-green sentiment is coalescing into a social movement of pro-industry, free-enterprise people who want to destroy the environmentalists by demonizing the greens ("bugger a hugger") and reframing the debate around confrontation rather than cooperation (Rowell 1996). Environmentalists point out that although trees may be renewable, forests are not (Maclean's, August 16, 1993). Aborigi-

nal nations counter that the issue is neither one of jobs nor one of environment, but one of human rights. Their priorities are the settlement of their land claims and recognition of them as a self-determining people. The government, in turn, must make compromises that satisfy the competing demands of various sectors, including rights, jobs, and the environment, without destroying the investment and material basis of the provincial economy. The government's decision to tighten environmental regulations in a province whose forests furnish 60 percent of exports has contributed to a loss of 18 000 jobs in the first half of 1997 alone (Bercusson and Cooper 1997). Nor can they ignore the bluster of forest companies who threaten to move to Brazil if their profit margins are imperilled. There, they are less likely to be inundated with sobriquets about "Brazil—the B.C. of the south."

1992). To be sure, many will blame the Developing World for economic ruin, but many of the world's economic problems stem from Western consumption patterns, obscene levels of waste and wastefulness, and obsession with the "cult of the immediate" (Attali 1990). In spite of this, the Third World is expected to disproportionately contribute to protection of the global environment—even if this means curbing local consumption or curtailing regional economic growth (Durning 1991). There is much to commend in balancing production with ecology, but those who point the finger at others should begin by first examining their own consumption patterns. Third, solutions to environmental problems are not simple. The relation of human beings to their environment is complex, with the result that changes in one area will affect another, even though there is no way of predicting precisely what will happen in each situation.

FOREIGN AID AND (UNDER)DEVELOPMENT

The global integration of national and multinational economies is an established fact. The magnitude and scope of this integration cannot be overestimated. Nor can there be any doubt about the unevenness of this process. These imbalances in the global process are especially evident by observing postwar trends in international assistance. Since the Second World War, First World countries have transferred billions of dollars of assistance to the Third World. The rationale behind these initiatives is quite simple. The average American and Canadian earned over $21 000 in 1991. Compare this with the average annual income of $120 in Ethiopia or $70 in Mozambique (Toronto Star, January 5, 1993). Not only is this disparity morally uncomfortable for many, it has the potential to disrupt the international status quo, with long-term repercussions for global survival. Only a reduction in this massive gap can stave off the threat of global confrontations or deter the movement of asylum-seekers in search of economic opportunity. In this sense, any move to secure greater global equality provides benefits for the rich as well as the poor.

One strategy for achieving this goal has focused on expanding initiatives in foreign aid and development. A package of short- and long-term programs has been implemented to bolster Third World standards to the level of developed countries. But after 40 years of development and assistance, the track record is mixed at best. On the one hand, life expectancy in the Third World has crept up to 63 years (compared with an average of 75 in the industrialized world). Much of this increase can be attributed to longer survival rates among children because of improved immunization programs. On the other hand, the downside is inescapable. Increases in life expectancy may compound the problem of overpopulation in many Third World countries, increasing demands on scarce resources and aggravating sprawling urbanization, dwindling accommodation, and skyrocketing crime rates. Once again we are reminded of certain truisms that apply to solving social problems, including that elements exist only in relation to others, changes in one area create changes in others because of this interconnection, and the complexity of these interrelations make it difficult to predict events or control outcomes (Jackson 1992). Solutions or problems rarely fit into an "either–or" category. Solving one problem can activate additional, often unexpected problems, whose combined impact could well undermine the original gains. Solutions that only temporarily cover up the problem before the problem reinstates itself must be replaced with long-term prevention strategies that link people with resources.

Even the very concept of foreign assistance has come under intense scrutiny. Criticism is mounting over the use of foreign aid. Megaprojects like superhighways or international airports have been criticized because of their adverse effect on local economies and the environment (Culpepper 1993). Not only is there concern about the rationale for foreign aid in addressing world poverty, overpopulation, ill health, and illiteracy, but the effectiveness of foreign assistance is also being questioned because of unacceptably slow or nonexistent rates of progress in coping with the social problems of receiving countries. That doubts are escalating should come as no surprise. A backlash against foreign aid is inevitable as the rich countries wrestle with their own downsizing demons. Resentment smoulders when governments are seen as helping others while ignoring the plight of the poor through domestic deficit reduction or job creation. Finally, public perceptions are playing a key role in cutbacks. Many believe developing countries to be irresponsible for neither accepting the blame for their own social problems, nor assuming responsibility for problem-solving initiatives. The Developing World is also criticized for not doing enough to reduce inequities, defuse ethnic animosities or religious strife, or curtail military spending that gobbles up scarce resources while frittering away productive potential. Thus, public support appears to be dwindling. Many perceive foreign aid and development as wastefully tossing money into a bottomless pit. As the former editor of the *New Internationalist* sarcastically put it, foreign aid "transfers money from the poor people of the rich country to the rich people of the poor countries" (quoted in Nicholson-Lord 1992).

In response to this criticism about its propriety and effectiveness, there has been a rethinking of developmental assistance in recent years. The shift to more human-centred assistance (focused on health, education, and ameliorating poverty) is widely touted, as is the emphasis on sustainability (locally owned development) and proactive initiatives (with an emphasis on preventing rather than curing). Increasingly, attention and funding are directed towards cooperative programs often involving women in collectives as catalysts for change. Still, questions remain about whether foreign aid reduces—or magnifies—the problems of the Developing World, and what Canadians can or should do about it.

Underlying Logic

Foreign aid is based on the concept of improving a country's economy by modernizing its services and production facilities. The philosophical underpinnings of developmental assistance reflect the success of the Marshall Plan in the late 1940s. Conceived by U.S. Secretary of State John Marshall, the plan provided for the redevelopment of war-ravaged Europe through massive airlifts of supplies and the provision of technical assistance. The plan was so successful that it provided a blueprint for all future assistance strategies. The less fortunate (the south) receive assistance from the privileged (the north) through the transfer of wealth (resources, skills, expertise) in hopes of accelerating economic modernization. The objective of this so-called munificence is threefold:

1) to reduce inequality by eliminating dependency (especially dependence on those aspects of culture and society that inhibit growth and progress),

2) to encourage development at local and national levels, and

3) to fortify the grounds for a stable, capitalist, and democratic society.

Its anticipated benefits are local and international in scope. On the assumption that continued prosperity at home is directly related to Third World prosperity, it stands to reason that foreign aid constitutes an investment in global security and international peace rather than an act of charity or chivalry (Culpepper 1993). A reduction in local inequalities may forestall global tension, avert massive migration, and arrest environmental destruction.

The rationale of most of these plans is based on improving the GNP or GDP of each society. By focusing on GNP, most foreign aid programs aim to increase domestic wealth through the transfer of capital and tools (resources, money, infrastructure, experts, and expertise). At one end are donations of emergency assistance when countries experience natural catastrophes such as floods or famines. At the other end are long-term investments, which can include donations of foodstuffs or finished products, investment and expertise for sustainable community development, bilateral trade exchanges, and infrastructure development related to roads, communication links, and hospitals. In recent years, the focus and scope of foreign aid and development has taken a new direction. From an earlier commitment to throwing money and experts at a problem, the underlying philosophy is now directed towards locally driven, sustainable development (best encapsulated in the aphorism "give people fish, and they will eat for a day; teach them how to fish and they will eat for a lifetime"). But what happens when the local fishing place becomes polluted or is depleted? What sounds good in principle, in other words, does not always work in practice.

For Whom, for What?

Canada is widely admired as a generous contributor to the international scene. Under the auspices of the Canadian International Development Agency (CIDA), billions of dollars have been sent to developing nations. Funding has been funnelled into a variety of programs, ranging in scope from megaprojects to the current endorsement of sustainable development. According to the 1997 federal report *Shaping Our Future*, Canada's policies were to be directed at the poorest countries in an effort to help people to help themselves. In reality, less than 20 percent of Canada's foreign aid is directed at the neediest, with many Eastern European countries in receipt of large sums. In 1994–95, the government set aside $2.6 billion for foreign aid, or 0.41 percent of the GNP (1998 figures stand at 0.24 percent). While a drop from $3 billion in 1992–93, this total kept Canada in the top 10 countries with respect to national wealth spent on foreign aid, in effect making Canada a major player in world affairs. Because of bilateral trade arrangements with target countries, however, nearly $0.60 of every foreign aid dollar is eventually spent in Canada. In terms of dollars per target country, Bangladesh received $90 million, followed by China at $63 million, India at $42 million, and Mozambique at $41 million (Barthos 1994). Taken together, 33 percent of all aid is directed at "geographic programs" (including everything from infrastructure to lines of credit), 16 percent consists of cash transfers to international financial agencies (such as the International Monetary Fund), 12 percent is for food, 9 percent matches funds from other agencies (such as Oxfam), and 6 percent is for administration.

Despite such seeming generosity, nearly a half century of assistance from the rich to the poor has done little to ameliorate inequities. Many have concluded that billions in foreign aid spending have had little net impact on the overall economic performance of the Developing World. Nor has it had much effect on the economic policies of the Developing World, despite the use of foreign aid as an incentive to reduce inflationary government spending, pare back subsidies, and eliminate bureaucracy (Blustein 1997). The gap between the rich and the poor is even widening in some ways rather than decreasing as might be expected. How do we account for this singular lack of success? Is foreign aid simply an inadequate response to global problems? Or is it a Band-Aid solution ill-equipped for dealing with fundamental issues related to structure and system? Are target populations inadequate to the task of assisting in their own development? Or is the problem one of politics; that is, is the transfer of wealth organized around the needs of the donor rather than the target country? Is foreign assistance a tool for encouraging independence and growth, or a trap for fine-tuning the bonds of dependency and underdevelopment? Consider the case of Bangladesh, which came into existence when India was partitioned in 1971, and to this day receives half its national budget from foreign sources. More than 90 percent of the government development budget— including everything from building bridges to paying teachers' salaries—originates overseas, while another $5 billion in foreign aid remains unspent, "stuck in the pipeline" (Miller 1991). This aid transfusion is viewed by some as a necessary prelude for self-management; others pounce on it as an example of how "well-intentioned waste" actually stunts local growth by reinforcing a welfare mentality and dependency syndrome. In other words, foreign aid can be interpreted as much as a problem as a solution. It also has the effect of catching Canadians and Americans in one of their cultural blind spots, that is, a belief that there's a definitive solution to every problem (Dickey 1997).

Perils and Pitfalls: "A Trojan Horse"

What conclusion can be drawn from this examination of disbursements under foreign assistance? On the surface, there is much to be said for the commitment to help others eventually help themselves. In reality, too much foreign aid is concerned with political or commercial issues rather than with poverty eradication (Knox 1996). The rationale behind foreign aid has historically focused on political leverage for helping "allies." Expediency dictated that enemies would be overlooked regardless of need or duress. Foreign assistance was rationalized on the grounds of stabilizing—and rewarding—countries that were friendly to the West, thus allowing capitalist expansion without fear of unnecessary unrest or unwelcome takeovers. Second, most aid could not be separated from economic considerations. Foreign aid often materialized as a disguised export subsidy for the donor country, with strings attached because of "bilateral" political or economic concessions. Under "tied" assistance, countries would receive benefits provided they purchased Canadian-made goods in return. While this was of obvious benefit to Canada, developing countries were forced to purchase unnecessary goods at inflated prices as a precondition to qualify for foreign assistance from Ottawa (Drohan 1996). Not surprisingly, the strings-attached mentality further ensnared the host country in the workings of a global economy (Nicholson-Lord 1992). Other aid is contingent on making structural adjustments to induce higher productivity in industry or agriculture through free market pricing, private ownership, inflation reduction, pared-away government expenditures, elimination of food subsidies, and reduced social services. These austerity measures may please World Bank donors, but they often incite riots when suffering becomes acute (Chege 1997). Third, the bulk of foreign aid is of an expedient rather than humanitarian nature. Generous offers of emergency assistance are often an excuse to discard surplus commodities without depressing the international commodity markets. This has happened in the past with embarrassing stockpiles of milk powder, butter, and wheat—all largely subsidized by a government unable to unload them on the free market. The fact that disaster relief may intensify the suffering of the victims (for example, sending powdered milk to relief victims who cannot comfortably digest milk enzymes) is unconscionable. That the government can get away with this and still look good in the process is called "politics."

The failure of foreign aid programs may also reflect differences in the ways people think about social problems. Take the concept of solutions, for example. A central theme throughout this and other chapters is the inapplicability of simplistic solutions to complicated problems. Social problems are related to solutions in ways that are ambiguous, contradictory, and unpredictable. The world we live in is too complex and too interconnected to allow us to confidently predict outcomes or to control the shape of events. We may even have to confront the prospect that some problems have no solutions. Still, we continue to be preoccupied by a quick-fix mentality. In times of rapid change, simple solutions take on a certain appeal to those who merely want to convey the illusion rather than the substance of change. However, our search for simple (as in simplistic) solutions may be partly the result of a dominant intellectual tradition that shapes how we think and experience reality (Rothenberg 1992). Our intellectual tradition emphasizes a "line" of thought that partitions the world into mutually opposed categories (opposition thinking), linear models (cause–effect relations that reflect single causes and predictable effects in a straight-line progression), and the existence of a hierarchy (with a ranking of differences on a scale).

There is nothing wrong with patterns of thought organized around a "line" that connects and moves in a straight direction between points. However, an exclusive reliance on such rationality makes it impossible to consider alternative forms of thought that acknowledge complexity, relationships, and contradiction. Such a linear style of thought spells disaster in the design and implementation of foreign aid programs. It also compounds problems of communication when the host and donor communities do not have the same priorities or think along the same lines. A mindset is required instead that allows the coexistence of mutually exclusive alternatives. Additional reasons relate to poor program design and implementation. Projects continue to be poorly planned by technical experts out of touch with the particular needs of a country. Efforts are sabotaged by poor delivery systems and a lack of communication with local experts about how best to modify Western-style programs for Third World consumption. Experts may be inclined by training to produce computer-based irrigation technologies when all the local community really needs is a hand-held well pump. The human factor is too often ignored. Lastly, problems of maintenance are rarely addressed. Sophisticated technology may require expensive upkeep and constant repairs, thus further alienating the masses from participation or benefit. In other words, the poor become poorer, partly because developmental programs deal with symptoms rather than causes, ignore the broader social and cultural context, and disregard the interconnectedness of society and the environment. This may not be the intent behind foreign aid; nevertheless the consequences of assistance actions are such that, despite good intentions, they inadvertently harm those who need help the most.

What Next?

The string of foreign aid failures is now legendary. That, in itself, is no reason to blame individual field workers for glitches in the process. There is even less reason to accuse the recipients of being lazy or corrupt. Rather, failure is often built into the principles and practices of foreign aid. As well, it is easy to criticize foreign aid and development as a disincentive to progress or growth. But few any longer deny the political and economic overtones of conventional assistance. Agencies such as CIDA have revised their mission to include sustainable development and community-based growth. Partnerships are being forged that focus on local projects and areas of poverty, with women increasingly targeted as the beneficiaries. There has also been a move to decentralize and deregulate the procedures by which programs and projects are designed and delivered.

Public reaction towards foreign aid and development remains as vocal as ever, especially by those who denounce the exercise as a waste of time and money. Many see foreign aid and development as a superficial solution that never gets to the root of the problem. Too much, they say, is spent on building bridges and roads but not in helping the poor, given that only 3 percent of foreign aid budgets are earmarked for health or education (Knox 1996). For some, the concept of foreign aid reflects an old-fashioned liberalism; one identified the problem, then called in the social scientists to analyze it, the technicians to solve it, and the government to finance the program (Economist 1996). By contrast, current neo-conservative thinking argues that there isn't a problem in the first place—social scientists have misunderstood it, technicians can't solve it, and any effort by the government would only make things worse. For others, the whole concept of foreign aid is morally repugnant since millions are supported without much concern for the consequences or quality of life. Even more galling is an awareness that foreign aid may unwittingly abet conflict or suffering by propping up murderous regimes by playing politics with peoples lives (Unland 1996). For still others it is the short-sightedness of foreign aid that rankles. A short-term problem is solved at the expense of creating a long-term solution or an additional set of problems. It is one thing to feed people during emergencies; it is quite another to furnish them with the tools to feed themselves; it is still another to appreciate how increased life expectancy will exert further pressure on dwindling resources and restricted land space. The likelihood of additional famine and suffering is real unless steps are taken to deal with these problems holistically.

What to do? The solution is not to discontinue foreign aid and development; after all, people need assistance to survive regardless of our moral qualms. The goal is to examine the problem in global terms and to apply local solutions that will sever dependencies and foster meaningful local development. This is accomplished in part by taking foreign aid out of official hands and putting it to use as directly as possible for those who need it most. For if there is one thing we have learned, it is that social problems are rarely solved by telling others what to do or by doing it for them. Problems are even less likely to be solved if solutions fail to come from within and focus on the structures that created the problem in the first place.

SUMMARY

1. The world as we know it is being transformed by political, economic, technological, and social upheavals. Globalizing forces for worldwide integration and central control are conflicting with centrifugal forces such as nationalism and ethnicity. Tension between the forces "pushing together" and those "pulling apart" provides for much of the conflict at the heart of contemporary societies.

2. The growth of an integrated global economy is restructuring Canada's own economy, forcing it to change from an industrial strategy based on government intervention to one motivated by the challenges of an intensely competitive free market. This restructuring creates profound problems for Canada's national unity and economic prosperity.

3. The penetration of capitalism to all corners of the world has created a world system. A kind of global gridlock has arisen from these relations of dependency and underdevelopment. The consequences foster an inequality between rich cores and impoverished peripheries, with wealthy dependencies in between.

4. As a rich periphery, Canada may be a victim of external global forces, but it is also a victimizer of countries weaker than itself. But whether it is considered the oppressor or the oppressed, Canada is irrevocably enmeshed in a matrix of global economic and political forces.

5. In the ongoing debate over markets versus the state, advocates of the market point to incentives for producers to produce high quality, competitively priced goods within an

innovative and dynamic framework of supply and demand. Advocates of state regulation accuse the market of being inegalitarian, unnecessarily competitive, and undemocratic to the point of tearing the social fabric of society.

6. Evidence to date reaffirms the notion of globalization as a two-headed axe, with a capacity to be swung in both directions, for good or bad, depending on the context or purpose. Competing claims about the pros and cons of the Free Trade Agreement reflect different perspectives about Canada with respect to wealth creation and its ranking in a global system.

7. Links between countries nowadays are orchestrated not so much through political alliances as through the relatively unimpeded circulation of capital and investment, much of it by powerful stateless corporations whose single-minded devotion to profits benefits a few but penalizes many. Multinational corporations now control a significant portion of the world's wealth, and are therefore a threat to its political stability.

8. The forces of colonialism and neo-colonialism contribute to uneven north–south relations in matters of overpopulation, urbanization, poverty, ethnic conflicts, and environmental degradation.

9. One of sociology's more important contributions to human thought lies in its insistence on looking at the "bigger picture" as a source of knowledge. Developments in Canada can only make sense in the global context of free market economies, trading blocks, and multinationals, together with various demographic, social, and political changes that have loosened Canada's conventional moorings and set it adrift in a sea of uncertainty.

10. The concept of foreign aid and development is paradoxical. Foreign assistance provides a solution for many First World problems, not for the problems of the Developing World, as would appear to be the case.

11. The potential of foreign aid and development as a means of solving global problems is contaminated by commercial and political concerns. That Canada is a contributor to Developing World problems because of the design and implementation of its benefit packages provides insight into the perils and pitfalls of north–south restructuring.

References

Abbott, Pamela and Claire Wallace (1990). *An Introduction to Sociology: Feminist Perspectives*. London: Routledge and Kegan Paul.

Abbott, Pamela and Claire Wallace (1992). *The Family and the New Right*. London: Pluto.

Abel, Sue (1997). "Shaping the News." *Waitangi Day on Television*. Auckland University Press.

Abella, Irving and Harold Troper (1982). *None is Too Many. Canada and the Jews in Europe 1933–1948*. Toronto: Lester and Orpen Dennys Ltd.

Abercrombie, Nichalas (1995). *Television and Society*. London: Polity Press.

Abley, Mark (1997). "Free Trade No Friend of Earth." *The Toronto Star*, May 3.

Abraham, S. and D. Llewellyn-Jones (1992). *Eating Disorders: The Facts*. New York: Oxford.

Abu-Laban, Yasmeen and Daiva K. Stasiulis (1992). "Ethnic Pluralism Under Siege. Popular and Partisan Opposition to Multiculturalism." *Canadian Public Policy* 18(4): 365–386.

Acton, W. (1857). *Prostitution*. London: John Churchill.

Adams, Scott (1996). *The Dilbert Principle*. NY: Harper Business.

Adler, Freda (1975). *Sisters in Crime*. New York: McGraw-Hill.

Addiction Research Foundation (1997). *Canada Profile* 1997. Toronto: Addiction Research Foundation and the Canadian Centre on Substance Abuse.

Agocs, Carol and Monica Boyd (1993). "Ethnicity and Ethnic Inequality." Pp. 330–352 in Jim Curtis, Ed Grab, and Neil Guppy (eds.), *Social Inequality in Canada*, 2nd edition. Scarborough, Ontario: Prentice Hall.

Ahenakew, David (1985). "Aboriginal Title and Aborginal Rights: The Impossible and Unnecessary Task of Identification and Definition." Pp. 24–30 in Menno Boldt and J. Anthony Long (eds.), *The Quest for Justice. Aboriginal Peoples and Aboriginal Title*. Toronto: University of Toronto Press.

Aitkin, Don (1997). "Sour Times and High Anxiety in Australia." Address to Staff at Australian National University, Canberra, May 7. Reprinted in *Education Gazette*.

Akyeampong, Ernest B. (1992). "Absenteeism At Work." *Canadian Social Trends*, Summer: 26–28.

Alberta Report (1991). "Coping with Criminal Kids: A plague of teen crime illustrates the failure of the Young Offenders Act." April 15: 44–47.

Albo, Gregory and Jane Jenson (1996). "Remapping Canada: The State in the Era of Globalization." In J. Littleton (ed.), *Clash of Identities*. Scarborough: Prentice Hall.

Albrow, Martin (1996). *The Global Age*. London: Polity Press.

Alfred, Gerald Robert (1995). *Heeding the Voices of Our Ancestors: Kahnawake Mohawk Politics and the Rise of Native Nationalism in Canada*. Toronto: Oxford University Press.

Allen, Charlotte Low (1992). "Teenage Birth's New Conceptions." Pp. 144–147 in Ollie

Pocs (ed.), *Human Sexuality 92/93*. Guilford, CT: Dushkin.

Allen, G., G. Sietland, J. Rogers, A. Nikisoruk, D. Burke, and S. Mcphee (1985). "The Ethics of AIDS." *Maclean's*, November 18: 48.

Allgeier, E.R. and A.F. Fogel (1977). "Coital Positions and Sex Roles: Responses to Cross-Sex Behavior in Bed." *Journal of Counsulting and Clinical Psychology* 46: 588–589.

Ambert, Anne-Marie (1983). "Separated Women and Remarriage Behavior: A Comparison of Financially Secure Women and Financially Insecure Women." *Journal of Divorce* 6: 43–54.

Ambert, Anne-Marie (1990). "Marriage Dissolution: Structural and Ideological Changes." Pp. 192–210 in Maureen Baker (ed.), *Families: Changing Trends in Canada*, 2nd edition. Toronto: McGraw-Hill Ryerson.

Andersen, Robin (1996). *Consumer Culture and TV Programming*. Boulder, CO: Westview Press.

Anderson, Margaret L. (1988). *Thinking About Women: Sociological Perspectives on Sex and Gender*. New York: Macmillan.

Ang, Ien and Joke Hermes (1994). "Gender and/in Media Consumption." Pp. 2–7 in J. Curran and M. Gurevitch (eds.), *Mass Media and Society*. London: Edward Arnold.

Annual Report (1997). *Canadian Heritage. Multiculturalism Division*. Ottawa: Government Printer.

Apple, Michael W. (1996). *Cultural Politics and Education*. Buckingham: Open University Press.

Armstrong, Louise (1986). *Kiss Daddy Goodnight*. Toronto: Doubleday.

Armstrong, Pat (1990). "Economic Conditions and Family Structures." Pp. 67–92 in Maureen Baker (ed.), *Families: Changing Trends in Canada*, 2nd edition. Toronto: McGraw-Hill Ryerson.

Arnup, Katherine (ed). (1995). *Lesbian Parenting: Living With Pride & Prejudice*. Charlottetown: Gynergy Books.

Asbury, Kathryn E. (1989). "Innovative Policing: Foot Patrol in 31 Division, Metropolitan Toronto." *Canadian Police College Journal* 13(3): 165–181.

Atkinson, Joe (1994). "The State, The Media, and Thin Democracy." Pp. 146–177 in Andrew Sharp (ed.), *Leap into the Dark. The Changing Role of the State in New Zealand since 1984*. Auckland: Auckland University Press.

Attali, Jacques (1990). "Can Eastern Europe Move From the 19th to the 21st Century?" *New Perspectives Quarterly*: 38–41.

Bala, Nicholas (1988). "The Young Offender: A Legal Framework." Pp. 11–36 in Joe Hudson, Joseph P. Hornick, and Barbara A. Burrows (eds.), *Justice and the Young Offender in Canada*. Toronto: Wall and Thompson.

Balakrishnan, T.R., K. Krotki, and E. LaPierre-Adamcyk, (1985). "Contraceptive Use in Canada." *Family Planning Perspectives* 17: 209–215.

Balthazar, Louis (1993). "The Faces of Quebec Nationalism." Pp 2–17 in A.G. Gagnon (ed.), *Quebec: State and Society*, 2nd edition. Scarborough: Nelson.

Balthazar, Louis (1996). "Identity and Nationalism in Quebec." Pp. 101–112 in J. Littleton (ed.), *Clash of Identities*. Scarborough: Prentice Hall.

Banner, Lois (1992). *In Full Flower: Aging Women, Power and Sexuality*. New York: Alfred A. Knopf.

Banton, Michael (1987). *Racial Theories*. London: CUP.

Barash, D.P. (1982). *Sociobiology and Behaviour*, 2nd edition. New York: Elsevier.

Barile, Maria (1992). "Disabled Women: An Exploited Underclass." *Canadian Women Studies*, Summer, 12(4): 32–33.

Barlow, Maude (1997). "Media Concentration is Reaching Crisis Levels." *The Toronto Star*, May 2.

Barlow, Maude and Bruce Campbell (1996). *Straight Through the Heart. How the Liberals Abandoned the Just Society*. Toronto: HarperCollins.

Barlow, Maude and Heather-Jane Robertson (1993). *Class Warfare: The Assault on Canadian Schools*. Toronto: Key Porter.

Barrett, Stanley (1994). *Paradise. Class, Commuters, and Ethnicity in Rural Ontario*. Toronto: University of Toronto Press.

Barrett, Stanley R. (1987). *Is God a Racist? The Right Wing in Canada*. Toronto: University of Toronto Press.

Barthos, Gordon (1994). "Two Faces of Foreign Aid." *The Toronto Star*, February 27.

Basow, Susan A. (1986). *Gender Stereotypes: Traditions and Alternatives*, 2nd edition. Monterey, CA: Brooks/Cole.

Bayley, David (1994). "International Differences in Community Policing" Pp. 278–284 in D.P. Rosenbaum (ed.), *The Challenge of Community Policing*. Thousand Oaks, CA: Sage.

Becker, H. (1963). *Outsiders*. New York: Free Press.

Becker, H. (1973). *Outsiders: Studies in the Sociology of Deviance*. New York: Free Press.

Becker, H. (ed.) (1964). *The Other Side*. New York: Free Press.

Becker, Howard (1971). "Reply to Riley." *American Sociologist* 6(1): 13.

Behrendt, Paul (1996). "Aboriginal Australians: A Mirror of Attitude and National Conscience." Pp 6–15 in A. Pattel-Gray (ed.), *Martung Upah: Black and White Australians Seeking Partnership*. Blackburn, Victoria: HarperCollins.

Belensky, Mary F., Blythe M. Clinchy, Nancy R. Goldberger and Jill M. Tarule (eds.) (1980). *Women's Ways of Knowing: The Development of Self, Voice and Mind*. New York: Basic Books.

Bell, Daniel (1972). "On Meritocracy and Equality." *The Public Interest* 29: 29–68.

Bell, N. (1984). "Abusing the Child." *Choice*, March: 931–939.

Belliveau, Jo-Anne and Leslie Gaudette (1995). "Chances in Cancer Incidence and Mortality." *Canadian Social Trends*, Winter, 39: 2-7.

Beltrame, Julian (1997). "Free Trade Boosts Jobs." *Kitchener-Waterloo Record*, July 9.

Benkov, Laura (1994). *Reinventing the Family: The Emerging Story of Gay and Lesbian Parents*. New York: Crown Publishers.

Benokraitis, Nijole V. (1996). *Marriages and Families: Changes, Choices and Constraints*, 2nd edition. Upper Saddle River, NJ: Prentice Hall.

Bercusson, David and Barry Cooper (1997). "Glen Clark's Hard Line on Fish and Firs Is All About Jobs." *The Globe and Mail*, July 5.

Berger, Brigette (1993). "Multiculturalism and the Modern University." *Partisan Review*: 516–530.

Bergman, Brian (1996). "When children are vicious." *Maclean's*, August 12, 109(33):12–13.

Bernard, Jessie (1981/1995). "The Good Provider Role: Its Rise and Fall." *American Psychologist* 36(2): 1–12. Reprinted as pp. 156–171 in E.D. Nelson and B.W. Robinson (eds.), *Gender in the 1990s: Images, Realities and Issues*. Scarborough: Nelson.

Berry, John W. (1993). "Cultural Relations in a Multicultural Society." Paper presented at a Community Psychology Seminar for

Wilfrid Laurier University, Waterloo, Ontario, March 30.

Berry, John W. and Rudolf Kalin (1993). "Multiculturalism and Ethnic Attitudes in Canada. An Overview of the 1991 National Survey." Paper presented to the Canadian Psychological Association Annual Meetings, Montreal, Quebec, May.

Berry, John W and Rudolf Kalin (1995). "Multicultural and Ethnic Attitudes in Canada. An Overview of the 1991 National Survey." *Canadian Journal of Behavioural Sciences* 27(3): 301–320.

Berton, Pierre (1975). *Hollywood's Canada*. Toronto: McClelland and Stewart.

Besch, E.L. (1985). "Definition of Laboratory Animal Environmental Conditions." Pp. 197–315 in G.P. Moberg (ed.), *Animal Stress*. Bethesda, MD: American Psychological Society.

Best, Joel (1989). *Images of Issues: Typifying Contemporary Social Problems*. New York: Aldine de Gruyter, Inc.

Best, Joel (1995). *Images of Issues: Typifying Contemporary Social Problems*, 2nd edition. Hawthorne, NY: Aldine de Gruyter.

Bibby, Reginald W. (1990). *Mosaic Madness. The Potential and Poverty of Canadian Life*. Toronto: Stoddart.

Bibby, Reginald W. (1995). *The Bibby Report: Social Trends Canadian-Style*. Toronto: Stoddart Publishing Company.

Biddiss, Michael D. (ed.) (1979). *Images of Race*. New York: Holmes and Meier.

Bienvenue, Rita M. (1985). "Colonial Status: The Case of Canadian Indians." Pp. 199–216 in Rita M. Bienvenue and Jay E. Goldstein (eds.), *Ethnicity and Ethnic Relations in Canada*. Toronto: Butterworths.

Biesenthal, Lorri (1993). "London Study Examines Police Charging Policy as a Deterrent to Wife Assault." *Justice Research Notes*, April, 5: 7–10. Ottawa: Department of Justice Canada.

Bindman, Stephen (1997). "Statistics are shifty, criminologists warn." *KW Record*, July 31: A3.

Bissoondath, Neil (1993/1994). "A Question of Belonging: Multiculturalism and Citizenship." Pp. 367–387 in William Kaplan (ed.), *Belonging. The Meaning and Future of Canadian Citizenship*. Kingston/Montreal: McGill-Queen's Press.

Bissoondath, Neil (1994). *Selling Illusions: The Cult of Multiculturalism in Canada*. Toronto: Penguin.

Blachford, Greg (1981). "Male Dominance and the Gay World." Pp. 183–210 in Ken Plummer (ed.), *The Making of the Modern Homosexual*. Totowa, NJ: Barnes and Noble.

Black, Debra (1993). "Canadian Women Get Short Shrift, U.N. says." *The Toronto Star*, June 29: B1.

Black, Ken (1991). "A Provincial Perspective on Drug Abuse: Alcohol, Individuals and Society." Pp. 11–20 in Douglas J. McCready (ed.), *Health Futures: Alcohol and Drugs*. Waterloo, Ontario: Interdisciplinary Research Committee, Wilfred Laurier University, Occasional Paper 8.

Blackwell, J.C. and Erickson, P.G. (1988). *Illicit Drugs In Canada: A Risky Business*. Scarborough: Nelson.

Blau, Peter (1963). *The Dynamics of Bureaucracy*, 2nd edition. Chicago: University of Chicago Press.

Blauner, Robert (1972). *Racial Oppression in America*. New York: Harper.

Blumstein, Philip and Pepper Schwartz (1983). *American Couples: Work, Money, Sex*. New York: William Morrow and Company.

Bly, Robert (1990). *Iron John: A Book About Men*. Reading, MA: Addison-Wesley.

Bly, Robert (1991). "The Need for Male Initiation." Pp. 38–42 in Keith Thompson (ed.), *To Be A Man*. Los Angeles: Tarcher Books.

Blythe, Martin (1994). *Naming the Other. Images of the Maori in New Zealand Film and Television*. Metuchen, NJ: Scarecrow Press.

Boismenu, Gerard (1996). "Perspectives on Quebec–Canada Relations in the 1990s: Is the Reconciliation of Ethnicity, Nationality, and Citizenship Possible?" *Canadian Review of Studies in Nationalism* XXIII(1–2): 99–109.

Bolaria, B. Singh (ed.) (1991). *Social Issues and Contradictions in Canadian Society*. Toronto: Harcourt Brace Jovanovich.

Bolaria, B. Singh and Peter S. Li (1988). *Racial Oppression in Canada*, 2nd edition. Toronto: Garamond Press.

Bolaria, B. Singh and Terry Wotherspoon (1991). "Income Inequality, Poverty, and Hunger." Pp. 464–480 in B. Singh Bolaria (ed.), *Social Issues and Contradictions in Canadian Society*. Toronto: Harcourt Brace Jovanovich.

Boldt, Menno (1993). *Surviving as Indians. The Challenge of Self-Government*. Toronto: University of Toronto Press.

Boldt, Menno and J. Anthony Long (1984). "Tribal Traditions and European-Western Political Ideology: The Dilemma of Canadian Native Indians." *Canadian Journal of Political Science* 17: 537–554.

Bonilla-Silva, Eduardo (1996). "Rethinking Racism: Toward a Structural Integration." *American Sociological Review* 62: 465–480.

Bowles, Samuel and Herbert Gintis (1976). *Schools in Capitalist America*. London: Routledge & Kegan Paul.

Bowring, Philip (1993). "Asia Faces Struggle to Reach Urban Dreams." *Manchester Guardian*, July 23.

Boyd, Monica (1984). *Canadian Attitudes Towards Women: Thirty Years of Change*. Ottawa: Minister of Supply and Services.

Boyd, Monica (1987). "Migrant Women in Canada: Profiles and Policies." Research Division, Immigration Canada and Status of Women Canada. Ottawa.

Boyd, Monica and Doug Norris (1995). "Leaving the Nest? The Impact of Family Structure." *Canadian Social Trends*, Autumn, 38: 14-176.

Boyd, Neil (1991). "Legal and Illegal Drug Use in Canada." Pp. 135–151 in Margaret A. Jackson and Curt T. Griffiths (eds.), *Canadian Criminology: Perspectives on Crime and Criminality*. Toronto: Harcourt Brace Jovanovich.

Boyd, Susan (1987). "Child Custody and Working Mothers." Pp. 168–183 in Sheilah L. Martin and Kathleen E. Mahoney (eds.), *Equality and Judicial Neutrality*. Toronto: Carswell.

Brannigan, A. (1981). *Crimes, Courts and Corrections*. Toronto: Holt, Rinehart and Winston.

Braroe, N.W. (1975). *Indian and White: Self-Image and Interaction In A Canadian Plains Community*. Stanford: Stanford University Press.

Braxton, Greg (1997). "Root Cause." *Starweek Magazine*, April 5.

Brecher, Edward M. (1984). *Love, Sex, And Aging: A Consumers Union Report*. Mount Vernon, NY: Consumers Union.

Brenner, Johanna A. (1987). "Feminist Political Discourses: Radical Versus Liberal Approaches to the Feminization of Poverty and Comparable Worth." *Gender & Society* 1(4), December: 447–465. © 1987 Sociologists for Women in Society.

Breton, Albert (ed.) (1995). *Nationalism and Rationality*. Cambridge University Press.

Breton, Raymond (1998). "Ethnicity and Race in Social Organizations: Recent

Developments in Canadian Society." In R. Helmes-Hayes and J. Curtis (eds.), *The Vertical Mosaic Revisited*. Toronto: University of Toronto Press.

Breton, Raymond, Wsevolod W. Isajiw, Warren E. Kalbach, and Jeffrey G. Reitz (eds.) (1990). *Ethnic Identity and Equality: Varieties of Experience in a Canadian City*. Toronto: University of Toronto Press.

Bridge, William (1995). *Job Shift*. Reading, MA: Addison-Wesley.

Bridges, Judith S. (1991). "Perceptions of Date and Stranger Rape: A Difference in Sex Role Expectations and Rape-Supportive Beliefs." *Sex Roles* 24(5/6): 291–307.

Brinkerhoff, David D., Lynn K. White, and Suzanne T. Ortega (1992). *Essentials of Sociology*, 2nd edition. St. Paul's: West Publishing.

Brinkerhoff, Merlin B. and Eugene Lupri (1988). "Interspousal Violence." *Canadian Journal of Sociology* 31(4): 407–434.

Brod, Harry (ed.) (1987). *The Making of Masculinities: The New Men's Studies*. Boston: Allen & Unwin.

Brodie, Janine (1997). "The New Political Economy of Region." In W. Clement (ed.), *Understanding Canada. Building on the New Canadian Political Economy*. Montreal/Kingston: McGill-Queen's University Press.

Bromley, Simon (1996). "Globalization?" *Radical Philosophy*, November/December, 80: 2–4.

Brown, David (1989). "Ethnic Revival: Perspectives on State and Society." *Third World Quarterly* 11(4): 1–17.

Brown, Lee P. (1988). *Community Policing: Issues and Policies Around the World*. Washington, D.C.: National Institute of Justice.

Brown, Lee P. (1988). "Preface." In International Association of Chiefs of Police, *Developing Neighborhood Oriented Policing in the Houston Police Department*.

Brown, Lester (1993). "Facing the Crisis of Too Many Mouths to Feed." *The Globe and Mail*, August 9.

Browne, Malcome (1994). "What Is Intelligence, and Who Has It?" *New York Times Book Review*, October 16.

Brym, Robert J. (1991). "Ethnic Group Stratification and Cohesion in Canada. An Overview." Pp. 49–78 in Robin Ostow et al. (eds.), *Ethnicity, Structural Inequality, and the State in Canada and the Federal Republic of Germany*. New York: Peter Lang.

Brym, Robert J. (1993). "The Canadian Capitalist Class." Pp. 31–48 in James Curtis et al. (eds.), *Social Inequality in Canada*, 2nd edition. Scarborough: Prentice Hall.

Bufe, Charles (1991). *Alcoholics Anonymous: Cult or Cure?* San Francisco: See Sharp Press.

Burgess, Michael (1996). "Ethnicity, Nationalism and Identity in Canada–Quebec Relations: The Case of Quebec's Distinct Society." *Journal of Commonwealth & Comparative Politics* 34(2): 46–64.

Burke, Mary Anne, Susan Crompton, Alison Jones and Katherine Nessner (1991). "Caring For Children." *Canadian Social Trends*, Autumn: 12–15.

Burke, Peter, Jan Stets and Maureen M. Pirog-Good (1988). "Gender Identity, Self-Esteem, and Physical and Sexual Abuse in Dating Relationships." *Social Psychology Quarterly* 51: 272–285.

Burstyn, Varda (1985). *Women, Class, Family and State*. Toronto: Garamond Press.

Bush, M. (1988). *Families in Distress: Public, Private and Civic Responses*. Berkely, CA: University of California Press.

CAFCA (Campaign Against Foreign Control) (1996). "News Media Ownership in New Zealand." Fact Sheet No 3.

Caldicott, Helen (1984). *Missile Envy*. New York: William Morrow.

Campbell, Murray (1996). "The Shifting Line Between the Haves and the Have-Nots." *The Globe and Mail*, October 12.

Campbell, Murray (1996). "Work in Progress. A Century of Change." A Six-Part Series. *The Globe and Mail*, November 28.

Canadian Associated Press (1997). "Protesters press for action on death toll among addicts." *KW Record*, July 16: D10.

Canadian Human Rights Commission (1997). *Annual Report*. Ottawa: Minister of Supply and Services.

Canadian Social Trends (1995). "Alcohol Use and Its Consequences." *Canadian Social Trends*, Autumn, 38: 18–23.

Canadian Social Trends (1997). "Canadian Children in the 1990s: Selected Findings of the National Longitudinal Survey of Children and Youth." *Canadian Social Trends*, Spring, 44: 2–9.

Capon, Noel, John E. Farley, James M. Hulbert and David Lei (1991). "In Search of Excellence Ten Years Later: Strategies and Organization Do Matter." *Management Decision* 29(4): 12–21.

Caputi, Jane (1989). "The Sexual Politics of Murder." *Gender & Society* 3(4): 437–456.

Cardozo, Andrew (1996). "Policy Works, Warts and All." *The Toronto Star*, October 14.

Carey, Elaine (1995). "Is Graying of Faculty Turning Universities into 'Boring Places'?" *Toronto Star*, September 25.

Carrington, Peter J. and Sharon Moyer (1991). "A comparison of the treatment of prostitutes and their customers by the police and courts in Toronto, 1986–7." Paper presented at the annual meetings of the Canadian Sociology and Anthropology Association, Kingston, Ontario.

Carter, C.S. and W.T. Greenaugh (1979). "Sending the Right Sex Messages." *Psychology*.

Castells, Manuel (1993). "The Information Economy and the New International Division of Labor." Pp 15–44 in M. Carnoy (ed.), *The New Global Economy in the Information Age: Reflections on Our Changing World*. Pennsylvania State University Press.

Castonguay, Claude (1994). "Why More Quebec Voices Aren't Arguing for Federalism." *The Globe and Mail*, July 25.

Cawsey R.A. (President) (1991). *Justice On Trial: Report of the Task Force on the Criminal Justice System and Its Impact on the Indian and Métis People of Alberta*. Edmonton: Solicitor General of Alberta.

CCSA/ARIF (1997). *1997 Canadian Profile*. Toronto: Addiction Research Foundation.

Chamber, George (1997). "The Hypertextual Sea Change." *NZ Educational Review*, July 9.

Chamberlain, Art (1997). "Teen drug use lowest in Metro." *The Toronto Star*, December 11, A28.

Chambliss, William J. (1973). "The Saints and the Roughnecks." *Society*, November–December.

Chan, Janet (1996). "Changing Police Culture." *British Journal of Criminology* 36(1): 109–133.

Chan, Janet B.L. (1997). *Changing Police Culture. Policing in a Multicultural Society*. Cambridge, UK: Cambridge University Press.

Cheal, David et al. (1997). "Canadian Children in the 1990s: Selected Findings of the National Longitudinal Study of Children and Youth." *Canadian Social Trends*, Spring, Catalogue 11-008-XPE: 2–10.

Chege, Michael (1997). "Time to Put Away the Heroic Stereotypes." *TLS*, January 3: 14–16.

Chiose, Simona (1997). "You're Going to Make it After All!" *The Globe and Mail*, March 1.

Chisholm, Patricia (1996). "The Role of Parents." *Maclean's*, August 12, 109(33): 13.

Chodak, Simon (1994). "Review Essay: Voices on National Divorce." *Canadian Journal of Sociology* 19(3): 379–389.

Chorn, N.H. (1991). "Organisations: A New Paradigm." *Management Decision* 29(4): 8–11.

Christie, Nils (1993). *Crime Control As Industry: Towards Gulags, Western Type?* London: Routledge.

Churchill, Ward (1994). *Indians Are Us? Culture and Genocide in Native North America*. Toronto: Between the Lines.

Clairmont, Don (1988). *Community-Based Policing and Organizational Change*. Occasional Papers. Halifax: Atlantic Institute of Criminology.

Clark, L. and D. Lewis (1977). *The Price of Coercive Sexuality*. Toronto: Women's Educational Press.

Clark, Wayne (1996). "Youth Smoking in Canada." *Canadian Social Trends*, Winter, 43: 2-7.

Clarke, David (1996). *Urban World/Global City*. London: Routledge.

Clegg, Jeremy (1996). "The Development of Multinational Enterprises." Pp. 103–134 in P.W. Daniels and W.F. Lever (eds.), *The Global Economy in Transition*. Harlow Essex: Addison Wesley Longman.

Clement, Barrie (1997). "Rise of the White Collar Factory." *The Independent International*, July 15.

Clement, Wallace (1997). "Introduction: Whither the New Canadian Political Economy?" Pp. 3–18 in W. Clement (ed.), *Understanding Canada: Building on the New Canadian Political Economy*. Montreal/Kingston: McGill-Queen's University Press.

Clement, Wallace (1998). "Power, Ethnicity, and Class: Reflections Thirty Years After *The Vertical Mosaic*." In R. Helmes-Hayes and J. Curtis (eds.), *The Vertical Mosaic Revisited*. Toronto: University of Toronto Press.

Cleveland, Harland (1985). "The Twilight of Hierarchy: Speculation on the Global Information Society." *Public Administration Review*, January/February, 45.

Cloninger, R., M. Bohman, and S. Sigvaardson (1981). "Inheritance of Alcohol Abuse: Cross-Fostering Analyses of Adopted Men." *Archives of General Psychiatry* 38: 861–867.

Cloward, Richard S. and Lloyd E. Ohlin (1960). *Delinquency and Opportunity: A Theory of Delinquent Gangs*. Glencoe, IL.: Free Press.

Cohen, Andrew (1993). "Canada Abroad." *Policy Options*, July–August: 77–81.

Cohen, Stan (1974). Review of E. Schur's *Crime Without Victims*. *New Society*, November, 21: 38.

Cohen, Stanley (1979). "Guilt, Justice and Tolerance: Some Old Concepts for a New Criminology." Pp. 17–51 in David Downes and Paul Rock (eds.), *Deviant Interpretations: Problems in Criminological Theory*. Oxford: Martin Robertson.

Cohen, Stanley (1980). *Folk Devils and Moral Panics*, 2nd edition, revised. Oxford: Oxford Bloom.

Columbo, John Robert (1996). *The 1996 Canadian Global Almanac*. Toronto: Macmillan Canada.

Comack, Elizabeth (1991). "Women and Crime." In Rick Linden (ed.), *Criminology: A Canadian Perspective*, 2nd edition. Toronto: Harcourt Brace Jovanovich.

Comack, Elizabeth (1996). "Women and Crime." In Rick Linden (ed.), *Criminology: A Canadian Perspective*, 3rd edition. Toronto: Harcourt Brace Jovanovich.

Coney, Sandra (1997). "The Beatification Begins." *Sunday Star-Times*, September 7.

Conlogue, Ray (1997). "Time has not yet healed deep referendum wounds." *Globe and Mail*, January 1.

Connor, W. (1972). "Nation-Building or Nation-Destroying." *World Politics* 24(3).

Conway, John F. (1990). *The Canadian Family In Crisis*. Toronto: James Lorimer and Company.

Cooper, Sandi (1986). "Women's History Goes to Trial: EEOC v. Sears, Roebuck and Company." *Signs*, Summer, 11(4): 751–780.

Corcoran, Terence (1996). "How Subsidies Ate Atlantic Region." *The Globe and Mail*, October 29.

Cordell, Arthur J. (1991). "The Perils of an Information Age." *Policy Options*, April: 19–21.

Cornell, Stephen (1988). *The Return of the Native: American Indian Political Resurgence*. New York: Oxford.

Cottle, Charles E., Patricia Searles, Ronald J. Berger, and Beth Ann Pierce (1989). "Conflicting Ideologies and the Politics of Pornography." *Gender & Society*, September, 3(3): 303–333.

Coyne, Andrew (1996). "We Need a Better Measure to Gauge Who is Living in Poverty." *The Toronto Star*, December 15.

Crane, David (1996). "Beware of Globalization Backlash." *The Toronto Star*, February 1.

Crane, David (1996). "Multinationals Must Be Held Accountable." *The Toronto Star*, September 26.

Crane, David (1997). "Building Backlash Over U.S. Globalization." *The Toronto Star*, April 3.

Crane, David (1997). "Let's Not Give Up Culture." *The Toronto Star*, February 9.

Crane, David (1997). "A Very Good State To Be In." *The Toronto Star*, June 27.

Crawford, Trish (1997a). "Sexual health programs are at risk." *The Toronto Star*, August 23, M1.

Crawford, Trish (1997b). "Birth control injection is here." *The Toronto Star*, August 23, M1.

Cregheur, Alain and Mary Sue Devereaux, (1991). "Canada's Children." *Canadian Social Trends*, Summer: 2–5.

Crisis for the Newborn (1986). Videotape. National March of Dimes Foundation.

Crompton, Susan (1993). "Facing Retirement." *Perspectives on Labour and Income*, Spring, 5(1).

Cryderman, Brian, Christopher O'Toole, and Augie Fleras (1998). *Policing in a Multicultural Society. A Handbook for the Police Services*. Markham: Butterworths.

Cuff, John Haslett (1991). "Civil Wars That Nobody Wins." *The Globe and Mail*, November 18: C3.

Cuff, John Haslett (1997). "Black Sitcoms Play on Stereotypes." *The Globe and Mail*, April 16.

Culpepper, Roy (1993). "Now is Not the Time to Forget Foreign Aid." *The Toronto Star*, July 28.

Cummins, Jim and Marcel Danesi (1990). *Heritage Languages. The Development and Denial of Canada's Linguistic Resources*. Toronto: Garamond/Our Schools—Our Selves Education Foundation.

Curran, James and Michael Gurevitch (ed.) (1994). *Mass Media and Society*. London: Edward Arnold.

Currie, Dawn H. and Valerie Raoul (1992). "The Anatomy of Gender: Dissecting Sexual Difference in the Body of Knowledge." Pp. 1–36 in Dawn Currie and Valerie Raoul (eds.), *Anatomy of Gender: Women's Struggle For The Body*. Ottawa: Carleton University Press.

Curtis, James, Edward Grab, and Neil Guppy (eds.) (1993). *Social Inequality in Canada*. Scarborough: Prentice Hall.

Curtis, Jim and Lorne Tepperman (1993). *Haves and Have Nots*. Englewood Cliffs, NJ: Prentice Hall.

Daisley, Brad (1996). "Alta. must pay for wrongful sterilization." *The Laws Weekly*, February 23, 15(39): 1, 7.

Daniels, P.W. (1996). "The Lead Role of Developed Countries." Pp. 193–214 in P.W. Daniels and W.F. Lever (eds.), *Global Economy in Transition*. Harlow Essex: Addison Wesley Longman.

Daniels, P.W. and W.F. Lever (1996). "Introduction." Pp. 1–10 in P.W. Daniels and W.F. Lever (eds.), *Global Economy in Transition*. Harlow Essex: Addison Wesley Longman.

Daniels, Pamela and Kathy Weingarten (1984). "Mothers' Hours: The Timing of Parenthood and Women's Work." Pp. 209–231 in Patricia Voydanoff (ed.), *Work & Family: Changing Roles of Men and Women*. Palo Alto, CA: Mayfield.

d'Aquino, Thomas (1997). "Outlook for Social Progress Bright." *The Globe and Mail*, January 1.

Darder, Antonia (1990). *Culture and Power in the Classroom: A Critical Foundation for Bicultural Education*. Critical Studies in Education and Culture Series. New York: Bergin and Garvey.

Dare, P. (1996). "Coming to a School Near You." *Kitchener-Waterloo Record,* January 29.

Darling, Carol A., David J. Kallen and Joyce E. Van Dusen (1984). "Sex in Transition, 1900–1980." *Journal of Youth and Adolescence* 13: 5.

Darrch, Wendy (1997). "Growing pot for medicine ruled legal." *The Toronto Star*, December 11, A1, A24.

David, M. (1985). "Motherhood and Social Policy—A Matter of Education?" *Critical Social Policy* 12: 28–43.

Davies, John (1996). *Educating Students in a Media-Saturated Culture*. Lancaster, PA: Technomic Publishers.

Davis, Kingsley (1936). "The Sociology of Prostitution." *American Sociological Review* 2: 744–755.

Davis, Kingsley and Wilbert E. Moore (1945). "Some Principles of Stratification." *American Sociological Review* 5: 242–249.

DAWN (1986). Proceedings: Founding Provincial Conference, May 21–23, Health Promotion Directorate of Health and Welfare Canada/B.C. Coalition's Self-Help and Advocacy Project.

DeKeseredy, Walter S. (1992). "In Defence of Self-Defence: Demystifying Female Violence Against Male Intimates." Pp. 245–252 in Ronald Hinch (ed.), *Debates in Canadian Society*. Scarborough, Ontario: Nelson.

DeKeseredy, Walter S. and Ronald Hinch (1991) *Woman Abuse: Sociological Perspectives*. Toronto: Thompson Educational Publishing.

DeKeseredy, Walter S., Martin D. Schwartz and Karen Tait (1993). "Sexual Assault and Stranger Aggression on a Canadian University Campus." *Sex Roles* 28(5/6): 263–277.

Dennis, Wendy (1992). *Hot and Bothered: Men and Women, Sex and Love in the 90s*. Toronto: Key Porter.

Department of Justice (1993). "How Do Canadian Crime Rates Compare to Those of Other Countries?" *Justice Research Notes*, April, 5: 17–18.

Dershowitz, Alan (1994). *The Abuse Excuse: And Other Cop-Outs, Sob Stories, and Evasions of Responsibility*. Boston: Little, Brown and Company.

deSilva, Arnold (1992). *Earnings of Immigrants: A Comparative Analysis*. Ottawa: Economic Council of Canada.

Desroches, Frederick J. (1992, original 1986). "The Occupational Subculture of the Police." Pp. 39–51 in Brian K. Cryderman and Chris N. O'Toole (eds.), *Police, Race, and Ethnicity. A Guide for Law Enforcement Officers.* Toronto: Butterworths.

Diamond, Jack (1997). "Provinces are Archaic. More Power to the Cities." *The Globe and Mail*, May 26.

Dickey, Christopher (1997). "As American As Apple Pie?" *Newsweek*, August 11.

Dimbleby, Jonathan (1997). "Give Charles a Chance to Shine." *NZ Herald*, September 9.

Dobash, R. Emerson and Russell P. Dobash (1981). *Violence Against Wives: A Case Against Patriarchy.* New York: Free Press.

Dobash, R. Emerson and Russell P. Dobash (1995). "Reflections on Findings From The Violence Against Women Survey." *Canadian Journal of Criminology* 37(3): 457-484.

Dobash, Russell P. and R. Emerson Dobash (1981). "Community Response to Violence Against Wives: Charivari, Abstract Justice and Patriarchy." *Social Problems*, June, 28: 563–581.

Dobson, Chris and Ian Jackson (1993). "Clayoquot Sound is Not Clearcut Sound." *Imprint*, October 8.

Doherty, William J. (1992). "Private Lives, Public Values: The New Pluralism—A Report from the Heartland." *Psychology Today*, May/June.

Doleschal, E. and N. Klapmuts (1973). "Towards a New Criminology." *Crime and Delinquency Literature* 5(4): 607–625.

Doone, Peter (1989). "Potential Impact of Community Policing on Criminal Investigation." Pp. 84–106 in J. Robinson et al. (eds.), *Effectiveness and Change in Policing.* Wellington: Victoria University Institute of Criminology.

Douglas, M. and A. Wildavsky (1982). *Risk and Culture: An Essay on the Selection of Technological and Environmental Dangers.* Berkeley: University of California Press.

Downes, David (1979). "Praxis Makes Perfect: A Critique of Critical Criminology." Pp. 1–16 in David Downes and Paul Rock (eds.), *Deviant Interpretations: Problems in Criminological Theory.* Oxford: Martin Robertson.

Downes, David and Paul Rock (1982). *Understanding Deviance: A Guide to the Sociology of Crime and Rule Breaking.* Oxford: Clarendon.

Drache, Daniel and Meric S. Gertler (eds.) (1991). *The New Era of Global Competition. State Policy and Market Power.* Montreal/Kingston: McGill-Queen's University Press.

Drohan, Madelaine (1996). "Dependency on U.S. Leaves Canada 'Vulnerable': WTO." *The Globe and Mail*, November 20.

Drohan, Madelaine (1996). "Rich Nations Urged to Cut Strings on Aid to Poor Countries." *The Globe and Mail*, September 20.

D'Souza, Dinesh (1996). *The End of Racism.* New York: Free Press.

Dua, Enakshi (1992). "Racism or Gender? Understanding Oppression of South-Asian Canadian Women." *Canadian Woman Studies*, Fall, 13(1): 6–10.

Duggan, Penny and Heather Dashner (1994). *Women's Lives in the New Global Economy.* The Netherlands.

Dunsford, Cathie (1997). "Martyr to the Beauty Myth." *Canta*, September 10.

Durie, Mason (1995). "Tino Rangatiratanga." *He Pukenga Korero* 1(1): 66–82.

Durkheim, Emile (1966). Sarah A. Solovay and John H. Mueller, trans. George E.G. Catlin, ed. *The Rules of the Sociological Method.* New York: Free Press.

Durning, Alan (1991). "Enough is Enough. Assessing Global Competition." *Annual Editions. Social Problems 93/94*. Guilford, CT: Dushkin Publishing. Originally published in *Dollars and Sense*. June.

Dworkin, Andrea (1974). *Woman Hating*. New York: Dutton.

Dworkin, Andrea (1981). *Pornography: Men Possessing Women*. New York: Penguin.

Dyck, Noel (ed.) (1985). *Indigenous People and the Nation-State. Fourth World Politics in Canada, Australia, and Norway*. St John's, Nfld.: Memorial University.

Dyer, Gwynne (1996). "Saying 'The World is a Mess' Is Just Not True." *New Zealand Herald*, September 4.

Eamon, Ross A. (1987). *The Media Society. Basic Issues and Controversies*. Markham: Butterworths.

Echols, A. (1984). "The Taming of the Id: Feminist Sexual Politics, 1968–83." Pp. 50–72 in C.S. Vance (ed.), *Pleasure and Danger: Exploring Female Sexuality*. London: Routledge and Kegan Paul.

Eck, John E. and Dennis P. Rosenbaum (1994). "The New Police Order: Effectiveness, Equity, and Efficiency in Community Policing." Pp. 3–26 in D.P. Rosenbaum (ed.), *The Challenge of Community Policing*. Thousand Oaks, CA: Sage.

Economic Council of Canada (1977). *Living Together: A Study of Regional Disparities*. Ottawa: Supply and Services Canada.

The Economist (1993/1994). "Towers of Babble." December 25–January 7.

The Economist (1996). "The Old New Right." September 14.

Editorial (1994). *The Globe and Mail*, March 11.

Editorial (1995). *The Globe and Mail*, March 1.

Editorial (1996). "Globalization and the Canadian Prospect." *BTH*: 2–5.

Editorial (1996). *Report on Business*, January.

Editorial (1997). "Let Tuition Fees Rise." *The Globe and Mail*, October 1.

Edwards, Susan (1981). *Female Sexuality and the Law*. Oxford: Martin Robertson.

Egan, Jennifer (1997). "The Thin Red Line." *The New York Times Magazine*, July 27: 21-25, 34, 40, 43-44, 48.

Ehrenreich, Barbara (1992). "Double Talk about Class." *Time*, March 2.

Ehrenreich, Barbara and Deirdre English (1974). *Complaints and Disorders: The Sexual Politics of Sickness*. London: Compendium.

Ehrenreich, Barbara and Deirdre English (1978). *For Her Own Good: 150 Years of the Experts Advice to Women*. Garden City, NY: Anchor.

Ehrenreich, Barbara and Karen Stallard (1982). "The Nouveau Poor." *Ms.*, July/August: 217–224.

Ehrenreich, Barbara, Elizabeth Hess, and Gloria Jacobs (1987). *Re-Making Love: The Feminization of Sex*. Garden City, NY: Anchor.

Eichler, Margrit (1984). "Sexism in Research and its Policy Implications." Pp. 17–39 in Jill McCalla Vickers (ed.), *Taking Sex Into Account: The Policy Consequences of Sexist Research*. Ottawa: Carleton University Press.

Eichler, Margrit (1988). *Nonsexist Research Methods: A Practical Guide*. Winchester, Mass: Unwin Hyman.

Eichler, Magrit (1989). "Reflections on Motherhood, Apple Pie, The New Reproductive Technologies and the Role of Sociologists in Society." *Society/Société*, February, 13(1): 1–15.

Eidham, Harald (1985). "Indigenous Peoples and the State: The Sami Case in Norway." Pp. 155–171 in Jens Brosted (ed.), *Native Power: The Quest for Autonomy and Nationhood of Indigenous Peoples*. Oslo: Universiteforlaget AS.

Eitzen, D. Stanley and Maxine Baca Zinn (1992). *Social Problems*, 5th edition. Toronto: Allyn and Bacon.

Eliany, Marc (1991). "Alcohol and Drug Use." *Canadian Social Trends*, Spring, 20: 19–26.

Eliany, Marc (1992). "Alcohol and Drug Consumption Among Canadian Youth." *Canadian Social Trends*, Autumn, 26: 10–13.

Elias, Robert (1986). *The Politics of Victimization: Victims, Victimology and Human Rights*. New York: Oxford University Press.

Eller, Jack David (1997). "Anti-Anti-Multiculturalism." *American Anthropologist* 99(2): 249–260.

Elliot, Patricia and Nancy Mandell (1995). "Feminist Theories." Pp 3–31 in Nancy Mandell (ed.), *Feminist Issues: Race, Class and Sexuality*. Scarborough: Prentice Hall Canada.

Elliott, Jean Leonard and Augie Fleras (1991). *Unequal Relations. Introduction to Race and Ethnic Dynamics in Canada*. Scarborough: Prentice Hall.

Ellis, L., D. Burke and M.A. Ames (1987). "Sexual orientation as a continuous variable: A comparison between the sexes." *Archives of Sexual Behavior* 16(6): 523–529.

Ellul, Jacques (1965). *Propaganda*. New York: Knopf.

Emmott, Bill (1993). "Multinationals. Back in Fashion." *Economist*, March 27: 5–13.

Engels, Howard (1996). *Lord High Executioner*. Toronto: Key Porter Books.

Epstein, Cynthia Fuchs (1988). *Deceptive Distinctions: Sex, Gender, and the Social Order*. New Haven: Yale University Press.

Ericson, Richard and Patricia Baranek (1982). *The Ordering of Justice: A Study of Accused Persons as Dependents in the Criminal Process*. Toronto: University of Toronto in association with the Centre of Criminology, University of Toronto.

Erwin, Greg (1992). "Recidivism among Homicide Offenders." *Forum on Corrections Research*, June, 4(2): 7–9.

Esses, V. and C.D. Webster (1986). *Physical Attractiveness, Dangerousness and the Canadian Criminal Code*. Unpublished manuscript, Clarke Institute of Psychiatry and the University of Toronto.

Esses, Victoria M. and R.C. Gardner (1996). "Multiculturalism in Canada: Context and Current Status." *Canadian Journal of Behavioural Science* 28(3): 145–152.

Estrich, Susan (1987). *Real Rape: How the legal system victimizes women who say no*. Cambridge, Mass.: Harvard University Press.

Evans, John and Alexander Himelfarb (1996). "Counting Crime." Pp. 57–90 in Rick Linden (ed.), *Criminology: A Canadian Perspective*, 3rd edition. Toronto: Harcourt Brace & Company.

Faludi, S. (1991). *Backlash: The Undeclared War Against American Women*. New York: Crown.

Fattah, Ezzat A. (1991). *Understanding Criminal Victimization: An Introduction to Theoretical Victimology*. Scarborough: Prentice Hall.

Fedorowycz, Orest (1994). "Homicide in Canada, 1993." *Juristat*, 14, 15. Ottawa: Canadian Centre for Justice Statistics.

Fekete, John (1994). *Moral Panic: Biopolitics Rising*. Toronto: Robert Davies.

Ferree, M. (1987). "The Superwoman Syndrome." In Christine Bose, Roslyn Feldberg, and Natalie Sokoloff (eds.), *Hidden Aspects of Women's Work*. New York: Praeger.

Fine, M. and A. Asch (1981). "Sexism Without the Pedestal." *Journal of Sociology and Social Welfare* 9(2): 233–249.

Finkelhor, David (1979). *Sexually Victimized Children*. New York: Free Press.

Finkelhor, David and Kersti Yllo (1988). "Rape in Marriage." Pp. 140–152 in M.B. Straus (ed.), *Abuse and Victimization Across the Life Span*. Baltimore: John Hopkins University Press.

Finkelhor, David and Kersti Yllo (1989). "Marital Rape: The Myth Versus the Reality." In James M. Henslin (ed.), *Marriage and Family in a Changing Society*, 3rd edition. New York: Free Press: 382–391.

Fischhoff, B. (1975). "Hindsight = Foresight: The Effect of Outcome Knowledge on Judgement Under Uncertainty." *Journal of Experimental Psychology: Human Perception and Performance* 1: 288–299.

Fishman, M. (1978). "Crime Waves as Ideology." *Social Problems* 25: 531–543.

Fiske, John (1987). *Television Culture*. New York: Routledge.

Fitzgerald, K.W. (1983). "Living With Jellinek's Disease." *Newsweek*, October 17: 22.

Fleras, Augie (1987). "Redefining the Politics over Aboriginal Language Renewal. Maori Language Schools as Agents of Social Change." *Canadian Journal of Native Studies* 7(1): 1–40.

Fleras, Augie (1989). "Inverting the Bureaucratic Pyramid. Reconciling Aboriginality and Bureaucracy in New Zealand." *Human Organization* 48(3): 214–225.

Fleras, Augie (1992). "Aboriginal Electoral Districts for Canada: Lessons From New Zealand." Pp. 67–104 in Rob Milen (ed.), *Aboriginal Peoples and Electoral Reform in Canada*. Toronto: Dundurn Press.

Fleras, Augie (1992). "Managing Aboriginality: Canadian Perspectives, International Lessons." Paper presented to the Australian and New Zealand Association of Canadian Studies, Annual Conference. Victoria University, Wellington. December.

Fleras, Augie (1994). "Doing What is Workable, Necessary, and Fair. Multiculturalism in Canada." In Mark Charlton and Paul Barker (eds.), *Contemporary Political Issues*. Scarborough: Nelson.

Fleras, Augie (1995). "'Please Adjust Your Set': Media and Minorities in a Multicultural Society." Pp. 281–307 in Benjamin Singer (ed.), *Communications in Canadian Society*, 4th edition. Scarborough: Nelson.

Fleras, Augie (1996). "The Politics of Jurisdiction." Pp. 178–211 in David Long and Olive Dickason (eds.), *Visions of the Heart*. Toronto: Harcourt Brace.

Fleras, Augie (1997). "Politicizing Indigeneity: Ethnopolitics in White Settler Dominions." In Paul Havemann (ed.), *New Frontiers*. Auckland: Oxford.

Fleras, Augie (1998). *Demystifying The Media: An Intellectual Self-Defence For the 1990s*. Palmerston North, NZ: Dunmore Press.

Fleras, Augie and Jean Leonard Elliott (1991). *Multiculturalism in Canada. The Challenges of Diversity*. Toronto: Nelson.

Fleras, Augie and Jean Leonard Elliott (1992). *The Nations Within. Aboriginal-State Relations in Canada, the United States, and New Zealand*. Toronto: Oxford.

Fleras, Augie and Jean Leonard Elliott (1996). *Unequal Relations: An Introduction to Race, Ethnicity, and Indigeneity in Canada*, 2nd edition. Scarborough: Prentice Hall.

Ford, C.S. and Beach, F.A. (1951). *Patterns of Sexual Behavior*. New York: Harper and Brothers.

Fournier, Pierre (1994). *A Meech Lake Post-Mortem: Is Quebec Sovereignty Inevitable?* Montreal/Kingston: McGill-Queen's University Press.

Francis, Daniel (1992). *The Imaginary Indian. The Image of the Indian in Canadian Culture*. Vancouver: Arsunal Pulp Press.

Frank, Jeffrey (1996). "15 Years of AIDS in Canada." *Canadian Social Trends*, Summer, 1: 4–10.

Frank, Jeffrey (1997) "15 Years of AIDS in Canada." *Canadian Social Trends*, Catalogue 11-008-XPE: 4-10.

Fraser, Sylvia (1987). *My Father's House: A Memoir of Incest and of Healing*. Toronto: Doubleday.

French, Marilyn (1992). *The War Against Women*. New York: Summit.

Frideres, James (1993). *Native Peoples in Canada. Contemporary Conflicts*, 3rd edition. Scarborough: Prentice Hall.

Friedman, M. (1985). "Bulimia." *Women & Therapy* 2: 63–69.

Frizzell, Alan and Jon H Pammett (eds.) (1996). *Social Inequality in Canada*. Ottawa: Carleton University Press.

Fuller, John (1996). *News Values: Identity for an Information Age*. University of Chicago Press.

Furedy, John (1995). "Salem Witch Hunts." *The Globe and Mail*, July 20.

Gabor, T. and J. Roberts (1992). "How the Innocent End Up Behind Bars." *Toronto Star*, February 12: A21. Reprinted as pp. 227–228 in Ian McDermid Gomme (1993). *The Shadow Line: Deviance and Crime in Canada*. Toronto: Harcourt Brace Jovanovich Canada Inc.

Gaffield, Chad (1990). "The Social and Economic Origins of Contemporary Families." Pp. 23–40 in Maureen Baker (ed.), *Families: Changing Trends in Canada*. Toronto: McGraw-Hill Ryerson.

Gagnon, Lysiane (1996). "Sorry to be boring, but Quebec loves its constitutional contradictions." *The Globe and Mail*, July 6.

Gairdner, William (1991). *The War Against The Family: A Parent Speaks Out*. Toronto: Stoddart.

Galarneau, Diane (1993). "Alimony and Child Support." *Canadian Social Trends*, Spring: 8–11.

Gallon, Gary (1997). "Five Years After Rio: Canada's Spotty Record." *The Globe and Mail*, June 23.

Galt, Virginia and Miro Cernetig (1997). "Two Schools, Worlds Apart." *The Globe and Mail*, April 26.

Gaskell, Jane, Arlene McLaren and Myra Novogrodsky (1989). *Claiming an Education: Feminism and Canadian Schools*. Toronto: Our Schools/Our Selves Education Foundation.

Gay, Katherine (1992). "Change Demands Treating Employees Like Adults." *The Financial Post*, November 11.

Gebhard, P.H. (1965). "Situational Factors Affecting Human Sexual Behaviour." In F. Beach (ed.), *Sex and Behavior*. New York: John Wiley.

Gelder, Lindsy Van (1987). "Addictions: The Surprising Dependencies of Independent Women." *Ms.*, February: 36–42, 73–75.

Ghalam, Nancy Zukewich (1993). "Women in the Workplace." *Canadian Social Trends*, Spring: 2–6.

Gherson, Giles (1997). "Atlantic Hampered by Benefits." *Kitchener-Waterloo Record*, June 20.

Gibbs, Jack P. (1966). "Sanctions." *Social Problems*, Fall, 13: 147–159.

Giddens, Anthony (1992). *The Transformation of Intimacy: Sexuality, Love and Eroticism in Modern Societies*. Cambridge, England: Polity Press.

Gilder, George (1973). *Sexual Suicide*. New York: Quadrangle.

Gilder, George (1974). *Male Nomads: Unmarried Men in America*. New York: Quadrangle.

Gilder, George (1978). *Visible Man: A True Story of Post-Racist America*. New York: Basic Books.

Gilder, George (1982). *Wealth and Poverty*. London: Buchan and Enright.

Gilder, George (1985). *The Spirit of Enterprise*. Harmondsworth: Viking.

Gilder, George (1986). *Men and Marriage*. Louisiana: Pelican.

Gillespie, Marie (1996). *Television, Ethnicity, and Cultural Change*. London: Routledge.

Gillies, James (1997). "Thinking the Unthinkable and the Republic of Canada." *The Globe and Mail*, June 28.

Gilligan, C. (1982). *In a Different Voice*. Cambridge, Mass.: Harvard University Press.

Gillmor, Don (1996). "The Punishment Station." *Toronto Life*, January: 46–55.

Giroux, Henri A. (1996). *Fugitive Cultures: Race, Violence, and Youth*. New York: Routledge.

Glazer, Nathaniel and Daniel P. Moynihan (1970). *Beyond the Melting Pot*. Cambridge: MIT Press.

The Globe and Mail (1992). "Community Standard Is Test of Tolerance." February 28: A2.

The Globe and Mail (1993). "Study finds 20 per cent condone forced sex: Male Grade 9 and 10 students in London, Ont., say action acceptable in certain circumstances." August 23: A8.

The Globe and Mail (1995). "Where Women Stand Now." August 12: A6.

The Globe and Mail (1996). "Poverty Rates Vary Wildly, Study Finds." June 26.

Goar, Carole (1996). "Canada Again Best Place in the World." *The Toronto Star*, July 16.

Goar, Carole (1997). "We're Losing the Tools to Make a Fair Society." *The Toronto Star*, April 19.

Goddard, John (1991). *The Last Stand of the Lubicon*. Toronto: Stoddart.

Goffman, Erving (1971). *The Presentation of Self in Everyday Life*. Garden City, NY: Doubleday Anchor.

Goldberg, David Theo (1993). *Philosophy and the Politics of Meaning*. Cambridge: Basil Blackwell.

Goldberg, David Theo (1994). "Introduction: Multicultural Conditions." Pp 1–44 in D.T. Goldberg (ed.), *Multiculturalism: A Critical Reader*. Cambridge: Basil Blackwell.

Goldberg, Steven (1973). *The Inevitability of Patriarchy*, 2nd edition. New York: Morrow.

Goldman, Robert (1992). *Reading Ads Socially*. New York: Routledge.

Goldscheider, Frances and Calvin Goldscheider (1994). "Leaving and returning home in 20th century America." *Population Bulletin*, March, 48(4): 2–33.

Gomme, Ian McDermid (1993). *The Shadow Line: Deviance and Crime in Canada*. Toronto: Harcourt Brace Jovanovich Canada Inc.

Goode, William J. (1971). *The Contemporary American Family*. Chicago: Quadrangle Books.

Gordon, Avery F. and Christopher Newfield (1996). *Mapping Multiculturalism*. St. Pauls: University of Minnesota Press.

Gordon, Michael and Penelope J. Shankweiler (1971). "Different Equals Less: Female Sexuality in Recent Marriage Manuals." *Journal of Marriage and the Family* 33: 459–466.

Gordon, Suzanne (1991). *Prisoners of Men's Dreams*. Boston: Little, Brown.

Gottlieb, Beatrice (1993). *The Family in the Western World from the Black Death to the Industrial Age*. New York: Oxford University Press.

Gould, Stephen Jay (1984). "Triumph of a Naturalist." Review of *A Feeling for the Organism: The Life and Work of Barbara McClintock* by Evelyn Fox Keller. *New York Review of Books*, March 29: 58–71.

Goyder, John (1990). *Essentials of Canadian Society*. Toronto: McClelland and Stewart.

Grab, Edward G. (1990). *Theories of Social Inequality. Classical and Contemporary Perspectives*, 2nd edition. Toronto: Holt Rinehart and Winston.

Grab, Edward G. (1993). "General Introduction." Pp. xi–xxix in James Curtis et al. (eds.), *Social Inequality in Canada*, 2nd edition. Scarborough: Prentice Hall.

Grabe, Marie Elizabeth (1997). "Tabloid and Traditional Television News Magazine Crime Stories: Crime Lessons and the Reaffirmation of Social Class Distinctions." *J&MCQ* 73(4): 926–946.

Graham, H. (1987). "Women's smoking and family health." *Social Science and Medicine* 25: 47–56.

Grasmick, H., R. Burskill and M. Kimpel (1991). "Protestant Fundamentalism and Attitudes Towards Corporal Punishment of Children." *Violence and Victims*, Winter: 283–298.

Gray, Herman (1995). *Watching Race: Television and the Struggle for Blackness*. Minneapolis: University of Minnesota Press.

Green, Melvyn (1986). "The History of Canadian Narcotics Control: The Formative Years." Pp. 24–40 in Neil Boyd (ed.), *The Social Dimensions of Law*. Scarborough: Prentice Hall.

Green, R. and J. Money (1966). "Stage Acting, Role Taking and Effeminate Impersonation During Boyhood." *Archives of General Psychiatry* 15: 438–439.

Greenberg, D. (1979). "Delinquency and the Age Structure of Society." Pp. 586–620 in S.L. Messinger and E. Bittner (eds.), *Criminology Review Yearbook*. Beverly Hills, CA: Sage.

Greenglass, E. (1982). *A World of Difference*. Toronto: John Wiley and Sons.

Greenspon, Edward (1997). "Economy Changing Faster Than People." *The Globe and Mail*, April 20.

Greenspon, Edward (1997). "Poverty Issue Requires Kid Gloves." *The Globe and Mail*, February 17.

Greenwald, H. (1958). *The Call Girl*. New York: Ballantine Books.

Grey, Earle (1996). "Separatists Trapped by Double Standard." In *Canadian Speeches: Issues of the Day*. November.

Griesman, H.C. (1984). "Social meanings of terrorism: Reification, violence and social control." Pp 34–44 in Jack D. Douglas (ed.), *The Sociology of Deviance*. Toronto: Allyn and Bacon.

Griffiths, Franklin (1996). *Strong and Free. Canada and the New Sovereignty*. Toronto: Stoddardt.

Griffiths, Curt T. and J. Colin Yerbury (1996). "Understanding Aboriginal Crime and Criminality: A Case Study." Pp. 381–398 in Margaret A. Jackson and Curt T. Griffiths (eds.), *Canadian Criminology: Perspectives on Crime and Criminality*, 2nd edition. Toronto: Harcourt Brace and Company.

Griffiths, Curt T., J.C. Yerbury and L.F. Weafer (1987). "Canada's natives: Victims of socio-structural deprivation? *Human Organizations* 46: 277–282.

Grindstaff, Carl F. (1995). "Canadian Fertility: 1951 to 1993, From Boom to Bust to

Stability?" *Canadian Social Trends*, Winter, 39: 12-16.

Grossman, Lawrence K. (1995). "Beware the Electronic Republic." *USA Today*, August 29.

Guibernau, Monsterrat (1996). *Nationalisms. The Nation-State and Nationalism in the Twentieth Century*. Cambridge, UK: Polity Press.

Gusfield, Joseph (1996). *Contested Meanings: The Construction of Alcohol Problems*. Madison: University of Wisconsin Press.

Gwyn, Richard (1996). "A Nation of Two Economic Solitudes." *The Toronto Star*, July 7.

Hacker, Sylvia S. (1992). "The Transition From the Old Norm to the New: Sexual Values for the 1990s." Pp. 22–29 in Ollie Pocs (ed.), *Human Sexuality 92/93*. Guilford, CT: Dushkin.

Hackler, James (1978). *The Prevention of Youthful Crime: The Great Stumble Forward*. Toronto: Methuen.

Hagan, John (1987). "Class in the household: A power-control theory of gender and delinquency." *American Journal of Sociology* 92(4): 788–816.

Hale, Sylvia (1990). *Controversies in Sociology. A Canadian Introduction*. Mississauga: Copp Clark Pitman.

Halleck, Seymour (1971). *The Politics of Therapy*. New York: Science House.

Hamilton, Vivian, Franque Grimard, Carey Levinton and Yvan St. Piere (1997). "The Poor and Cigarettes." *Policy Options*, June, 18(5): 16–18.

Handelman, Stephen (1996). "A Patchwork Piece." *The Toronto Star*, December 8.

Harman, Lesley D. (1992). "The Feminization of Poverty: An Old Problem With a New Name." *Canadian Woman Studies* 12(4): 6–9.

Hartnagel, T. (1992). "Correlates of Criminal Behavior." In Rick Linden (ed.), *Criminology: A Canadian Perspective*, 2nd edition. Toronto: Harcourt Brace Jovanovich.

Hartnagel, T. (1996) "Correlates of Criminal Behaviour." In Rick Linden (ed.), *Criminology: A Canadian Perspective*, 3rd edition. Toronto: Harcourt Brace Jovanovich.

Hawkins, R. and G. Tiedman (1975). *The Creation of Deviance*. Columbus, Ohio: Merrill.

Heath, Dwight B. (1988). "Emerging Anthropological Theory and Models of Alcohol Use and Alcoholism." Pp. 353–410 in C. Douglas Chaudron and D. Adrian Wilkinson (eds.), *op. cit.*

Helmes-Hayes, Rick and Jim Curtis (eds.) (1998). *The Vertical Mosaic Revisited*. Toronto: University of Toronto Press.

Henry, Frances (1968). "The West Indian Domestic Scheme in Canada." *Social and Economic Studies* 17(1): 83–91.

Henry, Frances and Effie Ginzberg (1993). "Racial Discrimination in Employment." Pp. 353–360 in James Curtis et al. (eds.), *Social Inequality in Canada*. Scarborough: Prentice Hall.

Henry, Frances, Carol Tator, Winston Mattis and Tim Rees (1995). *The Colour of Democracy*. Toronto: Harcourt Brace.

Henry III, William A. (1994). "In Defence of Elitism." *Time*, August 29.

Herman, Edward S. and Noam Chomsky (1988). *Manufacturing Consent: The Political Economy of the Mass Media*. New York: Pantheon Books.

Herman, Judith Lewis (1991). "Sex Offenders: A Feminist Perspective." Pp. 177–194 in W.L. Marshall, D.R. Laws, and H.E. Barbaree (eds.), *Sexual Assault: Issues, Theories and Treatment of The Offender*. New York: Plenum Press.

Hernnstein, Richard J. and Charles Murray (1994). *The Bell Curve: Intelligence and Class Structure in American Life*. New York: Free Press.

Hiller, Harry (1990). *Canadian Society. A Macro Analysis*. Scarborough: Prentice Hall.

Hills, Stuart L. (1980/1995). "Rape and the Masculine Mystique." Pp. 443–454 in E.D. Nelson and B.W. Robinson (eds.), *Gender in the 1990s: Images, Realities and Issues*. Scarborough: Nelson.

Hochschild, A. (1989). *The Second Shift: Working Parents and the Revolution at Home*. New York: Viking.

Hodgins, S. and G. Cote (1990). "The Prevalence of Mental Disorders among Penitentiary Inmates." *Canada's Mental Health*.

Hofferth, S.L., J.R. Kahn, and W. Baldwin (1987). "Premarital Sexual Activity Among U.S. Teenage Women Over the Past Three Decades." *Family Planning Perspectives* 19: 46–53.

Holly, Brian P. (1996). "Restructuring the Production System." Pp. 24–39 in P.W. Daniels and F.W. Lever (eds.), *The Global Economy in Transition*. Harlow Essex: Addison Wesley Longman.

Honderich, John (1996). "Referendum: One year later." *The Toronto Star*, October 26.

Hookham, Lynda and Nicole Merriam (1991). "The Caribou House Incident: Sexual Harassment of UBC Women." *Canadian Women Studies* 12(1): 58–59.

Horsman, Matthew (1993). "Canada in the World." *Policy Options*, May: 3–4.

Hotaling, Gerald T. and David B. Sugerman (1986). "An analysis of risk markers in husband to wife violence: The current state of knowledge." *Violence and Victims* 1(2): 101–124.

Hughes, John (1993). "31% favour legalized abortion under any circumstance." Press release. Toronto: Gallup Canada, Inc.

Hume, Christopher (1994). "A Jolt of Reality—Sponsored by Benetton." *Toronto Star*, January 20.

Hummel, Ralph (1987). *The Bureaucratic Experience*. New York: St Martin's Press.

Humphreys, Laud (1970). *Tearoom Trade: Impersonal Sex in Public Places*. Chicago: Aldine.

Hunter, Alf (1986). *Class Tells*. Scarborough: Nelson.

Hurrell, Andrew and Ngaire Woods (1995). "Globalization and Inequality." *Millenium: Journal of International Studies* 24(3): 447–470.

Hurtig, Mel (1991). "Canada. Love It or Leave It." *The Globe and Mail*, October 5.

Huston, A.C. (1983). "Sex Typing." In Paul H. Mussen (ed.), *Handbook of Child Psychology*, Volume 4, E. Mavis Hetherington, volume editor. New York: John Wiley and Sons.

Hutchins, Christopher (1997). "Nun Deliverer of Dogma." *Christchurch Press*, September 12.

Hutchison, Ian and Geoff Lealand (1996). "Introduction: A New Mediascape." *Continuum (Aotearoa/New Zealand: A New Mediascape)* 10(1): 7–11.

Ignatieff, Michael (1993). *Blood and Belonging: Journeys into the New Nationalism*. New York: Viking.

Illich, Ivan (1971). *After School, What?* New York: Harper & Row.

Interrogating the Internet (Study Group) (1996). "Contradictions in Cyberspace: Collective Response." Pp. 125–133 in R. Shields (ed.), *Cultures of Internet, Virtual Spaces, Real Histories, Living Bodies*. Thousand Oaks: Sage.

Ip, Greg (1996). "Job Cuts Despite Hefty Profits." *The Globe and Mail*, February 6.

Irving III, G.W. (1985). "Regulations and Guidelines For Animal Care: Problems and Future Concerns." Pp. 297–315 in G.P.

Moberg (ed.), *Animal Stress*. Bethesda, MD: American Psychological Society.

Irwin, Kathie and Irihapeti Ramsden (1995). *Toi Wahine. The Worlds of Maori Women*. Penguin.

Isin, Engin (1996). "Introduction. the Canadian Cosmopolis and the Crisis of Confederation." *New City Magazine* 17 (special issue): 5–8.

Israelson, David (1997). "Media Coming Out Shows Growing Clout of Gays." *The Toronto Star*, April 14.

Jackson, Chris (1996). "Measuring and Valuing Households' Unpaid Work." *Canadian Social Trends*, Autumn, 42: 25–29.

Jackson, Donna (1992). "The Return of Sexism." *New Woman*, January: 80–83.

Jackson, E. and S. Persky, (1982). "Victories and Defeats: A Gay and Lesbian Chronology 1964–1982." Pp. 224–247 in E. Jackson and S. Persky (eds.), *Flaunting It: A Decade of Gay Journalism from the Body Politic*. Toronto: Pink Triangle Press.

Jackson, Margaret A. (1991). "Search for the Cause of Crime: Biological and Psychological Perspectives." Pp. 173–196 in Margaret A. Jackson and Curt T. Griffiths (eds.), *Canadian Criminology: Perspectives on Crime and Criminality*. Toronto: Harcourt Brace Jovanovich.

Jackson, Susan E. and Marian N. Ruderman (1995) (eds.). *Diversity in Work Teams: Research Paradigms for a Changing Workplace*. Washington: American Psychological Association.

Jacobson, Bobbie (1988). *Beating the Ladykillers: Women and Smoking*. London: Victor Gollancz Ltd.

Jacobson, Jodi (1992). "The Global Politics of Abortion." Pp. 135–139 in Ollie Pocs (ed.), *Human Sexuality 92/93*. Guilford, CT: Dushkin.

Janis, I. (1972). *Victims of Groupthink*. Boston: Houghton Mifflin.

Jakubowicz, Andrew et al. (1994). *Racism, Ethnicity and the Media*. Sydney: Allen and Unwin.

Jakubowski, Lisa Marie (1997). *Immigration and the Legalization of Racism*. Halifax: Fernwood.

James, Carl E. (ed.) (1996). *Perspectives on Racism and the Human Services Sector*. Toronto: University of Toronto Press.

James, Steve and Ian Warren (1995). "Police Culture." Pp. 3–13 in Judith Bessant, Kerry Carrington, and Sandy Cook.

Jamieson, Roberta (1993). "Community, Diversity, Learning." Notes for Remarks. Address to St. Paul's United College 30th Anniversary Celebration, February 24, Waterloo, Ontario.

Janoff-Bulman, Ronnie, C. Timko and L. Carli (1985). "Cognitive Biases in Blaming the Victim." *Journal of Experimental Social Psychology* 23: 161–177.

Janoff-Bulman, Ronnie and Irene Hanson Frieze (1987). "The Role of Gender in Reactions to Criminal Victimization." Pp. 159–184 in Rosalind C. Barnett, Lois Biener and Grace K. Baruch (eds.), *Gender and Stress*. New York: Free Press.

Janson, C.G. (1989). "Psychiatric Diagnoses and Recorded Crimes." Pp. 127–133 in C.J. Janson and A.M. Janson (eds.), *Crime and Delinquency in a Metropolitan Cohort*. Stockholm: University of Stockholm.

Jaworski, John (1979). *A Case Study of Canadian Federal Governments' Multicultural Policies*. Unpublished MA thesis, Political Science Department, Carleton University, Ottawa.

Jellinek, E.M. (1960). *The Disease Concept of Alcoholism*. New Haven, CT: Hillhouse Press.

Jenson, Jane (1996). "Quebec: Which Minority?" *Dissent*, Summer: 43–49.

Jhally, Sut (1989). "Advertising as Religion: The Dialectics of Technology and Magic."

Pp. 217–229 in Ian Angus and Sut Jhally (eds.), *Cultural Politics in Contemporary America*. New York: Routledge.

Jhally, Sut and Justin Lewis (1992). *Enlightened Racism. The Cosby Show, Audiences, and the Myth of the American Dream*. Boulder, CO: Westview Press.

Johnson, Holly (1988). "Illegal Drug Use in Canada." *Canadian Social Trends*, Winter: 5–8.

Johnson, Holly (1996). *Dangerous Domains: Violence Against Women in Canada*. Toronto: Nelson.

Johnston, Steven (1997). "On the Information Highway." *Imprint*, January 31.

Kameny, F. (1972). "Gay Liberation and Psychiatry." Pp. 182–194 in J.A. McCaffrey (ed.), *The Homosexual Dialectic*. Englewood Cliffs, NJ: Prentice Hall.

Kamin, L. (1985). "Genes and Behaviour: The Missing Link." *Psychology Today* 19(10): 76–78.

Kaminer, Wendy (1992). *I'm Dysfunctional, You're Dysfunctional*. New York: Addison-Wesley.

Kanter, Rosabeth Moss (1976). "The Impact of Hierarchical Structures on the Work Behaviour of Women and Men." *Social Problems* 23: 415–430.

Kanter, Rosabeth Moss (1977). *Men and Women of the Corporation*. New York: Vintage.

Kanter, Rosabeth Moss (1995). *World Class: Thriving Locally in the Global Economy*. New York: Simon & Schuster.

Kaplan, Louise J. (1991). *Female Perversions: The Temptations of Emma Bovary*. New York: Anchor Books.

Kaplan, Robert D. (1994). "The Coming Anarchy." *The Atlantic Monthly*, February: 44–76.

Kaplan, William (ed.) (1993). *Belonging. The Meaning and Sense of Citizenship in Canada*. Montreal/Kingston: McGill-Queen's University Press.

Kastor, Elizabeth (1997). "At Home, Women See Their Mirrored Lives in Diana." *Washington Post*, September 7.

Katz, Jon (1997). *Virtuous Reality: How America Surrendered Discussion of Moral Values to Opportunists, Nitwits, and Blockheads Like William Bennett*. New York: Random House.

Keen, Sam (1991). *Fire In The Belly: On Being A Man*. New York: Bantam Books.

Keith, W.J. (1997). "The Crisis in Contemporary Education." *Queen's Quarterly* 94: 511–520.

Kelly, Liz and Jill Radford (1996). "'Nothing really happened': The invalidation of women's experiences of sexual violence." Pp 19–33 in Marianne Hester, Liz Kelly and Jill Radford (eds.), *Women, Violence and Male Power: Feminist Activism, Research and Practice*. Buckingham: Open University Press.

Kelsey, Jane (1986). "Decolonization in the First World: Indigenous Minorities Struggle for Justice and Self-Determination." *The Windsor Yearbook of Access to Justice* 5: 102–141.

Kelsey, Jane (1997). *The New Zealand Experience*, 2nd edition. Auckland: Auckland University Press.

Kennedy, Mark (1996). "Part Time Careers." *Kitchener-Waterloo Record*, February 26.

Kerckhove, Derrick de (1995). *The Skin of Culture: Investigating the New Electronic Reality*. Toronto: Sommerville House Publishing.

Kershaw, Anne and Mary Lasovich (1991). *Rock-a-bye Baby: A Death Behind Bars*. Toronto: McClelland and Stewart.

Kickingbird, Kirke (1984). "Indian Sovereignty: The American Experience." In

Leroy Little Bear et al. (eds.), *Pathways to Self-Determination: Canadian Indians and the Canadian State.*

King, Dave (1995). "A Year When the Internet Came of Commercial Age." *Dominion*, December 11.

King, Rebecca (1997). "Stalking: Criminal Harassment in Canada." *Canadian Social Trends*, Fall, 46: 29–33.

Kinsey, A., C. Pomeroy, W. Gebhard, and C. Martin (1953). *Sexual Behavior in the Human Female.* Philadelphia: W.B. Saunders.

Kinsey, A., C. Pomeroy, and C. Martin, (1948). *Sexual Behavior in the Human Male.* Philadelphia: W.B. Saunders.

Kirkham, G.L. (1971). "Homosexuality in Prison." In J.M. Henslin (ed.), *Studies in the Sociology of Sex.* New York: Appleton-Century-Crofts.

The Kitchener-Waterloo Record (1995). "Canadians Facing 'Ugly Destruction' of Environment." April 10.

Klein, Naomi (1997). "Academics Can't Give in to Corporate Agenda." *The Toronto Star*, April 28.

Kline, Marlee (1989). "Race, Racism and Feminist Legal Theory." *Harvard Women's Law Journal* 12: 115–150.

Knox, Paul (1997). "Canada Gets a Poor Grade on Reform." *The Globe and Mail*, June 21.

Koenig, Daniel J. (1996). "Conventional Crime." In Rick Linden (ed.), *Criminology: A Canadian Perspective*, 3rd edition. Toronto: Harcourt Brace.

Kong, R. (1997). "1996 Crime Trends." *Juristat*, Catalogue no.85-002-XPE, 17(8): 2-6. Ottawa: Minister of Industry.

Kornblum, William and Joseph Julian (1992). *Social Problems.* Englewood Cliffs: Prentice Hall.

Koss, M.P., T.E. Dinero, C.A. Seibel and C.L. Cox (1988). "Stranger and Acquaintance Rape: Are There Differences in the Victim's Experience?" *Psychology of Women Quarterly* 12: 1–24.

Koss, Mary P. and Sarah L. Cook (1993). "Facing the Facts: Date and Acquaintance Rape Are Significant Problems for Women." Pp. 104–119 in R.J. Gelles and D.R. Loseke (eds.), *Current Controversies on Family Violence.* Newbury Park, CA: Sage.

Krahn, Harvey J. and Graham S. Lowe (1994). *Work, Industry, and Canadian Society*, 2nd edition. Scarborough: Canada.

Kunz, Jean and Augie Fleras (1998). "Women of Colour in Mainstream Advertising: Distorted Mirror or Looking Glass?" *Atlantis*, in press.

Kurthen, Hermann (1997). "The Canadian Experience with Multiculturalism and Employment Equity: Lessons for Europe." *New Community* 23(2): 249–270.

KW Record (1997a). "Calgary arena cancels Marilyn Manson concert." July 9: B7.

KW Record (1997b). "Price cut boosts youth smoking." July 10: A2.

KW Record (1997c). "Child abuse prevalent among Ontario families, study finds." July 9: E4.

KW Record (1997d). "Job-sharing plans let women enjoy best of both worlds." July 17: E3.

Laab, Jennifer (1996). "Change." *Personnel Journal*, July.

LaPrairie, Carol (1990). "The Role of Sentencing in the Overrepresentation of Aboriginal People in Correctional Institutions." *Canadian Journal of Criminology* 32(2): 429–440.

LaPrairie, Carol (1997). "Reconstructing Theory: Explaining Aboriginal Over-Representation in the Criminal Justice System in Canada." *The Australian and New Zealand Journal of Criminology* 30(1): 39–54.

Larsen, David (1991). "Unplanned Parenthood." *Modern Maturity*, December 1990/January 1991: 32–36.

Latouche, Daniel (1995). "To Be or Not To Be a Province." *The Globe and Mail*, February 17.

Laux, Jeanne Kirk (1990/91). "Limits to Liberalism." *International Journal*, Winter, XLVI: 113–136.

Lawrence, M. (1982). *Fed Up And Hungry*. London: The Woman's Press.

Laws, Judith Long (1977). *Sexual Scripts: The Social Construction of Female Sexuality*. Hinsdale, IL: Dryden.

Laxer, Gordon (1991). *Open for Business*. Toronto: Oxford University Press.

Laxer, James (1991). "Teaching Old Leftists Some New Truths." *The Globe and Mail*, December 20.

Laxer, James (1993). "Buying into Decline." *Canadian Forum*, April: 5–7.

Laxer, James (1994). "Canada Can't Survive as a Union of 10 Equal Provinces." *Toronto Star*, August 7.

Laxer, James (1996). "Canada Just Doesn't Jibe with Neo-conservative Image." *The Toronto Star*, September 30.

Leach, Edmund (1967). *A Runaway World?* London: BBC Publications.

Lebsock, Suzanne (1984). *The Free Women of Petersburg: Status and Culture in a Southern Town, 1784–1860*. New York: W.W. Norton.

Lees, Susan (1996). "Unreasonable doubt: The outcomes of rape trials." Pp 99–115 in Marianne Hester, Liz Kelly and Jill Radford (eds.), *Women, Violence and Male Power: Feminist Activism, Research and Practice*. Buckingham: Open University Press.

Leighton, Barry N. (1994). "Community Policing in Canada: An Overview of Experience and Evaluations." Pp. 209–223 in D.P. Rosenbaum (ed.), *The Challenge of Community Policing*. Thousand Oaks, CA: Sage.

Leiss, William (1997). "Tobacco Control Policy in Canada: Shadow Boxing with Risk." *Policy Options*, June, 18(5): 3–6.

Lerner, Sally (1997). "The Future of Work." *Good Work News*, September, 50.

Leroux, T.G. and M. Petrunik (1990). "The Construction of Elder Abuse as a Social Problem: A Canadian Perspective." *International Journal of Health Services* 20(4): 651–663.

Lester, David (1988). "Genetic Theory—An Assessment of the Heritability of Alcoholism." Pp. 1–23 in C. Douglas Chaudron and D. Adrian Wilkinson (eds.), *op. cit.*

Levine, Allan (1997). "A Checkered History of Covering Federal Elections." *Media*, Spring: 11–12.

Levitt, Cyril (1997). "The Morality of Race in Canada." *Society*, July/August: 32–37.

Lewington, Jennifer (1997). "Grappling with an Eternal Question." *The Globe and Mail*, March 27.

Lewis, M. (1972). "State as an Infant-Environmental Interaction." *Merrill-Palmer Quarterly* 18: 95–121.

Lewis, Oscar (1964). "The Culture of Poverty." Pp. 149–173 in J. Tepaske and S. Fisher (eds.), *The Explosive Forces in Latin America*. Columbus, Ohio: University Press.

Lewycky, Laverne (1992). "Multiculturalism in the 1990s and into the 21st Century: Beyond Ideology and Utopia." Pp. 359–402 in Vic Satzewich (ed.), *Deconstructing a Nation*. Halifax and Saskatoon: Fernwood and Social Research Unit, University of Saskatchewan.

Li, Peter S. (1988). *Inequality in a Class Society*. Toronto: Wall & Thompson.

Li, Peter S. (1995). "Racial Supremacy Under Social Democracy." *Canadian Ethnic Studies* XXVII(1): 1–17.

Liazos, A. (1972). "The Poverty of the Sociology of Deviance: Nuts, Sluts and Perverts." *Social Problems*, Summer: 103–120.

Lindsay, Linda L. (1997). *Gender Roles: A Sociological Perspective.* Upper Saddle River, NJ: Prentice Hall.

Little, Bruce (1997). "Women Ahead in the Job Stakes of the Nineties." *The Globe and Mail*, April 14.

Little Bear, L., Menno Boldt, and J. Anthony Long (1984). *Pathways to Self-Determination. Canadian Indians and the Canadian State.* Toronto: University of Toronto Press.

Livingstone, Ken (1996). "Democracy Will Have its Day." *New Statesman*, June 7.

Lloyd, Sally A. (1991). "The Darkside of Courship: Violence and Sexual Exploitation." *Family Relations* 40: 14–20.

Loftus, Elizabeth and Katherine Ketcham (1991). *Witness for the Defence.* New York: St. Martin's Press.

Logan, Ron and Jo-Anne Belliveau (1995). "Working Mothers." *Canadian Social Trends*, Spring, 36: 24–28.

Long, David and Olive Dickason (1996). *Visions of the Heart.* Toronto: Harcourt Brace.

Long Laws, Judith and Pepper Schwartz (1977). *Sexual Scripts: The Social Construction of Female Sexuality.* Hinsdale, IL: Dryden Press.

Lopata, Helena Znaniecka (1993). "The Interweave of Public and Private: Women's Challenge to American Society." *Journal of Marriage and the Family* 55: 176–190.

Lorenz, Konrad (1967). *On Aggression.* New York: Bantam.

Love, John F. (1995). *McDonald's: Behind the Arches.* New York: Bantam

Lowe, Graham H. (1992). *Human resource challenges of education, computers and retirement,* General Social Survey Analysis Series, no. 7. Ottawa: Statistics Canada. Catalogue No. 11-612E.

Lowman, John (1992). "Street Prostitution." Pp. 49–94 in V. Sacco (ed.), *Deviance: Conformity and Control in Canadian Society*, 2nd edition. Scarborough: Prentice Hall.

Lowman, John, Robert J. Menzies and Ted S. Palys (1987). *Transcertation: Essays in the Sociology of Social Control.* Aldershot: Gower.

Lucas, Salome, Judy Vashti Persad, Gillian Morton, Sunita Albaquerque and Nada El Yassir (1991/1995). "Changing the Politics of the Women's Movement." Pp. 534–536 in E.D. Nelson and B.W. Robinson (eds.), *Gender in the 1990s: Images, Realities and Issues.* Scarborough: Nelson.

Lundy, Colleen (1991). "Women and Alcohol: Moving Beyond Disease Theory." Pp. 57–74 in Douglas J. McCready (ed.), *Health Futures: Alcohol and Drugs.* Waterloo, Ontario: Interdisciplinary Research Committee, Wilfred Laurier University, Occasional Paper 8.

Lundy, Katherina L.P. and Barbara D. Warme (1990). *Sociology. A Window on the World*, 2nd edition. Scarborough: Nelson.

Lupul, Manoly (1983). "Multiculturalism and Canada's White Ethnics." *Multiculturalism* 6(3).

Lurie, N.O. (1971). "The World's Oldest On-Going Protest Demonstration: North American Drinking Patterns." *Pacific Historical Review* 40: 311–332.

Luxton, Meg (1983/1995). "Two Hands for the Clock: Changing Patterns in the Gendered Division of Labour in the Home." Studies in Political Economy, Fall 1983, 12: 27–44. Reprinted as pp. 288–301 in E.D. Nelson and B.W. Robinson (eds.) (1995), *Gender in the 1990s: Images, Realities and Issues.* Scarborough: Nelson.

Lynch, Frederick (1997). "The Diversity Machine." *Society*, July/August: 32–37.

Maaka, Roger and Augie Fleras (1997). "Politicizing Customary Rights: Tino Rangatiratanga and the Re-Contouring of Aotearoa New Zealand." Paper presented to the Conference on Indigenous Rights, Political Theory, and the Transformation of Institutions. Canberra: August 8–10.

MacDonald, Finlay (1996). "I Shop Therefore I Am." *Metro*, October: 55–61.

Macionis, John, Juanne Nancarrow Clark and Linda M. Gerber (1994). *Sociology*, Canadian edition. Scarborough: Prentice Hall.

MacKenzie, Betsy (1990). "Therapeutic Abortion in Canada." Pp 130–134 in Craig McKie and Keith Thompson (eds.), *Canadian Social Trends.* Toronto: Thompson Educational Publishing, Inc.

Mackie, Marlene (1991). *Gender Relations In Canada: Further Explorations.* Toronto: Butterworths.

MacKinnon, Catherine A. (1987). *Feminism Unmodified: Disclosures of Life and Law.* Cambridge, MA: Harvard University Press.

MacKinnon, Catherine A. (1991). "Difference and Dominance: On Sex Discrimination." Pp. 81–94 in Katharine T. Bartlett and Rosanne Kennedy (eds.), *Feminist Legal Theory: Readings in Law and Gender.* San Francisco: Westview Press.

Macklin, Eleanor D. (1987) "Non-traditional Family Forms." Pp. 317–352 in M.B. Sussman and S.K. Steinmetz (eds.), *Handbook of Marriage and the Family.* New York: Plenum Press.

MacLean, Eleanor (1981). *Between the Lines. How to Detect Bias and Propaganda in the Press and Everyday Life.* Montreal: Black Rose Books.

Maclean's (1993). "When the boss is a woman." October 4, 106(40): 16–19.

MacLeod, Linda (1980). *Wife Battering in Canada: The Vicious Circle.* Ottawa: Canadian Advisory Council on the Status of Women.

MacLusky, N. and F. Naftolin (1981). "Sexual Differentiation of the Central Nervous System." *Science* 21: 1294–1308.

Magder, Ted (1997). "Public Discourse and the Structures of Communication." Pp. 338–359 in W. Clement (ed.), *Understanding Canada.* Montreal/Kingston: McGill-Queen's University Press.

Mallet, Gina (1997). "Has Diversity Gone Too Far?" *The Globe and Mail*, March 15.

Malvaux, Julianne (1985). "The Economic Interest of Black and White Women: Are They Similar?" *Review of Black Political Economy* 14(1): 4–27.

Manitoba (1991). *Public Inquiry into the Administration of Justice and Aboriginal People: Report of the Aboriginal Justice Inquiry of Manitoba.* Commissioners, A.C. Hamilton, C.M. Sinclair, Government of Manitoba.

Maracle, Brian (1996). "One More Whining Indian Tilting at Windmills." Pp. 15–20 in J. Littleton (ed.), *Clash of Identities.* Scarborough: Prentice Hall.

Marchak, Pat (1991). *The Integrated Circus. The New Right and Restructuring of Global Markets.* Kingston/Montreal: McGill-Queen's University Press.

Marshall, Katherine (1987). "Women in Male Dominated Professions." *Canadian Social Trends*, Winter: 7–11.

Marshall, Susan E. (1989). "Keep Us on the Pedestal: Women Against Feminism in Twentieth-Century America." Pp 567–580 in Jo Freedman (ed.), *Women: A Feminist Perspective.* Mountain View, CA: Mayfield.

Marshall, William and Sylvia Barnett (1990). *Criminal Neglect: Why Sex Offenders Go Free*. Toronto: Doubleday.

Martin, Daniel and Gary Alan Fine (1991). "Satanic Cults, Satanic Play: Is 'Dungeons & Dragons' a Breeding Ground for the Devil?" Pp. 107–123 in James T. Richardson, Joel Best and David G. Bromley (eds.), *The Satanism Scare*. New York: Aldine De Gruyter.

Martin, John A. (1990). *Blessed Are The Addicts: The Spiritual Side of Alcoholism, Addictions And Recovery*. New York: Villard Books.

Masson, J.M. (1985). *Assault on Truth*. New York: Penguin.

Masters, William, Virginia Johnson and Robert Kolodny (1985). *Human Sexuality*, 2nd edition. Boston: Little Brown and Company.

Matas, Robert (1996). "Reports of Work's Demise Appear Exaggerated." *The Globe and Mail*, October 17.

Matas, Robert (1997). "Breast-feeding in public a right, tribunal rules." *The Globe and Mail*, August 12: A4.

Matthews, Roy (1983). *The Creation of Regional Dependencies*. Toronto: University of Toronto Press.

Matthews, Roy A. (1993). "NAFTA: A Way to Save Canadian Jobs." *The Globe and Mail*, September 24.

Max, D.T. (1994). "The End of the Book." *The Atlantic Monthly*, September: 61–70.

McAllister, Matthew P. (1995). *The Commercialization of American Culture. New Advertising, Control, and Democracy*. Thousand Oaks, CA: Sage.

McArthur, Keith (1997). "Canada Puts Environment First." *The Globe and Mail*, March 15.

McDaniel, Susan A. (1988). "Women's Roles and Reproduction: The Changing Picture in Canada in the 1980's." *Atlantis*, Fall, 14(1): 1–12.

McDaniel, Susan A. and E. Roosmalen (1992). "Sexual Harassment in Canadian Academe: Explorations of Power and Privilege." *Atlantis* 17(1): 3–19.

McDougall, Alan (1988). *Policing: The Evolution of a Mandate*. Ottawa: Canadian Police College.

McEwan, B.S. (1981). "Neural Gonadal Steroid Actions." *Science* 21: 1303–1322.

McGregor, Judy (ed.) (1996). *Dangerous Democracy. News Media Politics in New Zealand*. Palmerston North: Dunmore.

McHutchion, Rob and David Crane (1996). "Dead End Kids." *The Toronto Star*, February 27.

McIntosh, Mary (1978). "Who Needs Prostitutes?" Pp. 53–64 in C. Smart and B. Smart (eds.), *Women, Sexuality and Social Control*. London: Routledge and Kegan Paul.

McIntyre, Sheila (1994). "Backlash Against Equality: The 'Tyranny' of the 'Politically Correct'." *McGill Law Journal/Revue de Droit de McGill* 38(1): 3–63.

McKague, Ormand (1991). *Racism in Canada*. Saskatoon: Fifth House Publishing.

McKie, Craig (1991). "The Social Consequences and Functions of the New Media." Pp 391–410 in B. Singer (ed.), *Communications in Canadian Society*. Scarborough: Nelson.

McKie, David (1997). "Taking Stock of Election Coverage." *Media*, Spring: 3–4.

McKinnon, Allison L. (1991). "Knowledge, Attitudes and Behaviours in Alberta." *Canadian Social Trends*, Winter: 25.

McLaren, A. (1990). "What Makes a Man a Man?" *Nature* 346: 216–217.

McLeod, Keith A. (ed.) (1987). *Multiculturalism, Bilingualism, and Canadian Institutions*. Toronto: University of Toronto Guidance Centre.

McLeod, Rosemary (1997). "Piquant Touch of Blood on the Lens." *Dominion*, September 6.

McLuhan, Marshall (1960). *Expolorations in Communication: An Anthology*. Boston: Beacon Press.

McLuhan, Marshall and Bruce Powers (1989). *The Global Village: Transformations in the World Life and Media in the 21st Century*. Toronto: Oxford University Press.

McMahon, Fred (1997). *Looking the Gifthorse in the Mouth: The Impact of Federal Transfers on Atlantic Canada*. Halifax: Atlantic Institute for Market Studies.

McMillan, D. (1991). *Winning the Battle against Drugs: Rehabilitation Program*. New York: Franklin Watts.

McNeely, R.L. and G. Robinson-Simpson (1987). "The Truth About Domestic Violence: A Falsely Framed Issue." *Social Work* 32: 485–490.

McQuail, Dennis (1987). *Mass Communication Theory: An Introduction*. Beverly Hills: Sage Publications.

McRoberts, Kenneth (1993). "English-Canadian Perceptions of Quebec." Pp 116–129 in A.G. Gagnon (ed.), *Quebec: State and Society*. Scarborough: Nelson.

McRoberts, Kenneth (1997). *Misconceiving Canada. The Struggle for National Unity*. Toronto: Oxford University Press.

McRoberts, Kenneth (1997). "Talking It Over." *The Globe and Mail*, January 4.

Media Watch (1987). *Adjusting the Image. Women and Canadian Broadcasting*. Report of a National Conference on Canadian Broadcasting Policy Held in Ottawa, March 20–22.

Medved, Michael (1996). *Hollywood's Four Big Lies*. London: Bloomsbury Press.

Mercredi, Ovide and Mary Ellen Turpel (1993). *In the Rapids. Navigating the Future of First Nations*. Toronto: Penguin Books.

Merton, Robert (1957). "Priorities in Scientific Discovery: A Chapter in the Sociology of Science." *American Sociological Review* 22: 635–659.

Messner, Michael A., Margaret Carlisle Duncan, Fay Linda Wachs (1996). "The Gender of Audience-Building: Televised Coverage of Women's and Men's NCAA Basketball." *Sociological Inquiry* 66(4): 422–439.

Michael, R.T., J.H. Gagnon, E.O. Laumann and G. Kolata (1994). *Sex in America: A Definitive Survey*. Boston: Little, Brown.

Mietkiewitz, Henry (1993). "Studies Link TV Violence and Viewer Aggressiveness." *The Toronto Star*, January 16.

Miles, Robert (1982). *Racism and Migrant Labour*. London: Routledge and Kegan Paul.

Miller, Alice (1988). *Thou Shalt Not Be Aware: Society's Betrayal of the Child*. New York: Meridian.

Miller, J.B. (1974). *Psychoanalysis and Women*. London: Penguin.

Miller, Jon (1991). "Is Bangladesh Hooked on Aid?" *The Globe and Mail*, December 16.

Miller, Walter B. (1958). "Lower Class Culture as a Generating Milieu of Gang Delinquency." *Journal of Social Interest* 14: 5–19.

Mills, C. Wright (1967). *The Sociological Imagination*. New York: Oxford University Press.

Mintzberg, Henry (1996). "The Myth of Society Inc." *Report on Business Magazine*, October: 113–117.

Mitchell, Alanna (1997). "Face of Poverty Ever-Changing." *The Globe and Mail*, July 8.

Mitchell, Alana (1997). "Tuition Squeeze Not Stopping Students." *The Globe and Mail*, September 30.

Mitchell-Powell, Brenda (1992). "Color Me Multicultural." *Multi-Cultural Review* 1(4): 15–17.

Mofina, Rick (1996). "Sex harassment in RCMP for 60% of women officers." *Edmonton Journal*, September 26: A3.

Moir, Peter and Matthew Moir (1993). "Community-Based Policing and the Role of Community Consultation." Pp. 211–235 in P. Moir and H. Eijkman (eds.), *Policing Australia*. Melbourne: Macmillan.

Mones, Paul (1991). *When A Child Kills: Abused Children Who Kill Their Parents.* New York: Pocket Books.

Money, J. and A.E. Ehrhardt (1972). *Man and Woman, Boy and Girl.* Baltimore: John Hopkins University Press.

Moore, Harry W. and Robert C. Trojanowicz (1988). *Criminal Justice in the Community*. Englewood Cliffs: Prentice Hall.

Moore, Maureen (1989). "Dual-Earner Families: The New Norm." *Canadian Social Trends* 4(2): 24–26.

Moore, Maureen (1990). "Dual-Earner Families: The New Norm." Pp. 161–163 in Craig McKie and Keith Thompson (ed.), *Canadian Social Trends.* Toronto: Thompson Educational Publishing.

Morgan, Gareth (1986). *Images of Organization.* Toronto: Oxford University Press.

Morris, Desmond (1968). *The Naked Ape*. New York: McGraw-Hill.

Morris, Merrill and Christine Ogan (1996). "The Internet as Mass Medium." *Journal of Communication* 46(1): 39–52.

Morrison, Nancy (1987). "Separation and Divorce." Pp. 125–143 in M.J. Dymond (ed.), *The Canadian Woman's Legal Guide.* Toronto: Doubleday.

Morrow, Raymond A. (1994). "Mass-Mediated Culture, Leisure, And Consumption: Having Fun as a Social Problem." Pp. 189–211 in Les Samuelson (ed.), *Power and Resistance.*

Mortimer, Jeylan T. and Jane London (1984). "The Varying Linkages of Work and Family." Pp. 20–35 in Patricia Voydanoff (ed.), *Work Family: Changing Roles of Men and Women.* Palo Alto, CA: Mayfield.

Morton, Mildred (1990). "Controversies Within Family Law." Pp. 211–240 in Maureen Baker (ed.), *Families: Changing Trends in Canada.* Toronto: McGraw-Hill Ryerson.

Mosher, William D. (1990). "Contraceptive Pattern in the United States, 1982–1988." *Family Planning Perspectives* 22(5): 198–205.

Moynihan, Daniel (1993). *Pandaemonium. Ethnicity in International Politics.* New York: Oxford University Press.

Murdock, George Peter (1949). *Social Structure.* New York: Free Press.

Murray, Charles (1977). *A Behavioural Study of Modernization, Social and Economic Change in Thai Villages.* New York: Praeger.

Murray, Charles (1984). *Losing Ground: American Social Policy 1950–1980.* New York: Basic Books.

Murray, Charles (1988). *In Pursuit of Happiness and Good Government.* New York: Simon and Schuster.

Murray, Charles (1990). *The Emerging British Underclass.* London: IEA Health and Welfare Unit.

Nader, Ralph, Nadia Milleron and Duff Conacher (1992). *Canada Firsts.* Toronto: McClelland and Stewart.

National Council of Welfare (1990). *Women and Poverty Revisited.* Ottawa: Supply and Services.

National Council of Welfare (1995). *Poverty Profile 1993.* Ottawa: Minister of Supply and Services.

National Council of Welfare (1997). *Poverty Profile 1995.* Ottawa: Minister of Supply and Services.

Nelson, Adie and Barrie W. Robinson (1994). *Gigolos & Madames Bountiful: Illusions of Gender, Power and Intimacy*. Toronto: University of Toronto Press.

Nelson, E.D. (1997). *Crime and Its Memorabilia*. In progress. SSHRC Standard Research Grants Program 410-96-0463.

Nett, Emily (1993). *Canadian Families: Past and Present*, 2nd edition. Toronto: Butterworths.

Nettler, G. (1984). *Explaining Crime*, 3rd edition. Toronto: McGraw-Hill.

New Internationalist (1996). "New Technology: Keynote." December: 7–10.

Ng, Roxana (1988). *The Politics of Community Services: Immigrant Women, Class, and the State*. Toronto: Garamond Press.

Nicholson-Lord, David (1992). "Aid, Debt, and the Poverty Trap." *Dominion (NZ)* (originally the *Independent*), December 10.

Nisbet, Michael (1994). "Theory 'X' Like Tuberculosis Is Making a Comeback." *The Globe and Mail*, February 16.

Nisbet, Robert A. (1965). *Emile Durkheim*. Englewood Cliffs, NJ: Prentice Hall.

Normand, Josee (1995). "Education of Women in Canada." *Canadian Social Trends*, Winter, 39: 17–21.

Normandeau, Andre and Barry Leighton (1990). *A Vision of the Future of Policing in Canada*. Police-Challenge 2000 Background Document. Policy and Security Branch. Ministry Secretariat. Solicitor General Canada. Ottawa: Minister of Supply and Services Canada.

Noult, Francois (1996). "Twenty Years of Marriage." *Health Reports* 8(2): 39–47.

Nuwer, H. (1990). *Steroids*. New York: Franklin Watts.

Oakley, A. (1972). *Sex, Gender and Society*. London: Temple-Smith.

Oakley, A. (1974). *The Sociology of Housework*. New York: Pantheon.

Oakley, Anne (1981). *Division of Labour by Gender*. Milton Keynes, Buckinghamshire: Open University Books.

Oderkirk, Jillian and Clarence Lochhead (1992). "Lone Parenthood: Gender Differences." *Canadian Social Trends*, Winter: 16–19.

Oettmeier, Timothy N. and Lee P. Brown (1988). "Role Expectations and the Concept of Neighborhood Oriented Community Policing." In International Association of Police Chiefs, *Developing Neighborhood Oriented Policing in the Houston Police Department*.

Okin, Susan Moller (1989). *Justice, Gender and the Family*. New York: Basic Books.

Olive, David (1992). "Fire at Will." Perspective *Report on Business Magazine*, March: 9–10.

Olmsted, A.D. (1988). "Morally Controversial Leisure." *Symbolic Interaction* 11: 277–287.

Olson, Mancur (1965). *The Logic of Collective Action*. Cambridge, MA: Harvard University Press.

Ontario Ministry of the Solicitor General (1989). *Report of the Race Relations and Policing Task Force*. C. Lewis, Chair. Ontario: Solicitor General of Ontario.

Orbach, Suzie (1984). *What Do Women Want?* New York: Coward-McCann.

Orbach, Suzie (ed.) (1986). *Hunger Strike*. New York: Norton.

Orpood, Graham and Jennifer Lewington (1995). *Overdue Assignment. Taking Responsibility for Canada's Schools*. Toronto: John Wiley and Sons.

Orwell, George (1984). *Animal Farm: A Fairy Story*. Harmondsworth: Penguin Books.

Osborne, Judith A. (1991). "The Criminal Law." Pp. 49–73 in Margaret A. Jackson and Curt T. Griffiths (eds.), *Canadian Criminology: Perspectives on Crime and*

Criminality. Toronto: Harcourt Brace Jovanovich.

Ostow, Robin et al. (1991). *Ethnicity, Structured Inequality, and the State in Canada and the Federal Republic of Germany*. New York: Peter Lang.

Owen, Rob (1997). *Gen X TV: The Brady Bunch to Melrose Place*. Syracuse University Press.

Pagelow, Mildred D. (1984). *Family Violence*. New York: Praeger.

Paglia, Camille (1990). *Sexual Personae*. New Haven, CT: Yale University Press.

Paglia, Camille (1992). *Sexual, Art, and American Culture: Essays*. New York: Vintage Books.

Paine, Robert (1985). "The Claim of the Fourth World." Pp. 49–66 in Jens Brosted (ed.), *The Quest for Autonomy and Nationhood of Indigenous Peoples*. Bergen: Universiteforlaget AS.

Palat, Ravi Arvind (1996). "Curries, Chopsticks, and Kiwis: Asian Migration to Aotearoa/New Zealand." Pp 35–54 in P. Spoonley et al. (eds.), *Nga Patai*. Palmerston North: Dunmore.

Palmer, Howard (ed.) (1975). *Immigration and the Rise of Multiculturalism*. Toronto: Copp Clark Publishing.

Parenti, Michael (1978). *Power and the Powerless*, 2nd edition. New York: St. Martin's Press.

Parenti, Michael (1992). *The Make-Believe Media: The Politics of Entertainment*. New York: St. Martin's Press.

Parizeau, Jacques (1996). "The object is sovereignty, not partnership." *The Globe and Mail*, December 19.

Parker, Graham (1991). "Crime, Law and Legal Defences." In Rick Linden (ed.), *Criminology: A Canadian Perspective*, 2nd edition. Toronto: Holt Rinehart and Winston.

Parris, Matthew (1997). "A Spider in the Bathtub." *Dominion*, September 15.

Parsons, Talcott (1942). "Age and Sex in the Social Structure." *American Sociological Review* 7: 601–616.

Parsons, Talcott (1949). "The Social Structure of the Family." Pp. 173–201 in Ruth Anshen (ed.), *The Family: Its Function and Destiny*. New York: Harper and Brothers.

Parsons, Talcott (1955). "The American Family: Its Relation to Personality and to the Social Structure." In Talcott Parsons and Robert Bales, *Family Socialization and Interaction Process*. Glencoe: The Free Press.

Parsons, Talcott (1959). "The School as Social System." *Harvard Educational Review* 29: 297–318.

Parsons, Vic (1995). "A Horrifying Account of Canada's Tainted-Blood Scandal." *The Globe and Mail*, May 13: C21.

Peart, Joseph and Jim Mcnamara (1996). *The New Zealand Public Relations Handbook*.

Peluso, Lucy and Emmanuel Peluso (1988). *Women & Drugs: Getting Hooked, Getting Clean*. Minneapolis, MN: ConCare.

Pendakur, Krishna and Ravi Pendakur (1995). "Earning Differentials Among Ethnic Groups in Canada." Social Research Group. Hull: Department of Canadian Heritage. Ref. SRA-34.

Penner, Keith (1983). *Indian Self-Government in Canada*. Report of the Special Committee chaired by Keith Penner. Ottawa: Queen's Printer for Canada.

Peplau, Letitia Anne and Steven L. Gordon (1985). "Women and Men in Love: Gender Differences in Close Heterosexual Relationships." In Virginia E. O'Leary, Rhoda Kesler Unger and Barnara Strudler Wallston (eds.), *Women, Gender and Social Psychology*. Hillsdale, NJ: Lawrence Erlbaum.

Perry, Martin, Carl Davidson, Roberta Hill (1995). *Reform at Work: Workplace*

Change and the New Industrial Order. Auckland: Longman Paul.

Peter, Karl (1978). "Multi-Cultural Politics, Money, and the Conduct of Canadian Ethnic Studies." *Canadian Ethnic Studies Association Bulletin* 5: 2–3.

Peters, Thomas J. and Robert H. Waterman (1982). *In Search of Excellence. Lessons from America's Best Run Companies.* New York: Harper and Row.

Pfohl, Stephen J. (1977). "The 'Discovery' of Child Abuse." *Social Problems*, February, 24(3): 310–323.

Pfuhl, E.H. (1978). "The Unwed Father: A Non-Deviant Rule Breaker." *The Sociological Quarterly* 19: 113–128.

Pictor, Garnett and John Myles (1996). "Children in Low-Income Families." *Canadian Social Trends*, Autumn, 42: 15–19.

Pike, J.A. (1967a). *If This Be Heresy.* New York: Harper and Row.

Pike, J.A. (1967b). *You and the New Morality.* New York: Harper and Row.

Pizzey, Erin and Jeff Shapiro (1982). *Prone to Violence.* London: Hamlyn Paperbacks.

Plapinger, L. and B.S. McEwan (1978). "Gonadal Steroid-Brain Interactions in Sexual Differentiation." Pp. 153–218 in J.B. Hutchinson (ed.), *Biological Determinants of Sexual Behaviour.* New York: John Wiley and Sons.

Pleck, E. and J. Pleck (eds.) (1980). *The American Male.* Englewood Cliffs, NJ: Prentice Hall.

Pleck, Joseph H. (1979). "Men's Family Work: Three Perspectives and Some New Data." *The Family Coordinator* 28: 481–488.

Pleck, Joseph H. (1985). *Working Wives/Working Husbands.* Beverly Hills, CA: Sage.

Pleck, Joseph and M. Rustad (1980). *Husbands' and Wives' Time in Family Work and Paid Work in 1975–76 Study of Time Use.* Unpublished paper. Wellesley College Center for Research on Women.

Plummer, Ken (1975). *Sexual Stigma: An Interactionist Account.* London: Routledge Kegan Paul.

Plummer, Ken (1979). "Misunderstanding Labelling Perspectives." In David Downes and Paul Rock (eds.), *Deviant Interpretations.* Oxford: Martin Robertson.

Pogrebin, L. (1983). "The Secret Fear that Keeps us from Raising Free Children." In L. Richardson and V. Taylor (eds.), *Feminist Frontiers: Rethinking Sex, Gender and Society.* New York: Random House.

Pollack, Andrew (1995). "Cyberspace's War of Words." *The Globe and Mail*, August 10.

Pollak, O. (1950). *The Criminality of Women.* New York: A.S. Barnes.

Pollay, Richard (1997). "Who Are They Kidding? Tobacco Marketing Targets Youth." *Policy Options*, June, 18(5): 7-11.

Ponting, J. Rick and Roger Gibbins (1980). *Out of Irrelevance: A Socio-Political Introduction to Indian Affairs in Canada.* Toronto: Butterworths.

Porter, John (1965). *The Vertical Mosaic.* Toronto: University of Toronto Press.

Porter, John (1979). *The Measure of Canadian Society.* Toronto: Gage.

Posluns, Elaine and Allen Tough (1987). "How Individuals Become Freer From Sex-Role Stereotyping." *Atlantis* 13(1): 169–176.

Postman, Neil (1985). *Amusing Ourselves to Death.* New York: Pantheon.

Postman, Neil (1995). *The End of Education: Redefining the Value of School.* New York: Knopf.

Poverty Profile Update for 1991, 1993. Ottawa: National Council on Welfare.

Powell, Thomas (1992). "Feel-Good Racism." *The New York Times*, May 24.

Presthus, Robert (1978). *The Organizational Society*, revised edition. New York: St Martin's Press.

Price, Christopher (1993). "School of Thought." *New Statesman and Society*, August 20.

Priest, Gordon E. (1993). "Seniors: 75+ Living Arrangements." *Canadian Social Trends*, Autumn: 24-26.

Propper, Alice (1990). "Patterns of Family Violence." Pp. 272–305 in Maureen Baker (ed.), *Families: Changing Trends in Canada*, 2nd edition. Toronto: McGraw-Hill Ryerson.

Qadeer, M.A. (1997). "Pakistan Broke Ground for Minority Nationalism." *Toronto Star,* August 14.

Qualter, Terence H. (1991). "Propaganda in Canadian Society." Pp. 200–212 in Benjamin D. Singer (ed.), *Communications in Canadian Society*. Scarborough: Nelson.

Quinney, Richard (1970). *The Social Reality of Crime*. Boston: Little, Brown.

Rado, Sandor (1933). "The Psychoanalysis of Pharmacothymia (Drug Addiction)."

Radzinowciz, L. (1961). *In Search of Criminology*. London: Heinemann.

Ramcharan, Subhas (1989). *Social Problems and Issues. A Canadian Perspective*. Scarborough: Nelson.

Ramsey, Lynn (1976). *Gigilos: The World's Best Kept Women*. Englewood Cliffs, NJ: Prentice Hall.

Rawson, Bruce (1991). "Public Service 2000 Services to the Public Task Force: Findings and Implications." *Canadian Public Administration* 34(3): 490–502.

Razack, Sherene (1993). "Exploring the Omissions and Silences in Law Around Race." Pp. 37–38 in Joan Brockman and Dorothy E. Chunn (eds.), *Investigating Gender Bias: Laws, Courts and the Legal Profession*. Toronto: Thompson Educational Publishing, Inc.

Reagan, Tom (1983). *The Case for Animal Rights*. Berkeley: The University of California Press.

Reality (newsletter of REALWOMEN of Canada) (1991). Fall, 9(3).

Reality (newsletter of REALWOMEN of Canada) (1991). Winter, 9(5).

Reality (1991). "Real Women of Canada Policies Supported by Majority of Canadian Women." Winter, 9(5).

Reform Watch (1997). "Hitting kids." http://www.vcn.bc.ca/refwatch/

Reinisch, June M. and Ruth Beasley (1990). *The Kinsey Institute New Report on Sex*. New York: St. Martin's Press.

Reiss, A.J. Jr. (1961). "The Social Integration of Queers and Peers." *Social Problems* 9: 102–119.

Reiss, Ira L. (1986). *Journey Into Sexuality: An Exploratory Voyage*. Englewood Cliffs, NJ: Prentice Hall.

Reiter, Ester (1992/1996). *Making Fast Food. From the Frying Pan into the Fryer*. Montreal: McGill-Queens University Press.

Reitz, Jeffrey and Raymond Breton (1994). *The Illusion of Difference: Realities of Ethnicity in Canada and the United States*. Toronto: C.D. Howe Institute.

Report (1991). *Towards Managing Diversity*. A Study of Systemic Discrimination at DIAND. The Deputies Council for Change and the Minister of Indian Affairs and Northern Development. Ottawa.

Rex, John and Beatrice Drury (eds.) (1996). *Ethnic Mobilisation in a Multi-Cultural Europe*. Aldershot, UK: Ashgate Publishing.

Richardson, C. James (1987). "Children of Divorce." Pp. 163–200 in K.L. Anderson et al. (eds.), *Family Matters: Sociology and Contemporary Canadian Families*. Toronto: Methuen.

Richardson, L.W. (1981). *The Dynamics of Sex and Gender*, 2nd edition. Boston: Houghton Mifflin.

Richardson, Laurel (1988). *The Dynamics of Sex and Gender: A Sociological Perspective*, 3rd edition. New York: Harper and Row.

Rifkin, Jeremy (1995). "Work: A Blueprint for Social Harmony in a World Without Jobs." *Utne Reader*, May/June: 53–62.

Rifkin, Jeremy (1996). "Civil Society in the Information Age." *The Nation*, February 26.

Riley, Diane (1993). "Is Drug Policy a Handy Check on the 'Dangerous Classes?'" *CCSA-CCALAT News Action*, May/June, 4(3): 3, 6.

Ritzer, George (1993). *The McDonaldization of Society: An Investigation into the Changing Character of Contemporary Social Life*. Newbury Park, CA: Pine Forge Press.

Rizvi, Fazal (1994). "The New Right and the Politics of Multiculturalism in Australia." In *Multiculturalism and the State*, volume 1, collected seminar papers no. 47. University of London: Institute of Commonwealth Studies.

Roberg, Roy R. (1994). "Can Today's Police Organizations Effectively Implement Community Policing?" In R.P. Rosenbaum, *The Challenge of Community Policing*. Thousand Oaks, CA: Sage.

Roberge Jr., Roger (1992). "Canada's Court System." *Canadian Social Trends*.

Roberts, J.V. and T. Gabor (1990). "Lombrosian Wine in a New Bottle: Research on Crime and Race." *Canadian Journal of Criminology* 32.

Roberts, Paul (1996). "Virtual Grub Reality." *Harper's*, June: 71–83.

Roberts, Robin (1990). "'Sex as a Weapon': Feminist Rock Music Videos." *NSWA Journal*, Winter, 2(1): 1–15.

Robertson, Ian (1980). *Social Problems*, 2nd edition. New York: Random House.

Robertson, Ian (1987). *Sociology*, 3rd edition. New York: Worth Publishing.

Robinson, Ira et al. (1991). "Twenty Years of the Sexual Revolution, 1965–1985: An Update." *Journal of Marriage and the Family*, February, 53: 216–220.

Robinson, Jan, Warren Young and Neil Cameron (eds.) (1989). *Effectiveness and Change in Policing*. Wellington: Victoria University Institute of Criminology.

Robinson, Richard (ed.) (1996). *Pathways to Asia: The Politics of Engagement*. Sydney: Allen & Unwin.

Robinson, William I. (1996). "Globalisation: Nine Theses on Our Epoch." *Race & Class* 38(2): 13–31.

Rochefort, David A. and Roger W. Cobb (1994). *The Politics of Problem Definition: Shaping the Policy Agenda*. Lawrence, KA: University Press of Kansas.

Rock, Paul E. (1992). *A View from the Shadows*. London: Clarendon Press.

Rodgers, Karen (1994). "Wife Assault in Canada." *Canadian Social Trends*, Autumn, Catalogue 11-008E.

Rodgers, Karen and Garry MacDonald (1994). "Canada's Shelters for Abused Women." *Canadian Social Trends*, Autumn, 34: 10–15.

Roiphe, Katie (1993). "Date Rape's Other Victim." *The New York Times Magazine*, June 13: 26, 28, 30, 40, 68.

Roiphe, Katie (1993). *The Morning After: Sex, Fear, And Feminism On Campus*. Boston: Little, Brown and Company.

Rose, Vicki McNickle and Susan Carol Randall (1982). "The Impact of Investigator Perceptions of Victim Legitimacy on the Processing of Rape/Sexual Assault Cases." *Symbolic Interaction* 5(1): 23–36.

Rosenbaum, Dennis (ed.) (1994). *The Challenge of Community Policing: Testing the Promises*. Thousand Oaks, CA: Sage.

Rosenthal, Carolyn J. (1987/1995). "Kinkeeping in the Familial Division of Labor." *Journal of Marriage and the Family* 47(4): 965–974. Reprinted as pp. 120–127 in Lorne Tepperman and James E. Curtis (ed.), *Everyday Life—A Reader*. Toronto: McGraw-Hill Primis.

Ross, David P., E. Richard Shillington and Clarence Lochhead (1994). *The Canadian Fact Book of Poverty*. Ottawa: Canadian Council of Social Development.

Roszak, Theodore (1994). *The Cult of Information: The Folklore of Computers and the True Art of Communication*. New York: Pantheon.

Roszak, Theodore (1996). "Dumbing Us Down." *New Internationalist*, December: 12–14.

Rothenberg, Paula S. (ed.) (1992). *Race, Class, and Gender in the United States. An Integrated Study*, 2nd edition. New York: St. Martin's Press.

Rothenberg, Randall (1997). "How Powerful is Advertising?" *The Atlantic Monthly*, June: 113–115.

Rowell, Andrew (1996). *Green Backlash. Global Subversion and the Environmental Movement*. New York: Routledge.

Rowland, R. (1986). "Women Who Do and Women Who Don't, Join the Women's Movement: Issues for Conflict and Collaboration." *Sex Roles* 14: 679–692.

Royal Commission on Aboriginal Peoples (1993). *Partners in Confederation. Aboriginal Peoples, Self-Government, and the Constitution*. Ottawa: Minister of Supply and Services.

Royal Commission (1995). *Aboriginal Self-Government: Legal and Constitutional Issues*. Ottawa: Minister of Supply and Services.

Royal Commission (1995). *Bridging the Cultural Divide*. Report of the Royal Commission on Aboriginal Peoples. Ottawa: Minister of Supply and Services.

Royal Commission (1996). *People to People, Nation to Nation*. Highlights from the Report of the Royal Commission on Aboriginal Peoples. Ottawa: Minister of Supply and Services.

Rubin, J.Z., F.J. Provenzano and Z. Lurra (1974). "The Eye of the Beholder." *American Journal of Orthopsychiatry* 44: 512–519.

Rubin, Lillian (1990). *The Erotic Wars: What Happened to the Sexual Revolution?* New York: Farrar, Straus and Giroux.

Ruesch, Hans (1985). *Slaughter of the Innocent*. New York: Civitas.

Rueters (1997). "India's caste violence outbreak kills 60." *Kitchener-Waterloo Record*, December 2.

Rushton, Philippe (1995). *Race, Evolution and Behavior: A Life History Perspective*. New York: Transaction.

Russell, D.E.H. (1982). "The prevalence and incidence of forcible rape and attempted rape of females." *Victimology* 7: 81–93.

Russell, Diana (1984). *Sexual Exploitation*. Beverly Hills, CA: Sage.

Russell, Diana and David Finkelhor (1984). "The Gender Gap." In D. Russell, *Sexual Exploitation*. Beverly Hills, CA: Sage.

Russell, Diana E.H. (1987). "The Nuclear Mentality: An Outgrowth of the Masculine Mentality." *Atlantis* 12(2): 10–16.

Sacco, Vince and Holly Johnson (1990). "Violent Victimization." *Canadian Social Trends*, Winter, 17: 10–13.

Sadker, Myra and David Sadker (1987). "Sexism in the Schoolroom of the '80s." Pp 143–147 in E.D. Salamon and B.W. Robinson (eds.), *Gender Roles: Doing What Comes Naturally*. Toronto: Methuen.

Safilios-Rothschild, C. (1974). *Women and Social Policy*. Englewood Cliffs, NJ: Prentice Hall.

Salamon, E.D. (1989). "Homosexuality." Pp 95–136 in Vince F. Sacco (ed.), *Deviance: Conformity and Control in Canadian Society*. Scarborough: Prentice Hall.

Salamon, E.D. and B.W. Robinson (eds.) (1991). *Gender Roles: Doing What Comes Naturally?* Scarborough: Nelson.

Salee, Daniel and William D. Coleman (1997). "The Challenges of the Quebec Question: Paradigm, Counter-Paradigm, and Sovereignty." Pp. 262–282 in W. Clement (ed.), *Understanding Canada*. Montreal/Kingston: McGill-Queen's University Press.

Salhotz, Eloise et al. (1992). "The Future of Gay America." Pp. 81–85 in Ollie Pocs (ed.), *Human Sexuality* 92/93. Guilford, CT: Dushkin.

Salutin, Rick (1997). "The Virtual Appearance of Humanity in the Media." *The Globe and Mail*, May 9.

Salutin, Rick (1997). "What Does the Word Racism Mean to Sportswriters?" *The Globe and Mail*, April 25.

Sandmaier, Marian (1992). *The Invisible Alcoholics: Women and Alcohol*, 2nd edition. Blue Ridge Summit, PA: Tab Books.

Sandor, G. (1980). "Fetal Alcohol Syndrome: Cardiac Malformations." *B.C. Medical Journal* 23: 326–327.

Sanger, W. (1910). *A History of Prostitution*. New York: Medical Publishing.

Satzewich, Vic (1991). "Social Stratification: Class and Racial Inequality." Pp. 91–107 in B. Singh Bolaria (ed.), *Social Issues and Contradictions in Canadian Society*. Toronto: Harcourt Brace.

Satzewich, Vic (1993). "Race and Ethnic Relations." Pp. 160-177 in Peter Li and B. Singh Bolaria (eds.), *Contemporary Sociology. Critical Perspectives*. Mississauga: Copp Clark Pitman.

Saul, John Ralston (1995). *The Unconscious Civilization*. Toronto: House of Anansi Press.

Saunders, Douglas (1997). "Adacity." *The Globe and Mail*, June 7.

Saunders, John and Casey Mahood (1996). "New Layout, Same Story." *The Globe and Mail*, May 4.

Saville, Gregory and D. Kim Rossmo (1995). "Striking a Balance: Lessons From Problem-Oriented Policing in British Columbia." Pp. 119–132 in K.M. Hazlehurst (ed.), *Perceptions of Justice*. Aldershot: Avebury Press.

Schaefer, Richard T., Robert P. Lamm, Penny Biles and Susannah J. Wilson (1996). *Sociology: An Introduction*, 1st Canadian Edition. Toronto: McGraw-Hill Ryerson Ltd.

Schellhardt, Timothy D. (1997). "Management? Forget About It." *The Globe and Mail*, April 4.

Schlesinger, Arthur M. Jr. (1992). *The Disuniting of America: Reflections on a Multicultural Society*. New York: W.W. Norton.

Schlesinger, Philip and Howard Tumber (1993). "Fighting the War Against Crime." *British Journal of Criminology* 33: 19–32.

Schoenborn, Charlotte (1993). "Health status and practices: Canada and the United States." *Canadian Social Trends*, Winter: 16–23.

Schoon, Nicholas (1997). "Global Warning—Too Much Hot Air." *The Independent International*, May 28.

Schur, Edwin (1989). *Americanization of Sex*. Philadelphia: Temple University Press.

Schwartz, Felice (1989). "Management Women and the New Facts of Life." *Harvard Business Review* 89: 65–76.

Schwartz, Richard D. and Jerome H. Skolnick (1962). "Two Studies of Legal Stigma." *Social Problems* 10: 133–143.

Scott, R.A. (1972). "A Proposed Framework for Analyzing Deviance as a Property of Social Control." In R.A. Scott and J.D.

Douglas (eds.), *Theoretical Perspectives on Deviance*. London: Basic Books.

Seagrave, Jane (1997). *Introduction to Policing in Canada*. Scarborough: Prentice Hall.

Secord, P. and C.W. Backman (1967). *Social Psychology*. New York: McGraw-Hill.

Sefa Dei, George J. (1996/97). "Beware of False Dichotomies: Revisiting the Idea of 'Black-Focused' Schools in Canadian Contexts." *Journal of Canadian Studies* 31(4): 58–69.

Seguin, Francine (1991). "Service to the Public: A Major Strategic Change." *Canadian Public Administration* 34(3): 465–473.

Seiler, Tamara Palmer (1996). "Multi-Vocality and National Literature. Toward a Post-Colonial and Multicultural Aesthetic." *Journal of Canadian Studies* 31(3).

Seitzinger, Jack and Michele J. Sabino (1988). "Training for Neighborhood Oriented Policing." In The International Association of Police Chiefs, *Developing Neighborhood Oriented Policing in the Houston Police Department*. Washington.

Seligman, Jean (1992). "Variations on a Theme." Pp. 77–80 in Ollie Pocs (ed.), *Human Sexuality 92/93*. Guilford, CT: Dushkin.

Sellin, Thorsten (1938). *Cultural Conflict and Crime*. New York: Social Science Research.

Sen, Amartya (1993). "The Threats to Secular Indian Society." *The New York Times Book Review*, April 8: 26–32.

Shalev, Carmel (1989). *Birth Power: The Case for Surrogacy*. New Haven: Yale University Press.

Shaw, Clifford R. (1938). *Brothers in Crime*. Chicago: University of Chicago Press.

Shaw, Clifford and Henry D. McKay (1942). *Juvenile Delinquency and Urban Areas*,

revised edition. Chicago: University of Chicago Press.

Shaw, Clifford R. and Henry D. McKay (1931). *Social Factors in Juvenile Delinquency*. Washington, D.C.: U.S. Government Printing Office.

Shaw, Margaret (1989). *Survey of Federally Sentenced Women*. Ottawa.

Sher, Julian (1983). *White Hoods: Canada's Ku Klux Klan*. Vancouver: New Star Books.

Shibley-Hyde, J. (1982). *One Half the Human Experience*. New York: McGraw-Hill.

Shibley-Hyde, J. (1985). *Half The Human Experience*, 2nd edition. Toronto: D.C. Heath.

Shields Rob (ed.) (1996). *Cultures of Internet. Virtual Spaces, Real Histories, Living Bodies*. Thousand Oaks, CA: Sage.

Shkilnyk, Anastasia (1985). *A Poison Stronger Than Love*. New Haven, CT: Yale University Press.

Shostak, Arthur B. (1991). "Abortion in America: Ten Cautious Forecasts." *The Futurist*, July/August: 20–24.

Shusta, R.M. et al. (1995). *Multicultural Law Enforcement: Strategies for Peacekeeping in a Diverse Society*. Englewood Cliffs, NJ: Prentice Hall.

Siddiqui, Haroon (1996). "Multiculturalism and the Media." Pp. 113–118 in J. Littleton (ed.), *Clash of Identities. Media Manipulation, and Politics of the Self*. Scarborough: Prentice Hall.

Sidorowicz, L.S. and G.S. Lunney (1980). "Baby X Revisited." *Sex Roles* 6: 667–673.

Silvera, Mikeda (1983). *Silenced*. Toronto: Williams-Wallace Publishers.

Silverman, Robert and Leslie Kennedy (1993). *Deadly Deeds: Murder in Canada*. Scarborough: Nelson.

Simon, W. and J.H. Gagnon (1967). "Homosexuality: The Formulation of a

Sociological Perspective." *Journal of Health and Social Behavior* 8: 177–185.

Sinclair, Peter R. (1991). "Underdevelopment and Regional Inequality." Pp. 358–376 in B. Singh Bolari (ed.), *Social Issues and Contradictions in Canadian Society*. Toronto: Harcourt Brace.

Singer, Benjamin (1986). *Advertising and Society*. Don Mills, ON: Addison-Wesley.

Singer, Peter (1976). *Animal Liberation*. New York: Avon.

Single, Eric, Anne MacLennan and Patricia MacNeil (1994). "Alcohol and Its Consequences." *Canadian Social Trends*, Catalogue 11-008-XPE: 18–23.

Sleeter, Christine E. (1991). *Empowerment Through Multicultural Education*. Albany: SUNY Press.

Slotnick, Lorne (1989). "Experiment with 'Quality.'" *The Globe and Mail*, September 12.

Small, Shirley Endicott (1985). "Why Husband-Beating is a Red Herring." Pp. 160–164 in Deborah Sinclair (ed.), *Understanding Wife Assault: A Training Manual for Counsellors and Advocates*. Appendix A. Toronto: Ministry of Community and Social Services, Family Violence Program.

Smart, Carol (1976). *Women, Crime and Criminology: A Feminist Critique*. London: Routledge and Kegan Paul.

Smart, Carol (1984). *The Ties That Bind: Law, Marriage and the Reproduction of Patriarchal Relations*. London: Routledge and Kegan Paul.

Smith, Elizabeth A. (1989). "Butches, Femmes and Feminists: The Politics of Lesbian Sexuality." *NWSA Journal*, Spring, 1(3): 398–421.

Sniderman, David et al. (1993). "Psychological and Cultural Foundations of Prejudice: The Case of Anti-Semitism in Quebec."

Canadian Review of Sociology and Anthropology 30(2): 242–267.

Solomon, R.R. and M. Green (1988). "The First Century: The History of Non-Medical Opiate Use and Control Policies in Canada, 1870–1970." In J.C. Blackwell and P.G. Erickson (eds.), *Illicit Drugs in Canada: A Risky Business*. Scarborough: Nelson.

Solomon, Robert and Lisa Constantine (1991). "The 'Miami Vice' View of Drugs: Identifying Canada's Real Drug Problems: Alcohol and Tobacco." Pp. 81–100 in Douglas J. McCready (ed.), *Health Futures: Alcohol and Drugs*. Waterloo, Ontario: Interdisciplinary Research Committee.

Solomos, John and Les Black (1996). *Racism and Society*. London: Macmillan.

Sontag, S. (1972). "The Double Standard of Aging." *Saturday Review*, September 23: 28–29.

Southerst, John (1994). "Now Everyone Can be a Boss." *Canadian Business*, May: 48–50.

Spade, Joan Z. and Carole A. Reese (1991). "We've Come a Long Way, Maybe: College Students' Plans for Work and Family." *Sex Roles* 21(5/6): 309–321.

Spallone, Patricia (1989). *Beyond Conception: The New Politics of Reproduction*. Granby, MA.: Bergin and Garvey Publishers.

Spector, Malcolm and John I. Kitsuse (1987). *Constructing Social Problems*, 2nd edition. Menlo Park, CA: Cummins.

Sperling, Susan (1988). *Animal Liberators: Research and Morality*. Berkeley: University of California Press.

Spoonley, Paul, David Pearson and Cluny McPherson (eds.) (1996). *Nga Patai: Racism and Ethnic Relations in Aotearoa/New Zealand*. Palmerston North: Dunmore.

Sprecher, Susan, Kathleen McKinney and Terri I. Orbuch (1987). "Has the Double

Standard Disappeared: An Experimental Test." *Social Psychology Quarterly*, March: 24–31.

St. Peter, Christine (1989). "Feminist Discourse, Infertility and Reproductive Technologies." *NWSA Journal*, Spring, 1(3): 353–367.

Stackhouse, John (1996). "Despite Progress, Woes Still Haunt Africa." *The Globe and Mail*, September 17.

Stamler, R. (1992). "Organized Crime." In R. Linden (ed.), *Criminology: A Canadian Perspective*, 2nd edition. Toronto: Holt, Rinehart and Winston.

Stasiulis, Daiva (1997). "The Political Economy of Race, Ethnicity, and Migration." Pp. 141–164 in W. Clement (ed.), *Understanding Canada: Building on the New Canadian Political Economy*. Montreal/Kingston: McGill-Queen's University Press.

Statistics Canada (1992). *Report on the Demographic Situation in Canada*. Ottawa: Minister of Industry, Science and Technology.

Statistics Canada (1996). *Marriages*. Catalogue 84-212. Ottawa: Ministry of Industry.

Stea, David and Ben Wisner (eds.) (1984). "The Fourth World: A Geography of Indigenous Struggles." *Antipodes: A Radical Journal of Geography* 16(2).

Steil, Janice M. and Karen Weltman (1991). "Marital Inequality: The Importance of Resources, Personal Attributes, and Social Norms on Career Valuing and the Allocation of Domestic Responsibilities." *Sex Roles* 24(3/4): 161–179.

Steinem, Gloria (1978). "Erotica and Pornography: A Clear and Present Difference." *Ms.*, November: 53–54, 75–76.

Steinmetz, Suzanne (1977–1978). "The Battered Husband Syndrome." *Victimology: An International Journal* 3–4: 499–509.

Stepan, Nancy (1982). *The Idea of Race in Science: Great Britain 1800–1960*. London: Macmillan.

Stets, Jan and Murray Straus (1989). "The Marriage License as a Hitting License: A Comparison of Assaults in Dating, Cohabiting and Married Couples." *Journal of Family Violence*, June, 4: 161–180.

Steward, Nicole and Augie Fleras (n.d.). "Couched in Compromise: Newspaper Coverage of the Third World in Canadian Mainstream Media." Unpublished paper.

Stewart, Jenny (1997). "Dismantling the State." *Quadrant*, April: 35–39.

Stimmel, Barry (1991). *Behavioral and Biochemical Issues in Substance Abuse*. New York: Haworth Press.

Stimpson, Catherine H. (1983). "Contemporary Women's Studies." Paper prepared for the Ford Foundation, September.

Stocking Jr., George (1968). *Race, Culture and Evolution: Essays in the History of Anthropology*. London: Collier-Macmillan.

Stoller, Robert (1985). *Observing the Erotic Imagination*. New Haven: Yale University Press.

Stoltenberg, John (1990). *Refusing to Be a Man*. New York: Meridian.

Stone, Sharon D. (1990) "Lesbian Mothers Organizing." Pp. 191–205 in Sharon D. Stone (ed.), *Lesbians in Canada*. Toronto: Between the Lines.

Stone, Sharon D. (1993). "Getting the Message Out: Feminists, the Press and Violence Against Women." *Canadian Review of Sociology and Anthropology* 30(3): 377–400.

Stossel, Scott (1997). "The Man Who Counts the Killings." *The Atlantic Monthly*, May.

Straus, Murray A. (1992). "Explaining Family Violence." Pp. 344–356 in James M. Henslin (ed.), *Marriage and Family in a Changing Society*, 4th edition. New York: Free Press.

Straus, Murray A. and Richard J. Gelles (1986). "Societal Change and Change in Family Violence from 1975 to 1985 as Revealed by Two National Surveys." *Journal of Marriage and the Family*, August, 48(4): 465–479.

Straus, Murray A. and Richard J. Gelles (eds.) (1990). *Physical Violence in American Families: Risk Factors and Adaptations to Violence in Families*. New Brunswick, NJ: Transaction.

Straus, Murray A., Richard J. Gelles and Suzanne K. Steinmetz (1980). *Behind Closed Doors: Violence in the American Family*. New York: Anchor/Doubleday.

Strauss, Marina (1997). "TV Violence Warnings Tune Teens into Ads." *The Globe and Mail*, May 1.

Strike, Carol (1991). "AIDS Into The 1990s." *Canadian Social Trends*, Winter: 22–24.

Strossen, Nadine (1995). *Defending Pornography*. New York: Scribner.

Sullivan, Terrence (1992). *Sexual Abuse and the Rights of Children: Reforming Canadian Law*. Toronto: University of Toronto Press.

Sutherland, Edwin (1940). *White Collar Crime*. New York: Dryden.

Swan, Neil and John Serjak (1993). "Analysing Regional Disparities." Pp. 430–448 in James Curtis et al. (eds.), *Social Inequality in Canada*, 2nd edition. Scarborough: Prentice Hall.

Switzer, Maurice (1997). "Indians are Not Red. They're Invisible." *Media*, Spring: 21–22.

Swyngedouw, Erik (1996). "Producing Futures: Global Finance as a Geographical Project." Pp. 135–163 in P.W. Daniels and W.F. Lever (eds.), *The Global Economy in Transition*. Harlow Essex: Addison Wesley Longman.

Symes, Marti (1994). "Why Workers Must Move From Being Sheep to Survivalists." *The Globe and Mail*, February 22.

Szasz, Thomas (1992). *Our Right To Drugs: The Case for a Free Market*. New York: Praeger.

Szekeley, Eva (1988a). *Never Too Thin*. Toronto: The Women's Press.

Szekeley, Eva (1988b). "Reflections on the Body in the 'Anorexia' Discourse." *RFR/DRF* 17(4): 8–17.

Tabakoff, Boris and Paula L. Hoffman (1988). "A Neurobiological Theory of Alcoholism." Pp. 29–61 in C. Douglas Chaudron and D. Adrian Wilkinson (eds.), *op. cit.*

Tangri, S.S. and M. Schwartz (1967). "Delinquency and the Self-Concept Variable." *Journal of Criminal Law, Criminology and Police Science* 58: 182–190.

Tannahill, Reay (1980). *Sex in History*. London: Hamish Hamilton.

Taras, David (1991). *The Newsmakers. The Media's Influence on Canadian Politics*. Scarborough: Nelson.

Tarter, Ralph E., Arthur I. Alterman and Kathleen L. Edwards (1988). "Neurobehavioral Theory of Alcoholism Etiology." Pp. 73–102 in C. Douglas Chaudron and D. Adrian Wilkinson (eds.), *op. cit.*

Tate, Eugene D. and Kathleen McConnell (1991). "The Mass Media and Violence." Pp. 299–321 in Benjamin Singer (ed.), *Communications in Canadian Society*. Scarborough: Nelson.

Tator, Carol (1997). "Anti-Racism Body Strengthened Social Fabric." *The Toronto Star*, April 25.

Tavris, C. (1992). *The Mismeasure of Women*. New York: Simon and Schuster.

Taylor, Charles (1993). *Reconsidering the Solitudes. Essays in Canadian Federalism and Nationalism*. Montreal/Kingston: McGill-Queen's University Press.

Taylor, Ian, Paul Walton and Jock Young (1975). *Critical Criminology*. London: Routledge and Kegan Paul.

Taylor, J.G. Rattray (1956). *Sex In History*. London: Thames and Hudson.

Tehranian, Majid (1996). "Communication and Conflict." *Media Development* XLIII(4): 3–5.

Tepper, Elliot (1988). *Changing Canada: The Institutional Response to Polyethnicity. The Review of Demography and Its Implications for Economic and Social Policy*. Ottawa: Carleton University.

Tepperman, Lorne and Michael Rosenberg (1991). *Macro/Micro. A Brief Introduction to Sociology*. Scarborough: Prentice Hall.

Thomas, Lyn (1995). "In Love with Inspector Morse." *Feminist Review* 51: 1–25.

Thompson, John Herd (1996). "Editorial: The Future of North America(n Studies)? *The American Review of Canadian Studies*, Summer: 169–176.

Thorne, Barrie (1982). *Feminist Rethinking of the Family: An Overview*. New York: Longman.

Thorne-Finch, Ron (1993). *Ending The Silence: The Origins and Treatment of Male Violence Against Women*. Toronto: University of Toronto Press.

Tobias, John L. (1976). "Protection, Civilization, and Assimilation. An Outline History of Canada's Indian Policy." *Western Canadian Journal of Anthropology* 6(2): 13–30.

Toch, H. and K. Adams (1989). *The Disturbed Violent Offender*. London: Yale University Press.

Tomovich, V.A. and D.J. Loree (1989). "In Search of New Directions: Policing in Niagara Region." *Canadian Police College Journal* 13(1): 29–54.

Tong, Rosemarie (1989). *Feminist Theory: A Comprehensive Introduction*. Boulder: Westview Press.

The Toronto Star (1993). "'Tele-sharks' feed on the gullible." August 15: A1.

The Toronto Star (1993). "Pushing the Crime Button." August 15: B1.

The Toronto Star (1993). "Politicians play law-and-order card." August 15: B5.

The Toronto Star (1996). "Divisive bill on gay rights is passed: 28 Liberals go against party line in free vote." May 10: A1.

The Toronto Star (1996). "Alternate families outweight traditional." June 20: A2.

The Toronto Star (1997). "Olson hearing new trial for families." August 11: A1, A4.

The Toronto Star (1997). "Province blamed for VLT addiction." December 14, A20.

Townson, Monica. (1995) *Women's Financial Futures: Mid-Life Prospects for A Secure Retirement*. Ottawa: Canadian Advisory Council on the Status of Women.

Trasov, I. (1962). "History of the Opium and Narcotic Drug Legislation in Canada." *Criminal Law Quarterly* 4: 274.

Trevethan, Shelly and Tajeshwer Samagh (1993). "Gender Differences Among Violent Crime Victims." *Juristat*, Winter, 12.

Troyna, Barry (1984). "Media and Race Relations." Pp. 157–160 in E. Ellis Cashmore (ed.), *Dictionary of Race and Ethnic Relations*. London: Routledge and Kegan Paul.

Turner, Richard (1997). "The Ad Game." *Newsweek*, January 20.

Turow, Joseph (1992). *Media Style in Society. Understanding Initiatives/Strategies/Power*. White Plains, NY: Longman.

Ungerleider, Charles (1997). "Multiculturalism." Letter to *The Globe and Mail*, April 9.

Unland, Karen (1996). "Documentary Predicted Ethnic Violence in Zaire." *The Globe and Mail*, November 12.

Valaskakis, Kimon (1990). *Canada in the Nineties. Meltdown or Renaissance?* Montreal: Gamma Institute Press.

Valaskakis, Kimon (1992). "A Prescription for Canada, Inc." *The Globe and Mail*, October 31.

Valette, B. (1988). *A Parent's Guide To Eating Disorders*. New York: Walker.

Vallee, Frank G. (1981). "The Sociology of John Porter: Ethnicity as Anachronism." *Canadian Review of Sociology and Anthropology* 18(5): 46–58.

Valpy, Michael (1993). "Tory View of Poverty Not Progressive." *The Globe and Mail*, June 9.

Vancouver Sun (1993). "Lesbian couple who want child denied sperm." July 22: A1.

Vanderbilt, H. (1992). "Incest." *Lear's*, February: 49–77.

Vasta, Ellie and Stephen Castles (1996). *The Teeth are Smiling. the Persistance of Racism in a Multicultural Australia*. Sydney: Allen and Unwin.

Vaugh, Diane (1985). "Uncoupling: The social construction of divorce." Pp 429–439 in James M. Heslin (ed.), *Marriage and Family in a Changing Society*, 2nd edition. New York: Free Press.

Vienneau, David (1997). "Fear and Shattered Dreams Plague Jobs, Task Force Study Says." *The Toronto Star*, July 9.

Villeneuve, Paul J. and Howard I. Morrison (1995). "Trends In Mortality from Smoking-Related Cancers 1950 to 1991." *Canadian Social Trends*, Winter, 39: 8-11.

Vivian, John (1997). *The Media of Mass Communication*. Needham Heights, Mass: Allyn and Bacon.

Vold, George (1958). *Theoretical Criminology*. New York: Oxford University Press.

Vold, George B. and Thomas J. Bernard (1986). *Theoretical Criminology*, 3rd edition. New York: Oxford University Press.

Wachtel, S.S. (1979). "H-Y Antigen and Sexual Development." Pp. 271–277 in H. Vakket and I. Porter (eds.), *Genetic Mechanisms of Sexual Development*. New York: Academic Press.

Waldram, James B. (1994). "Canada's 'Indian Problem' and the Indian's 'Canada Problem.'" Pp. 53–71 in L. Samuelson (ed.), *Power and Resistance*.

Walker, Christopher (1987). *The Victorian Community Police Station: An Exercise in Innovation*. Ottawa: Canadian Police College.

Walkom, Thomas (1997). "Canadians Turn Against Cuts." *The Toronto Star*, April 5.

Wallace, Iain and Rob Shields (1997). "Contested Terrains: Social Spaces and the Canadian Environment." Pp. 386–401 in W. Clement (ed.), *Understanding Canada*. Montreal/Kingston: McGill-Queen's University Press.

Ward, Sally K., Kathy Chapman, Ellen Cohn, Susan White, and Kirk Williams (1991). "Acquaintance Rape and the College Social Scene." *Family Relations* 40: 65–71.

Watkins, Mel (1997). "Canadian Capitalism in Transition." Pp. 19–42 in W. Clement (ed.), *Understanding Canada*. Montreal/Kingston: McGill-Queen's University Press.

Watson, William (1996). "In Redefining Poverty, Quebec is Better Off." *The Toronto Star,* June 29.

Watts, Thomas (1997). "Warning: Internet overuse can be hazardous." *The Toronto Star*, August 23, M1.

Weaver, Sally M. (1984). "Struggles of the Nation-State to Define Aboriginal Ethnicity: Canada and Australia." Pp. 182–210 in G. Gold (ed.), *Minorities & Mother Country Imagery*. Institute of Social and Economic Research Number 13. St. John's: Memorial University Press.

Webber, Jeremy (1994). *Reimaging Canada. Language, Culture, Community, and the*

Canadian Constitution. Montreal/Kingston: McGill-Queen's University Press.

Weber, Max (1947). *The Theory of Social and Economic Organization*. Translated by A.M. Henderson and Talcott Parsons. New York: Oxford University Press.

Wein, Fred (1993). "Regional Inequality: Explanations and Policy Issues." Pp. 449–469 in James Curtis et al. (eds.), *Social Inequality in Canada*. 2nd edition. Scarborough: Prentice Hall.

Weis, K. and S. Borges (1973). "Victimology and Rape: The Case of the Legitimate Victim." *Issues in Criminology* 8(2): 71–115.

Wells, J.A. (1982). *A Herstory of Prostitution in Western Europe*. Berkeley: Shameless Hussy.

Werth, Barry (1993). "The Terminator." *GQ*, July: 126–134.

West, Shearer (1996). *The Victorians and Race*. Aldershot, UK: Scolar Press.

Westoff, Charles F. (1983). "Fertility Decline in the West: Causes and Prospects." *Population and Development Review* 9(1): 99–104.

Weston, Kath (1991). *Families We Choose: Lesbians, Gays, Kinship*. New York: Columbia University Press.

Whitaker, Reg (1996). "Sovereign Division: Quebec's Nationalism Between Liberalism and Ethnicity." Pp. 73–88 in J. Littleton (ed.), *Clash of Identities*. Scarborough: Prentice Hall.

White, Patrick (1997). "Linguistic Vigilantes to Boost Québecois." *Otago Daily Times*, June 11.

Wigmore, J.H. (1940) *A Treatise on the Anglo-American System of Evidence in Trials at Common Law*, 3rd edition, volume III. London: Boxton, Little Brown.

Wilcox, Leonard (1996). "Saatchi Rap: The Worlding of America and Racist Ideology in New Zealand." *Continuum* 10(1): 121–135.

Williams, C.J. and M.S. Weinberg (1971). *Homosexuals and the Military: A Study of Less Than Honourable Discharge*. New York: Harper and Ross.

Williams, Joan C. (1991). "Deconstructing Gender." Pp. 95–123 in Katharine T. Bartlett and Rosanne Kennedy (eds.), *Feminist Legal Theory: Readings in Law and Gender*. San Francisco: Westview.

Williams, John E. and Deborah B. Best (1990). *Measuring Sex Stereotypes: A Thirty Nation Study*, 2nd edition. Beverly Hills: Sage.

Williams, Karen (1995). "A Good Mother." Pp 98–110 in Katherine Arnup (ed.), *Lesbian Parenting: Living with Pride and Prejudice*. Charlottetown: gynergy books.

Williamson, Judith (1978). *Decoding Advertisements: Ideology and Meaning in Advertising*. London: Marion Boyars.

Williamson, Linda (1997). "Who's afraid of Neitzsche with mascara? As a monster shock rocker Marilyn Manson is vastly over-rated." *Toronto Sun*, July 29: 12.

Wilson, E.O. (1975). *Sociobiology*. Cambridge, MA: Harvard University Press.

Wilson, James Q. and George L. Kelling (1989). "Making Neighbourhoods Safe." *The Atlantic Monthly*, February: 46–52.

Wilson, Margo and Martin Daly (1994). "Spousal Homicide." *Juristat*, March, 14(8). Ottawa: Ministry of Industry, Science and Technology.

Wilson, S.J. (1986). *Women, the Family and the Economy*. 2nd edition. Toronto: McGraw-Hill Ryerson.

Wilson, S.J. (1996). *Women, Families & Work*, 4th edition. Toronto: McGraw-Hill Ryerson.

Wilson, Susan J. (1991). *Women, Families and Work*, 3rd edition. Toronto: McGraw-Hill Ryerson.

Winter, Bronwyn (1994). "Women, the Law, and Cultural Relativism in France: The Case of Excision." *Signs* 19(4): 939–971.

Winter, James (1997). *Democracy's Oxygen. How Corporations Control the News.* Montreal: Black Rose Books.

Winzer, Margaret (1993). *Children With Exceptionalities: A Canadian Perspective.* Scarborough: Prentice Hall.

Wolf, Naomi (1991). *The Beauty Myth.* Toronto: Random House.

Wong, Jan (1997). "Preston Manning Reforms from Geek to Sleek." *The Globe and Mail,* May 22.

Woodley, Brian (1997). "A Blueprint with Blots." *The Weekend Australian,* March 3–4.

Worden, Alissa Pollitz (1993). "The Attitudes of Women and Men in Policing: Testing Conventional and Contemporary Wisdom." *Criminology* 31(2): 203–241.

Wotherspoon, Terry and Vic Satzewich (1993). *First Nations. Race, Class, and Gender Relations.* Scarborough: Nelson.

Wrong, Dennis (1992). "Why Do Poorer Get Poorer." *The New York Times Book Review,* April 30.

Yesalis, Charles E. (ed.) (1993). *Anabolic Steroids In Sport And Exercise.* Champaign, IL: Human Kinetics Publishers.

Yogis, John A., Randall R. Duplak and J. Royden Trainor (1996). *Sexual Orientation and Canadian Law: An Assessment of the Law Affecting Lesbian and Gay Persons.* Toronto: Emond Montgomery Publications Limited.

Zeitlin, Irving M. and Robert J. Brym (1991). *The Social Conditions of Humanity,* Canadian edition. Toronto: Oxford University Press.

Index

Abbott, P. 9, 15, 69, 70, 192, 251, 267, 268, 276
Abel, S. 294, 302, 303
Abella, I. 211
Abercrombie, N. 286, 291
Aboriginal peoples xv, xvi, 2, 238–247
  aboriginal rights 245–246
  and alcohol 54
  and capitalism 241
  and crime 109–110, 116–118
  the Department of Indian Affairs 242
  as peoples 238–239
  as social problem 240–-243
  and the environment 21–22, 402–404
  political responses 239
  self-determination 244–245
  socioeconomic status 240–241
  solution to problems 243–247
  youth 240
Aboriginal policy 243–247
Aboriginal rights 243–247
  definition of 245–246
  inherent 243–247
Abortion (*see also* Reproduction) 13, 80–84, 104
  abortion pill 82
  age of women 81–82
  fetal rights 80–81
  parental rights 80–81
  rates of 81–82
Abraham, S. 45
Absolute liability 106
Abu-Laban, Y. 226
Abuse
  of children xiii, 13, 18–19, 256–257
  of the elderly 102, 259
  of women, 2, 4, 9-10, 12–13, 52, 273–174, 258–261
  within families xvi, 4–5, 38, 116, 206, 250, 256–261, 277, 280, 282
Accomodating diversity
  (*see* Managing diversity)
Acton, W. 68–69
Actus reus 105
Addiction Research Foundation 39
Addiction xv, 28–61
  characteristics of 29
  definition of 29
  economic costs of 38–39
  effects on personal/social well-being 39–43
  enslavement hypothesis 53
  food addictions 29, 34, 45, 49–50, 53, 56, 192
  medical or disease model of 46–51
  sexual addictions 55–57
  structuration theory of 55–57
  tobacco 35-36, 40, 106–107, 276
  twelve-step programs 57–60
Adler, F. 116

Advertising (*see also* Mass media) 311–316
  and women 315–316
  Benetton 313–314
  logic behind 312–313
  problems with 315–316
Affirmative action (*see* Employment equity)
Africa 394–395
African-Canadians 207, 210–211
Agency
  vs structure 134
Agocs, C. 149–150, 229
Ahenakew, D. 246
AIDS 10, 34, 42-43, 66, 84–85, 253, 264, 271–272
Akyeampong, E.B. 197
Albert, T. 74
Alcohol 5–7, 28, 30, 32, 35, 38–41, 44–47
Alcoholics Anonymous 58–60
Alfred, G. 243
Allen, C.L. 79
Allen, G. 10
Allgeier, E.R. 65
Alterman, A.I. 46
Alternative measures 114
Ambert, A.M. 263, 278, 282
Anderson, C. 197
Androcentrism 15, 92, 178–179
Anti-racism (*see also* Race, Ethnicity) 164-165, 223–224
Anti-semitism 211
Apartheid 8
Apple, M. 292
Armstrong, L. 257
Armstrong, P. 262
Arnup, K. 252
Asbury, K. 368
Asch, A. 201
Ascribed status (*see also* Castes) 142
Assimilation
  and Aboriginal peoples 240–243
Atkinson, J. 287
Atlantic Canada (*see also* Regions) 153–157
Attali, J. 376, 394
Attitudes
  vs behaviour 218

Backman, C.W. 173
Badgley, R. 98, 104, 257
Baker, M. 254, 263, 273
Bala, N. 113
Balakrishnan, T.R. 78
Baldwin, W. 77
Bangladesh 396
Banner, L. 265
Baranek, P. 120
Barash, D.P. 178
Barile, M. 201
Barlow, J.P. 329
Barlow, M. 378, 385, 393
Barnett, S. 93

Barrett, S. 141, 143, 211
Basow, S.A. 192
Bayley, D. 354, 365
Beach, F.A. 64
Beasley, M. 65
Beattie, M. 50
Becker, H. 17, 24, 54–55, 68, 124
Belensky, M. 90
Bell, N. 256
Belliveau, J. 40, 195–196
Benkov, L. 252
Benokraitis, N. 90
Bergman, B. 114
Bernard, J. 173, 262, 269
Berger, R.I. 186
Bernard, T. 13
Bernardo, P. 98, 100–101
Berry, J. 145, 210, 225
Berton, P. 322
Besch, E.L. 20
Best interests of the child 278–279
Best, D.B. 172–173
Best, J. 5, 20
Beyer, C.A. 107
Bibby, R. W. 98, 108, 318
Bienvenue, R. 242
Biesenthal, L. 98
Bilingualism 231
Bindman, S. 102
Biological determinism 135, 215–217
Biology
  and inequality 135, 137, 174–182
Birth control (*see also* Reproduction) 76–80
Birth rate 265
  illegitimacy 266–267
Bissoondath, N. 225–226, 281
Blachford, G. 271
Black, C. 301
Black, D. 176
Black, K. 33, 38
Blackwell, J.C. 53
Blaming the victim 132, 135–137
Blau, P. 363
Blauner, R. 242
Blumstein, P. 263
Bly, R. 189–190
Blythe, M. 322
Bolaria, B. Singh 136–137, 144, 217
Boldt, M. 239, 244
Borges, S. 18
Bowles. S. 163
Boyd, M. (*see also* Agocs) 181, 201, 229, 283
Boyd, N. 34–35
Boyd, S. 280
Bradshaw, J. 28
Branch plant economy (*see also* Globalization) 384–387
Brannigan, A. 104
Braroe, N.W. 54
Breastfeeding 62–64
Brecher, E.M. 265
Brenner, J. 205–206

Breton, R. 144-145, 147, 149, 399
Bridges, J.S. 89
Brinkerhoff, M. 5, 259–260
Brinkerhoff, D. 141
Brod, H. 189
Brodie, J. 152–154, 156
Brooks, G. 86
Brown, L. 397, 399
Brown, L. 370
Brym, R. 131, 153, 173, 175–176
Bufe, C. 47, 58-60
Bureaucracy xvi, 368–369
Burger King 346–348
Burke, M. 90
Burke, M.A. 197
Burskil, R. 19
Burstyn, V. 72
Bush, M.M. 258

Caldicott, H. 187
Campbell, K. 172
Campbell, M. 157–159, 338–339
Canada
   and environment 400–404
   and foreign aid 405–410
   and free trade 383–393
   and multiculturalism 1, 225–230
   and multinationals 381–383
   mismanagement of race
    relations 207–213
Canadian Advisory Council on the
   Status of Women 2
Canadian Social Trends 6–7, 30–32,
   39–41, 275, 282–283
*Canadian Uniform Crime
   Reports* 120
Cannibis 29–31, 34, 38, 42, 54–55
Capitalism 12, 16, 138–140, 144,
   149–152, 223–224, 228–229
   interventionist vs free
    market, 392–393
Capital Punishment xiii, 108, 121
Capon, N. 334
Caputi, J. 12, 186
Carrington, P. 20
Carter, C.S. 177
Castells, M. 342, 379
Castles, S. 229
Cawsey, R.A. 2
Celebrity cults xiii, 295–300
Censorship 310–311
Chamberlain, A. 31
Chambliss, W. 119
Chan, J. 366, 370
Chesler, P. 280
Child abuse xiii, 10, 18–19, 256–257,
   282
Child custody 278–280
Chisholm, R. 42, 115
Chomsky, N. 316–318
Chorn, N.H. 334
Chretien, J. 333
Christie, N. 52
Cities (see Global Problems)
Citizenship 209
Citizenship-plus (see indigenous plus)
Clark, L. 91, 181
Clark, W. 35–36, 38
Class 140-144

and mobility 144
   definition of 140–141
   reproduction of 163
   typologies of 143–144
Clayoquot Sound 402–404
Clement, W. 131, 336, 393
Cloninger, R. 46
Cloward, R.S. 45
Cohen, A. 119
Cohen, S. 70, 126
Cold War 376
Collective rights 150–152, 239,
   243–247
Colonialism 394–396
Colour-conscious 150–152
Columbo, R. 201, 255, 265
Comack, E. 93
Communism (see Marxism)
Community policing (see also
   Policing, Work, Workplace)
   349–359, 365–370
   as Total Quality 349–350
   compared to conventional
    policing 358–359
   crisis in policing 353–354
   definitions of 354–355
   principles of 355–360
Computer-mediated
   communication (see also
   Mass Media) 323–330
Conflict Perspective xv, 13, 15–16
   on addictions 51–53
   on crime 123–124
   on family 267–268
   on inequality 133, 139–140
   on sexuality 71–73
Conflict Tactics Scale 258
Constantine, L. 35, 39
Constitution Act 232
Contested sites
   and education 168
   and multiculturalism 260
   and the workplace 335
Contraception 76–80, 272
Conway, J. 18–19, 78, 80, 82, 251,
   254, 266, 274, 276, 280
Cook, S.L. 90
Corcoran, T. 152–153, 390
Corporal punishment 18–19
Corporate culture (see also
   Workplace, Formal
   organizations) 348–349
Corporate subculture (see
   Organizational subculture)
Cote, G. 38
Cottle, C.E. 186
Coyne, A. 157
Cox, K. 446
Crane, D. 374, 377, 382–383
Crawford, T. 79
Cregheur, A. 191
Crime xv, 2, 16
   age 111–115
   correlates of crime 111–116
   dark figure of 120–121
   fear of crime 97–99, 102–103
   false convictions 120–121
   gender 110, 114–116, 258
   labelling theory 125

media depiction 99–102, 109–111
   maturational reform 112–113
   official statistics 120–121
   police 125
   race 109–110, 116–118
   sanctions 104, 107–109, 111,
    114–115, 126–127
   sex-role socialization thesis
    115–116
   socioeconomic status 118–120
   victimless 104–105
   white-collar 99, 120, 123–124
Criminal conversation 65
Criminal justice system
   racism in 109–111, 116–118
   and social class 118–120
Crompton, S. 197, 203
Cryderman, B. 145, 211
Crude marriage rate 255
Cuff, J.H. 321
Culpepper, R. 405
Culture
   and inequality 136–137
   and organizations 333–335,
    360–361
Cummins, J. 318
Curran, J. 291
Currie, D. 84
Curtis, J. 134, 144, 146
Cyberspace 327–329

D'Souza, D. 213
Daigle, C. 82
Daisley, B. 9
Daly, M. 259
Dangerous offenders 111
Daniels, P. 281
Darder, A. 163
Darling, C.A. 77
Dartana, A. 121
David, M. 173
Davis, K. 70–71
De-regulation (see Globalization)
Decarceration 126
Decolonization 243-247
DeKeseredy, W. 4, 90, 258
Dennis, W. 85
Department of Indian Affairs 209
Dependency theory, (see also Global
   Problems) 394–396
Dershowitz, A. 122
Desroches, F.J. 366
Developing World (see also Third
   World) 375, 394–410
Devereaux, M.S. 191
Diana, Princess of Wales 295–300
Disabilities (see Individuals with
   disabilities)
Discrimination xvi, 1, 2, 116–118,
   217–223
Divorce (see also Feminization of
   Poverty)
   changes in the laws of 272, 276–277
   custody and 278–280
   feminization of poverty 199–206
   rate of 255–256
   and remarriage 255–256
Dobash, R. 259–260
Dobash, R.E. 259–260

Doherty, W. 190
Doleschal, E. 119
Doli incapax 113
Double standard of aging 260
Double standard of sexual morality
76–78
Douglas, M. 51
Dowling, C. 222
Downes, D. 99, 124
Drache, D. 383–386
Drohan, M. 408
Drug abuse (*see also* Alcohol;
Tobacco)
alcohol 5–7, 28, 30, 32, 35, 38–41,
44–47, 104
and AIDS 42–43
and crime 33–35, 41–42, 104–107
and laws 32, 34–35, 51–52,
104–107, 126
and sports 32
continuum of 49–50
depressants 33
economic costs 38–39
hallucinogens 33
sedatives 33
social cost of 42–43, 45–46
stages of 53–54
steroids 32
Dua, E. 188
Duplak, R.A. 253, 279
Durkheim, E. 14, 17, 44, 118
Dworkin, A. 12, 72
Dyck, N. 239
Dyer, G. 375

Eamon, R. 316
Eating disorders 34–35, 45, 49, 50,
53, 56, 192
Echo boom 255
Echols, A. 187
Economic Council of Canada
152–153
Education xiii, 161–168
and class 163
and gender 140, 165, 171, 192–194
and mobility 163
business and 168
democratization and 166–167
in crisis 163–168
postsecondary 167–168
process-oriented 164–166
Edwards, K.I. 46
Edwards, S. 76, 88, 181
Egalitarian 140–141
Egan, J. 57
Ehrenreich, B. 76, 198, 205
Ehrhardt, A.E. 176–177
Eichler, M. 178, 183, 264, 266
Eidham, H. 238
Eitzen, D.S. 5, 136, 191
Electronic alienation 325–326
Eliany, M. 29, 30, 41
Elias, R. 8, 12, 101–103
Elliot, P. 188
Elliott, J.L. 79
Ellul, J. 306
Employment equity 11, 151–152
and firefighters 371
and pay equity 368

assumptions 366–368
criticism of 369–371
definition of 366
restrictions 368–369
Enemy blaming 9–10
Engels, H. 108
English, D. 76, 198
Enlightened Propoganda (*see also*
Propoganda; Mass Media)
Entitlements 151–152
Environment (*see also* Global
Problems) 2, 400–404
Clayoquot Sound 402–404
Epstein, C.F. 174
Equal Employment Opportunities
Commission (EEOC) vs.
Sears 184
Equality (*see also* Employment
equity, Managing diversity)
150–152
and aboriginal peoples 275
and multiculturalism 259–260
of opportunity 196
substantive vs formal 178, 195–196,
257–258, 333, 372–373
types of 195
Equalization payments 153
Equity 149–152
Ericson, R. 120
Erickson, P.G. 53
Erwin, J. 101
Essed, P. 224
Esses, V. 111
Estrich, S. 91
Ethnic Nationalism 375, 398–399
Ethnic stratification (*see*
Stratification) 144–148
Ethnicity xv, 207–248
and aboriginality 238–247
and global conflicts 398–399
and inequality 145–148
and multiculturalism 225–230
and Quebec 230–238
Eugenics 9
Evans, J. 120

Faint hope clause xiii, 108–109
False consciousness 139
Faludi, S. 80, 265
Families xvi, 285–327
abuse in 2, 4, 9, 10, 12–13, 38,
52–53, 87, 98, 173–174, 206,
250, 256–261, 280, 282
blended 282–283, 255–256
changing demographics of 254–256
child custody 278–280
common-law 255, 280–281
defining 250–256
dual-earner 272–274
essential functions of 264, 267
evolving 74, 250–256, 268–272
homosexual 74, 250, 252–254, 263,
272, 279
illegitimacy 74–78, 90, 276
nuclear 265–267
one-parent 77–78, 90, 250, 253,
274–278
power in 261–264
single-provider 250, 274–278

transitional 281–282
Fast foods 346–348
Fattah, E. 52–53, 101–102
Fear of crime xv-xvi, 101–102
Fedorowycz, O. 38
Fekete, J. 88, 92
Femicide 12
Feminism xvi, 5, 16, 20, 172
anti-feminist feminism 188–189
critiques of sociology 15, 182
cultural feminism 187
eco-feminism 187
feminism of difference 184–185
integrative feminism 187–188
liberal feminism 183–185
Marxist feminism 185
radical feminism 12, 186
socialist feminism 186, 205–206
Feminization of poverty xvi, xvii, 23,
171, 199–206, 250, 254–255,
275–276
Ferree, M. 262
Fetal Alcohol Effect (FAE) 5–7
Fetal Alcohol Syndrome (FAS) 5–7,
93
Fine, G.A. 3
Fine, M. 201
Finkelhor, D. 89–90, 282
First Nations (*see* Aboriginal peoples)
Fischhoff, B. 127
Fiske, J. 286, 291
Fitzgerald, K.W. 46
Fleiss, W. 181
Focal concerns 119
Fogel, A.F. 65
Folk devils 78
Food Banks 130, 158
Ford, C.S. 64
Foreign aid and development xvi,
405–410
CIDA 407, 409–410
crisis in 405–406
criticism of 407–408
logic behind 406–407
sustainable development 410
Formal organizations (*see also*
Culture; Work; Workplace)
332–371
and change 360–370
and uncertainty 333–337
as contested sites 337
Forward, S. 256
Francis, D. 391
Frank, J. 43, 84–85
Fraser, S. 257
Free Trade 388
FTA 387–393
GATT 387
NAFTA 388–390
vs protectionism 391–392
Freeman, G. 175
French-English Relations (*see also*
Quebec) 230–238
French, K. 101
French, M. 7–8, 83, 271
Freud, S.
stages of psychosexual
development 179–180
criticisms of 180–182

Frideres, J. 240
Friedman, M. 53
Friendly parent rule 277
Frieze, I.H. 115, 127
Frustration-aggression theory 116
Functionalist perspective xv, 13–15,
    138–139
  critiques of 15
  on addiction 43–46
  on crime 14, 122–123
  on the family 264–267
  on gender 182
  on sexuality 70–71
Functions
  latent 14, 47
  manifest 14

Gabor, T. 45, 109–110, 121, 124
Gaffield, C. 269
Gagnon, J. 74
Gairdner, W. 69, 79, 175, 251,
    253–254
Galarneau, D. 204–205
Gaskell, J. 193
Gaudette, L. 40
Gay, K. 360
Gebhard, P.H. 64
Gelder, L. 29
Gelles, R. 4, 259–260
Gender xv, xvi
  and biology 174–182
  and education 140, 171, 192–194
  and family 173–174, 191–192,
    251, 262–268, 273
  and language 172
  and work xvi, 171, 182–183, 185,
    194–199, 262–263, 273
  and violence, xvii, 3, 4, 173–174
  Freudian theory on 179–182
  feminist theories of 182–188
  and mass media 172
  perspectives on 174–176
  private troubles or public issues
    190, 199–206, 264–268
  socialization 191–194
  sociobiology 176–192
  stereotypes 172–173, 190, 278–279
Genocide 4
Gerbner, G. 305
Ghalam, N.Z. 194–197
Gherson, G. 132, 156
Gibbs, J.R. 17
Giddens, A. 29, 55–57
Gilder, G. 253
Gillespie, M. 134–135, 137, 141, 158,
    290, 400
Gilligan, C. 184
Gillmor, D. 362
Giroux, H. 163, 166, 307
Glass ceiling 333
Global problems 376–378, 394–410
  and Africa 394–395
  and Developing World 395–396
  environment xiv, xvi, 400–404
  ethnicity 399–400
  foreign aid 405–410
  overpopulation xvi, 397
  poverty 398–399
  urbanization 375, 397–398

Globalization xvi, 167, 374–411
  and Canada 377-378, 383–393
  and ethnicity 377–378
  and foreign aid xvi, 405–410
  and free trade 387–393
  and multinationals 381–383
  definition of 379–380
  state vs. market 384–385
Goar, C. 378
Goddard, J. 2, 117
Goffman, E. 54
Goldberg, S. 174
Goldscheider, C. 265
Goldscheider, F. 265
Gomme, I. 42, 53, 99, 105, 119
Goode, W. 264
Gordon, L. 53
Gordon, M. 76
Gottlieb, B. 251, 283
Gould, S. 174
Goyder, J. 174
Grab, E. 135, 141, 143
Grasmick, H. 19
Gray, H. 286
Green, M. 32, 52
Green, R. 75
Greenaugh, W.T. 177
Greenberg, D. 112-113
Greenglass, E. 180
Greenspon, E. 157
Greenwald, H. 69
Griesman, H.C. 123
Griffiths, C. 116, 118
Grindstaff, C. 266
Groupthink 121
Gwyn, R. 336, 338–339

Hacker, S. 78, 85
Hackler, J. 112
Hagan, J. 123
Hale, S. 363
Halleck, S. 9
Hamilton, V. 38
Hamner, J. 271
Harassment (*see* Discrimination)
Harman, L. 199
Hartnagel, T. 111–112, 115,
    117–118, 199
Hate literature 1
Hawkins, R. 173
Heath, D.B. 54
Hegemony 16
Helmes-Hayes, R., 143, 147
Henry, F. 145, 147
Herman, J. 282
Heroin 30–31, 33, 35, 39–40, 43
Herrnstein, R. 135
Herstory 268
Hess, E. 76
Hiller, H. 131, 144, 152, 154, 386
Hills, S. 38
Himelfarb, A. 120
Hinch, R. 258
Hindsight effect 127
Hobbes, T. 49
Hochschild, A. 196, 263
Hodgins, S. 38
Hofferth, S.L. 77
Hoffman, P.L. 46

Hollander, N. 199
Hollinger Inc. 301
Homolka, K. 100–101, 110
Homosexuality 10, 46, 65–67, 74–76,
    103–104, 250, 252–253, 263,
    270–271, 277, 279
Hookham, L. 91
Hotaling, G.T. 257
Hughes, J. 83
Human resources model (*see also*
    Formal organizations) xvi
  characteristics of 348–349
  evaluation of 355
Hummel, R. 363
Humphreys L. 74
Hurtig, M. 387
Husband-battering 4
Huston, A.C. 192

Ideology 9
  of motherhood 276
Ignatieff, M. 376, 399
Illegitimacy 74–75, 77–78, 90, 276
Illich, I. 167
Immigration 18, 209
Income (*see also* Class) 167, 184,
    187, 190
  by ethnic origin 174–175
  in the USA 187–189
India 163–166
"Indian" Problem (*see also*
    Aboriginal peoples) 238–247
  solutions to 243–247
Indigenous peoples (*see* Aboriginal
    peoples)
Indigenous Plus 243–244
Individuals with disabilities 201,
    256, 259
  and workplace 332
Inequality, xv–xvi, 129–170
  and Aboriginal peoples 131
  and class 140–144
  and education 161–168
  and equality 150–152
  and gender 152
  and poverty xvi, 156–161
  and race and ethnicity 131,
    144–152
  and region 152–156
  definition of 133–135
  sociological perspectives 134–137
  theories of 138–140
Infanticide 111–112
Inherent rights (*see also* Aboriginal
    rights, Aboriginal peoples)
    238–239, 243–247
Innes, H. 185
Institution (*see* Work; Workplace)
Institution-blaming 11–12
Institutional accommodation
    335–336, 360–364
Interactionist perspective xv, 16–17
  on addictions 59–63
  on crime 124–125
  on sexuality 73–75
Internal colonialism 273
Internet (*see also* Mass Media)
    327–328
  a new world order 329

Jacobs, G. 76
Jackson, C. 263, 267
Jackson, D. 376, 405
Jackson, E. 104
Jackson, M. 111, 252
Jacobson, B. 53, 80
Jaffe, P. 62, 89
Jamieson, R. 227
Janoff-Bulman, R. 115, 127
Janson, C.G. 38
Japan 375
Japanese-Canadians 211
Jaworsky, J. 228
Jellinek's Disease 46
Jellinek, E.M. 46
Jhally, S. 313
Job segmentation 23, 194–198, 262
Job-sharing 198
Johnson, B. 32
Johnson, H. 38–39, 42, 101, 125
Johnson, V. 68
Jones, A. 197
Juristic person 107
Juvenile Delinquency Act 113

Kahn, J.R. 77
Kallen, D.J. 77
Kameny, F. 74
Kamin, L. 179
Kaminer, W. 50, 53
Kanter, R.M. 182
Kaplan, L. 72–73
Kaplan, R. 394
Keen, S. 190
Kelling, G. 357
Kelly, L. 89
Kelsey, J. 378, 395, 392
Kennedy, L. 110
Kershaw, A. 111, 117
Ketcham, K. 100
Keynsian Economics 340
Kibbutz 140
"Killer cards" 99
Kimpel, M. 19
King, M. L. 3
Kinsey, A.C. 65–66, 73
Kirkham, G.L. 74
Kitsuse, J.I. 5, 20
Klapmuts, N. 119
Kline, M. 188
Koenig, D. 38, 101
Kolodny, R. 68
Kong, R. 98, 102, 125–126
Koss, M.P. 89–90
Krahn, H. 338
Krotki, K. 78
Ku Klux Klan 8, 211
Kunz, J.L. 319

Laab, J. 362
Labelling theory 17, 124–126
Lamphear, G. 3
LaPierre-Adamcyk, E. 78
LaPrairie, C. 117–118
Lasch, C. 256
Lashinger, J. 98
Lasovitch, M. 111, 117
Laux, J. 380
Laver, R. 386

Law of comparative advantage (*see
    also* Globalization) 380
Law of inertia 14
Lawrence, M. 53
Laws, J.L. 76, 191
Laxer, J. 380, 384, 389
Leach, E. 251
Lebsock, S. 184
Lees, S. 88
Leighton, B. 366
Leiss, W. 37
Lesbianism (*see* Homosexuality)
Lester, D. 46
Levitt, C. 147, 209
Lewis, D. 91, 181
Lewis, M. 191
Lewis, O. 136
Lewycky, L. 209
Li, P. 211
Liazos, A. 64
Liberalism 149–152
Life expectancy gap 265
Little Bear, L. 244
Llewellyn-Jones, D. 45
Lloyd, S. 90
Lochhead, C. 275
Loftus, E. 100
Logan, R. 195–196
London, J. 196, 273
Long, D.A. 240
Lopata, H.Z. 182
Lorenz, K. 116
Lowe, G. 203
Lowman, J. 71, 123, 126
Lubicon Cree 1–2
Lucas, S. 188
Lundy, C. 53
Lundy, K. 144
Lunney, G.S. 192
Lupri, E. 5, 259–260
Lupul, M. 228
Lurie, N.O. 54
Luxton, M. 276

MacDonald, G. 259
MacKenzie, B. 81
Mackie, M. 83, 173, 182, 193, 198,
    254, 267, 271–272
MacKinnon, C. 72, 88, 187
Macklin, E. D. 264
MacLean, E. 316
MacLeod, L. 2
MacLusky, N. 177
MacMillan-Bloedel 402–404
Macionis, J. 168
Mahaffy, L. 101
Mainstreaming diversity (*see*
    Managing Diversity; Work;
    Workplace) 335–336
Mala in se 105
Mala prohibita 106
Malvaux, J. 205
Management-labour relations
    344–360
Managing diversity (*see also* Work;
    Workplace) 225–230
Mandatory retirement 202–203
Mandell, N. 188
Mander, J. 378–379

Manitoba Aboriginal Justice
    Inquiry 2, 117
Maracle, B. 323
Marchak, P. 383
Maritimes (*see* Atlantic Canada)
Marshall, S. 79, 174, 271
Marshall, W. 93–93
Martin, D. 3
Martin, J.A. 43-44
Marx, K. 15–16, 19, 51, 56, 139
Mass communication (*see* Mass
    media)
Mass media 285–331
    and advertising 311–316
    and audience 290–291
    and gender 191, 315–316
    and minorities 318–323
    and Third World 328, 395
    as contested site 286–289
    as ideology 292
    commercial dimension 291–292,
        301
    computer mediated
        communication 323–329
    definition of 289–290
    depiction of crime 99–102, 109–111
    enlightened propaganda 292,
        316–323
    news media 288–290
    TV programming 304–311
Masson, J.M. 181–182
Masters, W. 64
Masters, W.H. 68
Matas, R. 64
Matthews, R. 152, 156
McDaniel, S. 89, 182
McEwan, B.S. 177
McGregor, R. 319
McIntosh, P. 63, 70
McIntyre, S. 151
McKague, O. 245
McKay, H. 122–123
McKie, C. 304, 329
McKinney, K. 75, 77
McKinnon, A. 85
McLaren, A. 176, 193
McLeod, K. 228
McLeod, R. 295–296
McLuhan, M. 324, 329
McMahon, M. 136
McMillan, D. 45
McNeely, R.L. 4
McQuail, D. 316
Media (*see* Mass media) 378
Men's liberation movement xvi,
    189–190
Mens rea 105–106
Menzies, R. 126
Mercredi, O. 247
Merit 157–160
Meritocracy 214
Merriam, N. 91
Merton, R. 44–45, 118–119
Metis (*see* Aboriginal Peoples) 238
Meyrowitz, J. 305
Michael, R.T. 66
Middle class measuring rod 119
Mietkietwitz, H. 308
Miles, R. 214

Miller, A. 181
Miller, W. 119
Mills, C.W. 4, 5
Minas, A. 74
Mind sex 193
Minorities 2, 242–282
    and inequality 144–148
    and media 318–323
    and police 253, 116–118, 361–363
    and workplace 161, 363–374
Misogyny 12–13
Mitchell-Powell, B. 227
Mitigated accountability 114
Mobility 144, 163
Modernization 271, 273
Mofina, R. 11
"Mommy track" 197–198
Mones, P. 122, 257
Money, J. 75, 176–177
Moore, H. W. 101
Moore, M. 273
Morgan, G. 363
Morris, D. 116
Morrison, H. 40
Morrison, N. 276
Morrow, R. 288
Mortimer, J.T. 196, 273
Morton, M. 277
Mosaic 144
    vertical 146–148
Mosher, W.D. 78, 85
Moyer, S. 20
Multiculturalism Act 209, 226
Multiculturalism 209, 225–230
    as symbol 228
    criticism of 381
    praise of 209, 226–230
Multinationals (*see also*
        Globalization, MacMillan-
        Bloedel) xvi, 381–383
    definition of 381
    impact of 383
    scope of 382
Murdock, G. 2, 86, 252
Murray, C. 69–70, 253
Myles, J. 2

Naftolin, F. 177
Nader, R. 36-37
Nansen Medal 1, 207
Narcotics Control Act 36, 39, 105
Nation-state, (*see also* Globalization)
        431, 432, 438–439, 444
*National Alcohol and Other Drugs
        Survey* 29
National Council of Welfare
        198–199, 203, 254, 273
*National Drug Intelligence Estimate
        1992* 39
National Organization for the
        Reform of Marijuana Laws
        (NORML) 126
"Nation within" (*see also* Self-
        government; Aboriginal
        peoples) 238–239, 243–247
Natural history of social problems
        18–22
Natural person 107
Nelson, A. 75-76, 78, 268–269

Nessner, K. 197
Nett, E. 203
Nettler, G. 112
Networked Society 323–329
New equality (*see also* Equality)
        149–152
Newcombe, C. 24
News (*see* Newscasting)
Newscasting xvi, 293–304
    as contested site 293
    as propaganda xvi, 316–318
    as social construction 300–304
    bias 300–304
    big business 300–301
    CBC 303
    collecting 302–303
    definition of 294
    gatekeepers 393
    "infotainment" 304
    libertarian vs socialist 316–317
    manufacturing consent (*see also*
        Herman) 316–318
    TV news 304
Nicholson-Lord, D. 406, 408
Normand, J. 194
Noult, F. 266
Novara, P. 222
Novogrodsky, M. 193
Nuclear mentality 187
Nuwer, H. 32

Oakley, A. 13, 276
Obscenity 71
Occupational subculture 366–368
Oderkirk, J. 275
Oettmeier, T. 352, 367
Ohlin, L.E. 45
Okin, S.M. 267
Olive, D. 344
Olmsted, A.D. 3
Olson, C. 19
Ontario Task Force on Race
        Relations and Policing 2
Opium Act 32
Orbach, S. 53, 192
Orbuch, T.L. 75, 77
Organizational change (*see also*
        Work; Workplace) 332–371
    barriers to 361–370
    organizations in crisis 360–361
Organizational subculture 360–363
Organizations (*see* Formal
        organizations)
Orpwood, J. 162, 164
Orwell, G. 8
Osborne, J. 106
Ostow, R. 145

Pagelow, M. 4
Paglia, C. 188
Paine, R. 238
Palys, T. 126
Parens Patriae 113
Parental Responsibility Act 114–115
Parenti, M. 8
Parizeau, J. 237
Parker, G. 110
Parricide 257
Parsons, T. 14, 192, 265

Parsons, V. 42
Patriarchy 186
Pay equity 23, 172
Peluso, E. 53
Peluso, L. 53
Pendakur, K. 131, 145, 148, 236
Pendakur, R. 131, 145, 148, 236
People of colour (*see* Visible
        minorities)
People with disabilities (*see*
        Individuals with disabilities)
Persky, S. 85, 104, 252
Person-blame approach 110
Peters, T. 360
Pfohl, S. 256
Pfuhl, E.H. 78
Pictor, G. 2
Pierce, B.A. 186
Pike, J. 68
Pizzey, E. 52–53
Plapinger, L. 177
Pleck, J. 196, 273
Plummer, K. 17, 73–74
Pogrebin, L. 73
Police (*see also* Community Policing;
        Organization change)
    and minorities 11, 116–118,
        357–358
Policy (*see also* Aboriginal peoples)
Polite discrimination 221–222
Pollak, O. 115
Pollay, R. 36, 40
Ponting, J. R. 242
Pornography 71–73, 105, 187
Porter, J. 131, 146–148
Posluns, E. 190
Postman, N. 304, 326
Poverty xvi, 2, 129–132, 156–161
    and Third World 398–399
    definitions of 156–160
    explanations of 160–161
    feminization of 199–206,
        254–255, 275–276
Preist, G.F. 203
Prejudice 12, 218
Presthus, R. 333
Price, J. 162, 167
Primitive society 161
Principle of least interest 262
Privilege
    white 258
Productive Loop 385–386
Proceeds of Crime Act 35
Propaganda (*see also* Mass media)
        316–323
    and minorities 318–323
Propper, A. 259
Prostitution 20, 70–71, 104, 126
Psychology
    and inequality 156

Quality circles 349
Qualter, T. 317
Quebec 230–238
    and federalism 232–234
    and sovereignty 235–238
Quinney, R. 102, 123–124

Race xv, xvi, 144–152

as social construct 213–214
typologies 214–217
Race and ethnic relations 144-152,
207–248
Racial discrimination 217–223
Racial minorities (*see* Visible
minorities)
Racism (*see also* Discrimination) 1, 2,
4, 10, 11, 12, 210–212, 219–229
definition of 219
types of 220–223
Radical non-intervention 126
Rado, S. 48–49
Ramcharan, S. 154, 156
Ramsey, L. 3
Randall, S.C. 129
Raoul, V. 84
Rape (*see* Sexual assault)
Rappeport, J. 105
Rappoport, G. 19
Rappoport, S. 19
Rational control 363–364, 368–369
vs social action 363–364
Rationality (*see* Rational control)
Rawson, B. 350
Razack, S. 188
Razovsky, L. 10
*RCMP National Drug Intelligence
Estimate 1992* 33-34
Reaction formation 119
Reagan, T. 20
Red-neck discrimination 221
Reese, C.A. 254
Refugees 297
Regionalism 153
Regions in Canada 152–156
and inequality 132, 155
Atlantic Canada 153–154
redressing inequality 156
Reinisch, J. 65
Reiss, A. 74
Reiss, I. 77
Reitz, J. 147
Reproduction (*see also* Abortion;
Contraception; Illegitimacy)
iv, 68, 186, 266–267, 271–272
Ressler, R. 100
Restructuring (*see* Globalization)
Richardon, C.J. 279
Richardson, L. 99, 191–192
Rieter, E. 345–348
Rifkin, J. 338–344
Roberge, R. 125
Roberts, J. 109–110, 121, 124
Robertson, I. xiii, xiv, 12, 16, 20,
75–78, 104, 119, 172, 265,
268–269
Robinson, B.W. 75–78, 104, 119,
172, 265, 268–269
Robinson, J. 353
Robinson, W. 378–380
Robinson-Simpson, G. 4
Rochlin, M. 67
Rock, P. 13, 99
Rodgers, K. 258–259
Roiphe, K. 88
Roosmalen, E. 89
Rose, V.M. 120
Rosenthal, C. 203

Ross, D.P/ 201, 203
Roszak, T. 325
Rothenberg, P. S. 334
Rowland, R. 172
**Royal Commission on Aboriginal
Peoples** 131, 211, 244–245,
355
**Royal Commission on the Status of
Women** 193
Royal Proclamation 244
Rubin, L. 76, 78, 270
Rubin, R. 191
Ruesch, H. 20
Rueters 142
Rushton, P. 109–110, 214, 215–217
Russell, D. 12, 89–90, 187, 282
Rustad, M. 273
Rwanda 397

Sacco, V. 101, 125
Sadker, D. 193
Sadker, M. 193
Safe sex 46, 84-86
Safilios-Rothschild, C. 189
Sakaiya, T. 350
Salamon, E. 172, 252
Saless, D. 231, 234
Salholz, E. 270–271
Samagh, T. 258
Sandmaier, M. 6, 53
Sandor, G. 6
Sanger, W. 68-69
Satzewich, V. 136, 156–157, 220
Schaef, A.W. 49–50
Schaefer, R.T. 252
Schlafly, P. 174
Schlesinger, A.M. 400
Schlesinger, P. 99
Schoenborn, C. 37
Schur, E. 88
Schwartz, F. 197–198
Schwartz, M. 55, 125
Schwartz, P. 76, 263
Scientific management (*see also*
Formal organizations;
Workplace) 347–348
Schooling (*see* Education)
Scott, R. 252
Scripting 253
Seagrave, J. 351, 367
Searles, P. 186
Second shift 196, 263
Secord, P. 173
Segregation 210
Seguin, F. 349
Seinfeld, J. 286
Seitzinger, J. 367
Self-determination
as self-government 244–245
(*see also* Aboriginal peoples)
Self-government definition of 276–277
(*see also* Self–determination)
Self-help 57–60
Seligmann, J. 253, 266
Sellin, T. 15
Sen, A. 142
Serial murder 99–101, 123
Sexual assault
against females 12–13, 18, 62, 65,
86–88

definition of 86–91
in high schools 89
on campus 89–91
sentences for 91–93
Sexual behaviour
attitudes towards 63, 282
committed virgins 77
coercive sexuality 86-91, 257
homosexuality xvi, xviii, 46, 72,
74, 77, 79, 83–85, 119–120,
250, 252–253, 270–271
premarital sex 69–70, 76–77
safe sex 84–86
sexual deviance 68–70
sexual scripts 68, 75, 88–89
sexually transmitted diseases
62–78, 84–86
trend towards conservatism 77
trend towards convergence 77
Sexual harassment (*see also*
Discrimination) 11, 91
Sexual Sterilization Act (Alberta) 9
Sexually Transmitted Diseases 62,
84–86
Shalev, C. 271
Shankweiler, P.J. 76
Shapiro, J. 52-53
Shaw, C. 122-123
Shaw, M. 122
Sher, J. 1
Shibley-Hyde, J. 178–179
Shkilnyk, A. 210, 240
Shostak, A.B. 80–83
Siddiqui, H. 318
Sidorowicz, L.S. 192
Silverman, R. 110
Simeoni, P. 239–340, 343–345
Simon, W. 74
Simpson, J. 230
Sinclair, P. 154–156
Singer, B. 409, 415
Singer, P. 20
Skolnick, J. 1 43, 125
Sleeter, C. 163, 165, 168
Slotnick, L. 359
Small, S.E. 5
Smart, C. 115–116, 259
Smith, E. 12
Smith, M. 5, 7
Social Class (*see* Class)
Social Darwinism 8
Social disorganization 14, 48
Social mobility (*see* Mobility)
Social problems
as conditions xiv, 5
as processes xiv, 5
Social reality of crime 123
Social structure (*see* Structure)
Socialism 161
Socialization
and inequality 156–157
Society building 220–230
Sociobiology 178–179
Sociological imagination 5
Sociological perspectives 13–15
on inequality 138–149
on poverty 160–161
Solomon, R. 32, 35, 39
Solomos, J. 388
Sontag, S. 265

Sovereignty (*see* Nation–state; First Nations; Quebec) 235–238, 246–247
Sowell, T. 370–371
Spade, J.Z. 254
Spallone, P. 271
Spector, M. 5, 20
Spencer, H. 14
Sperling, S. 21
Spiro, M. 139
Spoonley, P. 214
Sprecher, S. 75, 77
St. Peter, C. 271
Stallard, K. 205
Stamler, R. 38-39
Stasiulis, D. 145, 210, 225–226
State 229-230
    vs market 392–393
Stateless corporations (*see* Multinationals)
Stea, D. 238
Steil, J. 263
Steinem, G. 71
Steinmetz, S. 4, 260
Stephenson, C. 100–101
Steroids 32, 45
Stets, J. 90
Stevens, J. 98
Steward, N. 319, 395
Stimmel, B. 48
Stimpson, C.H. 174
Stoller, R. 72
Stoltenberg, J. 189
Stone, S. D. 252
Strain theory 17, 118–119
Stratification 140–141, 144–148
Straus, M. 4, 90, 256, 259–260
Strike, C. 46, 85
Strossen, N. 72
Structure 136-137
Subculture (*see* Organizational subculture) 15, 366–368
Subliminal advertising 312–313
Sudermann, M. 89
Sugerman, D. 62, 257
Sullivan, T. 81, 257
Superwoman Syndrome 262–263
Survey of Consumer Finances 275
Sutherland, E. 99
Suttee 13
Suzuki, D. 167, 401
Swan, N. 156
System-blaming 12–13
Systemic discrimination 117–118
    (*see also* Discrimination)
Szasz, T. 29, 50–51, 60, 124
Szekeley, E. 192

Tabakoff, B. 46
Tangri, S.S. 55
Tannahill, R. 68
Taras, D. 303–304
Tarter, R.E. 46
Tator, C. 224
Tavris, C. 49–50, 53, 177–178
Taylor, F. 344–346
Taylor, I. 124
Taylor, J.G.R. 76
Tele-sharks 102
Television 304–311

as reality 306–307
censorship 310–311
codes of 305–306
violence and 307–311
programming 304–307
Tender years doctrine 278–279
Tepper, E. 145
Tepperman, L. 144
Teratogens 6
Terrorism 123
Thomas, W.I. 51
Thorne, B. 267
Thorne-Finch, R. 82, 260–261
Thorsell, W. 342
Tiedman, G. 173
Timko, C. 127
Tobacco 35-36, 40, 106–107, 276
Tobias, J. 242
Toch, H. 38
Tong, R. 183, 185
Total quality management (*see* Human resources, Workplace) 349–350
Tough, A. 190
Townson, M. 199–204
Transnationals (*see* Multinationals)
Trasov, L. 10
Tremblay, J.G. 82
Trevethan, S. 258
"Tribalism" (*see also* Ethnicity) 399–400
Trojanowicz, R. C. 101
Troyna, B. 316
Trudeau, P. E. 1, 156, 208
Tumber, H. 99
Turkel, S. 338
Turner, R. 24
Turpel, M.E. 247
Turrow, J. 289
Tyson, M. 304

Underground economy 197
Unemployment 281, 332–333

Valaskakis, K. 377, 387
Valette, B. 45
Valpy, M. 159
Van Dusen, J.E. 77
Vasta, E. 229
Vaughan, D. 278
Vertical mosaic 146–148
Victimless crimes 104–105
Victims of Violence 19, 127
Villeneuve, P.J. 40
Violence xvii, 2, 9, 12-13, 18–19, 256–261
Violence-prone women 52-53
Visible minorities 11, 147–148
    and mass media xvi, 318–323
Vivian, J. 314, 324
Vold, G. 13, 16, 124

Wachtel, S.S. 176
Walkom, T. 393
Wallace, C. 9, 15, 69–70, 192, 251, 267–268, 276
Waller, W. 262
Ward, S. 90
Watkins, M. 139, 393
Weaver, S. 239

Weber, M. 167–168, 363
Webber, J. 162, 234
Webster, C.D. 111
Wein, F. 152–153, 155–156
Weinberg, M.S. 75
Weingarten, K. 281
Weis, K. 18
Wells, J.A. 268
Weltman, K. 263
Werth, B. 82–83
Westoff, C.F. 262
Weston, K. 252
White-collar crime 99, 120, 123–124
Wife-abuse 2, 4, 9, 12–13, 20, 173–174
Wildavsky, A. 51
Williams, C.J. 75
Williams, J.C. 184
Williams, J.E. 172–173
Williams, K. 252
Williams, T. M. 309
Williamson, L. 3
Wilson, E.O. 178
Wilson, M. 259
Wilson, S.J. 2, 183, 202, 254, 262
Winter. J. 300
Winzer, M. 6
Witt, S.H. 79
Wolf, N. 53, 192
Women (*see* Gender)
Work 332-337
    new work 341–344
    rethinking work 336–337
    transformations in 334–345
Workplace xvi, 332–371
    and diversity 335–335
    effects of computer 338–340
    Fordism 341–344
    gender stratification in xvi, 194–198
    human resources model 348–360
    mandatory retirement 202–203
    post-Fordism 341–344
    resistance to 360–370
    scientific management 344–348
    workerless factories 341–342
    workteams 348–349
Wotherspoon, T. 241, 273

Yerbury, C. 116
Yesalis, C.E. 44–45
Yllo, K. 90
Yogis, J.A. 253, 279
Young Offender's Act 112–114, 126

Zeitlin, I. 393
Zerbisias, A. 290
Zinn, M.B. 5, 22–23, 191